World Musics in Context

World Musics in Context

A Comprehensive Survey of the World's Major Musical Cultures

Peter Fletcher

OXFORD
UNIVERSITY PRESS

Great Clarendon Street, Oxford OX2 6DP

Oxford University Press is a department of the University of Oxford.
It furthers the University's objective of excellence in research,
scholarship, and education by publishing worldwide in

Oxford New York

Athens Auckland Bangkok Bogotá Buenos Aires Cape Town
Chennai Dar es Salaam Delhi Florence Hong Kong Istanbul
Karachi Kolkata Kuala Lumpur Madrid Melbourne Mexico
City Mumbai Nairobi Paris São Paulo Shanghai
Singapore Taipei Tokyo Toronto Warsaw and associated
companies in Berlin Ibadan

Published in the United States
By Oxford University Press Inc., New York

First published 2001

British Library Cataloging in Publication Data

Data available

Library of Congress Cataloging-in-Publication Data
Fletcher, Peter, 1936–
World's musics in context : a comprehensive survey of the world's
major musical cultures / Peter Fletcher.
p. cm.
Includes bibliographical references and index.
1. Music—History and criticism. I. Title
ML 160. F64 1997 780′.9—dc21 97–8042

ISBN 0–19–816636–2

1 3 5 7 9 10 8 6 4 2

Typeset in 12/13 WallbaumMT by Kolam Information Services Pvt.
Ltd, Pondicherry, India
Printed in Great Britain
on acid-free paper by
Biddles Ltd., Guildford & King's Lynn

Acknowledgements

'Generalist' books usually contain a distillation of the specialist work of others, and this book is no exception; it could not have been written without drawing on the publications of hundreds of individual scholars. To have listed all sources in the text would have made it unduly cluttered; individual scholars, therefore, have been named only when their *theories* have been presented at some length. This does not lessen indebtedness to the work of specialists, and all sources are recorded in the footnotes.

In the course of my travels, extraordinary help and kindness were afforded by many musicians, scholars, and institutions. A particular debt of gratitude is owed to the University of Hong Kong for a stay of two months as Rayson Huang Visiting Fellow, and to the Hong Kong Academy for Performing Arts, where eight months were spent as Dean of Music. Both institutions provided help and encouragement. The many individuals who assisted in Hong Kong include the composers Doming Lam and Chan Kambiu of the University of Hong Kong; Professor David Gwilt, Dr Tsao Pen-yeh, and Dr Chan Wing-wah of the Chinese University; Dr John Hosier, Dr Tong Kin-woon, Dr Wang Guo-tong, and Dr Carl Wolz of the Academy for Performing Arts; the composer Richard Tsang, and the folklorist, Dr Patrick Hayes. Students at the Academy for Performing Arts—some from other parts of Asia—were a constant source of inspiration, as well as of information.

In Taiwan, valuable assistance was received from Dean Chuang Pen-li, Professor Cheng Ye-yuan, and the conductor, Mark Graveson, all from the University of Chinese Culture, and from the pipa player, Wong Ping-ching. In Japan, Dr Fujita Fumiko of Kunitachi College of Music, Tokyo, provided invaluable organizational assistance; she herself gave generously of her knowledge, as did Professor Shinobu Oku of Nara

University of Education, and many staff members of Kunitachi College, Tokyo. In Korea, Professor Kim Chong-ja of Seoul National University, with the assistance of her willing students, was extraordinarily helpful in leading me to performances and ceremonies that would otherwise have been missed; she and other staff members of Seoul National University, and musicians at the Korean Traditional Performing Arts Centre, gave willingly of their time and advice.

The Thai musician Anant Narkong, now Head of Thai Music at Chulalongkorn University, Bangkok, prepared my visit to Thailand. His father (the sculptor, Apai Narkong) and Panya Roongruang of Chulalongkorn University were unremitting in their efforts to extend my knowledge and experience of Thai music and culture. In Burma, the Staff of the Cultural Attaché of the British Embassy gave directions. In Vietnam, Dr Trong Bang and Professor Vu Huong of the Hanoi Conservatory of Music first made possible experience of traditional music and theatre, and numerous performers of traditional and Western music have since provided assistance. In Laos, Zamphiou Buaphacanh, Minister of Arts and Culture, led to my experiencing Laotian music and dance; and Rattikone Thogphath, Director of the Indigenous Theatricals Centre, furnished valuable information and advice.

In Manila, Ma. Teresa Escoda Roxas, President of the Cultural Centre of the Philippines, provided helpful contacts and an entrée to many musical functions. Sister Mary Placid, Dean of Music at St Scholastica's College, offered valuable insights and introductions to helpful staff and students, both at the University of the Philippines and at the Asian Institute for Liturgy and Music. Dr Corazon Diaquino gave generously of her time in providing information on indigenous music.

Over the years, much advice has been received from musicians in India; and the Indian Council for Cultural Relations generously hosted visits in 1983 and 1984 when the Indian Music teaching project for Leicestershire was being developed. At that time, valuable help was received from Namita Chaterjee, Principal of the Saurabh Academy of Music and Dance in Calcutta, Pemlata Puri, Director of the Centre of Cultural Resources and Training in New Delhi, and Professor D. T. Joshi, Principal of the Burdwan Academy of Music. Professor Debu Chaudhury, Dean of Music at New Delhi University, who spent four months with the Leicestershire project, passed on many helpful insights. The brilliant young *kathak* dancer, Kumar Saswat, now resident in Leicestershire, has been an unfailing mentor in Indian music and culture. More recently, in Madras, Dr N. Ramanathan, Reader in Music at the University of Madras, B. Rajam Iyer, Principal of the Teachers' College of Music, V. R. Devika, Coordinator of the Madras Craft Foundation, Ranganayaki Ayyanger, Director of the Sampradaya, and Dr S. A. K. Durga, Director of the Centre for Ethnomusicology, all gave generously of their time in providing assistance.

Philip Mundey, Director of Examinations of the Associated Board of the Royal Schools of Music, steered me in useful directions in Kenya; and Trevor Wilshaw, Director of the Kenya Conservatoire of Music, Samuel Otieno of the Kenyan Presidential Music Commission, Dr Luzili Mulindi-King of Kenyatta University, and Richard Moss of the Nairobi Symphony Orchestra gave generously of their time and knowledge.

Professor Judith E. Grimes (of Indiana State University) opened many doors for me in Jamaica. Mrs C. Walden, Principal and Director of Sam Sharpe Teachers' College in Montego Bay, provided generous hospitality; her staff, and Mr Lloyd Whinstanley, Headmaster of Herbert Morrison Comprehensive School, contributed advice. In Kingston, Jamaica, it was my privilege to have discussions with Professor Rex Nettleford and Noel Dexter of the University of the West Indies. In Latin America, Guy Hunter-Watts, Rafael Mendez (broadcaster in Mexico), and many other individuals, too numerous to name, in Brazil, Peru, and Mexico, assisted understanding of many aspects of musical culture in Latin America. Coriún Aharonián, the Uruguayan composer, researcher, and educator, also provided valuable materials and insights on Latin American music.

In Bali, Nick Gray (leader of the Gender Wayang Group 'Segara Luadu') passed on many perceptive insights; but in Bali, as in Java (and indeed in Africa and Latin America), one need only use ears, eyes, and legs, and follow hunches, to be led to many delightful encounters. Perhaps most has been owed to chance meetings with people of all nationalities—at an airport, cruising down an African river—meetings that led to new insights, and new musical experiences.

As a musician coming late to the field, I acknowledge an incalculable debt to the UK Chapter of the International Council for Traditional Music (now renamed the British Forum for Ethnomusicology). Its many conferences have demonstrated different approaches from the standpoint of many nationalities, and have afforded valuable preliminary contacts.

Many scholars in the UK have provided assistance, in conversation, and in pointing me towards useful source material. Dr David W. Hughes, Centre for Music Studies, School of African and Oriental Studies, University of London, assisted in many ways. A particular debt of gratitude is owed to Dr Peter Cooke, School of Scottish Studies, Edinburgh University, Dr Ruth Davis, Corpus Christi College, Cambridge, Professor Hormoz Farhat, Trinity College, Dublin, Dr Jonathan Katz, Westminster College, London, Dr Josef Pacholczych, University of Maryland, and Harold Jones, Trinity College of Music, London, for reading, and giving critical advice, on chapters relating to their specialist fields.

The final text owes much to Laurence Picken. His detailed examination of the text stimulated new ideas; and he gave freely of his knowledge and experience. Few were better qualified to assist this essay to its conclusion.

Permission by the publishers to reproduce a few passages, substantially rewritten, from my earlier book *Roll over Rock* (Stainer & Bell, 1981) is gratefully acknowledged.

Finally, a debt of gratitude is owed to Elizabeth Agate, who assisted with the illustrations; to Bruce Phillips, Oxford University Press, for his continued support during the gestation and writing of the book; and to my son, Nic, who assisted tirelessly with computer technology at various stages of the book's production.

For errors and confusions the author takes full responsibility, and will be grateful to those who make known such shortcomings.

Contents

List of Plates

List of Maps

I . . . asked my audience to question carefully, even sadly if they wished, the future of a world whose cultures, all passionately fond of one another, would aspire only to celebrate one another in such confusion that each would lose any attraction it could have for the others and its own reasons for existing.

CLAUDE LÉVI-STRAUSS

We shall not cease from exploration
And the end of all our exploring
Will to be arrive where we started
And know the place for the first time.

T. S. ELIOT

Foreword

The context in which musics of the world are here to be examined is that of geography, history (in the old-fashioned sense of who did what to whom and when), and social structure (in the basic sense of who were at the bottom of the heap and who on top).

There are those who will say that so simple-minded a project should never have been attempted in a post-Claude-Lévi-Straussian-and-Charles-Seegerian world. Evidently, to attempt a necessarily brief account of the history of any one of the great cultural zones of the planet is hazardous in the extreme. Specialists themselves will differ about both 'facts' and their 'interpretation'; specialists, as they read, may wish to qualify virtually every statement made. Old charges once preferred in the history of ethnic-music studies will be revived. Like anthropologists of a previous generation, who referred (with touching possessiveness) to 'my people', many with extended, specialist knowledge of a particular region will be affronted by this invasion of their territory; many toes will be trodden on.

Such reactions are to be anticipated. It remains fact, however, that the approach adopted has revealed a worldwide positive correlation between the vicissitudes of what the ordinary person regards as 'history' and the character—in the broadest sense of that word—of music today in any such given cultural zone.

In any society under investigation, it is important to distinguish sharply between relationships of *correlation* between aspects of culture, and relationships of *causation*. Some decades ago, a crypto-hypothesis seems to have persuaded certain fieldworkers that the structure of a society, in the socio-anthropological sense, determined (in a manner never explained or defined) the organization of all aspects of music in that society. There are, indeed, areas of behaviour where social constraints—the required duration of ritual music in a particular ceremonial context, for example—may determine temporal limits, but this is scarcely to be equated with *causation* in the process of generating a music. For some workers it became sufficient to make parallel statements describing social organization, and the position of musicians in that society, on the one hand, and musical forms and institutions, on the other, without specifying the nature of any linkage between the two.

One of the most trenchant criticisms of ethnomusicological studies came in a letter (addressed to Charles Seeger) from Howard Becker, himself a sociologist.[1] The gist of his observations lies in this statement: '. . . ethnomusicology, as a field of scholarly endeavor, has in some ways painted itself into a corner, theoretically if not practically.' Listing Seeger's demands for a multidisciplinary approach, he argued that the job was not doable. What Becker believed could not be done will be stated at the end of this Foreword; but his prescription, for doing what is practicable, may be given here and now: in practice to 'subordinate multiple facts and approaches to one particular approach'.

As its name tells us, the science of ethnomusicology is the *logos* of the musics of other people. (Those who would construe this compound as meaning 'the ethnology of music' are mistaken.) To some extent, the difficulties of those investigating this particular *logos*—the difficulties of ethnomusicologists—are due to the character of music. It is the case that no cultural trait is invested with greater power to affirm cultural identity than is music; and yet we are unable to state in what that power resides.

Reaching the end of her study of music-making over the previous thirty years in an English town, a study embracing every category of music, Ruth Finnegan turned, in a final chapter, to examine the role of music, and the function of musicians, in an ordinary, down-to-earth, present-day, Western society.[2] She observes that 'musicians like priests and seers bear their necessary part in public events . . .'; that 'the participants in musical rituals can achieve a self-fulfilment conjointly with loss of self and of the everyday mundane affairs of life in a somehow transcendent and symbolic enactment'.[3] She notes an unspoken but shared assumption among the participants in local music that there was

[1] Howard Becker, 'Ethnomusicology and Sociology: A Letter to Charles Seeger', *Ethnomusicology*, 33 (1989), 275–85.

[2] Ruth Finnegan, *The Hidden Musicians: Music-Making in an English Town* (Cambridge: Cambridge University Press, 1989).

[3] Ibid. 338, 332.

something *sui generis*, something unparalleled in quality and in kind about music, which was not to be found in other activities of work or play; there was also something about music which for the participants set it apart—something akin perhaps to the spiritual meaning of religion.

With insight she continues: '... music is both similar to and different from language as a basic characteristic of humanity.'[4] Language is seen as a cognitive mode, its capacity deep in the mind, while music is not essentially cognitive, and extends beyond mind, beyond the body.

That music and language are not part of the same system is manifest in the absence of dependence of one on the other: musical skill is maintained in severe aphasia (loss of the ability to speak); and autists may combine musical ability with subnormal IQ and poor language function.[5] Moreover, the domains are spatially separate in relation to the cerebral hemispheres. Aphasias nearly always result from damage to the left hemisphere, while amusias (loss of musical ability) follow damage to the right hemisphere.[6]

Some Attributes of Music and Language

In the light of this antithesis, as restated by Finnegan, it may be helpful once more to consider, in general and very elementary terms, some of the attributes of music.[7] Very remarkably, its most distinctive attribute, that which sets it apart from all other arts except dance (with which it is inextricably linked), is never (or but rarely) mentioned in definitions. It is: that music exists only in time; it is a process. Many years ago now, in conversation, Alan Lomax said: 'Music is reality; it has to be lived through'—adding that, if, in our impatience, we switch to 'fast forward-wind', music is transformed or even destroyed.

[4] Ibid. 340.

[5] Rachel Gelman and Kimberley Brenneman, 'First Principles can Support both Universal and Cultural Specific Learning about Number and Music', in Lawrence E. Hirschfeld and Susan A. Gelman (eds.), *Mapping the Mind: Domain Specificity in Cognition and Culture* (Cambridge : Cambridge University Press, 1994), 375.

[6] Ibid. 376.

[7] In search of a general discussion in philosophical terms of theories of music, the reader is directed to Professor Malcolm Budd's critique: *Music and the Emotions: The Philosophical Theories* (London, 1985, 1992, 1994).

A perceptive essay by Ruth A. Solie on 'organicism and musical analysis' redressed the balance, and reminded us that Schenker himself regarded 'the concept of organic coherence' as 'the secret and source of the very being' of works by the great masters.[8] It is important, however, that we beware, lest we find ourselves embroiled with that 'entelechy'—that 'life-force'—that Schenker evidently found so seductive as an adjunct to 'explanation' of the creative process, but from which the biologists have found it so difficult to escape, once admitted as a concept. The concept of any 'force' driving the process is surely fallacious. The secret lies in the nature and details of the process, yet to be determined.

Commonly we tend to identify music with melody; but this equation is invalid, since whole areas of music are constructed from quasi-non-pitched or complexly structured sounds. Even where melodic music is concerned, we can recognize many musics of the world, from many different historic periods, on hearing a specimen of no more than a few seconds' duration—at times even less. In so doing we are (admittedly) identifying a brief sample; but nevertheless such a sample possesses extension in time, and it is proper, not withstanding the brevity of the sample, to speak of it as 'music'.

We tend to forget that not only the Great Apes, but all the Primates—and for that matter all the Vertebrates—possess systems of non-verbal, vocal communication, as well as all their other systems of non-verbal communication: odour, gesture, facial expression, bodily contact. Vocalization, independent of language, is part, too, of the Hominid scheme of communication. Let us briefly examine an aspect of neurological, anatomical structure in ourselves: Primates, genetically less than 2 per cent different from the Chimpanzee; indeed, more closely related to the Chimpanzee than is the Gorilla or the Orang-utan.[9]

The neural pathways that control vocalization in Primates (including humans), descend, from regions of the brain cortex (the anterior limbic cortex) that control emotional arousal, to a region of synaptic relay in the midbrain; and motor axons run thence to the larynx, tongue, and muscles of the face.[10]

[8] Ruth A. Solie, 'The Living Work: Organicism and Musical Analysis', *19th Century Music*, 4 (1980), 147–56.

[9] Desmond Morris, *The Human Animal* (London: BBC, 1994), 7.

[10] Terence W. Deacon, 'The Human Brain', *The Cambridge Encyclopedia of Human Evolution* (Cambridge: Cambridge University Press, 1992), 133.

On the other hand, pathways essential for human language originate in those superficial cortical areas of the forebrain (specifically of the left cerebral hemisphere) that control, in general, skilled behaviour; successively these paths too come to innervate face and jaw muscles, larynx, and tongue.[11]

In humans, these paths work together, so that the larynx is brought into play, both in cries and in speech. In humans, too, the pathways that function in Primate vocalizations in general are involved in 'innate calls' (shrieks, sobbing, weeping, laughter) and may affect speech intonation, tone, and rhythm of utterance. Under conditions of great emotional stress, such innate calls may (as we are all aware) usurp the function of language, so that, in a sense, we revert (as regards communication) to the condition of our speechless Primate relatives. Unlike them, however, we can weep; they cannot.

All such vocalizations (and indeed those other components of the non-linguistic system of communication) are manifested through time; and the sonic character of each vocalization exhibits change in form and content through time.

Music is not a language, in the sense in which we commonly use that term for speech, even though (in structural terms) it may be said to have a 'grammar', learned by all members of a given society in regard to its own music; but, as Primate studies have shown, the amount of information conveyed—by vocalizations—between members of a given species is enormous. Only in the assessment of the relative contribution of intention, cognition, and affect, in these exchanges, is there difficulty in making comparison with language itself. (Even in human speech, however, these aspects are difficult for an observer to assess.) Furthermore, it is important to be aware of the structural complexity of such vocalizations that frequently cover 'a broad frequency-band from a few hundred hertz up to near ultrasonic range (about 40,000 Hz)'.[12] A call lasting less than one second may manifest a highly variable temporal pattern in amplitude, superimposed on wide swings in frequency range, from audible to ultrasonic.

If our recognition of a music from a particular geographical region depends not on what a musician might mean by 'structural features' of a musical style, but on characteristics inherent in a sample of no more than a second-or-so's duration, it would seem likely that the domain of

[11] Ibid.

[12] Elke Zimmermann, 'Communication by Non-Human Primates', *The Cambridge Encyclopedia of Human Evolution*, 124.

music lies primarily in that region of brain function which is involved in the emotion-charged vocalizations of Primates in general. The 'language of music' is, in the simplest terms (it is suggested), the same kind of 'language' as weeping, sobbing, shrieking, laughing.

Staying for a while with this outrageous simplification in significance of the term 'music', it is conceivable that the 'otherness' of music, the universal acceptance of music as the medium of communication with the spirit world, becomes intelligible: for such vocalizations are indeed *our* 'other voice', *our* 'other language'—in evolution a primary medium of self-expression, not merely in intraspecific communication, but also (seemingly) in intercommunication between members of different orders of mammals.

On 31 July 1994 the evening programme of the British Broadcasting Corporation's BBC 2 included 'a light-hearted examination of the relationship between animals and music', in the first issue of a new magazine series on music (*The Score*), presented by David Pearl. This demonstrated the response of the canine inhabitants of the Dogs Home, Battersea (London, UK) to playback of a CD of *The Song of the Humpback Whale*. The demonstration made widely known a prior observation of the Dogs Home staff that a previously all-barking community of caged dogs falls silent under these conditions, save for tiny sound gestures—the whimpering that occurs when dogs are in a very particular state of mind. Under the influence of the whale's song, some dogs retired to their sleeping baskets; many cocked an ear to listen. As we shall see, in human societies also, the song of a different *class* of vertebrate may at times have profound emotional significance.

Even the smallest, one-second sample of a music may exhibit all the basic elements of what we usually imply when referring to a 'music': a structure in time, derived from periodic changes, in amplitude and frequency of vibrations in an elastic, oscillating medium.

Out of such microstructures, larger entities can be assembled, having greater temporal extension, structures that unwind at so slow a pace that we, as humans, can perceive temporal sequence, and change in content. We may look down the time axis (as in a diagram drawn in polar coordinates) and see the sequence of musical events as a uniplanar spiral about a centre: as *tablā*-improvisations have been represented by Hindustani musicians; as David Rycroft saw African songs;[13] as Andrea

[13] David Rycroft, 'Tribal Style and Free Expression', *African Music*, 1 (1954), 16–27; 'Nguni Vocal Polyphony', *Journal of the International Folk Music Council*, 39 (1967), 88–103; see also 'Africa', *The New Grove* (1980), i. 149.

Nixon summarized the pentatonic structure of Mongolian Long Song: *urtyn duu.*[14]

If, as suggested, music is primarily a process in which manipulation of changes in frequency and amplitude of air vibrations within the human auditory range occur, what might be meant by *causation* in these sequential changes?

Musical analysis commonly implies, and seeks to persuade, that the action of analysis discloses the mainspring of the creative process. It is here suggested that nothing of that kind is disclosed. Schenkerian Analysis displays, with great elegance and clarity, the stratified levels of analytical insight into the structure of Western art music; but (it may be argued) this is only description—progressively enhanced and refined description—of what is happening in time. In isolation, no detached moment is 'explained' by what precedes, or itself 'explains' what follows.

To have knowledge of *causation* we must know what (in a monody, let's say) determines the pitch and other characteristics of the note that follows a first note. It may be the case that the two notes together are themselves a gesture from a thesaurus of musical gestures, something 'given' in the mind of the tune-maker by virtue of being a member of a particular society; but, even if the gesture be subsequently completed, we still do not know what factor or factors determined its choice.

Clearly we are very far from possessing that sort of knowledge in respect of any musical culture. We may describe correlations, such as determine a liturgical sequence, say; but we may not maintain that social structures determine, in the detailed sense of moment-to-moment causation, the flux of music: what is happening in sound.

Nevertheless, a people's music symbolizes that people, perhaps more completely than does any other of their arts, or any other aspect of their culture. Perhaps, what we hear is the primal, Primate call, transformed by superimposition of a new, quasi-linguistic, intellectual modulation; a system of non-verbal, sonic communication evolved by humans, taking advantage of the existence in our species of both systems of communication, employing both in the creation of *our* music, as opposed, say to that of birds.

It would be impertinent to commend Professor Bruno Nettl's survey of the history, principles, and aims of ethnomusicology,[15] but it is surely

[14] Andrea Nixon, 'The Pentatonic Structure of Mongolian Long Song' (Part II Music Tripos Dissertation, 1980), private communication.

[15] Bruno Nettl, *The Study of Ethnomusicology: Twenty-nine Issues and Concepts* (Urbana, Ill.: University of Illinois Press, 1983).

permissible to express gratitude for, and indebtedness to, a work that summarizes so much of the changing attitudes, over time, of those interested in 'ethnic musics'; from the beginning, in the recognition of difference, to acceptance of the social-anthropological all-importance of cultural setting; from notions of the existence of universals to denial of such, and later to admission of the possibility of their presence.

His readers owe an enormous debt to questioners (fortunate enough to be present, along with him) at drinks parties where topics (unusual at parties for lesser mortals) were discussed. Perhaps an imaginary expostulation from an imaginary bibber may be introduced at this point: 'What! One second of music identifying an entire musical culture?'

The reply is 'Yes'; but there is of course more to be said. The one-second-or-less call of a Mouse Lemur (*Microcebus murinus*)[16] of Madagascar may be dismissed as a specimen of 'music' in any civilized sense; but the 'song' of the Humpback Whale (*Megaptera novaeangliae*) impresses even the man-in-the-street as song, though it be song of a disturbingly unusual kind. Lois and Howard Winn,[17] who have recorded songs of the Humpback for thirteen years in waters off Puerto Rico and the Virgin Islands, offer two initial impressions: 'some portions of the humpback song sound amazingly like birds chirping', and again: 'any one who has ever heard a group of humpbacks chorusing would find no difficulty in likening them to a heavenly choir.' The song may last from six to twenty minutes. One whale repeated its song for twenty four hours without interruption, and was still singing when recording ceased. Commonly the song is composed of six 'themes'; but in some years only four or five are used.

The song extends over three pitch levels. The highest pitch range is 4 Khz; but a majority of sounds are below 1 Khz. In all three pitch levels a number of types of call are distinguished; their variety (as expressed in onomatopoeic, verbal simulations) affords a glimpse of the acoustic complexity of the song. The 'Lows' are described as moans, groans, snores, and 'surface ratchets'; the middle range 'Modulateds' are characterized by frequency modulation; they include a majority of differentiated calls: waves, oos, ees, whos, wos, foos, yuos, mups, and ups, and are associated with particularly rapid frequency change. The 'Highs' embrace cries and chirps.

[16] Deacon, *The Human Brain*, 133.

[17] Lois King Winn and Howard E. Winn, *Wings in the Sea: The Humpback Whale* (University Press of New England for University of Rhode Island, 1985), 92.

Sonograms show 'themes' of up to twenty-five seconds' duration, with individual sounds ranging in duration from one to as much as five seconds.[18] Katy Payne is quoted as having observed that, in the Bermuda area, songs change from year to year.

The Humpback has no vocal chords, and song production must depend on valves, sacs, and muscles in the larynx. Interestingly, the Tongans of Polynesia claim that Humpbacks *talk*, not sing; and one can see from the Winns' sonograms why they take that view. It is to be emphasized, however, that these sonograms are at relatively low magnification and corresponding resolution. We prefer to regard them as music.

A Humpback Whale's song of twenty minutes' duration is a little longer perhaps than certain Brandenburg *Concerti*. In terms of total acoustic complexity, as opposed to musical grammar and style, there may be little difference in degree between them. Human attention is unaware of the complexity of whale sounds, just as it is unaware of the sound-spectral complexity of musical sounds in general, to be ignored in listening. What is perceived as *musical structure* (by a Western, musical, human listener to Bach) is indeed lacking in the whale's song. A more serious lack, from our point of view, stems from the fact that the whale's musical gestures, though disturbing, are not as 'meaningful' to humans as presumably they are to whales.

'Meaningfulness', of an absolute kind, undoubtedly exists for us in our own vocal and musical world, but is not to be equated with semantic meaning. Music is rather a paradigm of a culture in a historical context; a complex signal, gratifying to the hearer for cultural reasons. Its order may tempt us to think of it as para-linguistic; we refer to its temporal segments as 'phrases', as if indeed it were speech. It is not. It has none of the attributes of speech; its 'grammar' and 'syntax' are not those of a language, even though in some senses and to some extent analogous thereto. Nevertheless, the fact that we tend to use such terms, if only figuratively, might already suggest to us that, in the creation of music, our primal, Primate call is undergoing a restructuring that involves not just the anterior limbic cortex, and the region of synaptic relay in the midbrain, but also the cortex of the left hemisphere, responsible for language.[19]

[18] Ibid. 100, 101. [19] Deacon, *The Human Brain*, 133.

'Meaningful Melodies' in Mother-to-Infant Speech

There is now the best possible evidence that human vocal gestures exist that are musical universals, worldwide in their significance, irrespective of the language group of those who use them. As recorded by Anne Fernald and her co-workers,[20] Darwin recorded that his son of less than a year 'understood intonation and gestures';[21] and it was Ferguson who first remarked that adults speak to infants in a special way: syntax is simplified, and both phonological and lexical modifications are made in their speech.[22] The elevation of pitch, and the exaggerations in intonation, to which Ferguson drew attention have been observed across cultures: English, Spanish, Arabic, Comanche, Gilyak, and Marathi; Anne Fernald and her co-workers have extended the list to Japanese.[23]

Very precisely Fernald writes of 'meaningful melodies' in mothers' speech directed to infants of 12 months; 'very precisely' since the prosodic modifications show a higher fundamental frequency generated by the larynx: higher minima and maxima, greater variability; utterances are shorter, pauses longer. The 'melodies' relate to the categories of Attention, Approval, Prohibition, and Comfort. Fernald's frequency contours reveal surprising similarity in all languages, within each category, with rising contours to attract attention; bell-shaped contours to maintain attention; and falling (rather than rising) contours to comfort. This is indeed song: the fundamental frequency of phonation generated by the larynx is varied systematically. Song is nothing else.

In the light of these observations, it is the case that in humans, and between mother and pre-speech infant, there exist universally comprehensible music gestures, structured vocal utterances, that have meaning in the sense of conveying behaviour-modifying information. Again it is to be emphasized that these are melodies of but a second-or-so's duration (as judged from the length of the accompanying spoken texts in Fernald's diagrams).

[20] Anne Fernald, 'Meaningful Melodies in Mothers' Speech to Infants', in Uwe Jürgens and Mechthild Papousek (eds.), *Non-Verbal Vocal Communication: Comparative and Developmental Approaches* (Cambridge: Cambridge University Press, 1992), 262–82.

[21] Charles Darwin, 'A Biographical Sketch of an Infant', *Mind*, 2 (1877), 286–94.

[22] Charles Ferguson, 'Baby Talk in Six Languages', *American Anthropologist*, 66 (1962), 103–14.

[23] Fernald, 'Meaningful Melodies', 262–82.

The amplification of duration by a thousand times or more, in the organization of macro-musical forms, does not change the essential character of a musical utterance. In the axial direction of Time's Arrow—the direction in which, in a sonogram, the distribution of changing frequencies of vibration of the resonant medium extends—there is again a parallel between smaller-scale and larger-scale utterance. In speech, in phonation, the supra-laryngeal vocal tract filters the acoustic energy of the fundamental frequency, generated by the vibration of the larynx, and its higher harmonics. These filtered sounds are the unambiguous sonic elements that make possible the high rate of transmission of human speech; their essential feature is the formant-frequency pattern, a complex pattern of harmonics, changing in intensity and frequency, over time.[24] The duration of these individual patterns in speech is, of course, of the order of milliseconds, as compared with the maternal 'melodies' that last a second or so, in adult speech with infants; nevertheless, in recognizing a vowel in speech we are again identifying a sound that extends in time, a sound with a changing structure in both frequency and intensity—a 'chordal structure' on an infinitely small scale, a musical element.

What might be the fundamental difference between the song of the Humpback Whale and a Brandenburg *Concerto*, if we are now satisfied that the former, like other animal vocalizations, is music? It is, perhaps, a matter of the degree of organization of human sound-producing resources, imposed by the cerebral cortex of the left hemisphere: that cortical region, the actions of which seem to have been progressively extended and amplified in the evolutionary processes of language acquisition. Perhaps also primary gestures of pitch-inflection (of the same kind as those used in mother-and-infant melodies), used symbolically in adulthood, retain their capacity to generate states of mood, rather than control actions on the part of the listener. Furthermore, such gestures may acquire a symbolic life of their own, permitting display of private dramas, reflections of the emotional, non-verbal life of the composer.

The activity of the cerebral cortex would seem to be revealed by the frequency with which 'sophisticated' parts of the fabric of a musical structure may be inaudible in performance, so that the ingenuity of the builder is only evident in silent reading of the structure, as reflected in notation on the printed page.

[24] Philip Lieberman, 'Human Speech and Language', *The Cambridge Encyclopedia of Human Evolution* (Cambridge: Cambridge University Press, 1992), 134.

Recently Alexander Goehr suggested that unrestrained, aesthetic creativity, in such a work as Schoenberg's *Fourth String Quartet*, is revealed in relatively brief, episodic interludes, without evident contrapuntal, combinatorial justification.[25] Even in J. S. Bach's *Das wohltemperirte Clavier*, it is not difficult to find fugues (for example: Book I, *Fuga* viii, E♭ minor) where emotional release, provoked by episodic creativity, outweighs the satisfaction of *stretti*, of combinations of *recto* and *verso*, or the surprising use of augmentation, however well contrived. Or, as a more mature instance, in the 15th *Contrapunctus* of the *Kunst der Fuge*, three episodic bars (224–6) between the end of a *verso*- and the beginning of a *recto*-statement of the BACH subject. Head against heart; heart against head, perhaps.

Returning for a moment to Fernald's summary of her work on 'meaningful melodies' in the speech of mothers with pre-speech infants: 'Through this early experience of sharing feelings and intentions by means of prosody, speech first becomes meaningful to the infant... babies are learning "how to mean", when they express their desires and intention through intonation and gesture, before they express them through language.' The child in us continues to do so in music.

Thus far, non-verbal vocalizations have been considered only from the standpoint of *human* communication, as if their significance were entirely concentrated in the behaviour of the recipient. It is evident, however, as set out by Hartshorne,[26] that in animal utterances also, the emergence of rhythmic patterning, in calls ('song' as we understand it) is manifest, if only incipiently. He describes, for example, a frog varying the number of croaks in a 'stanza' and the length of pauses between. Apart from the mammalian order that includes the whales (*Cetacea*), 'birds are by far the closest of all creatures to man in their interest in sound patterns and skill in their production'.

Avian Music

It has, of course, been strenuously denied, and would still be denied by many, that birdsong is 'music'. Recently, Juri

[25] Alexander Goehr, in a Public Lecture on Schoenberg's *Fourth String Quartet*, given in the Concert Hall of the University Music School, University of Cambridge, with illustrations by the Endellion Quartet, 1994.

[26] Charles Hartshorne, *Born to Sing: An Interpretation and World Survey of Bird Song* (Bloomington, Ind.: Indiana University Press, 1973; Midland Book Edition, 1992).

Cholopow, in a valuable digest of the theories of Alexei F. Lossew[27] examined, in particular, his essay: 'Music as Object of Logic' (*Die Musik als Gegenstand der Logik*) (1927). Lossew is to be given credit for recognizing the all-importance of 'time', as a significant attribute of music, when he defines music as 'the structure of numbers in the flux of time' (*Die Zahlenstruktur im Zeitstrom—das ist die Musik*). In his essay, however, he takes opportunity to state: 'Accordingly, the song of the Nightingale, which so refreshes us, is no music; in this statement in sound, the Reason of Art is missing, that is to say, the essence of human Number' [that is, the essence of Number as employed by human beings, in the analytical description of the physical world] (*Darum ist aber der Gesang der Nachtigal, der uns erquickt, keine Musik; in diese Klangäusserung fehlt die Kunst-Vernunft, d.h. das Wesen der menschlichen Zahl*).

A major contribution to this discussion of the status of birdsong in relation to music was made by David Hindley (musician and composer), who, in the light of transcriptions from recordings (see p. 15), has shown that the fact that the music of the Nightingale's song moves at a speed beyond the capacity of humans to count, does not make it any less music.[28] Sixty-eight seconds of the Nightingale's song, slowed down by a factor of 4 (in a transcription by Hindley), become a 'modified strophic song' of 4.5 minutes' duration. A Skylark (*Alauda arvensis*), pouring out notes at the rate of 200 per second—discrete, pitched notes, in *staccato* delivery—sings, in fifty seconds, the equivalent of a through-composed work, in Western note values, of thirteen minutes' duration: thirteen minutes of *coherent, through-composed music*.

As we see, and will see again in greater detail later, the time scale (in which numerical attributes of frequency and amplitude are expressed in such 'music'—the fine-structure of music in time) is infinitely smaller than that of the slow-moving units of duration, of 'phrases', of 'notes' even, in which humans perceive musical performance. Birdsong *is* song, and at a yet higher degree of resolution it would necessarily exhibit the essential attributes of Lossew's definition. As Hindley points out: 'whereas the Blackbird's song has strophes of fairly contrasted and dislocated material, the strophes of the Woodlark's song have a consistent texture, each one derived out of a unique opening motif.' As Schumann might have said: *Der Musiker spricht!*—both of the bird and of the human musician who champions it.

[27] Juri Cholopow, 'Über die Philosophie der Musik von A. F. Lossew', *Acta Musicologica*, 66 (1994), 31–40.

[28] David Hindley, 'The Music of Birdsong', *Wildlife Sound*, 6 (1990), 25–33.

What frequently arrests attention, in human listeners to birdsong, is the 'purity' of notes, and the harmonious relationship between pitches, even though phrases may last no more than 2–5 seconds. Repetition with pauses may yield a song of fifteen or more notes 'with many distinct pitch intervals'. The ability to transpose is widely distributed; key may change; interval inversion occurs; harmonic relationships between pitches are evident: thirds, fourths, fifths, octaves; such devices as accelerando, ritardando, crescendo, diminuendo, are manifest, as well as techniques of theme and variations: all of these have been observed and recorded. Moreover, birds have been observed 'playing at sound-making' by dropping objects from the beak, or pushing them off the top of a house or off a desk-top. The birds so engaged show signs of 'listening' for the resultant impact.[29]

Human and Avian Musics

Birds sing when there is no evident stimulus to their so doing; when the bird is 'relaxed', 'free', or 'satiated'. These are conditions under which humans, too, frequently turn to the arts. That birds 'appreciate' song is suggested by the fact that one bird will imitate the song of another. That many birds create their song by a long-sustained process of improvisation, selective repetition, and reshaping of components has been known for many years. During this process, elements from neighbours of the same species, or from quite different species, may be incorporated, retained, or discarded after a while, as if the song, as a composition, were constantly under review and revision.

There is good reason, moreover, to suppose that the song of songbirds has also developed from a primary system of vocalization, dependent on regions of motor synaptic relay in the midbrain, coupled with accessory evolution of the *corpora striata* (the floor of the original, primitive forebrain of the vertebrates). This evolution is perhaps comparable with that of the cerebral cortex in mammals; it may be functionally responsible for the development of motor control of the syrinx (the distinctive sound-generating organ, unique to the birds); this in turn may be comparable with controls developed in humans, in relation to speech and language. (There is no evidence of *structural* asymmetry in the brain of songbirds, comparable with hemisphere-differentiation in

[29] Hartshorne, *Born to Sing*.

humans, apart from one minor feature of the brain-stem, but there may well be bilateral asymmetry in function.)

Surely, in the context of birdsong and music, one of the most remarkable ethnomusicological studies of all time is Steven Feld's *Sound and Sentiment.*[30] He presents sound as a cultural system in a society; a system of symbols of the Kaluli people of the four-membered Bosavi-group in Papua New Guinea. In general biological terms, however, it is much more than that. The focus of Feld's personal interest is the musical elaboration of human acts of lamentation, based on the calls of a bird; here, however, what engages our attention is the very fact of interaction between human being and bird. We learn from Feld what is offered, in bird calls, to listeners; and the relationship of that which is offered to musical forms of lamentation in a particular society. We come to see relationships with musical gesture elsewhere, and indeed to forms of lamentation elsewhere in other human societies.

It is one of the major problems now facing research, both in the humanities and in the sciences, that observations made, and recorded, by a previous generation are not readily available to researchers of a later generation. It is for that reason no criticism of Feld to mention that he seems not to have known of the first detailed examination of bird-song by Péter Szöke (observations made possible by slowing-down recorded tapes in playback, 16, and even 32, times); or Szöke's suggestion that humankind may have learned to sing from birds, precisely because, while the *syrinx* lends itself to the sequential generation of pitches in harmonic relationship, the *larynx* and the supra-laryngeal vocal tract of man, do not.[31]

Szöke states: 'only by tightening or slackening their vibrating vocal cords can human-beings change the pitch of their voices. This possibility is not regulated by any law that might give rise to something like a scale, such as the Law of the Harmonic Series which, on the whistle-principle, regulates note-production in birds.' He continues: 'Nevertheless, in all parts of the world, humans sing in systems of musical notes regulated by laws.' He adds that 'the elementary intervals of human melody coincide with the elementary intervals of avian melody'. In regard to birds he concludes that: 'The Law of the Harmonic Series

[30] Steven Feld, *Sound and Sentiment: Birds, Weeping, Poetics, and Song in Kaluli Expression* (Philadelphia: University of Pennsylvania Press, 1982, 1990).

[31] Péter Szöke, 'Zur Entstehung und Entwicklungs-Geschichte der Musik', *Studia Musicologica Akademiae Scientiarum Hungaricae*, 2 (1962), 33–85.

was the physico-acoustical pre-condition, for the inner physiological, and entire biological, development of birdsong.'[32]

In this same paper he had already transcribed, in full, a recording of the song of the Meadowlark/*Heidelerche* (*Lullula arborea*), marking passages that exhibit transposition of motifs by a fifth, a fourth, and a major second; and he drew attention to quasi-'pentatonic' motifs, consisting of major-second+minor-third tetrachords, with a note or notes added above, and/or below. These first observations on the existence of quasi-pentatonic motifs in birdsong were of course at speeds beyond the powers of human ears to perceive in song at normal speed. In this same paper, and at this relatively low-level of acoustic resolution, he commented on the ability of a bird to sing at a speed of 100 to 130 notes per second.

Other studies[33] have shown that birds are capable, in the course of developing their song, of transposing harmonics down, out of their position in the natural series, so that they become available in a lower octave; and that many birds—like the *muni* of the Kaluli—are making use of entire pentatonic note-sets, or smaller sets based on the same type of tetrachord.

Wept-Song Lamentation of Kaluli Women

Kaluli believe 'that birds are... "spirit reflections" of their dead'; 'their calls are vocal communications' from such 'spirit reflections'. Furthermore, a 'melodic, sung-texted weeping' by women is based on one phase of the song of a particular bird, *muni*: the Beautiful Fruitdove (*Ptilinopus pulchellus*). A group of species of this genus produce both 'high, human falsetto-like' and 'melodically descending sounds'. The first phase of the birdsong is described as a shriek; the second, as a sequence of distinct, descending pitches, represented as successive steps of tone, minor third, and tone. A tetrachord of this structure provides the entire musical material for laments, both by women and by men. While men, when asked about its character, respond with a naturalistic imitation of the first call: the *vibrato*-shriek; in response to a question about the second, they spontaneously sing the

32 Szöke, 'Zur Entstehung und Entwicklungs-Geschichte der Musik', 72, 73, 71.

33 Joan Hall-Craggs, Subdepartment of Animal Behaviour, Madingley, Cambridge, UK, private communication.

second phase in sustained notes, as set out by Feld, in minim values. (That doves should be involved in this human/bird musical relationship is highly reasonable,[34] inasmuch as the songs of doves commonly consist of relatively few notes, sung at speeds such that humans can readily imitate them.)

The structure of women's wept-song lamentation among the Kaluli shows verbal and musical creativity in the handling of the lower note of the minor third in descent. Verbalization tends to occur uniquely on this note, leaving the remaining three notes of the tetrachord as sustained minims; the first note of the three is stressed; and all three notes are sung (without verbalization) to the vowel [e]. The intimate, disciplined mixture of controlled weeping, and phonation of musical pitches, is surely compatible with the association, previously suggested, of music with the non-verbal vocal communication system. It is perhaps not without significance that the creative generation of text here in *women's song* is monotone in projection: a minimal intervention of speech pathways into emotional channels.

What strikes a biologist in this situation is: first, the overt recognition by the Kaluli of the source of this, their music for a major ritual of lamentation, in the song of a specific genus of bird; secondly, the intimate admixture of weeping and singing in the lamentation by women; thirdly, the choice of a descending musical phrase to carry the burden of grief—a choice encountered elsewhere in the construction of laments; and, lastly, the parallels between the responses to lamentation among this people and those recorded among other peoples in other contexts. The Kaluli exhibit to us, acted out, what Szöke proposed: humans imitating the song of a bird, and basing their most characteristic ritual music on the song of one particular bird.

In the lament tradition of Hungary (unknown to folklorists until accidentally discovered by Kodály in 1918, and subsequently shown to exist throughout Hungary[35]) it was found that all improvised laments, whether shorter or longer forms, invariably descend to the final. Fifteen per cent of all laments exhibit descending lines only; a majority, however, consist of descending lines + arched phrases + monotone recitative, but always with overall descent to the final. Weeping occurs as an

[34] Ibid.

[35] Lajos Kiss and Benjamin Rajeczky, trans. Imre Gombos, *Collection of Hungarian Folk Music/A Magyar Népzene Tara, V. Laments/Siratók* (Budapest: Akadémiai Kiadó, 1966), 118.

integral part of Hungarian lamentation,[36] and the described response of singers to playback of their own laments strikingly resembles that of the Kaluli.

From Feld's account it is evident that singers, as well as members of the original audience, derive satisfaction from listening to their own performance on playback. This was precisely the experience of the Hungarians, and that of Lucy Durán in Western Crete.[37] Indeed, the latter found that women could readily be brought to repeat their laments (for them to be recorded), in a group situation, if the fieldworker first spoke of bereavement, and while so doing began to weep.

It is suggested here that the process of lamentation brings its own satisfaction, its own purging, cathartic 'comfort'; and it may not be inappropriate to remember the comforting attribute of the falling, mother-to-infant, 'meaningful melodies', in the widely cross-cultural experiments of Fernald. The collective release (experienced by the people of the Kaluli longhouse) is surely that component which is life-sustaining and essential to the society, rather than the ceremonial confrontation with death and separation, though these too are both explicit and important. Who has not experienced the consoling, refreshing release, and renewal, of a good wake?

Rhythms of Song and of Dance and the Maternal Heartbeat

A further link with avian culture (among the Kaluli) is present in the dance of the male singer of a lament of the *gisaló*-kind, which is restricted to performance in the dark, in spirit-medium seances and funerary ceremonies. In this lament, all pitches of the *muni*-bird call become word-bearing. Here the bird overtly imitated in the dance is the Giant Cuckoodove *Reinwardtoena reinwardtsi*. This is the bird that itself '*dances gisaló*'. The bird bobs up and down; and the dancer too, pacing the central aisle of the longhouse from end-to-end, performs such a movement, bending at the knees, so that the mussel shells of the rattle attached to his waist touch and brush the floor as he

[36] Kiss and Rajeczky, *Collection of Hungarian Folk Music*, 118.

[37] Lucy Durán, Centre for Music Studies, School of Oriental and African Studies, University of London, UK, private communication.

progresses. The rattle provides a regular pulse at a frequency of 125 to the minute, the duration of the crotchet in Feld's transcriptions. This is about twice the resting frequency (60 per minute) of the heartbeat of an athlete. Athletic, the *gisaló*-dancer must surely be; and the numerical relationship between dance step and heartbeat is perhaps no coincidence.

It is the case, of course, that before birth the human infant is experiencing the pulse, varying in frequency, of the mother's heartbeat. Certainly, the auditory apparatus of the foetus is fully functional by the beginning of the ninth month of pregnancy; indeed, even seventh-month, extra-uterine foetuses respond, by movement, to a loud noise. Moreover, there can be no doubt that the foetus responds to changes in the maternal heartbeat rate. Whether it can distinguish between frequency increase due to climbing stairs, and that due to emotional disturbance, is not certain, but is very probable.[38] Before birth, therefore, an infant is aware that the rhythmic sound of the heartbeat may vary in frequency. It may also be aware that such changes are correlated with changes in internal physiological conditions that may be either soothing, or alarming. It is possible, therefore, that the maternal heartbeat supplies a standard of rhythmic frequency that is basic in all human musical utterance, and to all human musical experience.

If this is so, the same may be true for vertebrates in general. Meijler and others have shown that the averaged heart rate in two Humpback Whales was 'on the order of 30 to 35 beats/min'.[39] This means that the frequency is of the same order (that is, within a factor of 10) as that of adult humans. Perhaps this determines the fact that its song moves in time in 'meaningful' sound units perceptible as such by human, as well as by other, mammalian ears. The intra-uterine whale foetus may acquire an ingrained notion of a serial pulse from its mother's heartbeat; and it may be for the reason that our pulse frequency is of the same order that we perceive the Humpback's 'song' as 'music'.

That time—for birds (and for songbirds in particular)—flows at an altogether different pace than for humans has been known for many

[38] Information from Dr Abbie Fowden, Physiological Laboratory, University of Cambridge, 1994.

[39] F. L. Meijler, F. H. M. Wittkampf, K. R. Brennen, Verne Baker, Claes Wassenaar, and Earl E. Bakken, 'Electrocardiogram of the Humpback Whale (*Megaptera novaeangliae*), with Specific Reference to Atrioventricular Transmission and Ventricular Excitation', *Journal of the American College of Cardiology*, 20 (1992), 475–9. We are indebted to Mr Greg Donovan of the International Whaling Commission for finding this reference and supplying a xerox copy.

years. We are incapable of discriminating sounds shorter than 1/20th of a second, while birds can separate sounds of two-hundredths of a second's duration. R. J. Pumphrey commented that 'temporal discrimination in birds is probably ten times more acute than in humans',[40] and C. H. Greenewalt suggested that the factor may well be 50–100 times.[41]

Number and Music

Gelman and Brenneman have provided evidence that 'infants attend selectively to some fundamental aspects of number and music'.[42] They suggest 'the presence of innate, skeletal principles' in both domains, principles inherent in 'the structure of the information-processing mechanism'. Their coupling of the domains of number and of music chimes strikingly with the philosophical insights of Alexei Lossew and the latter author's definition of music as number structure in the flux of time. As evidence for the 'existence of a skeleton of nonverbal counting' in infants, they cite the fact that infants exhibit preference for 'one of a pair of slides that depicts the number of household objects *matching the number of drumbeats they hear*' (emphasis added). Here surely we are offered unmistakeable evidence that the domain of number is indeed linked with that of music, for the drumbeat is quite as much music as is a pitch sequence. It is apparent, however, that Gelman and Brenneman do not recognize the possibility of a music of pure percussion.[43]

We may perhaps also have been offered here the first evidence of the significance of the maternal heartbeat rhythm in furnishing a skeletal basis for the temporal framework of music. The heartbeat supplies an experience of sequence, with implications both for time/rhythm, and

[40] R. J. Pumphrey, 'Sensory Organs: Hearing', in A. J. Marshall, *Biology and Comparative Physiology of Birds* (London: Academic Press, 1961), ii. 69–86.

[41] C. H. Greenewalt, *Bird Song: Acoustics and Physiology* (Washington DC: Smithsonian Institution Press, 1968), 142.

[42] Gelman and Brenneman, 'First Principles', 369.

[43] They also reject the view that 'meaningful melodies in mothers' speech' are music, on the grounds that 'music is based on contours provided by the relationship between discrete notes', and infant-directed 'parent-ese' is characterized more by glissandi. Their hesitant 'more' is suggestive; were the distinction absolute, music would cease to be music whenever a singer executed a *portamento*. It is a matter (yet again) of time scale, and the effect of time scale on perception.

for the sequential enumeration of objects. Furthermore, the heartbeat establishes a pattern for all future experience of rhythm; indeed it is the child's first music and the child's first clock. In that experience is learned the possibility of variation in time's pulse, as well as the correlation of various affective states with such variation. Again, already in the womb, a paradigm of all *process* will have been established through the phenomenon of heartbeat. Nor must it be forgotten that the graded, frequency-sensitivity scale of the cochlea may be looked upon as furnishing a perceptual number series in frequency terms, on which inborn, intervallic gradations may already have begun to be registered.

'The beat'—that all-important component of popular music worldwide—is assuredly far more important than any melodic aspect, if popular music is to afford satisfaction to its listeners. Notwithstanding the fact that 60 per cent and more of the energy output of any mixed, instrumental ensemble comes from the percussion, it is evident to an observer that, when adjusting levels of amplification prior to a 'rave', what is important to the sound engineers is not amplification of melodic resources, but amplification of the heaviest items in the percussion battery. What is important (it is suggested) is this reflection (reminiscence, perhaps) of the maternal heartbeat. At a distance of, say, 250 to 500 metres, any melody line will be inaudible; only the percussion bass reaches the ear; and *that* is evidently the essential aspect of the music. Increase, not merely in intensity, but above all in frequency, of a drum beat can bring a crowd to a state of frenzied hysteria; DJs are aware that a beat frequency exists which may not safely be exceeded. Perhaps the use of chest-drumming by the Great Apes reflects *their* intra-uterine experience.

Mediational Ritual Role of Players and their Instruments

The relationships between man and animals in *Yurupary*—a secret men's cult of Northwestern Amazonia, examined by Stephen Hugh-Jones[44]—differ from such as Feld established in Papua New Guinea. A major difference is that avian, mammalian, and reptilian vocalizations and other natural sounds, such as thunder,

[44] Stephen Hugh-Jones, *The Palm and the Pleiades* (Cambridge: Cambridge University Press, 1979).

are simulated by means of 'sacred flutes and trumpets'. (The term 'Yurupary' itself conveniently covers 'sacred flutes and trumpets taboo to women'). Both sets of instruments are regarded as the living dead, and also as 'pets', since they are seen as animals, coming from the forest to live in the house. The 'trumpets' (in fact, megaphones = voice-disguisers) are used to amplify vocalizations of low pitch, equated with the sounds of jaguar and thunder, for example. The flutes are equated with birdsong, and are made from a tree that grows only in swamps, and itself could be said to mediate between sky, water, and earth, so that the flutes also are mediators: between water, earth, and sky.

A prime concept is that of *He* (open [e] as in 'hen'), a state of being, prior to, and now parallel with, human existence; a man–animal condition, from which the human emerges. At birth, humans leave the *He*; at death they return thereto.

Initiation of adolescents takes place in two stages, separated by a gap in time. The first extended ceremony: Fruit House, is an attenuated imitation of the second: *He* House. To a degree, this ritual retraces steps in the development of proto-humans to humans. The trumpets and flutes, despite their being man-made, are uniquely associated with the initiation ceremony of *He* House, and are themselves mediators, to be identified with shamans, jaguars, anacondas, and so on.

The absence of detailed information regarding musical aspects of the rites described prevents discussion in terms such as were possible in the case of Feld's studies. It is apparent, however, that certain vertebrate (non-human) and human (shaman) vocalizations are being used as the most secret (in the sense of most highly taboo) aspects of major rites of initiation. The use of an accelerando scalar descent, from long sustained notes to notes of minimal brevity, at the mid-afternoon playing of long flutes in the Fruit House ceremony, reminds one of the falling melodic character throughout the bird-based vocal music of the Kaluli; and (more generally) of the appeasing, comforting effect of such vocal gestures—on a very different time scale—in mother-to-infant 'meaningful melodies'.

Notwithstanding the implications of mortality, both in Fruit House and *He* House ceremonies, the overall impact on the condition of the community remains that of soothing, of confirming bonds, of regulating relationships between different age groups, of collective celebration of that which sets it apart from all other communities, something infinitely calming and reassuring. As noted by Hugh-Jones, the rate of change of groups of performers playing instruments is notably high, with three or four changes during the afternoon. This again suggests recognition by the society of the mediational role of the *players*, as well as that of the instruments played. Something of the spiritual rubs off on to those who manipulate the instrumental vehicles of spirit voices. 'Myth may exhibit order in thought, but it is through ritual that this order is manipulated to produce order in action and in society at large.'[45]

Limitations of Emic Description

The endeavour to envisage any aspect of a given culture in emic terms (in terms employed by bearers of the same culture) is both laudable and justified, to the extent that it enriches our perception of the value, to that community, of the particular cultural trait in question. Nevertheless, it is always important, for the understanding of a given cultural phenomenon, to have the benefit of observations made by those who stand outside the culture. Both in the instance of the Kaluli people, and of the Yurupary rites, we see that the purpose of the rites, both that which is overt to the enactors, and that which is symbolic, does not exhaust the significance of the rites in either culture. The general, tangential benefit to the communities is not spelled out in the emic description.

Reading ethnomusicological writings of the last decade, a biologist is at times saddened to witness the attempt to comprehend, and give definitive, all-embracing description, to complex ritual processes. Our minds are not equipped so to do; our most useful intellectual attribute is that of analytical discrimination. Comprehensive description, whether diachronic or synchronic, eludes us. The modern abusive use of the term 'reductionist' is symptomatic of the age. At times it seems to be used almost as if any analytical approach to any aspect of culture is to be regarded as 'racist'.

We need to be on guard against being frightened by the threat of appearing to be 'reductionist'. It is not the case that the analytical cast of mind is peculiar to the West, and therefore to be rejected in pursuit of a 'non-racist' approach. Those who would so argue forget, or ignore, the contribution of the Muslim–Arabic world, or the South Asian world, or the East Asian world, to mathematics, to analytical thought; forget the

[45] Hugh-Jones, *The Palm and the Pleiades*, 260.

remains of the giant astronomical observatories in Central Asia at Maragah (thirteenth century) and Samarqand (fifteenth century), in China (thirteenth century), in Korea (seventh century). All these bear witness to a zeal for 'reductionist', analytical, astronomical, and calendrical enquiry quite as strong as that of the West.

The values of the emic approach in assessing the significance of cultural traits are positive; but it should never be supposed that the etic (seen from the outside) analytical approach is to be dismissed. Let it be repeated: we have no other means of intelligent enquiry. To know the 'meaning' is not necessarily to 'understand'. The insights of Jakobson and Lévi-Strauss that led to a view of all aspects of a culture as a multidimensional grid were insights of genius; but it is necessary to remember that the structuralist grid is a construct of the observer; it is not a structure defined in emic terms by the society itself.

The Role of Music in Ritual

Perhaps the most moving accounts of societies and their musics come from opposite ends of the world: Feld in the rain forest of Papua New Guinea, and Anthony Seeger in the rain forest of Central Brazil.[46] Surely much of the appeal of these accounts is due, first, to the fact that both authors are highly musical; secondly, that both authors (and in Anthony Seeger's case his wife as well) lived with their hosts as participant members of the respective societies—the Kaluli in Feld's case, the Suyá in that of the Seegers.

The descriptions of extended rituals, given by both, are deeply moving, in particular the ending of the Mouse Ceremony of the Suyá, wherein (as Seeger states) in full darkness—as in the longhouse of the Kaluli, where men lament as birds—boy-initiates ('mice') become combinations of mice and men. The Suyá ceremony ends with each of the mice/men being 'wounded' by an arrow-thrust from a sister, through the woven crowns of their capes. The sisters then strip the capes from the dead mice/living men, and rinse the wearers with gourdsfull of cold water, before all the men, both old and 'new', bathe in the tepid river. After fourteen days of musical ceremony, and fifteen hours of singing on the final day, the ceremony of boy-initiation is completed; and, in the

[46] Anthony Seeger, *Why Suyá Sing: A Musical Anthropology of an Amazonian People* (Cambridge: Cambridge University Press, 1987).

regret of the chief ritualist—that it is indeed over—one glimpses, perhaps, the real 'meaning' of the ceremony for the community at large. It is: the bringing of a community to a physiological state that is far more than the mere termination of a process of verbalization.

What impresses here, as in Feld's account of lamentation and of a spirit-medium seance, is the sense of the engagement of an entire community and the role, in that engagement, of music as a means of extending the time dimensions of ceremony. In many respects, the basic musical materials of both societies are structurally similar. Their source in both types of society is overtly animal, but most explicitly—and indeed audibly—from a particular bird, among the Kaluli. Among the Suyá, music (through this extended period of time) is said to have 'helped express and create the euphoria that should characterise Suyá ceremonies'.[47]

Even though, in Kaluli ceremonies, the capacity to induce weeping seems to be the yardstick by which to measure the quality of a singer, it is plain from Feld's account that both lamentation and spirit-medium seance have other functions than the mere expression of grief. They are clearly cathartic, in the ancient sense; but they are also major ceremonies that serve to integrate their society; the esteemed singers are performers, quite as much as were actors in a Greek tragedy. The singers are aware of what they do in manipulating the feelings of members of the audience, and they are self-congratulatory in their estimate of their own success. In this there is similarity again with the attitudes of singers of laments in the Hungarian tradition, already described, as also in that of Western Crete.[48]

Were the *texts* of songs of the Kaluli and of the Suyá merely spoken, they would be recited complete in a matter of minutes. Even so, these texts themselves are surcharged with verbal redundancy; and that redundancy seems to be present in order to make possible the almost indefinite extension of meaningful, musical gestures in time. The use of song, as a bearer of text in words, makes possible the creation of an extended performance. This structure, however, is a structure in *the other voice*; not in the voice of speech, but in the voice of tears themselves.

Even a society such as that of the West, in part long divorced from cohesive, community binding ceremonies, hears and listens to this voice. We no longer have ceremonies in which the mythic structure of the immediate world, as well as that of the cosmos, is rehearsed and

[47] Ibid. 127. [48] Durán, private communication, 1994.

reimplanted. We have a framework of natural science that relieves us both of the need for mythic explanation, and of the consequent need for ritual enactment of the substance of myth; but, as Ruth Finnegan demonstrates, for those who participate in the creation (in any sense) of music, that act still engenders the catharsis of ritual.[49]

That which would begin to make sense of 'ethnomusicology' as a scientific discipline is a primary recognition and acceptance of the 'otherness' of music, as compared with language. Wordless song is capable of evoking, in us, an entire gamut of changes in mood, as in the birds, and probably in the Humpback Whales also. The weeping-inducing songs (of the Kaluli) exploit, in extended sequence, the weeping, falling gestures of the *muni*-bird; but we know from our earliest childhood that such pitch descents are fundamentally soothing and comforting.

Rituals are to be seen (in value terms) precisely as leading to a sort of purgation—using this term in a generalized way to designate the final physical and mental condition of the participants. Anthony Seeger came close to expressing this in his use of the word 'euphoria' to describe the end-condition. 'Well-being' is perhaps a better word, however, since 'euphoria' commonly carries with it an implication of 'over confidence' or 'over optimism', not applicable to the condition of the community at the close of ceremonies such as those here described.

The widely differing scenarios of myths, and of the rituals to which they give rise, are irrelevant from that standpoint; they are 'accidents'—almost in terms of scholastic theology. The reality, the 'substance', is quite other. By all means let rituals be recorded: the poesis of ritual is indeed a legitimate object of study and record; but its detail is irrelevant to the achievement of a particular, resultant, physiological state.

The role of music in such processes is twofold: (1) it greatly extends the duration of the process as compared with the time that would be occupied were a simple spoken recitation of the mythical content of the ritual to replace its musical presentation; (2) of itself, and in its use of universally meaningful sound gestures (with meaning already learned by the infant), music progressively induces the desired, essential, ultimate, physiological condition; and it does this, independently of any language content, through the physical work of dance, and through the by-no-means inconsiderable physical labour of singing.

To adopt the posture that all musics are so different—because of the difference in their ethnological, and detailed ritual, mythic contexts—

[49] Finnegan, *The Hidden Musicians.*

that no comparison between musics is legitimate is unsound. Of course, it is the case that rituals of all kinds enhance the stability of, and facilitate communal, structural renewal of, societies organized in a multiplicity of different ways; but those who describe ceremonies hardly ever seem to perceive the real outcome of ritual (in physiological and psychological terms); or to recognize that that final condition, and its achievement, is the purpose of ritual. It is because of this that the most tragic and grief-fraught occasions end in profound comfort and corporate renewal.

In his introduction to that remarkable study *Zen Training* (by the Zen Master, Katsuki Sekida), the zoologist A. V. Grimstone, who edited the text, refers to Sekida's 'writing of the physiology of zazen'.[50] (The term 'zazen' is the Sino-Japanese reading of Chinese *zuochan*: literally 'sitting meditation'). He continues: 'to describe a phenomenon in scientific terms is not necessarily to diminish it. The grandeur of the Alps is not reduced by giving an account of their geology; the two are separate, and can co-exist . . . I believe it would be possible . . . to mount a convincing refutation of the argument that the discovery of a physiological correlative of, say, the state of *samādhi* necessarily diminishes the value of that state.'[51] We would urge the same in putting forward the essentially physiological quality of the consummation of ritual.

There exists, however, an even closer parallel between the achievement of *samādhi* ['the condition of total stillness . . . "body and mind fallen off" ']52 and the climax of ritual. Both pupil and master approach that condition through a species of bodily 'music' in which, first, the breathing frequency begins to be actively controlled; a controlled rhythm of intake of breath and exhalation is established. Secondly, this is linked with counting of the breaths, breathing with the lips parted—that is, making a breathing sound—and either saying '*Mu*' (= non-existing), or slowly counting.[53] That is to say, the subject is vocalizing. A rhythm of controlled breathing has been established, a rhythm of sound generation (however minimal) has been added, and the pulse rate will be falling. Of course, this occurs on a very different time-scale from the Mouse Ritual of the Suyá; but it is nevertheless a ritual, with its own concomitant 'dance' and 'music'.

From the standpoint of a biologist, both anthropologists and ethnologists seem prone to attach too much importance to words, in ceremon-

[50] A. V. Grimstone, Preface to Katsuki Sekida, *Zen Training Methods and Philosophy* (New York. 1975).

[51] Ibid. 19, 21. [52] Ibid. 12. [53] Ibid. 66–8.

ies, and in descriptions of music-making by informants. The current recognition of the importance of 'body language', in human intercourse, is a timely reminder of the extent to which we daily depend on far more than spoken language in the evaluation of every kind of human encounter, even with those of our own language group. It is essential to look beyond how societies interpret their own behaviour; essential to observe what, in fact, people (in reality) do; and what, in fact, are the results of their actions, thinking all the time *in terms of their total behaviour as animals*. That includes much more than any verbalizations about conduct.

The motto chosen by the Royal Society of the United Kingdom, when a second charter was granted in 1663: *Nullius in verba*, was understood by the society as an expression of determination to withstand dogma and to verify all statements by an appeal to facts. Perhaps we may regard it also as an admonition never to accept that what is expressed as *words* is all, when it comes to evaluating human behaviour.

And what was it that Howard Becker said could not be done? He said that 'music in context' cannot be studied. He was speaking, however, of a study that incorporated the multiplicity of Charles Seeger's facets and approaches. What Peter Fletcher has done has been, virtually, to follow Becker's prescription: 'to subordinate multiple facts and approaches to one particular approach'. In fact, he permits himself one-and-a-bit approaches. His chief approach is through historical geography; but in addition, and to a small extent, he offers a minimal outline of social structure, though scarcely what might be called 'sociology', still less 'social anthropology'. His book is an extensive guide to sources of ethnomusicological study. It demonstrates that, as a formative influence on regional musical styles, history is at least as important as social structure. It offers ethnomusicology a path away from 'The Anthropology of Music' back to what—in a more literate age—those who invented the term 'ethnomusicology' meant by that term: 'the science of the music of other people'.

One of his general conclusions—that the inhabitants of Western Europe and their descendants in North America display musical affinity with peoples of Sub-Saharan Africa—runs parallel with recent data on blood-group genetics. As set out by W. W. Howells an evolutionary tree, based on the frequencies of fifty-five different blood-group genes, shows an East–West division, with Europeans and Africans opposed to Asians, Australo-Melanesians and native Americans.[54] It is to be emphasized,

[54] W. W. Howells, 'The Dispersion of Human Populations', *The Cambridge Encyclopedia of Human Evolution*, 395.

however, that the study of molecular patterns in human relationships is still in its infancy. Nevertheless, this coincidence is suggestive. If valid, these observations begin to tie musical character to the most profound level of biological organization, the level at which Schenker's 'life-force' is seen to be an aspect of molecular structure and behaviour.

It was the Greeks for whom *mousikē* was not *technē* ('craft'), but *mimēsis* ('imitation'), as were poetry and sculpture also. In music we are imitating—but what? Perhaps: remembered musical gestures in the first, meaningful sung melodies, addressed to us by our mothers, before we were capable of speech, before we had knowledge of words.

LAURENCE PICKEN

Introduction

Content and Format of the Book

Awareness of musical traditions other than those of Europe and North America has increased greatly in recent years: tourism has led to familiarity with once-distant lands and peoples, while ever-advancing technological developments have facilitated the wide dissemination, on tape, video, and film, of the sights and sounds of other lands and peoples. Irresistibly, different musics of the world have been forced on our awareness through radio and television. Simultaneously, the ethnic mix of peoples that now exists in most countries of the Western world has created its own imperatives, necessitating the adoption of a global view of cultures and their musics. This book adopts such a view. It aims to lead students and teachers, and also all those who practise Western music, towards a deeper understanding of the various musical traditions that contribute to the modern, multicultural environment. To this end it offers, among other things, a compendium of information currently available in a bibliography of global range.

The book is principally concerned with the development over time of the world's differing civilizations, the place of music in that development, and the relevance of that development today to music and culture. It does not address in detail a principal concern of ethnomusicologists: namely, the placing of living music in its contemporary social-anthropological context. From that latter standpoint, the living music of any culture is, in effect, contemporary music; and the historical process may appear unimportant or irrelevant. This book is concerned with an infinitely longer time-span of observations on human societies and their musics than that of the immediate social-anthropological context. Such a view does not in any way devalue the social-anthropological position, nor the immense increase in musical knowledge to which it has led. Rather, it complements that position by stressing the importance of historical process as a determinant of what is to be observed in music throughout the world today.

The book's structure was planned to encourage the making of connections in time and place, but the book itself is not a 'history'. Different cultures and their musics do not share a common history, even though common historical features may be present. Moreover, music itself is but one aspect of the integrated pattern of human behaviour that constitutes a culture; and musics of disparate cultural systems cannot properly be understood in isolation from other cultural traits. Necessarily, this book covers a wide field, embracing (where relevant) history, geography, religion, philosophy, language, other arts, and technology. Such an essay could not hope to be comprehensive, nor could it treat all the subjects covered in depth. The choice of subject matter must, to some extent, be personal; footnotes serve to direct the reader towards appropriate further study (as well as to document sources for particular statements). Music, in any case, is best understood by listening to it, and recordings of world musics are increasingly available. One aim of this book is to provide a useful complement to such listening.

Many of the footnote references are to articles in readily accessible sources, such as the *New Grove Dictionary of Music and Musicians* and *The New Oxford Companion to Music*; these afford relevant and at times detailed information, from acknowledged experts, summarizing their own original researches. Most of the books and journals referred to are to be found in any major academic library.

Part One of the book describes aspects of musical style and function in relation to the early development of the civilizations of West Asia, Egypt, India, Central Asia, and Europe, as a background to a study of later transformations. (Because China and South East Asia were relatively isolated from developments further west, they are treated as separate entities in Part Two.) Knowledge of the distant past is not a prerequisite for an understanding acceptance of musical genres and styles as performed today; but, to the extent that these genres and styles originated in antiquity, and acquired regional characteristics as they spread between different civilizations in Africa and Eurasia, knowledge of the distant past can contribute significantly to a world view of music. Specific sections in Part One may usefully be read in conjunction with corresponding chapters in Part Two.

Part Two describes the predominant musical traditions of Sub-Saharan Africa, West Asia, the Indian Subcontinent, South East Asia, and East Asia. Each of these regions displays sufficient unity of musical style to justify a synoptic approach, while each exhibits sufficient individuality of style to warrant treatment as a separate zone. Historical synopses are included, as these help to explain contemporary social and political contexts for music; and the synopses are combined with summaries of musical history, where clear evidence of such history exists. References to other aspects of culture serve to amplify the context, as appropriate. The depth in which these other aspects of culture are treated, and the order in which they are examined, varies from chapter to chapter, according to the cultural characteristics of the particular region. The sub-headings are designed to enable readers to locate topics of immediate interest, to assimilate varying amounts of detail, or to use the book for reference.

The musics described in Part Two developed as oral–aural traditions; in consequence, direct knowledge of performance style can come only from recordings, films, and videos made during fieldwork by musicologists and anthropologists. Knowledge of what the music sounded like in the past must be speculative (as must, to some extent, such knowledge of Western music). Nevertheless, in the case of the major traditions of the Chinese, Indian, and Persian–Arab spheres of cultural influence, the present is connected to an identifiable past not only by recorded history but also by theoretical writings on music (some of which date back to the first or second millennium BC), and also, in some cases, by ancient systems of musical notation. Although such literature does not of itself recreate the music, it provides some explanation of *why* the music sounds as it does now, and it encourages an informed, imaginative, effort of reconstruction. In the Indian and Persian–Arab traditions in particular, there is accord, in broad terms, between past theory and present practice. Thus, in describing the musical styles of these regions, some emphasis has been given to theoretical systems.

'Traditional' musics are sometimes talked about as though they exist in a pristine condition, patiently awaiting inspection by the tourist, traveller, or field-researcher. This is far from the case. In many parts of Africa and Asia, the Western traveller is as unlikely, casually, to encounter 'traditional' music in its 'traditional' context as is an African or Asian visitor to Britain to encounter traditional British folk-singing during hay making. Since the matter of tradition and change is complex, it is treated as a separate topic in Part Five, and is only referred to in Part Two where understanding of a particular 'tradition' requires consideration of this matter.

Because of the variety of styles that now coexist within the ambience of Western performing arts—popular, non-Western, and 'crossover', as well as 'classical', modern, and 'Postmodern'—it is sometimes held that the 'classical' music of Europe may be regarded as 'traditional', in the sense that, for example, un-Westernized music-making in Africa, or gamelan-performance in Central Java, is regarded as 'traditional'. Although there is some logic in this contention, the subject is more complex than this summary equation suggests. The development of relatively precise musical notation in Europe, *as an integral element of musical performance*, has enabled Western music from the past to be performed and heard—albeit under contemporary circumstances—in a consciously historical perspective. Study of world musics does not necessarily affect an individual's *reaction* to such music; but, in causing Western music to be perceived within a geographically wider musical framework, it encourages questioning of accepted practice. Wider understanding of performance styles in Africa and Asia, for example—in which use of vibrato is limited (favouring clarity of multi-part textures)—may well have encouraged acceptance of 'period' performances of Western music.

In the light of such considerations, Part Three is devoted to a study of the development of European musical styles, against their cultural and historical background, and in relation to music cultures elsewhere. This part examines Europe's intellectual debt to earlier civilizations in Africa and Asia, which later made possible Europe's subsequent political and cultural colonialism; it also emphasizes aspects of music and culture, peculiar to Europe, which subsequently influenced most other regions of the world.

Chapter 11 describes in some detail the development of European music during the Middle Ages and early Renaissance. This is necessary in part because knowledge of these periods of musical history (and of their political and social contexts) is not widespread, and in part because these periods illustrate important ways in which European music diverged from musics of other major cultural zones. Chapter 12 does not, however, detail the course of post-Renaissance music in the baroque and classical periods, since such knowledge is widespread, and information is readily available elsewhere. Instead, it deals with concepts of music and culture (peculiar to Europe during these periods) that shed light on attitudes to European music today. Chapter 13 deals more specifically with musical issues, and charts those aspects of nineteenth- and early twentieth-century music and culture that led increasingly to disintegration of the universality (in Western European eyes) of eighteenth-century cultural systems, and to the melée of musical styles that characterizes the 'global' musical culture of today. Chapters 12 and 13 both examine, *inter alia*, the relationship between the twin senses of cultural superiority and racial superiority that came to pervade the thought of post-Renaissance Europe.

Part Four examines the musical consequences of Europe's appropriation of the Americas. It pinpoints the differences between Latin America (where, notwithstanding the imitation of European ecclesiastical architecture and music during the seventeenth and eighteenth centuries, the 'high arts' of European culture did not take lasting root), and the USA (where, despite the absence of such early influence on material culture, these same arts did). It considers the idiosyncratic way in which European music was perceived in the USA, and how that idiosyncrasy enabled Africans there to create and develop jazz. It also examines the rise of American pop styles, and the divorce of these from 'classical' styles to which, in earlier times, they would have been complementary.

Tourism sometimes finds charm in poverty; and those areas of the world in which 'traditional' musics still survive in relatively un-Westernized conditions are also, regrettably, areas that suffer most from economic depression. Though it may be desirable to retain existing traditions in such areas, television has altered the expectations of peoples throughout the 'developing' world. For the first time in history, and whether for better or worse, there appears to be only a single, basic model of social organization for emulation; politics apart, economic advance, modernization, and Westernization prefigure a common goal. Part Five, accordingly, considers the nature of tradition and change, examines some African and Asian musical styles in their colonial and post-colonial contexts, and considers, in broad historical perspective, the effects of Westernization. Specific sections in this chapter may be read in conjunction with corresponding chapters in Part Two. In the final chapter, and in conclusion, the consequences *for the West* of global Westernization, and of increasing cultural interchange, are examined.

A book of this nature cannot deal equally with all regions of the world; nor can it deal with the multiplicity of folk musics that may exist in a given region. Folk musics usually influence, and are influenced by, classical styles developed over a wide geographical area; they have been described here only where such description serves to elucidate the development of those wider, classical styles. (The terms 'folk' and 'classical', as used in this book, are defined on p. 39.)

To avoid repetition, certain geographical areas, the musical styles of which overlap others treated elsewhere, have not been considered as separate entities. This is the case, for example, with Central Asia: the Islamic styles are described under West Asia, and more archaic styles in Chapter 4. It is also the case with East Europe: Balkan folk styles are described, briefly, under West Asia, and East European folk styles, under Western Europe in the context of nineteenth-century nationalism.

The difficulty of summarizing, in brief, a diversity of styles within a single region has likewise caused a number of important musical cultures not to be treated separately—those of Malaysia and the Philippines, for instance. Moreover, musical styles of Polynesians have not been treated at all; nor, with the exception of Aztecs and Incas, have those of Native Americans. This is partly because of the diversity of these styles, and partly because they have not borne directly on those wider traditions that form the backbone of the book. In Part One, for similar reasons of cultural diversity, Africa is treated less comprehensively than are other major cultural zones. The musics of Canada and Australasia do not receive mention—apart from a brief description of some aspects of the music of Australia's Aboriginal peoples—because, notwithstanding their intrinsic vigour, they are not seen as influencing the course of world musics.

This book need not be read consecutively: each chapter is complete in itself. Most of the place names mentioned in the text of Part Two are shown on maps that precede each chapter.

Musical examples are provided where these help to elucidate descriptions of musical systems. For the most part, however, detailed transcription of music from oral–aural traditions has been avoided. Such music is basically monodic in style; it did not evolve in the shadow of the printed barline; and the detail of content tends to vary from performance to performance. Indeed, the *manner* of performance is often *more* important in execution than is pitch and duration of notes. What Westerners call 'ornamentation' is frequently not an imposed device but, for the musician, an intrinsic aspect of the notes 'ornamented'.

Western musical notation provides not only a series of instructions to the performer, but a means by which skilled musicians can 'hear' the music in their heads, without its being performed. That sense of 'hearing' is heightened by the exactness of notation in terms of pitch and rhythm, and by the important role that harmony plays in the music. In the case of oral–aural traditions, Western notation enables musicians to 'hear' the music in that way only if they are familiar with the style of performance of the tradition notated. The notation does not convey timbre, and non-tempered pitch systems require additional signs that are neither exact nor easily imagined. Staff notation conveys only the bare bones of the music's essence and, to the non-specialist reader, may make the music itself seem disappointingly arid and uninteresting. Transcriptions of oral–aural musics are useful for musical analysis; but for the purposes of this book, preference has been given to describing musics in elementary terms, in the contexts in which they arise.

Notes on Terminology and Transliteration

A book about peoples, their cultural systems, and their musical styles needs a technical terminology; but since these same elements are seldom homogeneous throughout a major geographical region, terms used in classifying and comparing can be misleading. Increasing sensitivity to the variety of peoples and lifestyles of the world, and the consequent erosion of former hierarchical values, have caused many such terms, commonly used in the past, to sound pejorative today. Since terminological matters are germane to this book, a brief explanation of their use here may help clarify the text.

The mix of peoples that occurred from the start of the Neolithic makes meaningless the word 'race'; it does not have even the weight of 'variety'. The concept of 'race' in common speech is a cultural construct. It has no genetic validity.[1] Provided that parents are fertile, all 'inter-racial' crosses between humankind result in progeny. The word is here used sparingly, usually only in quotes, or in the context of racism. When used in conjunction with 'nation', 'race' is disinformative, since 'nation', too, is a construct, a political one that overrides ethnicity. The word 'nation' is used only in the conceptual sense of 'nation-state', and 'nationality' only in dialectic. 'Country' is used to define a geographical area currently recognized as an autonomous state. The word 'region' may be applied to a part of the world or a part of a country: it is used here in either way, where its indeterminacy is advantageous.

[1] See Steve Jones, *The Language of the Genes* (London: Flamingo, 1994), 245–63.

Cardinal allocations are used only adjectivally. 'The Far East', for example, was once 'far' and 'east' when viewed from the 'west'; but it is no longer 'far', and promises soon to be neither East nor West, but Central. In particular, no reference is made to 'the Middle East', except in quotes. It is a handy term for describing a geographical area within which Islamic musical systems predominate, but it is vague in terms of world geography; it renders unclear, for example, to which part of the 'east' the Indian Subcontinent belongs, and how much of North Africa is included. Moreover, use of the term detaches Sub-Saharan Africa from North Africa, and withdraws attention from the enormous contribution made by Africans to world cultures, in the past, and in the present.

For the most part, the words 'tribe' and 'tribal' have been avoided, because they are sometimes perceived, pejoratively, as antithetical to the words 'civilization' and 'civilized'. Besides, we all belong to some 'tribe' or other. The word 'civilization', from the Latin, *civitas* (city), still has meaning in so far as it refers to the *scale* of human integration, and it is only used in that sense. Its effects are described in Chapter 2, and its growth is described in subsequent chapters.

Where possible, the words 'white' and 'black' have been avoided as descriptions of peoples. The terms encourage a ridiculous assumption that people who are not 'white' are 'black', ignoring the extent to which different peoples have intermarried. It has sometimes been necessary to use this terminology in the context of the USA; but wherever possible the term 'African American' (as being the most generally acceptable) is used to describe US citizens of African origin. It is recognized, however, that some US citizens of African origin prefer to be called 'American African' or, simply, 'African', underscoring their African identity; and that some others prefer to be called 'American', thus emphasizing their acculturation in the USA.

'Culture' is an ill-defined and currently overworked word. In its early uses it was a noun of process, indicating cultivation, basically of crops and animals.[2] During the eighteenth century, it came also to indicate the process of change in human society. During the nineteenth century, it became synonymous with 'civilization', and acquired a plural usage in the context of 'national' and 'folk' cultures. Over the past century, 'culture' (like 'civilization') has tended to be equated with arts of the élite, in implicit contrast to popular arts. Recently, however, the word

[2] Raymond Williams, *Keywords: A Vocabulary of Culture and Society* (London: Flamingo, 1983), 87–9.

has come to embrace both élite *and* popular arts, and to encompass all facets of life in a particular society.

In an increasingly multicultural society, the application of the word 'culture' to a single society, country, or perceived 'nation' has less and less meaning. Here, the word 'culture' is used only as a noun when a limiting adjective is added; the common reference is to a 'cultural system', or 'systems', where the term 'system' indicates an integrated pattern of human behaviour. Since this book attests the continued existence of cultural systems, the overall character of which derives from ancient civilizations, the word 'culture' is at times applied to persistent, over-arching customs and achievements common to a particular time or to a broad category of people (for example, 'medieval'; 'Chinese'; 'Indian'). In no instance does the word carry élitist overtones.

'Tradition' is another overworked and vague term. It derives from the Latin *tradere* (to hand over or deliver) and is commonly used in the sense of transmission by 'handing down'.[3] Although, in one sense, a tradition may be established instantaneously, the word tends more often to be used in the sense of 'age-old' tradition, and to imply some element of ceremony, duty, and respect. The word is used here to contrast cultural systems that have changed little over centuries, or millennia even, with those that appear to be essentially modern. This issue is discussed in Chapter 18.

Louis Armstrong (among others) is accredited with the aphorism: 'All music's folk-music, leastways I never heard of no horse singing it.' A modern city subsumes, for example, 'folk' who attend traditional dancing classes, as well as 'folk' who attend opera performances, or rock concerts. Nevertheless, terms such as 'classical', 'folk', 'popular', and 'art' still have broadly accepted, if not precise meanings, when applied to musics in particular contexts.

The word 'classical' refers to styles acknowledged as yardsticks of excellence, in their time, and through succeeding generations; such 'classical' styles are recognized in a number of distinct geographical areas. (In no way is it implied that such yardsticks are, or are not, applicable to our own time.) The word 'folk' refers to styles practised in rural communities, where such communities are, or have been, distinct from urban communities. The word 'urban' refers to styles—usually, though not necessarily, modern—that originated and were (and are) popular in urban communities. The word 'popular' itself—as distinct

[3] Ibid. 319.

from the stylistic category of 'pop'—refers to music that is, literally, popular, usually contrasting with a 'classical' style that belongs essentially to an élite. Where a number of élite styles coexist, it is convenient to refer to 'art'-music. The word 'music' is only used in the plural when referring to a multiplicity of élite and popular styles that subsume individualities of style.

The use, on occasion, of the terms 'non-European' and 'non-Western' is necessitated by the extent to which European/Western cultural systems have come to influence, and dominate, virtually all others on the planet. The terms indicate no value-judgement or implication of disparity; the prefix 'non-' is used comparably in respect of other major cultural zones.

All categories overlap, and a purpose of this book is to indicate the extent of that overlap. The corollary, of course, is to indicate also the extent of their separateness. The inexactness of terms reflects the inexactness of the field of study; this said, however, the terms indicate broadly recognizable, and usefully discriminated, categories. *No value judgements are associated with them*, and they are used hereafter without quotes.

In the interests of thoroughness, instruments, styles, and genres have been referred to by local names, followed by translations in brackets. Because a profusion of such terms is generated by a text of this nature, the translation has been repeated when terms recur, rather than referring the reader to a glossary.

The profusion of terms is a consequence of a profusion of foreign languages, and the transliteration of such languages, for a general readership, is problematic. Scholarly transliterations often employ diacritic signs, many of which are only fully understood by specialists. In this book, commonly understood signs used regularly in European languages have been retained. Macrons widely employed in transliteration of non-European languages have also been retained, because their function of lengthening the sound of the vowel over which they are placed is readily appreciated. Other diacritic signs, less widely understood, have been replaced with 'Anglicized' forms of spelling. With regard to the Chinese language, the now customary *Pinyin* system of transliteration has been retained, without further explanation. No system for multi-language transliteration can be wholly effective for non-specialist readers, but it is hoped that this mixture of diacritic and phonetic transliteration will enable foreign-language words to be perceived, and pronounced, with relative accuracy.

A few specialist terms may be unfamiliar to those with experience only of Western cultural systems: 'autochthonous' ('sprung from the earth') describes the original, or earliest known, inhabitants or cultural traits of a country; 'acculturation' describes the process of adaptation to new cultural systems; 'enculteration' describes the process of absorbing, from birth, the cultural traits of a particular environment.

'Heterophony' is a musical term that contrasts with 'homophony'; it refers to melodic material performed simultaneously by different voices or instruments, in slightly different versions, appropriate to the particular voices or instruments concerned.

A tetrachord spans four notes in no specific intervallic relationship, but approximating to the interval of a perfect fourth. A pentachord spans five notes under similar conditions. When tetrachords are conjunct, the lowest note of the higher tetrachord is the *same* as the highest note of the lower tetrachord. When tetrachords are disjunct, there is an interval—normally a tone—between them.

A pentatonic scale contains five different pitches within the compass of an octave. A hemitonic pentatonic scale includes at least one interval approximating to a semitone; an anhemitonic pentatonic scale contains no such intervals; in an equi-pentatonic scale, the intervals are approximately equal. A 'gapped' scale contains one or more intervals larger than a tone.

The word 'ethnomusicology'—'the *logos* (study/science) of the music of other people'—has not been used. There seems no reason why, for example, the study of Javanese or Chinese music should be more 'ethnological' than the study of Italian or Russian music. Java, China, Italy, and Russia do not represent single ethnic entities; nor do any other nation states. The study of any style of music, other than study directed to proficiency in performance, is a form of musicology. To deny this is to deny even the *possibility* of a common musical language.

Listening to World Musics

Western musicians listening for the first time to musics outside their own tradition may need time to grow accustomed to aspects of quality markedly different from those of the West. Most conspicuous among these is timbre; indeed, by timbre alone it is often possible to identify the region of origin of a piece of music, within seconds of its start. The timbre of traditional singing styles can seem particularly alien to those accustomed to Western, classical voice production. Vocal music is often intended for open-air performance, where high notes carry further and more clearly than low notes, and where simultaneous, discordant notes carry better than do concords. Timbre itself depends on the complex set of harmonics of different intensities that constitutes a single 'note', whether sung or played; and voices are often focused in such a way as to generate a vocal sound rich in harmonics of a high frequency.

In some Japanese ritual music, flutes play in minor seconds or ninths, the acoustic beat adding stridency to the sound, enabling it to carry further and, perhaps, drive away evil spirits. In Serbia, Macedonia, Bulgaria, southern Albania, and northern Greece, vocal performance over a fixed or variable drone often incorporates the use of major or minor seconds, for initial, intermediate, and final notes, or even for parallel movement; to performers and listeners in these areas, the interval of the second is not perceived as a dissonance. Two- and three-part Lithuanian songs called *sutartine* ('concord', 'singing in concord') frequently feature parallel seconds throughout.[4]

Whether in indoor or outdoor use, the voice has usually been considered the paramount medium of musical performance; even in Europe, where instrumental music acquired an unusual degree of importance, vocal music was considered superior to instrumental music up to the early nineteenth century. In many music cultures, instruments are designed to 'shadow' a continuous vocal line by imitating the contour of the melody a little behind the vocalist. (A similar process occurred between congregation and priest in 'lining-out' singing of Nonconformist hymnody in both Britain and the USA during the nineteenth century (see p. 542).) Notably in the Hindustani music of North India, such a continuous vocal line may become an extended, virtuosic, wordless vocalization. To Westerners accustomed to musical statements in strongly marked rhythms, with varied articulation, India's frequent, continuous interlinking of often fast-moving vocal notes may appear monotonous, even absurd, until it is understood how precisely the music conforms to the intricacies of Indian modal systems and rhythmic cycles.

In many parts of Asia, important notes in a given mode are often highlighted by ornamentation. Wide vibrato (such as is practised in Indian and Islamic vocal and instrumental styles), yodelling effects

[4] A. L. Lloyd, 'Europe', *The New Grove* (1980), vi. 309–11.

(as in Persian classical, and Armenian folk styles), or slow glissandos of approximately semitone steps (as used in Indian *dhrupad* or Lamaist chant), may disturb Westerners accustomed to the aimless practice of vibrato on every note. In Western classical music, unusually, bowed string instruments have come to be favoured over plucked string instruments, because of their capacity for producing sustained notes; whereas in many parts of Asia, plucked lutes and zithers were, and still are, valued for their capacity to 'bend' the pitch of a note as the sound dies away. An astonishing range of ornamentation can be achieved in this way. By deflecting the string away from the fingerboard, and thus increasing its tension, the pitch of a note can be raised by as much as a perfect fifth, and such ornamentation may last for several seconds. Reversing this operation at times generates a vibrato so wide as to appear grotesque to some Westerners; but it is worth noting that in Europe, until the end of the nineteenth century, vibrato was not practised continuously, but was likewise regarded as a form of expressive ornament, as was portamento, still widely used by string players in the early twentieth century.

Outside Western Europe (and in Western Europe too, until about the twelfth century), both art and folk musics commonly consist of a single melodic line, at times supported by drones, or other notes, but never supported by functional harmony. In ensemble, such a line is performed in heterophony. In Europe, from the time of the Renaissance, musical instruments were designed in homogeneous size-sets to blend and 'symphonize' with each other in polyphony and harmony; outside Europe, however, heterogeneous sets of instruments often play a given melody together, each performing it in slightly different ways, according to the physical properties and characteristics of the particular instrument and individual musical taste. Heterophony is a common feature of East European folk music; Gaelic psalm-singing (in the island of Lewis) and Irish keening (lamentation for the dead) are instances of vocal heterophony nearer to home.

Westerners are sometimes disturbed by tuning systems that yield intervals alien to those resulting from the system of equal temperament. The equal-tempered system facilitated transposition, and provided Europeans with a flexible musical resource. In the process of its evolution, however, the linear possibilities for scalar sets in music were reduced to two modes only, major and minor. Outside Europe, musical systems are usually constructed from a multiplicity of modes, or 'note-sets', and on melodic cells derived from components of them. Except in areas where elaborate modal systems evolved, tunings of 'note-sets' are often peculiar to an individual society; they appear not to have developed as a result of any mathematical theory of acoustics, and do not necessarily contain a perfect fifth. Intervals sometimes vary considerably from those commonly used in the West.

There is no evidence that the human ear finds intervals with simple ratios (between the number of vibrations of each of their sounding notes) more agreeable than intervals with complex ratios: for example, the octave (2:1), perfect fifth (3:2), or perfect fourth (4:3), as opposed to the Pythagorean semitone (256:243—the difference between three pure octaves and five pure fifths). On the contrary, research indicates, for example, that the octave that musicians perceive to be consonant is usually slightly larger than the 'true' octave with a ratio of 2:1.[5] Indeed, on the piano, the number of vibrations of a note played near the top of the keyboard in relation to a note played five octaves lower is, in the practice of the professional piano tuner, considerably greater than five times the number of vibrations of the lower note. This tendency to 'stretch' octaves was known already to the Greeks.[6]

The concept of precise intonation would appear essential for notes used in a Western, harmonic context: but research has demonstrated that, for notes used melodically, the ear—in the West as well as elsewhere—finds acceptable considerable variations in intonation.[7] The similarity of pitches performed in different octaves appears to be a factor in most tunings of note-sets; but otherwise, the way in which humans *hear* music seems not to be intrinsically related to the arithmetical-acoustic laws of music, but rather to be a matter of habituation. It should not, therefore, prove difficult for ears trained to the Western system of tuning to adjust to other tuning systems.

It is not a purpose of this book to emphasize the *differences* between musical styles. The reader who follows through the accounts of these styles, and of the circumstances that contributed to their development, may be as much impressed by their similarities as by their differences.

[5] F. Fransson and P. Tjernlund, 'Statistical Tone Measurements of the Tone-Scale in Played Music', STL-OPSR, 2–3, Department of Speech Communication, KTH, Stockholm, 1970; E. Terhardt, 'Pitch, Consonance and Harmony', *Journal of the Acoustical Society of America*, 55 (1967), 1061–9; and Peter Cooke, 'Exploring Musical Pitch Systems', *ICTM UK Bulletin*, 27 (1990), 6–22.

[6] Natasha Spender, 'Psychology of Music', *The New Grove* (1980), xv. 398.

[7] J. A. Siegel and W. Siegel, 'Categorical Perception of Tonal Intervals: Musicians Can't Tell Sharp from Flat', *Perception and Psychophysics*, 21 (1977), 399–407; and Cooke, 'Exploring Musical Pitch Systems', 8.

Nevertheless, functional harmony—with all the musical contrivances that emanate from it—is deeply embedded in the subconscious of Westerners as a norm of musical statement, as is becoming the case throughout much of the rest of the world today. The same holds true for the timbres of Western voices and instruments. Only familiarity with other musical styles can free the mind from such conceptions, so that Western systems of musical construction are seen to take their place in a much wider community of musical languages.

Approaching Unfamiliar Cultures

Understanding of a foreign musical style is assisted by a willingness to view the world from an unfamiliar perspective. One such perspective is obtained by turning a map of the world upside-down. When considering human origins, this is not an illogical thing to do. Gravity ensures a respect for things that are 'high'; and societies do not, commonly, place their heaven in the underworld. As it happens, with the map upside-down, Australia bears down on Asia, Africa bears down on Europe, and South America bears down on North America. This makes a stimulating change from Mercator's view of the world with Europe (top left) bearing down upon Africa, and with Asia (top right) handy for the taking.

In the present, more sensitive, intercultural climate, the word 'ethnocentricity' has been adopted to denote the viewing of foreign cultural systems from the standpoint of one's own. Europeans in particular, with their five-century-long history of imperialism, are often accused of 'Eurocentricity'. 'Afrocentrists', on the other hand, point with pride not only to East Africa as the site of human origin, but also to Egypt as the source of civilization. Africans, they conclude, taught civilization to the rest of the world. Although the truth is more complex, this selective use of facts is no more disingenuous than that of many Western historians. Alexander, for example, is known to every Western school child as 'The Great', and his conquests are usually extolled as 'achievements'. In Persia, however, Alexander was dubbed 'The Accursed', because he killed priests and burnt palaces. He is seen in Europe as 'The Great', rather than 'The Accursed', because for the past five centuries the world has been dominated by Europeans, and it is Europeans who have drawn the maps and written the histories. 'Eurocentricity' largely accounts for Western cultural arrogance.

Nevertheless, it is hardly possible—or desirable—to discard wholly one's own cultural background, or to make value judgements outside one's own sphere of culture. How, for example, should a Westerner judge a string quartet composed on the principles of Western integral serialism, by a Korean, performed by Koreans in Korea? By what structural system should it be analysed? In fact, the Westerner is scarcely in a position to make any judgement at all; only Koreans—or, at least, Asians—can judge what, within their cultural sphere, appears to them to have artistic integrity, even though they may argue over the matter as much as do Europeans. In the modern, multicultural environment, value judgements need not be discarded; but they carry more weight when they relate to the cultural systems to which the valuer is enculterated, or fully acculturated.

Westerners commonly believe themselves to be uniquely conditioned to see threads, continuities, and patterns in things. The concept is invalid, even though linear analysis has been intrinsic to Western thought until the coming of multi-dimensional structuralism. Nevertheless, the Western penchant for analysis has entailed, *inter alia*, categorizing certain peoples according to their 'racial' lineage. In Latin America, for example, people of mixed European and 'Indian' descent are referred to as *Mestizo*, and people of mixed European and African descent are commonly known as *Mulatto* (a term also used in Europe). It may not occur to Europeans to seek also a term for those of mixed 'Indian' and African descent, though there is one ('Cafuso'). In reality, the genetic mix of peoples in Latin America—and in most other areas of the world—defies precise description and categorization. It may be hard for Westerners to abandon use of those tidy little boxes that the Renaissance bequeathed; but the attempt must be made, if there is to be a genuine understanding and acceptance of the diversity of peoples and cultural systems now to be observed.

It was essentially as an aid to unlocking some of those boxes that this book was written.

Part One

Genesis

1 Elemental Features of Music

A Primary Mode of Expression

From time immemorial, music has been one of humankind's most important resources. It has eased the burden of work, and coordinated its rhythms. It has helped people in love, and calmed their fever. It has cemented social rituals, recalled ancestral history, and shaped codes of conduct. It has been held to appease gods and ancestral spirits, and to induce rain, or drive it away. Nor are such attributes mere relics of ancient superstition. Music still soothes the spirit in sickness or in love. It can still condition human behaviour. It still has strong historical associations. All over the world, people still sing or listen to music as they work, and they still celebrate their harvest in elaborate ritual. And music is still one of the most fundamental elements in religious and social ceremony. As technology makes musical styles from all over the world accessible to us, their fundamental similarities are as evident as their differences.

Despite music's importance as a means of individual and collective human expression, rational grounds for explaining its varying effects on mental states remain elusive. Music is a non-representational art; and, unlike other arts, it creates its own material. It can only be responded to visually through the symbolic movements of musical performers or dancers (or by painting to it). The foetus learns an equal-pulsed, in frequency varied, rhythm from the maternal heartbeat; and, at a primary level, it is possible that the response of humans to the first perceived rhythm remains an element in the perception of music, and the response to it, even in the most exalted contexts.[1] The body makes music in time as rhythm, and in space as dance; such ordered structure in time is, as yet, the only living 'organism' that man can create. If, more

[1] See Foreword, pp. 18–20.

than any other art, music has been held to link the natural world with phenomena that appear 'super-natural', it is because of its non-verbal, non-rational effectiveness in communication, where words fail.

Music is, nevertheless, a non-conceptual art: it cannot generate a predicate. But it possesses an inherent capacity to heighten the meaning of concepts expressed in words, and thus to enhance the impact of social and religious ceremonies. In most non-urban, non-literate, societies, song provides the very framework of community life. Some societies believe that their songs are actual gifts from remote ancestors (human or other animal); and song is a principal means by which healers appease disgruntled ancestor spirits lodged in the heads of the sick, or by which, in trance, the spirits of healers depart their bodies seeking knowledge.

Within literate societies, music has acquired extra-musical, cosmological associations. Babylonians of the second millennium BC knew that a direct correspondence exists between music and number, and this knowledge appears subsequently to have reached other civilizations across Eurasia. Such knowledge led the Chinese, for example, to make repeated attempts—and as a matter of prime importance—to adjust the fundamental pitch of music to harmonize with elements of the cosmos; and this continued up to the Revolution of 1911. It led the Greeks to conclude that musical intervals provide a means for calculating the orbits of the planets, a conclusion promulgated in Europe until the sixteenth century. When post-Renaissance European music subsequently became a vehicle for self-expression, aestheticians spilled much ink in the attempt to find rational links between music and emotion. To this day, they have no more been able to establish such links than have anthropologists to pinpoint the origin of human songs from animals. The non-representational character of music renders it a disarmingly irrational medium, for its symbolic gestures are susceptible of multiple interpretation.

Like music, humankind may act irrationally, though apparently driven by rational motives. Our genetic inheritance has enabled us to learn to select, enquire, and construct, to gain mastery over our natural environment; but we do not control our destiny.[2] We are trapped between what is predictable and what is not. As human beings, we live with an inherent duality. On the one hand, we claim to be creatures of logic; on the other hand, our imagination may precipitate us into a

[2] J. M. Roberts, *Pelican History of the World* (London: Pelican Books, 1988), 54.

world of irrational fantasy. The logic that binds us and the imagination that frees us are concomitant, yet contradictory. Tension between what we think and what we feel contributes to our creativity.

For individuals and societies alike, there are points of disjunction between the natural and the 'super-natural', between certainty and uncertainty. The evolution of religions and philosophies has helped to mitigate this condition. Like art, religion helps to balance rational and irrational aspects of our nature. Religion and art are born of the same dichotomy. Of all the arts, music perhaps reflects this link between art and religion in the most profound way; it is the only artistic medium that, of itself, has been held to have direct contact with the divine.

All religious practice appears to emanate from man's ambivalent relationship with nature and the 'super-natural'. Many peoples acknowledge a single, supreme god, too distant and mysterious to be approached directly, whose will is made manifest through the agencies of lesser gods or spirits. This supreme god is usually seen as the source, not merely of the creation itself, but of a mythological, personified pantheon that helps to explain the apparently perverse manifestations of the natural world, and the source of good and evil in human nature. Throughout the world, societies observe rituals linked with the cycle of the seasons, with the human life cycle, and with the appeasement of gods and spirits associated with both. Music is intrinsic to these rituals, and their efficacy depends on the accurate presentation of intricate songs and dances.

Ancestor worship has been a common element in religious practice, particularly among societies of hunters and foodgatherers; and song has usually been the medium in which ancestral genealogy and history were preserved. The practice of ancestor worship implies belief in the existence of a natural continuum between the living and the dead; through death a person becomes an 'ancestor', but may in turn be 'reborn' into the living world. A dissatisfied or discontented ancestor may be the cause of death and disease; and for this reason ritual contact with ancestors is often made at graves, at sites of ancestral habitation, or at spirit boxes, where, just beyond the walls of individual dwellings, spirits may be appeased with ritual offerings of food or money. Rituals associated with the dead are carried out with utmost precision; any mistake, or break in the continuity of the music, could invite death, or disaster.

Among extant hunter-foodgathering societies, the non-Westernized Aboriginal peoples of Australia may be taken as a single, and striking, example of the close connection that still exists between music, religion, and social custom. Aboriginal peoples from many parts of Australia believe that their totemic ancestors—mythical beings who came from the sea, or rose from the land—travelled throughout the continent scattering trails of songs. Such songs are held to delineate ancestral tracks that define the 'Dreaming' sites: sacred lands where, at 'Dreamtime', people honour their ancestors and the lands bequeathed by them.[3] The songs are also held to describe the nature of the land over which the ancestors passed. They provide, therefore, a kind of tribal grid map of the ancestral land, and are usually performed at special ceremonies on 'Dreaming' sites.[4] New songs are still received from ancestors in replacement of discarded songs. The correctness of execution of dream-songs, in all aspects of their performance, is fundamentally important, and errors may demand retribution, even summary execution.[5]

Attitudes to music in Australian Aboriginal society may be reflected in terminology. Among autochthonous peoples of Central Australia and the Western Desert, for example, *imma* means not merely music (in our sense) but also its mythical associations and behavioural context, exemplified in song, dance, and the design of body-painting. *Imma* thus implies overlapping layers of information and meaning. *Mayu* indicates both musical sound *and* its 'flavour'; while their combination, *imma mayu*, refers to the melodic shape that encapsulates the 'flavour' of a particular ancestor. This 'flavour' is conferred by the pitch distance between pivotal melodic points, and by the length of time spent between them.[6]

Such attitudes are common to many cultures. The attribution of songs to 'super-natural' sources, for example, occurs also in the Americas, where autochthonous societies link the origin of their songs with the origin of their people; both are revealed in dreams.[7] In remote

[3] W. H. Edwards, 'The Aborigines', in *The Religions of the World* (London: Lion Publishing, 1982), 148.

[4] Alice M. Moyle, 'Australia', *The New Grove* (1980), i. 715.

[5] For an account of life in an un-Westernized Aboriginal society, see Douglas Lockwood, *I, the Aboriginal* (Australia: Rigby, 1962).

[6] Catherine I. Ellis, 'Australia', *The New Grove* (1980), i. 715. For detailed discussion of musical structure in relation to social structure, see Fiona Magowan, 'The Land is our *Märr*, It Stays Forever: The *Yothu-Yindi* Relationship in Australian Aboriginal Traditional and Popular Musics', in Martin Stokes (ed.), *Ethnicity, Identity, and Music: The Musical Construction of Place* (Oxford: Berg Publishers, 1994).

[7] Doris J. Dyen and Willard Rhodes, 'North America', *The New Grove* (1980), xiii. 70.

communities in Andean Bolivia, new tunes are collected from *sirinus*, demons that live in rocks or beside waterfalls.[8] The existence of overlapping layers of meaning in words for 'music' is also common to many cultures: the East African word *ngoma* denotes a combination of music, dance, and drama; the Indian word *sangīt* incorporates music, poetry, and dance; the Greek word *mousikē* implied both the music *and* the ethical values associated with it; the Chinese word *yue* referred to the complex of ritual song and dance and associated musical instruments and dance properties.

Pitched Vocalization

The common relationship between music and religion transcends all types of 'religious' belief. Many societies regard the singing voice as a magical, 'other-worldly' voice, and have reserved its use for invoking divinities, using the speaking voice for purely social occasions and ceremonies.

Voiced sounds are produced when the lungs and respiratory muscles generate a stream of pressurized air that activates the vocal folds of the larynx and produces sound waves, amplified in the resonating cavities of the pharynx and mouth. When, by skilled control of the respiratory system, the air pressure is regulated so as to produce sound waves in regularly repeated sequences, at a frequency between (approximately) 18,000 and 15,000 times a second, the ear perceives notes of definite pitch.[9] Pitched vocalization enables vowel sounds to be sustained in a way that they cannot in speech;[10] short sounds can be contrasted with long sounds, and speech can be extended in time, as song.

Various acoustic features of the vocal mechanism render the basic tone of sung notes susceptible of substantial modification. For example, the 'envelope' formation (the changes in amplitude of the complex of wave formations) associated with a given note varies according to pitch and vocal intensity; formants (changes in wave form as a note is

[8] Henry Stobart, 'The Sirens of the Andes', *Musical Times*, Feb. 1992.

[9] Johan Sundberg, 'Acoustics', *The New Grove* (1980) i. 83, and Charles Taylor, 'Sound', *The New Grove* (1980), xvii. 546.

[10] In speech, phonetic 'segments' (approximating to the letters of the alphabet) are transmitted at a very fast rate of up to 25 per second; see Philip Lieberman, 'Human Speech and Language', *The Cambridge Encyclopedia of Human Evolution* (Cambridge: Cambridge University Press, 1992), 134.

amplified) vary in the different vowel sounds; and formants are further modified by the different amplifications of the resonating cavities of the pharynx, nose, and mouth. Voices have different ranges, according to gender, physical type, and cultural norms; and within these ranges specific 'registers' are recognized. ('Registers' are groups of notes of similar tone quality felt to be produced in the same way.) Voices may also be 'focused' to yield different combinations of harmonic partials.[11] Pitched vocalization, therefore, enables the voice organ to be used in a variety of ways; and individual voice organs acquire distinctive musical personalities. As a consequence, special effects—such as nasalization, falsetto, the production of very low notes, and the use of voice distorters—have commonly been used to disguise the individuality of pitched vocal expression in the presence of the divine.

Although human societies usually develop their music *in conjunction* with language, the relationship between music and language is non-essential. In our own era, for example, Saint Augustine (in his *Confessions*, *c.*AD 400) suggested that singing without words expresses a joy too deep for words.[12] Wordless vocalization has been practised at least since the advent of *Homo sapiens*, since it is part of the system of communication of the Great Apes. Humans, therefore, may well have communicated through wordless vocalization before they communicated through structured language. It is known, for example, that the early hominoid Australopithicenes of East Africa were anatomically capable of singing.[13]

Music—in the broadest sense of ordered sound—is a means of communication common not merely to humankind but to all vertebrates. Animal sounds are extremely complex: their structure, in terms of harmonics, and the modulation of these in time while a sound is uttered, is such that highly specific information can be transmitted and understood. A gull in flight, returning towards a nesting site, can identify its own chick, amid hundreds, by the *detailed* structure of its call, even though all calls are in essence the same.[14] Specific words form part of the sound repertoire of certain monkeys, who have an unambiguous word for 'snake', for example. Among pygmy marmosets, trills containing

[11] Taylor, 'Sound', *The New Grove*, xvii. 546.

[12] Richard L. Crocker, 'Melisma', *The New Grove* (1980), xii. 105.

[13] Frank Livingstone, 'Did the Australopithicenes Sing?', *Current Anthropology*, 14/1–2 (1973), 25–9.

[14] W. H. Thorpe, *Bird Song: The Biology of Vocal Communication and Expression in Birds* (Cambridge: University of Cambridge Press, 1961), 41.

acoustic features which make them easy to locate are used when animals are widely separated; but trills of a pitch and harmonic structure difficult to locate are used when animals are close together.[15] The screams of juvenile *Rhesus* macaques vary in their acoustic features: certain screams are uttered exclusively in particular social situations, 'tonal' and 'pulsed' screams being used for relatives; and mothers appear to respond differently to the various types of scream from their offspring.[16]

Such matters are germane to the music of humans; humans, like other animals, categorize pitch, transforming in the process continuously varying acoustic signals into a set of meaningful auditory units.[17] The development of such units into specific 'note-sets' appears to have occurred independently, in general, of knowledge of the acoustical laws of music (see pp. 43–4). Many societies have adopted different note-sets for use with different social functions. In the Philippines, for example, some societies use hemitonic *and* anhemitonic note-sets, separately, for separate repertories with separate social and aesthetic applications;[18] in Byzantium, the *oktōēchos* ('eight melody types') was the basis for dividing the liturgical year into eight-week cycles; in eighteenth-century Europe, a whole repertoire of musical devices came to be associated with specific musical feelings (known as 'affects'); indeed, the 'major' and 'minor' scales used in Europe, as well as individual keys, often acquired emotional connotations. The assembling of pitched notes into patterns, with symbolic meaning, would seem to be a process that links the sounds of the Primates and early hominids with the music of humans today.

Vocalization and Language

Perhaps the most important factor in the development of music by humans was language, in the structure of which

[15] Robert M. Seyfarth, 'Vocal Communication and its Relation to Language', in Dorothy L. Cheney, Robert M. Seyfarth, Barbara B. Smuts, Richard W. Wrangham, and Thomas T. Struhsaker (eds.), *Primate Societies* (Chicago: University of Chicago Press, 1987), 445–7.

[16] S. Gouzoules, H. Gouzoules, and P. Marler, 'Rhesus Monkey Screams: Representational Signalling in the Recruitment of Agnostic Aid', *Animal Behaviour*, 32 (1984), 182–93; cited in Seyfarth, 'Vocal Communication', 448.

[17] J. A. Siegel and W. Siegel, 'Categorical Perception of Tonal Intervals: Musicians Can't Tell Sharp from Flat', *Perception and Psychophysics*, 21 (1977), 399–407.

[18] José Maceda, 'In Search of a Source of Pentatonic Hemitonic and Anhemitonic Scales in Southeast Asia', *Acta Musicologica*, III. 2 (Bärenreiter-Verlag, 1990), 208.

pitch is a crucial element. Many languages of the world—probably a majority—are 'tonal': that is to say, they incorporate segmental tone, whereby the meaning of a syllable depends on syllable melody and pitch, as well as on phonemic structure. Throughout much of East Asia and Africa, the shape of melody is conditioned, to greater or lesser extent, by the syllable pitches of language, a condition which may at times inhibit the development of a melodic style independent of such syllable melodies.

Humans have always made use of music as an extension of speech, even though music has a life of its own, independent of words. Epic stories, or linguistic constructs associated with rites, seem universally to be recited as syllabic chant. Such chant, when not strongly measured, usually employs no more than two, three, or four, different, short melodic phrases in its structure; and the overall compass of its notes tends to be no greater than a fourth. Yet there exists also an impulse to allow chanted music to break free of linguistic restraints: words, phrases, or ideas that require special emphasis are commonly enhanced by the use of melismas. (Melisma is Greek for 'song'.) Melismatic chant makes use of more than one note per syllable; and when melismas are introduced, the note-span of syllabic chant is often considerably enlarged.

Melismas intrude upon the natural speech relationship between words and music.[19] Melismatic singing often takes place *between* opening and closing syllabic statements, but it may also replace a final syllabic statement, or occur as a musical section reserved specially for its use. The performance of lengthy melismas is often assisted by inserting syllables without obvious meaning, or by adding extraneous syllables to the individual notes of a melisma (known as 'troping'). In *measured* declamation—usually associated with dance or with some other physical action—the span of pitch compass tends to increase in proportion with the *extent* to which melismatic singing is practised. Melismatic chant, therefore, may be regarded as an amplification of the wordless vocalization.

Song and speech are seldom far apart. Among the Suyá people of Brazil, for example (as Anthony Seeger has shown[20]), the telling of myths, to a group, is partly improvised, and is distinguished from

[19] Crocker, 'Melisma', *The New Grove*, xii. 105.

[20] Anthony Seeger, *Why Suyá Sing: A Musical Anthropology of an Amazonian People* (Cambridge: Cambridge University Press, 1987), 30, and ex. 2.1 on accompanying tape.

normal conversation by the use of stylized speech, in which segmental tone, timbre, tempo, sliding pitches, and phonemic variations are formal devices. On the other hand, ritual invocations, used primarily in healing and performed while blowing on the patient, are remembered precisely, and are recited quickly and quietly.[21] When, by contrast, instruction is imparted to a group in special ceremonies, the oration is usually in syllabic, single-note chant, descending by approximately a minor third at intermediate points and at ends of phrases.[22] The Suyá do not, however, regard such forms of instruction and invocation as 'song'. (This attitude towards religious chant is common: it obtains within Islam, for example, where the Qur'ān is not 'chanted' but 'read', and among *Theravāda* Buddhist communities in South East Asia.)

Apart from these recitations, the Suyá recognize two broad categories of 'song', sharing similar verse-forms and performance structures: 'unison' songs, sung communally, usually at low pitch and of limited range; and 'shout' songs, sung by individuals either solo or in group heterophony, often starting on the highest note with forced voice, and progressing in spiralling pitch descent. In each song type, meaningless 'song syllables' are inserted.[23]

Such distinctions between speech, chant, and song are common to many cultures. In societies differing widely in customs and beliefs, and in which *styles* of musical performance also differ widely, equivalent *forms* of musical construction, in relation to language, may be used, such that their musics are similar in function. This may be exemplified by a comparison of Suyá musical practices with those of medieval Christian Europe.

In the Divine Office, celebrated at regular hours in the churches of medieval Europe, priests intoned the scriptural 'lessons' in preference to reading them in the speaking voice, so as to secure clear delivery of the words.[24] The psalms, when delivered by a choir, were chanted, mainly on one note, in 'plainchant', but short melismas were inserted at beginnings, at endings, and on intermediate cadences, in melodic units rarely exceeding a fourth in compass. When psalms were chanted by soloists, however, cadences came to be expanded into elaborate melismas; and, in the Gradual of the Mass in particular, this led to

[21] Ibid. 35, and ex. 2.3 on accompanying tape.
[22] Ibid. 31–2, and ex. 2.2 on accompanying tape.
[23] Ibid. 40.
[24] David Hiley, 'Plainchant', *NOCM* (1983).

brilliant soloistic melismas, employing wide note-spans, with the occasional insertion of supplementary text. Measured rhythms were used, at first in conjunction with processionals, and later, in praise-hymns.

By such means, medieval European ecclesiastics developed specific musical styles: for reciting religious history and ethical instruction (as revealed in the Bible); for invocation of the divine (through the psalms); and for praising the divine (through hymns). Music was also used to accompany action (in processionals). Such functions are not dissimilar from those for which the Suyá developed their musical styles; indeed, they are to be observed worldwide. Comparable distinctions of function, and of syllabic and melismatic vocal style, occur in such different genres as Vedic and Buddhist chant, Japanese *Nō*, and European 'recitative and aria'; and the insertion of meaningless syllables into melismatic chant occurs in both religious chant and secular song throughout the world.

Pitch, Rhythm, and Timbre

Vocal music has usually been accorded greater importance than instrumental music; and this remains true today, for the singing voice is the lifeblood of popular music. Instruments have most commonly been employed to support the voice, or to act as surrogates for speech.

Non-Westernized Aboriginal peoples of Australia, for example, evidently still feel no need to make instruments yielding a scale of pitched notes. The instrument requiring the greatest skill in performance, the *didjeridu*, is primarily a rhythmic instrument, and is unique to the continent. It normally consists of a eucalyptus branch hollowed out by termites, or of a tube of bamboo, mostly over a metre in length. It is blown rather like a trumpet but without a mouthpiece: the deep fundamental tone is obtained by blowing with loosely vibrating lips; and the timbre is varied by changing the position of the tongue and varying the resonance of the mouth cavity. The basic sound is rich in harmonics, and particular overtones are emphasized (by superimposing vocal pitches on the blown sound) so as to perform complex rhythms.[25] (The name of the instrument is itself an onomatopoeic mnemonic that represents some of the mouth movements necessary

[25] Jill Stubington, sleeve note to CD, *Les Aborigènes: Chants et danses de l'Australie du Nord*, Arion ARN 64056.

for performance.) 'Circular' breathing (the ability to breathe through the nose, while blowing, using the cheek muscles to maintain pressure in the mouth cavity) ensures that the sound is continuous, an important aspect of performance when music is used to facilitate communication with spirits.

In many other parts of the world, wind instruments are used for their rhythmic as much as their melodic attributes: examples include African and Philippine stopped flutes, South East Asian mouth organs, and Andean pan pipes. The winds and percussion of Lamaist ensembles are mostly used rhythmically, without melody. Percussive instruments themselves, whether of definite or indefinite pitch, have conspicuous individual timbres, and are often used in a secondary capacity to add variety to the texture of a musical performance. In Africa, for example, metal jingles may be attached to the tip of a lute, to the rim or head of a drum, or to the wrists of a xylophone player.[26] In many areas, percussion instruments are used *without* melodic instruments: in South Asia, China, and Japan, for example, ritual, through-composed pieces for gongs and drums are still preserved. Percussive instruments of definite and indefinite pitch display conspicuous individual timbres, making possible an infinity of textural variety.

Variations in timbre can alter the perception of pitch; indeed, many instruments have tone-modifiers which reduce pitch perception and deliberately mask any beating caused by instruments not quite in tune with one another.[27] In India, individual notes (*svara*) and small adjustments to their pitch (*shruti*) were associated with timbre before they were fully identified with pitch (see p. 102).[28] In China, the names of the pitches originally referred to the positions occupied by particular instruments (in ritual music and dance) on either side of the king (see p. 332); only because these locations were associated with pitch-giving instruments did they come to refer to pitches. In Korea, an essential element in court music, as performed today, is *shigumse* ('living notes'), in which each note assumes its own life and shape as its pitch is altered gradually (by up to a semitone) and its timbre is subtly changed (see p. 378). The emergence of individual pitches for instruments appears to be a relatively late development, before which

[26] J. H. Kwabenia Nkeita, *The Music of Africa* (London: Gollancz, 1979), 70.

[27] Peter Cooke, 'Exploring Musical Pitch Systems', *ICTM UK Bulletin*, 27 (1990), 8.

[28] Lewis Rowell, *Music and Musical Thought in Early India* (Chicago: University of Chicago Press, 1992), 78–9, 82.

differently *textured* sounds—used, as it were, like jewels on the ephod—were music's substance. The European, modernist, obsession with musical texture is most probably a reversion—albeit subconscious—to an archetype.

Musical Materials in the Natural Environment

Instruments have always been constructed from natural materials and objects to hand: gourds, bamboo and other giant grasses, tree trunks, horns, bones, ivory, and membranes of various kinds. Once discovered, the same mechanical principle may be applied to different materials. Many instruments of similar type are to be found in different continents. The Australian *didjeridu* may be compared with the bark trumpets and other instruments worldwide, made from wood, cane, bone, bark, or bamboo (Pl. 1). Reed flutes, recorder-like flutes, and nose flutes are also widespread. Single-note, stopped flutes, without finger-holes, of different sizes, are often 'rafted' together to form pan pipes: these are to be found in widely separated areas: Africa, Oceania, and Latin America. In Latin America, as in Africa, trumpets are made of bone, gourd, bamboo, or hollowed wood; they may be used as megaphones, creating a 'non-human' voice. Worldwide are to be found bullroarers (flat pieces of wood or bone, attached by one elongated flat end to string or rawhide, and whirled through the air), the awesome sound of which, in many musical cultures, is the voice of a spirit.

Hollow wood is raw material for bell-like instruments, drums, and wind instruments. The slit drum—a hollowed, cylindrical log of wood with a meridional slit—is, properly speaking, a bell. Usually the lips (to right and left of the slit) are of different thicknesses, so that different pitches can be obtained from each; the instrument can then act as a speech surrogate for tonal language; messages may be transmitted over considerable distances. Slit drums exist across Africa, and in parts of Europe, Asia, and South America (Pl. 2).[29] Sometimes the instrument is adorned with a carved head, representing the spirit whose voice it utters. Musical instruments are often constructed from the same materials as other useful structures. A slit-drum may be compared

[29] Anthony Baines, *The Oxford Companion to Musical Instruments* (Oxford: Oxford University Press, 1992), 312.

1. (*above*) Bark trumpet from Solimoes, upper Amazon. Photo: Harald Schultz.

2. (*left*) Standing slit drums, in anthropomorphic form, from Melekula, New Hebrides

with a dug-out canoe, for example: both require the hollowing of a tree trunk; and both have arisen in a material culture that is essentially at one with nature.

Musical instruments may actually *derive* from useful structures. The San (Bushmen), and some other peoples of Africa, use the hunting bow as a very private musical instrument. This is played by striking the string with a small stick in the right hand, and touching it lightly with the left hand at various acoustic nodes, so that a sequence of harmonics is audible to the player, above the fundamental frequency of the string. Alternatively, an end of the bow may be held between the lips or teeth, and the mouth cavity then acts as a resonator; by varying the shape of the mouth cavity, different harmonics may be selected.[30] (In Gabon, in the equatorial forest zone of West Africa, where the mouth-bow technique is used, the stretched string of the musical bow symbolizes mediation between heaven and earth, and its vibrations are believed to connect a people with the 'word' of their first ancestor.[31]) Outside Africa, the mouth-bow technique is used in Taiwan, in Melanesia, and in North, South, and Central America.[32]

A similar technique, using the mouth cavity as resonator, is used to select harmonics from the spectrum of frequencies generated by the vibrating, narrow, flexible, lamella of the Jew's harp; this instrument is found in all the countries of Eurasia, from the Hebrides and beyond, to Polynesia. The technology of the free reed—a tongue vibrating a slot—seems first to have appeared in South East Asia, and has been used in mouth organs throughout the East Asian region. The mouth organ probably developed as a miniaturization of the Jew's harp.[33]

The close link between music, nature, and religion is not something peculiar to rural or animist societies; it is to be observed in folk and art music around the world. And around the world—notwithstanding the multiplicity of musical styles and the diversification of musical functions that have been generated—the essential methods of manipulating the musical impulse are the same. They seem to be inherent in the sonic medium itself.

[30] Baines, *Oxford Companion to Musical Instruments*, 214–15.

[31] Pierre Salée, 'Gabon', *The New Grove* (1980), vii. 53.

[32] Baines, *Oxford Companion to Musical Instruments*, 214; and Bruno Nettl, 'North America', *The New Grove* (1980), xiii. 302.

[33] L. E. R. Picken, 'The Music of Far Eastern Asia', *The New Oxford History of Music*, i (Oxford: Oxford University Press, 1957), 83–190.

From time immemorial, 'tune-smiths' have created musical 'organisms' by developing a given, minimal, musical statement. Like a bird-song, a musical statement makes a declaration about a personality, at a spot in a time in a specific mood from a particular cultural environment. This statement is extended into a musical construct by applying such devices as repetition, sequence, inversion, augmentation, diminution, transposition, ornamentation, and transformation of rhythmic shape. (Western triadic harmony makes possible the contrasting of *two* such statements in the same performance, but the distinction is essentially one of key—that is to say, transposition of mode.) These are all European terms, developed for the analysis of European music; but they are generally applicable to musics from Africa to China. They, and the note-sets on which such devices confer individual character, are intrinsic to the symbolic meaning of music.

Elemental features of music have been described in this chapter mainly in the context of rural, non-literate societies; but such features varied little as urbanization replaced the hunter-foodgathering way of life across Africa, Eurasia, and the Americas. Urbanization led to an enlargement in the *scale* of human integration; it encouraged, therefore, a corresponding enlargement in the *scale* of musical construction and performance, and imposed diversification of musical functions. More importantly, however, it altered the relationship between humans and their environment. Whereas in hunter-foodgathering and subsistence-farming societies, religious rites served—and still serve—to regulate a state of harmony between humans and their natural world, in urbanized societies, class-oriented work patterns and cash economies enabled humans (to greater or lesser extent) to impose their will upon nature, and in so doing to create conditions of disharmony in the environment. Religious practice came to be conditioned not merely by nature but also by human actions; and religious thought, to be expressed in philosophical terms, reflecting the need for obedience to human as well as divine rulers.

As élite classes encouraged soloistic performance, the individual aesthetic response to music intensified. Religious custom was disengaged from social custom, and music came to exist as much for the pleasure of humans as for the appeasement of gods and ancestors.

2 Aspects of Civilization

Peoples, Languages, and Culture

Fossil finds in East Africa suggest that the genus *Homo* emerged there some two million years ago. Modern humans are thought to have originated in Africa some 100,000 years ago: fossil finds in South Africa, Ethiopia, and Israel attest to the success and widespread dispersal of a new species.[1] These early humans made effective tools and weapons, and were probably able to communicate through some form of spoken language. With the later Stone Age (or 'Upper Palaeolithic') of some 40,000 years ago, such activities as orderly burial of the dead, and painting of wildlife scenes on cave walls and rock faces, bear witness to a more advanced capacity for structured thought. The development of language, the medium for such thought, may then be associated specifically with the development of *Homo sapiens sapiens* (anatomically modern humans).[2]

Over a space of time between 60,000 and 10,000 years ago, *Homo sapiens sapiens* colonized every continent except Antarctica. It is likely that this process began in Africa, and that, around 40,000 years ago, humans from Africa gradually replaced populations of earlier hominids in Europe and Asia; and it has been suggested that it was the use of language that enabled this species to displace the earlier species, *Homo neanderthalensis*, in Europe.[3]

[1] C. B. Stringer, 'Evolution of Early Humans', *The Cambridge Encyclopedia of Human Evolution* (Cambridge: Cambridge University Press, 1992), 248–51; and *The Times Atlas of World History*, ed. Geoffrey Barraclough (London, 1989), 32.

[2] Ibid. 34; and Colin Renfrew, *Archaeology and Language* (London: Penguin Books, 1987), 274.

[3] Jared Diamond, *The Rise and Fall of the Third Chimpanzee* (London: Vintage, 1992), 27–48.

The probability that all modern humans emerged from Africa undermines any concept of a world inhabited by genetically separate, and distinct, 'races'. Moreover, the concept of 'race' as a *determinant* of culture was long ago shown, by scientific evidence from population genetics, to be invalid: even a single, remote tribe was found not to constitute a genetic entity.[4] Miscegenation begins as soon as alliances between clans are formed, and is generally accelerated by large-scale movements of peoples. It is, of course, still possible to distinguish in broad anatomical terms between *varieties*—such as what have been called 'Negroid', 'Mongoloid', and 'Caucasoid' types—but all these are members of one species. And, whereas interbreeding between species does not (in general) occur, interbreeding between such types occurs freely. China embraces approximately one-quarter of the world's population; but there is no single, ethnically pure (Han) Chinese person. 'Race', culture, and nationality are not inherently interconnected.

A sense of nationhood is commonly fostered by language: linguistic boundaries are less readily changed by history than are political boundaries, as the existence of multilingual 'nations' attests. Belgium, for example, has been ruled in turn by Romans, Franks, Spaniards, and Austrians; it was not recognized as a nation state until 1839, and antipathy persists between speakers of Flemish (a Germanic language) and speakers of French (a Romance language). For India, a 'national' identity was scarcely even a concept, until English provided a language common to those who were educated. In Wales, the continued existence of a Celtic language alongside a Germanic language (English) furnishes a powerful stimulus to national consciousness, even though this irks many Welsh people who speak only English. Notwithstanding the popular association of language with 'homeland', language is no respecter of national boundaries. It cannot be *equated* with culture. Nevertheless, the structure of a language affects the style of music that supports it, and language is often a differentiating factor—indeed, at times the only such factor—between regional musical styles within a larger sphere of cultural influence.

There are many possible causes of linguistic—and by, extension, musical—change. When humans move into formerly uninhabited territory they bring a new language into the area; alternatively, when they move into sparsely inhabited territory, they cause a new language to displace, or blend with, an original. Interaction between neighbouring

[4] Claude Lévi-Strauss, *The View from Afar* (Oxford: Blackwell, 1985), 11–12.

communities, whether through trade or warfare, causes languages to intermingle; and changes in social mechanisms can create the need for new types of language (and new genres of song).[5] In our own day, jet travel and electronic communication have caused one language, English, to be spoken in various forms and degrees of complexity throughout the globe; indeed, workers worldwide, from peasants in the paddy fields to fishermen on the high seas, can listen to the latest pop-varieties of English as they go about their tasks.

Linguistic variants usually remain close to their neighbours, while becoming increasingly removed from the original, so that new languages develop from common roots but stay related to other languages within the 'family'. Uncertainties remain regarding the origin, spread, and development of languages; but because language is a key element in the development of any musical style, a brief description of certain widely accepted findings may provide a background to the provenance of musical styles, in relation to the spatial distribution of peoples.

Because *Homo sapiens sapiens* originated in Africa, it may be assumed that language originated there too. The principal language group of Sub-Saharan Africa is the Niger-Congo (using segmental tone), of which there are hundreds of varieties and some 300 million speakers. The largest branch of this group, the Bantu, constitutes one of the major language families of the world; it spread south with Bantu-speaking peoples during the first millennium AD, largely displacing the indigenous Khoisan languages. Bantu languages, of which there are now over 300 varieties, are spoken south of what has been called the 'Bantu line', extending from Cameroon in the west to Kenya in the east.[6]

Niger-Congo languages did not spread beyond Sub-Saharan Africa; Afro-Asiatic languages, on the other hand, established a link between peoples of Africa, Asia, and Europe. The Afro-Asiatic language group is thought to have originated in Africa to the west of the Red Sea.[7] It was here that the production of food crops and the use of domesticated animals began, as the retreat of the last Ice Age led to the development of rich savannah country. Moving through savannah lands with effective farming techniques, Chadic-speakers reached Lake Chad, the Berbers reached the Maghreb, Proto-Egyptians reached Upper Egypt, and speakers of Proto-Semitic settled in Ethiopia and moved on into Arabia

[5] Renfrew, *Archaeology and Language*, 121–3.
[6] Kenneth Katzner, *The Languages of the World* (London: Routledge, 1977), 6, 29–30.
[7] Roland Oliver, *The African Experience* (London: Weidenfeld & Nicolson, 1991), 38.

(then also savannah).[8] Semitic-speaking peoples moved into West Asia—possibly as early as the sixth millennium BC[9]—bequeathing other related languages to Babylonians, Jews, and Aramaens. (Aramaic—ancestral to Arabic—was the language of Jesus Christ.)

Afro-Asiatic languages met the family of Indo-European languages in West Asia. Indo-European languages are usually divided into two main branches, and their homeland has been a matter of constant controversy. A view that both emerged among farmers in Anatolia as early as the seventh millennium BC[10] now seems less probable than origin among hunter-fishing communities in the forest steppe or steppe zone of the Volga–Ural region.[11] The Western branch gradually spread west and south into Greece and Italy, east and north into Russia and parts of Scandinavia, and north-west as far as the British Isles.[12] It includes the Celtic, Germanic, Hellenic, Romance (derived from Latin), Slavonic, and Baltic languages. The second branch, usually called 'Indo-Iranian', travelled east and south into Iran and India and further east into Chinese Turkestan. This eastern branch includes the Iranian, Indic, and Tocharian languages. (Indic languages are separate from Dravidian languages, spoken widely in southern India and parts of Sri Lanka, and perhaps, at one time, over much of central, and even northern, India.) Indo-European languages, from Sanskrit and Persian to English and French, exhibit basic correspondences that suggest an early link between peoples from Ireland to the fringes of China.

The cultural link across Eurasia provided by the network of Indo-European languages was impaired during the first millennium AD, when successive peoples from the Altai mountains of Siberia and Mongolia adopted the nomadic way of life and moved into the steppe lands of Central Asia, each advance driving a previous wave onwards into some part of Europe and Asia. First came the Xiongnu, an alliance of nomad peoples who had dominated much of Central Asia between the third and fourth centuries AD; their successors, the Huns, pushed through southern Russia into the Danube Basin and eventually into Western Europe.[13] The Huns were followed in the mid-sixth century by

[8] Martin Bernal, *Black Athena, the Afroasiatic Roots of Classical Civilization* (2 vols.; London: Free Association Books, 1987), i. 11.

[9] Ibid. 11–14.

[10] Renfrew, *Archaeology and Language*, 168–74; Bernal, *Black Athena*, i. 11–14.

[11] J. P. Mallory, *In Search of Indo-Europeans: Language, Archaeology and Myth* (London: Thames & Hudson, 1989), 149.

[12] Katzner, *Languages of the World*, 10–11.

[13] *Times Atlas*, 60, 312.

the Avars, who caused the Indo-European-speaking Slavs—already pushed north and west from their original base in present-day Belorussia by the Huns—to spread south into the Balkans.

The Huns and Avars were succeeded by various Turkic peoples, headed by the Khazars (who were converted to Judaism *c.*AD 740 and are the likely ancestors of the East European Jews). When the Seljuk Turks—pushed west by the Mongols—eventually claimed suzerainty over what remained of the Byzantine Empire in the eleventh century, a wedge of Altaic languages severed the continuous chain of Indo-European languages.[14] The Altaic language family, believed to have originated in the Altai mountains of Mongolia, includes the Turkic and Mongolian languages; it is also related to the Uralic languages (such as Finnic and Hungarian) and, more distantly, to the languages of Korea and Japan.[15]

East of the Bay of Bengal, the languages spoken are mostly unrelated to those spoken to the west; the Bay itself appears to be situated at a point of cultural division. The Malayo-Polynesian (or Austronesian) language group, comprising some 800 different languages, is spoken from Malaysia and the Indonesian archipelago (in which countries it is dominant), through Taiwan, Malagasy, and the Melanesian islands, to Polynesia (including the Maoris of New Zealand, but excluding Australia and most of New Guinea). On the South East Asian mainland a mixture of language groups is spoken. Mons to the north, and Khmers to the south, established early empires and spoke Mon-Khmer languages. The Mons were subsequently displaced by the Thais and Burmese, and Mon is now a minority language; Khmer, however (which does not use segmental tone), remains the national language of Cambodia. Thais and Burmese brought differing versions of the Sino-Tibetan family (which does use segmental tone) to the area. The different but related scripts used by Burmese, Thais, and Khmers are thought to have originated in southern India.[16]

Chinese is the dominant sub-group of the Sino-Tibetan family and is spoken by approximately a billion people; it is a monosyllabic language, the script of which was originally pictographic. Both Koreans and Japanese may make use of the Chinese 'characters'; but both have developed 'syllabaries' that enable them to write their own polysyllabic languages

[14] *Times Atlas*, 60, 314.
[15] Katzner, *Languages of the World*, 19.
[16] Ibid. 24–5.

phonetically. (A syllabary differs from an alphabet in that each sign represents a vowel sound preceded by a different initial consonant.) The relationship of Vietnamese to Chinese is uncertain: it uses segmental tone, and nearly half its language is the same as Chinese; however, its use of Chinese characters was replaced in the eighteenth century by the Latin alphabet, together with a complex system of diacritical marks that distinguish certain vowel sounds and indicate tone.[17]

Autochthonous peoples of Australia and North and South America were isolated before the arrival of Europeans; on each continent a large number of separate languages were spoken, but in Australia and North America, English, and in South America, Spanish, are increasingly displacing these languages. English is now the principal language not only of the UK, USA, Canada, Australia, and New Zealand, but also of many newly independent countries in the Caribbean and of more than a dozen African countries. In India it has the title of 'associate official language'; and it is spoken with some degree of proficiency by peoples in all parts of the globe.[18] The spread of English as an 'international' language has, to some extent, been complemented by the spread of Western musical style; it provides living evidence of the extent to which the spread of language and musical style can cause each to acquire new dialects, increasingly removed from their originals.

The spread of a language does not imply a corresponding spread of other cultural systems. A particular language may be used over an area in which wide diversity of social customs or religious beliefs prevails. Both language and ethnicity are important aspects of culture, but neither *defines* culture. Culture is essentially about what people do, to and with themselves, and about what they do, to and with nature. A wide spectrum of traits distinguishes one cultural system from another.

The anthropologist Claude Lévi-Strauss has suggested that, from birth, 'things and beings' in an environment establish, for the inhabitants, an array of references that constitutes a system of 'conduct, motivation and judgement'; that this view is 'confirmed by an educationally reflexive view of the history of a particular culture or civilisation'; and that other cultural systems are perceptible to the inhabitants of a given environment only 'through distortions imprinted on them by the original system'. Although a 'cumulative history' can be achieved only when isolated peoples and their cultural systems come together,

[17] Ibid. 230–1. [18] Ibid. 43–4.

the tendency is for such peoples to preserve their individual cultural identity, and thus to distinguish themselves from adjoining peoples and cultural systems: 'Cultures are not unaware of one another, they even borrow from one another on occasion; but, in order not to perish, they must in other connections, remain somewhat impermeable toward one another.'[19]

Thus, if population movements cause cultural systems to combine, differing 'reference systems' are thrown into the same orbit. Intruding peoples may then absorb the 'reference systems' of those upon whom they intrude, or they may attempt to impose their own 'reference systems'. Whichever system dominates, the effect will be an enlargement of the cultural perspective, as different traits are tested and, for whatever reason, accepted or rejected. The dominant system will be that which has proved least permeable by the other. In such ways, for example, Chinese musical culture remained largely separate from the many foreign influences that bore upon it; Hindustani music remained distinct from West Asian classical music; and, in the climate of West Asian classical music, Turkey was more influenced (by Persia and Arabia) than influencing. In modern times, peoples worldwide are attempting to ameliorate overwhelming Western musical influence by infusing Western genres and styles with indigenous performance characteristics and sonorities.

The Development of Civilization

The most common causes of migration are population pressure and the need for new resources. The earliest widespread movements of peoples had their origins in farming: that is to say, the deliberate manipulation of natural systems in order to exploit favoured species.[20] With the melting of the last Ice Age around 8000 BC, a dramatic increase in population made scarce the wild plants and game that had formerly sustained small bands of hunter-foodgathering peoples. As a consequence, cereals that had originally grown wild in mountainous habitats came to be planted in surrounding valleys and plains. Subsequently, irrigation techniques for the distribution of river waters enabled human settlements to expand into drier, low-lying areas.

[19] Lévi-Strauss, *The View from Afar*, pp. xiv, 11, 18.
[20] *Times Atlas*, 38.

Different cereals, from many parts of the globe, contributed at different times to this process. Conspicuous among them were wheat and barley in West Asia—these spread west to Europe, and east as far as India—rice in South East Asia, rice and millet in China, and maize and beans in Mesoamerica.

Exploitation of plant species was complemented by exploitation of animal species, which, again, were isolated from their wild populations. It was found that certain mammals were a source of milk and wool, as well as of meat. Subsequently, animals were used to pull ploughs and carts, or to carry loads, and later, human riders. Farming led to the concept of land ownership;[21] and it gave rise to the familiar landscape of village communities as it survives in many parts of the world.[22] It provided the milieu from which sprang the myriad peasant musical styles associated with such communities.

The initial spread of settled farming was a slow process: new soil brought into cultivation was usually only a few kilometres distant. It has been estimated that the average movement of a farming family was one kilometre per year, or 1000 kilometres per millennium. Farming, however, was labour intensive, and caused populations to increase dramatically. In Europe, for example, it has been estimated that, among hunter-foodgatherers, there was one person for approximately 10 square kilometres; whereas among subsistence farmers there were approximately five people per single square kilometre.[23] Between 8000 BC and 4000 BC, the human population of the world is thought to have increased by some sixteen times.[24] The large-scale dispersion of new populations underpins the development of civilization.

Typically, farmers tend to establish village settlements. As populations increase in numbers, more land is required to feed them. Villages then join to form larger and denser settlements with a parallel increase in social power. Towns are then established, perhaps around a ford, a natural harbour, or a place where valleys meet; and shrines are erected for honouring and appeasing the local deity. Towns, often dominated by particular clans, develop into city states.[25] (Clans

[21] See Steve Jones, *The Language of the Genes* (London: Flamingo, 1994), 173; chs. 8 and 9 provide genetic evidence for the earliest migrations of *homo sapiens* and farming communities, respectively.

[22] *Times Atlas*, 30, 38.

[23] Renfrew, *Archaeology and Language*, 125.

[24] *Times Atlas* (1989), 30.

[25] J. M. Roberts, *Pelican History of the World* (London: Pelican Books, 1988), 65.

achieve and retain power by kinship rules restricting marriage, a system that still operates, for example, within surviving monarchies.) City states engender musical ceremonies associated with kinship.

Urbanization makes a given population more vulnerable to the natural elements: variations in rainfall, for example, acquire increased significance. Populations then become predatory: they need to conquer another's land.[26] Warfare leads to the creation of standing armies, commanded by local warlords who, if successful, acquire the trappings of kingship and found dynasties. When a state (or a nomadic people) from outside a given area establishes control over a large number of city states, and develops unified and cooperative systems of social and political control, a civilization with distinctive cultural systems may develop.

The word civilization (from *civitas*: city) implies a way of life qualitatively different from anything that preceded it. It creates new categories of non-agricultural occupations, such as artisan, merchant, priest, soldier, and king; and it generates a few large centres of settlement that dominate a sparsely inhabited hinterland. It encourages technological development, and generates long-distance trade. It leads to building on a larger scale and to sculptural decoration. It creates the need for writing. Writing leads to the development of larger lyric forms; and these, in turn, lead to the creation of new forms of music and dance. All this implies that human control over the natural environment makes possible significant change. This possibility in no way implies a value judgement on human behaviour, on the quality of life, or the quality of art or music: it is merely a comment on the *magnitude* of human intervention on the natural processes of the planet.

Around the middle of the fourth millennium BC, civilizations began to arise—apparently independently—in the 'Fertile Crescent' of the lower Tigris and Euphrates valleys (with expansion into Syria); in the Nile Valley; in the Indus Valley; in the Yellow River Valley, and, later, the Red River Valley (in Vietnam). During the second millennium BC, civilization spread from Egypt and Syria to Crete; and, by the beginning of the first millennium BC (if not much earlier), civilization was established in Mesoamerica. The influence of musical genres and styles associated with these early civilizations is still apparent in extant forms of music-making.

[26] Daniel Bates and Amal Rassam, *Peoples and Cultures of the Middle East* (Englewood Cliffs, NJ: Prentice Hall, 1983), 20.

Nomads as Culture Bearers

Until the fifteenth century AD, when the use of gunpowder changed long-established patterns of conquest, the greatest threat to established civilizations came from nomads. Nomad pastoralism emerged as a secondary development to farming in those arid steppe lands of Central Asia suitable for grazing but not for settled agriculture.[27] The domestication of the horse, and its use as a pack animal, made possible the movement of entire communities with livestock, from one pasture to another. Nomadic pastoralism generated its own distinctive musical genres and styles, involving only such instruments as could be easily and successfully transported, or fashioned quickly from surrounding natural materials. In western Central Asia, prior to Muslim influence, small two-string plucked lutes and two-string fiddles were commonly used by nomads. The strings of the latter are excited by a bow of slack horse hair threaded *between* the strings and tightened by finger tension, an arrangement that enabled horsemen to sling fiddle and bow safely together for transport.[28]

Nomad pastoralism existed in the Eurasian steppe lands during the third millennium BC, most probably originating in what is now the Ukraine, and spreading east into Central Asia. Based largely on the camel, it also became common in the semi-desert areas of North Africa and West Asia. Nomad pastoralists did not operate in isolation: their economy developed from mixed farming and herding, and they were usually dependent upon agriculturalists for the exchange of produce. Indeed, by lending livestock to indigent farmers, they could attract clients and achieve a degree of political dominance over them.[29] (Through such contacts, peasant and urban musical styles interacted.)

A more militaristic form of political dominance was made possible in the steppe by the development of the horse as an animal for *riding*. Mounted, nomad, pastoralists with an efficient, 'ranked' social organization, could then achieve political dominance through force of arms. The first clear evidence of this development is from the second millennium; the use of the chariot is attested from about 1600 BC, but

[27] Renfrew, *Archaeology and Language*, 198.

[28] Anthony Baines, *The Oxford Companion to Musical Instruments* (Oxford: Oxford University Press, 1992), 107.

[29] John Lamphear, 'Aspects of Early African History', in Phyllis M. Martin and Patrick O'Meara (eds.), *Africa* (Bloomington, Ind.: Indiana University Press, 1986), 81.

there is no evidence of the use of the horse for *riding* until about 1200 BC.[30]

The Eurasian steppe lands constitute a relatively arid, land-locked corridor, some 6,500 kilometres in length; they are bounded on the north by the forests of Siberia, and on the south by deserts, and by the mountainous plateaux of Iran and Afghanistan. Punctuated by oasis cities that lie between the rivers Oxus and Jaxartes—such as Bukhara, Samarkand, Kucha, and Khotan—the steppe lands provided a trade route from East to West; and, from the first century BC onwards, this route stretched from the borders of China to the Mediterranean. In effect, however, it was under the control of nomads, who frequently interrupted the passage of goods, and often made incursions into civilized regions of China, India, West Asia, and Europe.

The spread from China of the all-metal stirrup, around the middle of the first millennium AD, added to the effectiveness of mounted warriors. More stable in the saddle, riders could both use heavier weapons and wear armour; and the warrior-nomads of Central Asia never allowed the wearing of armour to impair their essential fleetness. For 2500 years, from about 1000 BC until the widespread use of gunpowder (invented in China, in the ninth century AD), these warrior-nomads were a recurrent influence in history. Mesopotamian chroniclers described them as 'peoples who had never known a city', and their 'onslaught' as 'like a hurricane'.[31] More recently the nomadic tribe has been described as 'a military machine in embryo whose impulse, if not to fight other nomads, is to raid or threaten the city'.[32] The nomads of Central Asia disrupted the developing course of civilizations, and tested their powers of endurance; but, by spreading ideas from one zone of civilization to another, they contributed to the dynamism of these same zones and, ultimately, to their durability.

The writer Bruce Chatwin—who spent much of his short life living with nomads—has neatly encapsulated the intrinsic historical function of such peoples:

> Settlers, since the beginning of history, have recruited nomads as mercenaries: either to stave off a nomad threat ... or to fight other states.... It can be argued that the State, as such, resulted from a kind of 'chemical' fusion between herdsman and planter, once it was realised

[30] Renfrew, *Archaeology and Language*, 138.
[31] Francis Watson, *A Concise History of India* (London: Thames & Hudson, 1974), 30.
[32] Bruce Chatwin, *The Songlines* (London: Picador, 1987), 225–6.

that the techniques of animal coercion could be applied to an inert peasant mass.... The masses are to be corralled, milked, penned in (to save them from the human 'wolves' outside), and, if need be, lined up for slaughter. The City is thus a sheepfold superimposed over a Garden.[33]

New Tasks for Musicians

The movement towards civilization had important consequences for music. A cash economy makes possible a variety of work patterns, based on hierarchical structures. Priesthood often becomes an exclusive profession, and artists may then be *employed* for the *adornment*—rather than for the enactment—of religious rituals. They may also be employed for the glorification of political rulers. Civilization makes possible the *profession* of music.

As civilization develops, the primary relationship between music and religion changes its character. Civilization usually brings a religious development from multifold animism to a form of systematic theology, expressed in writing. With any such enlargement of the religious perspective, music tends to become *associated with* rather than *intrinsic to* religion. In religious chant, the text takes precedence—and music tends to become soloistic. This is where music usually develops a complementary, secular function, with a courtly, rather than a religious, role.

The development of large-scale cultural systems leads, at some point, to a cleavage between the roles of priest and ruler. The ruler may regard himself as a god-king, as in Pharaonic Egypt; as having a Mandate from Heaven to rule, as in Imperial China; or he may, as is most often the case, acquire his position by brute force and superior technology. In any event, it is unusual for a ruler to consider himself subordinate to his priests. Accordingly, from musical structures used hitherto primarily in the cause of religion, musicians develop a musical ritual to adorn *court* procedures. The tendency is then for the stylized music of court ceremony to be replicated in religious ceremonies, now executed in large and ornate buildings. Meanwhile, popular music, often based on amorous lyrics, comes to be regarded as the proper preserve of secular entertainment and dance; it emerges in various styles, for performance at court, or among the 'folk'.

[33] Ibid. 225–6.

Such areas of activity are never self-contained, however; cross-fertilization between them occurs. In particular, the art music of a centre is frequently fashioned from the folk music of its peripheral regions. Nevertheless, the primal psychic concordat between life, religion, and art has been lost. Music gradually evolves from natural ritual to human artifice; and its stylistic traits become specific to particular areas of cultural influence.

3 Early Oligarchies in Mesopotamia and Egypt

Ancient Mesopotamia

Civilization appears first to have developed in what is known as the 'Fertile Crescent' of Mesopotamia. The name Mesopotamia means 'between rivers', and indicates the land drained by the rivers Tigris and Euphrates. The irrigation techniques needed to control these rivers had evolved elsewhere;[1] but it was in Mesopotamia that writing first developed, and writing enabled the peoples of this area to create the administrative apparatus needed for a political structure of evolving city states, and thus to meet the challenge of their physical environment. Writing also enabled a record to be left of a remarkable understanding of the relationships between string lengths and pitches in the generation of musical sound.

Who were the peoples of Mesopotamia? The question is pertinent, for its answer indicates the extent to which, from earliest times, the peoples and cultural systems of Africa, Asia, and Europe interacted in this area. The origin of the Sumerians, after whom the first empire is named, is still in dispute. They may have been indigenous to the land: Sumer is an ancient name for Mesopotamia. Alternatively, they may have arrived from the north-east, at the beginning of the fourth millennium, and mingled with Semitic-speaking peoples who had already moved there from East Africa via Arabia, following the desiccation of the Sahara. In any event, it seems clear that Mesopotamian civilization was built on foundations laid by Semitic-speaking peoples: texts from Uruk indicate that both Semitic and Sumerian languages were in use by *c.*3000 BC.[2]

The Sumerians were extremely inventive. They brought architecture, stone sculpture, and metalwork to the level of mastery. They laid

[1] Martin Bernal, *Black Athena, the Afroasiatic Roots of Classical Civilization* (2 vols.; London: Free Association Books, 1987), i. 12.

[2] Ibid., and *The Times Atlas of World History*, ed. Geoffrey Barraclough (London, 1989), 54.

the foundations of mathematics. By 3000 BC, their pictographic script had been replaced by the phonetic *cuneiform* script. This form of writing—in which nail-shaped wedges were pressed into wet clay in the formation of different signs (*cuneus* means 'wedge')—was used throughout Mesopotamia, and quickly spread to the Indus Valley. (It was to become the basis of the Arabic alphabet.) Flexible, syllabic writing not only eased the essential tasks of irrigation, harvest, and storage; it made possible the communication of knowledge and ideas.[3] The naming of harp strings in Old Babylonia, for example, reflected Sumerian tradition: it has been argued that the Sumerians themselves made use of scales of five notes.[4]

The Sumerians were probably the first to develop their religious ideas in a literary form. The story of Gilgamesh is the oldest surviving epic in the world, and it concerns a king of Uruk, known to have lived around 2700 BC. From it we have received the symbol of a flood as a godly punishment, and the legend of a favoured family who survive in an ark, from which a new 'race' will emerge.[5]

A society subsisting on agriculture is at the mercy of the nature-gods. The Sumerians built elaborate temples for their gods; the tower of the Temple of the Moon still rises above the ruins of Ur. Each temple was raised on a solid platform, above the level of the houses, and each contained a holy room for the statue of a particular god. Temples demanded decoration; and the Sumerians were the first to give artistic expression to the details of human features.[6] The list of staff at the Eshumesha Temple at Nippur includes no fewer than thirty-eight categories of people employed, divided into three main groups: cultic, administrative, and domestic (including craftsmen).[7] A total of 180 'musicians' and sixty-two 'lamentation priests' is reported at temples in the Lagash area.[8]

The Sumerians developed extensive trading networks; they used lead, silver, and tin from as far away as Hungary. Trade encouraged the spread of literacy; and, as early as the third millennium BC, there

[3] J. M. Roberts, *Pelican History of the World* (London: Pelican Books, 1988), 66–7.

[4] Marcelle Duchesne-Guillemin, 'La Théorie babylonienne des métaboles musicales', *Revue de Musicologie*, 55/1 (1969).

[5] Roberts, *Pelican History of the World*, 67.

[6] Ibid. 70.

[7] J. N. Postgate, *Early Mesopotamia: Society and Economy at the Dawn of History* (London: Routledge, 1992), 126, 127.

[8] L. J. Gelb, '*Homo ludens* in Early Mesopotamia', *Studia Orientalia*, 46 (1975), 43–76; see table (pp. 47–9), *Nar* 'singer/musician' (pp. 57–60), and *Gala* 'cantor' (pp. 64–74).

was cultural contact between Mesopotamia, the Levant (the eastern Mediterranean, with its islands and shores), Egypt, the Aegean, and the Indus Valley. A powerful civilization then developed in the Levant; and the schools of Ebla (in Syria) attracted students from Mesopotamia.[9] Writing was already used in Anatolia and the Aegean region, during the second millennium BC.

About 2000 BC, Semitic-speaking Amorites from Syria destroyed the city of Ur; they established dynasties in many parts of Syria and Mesopotamia, of which the most significant were to be those of Babylon (in the south) and Assyria, based on Nineveh (in the north). It was during the reign of Hammurabi (1792–50 BC)—famous for establishing some 282 articles of Mesopotamian law—that Babylon emerged as the pre-eminent city state; the Old Babylonian empire subsequently became the first to embrace the whole of Mesopotamia. The science of astronomy was founded in Babylonia, and made possible the prediction of lunar eclipses and the plotting of the positions of the planets. Old Babylonia developed the circle of 360 degrees and the hour of sixty minutes;[10] it also established the musical system of seven diatonic modes.

Around the seventeenth century BC, the Hittites, who wrote in a language that is a distinct branch of Indo-European, established a powerful empire in Anatolia. As they moved southwards into Syria they encountered the Egyptians (whose empire had expanded thus far north) and forced the great Pharaoh, Thutmosis III, to pay tribute. In 1595 BC, they marched down the Euphrates and sacked Babylon. Shortly thereafter, Babylon was taken by a people from the Zagros mountains of Iran, the Cassites, who assimilated Babylonian culture and ruled the empire for approximately four centuries.[11]

The Cassites were within the cultural sphere of the Elamite civilization that had developed in present-day Khuzistan and in parts of the Iranian highlands, before the arrival of Iranian-speakers in the second millennium BC.[12] Elamite is now thought to have belonged to the Dravidian language family that existed in South India, and the Elamites appear to have had the darker skins characteristic of many South Indians. Greek traditions link the Elamites with Ethiopians (*Aithiopes* means 'those with burnt faces'); the area may have been settled by expeditionaries in the Egyptian army, but the claim is unproven.[13]

[9] Bernal, *Black Athena*, i. 16.

[10] Roberts, *Pelican History of the World*, 77–8.

[11] *Times Atlas*, 55; Bernal, *Black Athena*, ii. 642.

[12] Bernal, *Black Athena*, ii. 254.

[13] Ibid.

During the early thirteenth century BC, the Hittite empire collapsed. This enabled the Phrygians, an Indo-European-speaking people from Thrace (today the province of Turkey on the European side of the Bosphorus), to occupy central Anatolia, and the Semitic-speaking Aramaeans (prominent traders, and the first major users of the camel) to occupy parts of Syria and northern Babylonia.[14] The Assyrians, however, assisted by iron-working techniques adopted from the Hittites, became increasingly imperialistic: by the ninth century BC, they were dominant in Syria; and by the seventh century BC, they had established an empire that extended from northern Egypt to western Iran.

Assyria's ascendancy was cut short by the entry into recorded history of two Indo-European-speaking peoples from the high plateau of Iran: the Medes and the Persians. This entrance was itself caused by the arrival from Central Asia of the first Indo-European-speaking nomadic *horsemen*. An offshoot of the Xiongnu, known as Scythians, they bore down on Iran from the Caucasus, driving the Medes onwards; but an alliance was struck between the two, and, together, in 612 BC, they sacked the great city of Nineveh. The Medes went on to rule the north as far as Anatolia, and drove the Scythians back into the steppes.

The Persians, meanwhile, had settled near the Gulf in Khuzistan. Their king, Cyrus, conquered the Medes; and in a historic encounter, made famous by the Bible, and by the composers Handel and Walton, defeated the apparently debauched and insouciant Babylonians in 539 BC. He went on to create the largest empire the world had yet seen; it extended from the Hindu Kush (in Afghanistan) to the Levant, and included the whole of Syria, Iran, and Iraq. His son added Egypt. Compared with the Assyrian empire, Cyrus's empire was tolerant, and respectful of traditions; it commanded a new type of loyalty from vassal states, and encouraged cultural assimilation. It also marked the onset of a new imperialism. For over 1,000 years thereafter, Persians were to harry successive empires in Greece and Rome.

Music and Musical Instruments in Ancient Mesopotamia

Evidence of musical practices in ancient Mesopotamia suggests topics that will recur time and again in these pages;

[14] *Times Atlas*, 56.

indeed, some have already appeared. Secrecy is one such. Music was intrinsic to religious observance, and, since the priests had a monopoly of religious knowledge, it was important that certain tunes were taught only to future priests. Storytelling is another. New Year festivals had obvious importance to a society in which nature-gods were still worshipped; there is evidence that a creation myth was recited (probably in chant) on such occasions.[15] Fertility rites included special dances, and it is probable that dance was used to enact religious myths at some point.

Music existed essentially to honour the gods, and music-making was itself a religious activity; instruments were objects of veneration and were most probably (as in many cultures today) regarded as possessing magical *personae*. Religious texts were intoned solo, chorally, or antiphonally, with or without instrumental accompaniment. Musicians were employed in the performance of daily liturgies in the temples, and musical performance was governed by precise rules. Music, therefore, was a fundamental aspect of the training of priests in the temple schools, schools that had existed since Sumerian times. Their training extended over three years, at the end of which the trainee was examined. As the divergencies between the roles of king and priest became wider, special music schools were set up in the palaces; they eventually became academic institutions. Musical training would have included theory as well as practice, for, by Babylonian times, music had become linked with cosmology.[16]

The Old Babylonians of the early second millennium were expert mathematicians. In the process of tuning a type of nine-string lyre, they appear to have discovered the arithmetical relationship between the length of a string and its pitch. They made use of the fact that a string of two-thirds the length of another sounds a fifth higher in tuning a basic, heptatonic, diatonic octave (plus one note), identical with our major (untempered) scale. They also systematized a tuning procedure for modulating from any one of the seven diatonic modes to another adjacent mode, by sharpening or flattening one of the outer strings of the tritone. All this is set out in cuneiform texts impressed on tablets of clay.[17] This tonal system may have supplied a theoretical basis for those that developed subsequently in Greece, India, and China. As in Greece

[15] Wilhelm Stauder, 'Mesopotamia', *The New Grove* (1980), xii. 199.

[16] Ibid. 200.

[17] M. L. West, 'The Babylonian Musical Notation and the Hurrian Melodic Texts', *Music and Letters*, 75 (1994), 161–79.

(at a later date), the Old Babylonians generated different modal octave sets within one and the same octave.[18]

The two most important string instruments of ancient Mesopotamia were the harp and the lyre. The remains of large, free-standing boat-shaped harps, with eleven to fifteen strings, secured by gold or copper pegs, found in the Royal Cemetery at Ur, suggest the religious importance attached to these instruments. Indeed, it is possible that musicians were buried alive while playing with their dead monarch.[19] Boat-shaped harps were sophisticated versions of arched harps. These consisted of three basic components: a curved neck (the 'bow') that carried the strings; a resonator (to which the neck was attached); and the strings. Arched harps were in use in Mesopotamia as early as 3400 BC, but there is little evidence of their use there after the second millennium; they appear in India, however, in the second century BC, in China by the fifth century AD, and in Burma by the sixth century AD, where they still survive.[20] (In less ornate form, they are also still in use in Central Africa.)

During the second millennium, the *angled* harp appeared in Mesopotamia. This harp has a *straight* neck jutting from the soundbox. Playing techniques differed according to the position in which the instrument was held. By the first millennium, horizontal angled harps were being held under the left arm, so that the player could use one hand to stop the strings and the other to pluck the strings with a plectrum (in essence, the basic technique of the guitar).[21]

The other important string instrument of ancient Mesopotamia, the lyre, is fundamentally different from the harp in that its strings run to a crossbar (or 'yoke'), supported by two arms that lie in the plane of the surface of the soundbox; a bridge rests on the soundbox and the strings are either attached to this or pass over it for attachment further down.[22] The lyre was associated with the bull, symbol of fertility and of divine power: a lyre embellished with a bull's head was found in the Royal Cemetery at Ur. Sumerian lyres were either free-standing or portable; usually they were comparatively large and held upright.

[18] L. E. R. Picken, *Folk Musical Instruments of Turkey* (Oxford: Oxford University Press, 1975), 606–9.

[19] Robert Anderson, 'Ancient Mesopotamian and Egyptian Music', *NOCM* (1983).

[20] Ann Griffiths and Joan Rimmer, 'Harp', *The New Grove* (1980), viii. 191.

[21] Stauder, 'Mesopotamia', *The New Grove*, xii. 197.

[22] Anthony Baines, *The Oxford Companion to Musical Instruments* (Oxford: Oxford University Press, 1992), 200.

Babylonian lyres, however, were smaller, and always portable. The instrument was held in a tilted position that enabled it to be played in the same manner as the angled harp. (This method of playing spread to Egypt, Greece, and Rome.)[23]

The long-necked lute appeared in Mesopotamia as early as the third millennium BC and is thought to have originated in Syria. It subsequently became popular in Babylonia, where perhaps it was used in measuring string lengths in relation to pitch. Its soundbox was small, either oval or round, with skin stretched over it.

Ritual dance in the ancient Mesopotamian area was accompanied initially by clappers, held in each hand. In time, clappers were superseded by the frame drum. A large goblet-shaped drum became an important cultic instrument during the second millennium. Cymbals are attested in the Babylonian period; but the earliest evidence of their being clashed *vertically*, as in European use, is on a Babylonian plaque of *c.*700–600 BC.[24] Single- and double-pipe instruments first appear during the second millennium, though they may have existed earlier; it is not clear whether they were played with single or double reeds (Pl. 3). These pipes were subsequently adopted by the Egyptians and, later, by the Greeks; descendants have spread to the limits of eastern Asia. In a later era, shawm and frame drum would become ubiquitous in the Islamic world (Pl. 4).

It was not only the *musical* traditions of ancient Mesopotamia that spread to other developing civilizations. Many aspects of religious thought appear first in Mesopotamia. Reference has already been made to the association between the lyre and the bull cult: the resonators of early Sumerian lyres were actually modelled on the body of a bull, and the symbol of the bull links many peoples of the ancient world. It appears in Zoroastrianism and Hinduism. The bull-god was the divine patron of a succession of Nubian Egyptian pharaohs, during the second millennium. Although the cult subsequently died out in Egypt, it travelled from Egypt to Crete and thence to Greece.[25] The cult was popular in Rome, as late as the second century AD, in the worship of Mithras, the bull-slayer; and Mithraism itself may have been a form of Zoroastrianism.[26] Christians abjured Mithraism; nevertheless the date

[23] Stauder, 'Mesopotamia', *The New Grove*, xii. 197.
[24] James Blades, 'Cymbals', *The New Grove* (1980), v. 113.
[25] Bernal, *Black Athena*, i. 18.
[26] *Times Atlas*, 72.

3. (*left*) Assyrian musicians: relief (seventh century BC), from the palace of Ashurpanibal, Nineveh

4. (*below*) Moroccans playing shawm, barrel drum, and frame drum. Photo: Jean Jenkins.

of Mithras' birth was adopted for that of Jesus, and the coming of the Magi is a legend first linked with the infant Mithras.[27] Europe as far as Britain is known for Roman monuments, and perhaps the number of country inns that still bear the name 'Bull's Head' is an echo of that same cult.

Egyptian Cults and their Influence

The civilization of Mesopotamia, watered by two rivers, was paralleled by that along the Nile, where exceptionally fertile soil enabled agriculture to be practised with a minimum of manual labour. As early as the mid-fourth millennium, settlements along the banks of the Nile were merging into towns; and by the beginning of the third millennium, a population of some two million lived in the habitable areas of Egypt. As the Nile provided an easily navigable highway, Egypt was relatively easy to govern, and to control; and huge fiscal returns from food surpluses enabled the pharaohs to mobilize enormous human forces.[28]

It appears that, during the early second millennium, an Egyptian army penetrated as far north as the Balkans, and on into the Caucasus.[29] Later, during the fifteenth century BC—as already noted—Egyptian armies advanced up the Levantine coast to the northern tip of Syria; they exercised suzerainty there and in the Aegean for over a century. Clearly, Egyptian civilization interacted with, and influenced, other civilizations to its north. But human resources in Egypt were also used for civil purposes: the great, 150-metre-high pyramid of Khufu (commonly known as 'Cheops'), at Gizeh, for example, is estimated to have cost the labour of 100,000 people for twenty years. Pyramids were built for dead pharaohs; and, as Egyptians came to believe that life would be lived *after* death very much as it had been lived *before*, great care was taken in preparing tombs, and in conducting the deceased to their eternal resting-place. (To this day, families in Cairo may still invest in houses that are specifically intended for the burial of their relatives, who continue to be visited on particular occasions.)[30]

[27] John Hinnells, 'Mithraism: Cult of the Bull', *The Religions of the World* (London: Lion Publishing, 1982), 88.

[28] Roland Oliver, *The African Experience* (London: Weidenfeld & Nicolson, 1991), 51–5.

[29] Bernal, *Black Athena*, ii. 187.

[30] Ali A. Mazrui, *The Africans* (London: BBC, 1986), 45.

The Egyptian pantheon numbered some 2,000 gods, many originating as animal deities; gradually, the animals became humanized, as artists added human bodies to animal heads. Horus, for example, the falcon-god from whom the pharaoh derived his power, became transformed into the son of Osiris, to be portrayed as a babe-in-arms, in the manner of later Christian iconography.[31] Osiris was the god of fertility and of resurrection and, according to early Egyptian mythology, was murdered by an evil brother, Seth; but the fragments of his mutilated body were reassembled by his sister, Isis; the god Horus was born of their incestuous union. Such fertility myths passed from Egypt to Greece, where Dionysos and Demeter equated with Isis and Osiris. Alexander the Great saw himself as the Son of Amon—that is, of Osiris/Dionysos.[32]

Pharaohs were regarded as god-kings; and, as those of the Old Kingdom (*c.*3100–2180 BC) were held to be the living embodiment of the falcon-god Horus (and therefore divine), an afterlife was a privilege reserved to them alone. During the Middle Kingdom (*c.*2080–1640 BC), the possibility of an afterlife was extended to all people, provided they could present a convincing case before Osiris after death. (Not until the New Kingdom—1570–1075 BC—did fear of purgatory enter Egyptian thinking.[33]) The journey thither was fraught with difficulties: demons, and other obstacles, could be bypassed by possession of the 'Book of the Dead', a collection of placatory incantations, frequently buried with the mummified corpse.[34] Through initiation into the Mysteries, a person could, like Osiris, undergo a symbolic death and be 'born again' as an immortal. The Egyptian 'Book of the Dead', current in the eighteenth century BC, has been equated with the Homeric *Odyssey*.[35] Cultural systems of Egypt interacted with those of Mesopotamia and passed, through Crete, into Greece.

It was during the second half of the first millennium BC that Egyptian documents, relating to magic and philosophy, were first assembled into what later became known as the Hermetic Texts. These were subsequently translated into Coptic in the early centuries AD. Hermeticism was the source both of Gnosticism and of Neo-platonism—both being

[31] Roberts, *Pelican History of the World*, 89.
[32] Bernal, *Black Athena*, i. 70, 115.
[33] Paul Jordan, *Egypt, the Black Land* (London: Phaidon Press, 1976), 42.
[34] John Ruffle, 'Ancient Egypt, Land of the Priest-King', in *The Religions of the World* (London: Lion Publishing, 1982), 78.
[35] Bernal, *Black Athena*, i. 70, 87, 139.

non-Christian heresies—that embodied notions of the pre-existence of souls and of their transmigration from one body to another.[36] Hermeticism also lay behind much medieval European heresy, and it re-surfaced during the European Renaissance. Subsequently it became the basis of Freemasonry;[37] and Freemasons believed Egypt to be the home of Geometry and of the craft of the Mason. Indeed, it is in the context of Freemasonry that Isis and Osiris are invoked by Sarastro in Mozart's *Die Zauberflöte*.

The variety of cults in Egypt led to a decentralization of religion, and this perhaps accounts for the evidence of a vigorous musical life, outside the confines of palace and temple. Surviving Egyptian literature makes frequent reference to music and to itinerant musicians; and, in contrast to Mesopotamia, texts for love-songs, shepherd songs, work songs, and banquet songs survive.[38] Many tomb paintings attest the prevalence of music-making among ordinary people, just as they depict—with persuasive naturalness—pastoral scenes of farming, fishing, and hunting (Pl. 5). The main musical instruments of the Old Kingdom appear to have been end-blown flutes, single- and double-pipes with single-beating, clarinet-type reeds, and arched harps. (Double-pipes of this sort are common in Egypt and the Levant today.) The sistrum (a metal rattle) first appears during the Middle Kingdom, as does the lyre. Lutes appear first in the New Kingdom, when also the first evidence of double-reed pipes appears. Lutes, lyres, and harps existed in various shapes and sizes.[39]

There is no direct evidence of the character of scales and tunings in ancient Egyptian music. Nevertheless, it is evident that musical instruments used in West Asia were also used in Egypt; it is thought that Pythagoras, in addition to visiting Babylon, investigated musical standards in Egypt; and it is known that, later, Plato extolled the excellence of Egyptian music.[40] It may be supposed, therefore, that Egypt developed a system of scales/modes similar to that of Old Babylonia. Nevertheless, the probability is that, away from court influence, Egyptian societies, like others throughout the world, adopted tunings not based on any mathematical, acoustic system, such as the cycle-of-fifths procedure.

[36] Ibid. 133.
[37] Ibid. 24–6, 514.
[38] Robert Anderson, 'Egypt', *The New Grove* (1980), vi. 70.
[39] Anderson, 'Ancient Mesopotamian and Egyptian Music'.
[40] Anderson, 'Egypt', *The New Grove*, vi. 70.

5. Egyptian musicians: tomb painting from Thebes

Egyptian civilization did not, in the long run, prove durable. It was not subject to the turbulence, associated with the dynamism of West Asia, that generated change and technological development. Decline was due largely to its very changelessness and stability. Yet stability, unity, and longevity gave the Egyptians a strong sense of national identity which to this day largely transcends the claims of Islam and pan-Arab nationalism.[41]

Religion and Civilization

The comings and goings of the peoples of the ancient world have significance in the context of this book. They demonstrate that history denies any sharp distinction between East and West, that the polarized use of these terms is misleading, and that there can be no neat categorizations of 'race' in relation to culture.

From 'the dawn of civilization', the cultural systems of Africa, Europe, and Asia have interacted. Greek culture rested heavily on West Asian and Egyptian foundations; and, while the histories of Europe and

[41] Daniel Bates and Amal Rassam, *Peoples and Cultures of the Middle East* (Englewood Cliffs, NJ: Prentice Hall, 1983), 23.

Africa were to be different, West Asia—in relation to both—remained a great crucible of cultural development. The three monotheistic religions played out their formative histories in these lands, as did successive empires. The foundings of Seleucia (capital of the Persian Seleucid dynasty) and of Baghdad (capital of the Islamic Abbāsid dynasty) were separated in time by some thousand years, but the cities were built within a few miles of each other on the banks of the Tigris.

A feature common to all ancient civilizations has been the dependence of kings upon some form of religious endorsement; indeed, monarchs commonly claimed semi-divine status. Priests have had a healthy respect for the secular power of monarchs; and it will have behoved the priesthood to ensure that the gods anticipate the royal will. Priests might escape censure, however, where godly guidance came through oracles. Priests gathered to themselves extraordinary powers and privileges as custodians of the secrets of divination, and of the special forms of sacrifice and of chant which this entailed.[42]

It was perhaps as a reaction against the power of the priesthood that, from around the middle of the first millennium BC, there was a gradual transformation of religious and philosophical consciousness throughout the major civilized zones of Eurasia. In China, ethical world-views—the 'philosophies'—came into being. Further west, the religions of Zoroastrianism, Judaism, Hinduism, Jainism, and godless Buddhism reached definitive stages of development.[43] The Orphic cult entered Greece from Egypt: like the *philosophia* of the Pythagoreans—another product of Egypt—with which it was associated, it concerned the transmigration of the soul.[44]

Such developments were not sudden: each drew on older traditions. Indeed, to some extent they accentuated the correspondences that had already existed within the major civilizations of Eurasia. All these civilizations, for example, were dependent upon agriculture for subsistence; and for energy, all were dependent upon wind, running water, and the muscles of animals and humans.[45] All these civilizations were hierarchical, warrior societies. Within the Indo-European-speaking region, the Indian *Rigveda*, the Persian *Avesta*, and the Homeric epics—like the later Irish and Welsh epics—all reflect heroic societies

[42] Robert Brow, 'Origins of Religion', in *The Religions of the World* (London: Lion Publishing, 1982), 42.

[43] Ibid.

[44] Bernal, *Black Athena*, i. 71–2, 104.

[45] Roberts, *Pelican History of the World*, 305.

that glory in feats of arms; so too, in the Hebrew-speaking region, does the Jewish Old Testament. These epics had come into being orally, in Indo-European-speaking societies, as they approached a state of literacy.[46] Horse-riding had encouraged contact between the Eurasian zones of civilization; and the establishment of the Silk Road during the first century BC would, for a few hundred years, bring the material culture of China into contact with that of Rome.

In other respects, however, contacts led to the accentuation of differences that had long been present in the cultures of Eurasian civilizations: for example, the awareness of different flora and fauna, distinctive metallurgical techniques, and differences in funerary practices, in pottery decoration, and in writing-systems. There were differences between types of musical instruments and modal practices. When distinctive religious views came to be expressed in writing, variation quickly led to marked divergence in cultural traditions.

Whereas, for example, Indian Hinduism—of which Buddhism was itself an offshoot—held that all material things are different manifestations of the same divine being, Persian Zoroastrianism (as preached by Zoroaster's disciples) held that the world was a battleground between the Good (Ahurā-Mazdā) and the Bad (Ahriman). Zoroastrianism offered individual responsibility in making the choice between good and evil: those choosing the good might expect resurrection, and life everlasting in paradise. This 'dualistic' theology was closer to Judaism (and thus to Christianity and Islam) than were the essentially 'monistic' theologies of Egypt and India. It was disseminated by the Magi, priests of a long tradition of West Asian seers (the 'kings' of Saint Matthew's gospel). It remained the basis of Persian religious belief for the next 1,000 years.[47] As already indicated, the religion spread west in the form of Mithraism, but, with the later ascendancy of Islam, it survives in Asia today mainly in the small Indian sect of the Parsees.

Zoroastrian Chant

The Zoroastrian scriptures, the *Avesta*, were composed over a period of some 300 to 400 years from around the beginning of the sixth century BC (when Zoroaster most probably

[46] Colin Renfrew, *Archaeology and Language* (London: Penguin Books, 1987), 255.

[47] Hinnells, 'Mithraism', 81–2.

preached); but they incorporated Avestan hymnal poetry that predated Zoroaster by some centuries. The scriptures were not written until the fourth to sixth centuries AD, when the form of Avestan in which they were written was devised for this purpose, Avestan being by then a dead language. Until the fifth century BC, Avestan scriptures had been composed in isometric, octosyllabic verse. The occurrence also of *heterometric* verse in the written *Avesta* has raised doubts as to the authenticity of such texts, and questions as to the correct manner of their execution as chant.[48]

A likely solution to the problem emerged from principles that hold good for measured, syllabic, verse-settings as song, throughout the world. If the metrical framework of a syllabic song is filled out with notes of more than one time value, arranged in different patterns in the several musical lines, the verse may be isometric or heterometric, without disturbing the equal lengths of musical lines. In other words, the setting to music of heterometric verse does not necessarily require that the tunes to which they are set be metrically irregular.[49]

Ex. 3.1*a* (after Picken) shows a precise transcription of a Zoroastrian prayer with verse-lines of 9–8–8 syllables, as sung by a Zoroastrian priest in Bombay during the mid-1960s. The prayer translates: 'Truth is the best possession: spontaneously Truth belongs at (his) wish to him who is best towards truth.'[50] In this most sacred prayer—a succinct praise of truth—both the prayer *and* the Avestan diction are sacrosanct. Singers, when not supported by the beat of dance or of an instrument, are apt to perform the same piece differently, on different occasions, according to mood and circumstance; and it is likely that the original form of the prayer was as in Ex. 3.1*b*. A tune with the same metric structure and with similar melodic shape, but suited to Avestan poetry with verse-lines of 8–7–7 syllables, is shown at Ex. 3.1*c*.[51]

Parsee priests undergo a rigorous apprenticeship that includes memorizing the sacred texts in the musical form in which they are believed to have been recited; and they live in closed communities, guarding

[48] Ilya Gershevitch, 'The Sound of Avestan Verse-Lines', *Ratanbai Katrak Lectures*, unpublished, Oxford, 1968.

[49] Ibid., and L. E. R. Picken, 'Secular Chinese Songs of the Twelfth Century', *Studia Musicologica Academiae Scientiarum Hungaricae*, 8 (1966), 130–1.

[50] Ilya Gershevitch, in an appendix (pp. 75–82) to Nicholas Sims-Williams, 'The Sogdian Fragments of the British Library', *Indo-Iranian Journal*, 18 (1976), 43–82; translation discussed at p. 81.

[51] Laurence Picken, unpublished transcription from the recitation of Jamsīd Katrak in Bombay.

Ex. 3.1a

Ex. 3.1b

Ex. 3.1c

jealously their ancient traditions. It is possible, therefore, that such melodies are stylistically akin to those associated with Avestan verse-lines in the fifth century BC. The style revealed is syllabic (but not equi-syllabic), and the musical lines are of equal length. This syllabic style contrasts with the rhythmically freer, more ornamented and melismatic style of chanting the *Sāmaveda*, used by Hindus in India (see p. 102); but the use in both styles of varied reiterations of simple three- or four-note melodies, within a compass of approximately a fourth, is common in epic and scriptural chant throughout the world.

The particular musical styles that have come to be associated with particular Eurasian zones of civilization vary not so much in their musical structures as in their *treatment* of such structures. Fundamental elements of structure, such as the placing of auditory units of definite pitch into note-sets, syllabic and melismatic chanting of texts, measured song and dance, and variation-making, are common to musics world-wide. Differences are more evident in such matters as the use of pitch in relation to language, timbre, and tessitura of the singing voice, the *method* of combining melodic and rhythmic strands into musical constructs, the materials used in the construction of musical instruments, the various techniques used in handling musical instruments, and above all—and consequent upon all these matters—variety in musical timbre and texture.

4 Diverging Traditions 1: South and Central Asia

The Aryas

Within present-day Europe and the USA, there is widespread appreciation of the music and culture of the Indian Subcontinent. Although this is a recent phenomenon, its roots lie in nineteenth-century European linguistics.[1] Following the discovery of affinities between the dead languages of Sanskrit, Latin, and Ancient Greek in 1786 (by Sir William Jones, serving in India at the High Court of Calcutta), subsequent linguists, mistakenly equating language with 'race', held Indian culture to have derived from the 'Aryans'. The 'Aryans' came to be imagined as a superior 'race' of conquering nomads from the Central Asian highlands, ancestors of both Europeans and Brahmans.[2] (The German natural history professor J. F. Blumenbach first publicized the idea that they were descended from the 'Caucasus' in 1795.[3]) Subsequently, German romantics imagined the 'Aryans' as a blond, blue-eyed 'master-race', originating in northern Europe. Such imaginings are all nonsense; but they remained popular into the second half of this century, and still persist in the popular imagination. The origins of Indian civilization, and of Hinduism, the direct source of India's classical traditions of music and dance, are still worth investigating, if only briefly.

Shortly after 3000 BC, an advanced civilization flourished in the fertile flood plains of the Indus Valley. The Indus culture was literate,

[1] The racist attitudes that (in general) underlay European veneration of India are discussed in Chapter 13.

[2] Colin Renfrew, *Archaeology and Language* (London: Penguin Books, 1987), 9, 13.

[3] Martin Bernal, *Black Athena, the Afroasiatic Roots of Classical Civilization* (2 vols.; London: Free Association Books, 1987), i. 219.

and its stratified society included artisans skilled in fashioning pottery and bronze. The collapse of this civilization towards 1800 BC has been widely attributed to invasion by Indo-European-speaking Aryas, a people now thought to have come from northern Iran, and to have broken away from the main nomad groups of the steppe. (The word 'Aryan' is used, properly, only as an adjective derived from 'Arya'.)

The Aryas figure prominently in the *Rigveda*, a remarkable body of hymns in Vedic Sanskrit, dating from about 1200 to 1000 BC. The Vedic Sanskrit of the *Rigveda* shows correspondences with the Old Iranian language of the *Avesta* (the Persian scriptures); and both show correspondences with Hittite. Given that the *Rigveda* attests the use of horses, it seems clear that there was interaction between the peoples of these three lands during the second millennium BC. On the other hand, as Colin Renfrew has indicated, the *Rigveda* portrays the Aryas not as a *nomadic* society of horse-riders, but as a warrior society, using the horse-pulled chariots known to have developed in West Asia. It seems probable, therefore, that the Aryas emerged as a 'chiefdom' society in the wake of the collapse of the Indus civilization, rather than that they were the cause of that collapse. Their origin cannot as yet be attested with certainty; but it is likely that they, and the *Rigveda*, were native to India.[4]

Over many centuries, the Aryas spread west into the Gangetic plain, and their culture, south into the Indian peninsula. The *Rigveda* depicts them as fighting the *dāsa*. Who the latter were is uncertain; but peoples thought to have been well established in India as early as the third millennium BC are Negritos, Proto-Australoids, Mediterranean peoples (now mainly associated with Dravidian culture), and Mongoloids (on the north and north-east fringes).[5]

Early Aryan society was divided into three classes: warriors or aristocracy, priests, and common people. All were subject to the king. Hereditary 'castes' were then unknown, and intermarriage between classes was not forbidden. A four-class system (*varna*) was subsequently incoporated into the *Rigveda*, comprising *brāhman*s (priests), *kshatriya*s (warriors), *vaishya*s (peasant farmers), and *shūdra*s (serfs). These classes were likened (in the *Purushasukta* hymn of the *Rigveda*) to a giant organism, with *brāhman*s at its head, *kshatriya*s its arms, *vaishya*s its trunk, and *shūdra*s its feet. Although the *dāsa* were excluded from the

[4] Renfrew, *Archaeology and Language*, 178.
[5] *The Times Atlas of World History*, ed. Geoffrey Barraclough (London, 1989), 64.

first three classes, the fact that the *varna*-system was originally conceived as an organism indicates that, for practical purposes, the four classes were interdependent. Interaction between *brāhman* and *kshatriya* was of particular significance; the priest was dependent upon the king for material wealth, but the king was dependent upon the priest for consecration of his power. The superior *ritual* status of the priest was to influence profoundly the structure of Indian society, as the four-class *varna*-system subsequently fragmented into a myriad 'castes' and 'subcastes' (see pp. 228–9).

Hinduism

The *Vedas* are the fount of Hinduism. (The word Hindu means 'belonging to the Indus'; and Hinduism implies no more than the religion of peoples of India.) They embody the concept of a cosmic law, and suggest that even the Aryan nature-gods were regarded as different manifestations of a single divine force. Nevertheless, the *Vedas* constitute a record, more than an interpretation, of religious experience; and because they came to be thought of as revelations from the Supreme Being, they were known as *shruti* (that which has been heard). Later religious texts, by contrast, applied reasoning to the experiential world of the *Vedas*, and were known as *smriti* (that which has been remembered).

Foremost among the *smriti* were the *Upanishads*, a body of literature that overlapped the later *Vedas* and evolved over many centuries, from about the fifth century BC. Whereas those who revealed the *Vedas* were known as *rishi* (sages), the authors of the *Upanishads* were known as 'forest teachers', *yogin*, or ascetics. (*Upanishad* means literally 'sit down near'.) The *Upanishads* gradually introduced a monistic doctrine that denied (in contrast to Zoroastrianism) the existence of a world separated from God. A new, questing spirit becomes evident: 'What', asks the author querulously 'is this universe? From what does it arise? Into what does it go?' And equivocally the answer comes: 'In freedom it rises, in freedom it rests, and into freedom it melts away.'[6] Here already is the beginning of the Hindu concept of the unreality of individual existence, and of its being ultimately subsumed in the Absolute.

[6] Cited in Jawaharlal Nehru, *The Discovery of India* (1946; Delhi: Oxford University Press, 1981), 92.

Gradually, the *Upanishads* developed the concept—central to the Indian world-view—of *Ātman*, the breathing individual Soul that must eventually merge with *Brāhman*, the indivisible Supreme Being. *Brāhman*, therefore, combined with *Ātman* to yield the unity of the Absolute; for notwithstanding all the diversity that is evident in the world, *Brāhman* constituted the one and only fundamental reality: that in which duality ceases. The Indian mystic aimed to identify his soul, or inmost self, totally—and finally—with *Brāhman*; and a principle means of achieving this was the practice of *yoga*: the partial, or complete, arrest, or cessation, of the mental states.[7] The mysticism of the *Upanishads* came to be reflected in the four stages of life that still characterize Hinduism: one of education, two of worldly preoccupation, and—in preparation for death—one in which all worldly goods were abnegated in favour of a hermitic life as a *sādhu* (the stage at which the meaning of life may be discovered).

Another Upanishadic key concept was that of *samsāra*, the transmigration and reincarnation of the soul. *Samsāra* implied a direct causal link between conduct while alive (*karma*), and status as a reincarnated being. (At a purely practical level, it also deterred protest against oppression, for misery could be attributed to past misdeeds.) Because the Soul was held to transmigrate until its identity was lost in the Absolute, human life and values came to be regarded as being essentially unreal. (This attitude featured strongly in the writings of the ninth-century teacher, Shankara.)

The culminating utterance of the *Upanishads* was the *Bhagavadgītā*, which recounts the advice given by the god Krishna to the great Arjuna, who hesitates, before waging battle against his kinsmen (as already told in the *Mahābhārata*). Krishna urges him on. The performance of duty does not incur guilt: in action without self-interest the believer is detached from the material; knowledge, work, and devotion are paths to the goal of self-realization. The narrative makes plain, however, that the true seer (in this case, Arjuna), after attaining the highest moral perfection, is still expected to continue to perform the duties allotted to his particular station in life.

As the concept of *samsāra* became pervasive in Indian life, gods were personalized and came to represent the great variety of human needs. The chief nature-gods of the Aryas were replaced by the 'Trinity' of

[7] S. N. Das Gupta, 'Philosophy', in A. L. Basham (ed.), *A Cultural History of India* (Oxford: Oxford University Press, 1975), 111, 115–16.

Hindu gods: Brahma the Creator, Vishnu the Preserver, and Shiva the Destroyer (and generator of new life); and all gods came to represent different aspects of the Supreme. Vishnu, who was held to have taken human form in order to save the world from disaster, was worshipped largely through his incarnations, Rama and Krishna, both of whom inspired a great body of mythology. Shiva was believed to dwell on Mount Kailāsa, with his beautiful wife, Pārvatī, his bull Nandi, and his two sons, the elephant-headed Ganesha, and the six-headed Kārttikeya; he became lord of the forest teachers, and of the cosmic dance of creation and destruction.

The texts of the great Indian epics, the *Mahābhārata* and the *Rāmāyana*, probably assumed their present shape (through oral tradition) in the middle of the first millennium BC; and they form part of a great body of mythic literature known as the *Purānas*, completed about 500 AD. While the *Mahābhārata* ponders deteriorating standards of human behaviour, and the necessity for detachment in the course of duty, the *Rāmāyana* extols faithfulness in marriage, and the triumph of good over evil. The outline of the *Rāmāyana*, which concerns the exploits of a deified ruler (Rāma) in the recovery of his beautiful wife (Sātā), abducted by a demon king (Rāvana), matches that of the Iliad, with which it is roughly contemporary.[8] Adoration of the Rāma story still unites Hindus; and it is also revered—and represented in art and music theatre—in many parts of South East Asia, where Hinduism shaped distinctive cultural systems before the arrival of Buddhism and Islam.

Indian Cosmology and Ritual

Not only the *Vedas*, *Upanishads*, and epics, but also an array of philosophical and specialized texts, display the complex, Indian, cosmological system, in which music and the arts are correlated with all aspects of the phenomenal world.

Central to the Indian world-view is a sense of the interconnectedness of all things, in particular between man (the human body and its senses) and the cosmos. The *Vedas* describe the creation of man from the waters, and of natural phenomena, from parts of the human body. Many Vedic hymns liken the 'navel' of the human body to the 'navel' of the earth—

[8] Francis Watson, *A Concise History of India* (London: Thames & Hudson, 1974), 35.

for, although natural phenomena flow from the body and senses, they also return to *affect* the body and the senses.[9]

Interconnection between the human body system, cosmic energy, and specific elements facilitated focus of the senses both outward on external objects, and inward, on the soul; indeed, it was experience of the formless, internal world of sense and awareness that enhanced the appreciation of the external world of form. The idea of a still centre, where tension and conflict cease to have meaning, is fundamental to the original concept of *yoga*. It was this possibility of 'opening-out' and 'closing-in' that enabled the senses to transcend the world of transient, manifold phenomena.[10] Man was imagined, in space, as a microcosm at the heart of a concentric universe, itself a 'macrocosm', capable of both infinite expansion and maximal contraction.[11]

From this concept of man in relation to the cosmos flowed two geometrical images, both pervasive in ancient Indian texts.[12] One was that of a sacred pillar (*stambha*), connecting earth and sky (the finite with the infinite); lasting communication between earth and sky was held to be essential to human existence. The *stambha* acquired cosmic significance as the *axis mundi*. (Legend has it that Shiva emerged from a pillar of fire to bestow knowledge on warring Brahma and Vishnu; he is still worshipped through the *lingam*—a much formalized phallic symbol—believed to represent this *stambha*.)

The other pervasive image was that of the wheel of a chariot, with a hub, or 'nave', connecting rim to centre. The wheel represented the constant movement of time; but it was also a generative force, the origin of all ritual action (Pl. 6).[13] Time itself was cyclical, as manifest in the rhythms of life; and the ordering of such rhythms was ensured by sacrifice and by the chanting of sacred formulas. It was the cyclical rhythms of life, therefore—and, by extension, those of music—that made the ritual act of sacrifice possible; but it was sacrifice that, in turn, established time/music in its proper course.

The Vedic and Brāhmanical concept of sacrifice (*yajna*) complemented these images of pole and wheel, by demonstrating man's capacity to

[9] Kapila Vatsyayan, *The Square and the Circle of the Indian Arts* (New Delhi: Roli Books International, 1983), 13.

[10] Ibid.

[11] Lewis Rowell, *Music and Musical Thought in Early India* (Chicago and London: University of Chicago Press, 1992), 16–17.

[12] Vatsyayan, *The Square and the Circle*, 23.

[13] Ibid. 10.

6. Eight-spoked *stūpa* of Nāgārjunakonde

establish a relationship with the cosmos, and by synchronizing annual time with solar time.[14] Thus the site selected for consecration becomes a finite symbol of cosmic space. A sacrificial pole, part buried beneath the earth, represents the *axis mundi*. (This element is still central to many theatrical traditions in India, where preliminaries revolve around the installation of a pole.) Bricks used in the construction of the fire altar conform to specific shapes, and number 360, so as to represent the days of the year; in their correspondence with a 360-degree circle, they further represent cyclical time. The bricks were laid out so as to represent the human body—the 'microcosm' at the heart of the 'macrocosm'.[15]

Gradually, in Upanishadic thought, this cultic, externalized concept of time came to be complemented by a division-less, internalized view of time. The cyclical rhythms of life may embody the creative force necessary for their perpetuation; but, in human experience, time is not so much continuous as illusory—a constantly limiting factor that must be mastered through control of the senses and actions (the path

[14] Vatsyayan, *The Square and the Circle*, 23. [15] Ibid. 23–30.

of the *yogin*). Internalized time, therefore, came to be seen as a source of personal self-discipline. Sacrifice, correspondingly, came to be associated with internal activity; and respiration—interpreted as sacrifice—came to supersede fire as the vital element of sacrifice.[16] Control of respiration frequency is essential to achieving the tensionless state of being that lies at the heart of *yoga*; but it is also a form of bodily music (see p. 97), and a primary source of rhythm. The controlled emission of vocal sound, therefore, enabled the priest to manifest true, inner—continuous—time.

Vedic Chant, and Theatre

Chant was crucial to all forms of sacrifice; and central to such chant was the recitation of the sacred syllable, *om* (more accurately spelled *aum*), intoned at the beginning and end of every Vedic lesson and recitation. In the *Māndūkya Upanishad*, the three phonetic elements of *aum* are held to represent threefold time (past, present, and future); a fourth phonetic element, the 'silence that follows and surrounds the syllable', represents the 'unthinkable and ungraspable'. *Om* symbolized the entire phenomenal universe, from which it was believed all audible sounds proceeded, and to which all sounds must ultimately return.[17] As Lewis Rowell has expressed it, 'When [the priest] began his recitation by intoning the sacred syllable *om*, he symbolically inhaled the whole world of phenomena, and with the mantras that he uttered, he exhaled vital substance that became one with the universal continuum of spiritual energy.'[18] Thus the *brāhman* priest represented the microcosm of the macrocosmic *Brāhman*.[19]

The four primary *Veda*s contain not only the texts for sacred chant, but also rules for its performance; these are the earliest on known record. The *Rigveda* is an enormous collection of 1,028 hymns

[16] Rowell, *Music*, 183–6.

[17] Ibid. 17. That the concept of *om* still has meaning is indicated by the fact that, at noon on 21 August 1994 (as reported in the *Straits Times*, Malaysia, 23 August), thousands of people in forty-two countries, led by some 10,000 people in London's Wembley arena, joined in a world chant of the *om*; the intention was to 'bring the earth to peace, harmony, love, and light' in its final evolutionary stage, before 'moving into a perfect fusion of spirit and matter'. By contrast, a secret cult in Japan, *Aum shinri kyō*, has attempted to overthrow the state government.

[18] Ibid.

[19] Richard Lannoy, *The Speaking Tree: A Study of Indian Culture and Society* (Oxford: Oxford University Press, 1971), 143.

addressed to the Indo-Aryan nature-gods. Derived from it are: the *Yajurveda*, in which verses from the *Rigveda* are rearranged for ritual purposes, and additional prayers and sacrificial formulas inserted; and the *Sāmaveda*, a manual for 'singer-priests' (*sāmaga*), in which verses from the *Rigveda* are arranged in a more musical, melismatic, form. The *Atharvaveda*, a more popular collection of magical spells, incantations, and prayers, represents an independent tradition.

The *Rigveda* were recited as syllabic chant, restricted in pitch compass.[20] The *Sāmaveda*, on the other hand, were conceived and rendered in specifically musical terms, and had a pitch compass of up to an octave; performances were preceded by melismatic vocalises on syllables (*stobha*) not obviously meaningful, a practice reflected today in the *ālāpana* that precedes performances of Indian song. The *Nāradīyashikshā* (*c.*AD 500), a short phonetic manual pertaining largely to the chanting of the *Sāmaveda*, uses the word *svara* (note) in three different—and revealing—ways: as 'accents', of which there were three (involving both metrical stress and musical pitch); as scale degrees, of which there were seven; and as 'shadings' (*shruti*), of which (in this instance) there were five.

The *Nāradīyashikshā* also provides names for the seven *svara*, the initial syllables of which are still used as the Indian sol-fa (*sargam*: see p. 248). Nārada describes the first three *svara*—*sa*, *ri*, and *ga*—as follows:

> Because *shadja* arises from the combination of nose, throat, chest, palate, tongue, and teeth, it is known as 'six-born'. When air, rising from the navel, and united with the throat and the head, bellows like a bull, the sound is called *rishabha*. When air, rising from the navel, and united with the throat and the head, carries fragrance to the nose, the sound is rightly known as *gāndhāra*.[21]

To such pitch concepts, Nārada added the five Vedic *shruti*, as representing brilliance, extension, sorrow, softness, and moderation.[22] For him, *shruti* were qualities of *timbre*, distinct from the twenty-two *shruti* used by musical theorists as units of intervallic measurement. This suggests that, in the recitation of chant, pitch was still not clearly distinguished from dynamic and timbral differences.

To ensure that a sacred text might be performed without error, trainee priests underwent strenuous memory-building routines.

[20] Rowell, *Music*, 58–9. [21] Ibid. 78–9. [22] Ibid. 82–3.

Memory was reinforced by the use of *mudrā* (hand gestures), linked with musical aspects of performance. The right hand provided tonal indications: individual *svara* were denoted by touching specific finger joints with the tip of the thumb; other finger actions indicated melodic sequences, tonal prolongations, and shakes. The left hand provided temporal indications: long syllables, the three Vedic 'accents', and the correct number of repeated words or syllables. Exact rendering of hand gestures was considered of greater importance than correct delivery of the poetic text.[23] Such gestures are surely reflected in the claps, finger actions, and silent waves that accompany Indian music today.[24]

Contrasting with the inner, spiritual world of sacrifice was the outer, secular world, as represented in the ritual of theatre. Theatre existed for the whole of society, and portrayed the entire phenomenal world. The theatrical director, therefore—the *sūtradhāra* ('he who holds the strings')—saw the world from without, and controlled (through the medium of theatre) the thoughts, feelings, and actions of Indian society. Music enabled him to time and coordinate all aspects of performance, and thus to induce specific emotions (*rasa*) in the audience.[25] (The term *sūtradhāra* may have referred to the puppeteer; in Indonesia, to this day, the puppeteer—the *dalang* of priestly status—performs a comparable function.)

The aesthetic theory of *rasa* arose from the condition of *sādhāna* (discipline), achieved through *yoga* and *yajna*; indeed, only through *sādhanā* could an artist achieve that intuitive understanding of an experience that was a prerequisite for its manifestation in art. *Rasa* theory was initially associated with theatre and poetry; it referred both to the state of bliss induced by artistic creation, and to the transitory states of being such creation induced in an audience.[26] Traditionally,

[23] Ibid. 64–6, 186.

[24] Abhinavagupta (a commentator on ancient treatises, *c.*1000) linked *tāla* with ritual action by suggesting that the hand gestures used in musical performance originated in gestures used in ancient sacrifice (Rowell, *Music*, 186). Sharngadeva, in the *Sangītaratnākara* ('Mine of Musical Jewels', *c.*1250), defined hand and finger gestures as metric markers, where the hand is either closed, as a fist, or open, with fingers extended in the plane of the palm. And a Chinese account of a formal embassy with thirty-five musicians sent to the Chinese court in 802 notes (in regard to their performance): 'At each enactment of a piece, all sang notes that were all alike. Each of them all alike opened, and all alike closed, the ten fingers of the two hands to give shape to their marking of the time: now up, now down, they were never in disagreement. (L. E. R. Picken, 'Instruments in an Orchestra from Pyū, Upper Burma, in 802', *Musica Asiatica*, 4 (1984), 262–3).

[25] Rowell, *Music*, 17.

[26] Kapila Vatsyayan, 'India', *The New Grove* (1980), ix. 160.

there were eight *rasa*, linked with deities, colours, and the eight permanent emotions: love, laughter, sorrow, anger, energy, fear, disgust, and surprise.

At conceptual and technical levels, rules gradually evolved that governed the proportional use of the elements in a particular artistic medium, inducing a particular *rasa*: mass, weight, and space in architecture; colour and perspective in painting; division of parts of the body, and their movements, in dance; the use of *svara*, *shruti*, and rhythm in music.[27] *Rasa* theory appears already in the *Nātyashāstra*, 'Treatise on Drama', *c*.AD 500, attributed to the sage, Bharata. As music is a non-representational art, however, the relationship of *rasa* theory to music has been the subject of constant discussion and controversy, over the ages.

It is not difficult to see in the performance of Indian music, dance, and theatre today, connections with ancient theories of space, time, gesture, and emotion; and, in South India, some Brāhman families still devote their lives to perfecting recitation of texts associated with sacrifices. Many different traditions of chant remain extant; and Brāhmans still guard strictly, and secretly, their particular tradition, believing inaccurate performance may disturb the balance of the universe. (Vedic recitation is itself believed to symbolize the *axis mundi*.) Ex. 4.1 (after Jairazbhoy) shows a verse from the *Rigveda*, with one of the Sāmavedic melodies to which it is sung by Brāhman Tamils; the chant is characterized by limited range, melismatic ornamentation, and the interpolation of vocalises. (The contraction of the 'consonant' interval, C–F, by nearly a semitone, in this performance, may be an unconscious means of preserving vocal energy; the full, seven-note, Sāmavedic chant extends the pitch range by approximately a tone above and below that of the example shown here.[28])

Such melismatic chant contrasts with the plain, syllabic, style of Parsee, Zoroastrian chant, shown earlier in Ex. 3.1. The texts of both are in 'dead' languages, but the use of ornamentations and melismas, in Indian secular and popular musics, as well as in devotional song, suggests that the performance and style of Sāmavedic chant reflect popular taste, in a way that Zoroastrian chant does not.

[27] Vatsyayan, 'India', *The New Grove* (1980), ix. 160.

[28] N. A. Jairazbhoy, 'An Interpretation of the 22 Srutis', *Perspectives on Asian Music: Essays in Honor of Dr Laurence E. R. Picken* (*Asian Music*, 6/1–2 (1975)), 51. This article provides detailed information on the performance of Vedic chant.

Ex. 4.1

Buddhism

While Hinduism was concerned with the nature of human existence in relation to the Absolute, the Buddha (Gautama Siddharta)—the 'Enlightened One'—perceived the need for escape from the perpetual cycle of rebirth. Gautama was born into an aristocratic family, near present-day Nepal, around 560 BC, at a time when India's iron age had created urbanization, and had led to increased disparity between rich and poor. In keeping with the emergent cult of homeless asceticism (as a means of seeking spiritual truth), he forsook power and worldly goods; and, after an increasingly ascetic mode of life, and lengthy meditation, he achieved 'enlightenment'. On the path thereto, Gautama apprehended that quiet meditation was more valuable for the acquisition of spirituality than is extreme asceticism: the only route of escape from the intolerable chain of suffering, brought about by endless rebirth, was to break free of earthly desire. Gautama applied a moral code to the evolving metaphysics of Hinduism; and, ousting the gods from their role as the petitioned, he gave the world its only atheistic religion.

Buddhism originated, in effect, as a reformist movement within Hinduism. Gautama accepted the concept of *karma* allied to reincarnation; but he adapted *dharma* (the Hindu code of conduct) so as to reconcile concepts of predestination with his own understanding of natural justice. He developed the Hindu concept of the essential unreality of individual life into a Law of Impermanence, with recognition that everything in the phenomenal world is subject to change. He also propounded the Law of Causality: that nothing happens fortuitously. From this position, Gautama went on to advocate the Four Noble Truths: that suffering is the result of *karma*; that suffering arises from desire; that suffering is preventable; and that prevention lies along the Eightfold Path. This path presumes right knowledge, right thought, right speech, right action, right living, right effort, right mindfulness, and right composure. Through the truths, and by the path, people could escape reincarnation through *nirvana*—a transformed mode of consciousness, in which desire is annihilated, and Buddhahood achieved. After enlightenment, Gautama assembled a body of disciples, and taught for forty-five years.

About 500 years after the Buddha's death, differences in the interpretation of his teaching resulted in the emergence of two main schools of Buddhism: *Hīnayāna* ('small vehicle'), now usually called *Theravāda* ('doctrine of the elders'), and *Mahāyāna* ('great vehicle'). *Theravāda* Buddhism is said by its adherents to reflect more closely Gautama's teaching. It conforms precisely to the *Tripitaka* ('Triple Basket'), canonical texts written in Sri Lanka, in Pali, the sacred language. The three baskets contained, respectively: the rules for monastic discipline; the legends and teachings of the 547 previous existences of the Buddha (*jātakas*); and specialist 'higher learning'. (Stories from the *jātakas*, like those from the Hindu *Mahābhārata* and *Rāmāyana*, were often set to music and enacted.)

Mahāyāna Buddhism was articulated during the first century AD in Gandhāra (in present-day Pakistan), where Persian and Vedic religious traditions had mingled, with Cyrus's thrust into India. The capital of Gandhāra—subsequently known to the Greeks as Taxila—had become an intellectual centre, a crossroads in the flow of ideas; and it was here that the classical form of Sanskrit had developed, probably during the fourth century BC. It was here too that, after Alexander's conquest, the Buddha was first represented in human form, with a recognizably Greek face, and in Roman clothing. *Mahāyāna* Buddhism was to become a tolerant, syncretic religion that allowed those qualified for Buddhahood to remain on earth, as 'Bodhisattvas', assisting others on the path to enlightenment.

Arising as it did from Hinduism, Buddhism made slight impact in the land of its birth, even though, in the third century BC, King Ashoka attempted to propagate the religion far and wide; in India, the Buddha was soon absorbed into the pantheon as an incarnation of Vishnu.

Elsewhere, however, Buddhism had a considerable influence. Sri Lanka became wholly Buddhist, and is still regarded as the hub of *Theravāda* Buddhism. *Mahāyāna* Buddhism became associated with animistic religions in Nepal, Sikkim, Bhutan, Tibet, China, Japan, and Korea, while *Theravāda* Buddhism established itself *alongside* spirit worship on the mainland of South East Asia.

The Music of Buddhism

It is likely that early Buddhist music drew heavily on existing Vedic musical practices. The conch was an important ritual instrument and became emblematic of Buddha's preaching (conchs are trumpets made from the very large, whelk-like shells of marine univalve molluscs). Bells and gongs, iron chimes, drums, and various types of woodblock also acquired emblematic associations: in East Asia the notched fin of a wooden fish came to represent water-borne creatures; in Tibet, however, short metal trumpets, with bells flared in the shape of mythical water creatures, fulfilled this function. An early Indian relief (second century BC) shows celestial dancers accompanied by drums and arched harps; a later relief (first century AD) shows pilgrims accompanied, as they process, by drums, conch, and flutes.[29] Various types of trumpet, shawm, and flute, were added to the Buddhist instrumentarium.

While *Theravāda* Buddhism placed emphasis on the recitation of texts, in Pali (the sacred language), *Mahāyāna* Buddhism developed rich traditions of ritual, with texts in Sanskrit and/or the local vernacular language; musically, therefore, *Mahāyāna* Buddhism has usually been the more elaborate. *Mahāyāna* ceremonies may include instrumental music; in China, for example, where Buddhist music was Sinicized during the third to sixth centuries BC and subsequently interacted with folk music, melodic instrumental music for use in Buddhist ritual exists that can be dated back to Tang times (seventh to ninth centuries), when such music was widely popular.[30]

[29] Peter Crossley-Holland, 'Buddhist Music', *The New Grove* (1980), iii. 418.

[30] Qing Tian, 'Recent Trends in Buddhist Music Research in China', trans. Tan Hwee San, *British Journal of Ethnomusicology*, 3 (1994), 67; see also Stephen Jones, *Folk Music of China: Living Instrumental Traditions* (Oxford: Oxford University Press, 1995), 215.

Since the heart of Buddhist practice is meditation, chant tends to be slow, often with gradual portamento from one note to another. Sutras ('threads' of discourse) are usually intoned, simply, in unmeasured chant. Hymns, on the other hand, are more often intoned in a florid, melismatic style of chant, with measured pulse; and such chanting can become a skilled, soloistic art. Percussion instruments usually accompany the chant, or punctuate the verses; and a gong or drum is used to signal specific routines of the service.

In many areas, the voice is disguised to give the chant a non-human, quasi-divine character. This may be achieved: by means of nasalization, as in Cambodia; by use of falsetto, as in parts of Vietnam and Thailand; or by use of a forced low register, with conspicuous high harmonics, as in Tibet.[31] Moreover, as with Islam, Hinduism, and many animistic religions, even the most elaborate chanting, because of its religious nature, is not usually regarded as 'song' or 'music', such terms being reserved for entertainment occasions.

A striking, surviving example of *Mahāyāna* Buddhist ritual—unusually containing elements of dance and dance music—is provided by the *Yongsanjae* ritual practised in Korea, where adaptable *Mahāyāna* Buddhism blended readily with indigenous shamanism. All *Mahāyāna* Buddhist rituals are performed with the dual purpose of urging the spirits of the deceased towards a higher plane of existence, and cleansing the minds and bodies of the living who are present. The name *Yongsanjae* derives from Mt Grdhrakuta, where the Buddha delivered the Lotus Sutra, and the ceremony is a symbolic re-enactment of that occasion.

The *Yongsanjae* is usually performed outdoors on the concourse of a temple. The spirits are carried to the temple entrance in a palanquin, where they 'prepare' to receive the Buddhas and Bodhisattvas. They are then brought before the Buddha for a symbolic cleansing, before hearing the sermon. A huge Buddha painting is mounted in the performance arena, after which guardians and other deities are petitioned to cleanse the site by their presence. During a long, sung incantation, Buddhas and Bodhisattvas are induced to come and hear the sermon, by means of offerings. These include: the cymbal dance (danced by priests with large cymbals, held with arms extended) (Pl. 7); the drum dance (danced with barrel drum attached to the waist); and the butterfly dance (danced with masks). The sermon is followed by more dances,

[31] Crossley-Holland, 'Buddhist Music', *The New Grove*, iii. 418.

7. Korean Buddhist priests performing the cymbal dance in the *Yongsanjae* ritual, in Seoul. Photo: Ven Sonam.

and then by a communal feast. Subsequently, solo chants urge the spirits into paradise, raising the level of spiritual consciousness of those present. Finally, Buddhas, Bodhisattvas, and their divinities are dismissed; and a ceremonial burning of all the accoutrements used in the ritual ensures that the spirits return to the void, and that everything returns to the four elements: fire, earth, air, and water.

The dances are accompanied by a band similar to that used for Korean Shaman dances and farmers' dances (see p. 384): flutes, double-reed bamboo pipe, two-string fiddle, and hourglass drum—with shawm, horn, and conch in attendance, to play at appropriate points in the ceremony. Four other instruments important to Buddhism are also played: a large bell (for beings in the underworld), iron chimes (for airborne creatures), the serrated back of a wooden fish (for water-borne creatures), and a large drum (for earthbound creatures).[32]

Two types of Buddhist chant are used in Korean Buddhist ceremonies: *yombul* and *pomp'ae*. (In Korea, a third type, in the vernacular, *hirach'ong* is commonly used away from the temples.) *Yombul* (literally

[32] Cited in the Venerable Sonam, *The Yongsanjae Ritual*, published privately in Korea.

Ex. 4.2

'praying to Buddha') is a simple, syllabic recitation of sutras, in Chinese and Sanskrit, used by all monks. *Pomp'ae* (literally 'sacred chanting') originated in China in the third century AD and derives from Sanskrit and Brāhman chant. There are two types of *pomp'ae*, long and short, of which the 'long chant' (*chissori*) is the more elaborate, and its technique requires substantial training. As exemplified in Ex. 4.2 (after Byong Won Lee), *chissori* is characterized by glissandi upwards from the reciting note to a firm pitch (often in falsetto), followed by an octave leap.[33]

Within *Theravāda* Buddhist ceremony, chant also varies between a simple syllabic style and one involving complex melismatic ornamentation. Sutras are intoned in Pali, the original sacred language, but this is a 'dead' lanugage, often not understood by the monks who intone it.

[33] Byong Won Lee, 'Korea', *The New Grove* (1980), x. 206.

Ex. 4.3

Moreover, Pali is a non-tonal language, whereas in Thailand, Laos, and Burma—where *Theravāda* Buddhism is widely practised—languages use segmental tone. In Thailand, texts are now written phonetically in the vernacular, and the two-, three-, and four-note scales on which the chant is normally intoned reflect the segmental tones of the language.[34]

In contrast to sutras, sermons are chanted in the vernacular; but those appropriate to merit-making occasions are usually delivered in a style similar to that used for chant in Pali. Often, however, sermons recount stories from the *Jātaka*s, most popularly the story of the exceptionally

[34] Terry E. Miller, 'A Melody not Sung: The Performance of Lao Buddhist Texts in Northeast Thailand', *Selected Reports in Ethnomusicology* (1992), 162–5.

meritorious Prince Wetsundawn (the penultimate incarnation of the Buddha). Although such preaching is not, strictly speaking, considered 'entertainment' (and its intonation is not considered 'music'), in practice the melismatic style of recitation can reach exceptional levels of artistry. Ex. 4.3 (after Miller, from north-east Thailand), exhibits extravagant melismas on key words of the text; they rise from the reciting note, and employ the notes of an anhemitonic pentatonic scale.[35]

Archaic Musical Forms in Central Asia

In Tibet, *Mahāyāna* Buddhism became blended with Tantric, *Vajrayāna* Buddhism, which had spread thither from India during the seventh century AD. *Vajra* originally meant the thunderbolt of the god Indra; later it came to mean a substance as bright, and indestructible, as a diamond.[36] The Tantra are esoteric texts which, Tibetans claim, are exceptionally efficacious in the attainment of enlightenment.[37] Tantrism makes use of magic charms and esoteric rituals to achieve enhanced states of meditation.

Mahāyāna Buddhism and *Vajrayāna* Buddhism gradually merged with the traditional Bön religion of Tibet to form the highly syncretic religion, Lamaism. This distinctive form of Buddhism reached Mongolia in the thirteenth century, where it became the religion of the empire. By the seventeenth century, it had reached Siberia, where it blended with local shamanism. Mongolia remained actively Lamaist until the 1920s.

The eastern zone of Central Asia now embraces the Tibeto-Burman-speaking Tibetans, and associated Himalayan peoples, as well as Altaic-speaking peoples of southern Siberia and Mongolia. From the seventh century to the tenth century, a Tibetan empire embraced the whole area; and at the beginning of this period the Indian alphabet was adapted for the writing of Tibetan. From the tenth to the fourteenth centuries, what had been a Tibetan empire became a Mongolian empire. When that empire crumbled in the sixteenth century, Tibet allied with Mongolia to regain its autonomy.[38] In eastern Central Asia, archaic musical

[35] From the story of Prince Wetsundawn, chapter 14, sung by Mr Jundee Juntawan, age 26, at Wat Glang-gosum in Kosum-pisai, Thailand, in 1973 (Miller, 'A Melody not Sung', 173–4).

[36] Wulf Metz, 'One God, Many Paths', in *The Religions of the World* (London: Lion Publishing, 1982), 237.

[37] Andrew Powell, *Living Buddhism* (London: British Museum, 1989), 38.

[38] Peter Crossley-Holland, 'Central Asia', *The New Grove* (1980), iv. 61.

traditions are to be observed, suggestive of musical prototypes, elsewhere developed and merged with more recent traditions.

Lamaist monks spend much of their lives chanting, or playing instruments, for Buddhist services. Styles of Lamaist chant include: unmeasured syllabic recitation (usually solo, in short, introductory passages); more elaborate, measured, hymns (usually in duple, or asymmetrical metre, with restricted pitch range); and slow sustained chant (*dbyang*). In *dbyang* the voice is extremely low, somewhere between *f* and *d* (the lowest register of the bass voice). The chants may be in 'long' or 'short' style; in either, the voice is pitched profoundly low, and this monotone is embellished by occasional slides: the voice seldom strays more than a tone from the initial pitch. The extreme duration of individual sung syllables destroys all sense of metrical division. Sometimes the deep tone is used as a fundamental tone and, by means of a special vocal technique known as 'throat music' (in Mongol, *xöömii*), high harmonics are selected, and reinforced by head cavities.[39]

Instrumental ensembles are often employed to alternate with the chanted sections of the services. Lamaist instrumental ensembles usually include conchs, short trumpets of bone or metal, long end-blown trumpets of brass or copper (up to three metres in length), shawms, handbell, cymbals, and double-headed frame drum. The wind instruments play in pairs; long trumpets sound the fundamental and a few other harmonics with considerable pitch variation; the shawm melody tends to be restricted in range, and is treated heterophonically between the two instruments. The percussion instruments yield sounds in a variety of timbres to point the lines of the text.[40] Except for the shawms, wind instruments are used like percussion, without melody. Timbral and textural variation, therefore, are more conspicuous than melodic variation.

Similar techniques of chant and instrumental playing are used for the New Year Mystery dance drama (*'cham*), performed and danced by masked priests in the forecourt of a monastery (Pl. 8); instrumentalists use special timbres to represent signals, calls, and wails, and chanters represent both celestial and demonic choirs.[41] More popular are the

39 Peter Crossley-Holland, 'Tibet', *The New Grove* (1980), xviii. 803.

40 CD, *Ladakh: Musique de monastère et de village*, Le Chant du monde LDX 274662, CM 251.

41 Crossley-Holland, 'Tibet', *The New Grove*, xviii. 804. For a discussion of court ceremonial music in Tibet, in relation to surviving traditions in Ladakh (in northern Kashmir), see A. Mark Trewin, 'The Court Ceremonial Music of Tibet', *CHIME*, 8 (Spring 1995), 4–31.

8. (*above*) New Year Mystery dance drama (*'cham*), performed by masked priests in the monastery of Himis, Western Tibet

9. (*left*) A masked Nepalese peasant carries a trumpet, formed from a human thigh-bone with which to summon the demons

'devil dances' (also performed by masked dancers), performed outside the monasteries (Pl. 9). Both are apotropaic rituals serving to banish evil spirits at the end of the Old Year and to propitiate the guardian spirits that bring luck in the New Year.

The Bön religion of Tibet derived from the pre-Buddhist system of shamanism, prevalent in Central and Northern Asia. The shaman achieves 'possession' and 'ecstasy' when his or her spirit departs from the body on receipt of power from the cosmic tree at the centre of the world. The spirit proceeds to the sky, or the underworld, in order to communicate with appropriate spirits, in search of information. Shamanism is not so much a religion, as a technique of ecstasy placed at the service of any religion, a fact which may account for its survival in areas practising different religions.[42]

In Siberia, the enabling instrument of 'ecstasy' has usually been a large frame drum, carved from special wood and making use of particular animal skins. The drum was often sanctified with water or a herbal potion.[43] (Occasionally the drum has been replaced by a musical bow; in shamanistic cultures of Africa and the Americas, the enabling instrument is frequently a rattle.) Songs, chants, and incantations—usually consisting of varied repetition of short melodic phrases—are essential to the attainment of 'ecstasy'. As song is the means by which the spirit finds its way back to earth, the music has to be continuous. There is much imitation of animal sounds, for these are held to indicate the migration of the spirit, and its return with relevant information.

In Mongolia and Tibet, the flight of the spirit is associated with a flying steed. Mongol legend attributes a magical origin to the characteristic fiddle—the *morin xuur*—through its association with the horse and with shamanism. The scrolls of Mongolian and Tibetan fiddles are finished with carved horses' heads; and the association with the horse is further indicated by the use of horsehair as bow and string on the instrument. Because the peoples of Central Asia were known, and feared, for their skill in horse-riding, the horse plays a dominant symbolic role in their culture;[44] traditionally, tent-dwelling nomads display a horse's skull or carved horse's head. A man unable to sing to, and play, the horse-head fiddle in a Mongolian festival might be

[42] Mircea Eliade, *Shamanism: Archaic Techniques of Ecstasy* (London: Penguin, 1964), 168–76.

[43] Ibid. 173–6.

[44] Mark Slobin, 'Central Asian and Siberian Music', *NOCM* (1983).

required to swallow bowls of fermented mare's milk,[45] reducing him to a state of drunkenness. The horse-head fiddle was popular among all nomadic peoples of Central Asia.

Among tent-dwelling nomads in Mongolia, performance of *xöömii* (throat-music) developed as a secular tradition; melodies are formed from the upper harmonics. This effectively superimposes a melodic line over a drone, a characteristic of musical performance found throughout much of East Europe and West, South, and Central Asia. In Mongolia, simultaneous performance of melody and drone is also accomplished on a three-holed vertical flute (*tsuur*), through which the performer plays a melody while simultaneously producing a low-pitched vocal drone.[46] The difficult technique of *xöömii* is now practised in Mongolia as a professional folk-art. (It has also been adopted by the composer Stockhausen, and by the New Age movement in the USA, and similar groups elsewhere in the West, as an aid to meditation.)

Other forms of Mongolian folk music include 'long songs' (melodic and highly ornamented with skilled control of tremolo) and epics. The principal epic of the region, *Gesar Sprungs* ('History of Gesar'), has been called the 'Iliad of Asia'. It has been—and in some places still is—sung in Tibetan, Mongolian, and Siberian versions, by illiterate, wandering storytellers, in a state of semi-trance, claiming inspiration from the hero of whom they sing.[47] Epics are sometimes performed in a deep, declamatory, non-melodic style related to the deep sounds of *xöömii*.[48] Throughout the region, melodies are thought to carry their words like a steed—they are referred to as *rta* (horse)—and epic is traditionally accompanied on the horse-head fiddle.[49]

Epic-singing also features strongly in the music cultures of western Central Asia, where a popular epic is that of *Manas*. Some 300,000 verses long, it has been sung by Kirghiz scholar musicians, claiming to be called to their profession by Manas himself (rather as shamans claim to have been called through visitations by spirits).[50] Characteristically in epic-singing, musical formulas are correlated with the prosodic

[45] Roberte Hamayon, 'Mongol Music', *The New Grove* (1980), xii. 483.

[46] Carole Pegg, 'Mongolian Conceptualizations of Overtone Singing (Xöömi)', *British Journal of Ethnomusicology*, 1 (1992), 32, 41, 46–8. Such simultaneous performance of melody and drone is also common in much of Eastern Europe, particularly among pastoral communities; see A. L. Lloyd, 'Europe', *The New Grove* (1980), vi. 309–11.

[47] Crossley-Holland, 'Tibet', *The New Grove*, xviii. 808.

[48] Pegg, 'Mongolian Conceptualizations', 47.

[49] Crossley-Holland, 'Tibet', *The New Grove*, xviii. 808.

[50] Slobin, 'Central Asian and Siberian Music'.

structure of the text. Text-lines with constant or minimally varied numbers of syllables are sung to a single musical line (commonly one note per syllable); and this musical line is subjected to minor variants during the course of a substantial number of repeats, until the topic changes, and a new musical formula is presented. Singing may be without accompaniment, accompanied by a frame drum, or by a string instrument. This last may also provide interludes during which the singer can draw breath and mentally rehearse the forthcoming text-lines. Bardic-singing is still revered among many Kirghis, Tajiks, and Uzbeks; and oral traditions of epic-singing still exist in many areas of Russia and Eastern Europe.

For over two millennia, the western zone of Central Asia stimulated cultural exchange and interaction across Eurasia. (This zone consists of: the Chinese province of Xinjiang; Afghanistan; and the former Soviet Republics of Uzbekistan, Turkmenistan, Tajikistan, Kirghizia, and Kazakhstan; with the exception of the Persian-speaking Tajiks, all speak Turkic-Altaic languages.) Its musical traditions are linked with folk styles of Iran, Turkey, and the Balkans, while its own traditions have, in turn, absorbed traits from the classical music styles of the Islamic world. (Islamic classical music styles will be described under West Asia, in Chapter 7.)

The musical and dramatic forms of Central Asia, with their roots in religion, legend, and superstition, have strongly interacted with those of major zones of civilization, and their influence is to be observed in performing practices and ceremonies, still practised across Asia.

5 Diverging Traditions 2: Europe

The Foundations of Greek Culture

The civilization that emerged in Europe was, ultimately, to prove more adaptable to change, and thus to show greater powers of evolution, than ancient civilizations to the east and south that preceded it. It developed, nevertheless, along familiar lines, with the progressive development of farming, pottery, writing, and monumental architecture. Until recently, it was widely accepted that its origin was in Crete, but recent studies suggest that it originated in the ancient civilizations of Egypt and West Asia.

A Proto-Indo-European speech spread into Greece and Crete, from southern Anatolia, about 7000 BC, with the spread of farming.[1] The origins of Greek itself are still contentious. The view that it 'arrived' in Greece with Indo- European-speaking Dorian invaders, during the late second millennium, was compromised when the Cretan 'Linear B' tablets, dating from about 1450 BC and deriving from earlier models, were deciphered on the basis of Greek.[2] In fact, invasions on the Greek mainland during the second millennium arrested the development of civilization there, while in Crete civilization was able to flourish.

Geographically, Crete lay between the West Asian and Egyptian spheres of cultural influence. Agriculture and pottery entered Crete from Anatolia; but iconography, burial customs, and various other forms of material culture suggest powerful influence from Egypt and the

[1] Martin Bernal, *Black Athena, the Afroasiatic Roots of Classical Civilization* (2 vols.; London, Free Association Books, 1987), i. 13.

[2] Colin Renfrew, *Archaeology and Landscape* (London: Penguin Books, 1987), 62.

Levant.[3] About the twenty-first century BC, palaces showing Egyptian influence emerged in Crete, their social organization based on Levantine models.[4] Between roughly the mid-third and early second millennia BC, Cretans colonized and settled much of the Aegean, including Miletus in Anatolia and possibly part of the Greek mainland.[5]

About 1730 BC the three major palaces of Crete were destroyed, and new palaces were built; and about 1628 BC—the date remains controversial—a massive volcanic eruption occurred on the neighbouring island of Thera (Santorini). This eruption—until recently dated some two centuries later—was popularly linked with the ending of Minoan civilization in Crete, and the start of the mainland-dominated, Mycenaean age. (A tidal wave in its wake has caused it also to be linked with the departure from Egypt of the Israelites.[6]) Mycenaean civilization—that of which Homer wrote, and which has provided the mythology that inspired much of European music drama—was named after the spectacular objects found in the shaft graves excavated at Mycenae.

Dating from the early seventeenth century BC, the Mycenae grave goods appear to emanate from the Aegean, Anatolia, the Levant, and Egypt; and some bear resemblances to the nomad art of the steppe. The varied ancestry of these grave goods has caused controversy over the origin of Mycenaean culture. It has been linked with possible invasions of Cretans from the Aegean, of Dorians from the north, of Phoenicians from the east, and of peoples from Egypt. More recently, Martin Bernal has argued persuasively that Mycenaean culture, both in the mainland *and* in New Palace culture in Crete, resulted from invasions by the Hyksos—a nomadic, predominantly Semitic-speaking people, who invaded Lower Egypt, probably in the eighteenth century BC, where they set up a pharaonic dynasty.[7] Cretan New Palace art incorporates emblems thought to be linked with Hyksos royalty and conquest;[8] and the material finds at Mycenae also show strong affinities with Hyksos material culture (suggesting that the shaft graves were those of Hyksos princes). It is possible, therefore, that the Hyksos invaded Greece during their ascendant period in Egypt, introduced to the mainland the West

[3] Bernal, *Black Athena*, ii. 69; and *The Times Atlas of World History*, ed. Geoffrey Barraclough (London, 1989), 66.
[4] Bernal, *Black Athena*, ii. 185.
[5] *Times Atlas*, 66.
[6] Bernal, *Black Athena*, ii. 355.
[7] Ibid. 361.
[8] Ibid. 380, 364.

Asian palatial system, and founded the 'heroic' dynasties that lasted from about the seventeenth to the thirteenth centuries BC.[9]

During this period, the Greek mainland became the focal point of a distinctive civilization, with a sphere of cultural influence extending to Sicily, Italy, Anatolia, and the Levant, as well as throughout the Aegean. It lasted until the twelfth century BC, when disruption of Mediterranean trade by 'Invasions of Sea Peoples', and Dorian attacks on southern Greece from the north-west, caused widespread devastation. (The Dorians claimed to be 'Heraklids' or of Egypto-Phoenician ancestry, Herakles being originally an Egyptian god, whose semi-divine conquests were associated with Middle Kingdom pharaohs; and later Spartan kings claimed kinship with the Jews, whose leaders were said to have been Hyksos princes.[10])

The enduring legacy of Greece's 'heroic age' is the *Iliad*, written around 900 BC from oral tradition of events that occurred some 300 years earlier. The siege of Troy and the fall of Thebes—the seat of the last of the Hyksos dynasties—marked the end of the Bronze Age Mycenaean civilization. The commitment to writing of the *Iliad* resulted in a surge of Greek national awareness;[11] by the ninth century BC, new Greek cities that would become the basis of the *polis*, or city state, were being constructed.

The Culture of Ancient Greece

The mainland of Greece consists largely of small plains separated by mountain barriers; the small city states that emerged on the plains became relatively independent, politically self-contained units. Pan-Hellenic consciousness was encouraged by such means as the establishment of the Olympiad (in 776 BC) and the enhancement of the status of the Delphic oracle. ('Hellenes' was the name used for all Greek-speaking peoples of the Aegean; the word 'Greek' was first used by the Romans.) Like many empire-builders, the Greeks regarded themselves as superior to others, whose unintelligible 'bar-bar' form of speech led to their being called 'barbarians'.[12]

It was their general attitude of intellectual scepticism that made the Greeks unique among Mediterranean peoples: they were never afraid to

[9] Bernal, *Black Athena*, ii. 41–2, 363. [10] Ibid. 60, 115.
[11] J. M. Roberts, *Pelican History of the World* (London: Pelican Books, 1988), 179.
[12] Ibid. 176.

pit one argument against another.[13] Pythagoras (*c*.570–500 BC), as already indicated, learnt his geometry in Egypt. From Old Babylonian times, savants had been preoccupied with number, and Pythagoras inherited the Babylonian interest in the arithmetical proportions inherent in the harmonic series. Pythagoras was a pioneer in linking number with geometry.[14] Investigation into the numerical properties of shapes led to awareness of the arithmetical relationship between numbers and arithmetical series. The power of number gave the possibility of creating an entire numerical framework for the analysis of the various phenomena in nature, and to the possibility of the existence of a numerological order of the universe. (This had already been important to the Sumerians, as early as the third millennium.) Pythagoras' conclusion that all regularities in nature are musical led to the belief that the movements of the heavens are the music of the spheres.

For all their interest in science, the Greeks were concerned to *relate* this empirical world with the intuitive world of the senses. A century and a half after Pythagoras, Plato distinguished between reality and appearance, between ideas and sensible objects, and between reason and sense perception, considering the first of each pair superior to the second.[15] Knowledge, Plato maintained, lay in the mind and arose from observation, whereas opinion was connected with the ephemeral world of the senses. This separation of mind and senses was to become the cornerstone of Cartesian philosophy, and of eighteenth-century European aesthetics.

The most important aspects of Greek education, according to Plato, were 'gymnastics for the body and music for the soul'.[16] The importance placed on gymnastics by the Greeks reflected a long-held belief in the 'moral' attributes of a fully developed physique in which beauty and strength combine. Throughout the Archaic period, the Greeks carved *kouroi*, statues of young men, recognizably Greek, but clearly betraying Egyptian origins. They were carved to a traditional formula by artisans whose work was called *technē*: art in the sense of skill or cunning, the work of a professional.

[13] Kenneth Dover, *The Greeks* (London: BBC, 1980), 7–12.

[14] J. Bronowski, *The Ascent of Man* (London: BBC, 1973), 157.

[15] Bertrand Russell, *History of Western Philosophy* (Woking: Allen & Unwin, 1946), 156.

[16] Oliver Strunk, 'Plato', *Source Readings in Musical History from Classical Antiquity through the Romantic Era, Selected and Translated by O. Strunk* (New York, 1950: London: Faber Paperbacks, 1981).

From about 570 BC onwards, a new naturalism in art developed, due partly to the invention of hollow bronze-casting from clay models; such models were constructed not by *removing* material from a block (as in sculpting from marble), but by *joining* different parts of the figures together.[17] This relieved sculptors of the need to work from outline drawings on the surface of the block (which had enshrined the traditional element in archaic Greek art); and it gave artistic sanction to a new, timeless, concept of ideal perfection, rather than to precedent. Humans themselves came to be seen as copies of ideal archetypes; and physical beauty came to be linked both with art and with divinity. This exalted sense of the holiness of beauty was peculiarly Greek, and was to exert a profound influence on the course of Western art. It made possible the concept of artwork as a source of empathy between an artist and those who experienced his work.[18]

A principal cause of this elevated status of human beauty was the attribution, from Homeric times, of *human* characteristics to gods. The Greek gods took sides in the Trojan war, and were susceptible to such human failings as theft, adultery, and deceit. Effectively, Greek gods assumed the divine aspects formerly claimed by semi-divine kings; thus the mortal heroes of Greece did not acquire the fearsome aura of divinity, characteristic of their Mesopotamian and Egyptian forebears. As Kenneth Dover has put it: 'Democracy was a logical consequence of irreverence.'[19]

The concept that made possible the idealized statues of the Parthenon friezes, for example, where gods are indistinguishable from humans, was *mimēsis*.[20] Literally, the word means 'imitation'; but because it came to refer to painting, poetry, and music, as well as to sculpture, the term (as used from Plato onwards) served to separate these arts—which eighteenth-century Europeans would call the 'fine arts'—from other arts that demanded only *technē*.[21] The essence of Greek humanism lay in this discrimination.

In their search for a rational order in their world, the Greeks, uniquely, concluded that things *could* be explained, and that human destiny did *not* rest on the unpredictable actions of gods and demons. At

[17] Peter Kidson, 'The Figural Arts', in M. I. Finley (ed.), *The Legacy of Greece* (Oxford: Oxford University Press), 412.

[18] Ibid. 413–14.

[19] Dover, *The Greeks*, 10.

[20] See also Foreword, p. 29.

[21] Kidson, 'The Figural Arts', 415.

the heart of the Platonic doctrine lay the belief that, behind the accidents of this world, an underlying order exists. This viewpoint was subsequently to be reflected in Christianity; and in seventeenth-century Europe it was to become the touchstone of the *Scienza Nuova.*[22]

Such a viewpoint was no doubt encouraged by the Greeks' victory over the Persians at Marathon in 490 BC and at Salamis ten years later, and by the burst of creativity that followed these events—one of the most extraordinary such bursts in human history. From it, in the fifth century BC, came the superbly proportioned architecture of the Parthenon, the exemplary sculpture of Pheidias, Polyclitus, and Myron, the wonderful 'red-figure' vases, the tragedies of Aeschylus, Sophocles, and Euripides, the comedies of Aristophanes, the histories of Herodotus and Thucydides, and the teachings of Socrates, built upon by Plato and Aristotle in the next century. Great festivals of theatre, music, and dance were staged in honour of Dionysos, the god of wine. He was counterbalanced by Apollo, god of music, archery, and prophecy, who presided over the oracle at Delphi. Such festivals were fiercely competitive: this was an age of individualism.

Investing gods with human characteristics inevitably presupposed that humans themselves could be god-like.[23] Ultimately, this led to the collapse of godly authority. Aristophanes ridiculed the gods, in his comedy *The Birds.* That he survived, and succeeded, may say more about the respect for playwrights as social commentators than about the tolerance of Athenian society; for in 399 BC that same society demanded the death of its most famous philosopher, Socrates, who also had been ridiculed by Aristophanes in his comedy *The Clouds.* This was in 423 BC, when Athenian confidence was already on the wane: Pericles, the great statesman, had died; and democratic Athens had embarked on a disastrous war with oligarchical Sparta. New heresies were challenging old assumptions. Protagoras had denied the importance of the gods, and Anaxagoras had declared all matter to be indestructible.[24] Foreigners from Sicily were teaching a new art called 'rhetoric'. Such inventiveness is not necessarily conducive to stability. Socrates, who was killed for 'corrupting the young', had in fact done nothing more than encourage his students to find rational grounds for accepting the new ideas.[25]

[22] Bryan Appleyard, *Understanding the Present: Science and the Soul of Modern Man* (London: Pan Books, 1992), 87.

[23] Roberts, *Pelican History of the World*, 178.

[24] Dover, *The Greeks*, 42.

[25] I. F. Stone, *The Trial of Socrates* (London: Jonathan Cape, 1988), *passim.*

The idealism at the heart of the Greek achievement was relatively short lived.

The Greek View of Music

The Greeks were musicians as much as they were sculptors, architects, playwrights, or philosophers. Musical performance was essential on all important occasions, and competitions in amateur choral singing and in professional instrumental playing took place alongside competitive sporting festivals. Winners were keen to erect stone epitaphs to their victories to remind the gods of their artistic pre-eminence.[26]

We know very little concerning the actual music the Greeks performed; some fifty short fragments are all that have come down to us. We do know, however, that choral singing by choirs of men or women, boys or girls, was highly regarded, that it became the kernel of Greek theatre, and that singing was usually accompanied on the lyre. We know that the bowl lyre was, in general, the instrument of the amateur, while a more sophisticated form of box lyre (*kithara*), and a reed wind instrument played in pairs (*aulos*), were the instruments of the professionals (Pl. 10).[27] (The reeds used are thought to have been double reeds.[28]) We know that the music was homophonic, with drones and occasional heterophony, supported by tambourines, cymbals, and castanets. We can only conjecture the extent to which it was influenced by Asian musical traditions. There was certainly a tradition of epic-singing to the lyre, and it is probable that the *Iliad* and *Odyssey* were chanted, as were the epics of Gilgamesh in Mesopotamia, and of Manas and Gesar in Central Asia. The semi-legendary Olympus, the Mysian, himself part-Asian, was said to have been the first to play the *aulos*, likely to have been of Mesopotamian origin.[29] And—as already indicated—the complete system of seven diatonic scales was in use in Mesopotamia in the early second millennium BC.

About the philosophy and theory of Greek music we know considerably more. Music was held to affect both the feelings and the actions of

[26] H. I. Marrou, *A History of Education in Antiquity* (London: Sheen & Ward, 1966).
[27] R. P. Winnington-Ingram, 'Greece', *The New Grove* (1980), vii. 660.
[28] M. L. West, *Ancient Greek Music* (Oxford: Oxford University Press, 1992), 82–5.
[29] J. F. Mountford and R. P. Winnington-Ingram, 'Ancient Greek Music', *NOCM* (1983).

10. Revellers with (from left) *barbiton* (long-armed bowl lyre), *kithara*, clappers, and *aulos*: black-figure amphora (late sixth century BC)

humans.[30] During the mid-fifth century, for example, Damon of Athens declared that, as musical activity arises from the soul, it can affect human nature favourably or unfavourably. Indeed, Plato attributed to Damon the claim that changes in musical style were always accompanied by changes in the laws of the state.[31] This kind of notion reflected music's inseparable connection with *ēthos*, for music was considered the primary means of conveying 'good states of mind', which 'alone are good ends', according to Plato. Greek *mousikē* combined the moral function of *ēthos* with the artistic function of the muses, the deities who inspired artistic creation.

The modes of Greek music were referred to as *harmoniai* ('tunings', 'attunements', involving separate tunings of the lyre), and aesthetic differences between them were linked with human behaviour.[32] Harmony, however, was perceived not only as a musical phenomenon but also as the dominant metaphysical principle of the universe; it was defined by the Pythagoreans as 'the harmonization of opposites, the unification of disparate things, and the conciliation of warring states';[33] and it was manifest in such matters as a healthy human life, and social intercourse. Heraclitus equated the hunting bow and the lyre, asserting

[30] West, *Ancient Greek Music*, 31–6.

[31] Warren Anderson, 'Ethos', *The New Grove* (1980), vi. 284. A comparable situation obtained in China where, with each new dynasty, the state mode, and the pitch of its final, changed (see p. 332).

[32] West, *Ancient Greek Music*, 177.

[33] Lewis Rowell, *Music and Musical Thought in Early India* (Chicago and London: University of Chicago Press, 1992), 53–4.

that 'the hidden harmony is better than the obvious'; indeed, he quipped (of the tensed string of the musical bow) that 'its name is life but its work is death'.[34] Where Indians believed that sound emanates from immaterial ether, Greeks believed that sound emanates from impact; music, therefore, was conceived as a nexus of clearly articulated points, rather than as a smooth continuum.[35] To the Greeks, it was *form*, rather than substance, that caused things to act on one another.

According to Greek theorists, all scales were built from tetrachords; and the octave of a heptatonic scale might comprise two disjunct tetrachords, or two conjunct tetrachords plus a tone. The outer notes of tetrachords within a scale were invariable in pitch, and were called 'standing notes'; inner notes, however, were variable, and were called 'moving notes'. (Variability of the inner notes of a tetrachord or pentachord is still the common basis of modality in traditional music throughout most of Asia.)

Variations in pitch of these inner notes accorded with one of three *genera* or 'kinds': *enharmonic*, *chromatic*, or *diatonic*; all were four-note tetrachords, derived (apparently) from a three-note tetrachord, itself divided into a semitone and a major third[36] (corresponding, for example, to E–F–A on the keys of a piano). In the *enharmonic* ('in tune') *genus*, the semitone of the basic tetrachord (E–F) was subdivided into two quarter-tones; this *genus* was (as its name implies) the standard *genus* during the classical period, and was said to have been that used by Olympus on the *aulos*. The *chromatic* ('coloured') *genus* was a variation on the *enharmonic*; here, the basic tetrachord was divided into a tone and a minor third (E–F♯–A), with the tone further divided into two semitones (E–F–F♯–A). The *diatonic*—less popular than the *enharmonic* and *chromatic* until the late fourth century BC—comprised a tetrachord divided into a semitone and a minor third, with the latter subdivided into a semitone and tone (E–F–G–A).[37] Clearly the terms *enharmonic*, *chromatic*, and *diatonic* acquired meanings in Ancient Greece very different from those attributed to them in modern Europe.

[34] Heraclitus, *The Presocratics*, trans. Philip Wheelwright (New York: Odyssey Press, 1966), 78.

[35] Rowell, *Music*, 53.

[36] West, *Ancient Greek Music*, 163–4.

[37] Ibid. 160–4.

Greek modes—like many others worldwide—were named after ethnic groups: among those most frequently mentioned are Dorian, Phrygian, and Lydian. The different *eidos* ('aspect') of modes is revealed if presented in different octave species—that is to say, in the seven different scales obtained by taking each note of a heptatonic scale, in turn, as a tonic. Octave species could exist in different *genera*, and were labelled with names borrowed or adapted from traditional modal names; but it is not known what modifications to their structure were made in the process of adaptation.

The most important surviving Greek treatise on music is that by Aristoxenus (early third century BC). Unlike the Pythagoreans and Harmonists before him, who had concentrated on tracing numerical relationships in concordant intervals, Aristoxenus attempted to establish a comprehensive theory of music.[38] He postulated three main 'systems' of tetrachords: the Lesser Perfect System, comprising three conjunct tetrachords and a tone (A–B–C–D–E–F–G–A–B♭–C–D); the Greater Perfect System, comprising four tetrachords in two conjunct pairs separated by a whole tone (B–C–D–E–F–G–A–B–C–D–E–F–G–A); and a Perfect Immutable System, combining features of both. (This last was so named because it represented an attempt to accommodate a variety of modes within the framework of one master scale.[39]) When it became necessary to transpose these systems to specific pitches, in order to accommodate particular vocal and instrumental ranges, scales were given a specific starting pitch, and—like the octave species—were labelled with traditional modal names. No clear relationship between key and mode was defined, however.

Theoretical preoccupations of this kind were subsequently to be characteristic of Islamic musical theorists who inherited the Greek mantle; and it is clear that Aristoxenus' system had more in common with West Asian modal systems (see pp. 203–5) than with the systems that evolved in Europe.

There is no way of knowing how far musical theory was put into practice, though some folk-songs of the present day have been shown to accord with tetrachordal theory, as have the steps of some folk-dances with classical metres. It is clear, however, that an innovative style of music-making was developed during the fourth century BC by soloist-composers such as Timotheus of Miletus (*c*.450–360 BC). The melodic

[38] Mountford and Winnington-Ingram, 'Ancient Greek Music'.

[39] West, *Ancient Greek Music*, 185.

contours of Greek music had formerly tended to follow the speech melody of the language; and rhythms were commonly based on the natural quantities of syllables, in units of feet rather than bars (including asymmetrical rhythmic patterns of various unitary lengths).[40] The new style appears to have involved modulation between modes, enlivened, perhaps, by greater ornamentation and rhythmic freedom.[41] Timotheus himself, in the epilogue to his *Persians*, criticizes 'out-of-date music spoilers ... maulers of songs, who strain and yell with far-ringing crier's voices'; and Aristoxenus states later that 'older musicians ... valued rhythmic intricacy ... whereas the moderns are lovers of melody'.[42]

This 'modern', virtuosic, style of music-making lasted throughout the Hellenic period, but was subsequently abjured by both Jews and Christians.

Hellenism, and the Music of Rome

The idealism at the heart of the Greek achievement was soon overtaken by the individualism to which that achievement gave rise. Already during the Peleponnesian war (431–404 BC) Athenian democracy had become tainted with imperialism; and, as democracy waned, so the Greek cultural achievement declined. Scepticism gave way to dogma. The new breed of teachers from Sicily, the Sophists, dealt not in ideals but in rhetoric: that form of public oratory which aimed to *persuade* people of the truth of what is said rather than to *seek* the truth itself. Sculpture became personalized as it imitated successful rather than ideal man.

The genius and—ironically—the ultimate undoing of the Greeks lay in their ability to see both sides of a question. This prevented them from taking decisive action in the face of danger, a problem not unknown to modern democracies. Demosthenes, the last great agitator of Greek democracy, warned of the threat to Athens from the 'lousy' Macedonians.[43] His warnings were in vain: in 338 BC Philip of Macedon forced the League of Corinth to agree to wage war against Persia, under

[40] Dimitri Conomos, 'Greece', *The New Grove* (1980), vii. 660; and West, *Ancient Greek Music*, 129–53.

[41] Winnington-Ingram, 'Greece', *The New Grove*, vii. 661.

[42] West, *Ancient Greek Music*, 154, 361.

[43] Dover, *The Greeks*, 19.

11. Musicians dancing, and playing *tibia*, cymbals, and frame drum, by Dioskourides of Samos: Roman mosaic (first century BC), from the Villa of Cicero

Macedonian leadership. A subsequent Greek rebellion was crushed by Philip's son and successor, Alexander the Great. A further rebellion after Alexander's death ended with Demosthenes taking his life and Athens being ruled by an oligarchy. A brief, but exceptionally influential, episode of history was at an end.

It was not only the West that was to be influenced by Greek culture. Alexander's conquest of Egypt, West Asia, and parts of India brought these regions into a new interrelationship. Through 'Hellenization'—the founding of cities on the Greek model—vast areas of North Africa and Asia became imbued with Greek culture, and Greek became their official language. Alexander's dream had been to unite his Greek and Persian empires; in the event, on his way back from his conquests, he died in Babylon in 323 BC, leaving no competent successor. Two Persian dynasties, the Seleucid and the Sassanian, were to harry Europe for the next 700 years; and it was Rome, not Persia, that inherited the mantle of Greece.

Hellenistic musical traditions survived under the Romans, and music continued to have an important place in public life. Following the Roman conquest of Macedon in 167 BC, large numbers of Greek artists entered Italy, including poets, actors, singers, and players of the *kithara* and *tibia* (Greek *aulos*) (Pl. 11). Greek artists first appeared in the triumphal games of Roman generals, but subsequently they participated in musical and theatrical festivals. Musicians sang settings of Latin verse, accompanying themselves on the *kithara*; and various genres of lyric song were cultivated. By the first century AD, outstanding Greek actor-singers, and *kitharōdes*, received large fees for the performance of praise-hymns and dramatic solos, in musical competitions such as were established (at Rome) by Nero (in AD 60). Senators and emperors were among those who emulated their performance; Nero himself participated in the competitions.[44]

During the same period, pantomime became popular throughout Italy. (*Pantomimus* referred to an actor who specialized in mime, accompanied by instrumental music and a chorus.) The genre was of native origin; as early as the mid-fourth century BC, Etruscan actor-dancers had performed pantomimic dances in Rome, to the accompaniment of *tibiae*. During the first century BC, Greek musicians and foreign solo dancers helped to develop and establish pantomime as a substantial form of entertainment;[45] by the second century AD, miming of everyday events, as well as of themes from Greek comedy, was the most popular form of theatre, among slaves, freedmen, and citizens alike. *Pantomimi* were accompanied by *tibiae*, *syrinx* (pan pipes), and *kithara*, the ensemble being led by *tibia* players with foot-clappers. Female dancers from Egypt, Syria, and Spain enlivened the performance. Their art was also practised in taverns, and on the streets; dancing, both exhibitional and social, became popular at all levels of society, despite condemnation by both conservative Romans and Christians.

Although the Romans valued Greek artistic traditions, they did little to develop them: it was gladiators, rather than actor-musicians, who performed in the vast arenas of the *colossea*. Roman culture was severely practical, and often brutal, with its principal accomplishments in law and administration. But there was one field in which the Romans surpassed the Greeks: that of engineering; it is perhaps characteristic of the Romans that they did not distinguish this science from architecture. Their invention of concrete, and their use of the arch and of the vaulted dome, led to the creation of a new architectural environment.[46] Concrete made possible the manipulation of volume and light, so

[44] Günter Fleischhauer, 'Rome', *The New Grove* (1980), xvi. 150.
[45] Ibid.
[46] Roberts, *Pelican History of the World*, 247.

characteristic of Christian basilicas. The model was to be refined by the Muslims, and then appropriated by the Normans, in a style subsequently known as 'Romanesque'. Graeco-Roman architectural remains are to be found as far apart as the Black Sea coast, northern England, and the Atlas mountains; and because of the subsequent dominance of Europe, two classical buildings—the Parthenon in Athens and the Pantheon in Rome—have been imitated in municipal architecture in cities throughout much of the modern world.

The Romans and Christianity

That Graeco-Roman culture survived was due to its fusion with a tradition that had taken root in Palestine in the first century AD. By virtue of a special covenant with Jahwe, the Jews considered the land to be theirs. The covenant had been made with Abraham, and it acquired renewed significance when the impact of Hellenism eroded Jewish insularity. Although for a brief period the Jews gained independence, hopes of nationhood were shattered in 63 BC, when Palestine fell to the armies of Pompey, and Roman rule was imposed.

When Jesus was born (in 7 BC),[47] many Jews believed that, according to prophecy, a 'Messiah' would be born who would deliver them by force from the Roman yoke. The role of the historical Jesus remains controversial, but the religion that arose from it came to be based on the Pauline interpretation of Jesus as Son of God, preaching reconciliation rather than rebellion. With economic conditions deteriorating within the Roman Empire, 'the Kingdom of God' became increasingly attractive to common people who had lost hope in the secular world. The establishment of Christianity was to have incalculable consequences for the future of music in Europe.

At the height of its power in the first century, the Roman Empire embraced the whole of the Mediterranean littoral and southern Europe; to the north-west it extended as far as Britain, and to the north-east over Mesopotamia, Armenia, and Assyria. The empire was overextended; when Diocletian became emperor in 284, he divided it into two halves. Ironically, this action by a Christian-hating emperor augured the division of Europe into rival Roman and Byzantine empires, each espousing

[47] Barbara Thiering, *Jesus the Man* (London: Corgi Books, 1992), 283.

different versions of Christianity, with different liturgies, leading to different traditions of religious music. When, in 313, the Emperor Constantine moved his court from Rome to Byzantium (to be renamed Constantinople), and from the many religious cults of the time singled out Christianity for 'compensation from our benevolence', he established himself as *dominus* (lord), an absolute ruler at the head of a vast bureaucracy.[48] Constantinople (later, Istanbul) was to become one of the world's great cities, culturally Greek, and rivalling the splendour of Rome.

Following Constantine's 'conversion', Christian worship became public and state-supported, and liturgical chants, such as the Introit, Offertory, and Communion, were developed.[49] The perpetual *anamnēsis* (commemoration) of the Last Supper in the Eucharist (termed the Mass in the West) was to provide the basic liturgies of both Byzantine and Roman Catholic rites. By the fourth century, many distinct forms of Eastern (Greek) and Western (Latin) rites emerged, each local rite having its own liturgy and music.[50] Common to them all was the primacy of the word over music, for the Church Fathers needed to distinguish Christianity from current mystery cults. Although at first, sung, improvised prayer was encouraged, chromatic modes, and instruments, were forbidden; and the rhythmic style of Hellenistic popular music appears not to have influenced early Christian music.[51]

The Christian Church modelled its structure on that of the Roman Empire, and its dioceses reflected the administrative divisions of Diocletian. The greatest centres were accorded special dignity; chief among these was Rome, the see of Peter, but its diocesan bishops shared power with those of Antioch, Alexandria, Constantinople, and Jerusalem.[52] When Rome was sacked by the Ostrogoths in 410, the imperial government was moved north to Ravenna, leaving the Bishop of Rome as the sole officer of rank in the former imperial capital. It fell to Leo 'the Great' (in office 440–61) to assume the defunct, Roman, urban title of *pontifex maximus* (originally the head of a guild of priests), 'Supreme Pontiff'—of Western Christendom.[53]

In fact, the sack of Rome shook the confidence of Western Christians and led to a crisis of ideas; although St Augustine of Hippo, in his *The*

[48] *Times Atlas*, 88, 100.

[49] David Hiley, 'Plainchant', *NOCM* (1983).

[50] Kenneth Levy, 'Plainchant', *The New Grove* (1980), xiv. 800.

[51] Christian Hannick, 'Christian Church, Music of the Early', *The New Grove* (1980), iv. 364.

[52] *Times Atlas*, 93.

[53] Clyde Curry Smith, 'The Ancient Religions of Greece and Rome', in *The Religions of the World* (London: Lion Publishing, 1982), 112.

City of God, promoted the doctrine of original sin and the necessity for divine grace, Western Christendom at the time was all but submerged by doctrines heretical to its teaching. Manichaeanism, for example, which arose in Persia, asserted that Jesus was mortal, and did not die on the cross. Although Manichaeans were persecuted viciously, the religion spread rapidly, and by the time of the Crusades there were Manichaean sects in Spain, southern France, Italy, and Bulgaria.[54] (St Augustine, a North African, had himself been a Manichaean in his youth.[55]) Arianism, which arose in Alexandria (in the early fourth century) as a compromise with the old Egyptian religion, still espoused by Egypt's Hellenized élite, likewise denied the divinity of Christ; during the fifth century it became the dominant religion in Spain, the Pyrenees, and what is now southern France. (It would subsequently lie behind much medieval heresy, and surface again during the sixteenth century in the form of Unitarianism.)

That the Roman Church survived was due to its forming an alliance with the Frankish Merovingians, who had taken over the administration of the Roman Empire after its collapse in 476, and had presented themselves as heirs to the Judaeo-classical tradition.[56] In 496 the Merovingian king, Clovis, accepted baptism into the Christian Church in return for the title 'Novus Constantinus', and then won much of Western Europe for Rome. Some three centuries later, on the basis of a forged document,[57] the pope in Rome usurped a secular prerogative by anointing a non-Merovingian, Pippin, as King of the Franks. And in the year 800, Pippin's son, Carolus Magnus (Charlemagne), was lured to Rome, where a crown was placed on his head, and the populace declared him 'Charles Augustus, crowned by God, the great and peace-loving Emperor of the Romans'.[58] This 'peace-loving' emperor went on to create the largest 'Roman' empire that had been seen since the fifth century. The Church then had no spiritual rival, and Rome could set

[54] Michael Baigent, Richard Leigh, and Henry Lincoln, *The Holy Blood and The Holy Grail* (London: Corgi Books, 1982), 405–9.

[55] Roberts, *Pelican History of the World*, 288.

[56] The Merovingians claimed descent from Troy and Arcadia (Baigent, Leigh, and Lincoln, *The Holy Blood*, 282–91); and they christened their cities with such names as Troyes and Paris. Homer has the Arcadians present at the Siege of Troy, and later Greek historians claim that Troy was founded by settlers from Arcadia. Moreover, there is clear evidence in the Apocrypha (Maccabees I) of a Jewish migration to Arcadia.

[57] *The Donation of Constantine*, Roberts, *Pelican History of the World*, 389.

[58] Einhard, *The Life of Charlemagne*, trans. in Lewis Thorpe, *Two Lives of Charlemagne* (Harmondsworth: Penguin, 1979), 81.

about unifying its new empire. An important means of achieving this was to be the promulgation of a common form of liturgical chant.

Significantly, the centre of Charlemagne's Holy Roman Empire was Aix-la-Chapelle (Aachen), not Rome, and scholars were imported from Ireland and England. The crowning of Charlemagne proved a decisive step in the movement of a nascent civilization northwards into the heart of Europe. It marked the triumph of the Roman Church over the 'barbarian' world with which it had lived for so long; and with it we have a first, momentary, glimpse of the Europe of the future.

Europe had recently held at bay a heresy more threatening than any so far seen, the progress of which had even cut short the advance of the warrior-nomads of Central Asia. Originating in Arabia, the other great centre of nomadism, another spiritual force was to reorder the cultural map of the northern hemisphere. It, too, held that Jesus was merely a prophet, but a prophet of secondary status to that of Muhammad. Islam was to permeate West Asia, would reach into the heart of Africa, into southern Europe, into Central and South East Asia, and across the borders of what is now China. It was to engender a prominent civilization that would preserve Greek literature and learning for posterity and have a profound influence on European culture.

Nevertheless, the heresies that beset the Roman Church worked ultimately to Europe's advantage. They imbued its culture with the contradictions that challenge traditions, that cause change, and that prevent the inertia that stifles creativity. They led, ultimately, to the secularization of the artistic, making possible in Europe a freedom of creative invention denied other great civilizations.

The Jewish Musical Tradition

Many traditions contributed to a cultural synthesis in Europe, before Islamic scholarship and technology made possible Europe's world dominance. One of the oldest traditions was that of Jewry. There are frequent references to music in the Old Testament. The instruments mentioned are basically those used throughout the ancient civilizations of Egypt and Mesopotamia: horns and trumpets, flutes and reed instruments, harps and lyres, cymbals, drums, clappers, and rattles. Many instruments had special significance. The *halil* (a generic name for flutes and, probably, reed instruments) had age-old phallic associations, symbolizing fertility, life, and resurrection; *halil*s were played at weddings and funerals, and to accompany prayers for rain.[59] String instruments appear to have retained ancient associations with males and with nobility; they were considered the instruments best suited to divine worship, and constituted the basis of the temple orchestra.[60]

Pitched instruments could also be used non-melodically. The name of Jubal, the mythical inventor of instrumental music, is related to the Hebrew word *yovel* (ram) and to the word 'jubilee', the occasions when the ram's horn was used. (The parallel with the use of the conch as an emblem of Buddha, and of the kudu horn in Sub-Saharan African ritual, is striking.) The young Saul, we are told, was made 'a new man' by the combined sounding of harp, drum, flute, and lyre; but in the melancholy of his old age he was soothed by the lyre alone. Around the end of the first millennium BC, King David granted a royal charter to the Levites, the professional musicians of the Temple in Jerusalem.[61] Their fame as musicians was legendary, and they were employed as far away as Egypt and India.

Hebrew poetry is rich in allusions to musical practice, and rabbinic theological literature makes frequent reference to musical matters. Despite this, however, no attempt was made to notate Jewish synagogue music. (Most of the synagogue music was notated only from the mid-eighteenth century onwards.) The tradition is therefore oral, originally passed down in the master–disciple tradition common throughout Asia. The structure of much of the synagogue music performed today—albeit in styles that vary with the region—dates back to the early centuries AD.[62]

The destruction of the Temple in Jerusalem in AD 70 led to the disappearance of all Levitical functions, including the provision of music for the sanctuary; and the rabbis replaced the Levites as custodians of liturgical practice. Isolated in a Roman world, the Jews had come to abjure Hellenistic music, and the rabbis banned all instruments from the synagogue, except for the *shofar* (horn of ram or ibex), which had special ritual connotations; to this day, instruments are not used in Orthodox Judaism. Great importance was attached to the chanting of sacred texts, however. Psalmody was intoned *senza mizura*, following

[59] Hanoch Avenary, 'Jewish Music', *NOCM* (1983).
[60] Eric Werner, 'Jewish Music', *The New Grove* (1980), ix. 618 ff.
[61] Avenary, 'Jewish Music'.
[62] Ibid.

speech rhythm, usually on a single pitch; but melismas, in the form of short melodic motifs, were used in cadential patterns attached to the middles and endings of verses. The form was antiphonal or responsorial, for the verses of Jewish poetry fall naturally into two halves, each echoing the other in 'rhymes of thought'.

The recitation of biblical texts and prayers was originally performed in a manner similar to that of the psalms; the Levites, who originally performed the liturgy, were given a rigorous five-year training that left little room for spontaneous invention. After the destruction of the Temple, however, prayers, psalms, and meditations came to involve a degree of improvisation within one particular mode, while biblical recitation came to employ a number of different modes, indicated by accent signs in the text.[63]

Modes, in this instance, must be interpreted in an Asiatic sense rather than in the sense in which they came to be used in Europe. Indeed, the difference between the two approaches to mode is what most marks the development of European music from that of developing Asiatic traditions. In medieval Europe, 'mode' came to refer to particular orderings of intervals, around which different scales could be assembled. In early Europe and throughout much of Asia, however, 'mode' referred to a series of orally transmitted melodic patterns, usually within a consistent, intervallic framework, and often within the span of a mere tetrachord or pentachord. *Modus* refers to both manner and mood. In many areas of the world—Greece, Persia, India, for example—modes were named after peoples or places; indeed, they arose as local musics. Modal systems were often collections of local musical manners.[64] In Hebrew biblical cantillation, certain modes were felt to be appropriate to certain sentiments, and particular melodic modes came to be related to particular word groups.

Notwithstanding its basic simplicity, Jewish synagogue music absorbed much of the Muslim–Asiatic tradition; and the improvisation of prayers came to resemble the Muslim rendering of *maqām* (the Arabic modal/melodic system). During the sixth century, metrical hymns were introduced, to be sung alongside the psalms. Originally these hymns used the free rhythm of biblical poetry and old Hebrew music, but gradually they also adopted some of the rhythmical patterns of Arab verse. (The attempt to strike a balance between the rhythmic

[63] Avenary, 'Jewish Music'.

[64] For a full discussion of this subject, see Harold Powers, 'Mode', *The New Grove* (1980), xii. 377.

freedom of Hebrew music and the measured rhythms of Arab and other host musical cultures was to be an enduring characteristic of Hebrew music.[65])

The new hymns required professional poet-musicians for their execution and transmission. The *hazan*, who as precentor had taken over the function of the chorus of Levites, now became a composer and arranger; he taught the whole community. Indeed, through the *hazan* many aspects of the synagogue musical tradition have been transmitted orally to the present day. Synagogue music still includes improvisation in modes that are determined in relation to their ethos, with chanting that incorporates inflections similar to those used in Islamic cantillation.

Music of the Early Christian Church

A system of eight modes was once common to Jewish, Roman, Byzantine, Syrian, and Armenian chant; it is possible that the biblical psalms were originally intended to be sung to an eight-mode system.[66] Christianity developed from Judaism, and Christians took from the synagogue the Jewish style of chanting the psalms and canticles, in both responsorial and antiphonal forms. Correspondences between Jewish and Gregorian melodies have been shown to exist, and the Christian *cantor* or *precentor* came to occupy a role similar to that of the Jewish *hazan*.

By the eighth century, an arrangement of eight modes, subsequently known as *oktōēchos* ('eight melody-types'), was in use in Byzantium. It probably originated in Syria. It became so firmly entrenched that the Byzantine liturgical year was itself divided into eight-week cycles, with the rotation of 'common' modes governing the choice of hymns for each week.[67] Modes in Byzantium followed Asiatic usage: each mode had its own melodic implications as well as intervallic structure.

The notion of Pope Gregory as the author of 'Gregorian' chant derives from medieval illustrations depicting the Holy Spirit whispering the divine message into the pontiff's ear, while the pontiff sings to an attendant scribe.[68] In fact, the classification of modes, and the

[65] Avenary, 'Jewish Music'.

[66] Werner, 'Jewish Music', ix. 623 ff; the evidence is not universally recognized as conclusive.

[67] Levy, 'Plainchant', *The New Grove*, xiv. 803.

[68] Ibid.

establishment of so-called Gregorian chant, did not develop until the late eighth century, when the intention was clearly to standardize forms of worship throughout the Frankish kingdom.

The form adopted was said to be based on Roman usage; regional styles such as the Gallican in France, the Mozarabic in Spain, and the Ambrosian in Milan were suppressed as far as possible. Nevertheless, Byzantine influence remained strong: recent scholarship indicates that Roman chant, as practised in the eighth century, differed substantially in style from that which subsequently became known as 'Gregorian'; it followed Byzantium in the use of ornamentation and, probably, a vocal drone to facilitate modal transposition.[69]

Carolingian musical theory derived not only from the Byzantine *oktōēchos* but also from the theorizing of late Greek ideas—in particular the work of an early, sixth-century theorist, Boethius (*c*.480–*c*.525), a speculative thinker in the Greek philosophical tradition. In *De institutione musica*, Boethius classified music into three types: *musica mundana* for the ordering of the cosmos, *musica humana* for a healthy body and soul, and *musica instrumentalis* for music that is actually audible. For audible music to be understood, it had to be translated into number.[70]

Boethius classified intervals as consonant or dissonant according to the complexity of their mathematical ratios. (This was determined by the use of a monochord, a one-string instrument with a movable bridge.) The perfect consonances of the fourth, fifth, and octave were identified. Boethius defined the system of seven diatonic scales and gave to them the Greek ethnic names used by Aristoxenus. This means of musical standardization was the more appealing to the Carolingians because Boethius related music to morality as well as to knowledge; he maintained that, in order to control human nature, it was necessary to understand and control the elements of music. Boethius' *De institutione musica* survived to become a standard text for university reading until the seventeenth century.[71]

Boethius' musical world had little place for feeling: music was to be judged solely on the basis of prescribed theory. This was a far cry from the Jewish tradition that had incorporated improvisation and measured rhythm into its practice, or indeed from Persian and Indian traditions,

[69] Marcel Pérès, 'Old Roman Chant, 7th–8th Centuries', sleeve-note to *Chant de L'Église de Rome*, performed by Ensemble Organum, Harmonia Mundi 901218.

[70] Calvin Bower, 'Boethius', *The New Grove* (1980), ii. 844–5.

[71] David Hiley, 'Mode', *NOCM* (1983).

in which performance practice overrode theory. As with the Jews, the Church Fathers forbade the use of instruments. Unlike the Jews, however, they had no long history of religious cohesion, substantiated by historical writings. Unlike the Jews, too, they were constantly contending with heresy. The early Christian Church Fathers feared music's potential for sensuality: as early as the third century, St John Chrysostom was warning Christians not to lapse into 'the Jewish manner of prayer'.[72] It was not until the eleventh century that a rhythmical song, the *conductus*, would enter the Church through liturgical drama.

By that time, 'Gregorian' chant had been elaborated through a number of devices. *Organum* involved singing the chant in parallel fourths and fifths; later, these intervals would be varied for artistic purposes. 'Troping' involved the addition of supplementary phrases of words and music to the Proper of the Mass, or of 'texting' extravagant melismas, most particularly the Alleluia. (Both probably arose as an aid to memorizing increasingly lengthy melismas.) Sequences were entire hymns that—deriving from Byzantine practice—were added to the liturgy for use on feast days. In contrast to the music of the Jewish synagogue, elaborations of this kind were not improvised, but were recorded in musical notation. Such devices were to lead to structured counterpoint.

The evolution of ordered counterpoint and of functional, triadic harmony—the aspects of European music that were to make it unique among the musics of the world—was indebted to the early medieval concern with theory; indeed, it was largely justified through theory. There was perpetual debate, for example, over the merits of perfect and imperfect numbers: the metaphysical superiority of three over two in relation to the Trinity (a rare European example of a sociological factor impinging upon musical structure). The frequent use of triple-time in art music was to be a conspicuous feature of European music. Theory was complemented by an increasingly sophisticated form of musical notation, and the new complexities of ecclesiastical music resulted as much from accurate systems of notation as from delight in the actual sound. Only in the late thirteenth century did Franco of Cologne's *Ars cantus mensurabilis* attempt to reconcile a fully rational theory with current practice, so that, by the fourteenth century, the sound of music, rather than its theory, could actually influence musical composition.

When a form of Greek humanism resurfaced during the Renaissance, the corpus of medieval theory was to prove a valuable enabling resource.

[72] Werner, 'Jewish Music', *The New Grove*, ix. 615.

The pull between prevailing musical theory, and the composer's inclination to adapt or disregard it, would characterize the course of European music, sustaining the notion of 'progress', and giving rise to the concept of individual 'genius'.

Changing Patterns of Cultural Diffusion

North of the Alps, a European civilization emerged with distinctive cultural systems between one and two millennia later than comparable civilizations in Asia. When it emerged, its assault upon the world was to change the course of human history; it was also to change the manner of cultural diffusion.

Up to the sixteenth century, the slow process of cultural diffusion, through trade, conquest, or migration, usually led to a process of gradual cultural absorption. When empires spread outwards, they usually absorbed the cultural systems of the regions over which they spread. When nomadic groups, or city or nation states, preyed upon the lands of long-established civilizations, their cultural systems were usually absorbed into the systems of the civilizations they invaded. It can be argued, of the Romans in Greece, of the Moghuls in India, or of the Mongols in China, that their cultural systems were more changed by those of the countries they invaded than were those of the invaded countries by theirs. The assimilation of foreign cultural elements strengthened the cultural systems of the civilizations invaded, and increased their durability, while the cultural identity of the invaders was often compromised.

Early cultural diffusion and cultural assimilation was usually due more to trade and conquest than migration, which, as already noted, was a very slow process. Because the lands of conquering and conquered peoples were usually contiguous, common cultural 'reference systems' (see p. 70) developed within particular regions. The existence of such 'reference systems' is an important factor affecting political and social stability. When cultural diffusion by sea involved relatively long distances—as, for example, with the Malayo-Polynesian voyages to Malagasy in the early centuries AD—it arose more from peaceful trading than from conquest. But it contained within it the possibility of bypassing contiguous cultural 'reference systems'.

The first conspicuous *collision* of cultural systems through diffusion by sea coincided with the effective use of gunpowder at the end of the fifteenth century. This was the European conquest of the New World; it was to prove one of the most important events in human history. It led to a global redistribution of peoples, bringing into the same environment those of African, Asian, and European stocks; it brought together different civilizations at differing stages of their cultural development, each having differing forms of religious belief; and, in bringing together different musical systems, it eroded the sense of identity established, sometimes over thousands of years, between a people and its music.

During the second half of this present century, the introduction of jet aircraft, along with magnetic tape, television, video, and the microchip, has again changed the nature and scope of cultural diffusion and interaction. Peoples with distinctive cultural traditions from widely separated regions of the globe have been brought together with unprecedented speed, and mass movements of peoples are taking place to an ever greater extent.

Between 1880 and 1920, immigrants from the poorer fringes of Europe—Ireland, Scandinavia, Sicily, the Balkans, and Eastern Europe—passed into the USA. Following the Second World War, similar 'poor and huddled masses' moved from the Caribbean and the Indian Subcontinent to Britain, from the Maghreb to France, and, later, from Mexico, Central America, and East Asia to the USA. More recently, Vietnamese have sought refuge in Europe, the USA, and Australia, while poorer Asians and Africans have migrated to and from the oil-rich Arab states. In the 1990s, political disturbances, and growing disparities between rich and poor, are creating a desire to migrate on a scale that is without precedent.

During the course of this book, it will emerge that many of the cultural systems thus being thrown together are intrinsically incompatible. Nevertheless, it is a fact of modern life that the political ambience in which they coexist encourages assimilation. The unprecedented speed with which such assimilation is occurring is tending to weaken individual cultural systems. Music is particularly vulnerable to such dilution. It developed in Europe in ways very different from those in Africa and Asia; and because European musical styles are now influencing those elsewhere to an even greater extent than they did during the period of European colonisation, musical traditions that have become established over long periods, with relatively little change, are disappearing. Radically changed contexts, both for performing music and listening to it, are undermining traditional roles of music. Appreciation of the musical problems—and opportunities—brought about by the global interaction of peoples will be assisted by a thorough understanding of the distinctive musical systems now being brought, so suddenly, into new, proximate relationships.

Part Two

Traditional Musics of Africa and Asia

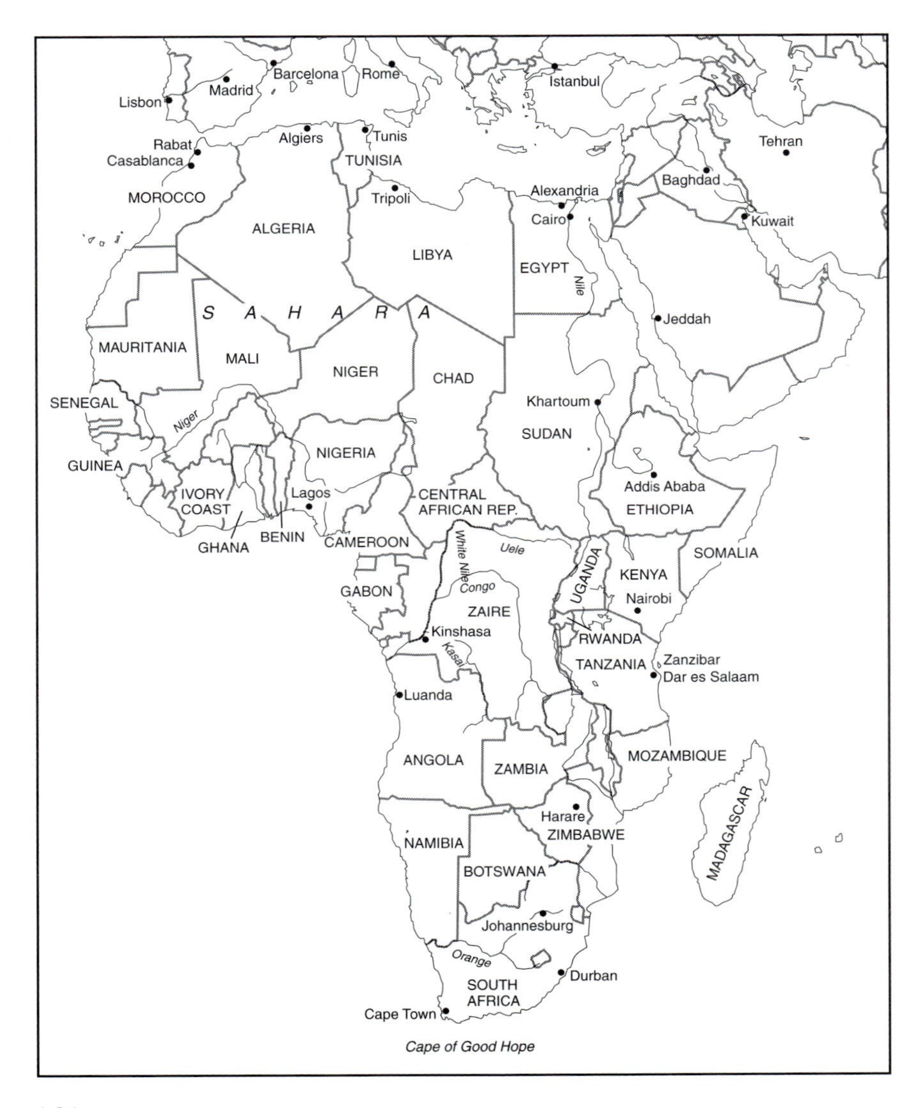
Lisbon
Madrid
Barcelona
Rome
Istanbul
Rabat
Casablanca
Algiers
Tunis
TUNISIA
Tehran
Baghdad
MOROCCO
Tripoli
Alexandria
Cairo
Kuwait
ALGERIA
LIBYA
EGYPT
Nile
S A H A R A
Jeddah
MAURITANIA
MALI
NIGER
CHAD
SENEGAL
Niger
Khartoum
SUDAN
NIGERIA
GUINEA
IVORY COAST
Lagos
CENTRAL AFRICAN REP.
Addis Ababa
ETHIOPIA
GHANA
BENIN
CAMEROON
White Nile
Uele
UGANDA
SOMALIA
KENYA
GABON
Congo
ZAIRE
Nairobi
Kinshasa
RWANDA
Kasai
TANZANIA
Zanzibar
Dar es Salaam
Luanda
MOZAMBIQUE
ANGOLA
ZAMBIA
MADAGASCAR
Harare
ZIMBABWE
NAMIBIA
BOTSWANA
Johannesburg
Orange
Durban
SOUTH AFRICA
Cape Town
Cape of Good Hope

Africa

6 *Africa*

Africa's Cultural Dilemma

It is fitting that this survey of traditional musics should start with Africa, for Africa gave birth to the first human beings and—we may assume—to the first human song. Africa also gave birth, along the Nile, to one of the first civilizations. Africa retains some of the oldest extant musical traditions, features of which have been used to reinvigorate tired musical traditions in the West; and, as Africans throughout the Diaspora have united, aspects of African and European music have combined to form new styles of popular music throughout the globe.

Africa is a huge and varied land mass, larger than China and India added together. Throughout recorded history, the Sahara desert, spanning the width of the northern bulge of Africa, has caused the peoples to the north and the south to develop separately and—to that extent—differently. To the north now lie Muslim states, the African identity of which has been, in various degrees, overlaid by cultural influences from West Asia; to the south, Muslim and Christian states, the majority of whose peoples follow a way of life still heavily conditioned by indigenous religion.

Until just over 100 years ago, most of the peoples of Sub-Saharan Africa had no native tradition of literacy; and this made for a rich oral–aural culture, linking peoples with their environment and their religion. Traditional African music is tied to religious and social custom and is as purposeful and disciplined as any in the world. Nevertheless, in the wider cultural context, the lack of literacy proved ultimately to be an impoverishment, for in its restriction of the dissemination of information it weakened consolidation of government.

That indigenous cultural systems continue to exist over large swathes of Sub-Saharan Africa is due to a prolonged history of abuse and spoliation of the weaker by those stronger. Arabs had long exported slaves from Africa to West Asia when Europe's conquest of the Americas led to the shipment of some ten million of Africa's most skilled farmers and miners across the Atlantic. Europe's subsequent infiltration and colonization of Africa undermined indigenous social and political institutions, milked the continent's resources, and generated conditions of wage labour sometimes more inhumane even than slavery itself. Had none of this despoliation taken place, and had Africa been in a position to sustain normal trading relations with Europe and Asia, literacy might have spread widely 400 years earlier; and continued indigenous development might have led to modern political structures, able to compete on more equal terms with the rest of the world. There would certainly not now be a conglomeration of African nation states, delineated by Europeans according to the vagaries of conquest rather than to traditional cultural and linguistic boundaries. Nor would these states be suffering the economic and technological underdevelopment bequeathed to them by Europeans, or attempting to reconcile entrenched kinship ties with the political organization necessary for the successful implementation of Western-style democracy.[1]

European colonization not only paralysed indigenous institutions; it reinforced a widespread belief among educated Africans that their traditional systems were inimical to 'progress' and 'modernization'. Such belief originated in consequence of the deprivations of the slave trade; it gained ground during the first half of the nineteenth century, in particular among 'recaptive' Africans: victims of slave-smuggling, rescued from illegal slave ships by British naval patrols (after the slave trade had been made illegal in 1807). Converted to Christianity, many of these 'recaptives' and their descendants achieved positions of distinction in what became creole-speaking, bourgeois communities in various towns along the west coast; and they naturally looked to

[1] Basil Davidson, *The Black Man's Burden: Africa and the Curse of the Nation-State* (London: Times Books, 1992), 226–9. What Davidson calls 'kinship corporations' evolved to provide protection against the violence created by the slave trade and, much later, against 'the predatory nature of the post-colonial or neo-colonial state in Africa'.

European models for national renewal, even though many believed that Africans must be free to develop in their own way, according to their own cultural traditions.[2]

In the event, European colonizers did little to encourage development of any sort, as the following educational statistics from the late 1950s demonstrate. In Tanzania after forty years of British administration, only 318 pupils in a population of some ten million were able to attend the fourth and final year of secondary schooling. In the three British-controlled East African states of Tanzania, Kenya, and Uganda, combined, only one child in 12,000 achieved a school certificate. In Southern Zimbabwe, exactly thirteen children out of a total population of three million entered the final grade of secondary school. Over Sub-Saharan Africa as a whole, less than 5 per cent of children attended any school.[3] Schooling is still a privilege in many parts of Africa. It is against a background of such facts as these that today's Africans view the continuance of their traditional social and artistic culture.

The inherent conflict between tradition and modernization, caused both by the deprivations of the slave trade and by the dispossessions of colonization, haunts Africa to this day; culture and politics remain in a critical state of conflict. Traditional cultural systems cannot be preserved in a 'museum' context while, manifestly, they still abound; yet to eliminate traditional systems, as is happening in urban areas, is to eliminate an essential element of African identity. Africans today seek to retain their cultural roots while improving the economic infrastructure of their societies. Not the least of the problems associated with the retention of traditional music is the extent to which, in Sub-Saharan Africa in particular, music is tied to its social context.

The Social Contexts for Music in Sub-Saharan Africa

Central to the mores of Sub-Saharan society is the belief that the moral life of a community is watched over by its ancestors. Symbolically, the ancestors communicate with the living

[2] Ibid. 26, 35–7. Notable among educated, articulate, writers was James 'Africanus' Horton, himself the son of a 'recaptive', whose line of thought was developed most notably in his *West African Countries and Peoples* (1868).

[3] Basil Davidson, *Africa in History* (London: Paladin Books, 1984), 304.

through music; the drum, in particular, is regarded as the 'voice' of the ancestors. Music, therefore, strengthens the moral values that inform community life.[4] Music deters individual or community misfortune, and it is intrinsic to the age-set ceremonies that are still an important aspect of community life. Music is a means of *obtaining* happiness rather than of expressing it: a village that is without organized music, that neglects traditions of singing, drumming, or dancing, is considered to be 'dead'.[5]

Most music-making is linked to some aspect of religious or social activity, and Africans judge musical performance not so much by its entertainment value—though entertainment may be one by-product of it—as by its social relevance. In village life, few activities take place without music, and specific songs, instruments, and musical styles are associated with each. There are songs for work situations, such as hoeing, pounding millet, chopping a tree, drawing water, or hauling fishing nets; a person paddling a canoe may have a different song for paddling with and against the tide. There are songs to cure bedwetters, and songs to ease the pain of cutting teeth. There are songs of love and songs of insult, which may be specially commissioned.[6] A singer-actor may take the occasion of a village festival to draw attention to social problems within the community.[7]

African children gain some of their earliest musical impressions in a tactile manner, because they spend much of the first two years of their lives on their mother's hips or back. They feel their mother's muscular movements when working, walking, or dancing, and they also feel the vibrato of her voice, in speech and song. Bells are often attached to babies' legs as soon as they are able to walk; thus children learn dance steps from the sound of the rhythm produced by their feet, while mothers are enabled to keep track of their children's whereabouts. In such ways, music fulfils both practical and aesthetic functions.

As in many societies worldwide, African kings and chiefs are extolled in music, not so much to satisfy their vanity as to establish their legitimacy within the context of their society's kinship laws. 'Praise-singers' (known in parts of West Africa as 'jalis' or by their French title

[4] John Miller Chernoff, *African Rhythm and African Sensibility* (Chicago: University of Chicago Press, 1979), 150.

[5] J. H. Kwabena Nketia, *Music in African Cultures: A Review of the Meaning and Significance of Traditional African Music* (University of Ghana, 1966), 20.

[6] Chernoff, *African Rhythm*, 34.

[7] Klauss Wachsmann and Peter Cooke, 'Africa', *The New* Grove (1980), i. 148.

12. Lamellaphone from Zaire; the entire torso of the dancer acts as the sounding chamber for the instrument

griots) guard jealously their knowledge of ancestral lineage and history, which they recite in music on ceremonial occasions. Such knowledge is usually passed down from father to son, as are the techniques of royal drumming, flute-playing, and trumpeting. In many societies, drums—acting as surrogates for speech—are used to 'recite' the ancestral lineage. (Drums are made to 'talk' by matching their pitches and rhythms to the syllable melody of the language.) It is of paramount importance that the names of the ancestors are rendered accurately; in former times a drummer who made a mistake in ancestral drumming could incur capital punishment.[8]

African instruments are often marvellously sculpted with human or animal decoration, indicating the dedication of an instrument to a specific deity or ancestral spirit. Human figures may crown or support many types of instrument, or are depicted in high or low relief on the instrument's surface. Sometimes it is the carved human figure, rather than the performer, who is seen to be making the music. A pair of figures may face each other from one side of an instrument to another; a bell may assume the form of a human head; the necks of arched harps may assume the shape of a slender human body, with a head carved above the strings; a lamellaphone (thumb piano) may form the torso of a carved figure (Pl. 12).[9]

In most states of Africa today, there is sharp contrast between city areas, where modernization and Westernization have largely eroded traditional culture, and rural areas, where traditional cultural systems are maintained, sometimes only marginally under Western influence. Nevertheless, even in heavily Westernized city areas, a strong sense of African cultural identity prevails, for Africans have benefited from centuries—probably millennia—of cultural continuity. A brief historical survey of the African continent may help to explain both the commonality and variety of musical style and usage that are to be observed today.

North Africa before Islam

The very concept of an African *continent* presents a dilemma to historians. The name 'Africa' was first used by the Romans; this was subsequently Arabized to *Ifriqya* to refer specifically to what is now Tunisia, where Carthage was an important trading city. Africa's boundaries—for example, its division from Asia by the cleft of the Red Sea—were defined by Europeans, as was Africa's appearance on the map of the world. Mercator's technique of moving lines of latitude further apart the nearer they are to the North and South Poles dimin-

[8] Chernoff, *African Rhythm*, 35.

[9] Marie-Thérèse Brigand (ed.), *Sounding Forms: African Musical Instruments* (American Federation of Arts, 1989).

ished the apparent size of the continent, and exaggerated its distance from southern Europe. Africa is in fact the second largest of the world's continents.

Throughout antiquity, 'Africa' referred essentially to the fertile lands north of the Sahara desert that were sucked into the trading networks of West Asia, the Aegean, and southern Europe. Only with the rise of northern Europe in the sixteenth century did the Mediterranean become any sort of cultural divide; before that time, with Mediterranean Africa a natural partner in Eurasian cultural and trading systems, knowledge of the geography and peoples of Sub-Saharan Africa was fragmentary, and there was no clear understanding of the overall shape of the African continent.

Although the Sahara caused the peoples to its north to be separate, geographically and culturally, from those to its south, the divide was never more than partial; despite the difficult terrain, international trade routes crossed the desert regularly. The Sahara was, in fact, a primary cause of African cultural unity.

Between the sixth and second millennia BC, the Sahara was a fertile area of grassland and scrub vegetation with large, shallow lakes, well suited to the hunter-fisher-foodgathering peoples who came to it from continental Africa, North Africa, and the Nile Valley. These peoples are thought to have shared cultural affinities;[10] and it is probable that predynastic Egypt was largely peopled from this mixed community.[11] During the third millennium BC, the Sahara began to lose rain, and a process of desiccation set in. (It still continues at an alarming rate.) The peoples who then inhabited the Sahara were forced to migrate east, north, or south.

Those who moved eastward confronted the peoples of the Nile, where, at the beginning of the second millennium, Egyptian pharaohs ruled from a strong power base at Thebes, dominating a large region that included the gold-rich lands of Nubia. As Egyptian power grew weaker, towards the end of the millennium, pressure from the Saharan migrants became increasingly intense, until, in 935 BC, Libyans took over the Egyptian throne. They, in turn, were ousted by the Kushites from Nubia, and the Kushites by the iron-clad armies of Assyria. Egypt was subsequently overrun successively by Persians, Greeks,

[10] Patrick J. Munson, 'Africa's Prehistoric Past', in Phyllis M. Martin and Patrick O'Meara (eds.), *Africa* (Bloomington, Ind.: Indiana University Press, 1986), 52, 55.

[11] Davidson, *Africa in History*, 29.

Macedonians, and Arabs. Its peoples were influenced by Greece and Rome, before they accepted Islam: Alexandria had been an unrivalled centre of Hellenistic culture, as well as the seat of a Christian Patriarch.

The migrants who moved northward from the Sahara mingled with indigenous peoples of North Africa, and with other Mediterranean-type peoples, eventually emerging as the Berber-speaking peoples of the Maghreb (Tunisia, Algeria, and Morocco). Long before Heroditus brought these peoples into recorded history, they had a script of their own, still used by the Tuareg nomads of the Sahara. They made contact with Bronze Age Spain and established a thriving Bronze Age culture in North Africa; later, they were drawn into the trading systems of the Roman Empire. They became famous as horsemen, dominating trans-Saharan trade, and bringing wealth to the great trading cities of the Mediterranean littoral.[12] When, in 31 BC, the North African littoral, as far as Morocco, was drawn into a unified Roman Empire, the Berbers cooperated with the Romans; and the prosperous cities of the littoral became gateways to huge Roman markets.

Berber control of trans-Saharan trade encouraged cultural interchange between peoples north and south of the Sahara, and made the north, to some extent, resistant to outside influence. When Christianity spread to Egypt in the first century AD, its impact was slight, except in the important cities (in Alexandria, it mingled with Hellenistic traditions to spearhead the Gnostic and Arian heresies); and when Islam became the dominant religion in the seventh century, only two small Christian enclaves remained in Africa: the isolated Ethiopians, and the Copts of Egypt (successors to the Gnostic heretics). (The Copts now number between 5 and 7 per cent of the Egyptian population.[13])

Islam in North Africa

The Arab conquest began in 641 with the seizure of Byzantine Babylon, later to become the great Fatimid city of al-Kahaira (modern Cairo). By 683 it had reached the Atlantic coast, and by 711 it had engulfed Spain. The Arabs had been preceded by the Vandals, who, emanating from Scandinavia, moved via Spain and Tunisia to Italy, destroying Roman systems of government. Following

[12] Davidson, *Africa in History*, 62–7.

[13] Daniel Bates and Amal Rassam, *Peoples and Cultures of the Middle East* (Englewood Cliffs, NJ: Prentice Hall, 1983), 23.

Vandalization, Islam appeared to offer unity and a measure of social justice. It brought literacy and, with it, a tradition of fine poetry and architecture; it brought Greek science; it led to improvements in techniques of trade and barter, and it reduced ethnic conflict. But it brought neither unity nor social justice. Instead, it adopted hierarchical systems that often led to despotic oligarchies.[14]

In 973, the Fatimid caliphate established a new capital in Cairo and extended its rule into Syria. This eastward expansion led to the creation of new and rival kingdoms to the west (in Tunisia and Algeria) which, with Fatimid encouragement, were constantly raided by Bedouin nomads. A divide then occurred between Egypt and the Maghreb, one still evident musically, in different styles of classical-music genres (see p. 186).

While the Berbers of Tunisia and Algeria were being Arabized, the Almoravid Berbers of Mauretania, tired of the social injustices to which prevailing Islamic rule had given rise, swept through Morocco and thence into Spain, in the early eighth century. They aimed to restore an egalitarian order, true to what they regarded as the original ideals of Islam.[15] The Almoravids were followed by the Almohads, also from Morocco; but these Berbers were unable to resist the persistent onslaught of Christian armies from the north, and most eventually returned to the Maghreb.

Islam brought a different face to African cultural systems north of the Sahara, but it did not swamp traditional African attitudes and beliefs; rather, it had to adjust itself to them. It led to a synthesis of Islamic and African mores, in which Arabs were as much influenced by Africans as Africans by Arabs. Nevertheless, the Arabization of North Africa meant ultimately that its peoples became to some extent isolated; for, with the rise of Christian Europe as a world power, the Mediterranean became a divide between a technologically advanced Europe and an ideologically bound North Africa—with Sub-Saharan Africa pursuing a somewhat separate course, further south.

The Development of Sub-Saharan Africa

The peoples who travelled southward from the desiccating Sahara spread a Neolithic way of life south-east into the

[14] Davidson, *Africa in History*, 132–6. [15] Ibid. 98–9, 137–8.

Ethiopian plateau and East Africa, and then across the Sudanese fringes of the Sahara to the west. From there they continued south to the forests of the tropical rain belt, where the natural abundance of fruit and vegetables gave to farming no great advantage over gathering.

This situation changed with the use of iron, which arrived in Nigeria about the fifth century BC, and led to improved cultivation, superior weaponry, and mastery of the forest lands.[16] The spread of iron-working is associated with the Bantu-speaking peoples, who appear to have emerged along the southern margins of the forest zone, during the first millennium BC. It is known that the Bantu used root and tree crops from South East Asia; and it is possible, therefore, that their knowledge of iron-working came from Arab and Malayo-Polynesian traders, rather than from North Africa. At the start of the first century AD, Bantu peoples spread throughout the remainder of the central forest zone, and then through the east and west Congo grasslands to the south Congo basin; from thence they moved through the plateau grasslands of Angola and Zambia to neighbouring lands in the south. Eventually the Bantu replaced or surrounded the indigenous Khoisan peoples.[17]

The Bantu spread was very slow: it was not until the start of the ninth century AD that an iron culture was thriving across continental Africa. Gradually, however, the migrations led to a substantial increase in population, and to an expansion of the family of Bantu-speaking peoples who now inhabit most of Sub-Saharan Africa. To these Bantu migrations must largely be attributed the fact that the musical traditions of this vast area are interrelated in many aspects of style and usage. (To a surprising extent, they are also related to musical styles and usages across the breadth of Eurasia.)

A more complex pattern of migration emerged in East Africa, where the Rift Valley enabled original migrants from the desiccating grasslands to move further south into savannah country. Kushitic, Sudanic, and Nilotic peoples all mingled in this area before Bantu peoples arrived; there is still a greater mix of peoples in East Africa than in the west.

The 'Bantu' spread was made possible by improved food supply, which led to urbanization and the emergence of specialist professions; as early as the fourth century AD the people of Zimbabwe were skilled in

16 Davidson, *Africa in History*, 31–2.

17 John Lamphear, 'Aspects of Early African History', in Martin and O'Meara (eds.), *Africa*, 78–86.

metal-working and gold-mining. By the tenth century, Zimbabwe had developed into a powerful kingdom, thriving on trade in gold; and by the fourteenth century it was the centre of a great trading state with connections reaching as far as China. Other states emerged throughout Sub-Saharan Africa: near the Congo estuary was the prosperous kingdom of Kongo; and to the south of the forest belt were Bantu-speaking kingdoms, such as Luba and Lunda. In the fertile lands between the lakes of East Africa, pastoralists from the north and north-east established ruling hegemonies over the Bantu, leading to a string of states, of which the most prominent were Rwanda, Bunyoro-Kitara, and, later, Buganda.[18] Such states were often brought together through trade; their kings and chiefs then derived substantial income from taxes and tributes.[19]

Islam South of the Sahara

Islam spread into Sub-Saharan Africa between the eleventh and sixteenth centuries; first down the Nile into the Christian kingdom of Nubia; then along the coasts of the Horn; and from thence across the Sudanic belt (stretching along the southern fringes of the Sahara from the Nile to Senegal). It also reached states in the west of the Sudan through trade with the Berbers. Trade in gold and slaves brought great wealth to the region, and states developed into great empires.

Ghana flourished between the eighth and twelfth centuries until, weakened by Berber disruption, it gave way to Mali, a vast empire that flourished from the twelfth to the fifteenth centuries. Mali was followed at the beginning of the sixteenth century by Songhay, centred on the cities of Gao and Timbuktu on the River Niger. The Kanem Borno empire developed to the east of Songhay, as did the Hausa states. To the south, by 1500, a group of 'forest states' emerged, of which Oyo, Benin, and Akan were particularly noteworthy.

As Islam spread into western states, African languages, such as Hausa, Fulani, and Yoruba, came to be written in something approaching an Arabic script. Great mosques and universities adorned the principal cities: Timbuktu, for example, was celebrated as a centre of

[18] *The Times Atlas of World History*, ed. Geoffrey Barraclough (London, 1989), 166.
[19] Lamphear, 'Aspects of Early African History', 81.

Islamic learning. During the fourteenth to sixteenth centuries, rulers of Sudanic states were often designated supreme representatives of Islam in the area, and were renowned throughout Europe and Asia for their wealth.

Despite the brilliance of these Islamic courts, Islamization throughout West Africa was never more than partial. Conversion was as much a matter of convenience as of conviction; often it was to avoid the slave trade. Only during the nineteenth century were there serious attempts to Islamize partly Islamized communities. During the 1800s, a *jihad* (holy war) led to an Islamic empire around what is now Nigeria; and during the 1870s and 1880s a further *jihad* led to an Islamic empire in the western states. The long-term, religious effect of these *jihad*s, however, was mitigated by subsequent European intervention.

Islam reached East Africa directly from Egypt, and its spread encouraged trading in slaves. The export of slaves from East Africa, via the Persian Gulf, to work the sugar plantations in the Fertile Crescent intensified under Islamic patronage. During the twelfth to fourteenth centuries, the slave-trading islands of Pemba and Zanzibar, and the ports of Mombassa and Kilwa, grew in prosperity with increasing Arab settlement.

As in West Africa, Islamization in East Africa was only partial: it was confined largely to the coastal areas. Intermarriage between Arab settlers and Africans led to an indigenous blend of Arab and Bantu elements, exemplified in the growth of a new language, Swahili ('coastal'); this, in turn, led to a distinctively Swahilian repertoire of legends and folk-tales relating to Islamic belief.[20] Swahili civilization was reaching a peak when Europeans started intervening in Africa; in the late fifteenth century, Portuguese mariners, on their way to the Indian Ocean, discovered and looted the Swahili trading cities. (They were subsequently ousted by Omani Arabs in the early eighteenth century.)

European Intervention

The original purpose of the Portuguese mariners was to divert the trans-Saharan gold trade. A later purpose was to establish sugar plantations (initially on the Cape Verde islands) with

[20] Jan Knappert, *Myths and Legends of the Swahili* (Kenya: Heinemann, 1979).

West African slave labour. Initial contacts between Africans and Europeans led to a trading partnership in which Europeans were guaranteed safety, and facilities for building forts, in return for defending agreed African trading rights against rival European predators.

African-European trade had little effect on interior regions until European plantation economies in the Americas created a demand for African slave labour. The ensuing slave trade was in practice supported by many Africans. One reason for this was the dependence of African rulers on Western luxuries, particularly alcohol; in return for alcohol, local chiefs would wage war on neighbouring societies to obtain slaves for Europeans. Another reason may have been a drought that lasted from the mid-seventeenth to the mid-nineteenth centuries; drought and famine would have encouraged societies to part with their own members. At the same time, unscrupulous African merchants exploited traditional social ties, while purchasing armed retainers to safeguard themselves from sanctions.[21]

Slaves were not only sent to the Americas; some 7.5 million slaves crossed the Sahara between the mid-seventeenth and the mid-nineteenth centuries. During the eighteenth century, the Omani and Swahili peoples jointly developed caravan routes across East Africa, bringing captives to the coast in increasing numbers; and during the nineteenth century, Sudanese and Egyptian slavers ravaged peoples of the Upper Nile.

The immediate outcome of this iniquitous trade was the destruction of Africa's developing system of centralized states and rural communities; many societies disintegrated completely. Such devastation was compounded by the transmission of diseases: caravans carried smallpox and cholera to the interior; in southern Africa—the only area settled by Europeans before the nineteenth century—diseases were transmitted from ships anchoring at the Dutch East India Company's 'refreshment station' on the 'Cape of Good Hope'. Those Khoikhoi and San peoples ('Hottentots' and 'Bushmen') who survived European diseases were driven ever deeper into the interior by land-hungry *trekboers*. Other groups, notably the Zulu and the Ndebele, reacted to this encroachment by developing as unprecedentedly militaristic societies. During the 'Great Trek' of the Boers between 1835 and 1843 the might of both peoples was compromised, but the legacy of that might is still with us.[22]

[21] George E. Brooks, 'African "Landlords" and European "Strangers": African–European Relations to 1870', in Martin and O'Meara (eds.), *Africa*, 106–20.

[22] B. G. Martin, 'The Spread of Islam', in Martin and O'Meara (eds.), *Africa*, 104.

This despoliation of Africa's political and social systems was completed with Europe's unseemly 'Scramble for Africa' in the late nineteenth century. The racist tendencies in Europe that allowed this peak in European acquisitiveness to be legitimized by the Berlin Conference of 1884–5 will be considered in Chapter 12. Politically, the scramble was caused by Europe's need to expand its markets, and by rivalries between European states. The military occupation of Africa began with the British invasion of Egypt in 1882, done to effect control over the Suez Canal, and thence of the sea routes to Asia. Britain, as the major industrial power, obtained the most valuable agricultural lands in East Africa. France, in return for the loss to Germany of Alsace and Lorraine during the Franco-Prussian War, was granted huge areas of North and West Africa, amounting approximately to one-third of the African land mass. The Belgians committed outrageous atrocities in the Congo. Only the states of Ethiopia and Liberia retained their sovereignty.

Colonization frequently set Africans against each other; weaker rulers would ally with Europeans for protection against more powerful neighbours, and it was not unusual for European armies to include large numbers of Africans. The irrelevance to African societies of Europe's partitioning of the continent further compounded the problem. It was not until after the Second World War that African states were in a position to demand independence from European domination. Many did not achieve it until the 1960s or 1970s.[23]

Aspects of Vocal Music in Sub-Saharan Africa

Over 3,000 different societies and over 1,000 distinct languages have been identified in Sub-Saharan Africa.[24] Inevitably, over such a large area, considerable variation in musical style and usage is to be observed. The musical resources and styles of pastoralist societies in desert areas, for example, differ considerably from those of agriculturalists in savannah areas; and these in turn differ from the musical resources and styles associated with the courts of states and kingdoms. Moreover, European traditions have been more influential in some areas than in others. Nevertheless, across Sub-Saharan Africa as a

[23] *Times Atlas*, 240, 276.

[24] Helen Myers, 'African Music', *NOCM* (1983).

whole there are also remarkable correspondences, and it is essentially these that will be described here.

Vocal music occupies a predominant place in all African societies, since belief is central to religious practice, and it is song-words that express belief. The bond between language and music is particularly intimate in Africa, where music closely follows both the melodic and rhythmic contours of speech, and where instrumental melodies, and percussion at different pitches, frequently act as speech surrogates. Africans do not distinguish between melody and rhythm, for rhythms are as much melodic as they are rhythmic. (African melodies are often referred to as 'melo-rhythms'.) The rhythmic structures of African songs are designed to enable poet-singers to incorporate improvised words into their music, in accordance with natural speech rhythms.

Songs are usually built from short phrases, and these are reiterated, and varied, continuously and cumulatively. Most songs are performed antiphonally, and follow a structure in which a 'call' from the leader is answered, antiphonally, by a 'response' from the group. 'Call-and-response' is an important structural element in African music. The 'response' normally repeats the melodic contours of the 'call'; it may repeat the 'call', more or less exactly, or it may vary it substantially. Alternatively, the 'call' may be in a stanzaic style of verse, in which case the 'response' will take the form of a refrain.[25] Sometimes the 'call' overlaps, or incorporates, the 'response'. Most frequently, however, the 'call' is varied or elaborated according to the requirements of the text—parts of which may be invented during performance to fit a particular social context—while the 'response' remains largely unaltered. Any variation to the basic melody is due to the need to accommodate differences in the natural syllable melody of the words.[26] The essence of 'call-and-response' lies in the manner in which either element responds to the other.

The relationship between 'call' and 'response' often reflects the social function of the music. In storytelling songs, for example, the 'call' may predominate, whereas in songs used on ceremonial occasions, the 'response' may predominate, as an affirmation of group solidarity.[27]

[25] J. H. Kwabena Nketia, *The Music of Africa* (London: Gollancz, 1974), 141.

[26] Peter Cooke, *Play Amadinda: Xylophone Music from Uganda* (Edinburgh: K. and C. Productions, 1990), 6.

[27] Robert A Kauffman, 'African Rhythm: A Reassessment', *Ethnomusicology* (September 1980), 403–4.

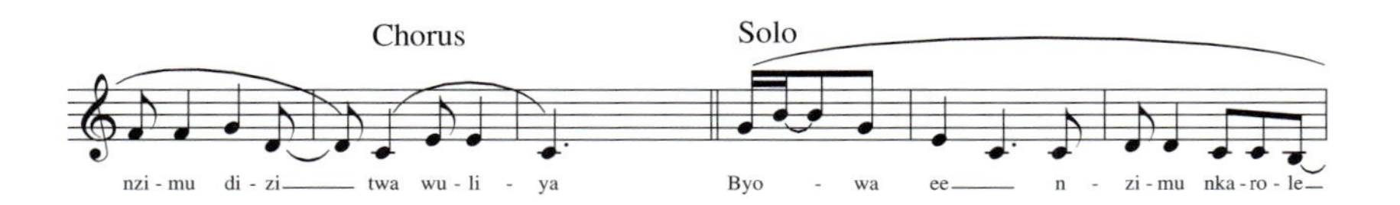

Ex. 6.1a

Ex. 6.1*a* (after Nketia) shows a short 'response'; Ex. 6.1*b* (after Nketia) shows a more elaborate response, sung in thirds, and overlapping the call.[28] The 'call-and-response' structural duality is also evident when a solo singer plays interludes on an accompanying instrument between vocal lines.

The melodic shape of songs is determined, in the first instance, by the tuning of note-sets used in a particular society. The notes may be in sets of five, six, or seven; and tunings may be more or less diatonic, anhemitonic, or equidistant. Scales and tuning systems, however, are usually consistent within a particular society; and the shape of a melody is largely determined by the syllable melody of the words, whatever the tuning used. Moreover, in speech, sentences tend to fall in pitch as they are uttered (a feature linguists call 'downdrift'), and a high tone at the end of a sentence is often lower than a low tone near the beginning. This may account for the prevalence of melodies incorporating downward spirals, to be observed not only in Africa but in many folk-music styles, worldwide.

The melodic structures of both 'call' and 'response' in African vocal music lie within a rhythmic cycle; and particular rhythmic cycles are associated with particular songs and functions.

[28] Nketia, *The Music of Africa*, 142.

Ex. 6.1b

A song comes to life when a professional poet-singer varies the standard words in accordance with a particular social situation, and varies the standard melodic pattern so as to enhance the new meaning. An actor, for example, might draw attention to particular problems in his society; a politician might allude to social and historical circumstances peculiar to a given society, perhaps drawing on local myth, or invoking the spirits of important ancestors.[29] The social or political point is made by departing, in some way, from the expected melodic pattern.

Such deviations may involve: extending the melodic range at a particular moment; retaining a pitch when it is expected to rise or fall; reducing the length of the vocal line within the cyclical pattern of beats; extending the vocal line to overlap the response; abandoning the initial

[29] Francis Katamba and Peter Cooke, 'Ssematimba ne Kikwabanga: The Music and Poetry of a Ganda Historical Song', *The World of Music*, 2 (1987), 57, 60.

tonality of the song; abandoning traditional variations; or inserting ululations. Additional layers of meaning may be provided by the drummer, using melo-rhythms associated with words *outside* the context of the performance. To Westerners, accustomed to music that explores a wide span of dodecaphonic octaves, such variations may seem slight; but in the context of African singing, and in relation to the mores and aspirations of a community, they have enormous significance.[30]

Sometimes a group refrains from singing a 'response', in deference to the artistry of a great singer. In such instances a melody instrument, such as a flute, maintains the continuity and identity of the song.[31]

In some African societies, vocal groups sing in polyphony, moving in parallel seconds, thirds, fourths, or fifths, according to the tuning systems in use. Where, less commonly, polyphony involves a contrapuntal texture, this usually results from quasi-canonical 'spacing'—the starting of individual lines at different points in the melodic-rhythmic cycle. Considerable complexities may evolve from this type of singing, found mainly among the Zulu, Xhosa, Swazi, and Pygmy peoples.[32]

Aspects of Rhythm in Sub-Saharan African Music

The structure of African music is largely defined by its rhythm; indeed rhythm has been described as the 'organizing force' of all African creative expressions.[33]

African rhythms derive from speech, and drummers often represent a specific speech-text, by simulating not only the rhythms but also the syllable pitch of speech; drums are made to 'speak' the language of the particular society in which they are in use. Thus the melodic attributes of drums are as important as their rhythmic attributes; and variations in pitch are critical in clarifying layers of rhythm within an ensemble. Drummers, literally, 'talk' through their drumming, and can pass *quasi*-verbal messages to passers-by, or to the community.[34]

[30] Katamba and Cooke, 'Ssematimba ne Kikwabanga', 57, 60–1.

[31] Ibid. 63.

[32] Nketia, *The Music of Africa*, 160, and Peter Cooke, 'Pygmy Music', *The New Grove* (1980), xv. 482.

[33] Senghor Léopold, cited in Kauffman, 'African Rhythm', 227–49.

[34] Chernoff, *African Rhythm*, 75.

Although rhythms act as speech surrogates, the essence of African music lies in the interplay of cross-rhythms. When cross-rhythms occur in *Western* music, they usually do so in a context in which there are predominantly two or three beats in a bar; and the predominant metre is usually resumed, after it has been 'crossed' with another. This is true, for example, of a typical eighteenth-century *courante*, where the interplay of 3/4 and 6/8, or of 3/2 and 6/4, is referred to as *hemiola*.

To Africans, rhythms involving two against three are as natural as rhythms in which all beats and their subdivisions coincide. Vertical (simultaneous) *hemiolas*, therefore, are a common characteristic, not just of special passages in the music, but of a continuing rhythmic complex. In the rhythmic complex shown in Ex. 6.2 (after Koetting), for example, 'simple' and 'compound' time are superimposed, but neither predominates.[35] In this example, the upper line is in groups of three, but it could be accentuated in performance as two bars of 3/4. The 'resultant'—the combination of the two rhythms—is in neither two nor three, and provides the basis for a rhythmically asymmetrical ostinato.

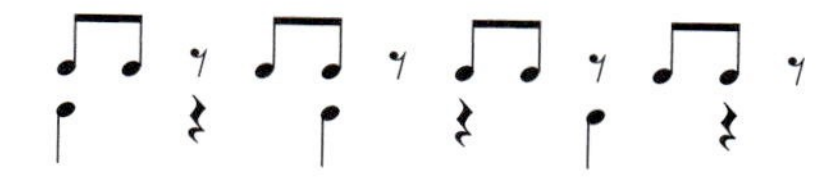

Ex. 6.2

Westerners tend to refer to the interplay of African rhythms as 'polyrhythmic'; but Ex. 6.2 indicates that 'polymetric' is a more suitable term. The ability to hear two metres concurrently—and, in particular, their 'resultant' rhythmic patterns, or 'inherent' rhythms—is fundamental to African music-making. In African music, at least two different rhythms are usually being sounded at the same time: a single rhythm makes little sense without the reciprocity of a second rhythm. A rhythmic pattern invites a response, an engagement in musical 'conversation'.[36]

Westerners think of a regularly recurring beat as the driving force of music—an attitude exemplified, for example, in the concept of the conductor. African musicians would regard a conductor as superfluous,

[35] James Koetting, 'What Do We Know About African Rhythm?', ed. Roderic Knight, *Ethnomusicology*, 30/4 (1986), 59–60.

[36] Chernoff, *African Rhythm*, 51–3.

not only because they can manage without a conductor, but because a regularly recurring beat—or even irregularly recurring beat—is not what drives the music. To think of African music in this way makes it seem more complex than it is.

Time signatures make little sense in transcribing African music. In Ex. 6.3 (after Chernoff) the rhythms, though tightly interlocked, do not meet at any point. Moreover, one rhythm is in what Westerners call 'compound' time, and the other is in 'simple' time. African drummers will be keenly aware of the 'resultant' patterns, as the relationships between the two rhythms change, and as each appears alternately to compete for attention.[37] In essence, African rhythmic structures are straightforward, consisting of combinations of relatively simple rhythms, in some version of 'duple' or 'compound' time.

Ex. 6.3

Ex. 6.3 illustrates another important aspect of African rhythm, sometimes called 'spacing' or 'apart-playing', in which a performer adds a *complementary* rhythm to the basic rhythm, at varying points in the cycle. The two rhythms together create a 'resultant' rhythm that is effectively a variation on the basic rhythm. 'Apart-playing' is essentially a form of 'call-and-response': the basic pattern acts as the unvarying response, while the new pattern takes the lead in making variations on it. Usually the second part will not enter until the rhythmic structure of the first part has been established.[38] 'Spacing' is characteristic also of vocal polyphony.

While Westerners think of the first beat of a bar as a point of emphasis, Africans tend to emphasize what Westerners call the 'off-beat'. Thus, although there is a 'theoretical' framework of beats in a rhythmic cycle, the beats may well occur at points where there is little

[37] Chernoff, *African Rhythm*, 46–7. [38] Ibid.

or no sound, even in complex polymetric drumming. The beats do not, in other words, regulate the rhythm.[39] Nor are they usually tapped by the performers, as this would eliminate the true rhythmic conflict within the music. Instead, they are indicated by the *audience*, through hand-clapping, dance, or other body movement; and it is the task of the audience to *find* the beat, and so make sense of the music. Audience involvement of this kind is an essential aspect of musical performance.[40]

The Shona 'Praise Song for a Chief', shown in Ex. 6.4*a* (after Kauffman), might be interpreted instinctively by Westerners as in this example. By the Shona it is interpreted according to the scheme shown in Ex. 6.4*b*, where the third beat is silent, and the natural accent falls on the fourth quaver.[41]

Ex. 6.4a

Ex. 6.4b

(The avoidance by African performers of tapping the beat contrasts with jazz, where a fusion of the asymmetries of African rhythm with the symmetries engendered by the Western barline makes the beat a determining factor of rhythm. As will be shown in Chapter 14, however, this is not necessarily true of Latin American music, where, in Cuban music, for example, African polymetres abound.)

In Africa, all ritual and recreational activities have specific time structures to which music must conform. Rhythmic structures, therefore, are usually built around a 'basic pattern'; this is associated with a

[39] Kauffman, 'African Rhythm', 410.
[40] Chernoff, *African Rhythm*, 50.
[41] Kauffman, 'African Rhythm', 408.

short speech pattern which, in turn, defines the function for which the music is used.[42] In many areas (West Africa in particular) the 'basic pattern' is complemented by a short ostinato rhythm—often referred to as the 'time-line'—that serves to sustain musical motion.[43] As the 'time-line' is usually played on a bell it is not a 'melo-rhythm', and one 'time-line' can serve for a number of musical functions. Sometimes, however, the 'time-line' acts as a 'basic pattern'.

One particular 'time-line' has been found to be ubiquitous throughout Africa, and is sometimes known as the 'standard pattern' (Ex. 6.5).[44] The metrical structure of this pattern is usually interpreted as 2+2+3+3+2=12. Other common metrical structures in African music are:

2+2+2+2=8
3+3+3+3=12
3+3+2=8
(2+2+2)+(3+3)=12
(2+2+2+3)+(2+2+3)=16
2+2+2+3=9
3+3+4+2+4=16[45]

Ex. 6.5

Importantly, all these structures are exactly divisible by two, three, or four; this contrasts with the 'limping' (*aksak*) structures of some Turkic and Balkan folk musics and some Indian *tāla*s, which may form indivisible lengths of 5, 7, 11, 13, or 17. The metrical structures of African music are determined by their internal organization, rather than by their total length.[46]

The 'basic pattern' (sometimes supported, or replaced, by an unpitched 'time-line') usually remains unvaried throughout a performance. Around it, other 'supporting' rhythms are played, sometimes composed of differing metric units; and such 'supporting' rhythms vary little in performance. Ex. 6.6 (after Chernoff) shows a 'time-line',

[42] Kauffman, 'African Rhythm', 403.
[43] Nketia, *The Music of Africa*, 132.
[44] Named by A. M. Jones as the 'Standard Pattern'; see Kauffman, 'African Rhythm', 397.
[45] Kauffman, 'African Rhythm', 409.
[46] Ibid.

Ex. 6.6

supported by rattles, handclaps, and a variety of drums, all playing in a variety of metres, from a slow Ewe dance from Ghana.[47]

When such a structure has been established, the leading drummer (or 'master drummer') improvises new material, in the manner of 'apart-playing'. The 'basic pattern' then acts, in effect, as a 'response' to the leading drummer's 'call'. The leader alters the impression of a cyclical rhythm by striking a new rhythm that cuts against it. Ex. 6.7 (after Chernoff) shows how the even strokes of a lead drummer can seem uneven, and the repetitions of a support pattern can seem inexact, when the two are heard in combination.[48]

A rhythm that cuts in on another rhythm must enable that other rhythm to be heard clearly. A good master drummer, through many years' experience of playing 'supporting' rhythms, will have amassed a large vocabulary of rhythms. He will use this experience, not to give emphasis to his own individual part, and still less to establish his virtuosity: his principal concern will be to focus the ensemble, by drawing attention to the various parts that make up the whole. His freedom to invent will be limited by the music's formal structure; and his skill resides in his ability to exploit and give life to that structure.[49] African music is, indeed, most tightly organized. The variations

[47] Chernoff, *African Rhythm*, 49. [48] Ibid. 97. [49] Ibid. 60, 88.

Ex. 6.7

introduced by the master drummer may be in response to the progress of a dance, or of some other social function upon which the performance is attendant; but his variations are mainly worked out—and communally approved—beforehand, according to time-honoured tradition.

Musical Instruments in Sub-Saharan Africa

Drums appear in many sizes and shapes throughout Africa. They are usually carved from solid logs of wood, but may also be made from strips of wood bound together with iron hoops. Earthenware vessels, calabashes, and large gourds are also used as drum shells; and a rim-potsherd is sometimes used as a hoop in constructing round frame drums. Drums with conical, cylindrical, semi-cylindrical (with a bulge in the middle, or a bowl-shaped top), vase-, goblet-, and hourglass-shapes are to be observed; frames may be round or square, and drums may be single- or double-headed (Pl. 13).[50] Notwithstanding this collective variety, each society usually specializes in a small number of drum types.

It should be noted, however, that not all African societies use drums; nomadic peoples, in particular, often use only stamping sticks, or hand-clapping, and foot-stamping, for percussive effect, though this does not necessarily imply a lack of rhythmic excitement in their music (Pl. 14).

Kettledrums, with bowl-shaped, bronze or wooden shells, played in pairs, with heavy wooden beaters, and mounted on camel or horseback, came from the Maghreb; they were used at the Islamic courts in ensembles, with shawms and long trumpets (end-blown, with mouth-piece). In Ethiopia too, large kettledrums, with a skin made from an entire animal hide, were mounted on horseback and beaten during

[50] Nketia, *The Music of Africa*, 85–6.

13. (*above*) Village drummers, Kende, near Kenema, Sierra Leone. Photo: Jean Jenkins

14. (*left*) Arussi stick dance, Ethiopia. Photo: Jean Jenkins

royal processions.[51] Such instruments were retained in Sub-Saharan Africa after they disappeared in the Maghreb.

[51] Roger Blench, 'The Morphology and Distribution of Sub-Saharan Musical Instruments, of North African, Middle Eastern, and Asian Origin', *Musica Asiatica*, 4 (1984), 161.

Particular drums are associated with particular occasions, and may have profound symbolic significance. Royal drums, for example, are representative of semi-divine power, and must be 'initiated' at special ceremonies. (Instruments are regarded as primarily inanimate objects that need to be invested with life before use by human beings.) A chief or king might be reluctant to travel without his drums, for their destruction would augur the loss of his power. Normally, however, the 'divinity' of his drums outlives that of the king.

In Uganda, there is a shrine that houses the remains of instruments of a *kabaka* (king) of Buganda who died around 1770. When Idi Amin's army attacked the palace in 1966, royal drum-makers described these drums as having 'committed suicide', and they were unwilling to perform on substitute drums, unless their use be sanctioned—with appropriate rituals—by a successor to the royal line.[52] This sanction arrived, in fact, in August 1993, with the investiture of King Ronnie of Buganda, and royal drums were sounded for the first time in twenty-seven years. Over 200 drums had been kept, in varying conditions of repair, in the royal palace; all would have needed new heads, for the old head is regarded as the corpse of the old *kabaka*. The huge sound of hundreds of drums, played simultaneously, is its own authority.

Idiophones (self-sounding instruments, made from materials that do not require tension to bring them to sounding on impact) are ubiquitous throughout Africa. Rattles of many kinds are shaken in the hand, attached to parts of the bodies of performers and shaken by their movements, or attached (as sound modifiers) to instruments. Struck or concussed idiophones include: multiple rock gongs, stick-clappers, and wood and iron bells, with or without clappers; linked, iron, one-hand clappers (probably from the Maghreb); and slit drums. Other idiophones include scrapers, stamping sticks, and stamping tubes. Prominent among tuned idiophones are xylophones and lamellaphones (to be described in the following section).

Flutes are usually made from materials with a natural bore, such as giant grasses, the husk of cane, the stalks of millet, the tip of a horn, or the neck of a gourd. They are made open or stopped, with or without finger-holes, and are played in vertical or transverse position; vertical, and end-blown flutes are made with round or notched embouchures. Single-reed pipes are used in the savannah belt of West Africa, and

[52] Andrew Cooke, 'Reconstructing the Etamiivu Ensemble', unpublished paper presented to ICTM UK, 1992.

15. Side-blown gruru horns, Ivory Coast. Photo: Jean Jenkins.

double-reed pipes appear in areas with Islamic traditions. Horns and trumpets are constructed from animal horns or elephant tusks and are usually side-blown (Pl. 15). Trumpets are also constructed from lengths, or composite sections, of gourd, or from a piece of cane to which a bell made from gourd is attached. Trumpets may also be constructed from giant grasses, or metal, or carved from wood.[53]

Plucked string instruments include musical bows (see p. 62), zithers of many kinds, lutes, harp lutes, arched harps, and lyres. Single-string zithers may be constructed from sticks (certain species of grass, or stalks of millet), the surface layer of which is lifted with a knife in a strip, to form a string, supported on bridges at either end. A number of such sticks may be tied together to form a 'raft zither'.[54] Stick zithers (where the string-bearer is a flat piece of wood), and tube zithers (where the string-bearer is a tube, such as a hollow stem) are also widespread. (Similar zithers are found in India and South East Asia.)

Straight-necked lutes (with strings running parallel to the neck) occur in many sizes, with different numbers of strings, both in plucked and bowed varieties. Plucked lutes are found mainly in West Africa, and may be one-string instruments, or with two to five strings; resonators are hemispherical, of gourd, covered with skin; or may be elongated and carved from wood. Bowed lutes are usually one-string fiddles, though

[53] Nketia, *The Music of Africa*, 92–7. [54] Ibid. 99–100.

bowed lutes with two and four strings have been observed in East Africa.[55]

Spike-bowl-fiddles are common throughout West Africa, and were probably transmitted from the Maghreb by Berber traders. The resonator is normally made from a hemispherical or oval gourd, with a lizard-skin table glued over an aperture; the cylindrical string-bearer passes *through* the resonator, so that the lower end of the string can be tied to its tip; both string and bow are usually made of horsehair.[56] A similar fiddle, but with an oblique, quadrilateral resonator, of wood, covered with goatskin, is used in Ethiopia, sometimes in ensembles of up to twenty players.[57] A further fiddle type, found in east and central Africa, has a tubular resonator with a skin-table pegged to it.[58]

Two other African lutes types exist: the bow lute (or 'pluriarc'), made by attaching a number of 'musical bows' to a single resonator, so that each string has its own string-bearer; and the harp lute, or 'bridge harp' (to be described in the next section).

Arched harps (or 'bow harps') are used in Central Africa; the strings run from a curved neck, at an angle, into the surface of the soundbox. Lyres of various kinds are used in East Africa; their strings run from a transverse yoke to a resonator.[59]

Aspects of Ensemble Playing in Sub-Saharan Africa

String instruments are most commonly used singly, as solo or accompaniment instruments; trumpets, stopped flutes, xylophones, and lamellaphones, on the other hand, are frequently used in ensembles, usually in homogeneous sets of instru-

[55] Nketia, *The Music of Africa*, 102–3.

[56] Blench, 'Morphology and Distribution', 171.

[57] Nketia, *The Music of Africa*, 102.

[58] Blench, 'Morphology and Distribution', 172. Such fiddles are similar, in design and construction, to the two-string fiddles found in North Africa, Central Asia, China, Korea, South East Asia, and West Asia, and to the Islamic *rabāb*. The earliest known visual representations of use of the horsehair bow are from Byzantium and Spain in the tenth century, and the earliest known literary account is from Baghdad, also in the tenth century; it is probable, however, that bowing originated among Central Asian nomads. (Werner Bachmann, *The Origins of Bowing*, trans. Norma Deane (London: Oxford University Press, 1969), *passim*; and Anthony Baines, *The Oxford Companion to Musical Instruments* (Oxford: Oxford University Press, 1992), 40.)

[59] Nketia, *The Music of Africa*, 104–7.

16. Xylophone players, Ivory Coast. Photo: Jean Jenkins

ments. Comparable techniques of ensemble performance are in use in many areas of the continent, usually so organized that all players are equally involved in creating a variety of interlocking melo-rhythmic structures. Because the melo-rhythms usually derive from speech, singers and drummers often contribute to ensemble performance. The general principle may best be illustrated by xylophone ensembles.

Xylophones appear in Africa in a variety of sizes: they may consist of one or more wooden slabs mounted on some elastic substance, over a hole in the ground, over boxes, or over clay pots. Alternatively, they may be elaborate instruments, of up to twenty-two slabs, mounted over a wooden frame, below which are suspended gourds, their sizes and resonance related to the pitches of the notes yielded by the slabs.[60] Xylophones are also made to be slung around the shoulders and played while standing or moving (Pl. 16).

Xylophones are usually played in pairs, or by two or more players seated at one xylophone. Among the Chopi of Mozambique, however, they are usually performed in ensembles of between fifteen and thirty

[60] James Blades, 'Xylophone', *The New Grove* (1980), xx. 563.

17. *Amadinda* xylophone, Uganda

instruments, comprising treble, alto, tenor, bass, and contrabass ranges.[61] Although a single player is sometimes to be observed playing a xylophone in two-part counterpoint, most xylophone music is based on interlocking melo-rhythms, produced by *pairs* of players. This may be illustrated by reference to one particular tradition of xylophone-playing, maintained by the Ganda people of Uganda, who name it after the type of log xylophone on which it is performed: *amadinda* (Pl. 17).[62]

Amadinda xylophone music consists of uninterrupted streams of notes that reproduce, essentially, the melodic structures of traditional songs, based on the 'call-and-response' pattern. The melody is filled out, so that every single syllabic unit acquires its own note; 'long' syllables receive two notes. When a song melody has been adapted in this way for xylophone usage, the units of the melody are shared between the players, in a manner that reflects the functions of the 'time-line', supporting rhythm, and 'lead' rhythm of drumming ensembles. In the *amadinda* xylophone tradition, the corresponding elements are usually termed 'starter', 'mixer', and 'binder'. First, the 'starter' establishes a pattern based on *alternate* notes of the unitarily adapted melody; the 'mixer' then joins in with the complementary alternate notes. The 'binder' is usually restricted to two notes of the xylophone, and creates

[61] Andrew Tracey, 'Mozambique', *The New Grove* (1980), xii. 663.
[62] Cooke, 'Reconstructing the Etamiivu Ensemble', 2.

a rhythmic pattern by playing these notes, as reinforcement, concurrently with their appearance in the melody.[63]

This process is performed at considerable speed. Xylophone playing, therefore, is a highly skilled art, involving sure knowledge of the repertoire and an ability to hold an interlocking part without faltering. Both 'starter' and 'mixer' parts are played by the two hands of each player in simultaneous octaves. (Xylophones are also played in this way in South East Asia.) The performers sit opposite each other at the same instrument, striking the ends of the bars; thus, to one player, the keys of the xylophone will run from *left to right* in ascending order of pitch, while to the other player they run from *right to left* in ascending order of pitch.

In Ganda usage, the *amadinda* xylophones have twelve bars, tuned (approximately) to an *equi*-pentatonic scale. The 'starter' and 'mixer' players (facing each other) each use ten bars (two octaves); but, because they each play in simultaneous octaves, they can perform their parts only over a single octave. The top two bars of the xylophone are reserved for the 'binder'. Sometimes, songs are transposed, in order to accommodate different vocal registers. This means that the relationship between certain notes of the melody, up or down, may alter. Moreover, as the intervals of the pentatonic scale are not exactly equal, the tonality (as well as the order of ascent and descent) of the song will appear (to Westerners) to alter.[64] Africans, however, appear to perceive no alteration, since the two interval classes 'whole tone' and 'minor third' do not exist for them.

Interlocking patterns of this kind are reflected in other instrumental techniques. The lamellaphone (thumb piano), for example, is used as an ensemble instrument (as well as a solo instrument) in many parts of Africa. It comprises a set of tuned bamboo or metal tongues (lamellae), attached to a resonator (usually a box, calabash, or wooden board). The tongues are attached at one end only, so that the other end is free to vibrate; and the instrument itself is held with the tongues facing the player, so that they can be plucked with the two thumbs (Pl. 12). Usually the lowest note is located at the *centre* tongue, and ascending notes *alternate* on either side of it. Each side, therefore, is effectively a set of ascending thirds or fourths, depending upon the structure of the scale. As with the two sides of the xylophone, the ascending patterns of notes on each side of the centre tongue are perceived from right to left, and from left to right, respectively.

[63] Ibid. 6–8. [64] Ibid. 10–11.

Since the *left* thumb plays on the *left* side of the lamellaphone in alternation with the *right* thumb on the *right* side, the result is an interlocking pattern of notes similar to that generated by two players on one xylophone. The lamellaphone has indeed been referred to as a portable equivalent of the xylophone.[65] (In the more complex lamellaphones, to be found in south-east Africa, individual notes are sometimes replicated on both sides of the centre tongue, and additional layers of tongues enable the pitches to be sounded at different octaves.)

Similar playing techniques apply to the harp, where the fingers of each hand play from opposite sides of the strings. The *kora*, a twenty-one-string bridge harp, found among the Manding peoples of West Africa, has two sets of strings hooked over the two *sides* of a vertical bridge. The strings are usually tuned in ascending, interlocking thirds, so that each set of thirds is played by a different hand.

Interlocking principles also apply to ensembles of wind players. 'Stopped-flute ensembles', for example, such as are found in South Africa, Zaire, Mozambique, Uganda, and Ethiopia, consist of end-blown flutes, mostly stopped by natural nodes or by movable tuning plugs. Usually they yield one pitch only, and are performed while dancing to the accompaniment of singing and drumming.[66] The ensemble functions like a large set of pan pipes, with each performer playing a separate note; and the individual players are required to insert their single-note contributions at specified points, creating what, in European terminology, has come to be known as 'hocket' technique. This technique symbolizes the cooperative role of individuals in society. The same 'hocket' technique is used for trumpet ensembles, usually associated with royalty (Pl. 18).

The Nyungwe of Mozambique use three- or four-note pan pipes. Played by twenty or thirty men, they extend over three seven-note octaves. The men dance as they play, and intersperse blown, with sung, notes; by interlocking of parts, they generate a continuous stream of blown and sung notes.[67] (Flutes often have phallic significance and are then played only by males; for this reason, flute ensembles are often used to promote courage and solidarity in battle.)

[65] Robert A. Kauffman, 'Lamellaphone', *The New Grove* (1980), x. 402.
[66] Peter Cooke, 'Stopped Flute Ensembles', *The New Grove* (1980), xviii. 178.
[67] Tracey, 'Mozambique', *The New Grove*, xii. 666.

18. Members of a specialist clan of trumpeters to the chiefs of Busoga (Uganda) displaying their *Ebigwala* gourd trumpets. Tuned pentatonically, the five different trumpets in each octave-set play in 'hocket' fashion, each sounding one note to make up the praise melodies. Photo: P. R. Cooke, 1994

It was noted earlier that the Bantu-speaking peoples use food crops introduced from the early centuries AD by Malayo-Polynesian mariners. An instrument made from a green banana-leaf petiole, in which three tongues are liberated from the surface and emit a clattering sound when a hand is drawn over them, has been observed in Zaire and the Congo. An exactly similar instrument has been recorded in Malaysia.[68] The correspondence between musical instruments and techniques in Africa and South East Asia seems almost too close to be coincidental (see Chapter 9). The possibility that, for example, xylophone and 'hocket'-ensemble techniques came to Africa from South East Asia cannot be discounted. Equally, however, it is conceivable that musical culture flowed in the opposite direction; Zimbabwe, it should be remembered, was trading with China as early as the fourteenth century. The African system of transforming songs into instrumental pieces has a logic and coherence on which the greater elaboration of South East Asian musical structures could well be an overlay. The insularity of Sub-Saharan Africa may be exaggerated.

[68] Blench, 'Morphology and Distribution', 160.

The Music of Ethiopia

If there was cultural transmission from South East Asia to Sub-Saharan Africa at an early stage, there was also strong cultural transmission from Egypt. Kingship, for example (and with it, probably, trumpet-playing), is thought to have spread southward from the kingdoms of the Upper Nile, westward across the southern edge of the Sahara to the mouth of the Senegal, eastward to the Red Sea, and southward down the central-highland spine to Zimbabwe. Ethiopia, in particular, source of the headwaters of the Blue Nile, became a melting-pot of cultural traditions. Its early contacts with Byzantium and West Asia caused elements of Jewish and Christian culture to be absorbed into its indigenous cultural systems, in addition to cultural influences from ancient Egypt and Islam. Many Jews of Ethiopian extraction believe they are descended from the twelve eldest sons of the twelve nobles of King Solomon, sent to accompany Menelik I on his return journey to Ethiopia; and Menelik I was claimed, both by Ethiopian Jews and Ethiopian Christians, to have been the son of King Solomon and the Queen of Sheba.[69] (More recently, and in particular since the mid-1980s, the Ethiopian Jews have migrated to Israel, to whose cultural systems they have brought many alien traditions.)

The musics of Ethiopia represent, in a microcosm, the diversity of traditions within Africa. Many musical genres, characteristic of Sub-Saharan Africa, have been recorded in the central highlands: for example, praise-songs, battle-incitement songs, historical songs, funeral laments, shepherd flute arabesques, and 'hocket' ensembles. Vocal styles include the use of meaningless syllables and drones, onomatopoeic sounds, shouts, cries, and ululations, as well as trills, buzzing, and humming. In desert areas, Muslim nomads have been recorded performing songs over cyclical rhythms, with 'spaced' vocal entries, at times in parallel fourths, fifths, or even seconds, or in polyphony; the songs may be accompanied by hand-clapping or heavy breathing; and polyphonic songs directed by a leader dancing with a staff have been observed.[70] Muslim traditions have been recorded in Eritrea, often syncretized with Sub-Saharan African characteristics: prayers in 'call-

[69] Marilyn Herman, 'Ethiopian Zefen and the "Band of Blossoming Hope" in Israel', unpublished paper presented to ICTM UK, 1992.

[70] Christian Hannick, 'Ethiopia', *The New Grove* (1980), vi. 268.

and-response' form, for example, or all-night trance ceremonies, using Arabized styles of vocal technique.[71]

Around Aksum, Christian priests and congregations have been recorded performing the fourth-century liturgical chant of the Syrian Antioch church. This is probably the oldest Christian chant of which we have aural evidence; the vocal style is syllabic, with melismas, clearly pitched, but with considerable ornamentation. Priests pound a large barrel drum, and also break into dance (a practice that exists in Buddhist rituals as far away as Korea); and members of the congregation sound the sistrum (a delicate rattle of metal jingles) a favourite instrument of ancient Egypt.

North African Music

The music of North Africa also shows diverse musical influences: Sub-Saharan African, European, Berber, and Arab. The *zar* trance ceremony, for example, still popular in Egypt, had its origins in Sub-Saharan Africa, and the *gnawa* trance ceremony of Tunisia and Morocco had its origins in the slave communities of the Sudanese empire. Both are used to exorcise evil spirits. European influence may account for the diatonic tunings found among the Berbers of Algeria.[72] It is Arab musical traits, however, that predominate in most social contexts; such traits are considerably more conspicuous in North Africa than in the Islamized areas of Sub-Saharan Africa.

Despite Islamic influence, music continued to be rooted in village-based social systems. In Egypt, which became a principal centre of Islamic learning, and where the singing of courtly genres such as the *qasīda* is still revered,[73] rural traditions with their roots in the pre-Islamic world are ubiquitous. In the lands of the Upper Nile Valley, former slaves from Nubia, gypsies, and other minority groups intermarried; and semi-professional musicians from such groups provide music for rituals and for entertainment to sustain village life.[74] Vestiges

[71] *Music of Ethiopia*, collected by the late Jean Jenkins of the Horniman Museum, London, Tangent Records TGM 101, 102, 103; and *Ethiopie: Musiques vocales et instrumentales*, Ocora/Harmonia Mundi, C580055/56.

[72] Salah El Mahdi, 'North Africa', *The New Grove* (1980), xiii. 287.

[73] Performances of the legendary singer, Oum Kaltsoum, are preserved on CD: CDA 401 (*Club du disque Arabe*, 125, Boulevard de Ménilmontant, 75011 Paris).

[74] Recorded by WOMAD for Real World, RWMC8/410 288–630, *The Musicians of the Nile*.

of ancient Egyptian tradition remain: for example, the *ārghūl*, a double clarinet incorporating a melody pipe and drone pipe, originated in the reed pipes of dynastic times; the *tunbūr* (long-necked lute) is a widely used instrument of ancient origin. Other instruments include the two-string *rebāb*, and the shawm, the latter usually played with 'circular' breathing. A popular percussion instrument is the *darabukka*, a goblet-shaped drum with a fish-skin head.

The Maghreb, down to the fringes of the Sahara, is occupied by Berbers and Arabs, related to each other through the Arabic language. The Berbers are found mainly in rural areas, while the Arabs tend to occupy the cities.

Near the edge of the Sahara are to be found Arabs descended from early Muslim conquerors; their music displays structural characteristics to be observed in many societies, worldwide. Songs are formed on tetrachordal and pentachordal structures, and are based on modal patterns. They may be improvised around a known melodic theme; alternatively, a melody, composed on the basis of a given rhythm, may subsequently be used as a pattern for improvised words. Poetry is usually sung to a simple melodic phrase, suited to the prosodic structure of the verse; such singing is to be found throughout North Africa, and is usually accompanied by instruments such as lute, fiddle, and percussion.[75]

In the Sahara itself are to be found the Tuaregs, nomads who are thought to be related to the Berbers; their music combines features of both Berber and Sub-Saharan African musical styles. The men improvise in lyrical and sometimes virtuosic fashion around traditional melodies, extolling the women they love or important events in their own lives. The women perform heavily ornamented phrases of restricted range, in praise-songs, songs of exorcism, and songs for social ceremonies, accompanied by a goblet drum. An entire community is involved in performance through hand-clapping, responsorial singing, and ululations. A favourite Tuareg instrument is the one-string fiddle, with hemispherical gourd resonator, covered with goatskin.[76]

The Berbers of the Atlas mountains maintain many traditional genres; and groups of musicians still travel from Tafraoute (in Morocco) to Marrakech to perform at social and ritual gatherings. Indeed, throughout Morocco, itinerant poet-musicians perform professionally,

[75] Mahdi, 'North Africa', *The New Grove*, xiii. 288.

[76] Tolia Nikiprowetzky, 'Tuareg Music', *The New Grove* (1980), xix. 236.

19. Dancing with drums, Ouzad, Morocco. Photo: Jean Jenkins

in souks, or for particular social occasions, such as circumcision and marriage ceremonies. The strategic role of the Berbers in African history brought many influences to bear on Moroccan music. Egyptian instruments and performance styles, for example, arrived in Fez from the Guinea coast via Islamic cities, such as Timbuktu.[77] In the Atlas mountains, 'call-and-response' forms that involve an entire community indicate influence from Sub-Saharan Africa (Pl. 19); and the use of foot-stamping by dancers suggests influence from Spain—or, indeed, African influence on Spain.[78]

North African Arabs and Berbers formed part of the intellectual élite that created the flowering of Islamic court music in Cordobá, during the twelfth to fourteenth centuries. With the Christian *reconquista*, begun in the twelfth century, Muslims increasingly migrated back to North Africa. 'Andalusian' court music—or so its modern proponents claim—then became the basis of the classical-music genres of Morocco, Algeria, and Tunisia; this music, based on West Asian models, will be discussed in the following chapter.

This survey of African music has focused on unity rather than diversity, for diversity is so extensive that it would require the researches of numerous musicologists to provide a comprehensive

[77] Theodore Grame, 'Morocco', *The New Grove* (1980), xii. 588.
[78] Mahdi, 'North Africa', *The New Grove*, xiii. 287.

survey. Moreover, it would be difficult to determine whether such a survey should be presented in the past or present tense. In urban areas, Africa's musical traditions have changed into modern, quasi-European forms; and those areas in which musical traditions survive, in context, tend to be among the least advanced, economically. It is difficult for many Africans to dissociate 'tradition' from 'backwardness'.

Nevertheless, Africa's musical traditions have had a lasting, positive, influence on music in the New World and, more recently, in Europe; and, in all the arts, Africa itself is developing modern styles, of which the relationship to traditional cultural systems is as immediate as it is stunning. Modern African music is now influencing popular music styles across the globe. In the ensuing account of traditional musics across Asia, Africa will disappear—temporarily—from view; but it will find an important place in the subsequent consideration of music in the Americas, and in the multicultural mêlée that is gradually engulfing the planet.

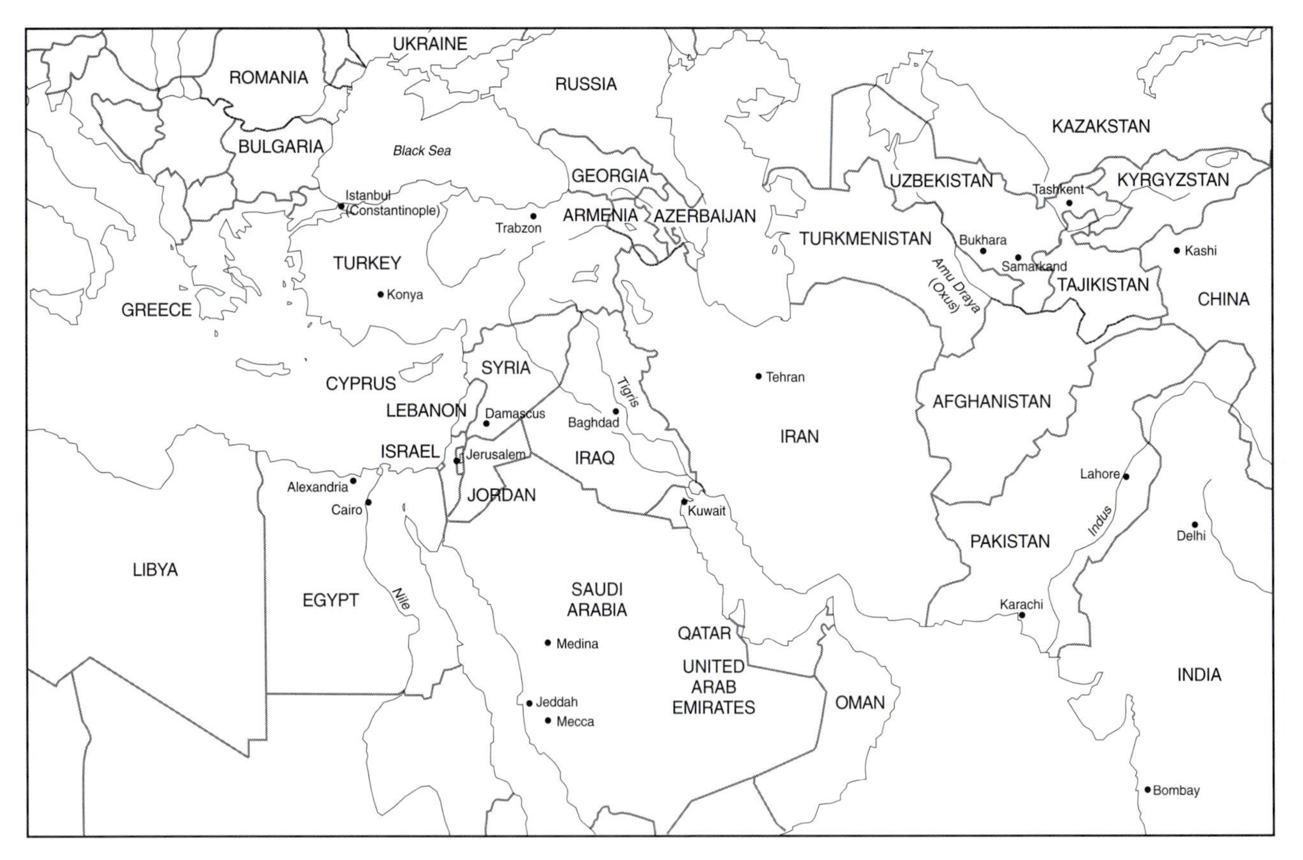
UKRAINE
ROMANIA
RUSSIA
KAZAKSTAN
BULGARIA
Black Sea
GEORGIA
UZBEKISTAN
Tashkent
KYRGYZSTAN
Istanbul
(Constantinople)
Trabzon
ARMENIA
AZERBAIJAN
TURKMENISTAN
Bukhara
Kashi
Samarkand
TURKEY
Amu Draya
(Oxus)
TAJIKISTAN
Konya
CHINA
GREECE
SYRIA
Tehran
CYPRUS
Tigris
AFGHANISTAN
LEBANON
Damascus
Baghdad
IRAN
ISRAEL
Jerusalem
IRAQ
Lahore
Alexandria
JORDAN
Cairo
Kuwait
Indus
Delhi
PAKISTAN
LIBYA
SAUDI
ARABIA
EGYPT
Nile
Karachi
QATAR
Medina
UNITED
ARAB
EMIRATES
INDIA
Jeddah
OMAN
Mecca
Bombay

West Asia

7 *West Asia*

Unity and Diversity

The most conspicuous cultural feature of West Asia today is Islam. Between a sixth and a seventh of the total population of the globe now adhere to this faith. The majority of Muslims are presently to be found, however, not in West Asia but in Indonesia, Bangladesh, Nigeria, India, and Egypt: West Asia's vast areas of desert, mountain, and high plateau make it a sparsely and unevenly populated part of the world. Nevertheless, West Asia is Islam's heartland. It was here that Islam arose, that its formative caliphates were situated, and from whence the spread of the faith—along with the Arabic language—led to the formation of a distinctive Islamic civilization.

Islam brought a measure of unity to many diverse cultural systems, the dynamics of which had been shaped in the ancient world. The religion itself was based largely on Judaic and local nomadic traditions. In Africa, South Asia, and South East Asia, Islam contributed to existing cultural systems, but was ultimately assimilated by them. In Egypt, the Levant, Iraq, and Iran, it blended with the cultural systems of Persia and Byzantium. As Islam spread, it absorbed elements of Jewish, Zoroastrian, Hellenic, Christian, and Hindu thought. In the end, it was a synthesis of all these elements, and in that lay its appeal: Islamic culture transcended the religion that generated it.

In music, the Arab conquest led to the formulation of a theory of music that became common to musical cultures across North Africa, West Asia, and Central Asia as far as Xinjiang Province in China. The style is also to be found in Kashmir. Musically, this huge area has been referred to as 'The *Maqām* World'. (In music, the word *maqām* is taken to mean 'mode', and, in some areas, 'suite'; primarily, however, it means 'place', and hierarchical offices associated with it.) The music came to be performed in huge suites of songs and instrumental pieces that survive in Xinjiang, in Uzbekistan, and in Tajikistan, as well as throughout West Asia and North Africa. A distinction in style is usually made between the 'western', Andalusian, style of suite performed in Morocco, Algeria, and Tunisia, and the 'eastern' style performed in Egypt and Syria. Further distinctions exist between styles in Iraq, Iran, and the zones of Persian influence in Central Asia, and in Turkey.[1]

The word *nawba*, used in the meaning of 'suite' in the Maghreb (see n. 1), was also used to describe 'loud' ensembles of shawms, kettledrums, and straight trumpets (playing one or two natural harmonics as alternating drone), at times also including horns, double-headed drums, and cymbals. Such ensembles were associated with royalty, and came to play, periodically, on the terraces and balconies of palaces and fortresses, and on city gates and towers, to announce the hours of the day or herald the arrival of visiting dignitaries. 'Loud' *nawba* ensembles were common throughout West Asia from the tenth century, and spread to India with Muslim conquests in the fourteenth century, and to Malaysia in the fifteenth century (Pl. 20). *Nawba* referred both to the ensemble and to the music performed.[2]

The historical currents that shaped what Westerners now call the 'Middle East' are complex. The fact that it was Arabs who spread the religion of Islam has tended to suggest synonymy between the words 'Arab' and 'Islam', but this association represents a mere fraction of a wider reality; in particular, it ignores the contribution to Islamic cultural systems made by the Persians. To appreciate the unity and diversity in musical styles and genres of West Asia, there must be prior understanding of Islamic culture and history; of its African, Persian, and Byzantine roots; of the interaction of the different peoples who followed the faith; of the cultural diversification that transformed the Islamic world from the eleventh century onwards; and of more recent history that resulted in the existence of a mêlée of peoples and cultural

[1] Terminology varies throughout the area. The term for mode is: in Egypt, Iraq, Syria, and Azerbaijan, *maqām*; in Morocco, Tunisia, and Algeria, *tubu*; in Turkey, *makam*; in Persia, *gusheh* (also a section of a suite). The word for suite is: in Egypt, *wasla*; in Iraq, *maqām* (the same as mode); in Azerbaijan, *mugam*; in Syria, Morocco, Tunisia, and Algeria, *nawba*; in Turkey, *fasil*; in Persia, *dastgāh*. In Kashmir, Uzbekistan, Tajikistan, and Xinjiang, *maqām* means both mode and suite.

[2] Carol Tingey, *Heartbeat of Nepal: The Pancai Baja* (Royal Nepal Academy, 1990), 14–18; John Levy, recording of *Music from the Shrines of Ajmer and Mundra*, Tangent Records, TGM105.

20. A *nawba* ensemble performing at the court of Emperor Akbar of India; from the *Akbarnāma* (late sixteenth century)

systems within artificially delineated boundaries. It will be necessary to address these matters in some detail.

The Backdrop to Islam

The word 'Arab' initially appears on an Assyrian cuneiform tablet from 853 BC, and seems to have referred to nomadic pastoralists.[3] From ancient times Arabs were enterprising traders,

[3] Daniel Bates and Amal Rassam, *Peoples and Cultures of the Middle East* (Englewood Cliffs, NJ: Prentice Hall, 1983), 24.

linking Mesopotamia with the Indus Valley, and carrying merchandise from East Africa to Egypt.[4] Subsequently, Arabs spread across West Asia from the south of the Arabian peninsula to the north of present-day Syria, and developed important trading centres such as Petra and Palmyra.

In Arabia itself, a number of sea-coast kingdoms flourished in the early centuries AD; but they subsequently disappeared, whereupon Arabia reverted to being a tribal society, its affairs regulated by patriarchal and kinship laws. This encouraged a migration from the south to the north, and led to prosperous trading oases (such as Mecca) acquiring larger populations than the traditional social system could support. Social conditions became progressively unstable and inequitable; and the nature-gods of the Arabs came to appear increasingly anachronistic beside the gods of Jews and Christians who had begun to settle in the same area.

Muhammad received his revelations from an apparition he identified as the Archangel Gabriel, in Mecca, in 610. Mecca was then an important junction of caravan routes between southern Arabian and Mediterranean ports; it was also an oasis, and a major centre of religious pilgrimage. Muhammad's monotheistic message posed a threat to this latter aspect of Mecca's trading interests; and the resultant hostility caused Muhammad and his followers to move to Medina, a little over 400 kilometres to the north-east. This *hijra* (migration)—on 16 July 622—marks the beginning of the Islamic era and of the Muslim calendar.

Muhammad did not claim to found a new religion, but rather to be bringing, to the Arab peoples, the old religion of One God. He did not expect Jews or Christians to convert to Islam; he recognized that they had received their own revelations and, moreover, that those revelations were set down in holy books. His achievement was to present the Arabs with their own holy book of revelations.[5] The Prophet of God died in 632, having won Mecca to his faith, and having consolidated his position over most of Arabia. Within ten years of his death, his armies defeated those of the Byzantines and of the Persians, spreading the faith, and, with it, the Arabic language.

When the Arabs defeated the Persians, that great empire had been in conflict with the West for over a thousand years. The conflict had been

[4] J. M. Roberts, *Pelican History of the World* (London: Pelican Books, 1988), 314.
[5] Ibid. 315.

brought to a head when, in the early seventh century, the last, great Sassanid emperor, Chosroes II, had pushed his armies south into Egypt and north to within 2 kilometres of Constantinople. In the event, Byzantium was saved—though in a precarious state—for another thousand years, by the military genius of the Emperor Heraclius. Nevertheless, this Persian conquest marked the end of Hellenistic urban civilization in Asia: before he died in 641, Heraclius was to see Arabs overturn virtually all the conquests made by him for Byzantium. Then, in 643, Arabs overran Persia itself. Persia and Rome had reciprocally both fascinated and exhausted each other, leaving a vacuum to be filled by Islam.[6]

Arabs progressively inherited the cultural systems of Persia, Rome, and Byzantium; and from Alexandria they acquired knowledge of the corpus of Greek learning. Significantly, the oldest Islamic monument is the Dome of the Rock, built at Jerusalem in 691. On this site Abraham was said to have offered his son, Isaac, as sacrifice; and Muhammad was said to have been taken therefrom, to heaven.

The Umayyad and Abbāsid Dynasties

Muhammad died without naming a successor. Following tribal custom, his closest associates met in council and chose, from among them, Abu Bakr to be the Prophet's khalifa (deputy). A minority group, however, believed that the leadership should remain within Muhammad's family; they favoured his cousin and son-in-law, 'Ali, and became known as the *shi'at 'Ali* (partisans of 'Ali). The issue was of fundamental importance because it created two opposing principles of political legitimacy that haunt Islam to this day: does licence to rule—and so to interpret the Qur'ān—reside in the will of the people; or is it determined by right of descent?[7]

Twenty-four years after the caliphate of Abu Bakr, 'Ali was elected to power, but not before his two immediate predecessors had been murdered (though not by his hand). In 661 he himself was murdered, and Mu'awiya, Governor of Syria and a lifelong opponent of 'Ali, set himself up as caliph. Three consequences of this were to be of lasting importance: the caliphate became dynastic; the Shi'ites ('the Partisans')

[6] Ibid. 307. [7] Bates and Rassam, *Peoples and Cultures*, 41.

became a separate, underground political faction; and power moved out of Arabia.

Mu'awiya founded the Umayyad dynasty, the first of two that were to give Arab peoples ascendancy in West Asia and North Africa for three centuries. The caliphate was based at Damascus, in the heart of the Mediterranean, thereby presenting itself as successor to the classical empires of Rome and Byzantium. The Umayyads did not greatly alter existing administrative structures: the process of Arabization was gradual. But, as the numbers of non-Arab converts grew, these non-Arabs felt increasingly alienated from the Arab élite; and the Shi'ites were not slow to exploit their disaffection, strongest in Iraq. In 749 a new caliph established his authority in Kufa, defeated and executed the last Umayyad, and, with the support of the Shi'ites, inaugurated the Abbāsid dynasty, with its capital in the newly founded city of Baghdad.[8]

The move to Baghdad was significant, for Baghdad lay on the banks of the Tigris, at the heart of the old Persian empire. Baghdad became a huge cosmopolitan capital city of an empire that encompassed a diversity of peoples and cultural systems. Increasingly, these peoples became Arab-speaking. (Of the Aramaic-, Greek-, and Persian-speaking populations within the empire, only Persia retained its linguistic identity.) Although the ruling castes of the Abbāsid dynasty were Arab-speaking, however, they were not necessarily of Arabic stock; and they were tolerant of the mores of their tributaries.

Islamic culture reached a peak in the tenth century. It was under the Abbāsids that the works of Plato, Aristotle, Euclid, and Galen were translated into the Arabic language, leading to developments in science, commerce, and the arts that would subsequently influence Europe. The words 'tariff', *douane*, and 'magazine', for example, are Arabic words; but so also are 'lute' and 'rebec'. It was also under the Abbāsids, however, that loyalty to the dynasty became more important than loyalty to *umma* (the Brotherhood of believers). Although, nominally, Abbāsid rule lasted until 1259, the empire was soon to be split between rival caliphates in Spain, Egypt, Iran, and Iraq.

As early as 756, in Spain—which had been conquered by the Arabs in the early eighth century (see p. 489)—an Umayyad prince ignored the Abbāsid succession and declared himself *emir* (governor) of El-Andalus. As noted in the context of Africa, this emirate was later joined by reformist, Almoravid Berbers from the Maghreb; the Umayyad dynasty

[8] Roberts, *Pelican History of the World*, 322.

in Andalusia reached its cultural flowering in the eleventh and twelfth centuries. In Cairo, in 973, the Shi'ite Fatamids set up an independent caliphate and extended their influence into Syria, gaining control of the holy places in Mecca and Medina. Three other caliphates exercised tenuous control in various parts of (present-day) Iraq, Iran, and Trans-oxiana ('across the Oxus', present-day Uzbekistan, and northern Tajiki-stan). Into this mêlée was to arrive another horde of nomadic invaders from Central Asia: the Turks.

The Arrival of the Turks

The Turks had established the first nomadic empire to span Central Asia; its importance was such that, during the seventh century, four of the world's contemporary civilizations—China, India, Byzantium, and Persia—felt it necessary to establish relations with the Turkish khans.[9] Their empire was weakened by the resurgence of Chinese power under the Tang, and shattered when Arabs invaded Transoxiana in 667. In the tenth century, however, just when the Islamic world was beginning to fracture, the Tang dynasty collapsed. This enabled the Turks to establish a second empire, headed by a clan already converted to Islam, the Seljuks.

Pushed westwards by the re-establishment of Chinese power under the Song, the Seljuks crossed the Oxus and went on to conquer Iran, Iraq, the Levant, and Anatolia, and to inflict a severe defeat on the Byzantine army at Manzikert (in present-day east Turkey) in 1071. After this, large numbers of Turks settled in what is now Anatolia, both as nomadic pastoralists and as mercenary warriors. Gradually, the whole of Anatolia was converted to Islam. The Seljuks ruled from Konya in the name of the Abbāsids, but they called their empire the sultanate of Rum, for they saw themselves as successors to Rome.[10] They did not only bring with them traditions from Central Asia, for during their migrations they had rubbed shoulders with Slavs and Bulgars, and had absorbed cultural traditions now common throughout the Balkans.

Being newly converted to Islam, the Seljuks were intolerant of other religions. (It was in part this, along with their incursion into the old Roman Empire, that sparked the crusading spirit in the West.) But their

[9] Ibid. 354. [10] Ibid. 313, 354.

settlement in the heartland of the Islamic empire helped to make possible, among the diverse peoples of West Asia, a measure of cultural unity; and that culture now included elements common to the civilizations of China, India, Persia, and Byzantium.

The Mongols and the Ottomans

Islamic unity was soon to be tested by the last, and most terrible, of all assaults on civilization to come from the steppe. Genghis Khan began his eastwards attack on China in 1211. By 1241 his son had pushed west as far as Austria; and only a dispute over succession to the Mongol Khanate saved Europe. By 1259 Mongol armies had captured Baghdad; but Muslim Asia was saved by another dispute that caused the greater part of the Mongol force to be concentrated in what is now north-west Iran. In 1260 an Egyptian army seized the opportunity and laid to rest the legend of Mongol invincibility, in a decisive battle at Ain Jalut, near Nazareth.

The Mongol onslaught put an end to the Seljuk sultanate of Rum; but because Mongol armies were composed largely of Turkic mercenaries, their assault resulted in increased numbers of Turks in West Asia and North Africa. In the wake of the Seljuk sultanate, Muslim petty princes of Turkic extraction, occupying lands adjacent to the Byzantine Empire, sought to extend their power. One such was Osman, who, in about 1281, founded the Ottoman dynasty; his son, Orkhan, the first to take the title of 'Sultan', founded the 'Janissaries', the 'new soldiers' (*yeni ceri*), family-less, captured Christian boys, loyal to the death to the Sultan who fed them. These provided armies of infantrymen for use against Europeans, and from which European music was to acquire the 'Jingling Johnny' (see p. 450), valveless trumpet, shawm, bass drum, cymbals, and the concept of the 'military band' (Pl. 21).

The Ottomans went on to create an empire that was to threaten the continued existence of European civilization. In 1453 they captured Constantinople and rang the death knell of Byzantium ('the second death of Homer and Plato' as one Pope called it).[11] In 1461 they dealt the *coup de grâce* to Hellenism, when at Trabzon, a trading centre on the south-east shore of the Black Sea, the last Hellenic city fell before the

[11] Roberts, *Pelican History of the World*, 366.

21. March of the *mehteran* (military band), with trumpets, cymbals, cylindrical drums, and kettle drums; miniature from *Surame-i Vehbi* (written and illuminated for Ahmed III (reigned 1703–30))

Ottoman Janissaries. At this point the Ottomans had already created an empire not dissimilar in size and situation to that of Byzantium. By 1683 they would be laying siege to Vienna.

Notwithstanding their military ruthlessness, Ottomans showed a tolerance towards non-Muslims that was seldom shown to Muslims by Christians. They devised a system that permitted specific non-Muslim peoples or communities, usually sharing a common religion, to manage their own civil and religious affairs; such designated communities were known as *millet*s. The device enabled non-Muslims to be absorbed within the Sunnite state, while it exposed and reinforced their sectarian identity. By the nineteenth century, no less than seventeen different *millet*s were recognized by the Ottoman government. Only with the rise of Arab nationalism towards the end of the nineteenth century was this system called into question.[12]

Shi'ism and Safavid Persia

By making itself adaptable to differing polities, Sunnism proved an essentially stabilizing institution. Shi'ism, on the other hand, had always proved attractive to dissident forces within the Sunnite hegemony, being tolerant of local practices, and operating largely as a folk cult. It became a lasting political force when Shah Ismael seized the throne of Persia in 1501, founded the Safavid dynasty, and made Shi'ism the state religion.[13]

From the start, the split between Sunnites and Shi'ites had been a potential source of disunity in Islam. The dynastic principle embodied in Sunnism allowed the ruling élite to exercise political authority over the state; and the *ulama* (educated, religious élite) tended to work closely with the ruling élites, the *imams* being confined to leading the prayers in the mosque. *Imams* of the Shi'ite faith, however, are regarded as direct descendants of 'Ali, and therefore to be endowed with special powers. They are regarded both as agents of Divine Illumination, and mediums of Divine Revelation; indeed, to Shi'ite Muslims, belief in the *imam* constitutes a special tenet of religion.[14] Collectively, the descendants of 'Ali are known as *sayyids*, and they still constitute a caste-like group, enjoying special privleges. The black turban worn by many Shi'ite clergy—such as the late Ayatollah Khomenei—symbolizes a blood relationship with the Prophet.

The majority of Shi'ites belong to the *Imami*, or 'Twelvers' sect, that acknowledges an unbroken line of twelve *imams*, starting with 'Ali, and ending with Muhammad al-Mahdi, who disappeared while a child (and was thought to have been murdered by the ruling Abbāsids). The twelth *imam* is still regarded as the 'hidden' imam, and is expected to return as the *Mahdi*, or 'Rightly-Guided One'. By contrast, the *Ismaili* sect, or 'Seveners', acknowledge the seventh imam, Isma'il, as the last *imam* and 'hidden' saviour. All Shi'ites regard 'Ali's son, Hussein, as the Lord of Martyrs; and in Iran and other Shi'ite areas, his martyrdom is re-enacted annually in processions and Passion plays, often with *sayyids* playing the leading roles. The authority by which the Shi'ite clergy

[12] Bates and Rassam, *Peoples and Cultures*, 94. [13] Ibid. 61–2. [14] Ibid. 62–7.

interpret the Qur'ān—and thus also the law—has proved continually to be a powerful source of subversion. (Shi'ites now predominate in Iran and southern Iraq, in rural Turkey, and in Syria and Lebanon, often in the more depressed regions.[15])

The (Shi'ite) Safavids were in fact of Turkic rather than Persian origin, and were naturally opposed to the Ottomans. Significantly, the core of the Ottoman Empire was what is now Turkey; and its historical heart—and prize—was Constantinople, now Istanbul. Anatolia's historical traditions were those of Byzantium; and the natural thrust of Ottoman expansion was to the west and south—into the former Roman Empire—rather than to the east. When the Safavids rose to confront the Ottomans, the ensuing conflict reflected the historical rivalry between Rome and Persia.

The Persian adoption of Shi'ism drove a wedge into the Muslim world; but in devolving power to the clergy, the empire's decline was hastened. In 1638 Baghdad was lost to the Turk. By the beginning of the eighteenth century, Shi'ite Persia was at war with a newly resurgent Sunnite Afghanistan; and in 1722 the Afghans forced the resignation of the last Safavid Shāh. Afghan power was short-lived: two years later, it was Ottomans and Russians who were carving up Persia between them.

The Decline of Ottoman Power

By then, however, the Ottoman Empire was in decline. Its economy had been undermined by European maritime activity during the seventeenth century (brought about, ironically, by the Ottomans' successful sealing-off of Europe from Asia); subsequently, Russia's expansion encroached on its territory. Napoleon's expedition to Egypt in 1798 led to increasing European involvement there and throughout West Asia. This, and ineffective Ottoman rule, created conditions for the rise of Arab nationalism which, in turn, furnished an excuse for Europeans to interfere in West Asia's affairs, ostensibly to protect Christian minorities; by 1914 most of West Asia was enmeshed in the European net. The ending of the First World War saw new nationalisms, new interferences, and new compromises, the effects of which are still with us.

[15] Ibid. 63, 66.

Persia survived as an independent kingdom but was partitioned into British and Russian 'spheres of influence' in 1907. In 1935, following the curtailment of British oil interests, the Persian government required that the country's internal collective name, Iran, should be adopted by the world outside. Iraq was formed out of an uneasy combination of the three Ottoman provinces of Basra, Baghdad, and Mosul. Syria, which formerly included Israel, Palestine, Lebanon, and Jordan, operated within its present boundaries under a French mandate from 1920. By 1926 the Saudis had come to control most of the Arabian peninsula. Turkey had allied itself with the Germans during the First World War, and what was left of it was subsequently partitioned into British, French, and Italian 'spheres of influence'; a resistance movement enabled it to negotiate independence within its present borders in 1923.[16]

After five millennia at the crossroads of Eurasian civilization and, in the 1990s, torn by strife as never before, West Asia may still be viewed as a culturally homogeneous unit bonded by Islam. Yet it is also a group of nation states imposed upon a variety of distinctive peoples and cultural traditions; and, because the area remains physically much as it was 5,000 years ago, it is also a patchwork of nomadic, agriculturalist, and urban peoples. The Semitic, Mediterranean, and Central Asian cultural systems of its peoples have to some extent merged, though language and, in some cases, religion still separate minority groups, such as the Kurds, Baluch, and Turkmen from the dominant groupings of Persians, Arabs, and Turks.

Islamic Religious and Artistic Culture

The assertion of Islamic fundamentalism in recent years has drawn widespread attention to the imperatives of the Islamic religion. These are more restrictive among Shi'ites than Sunnites; nevertheless, all devout Muslims observe five Islamic duties: to pronounce the creed; to pray fives times a day; to give alms; to fast throughout the month in which the Qur'ān was revealed to Muhammad (*Ramadan*); and to undertake pilgrimage to Mecca (*hajj*). Circumcision before puberty is an essential rite-of-passage; usually performed between the ages of 4 and 7, it marks entry of the boy into communal life in the society.

[16] *The Times Atlas of World History*, ed. Geoffrey Barraclough (London, 1989), 228.

The basis of religious education is the revealed Qur'ān. (The word derives from *qira'a*, reading, and therefore implies a written document.) Because Muhammad received his revelations in the Arabic language, the Qur'ān may not be translated out of Arabic: it must be memorized even by non-Arabic speakers (who memorize it without having a speaking knowledge of Arabic). Muslims also revere the *hadith*, a collection of stories recording the sayings and deeds of the Prophet (the counterpart of the Buddhist *Jātaka*s). From these two sources comes the *shari'a* ('divine law'), which, because of its divinity, is held to be unchangeable. Nevertheless, interpretation—then, as now—often varied, and differences defined various sects both of Sunnites and Shi'ites.

An escape from the legalistic demands of the *shari'a* was provided by Sufism, a mystical branch of Islam that sought to free the religious experience by allowing each individual to choose his or her own individual spiritual path.[17] By appealing more to the intuitive than the rational side of the human psyche, Sufism assisted Islam's spread into Africa, India, and Central and South East Asia. Its goal, like that of Buddhism—with which it had to find accommodation elsewhere in Asia—was the transference of consciousness from the Self to Truth (defined as 'Ultimate Reality'). The movement started in the eighth century, when travelling mystics began to preach asceticism as a means of achieving ecstatic communion with God. By the thirteenth century, it had become a popular movement, with an institutional structure of individual orders, influenced by the teachings of individual mystics.

Sufism derived from Gnosticism, itself a synthesis of Christian theology, Greek philosophy, and mystery-cults of the ancient world. (Gnostics claimed to possess an esoteric knowledge of the inner meaning of religion—the *gnōsis*—leading to illumination and immortality.) In Sufi thought, a higher state of consciousness may be achieved by means of a seven-stage path (repentance, abstinence, renunciation, poverty, patience, trust in God, and acquiescence in the will of God). In this state, the one who knows and the known are indivisible. From this perception, some mystics went so far as to suggest that the universe and its creator are, likewise, indivisible (a doctrine echoing Egyptian, Hindu, and Daoist world-views). Yet others believed that the supreme experience of union with God could not be expressed in words at all.

From their inception in the eighth century, Sufi orders included dancing and listening to music in their ecstatic rituals; indeed, many

[17] Bates and Rassam, *Peoples and Cultures*, 70.

regarded listening to music as the most potent means of achieving divine ecstasy. (It was the Sufis who established the art of *zikr*—the naming of God—a circular breathing technique whereby the *zikr* could be repeated silently, spoken aloud, sung, and at times danced, to a rhythmical melody.) During the eleventh century, a distinction was made between those who hear the *material* sound of music and those who appreciate its *spiritual essence*; the latter were held to be unable to hear individual notes, melodies, beats, and rhythm, but to hear only music, *per se*. In an echo of Platonic thought, the eleventh-century Sufi mystic, Ibn Zaila, suggested that 'sound produces an influence on the soul in two ways; one on account of its musical structure and the other because of its similarity to the soul'.[18]

The ecstatic dances of Sufi orders provoked controversy, among Islamic legists, over definitions of 'admissible' and 'inadmissible' music. Legists discouraged artistic expression, but they never actually proscribed secular music, considering Qur'ānic chant and hymn-singing to be quite separate from *mūsīqī*. They accepted secular music if it served a social function, but not if it was thought to provide sensual pleasure. They tended, however, to proscribe *listening* to music, in part to counter pre-Islamic ideas expressed in sung poetry, in part perhaps to discourage to heretical tendencies within Sufism; and this caused the music of Sufi orders to come under constant interdiction, by orthodox Shi'ites and Sunnites alike. Despite the disapproval of the orthodox, however, Sufi monasteries in many areas acquired the function of disseminating 'secular' musical styles among the populace, and they became important custodians of traditional Islamic musical genres and styles.

The most important medium for Sufi sentiment, however, was not music, but poetry. Poetic literature had flourished in pre-Islamic times, being the principal mode of expression of pre-Islamic soothsayers; and although much of the Qur'ān was written in rhyming prose (*saj*), and not poetry—possibly to dissociate the revelations of Muhammad from the pronouncements of soothsayers—poetry continued to be a principal artistic outlet in Islamic society as a whole. Other forms of artistic expression, however, were discouraged: not merely 'sensual' music, but also (for example) theatre (except for the Shi'ite Passion plays), and the representation of human likeness in art. Such discouragement met with varying degrees of success: representation of humans, for example, was

[18] George Henry Farmer, 'The Music of Islam', *The New Oxford History of Music*, i (Oxford: Oxford University Press, 1957), 440.

abundant in the miniature painting of Andalusia, Persia, and North India. Nevertheless, Islamic art became manifest largely in decoration; and such decoration was wonderfully intricate, whether applied in calligraphy, ceramics, metalwork, weaving, architecture—or music.

'Arabesque' has long been an accepted word in the English vocabulary; it is applied to ornamental friezes, to borders of intertwined scrolls, to musical compositions that are thought to reflect this kind of structure, and to the ballet dancer's pose on one foot with the other leg extended behind. The Arab filigree style developed from the cursive Arab script. Here text was sometimes scarcely distinguishable from the sumptuous patterns of its decorations. This decorative style was reflected in ceramics, particularly in ceramic tiles on the walls of mosques, where floral patterns, accompanied by ornamented inscriptions, are formed out of colour-glazed ceramic tiles. (The use of glazed ceramics dates back to ancient Mesopotamia.) Arguably, the abstract decoration of tile and stone in monumental Islamic architecture has never been equalled elsewhere.

Within Arabic art, any number of motifs may be combined to form an arabesque; but the essence of the art lies not in the motifs themselves but in the *structuring* of the motifs, to produce an arabesque. Ornamentation lies at the heart of this process. Ornamentations are not dispensable additions to given motifs, but themselves become the material from which infinite patterns are made. The same is largely true of Islamic musical art, in which ornamentation of a modal melody type may become so pervasive as itself to become 'melody'. By such means as note repetitions, sequences, glissandos, tremolos, shakes, vibratos, shifts of accent, or shifts of octave, musical motifs are structured into a seamless web of melodic patterning.[19]

Despite the interdictions of Islamic legists, a refined style of Islamic art music developed; but it did so as a private, soloistic art, at court, and in élite households, and professional musicians came to be paid huge sums of money for their performances. Only in North Africa did the style spread widely outside the courts and influence popular genres.

Islamic Cantillation

No attempt was made to notate Arab music, and no fixed rules were formulated for the recitation of the Qur'ān, other

[19] Lois Ibsen al-Faruqī, 'Ornamentation in Arabian Improvisational Music: A Study of Interrelatedness in the Arts', *The World of Music*, 20 (1978), 17–28.

than that the words, and their natural rhythms, should be clear, and that the chant should not be based on a secular melody.[20] Imposition, therefore, of given melodies or of rhythmic patterns is still forbidden; and, because to recite all verses the same way would be regarded as melody-making, the reciter has to rely on spontaneous melody, inspired by the text and the occasion.

In some areas, in the Qur'ān-reading schools of Egypt, Turkey, and Iran in particular, the chant uses modal structures and ornamental melismas, deriving from classical music, and absolute control of vibrato, in amplitude and frequency, from zero upwards, is often a prime feature of vocal training. Encouraged by the devotional—and sometimes vocal—response of the listeners, the reciter may by moved to considerable feats of virtuosity.[21] In most rural areas, however, a simpler version is used, and is learnt by children in primary schools, often from itinerant teachers.

As with Qur'ānic recitation, no rules were laid down for the call to prayer (*adhān*, or in some places, *azān*), sounded by the muezzin from the top of the minaret five times a day. (The high profile of this call was originally intended to distinguish it from similar practices of Jews, Christians, and Zoroastrians.) The muezzin's call became a considerable art in many areas, acquiring regional styles and, indeed, regional schools. Large mosques would employ up to twenty muezzins at any one time; and in Turkey muezzins formed their own guilds.[22] In modern times, *adhān* is increasingly committed to tape, and the muezzin no longer climbs the minaret five times a day, but sits at the foot with a microphone.

Within the mosque services themselves, the number and ordering of sung prayers, supplications, and praises to Allah are determined by local orders and sects. In Turkey, where—until the onset of Atatürk's modernizing reforms in 1924—the Sufi orders were influential, elaborate compositions were accepted for use on special occasions. There, and in other Sunnite Arab countries, *na't* (hymns in praise of the prophet) are frequently used, and may be sung in a style that reflects rural or court

[20] Eckhard Neubauer, 'Islamic Religious Music', *The New Grove* (1980), ix. 342. G. H. Farmer (in *A History of Arabian Music to the XIIth Century* (London: Luzac, 1929), 33) notes: 'We are assured by Ibn Qutaiba (died *c.*889) that Qu'ran was sung to no different rules than those of the ordinary artistic songs (*alhan al-ghina*).'

[21] Kristina Nelson, 'Reciter and Listener: Some Factors Shaping the Mujawwad Style of Qur'anic Reciting', *Ethnomusicology* (January 1982).

[22] Neubauer, 'Islamic Religious Music', *The New Grove*, ix. 342.

traditions. In Turkey, such hymns are sometimes sung, by special *na't* singers, before prayers; and in the home, religious women may visit to sing simple hymns (*ilâhi*), at times of bereavement, for example.

Shi'ite Muslims oppose music more vociferously than do Sunnites. Shi'ite 'music' is restricted to Qur'ān-recitation, *adhān*, religious verses, and chants associated with the lives of the martyrs. The first martyr, Hussein, was murdered in the month of Muharram, which became a month of mourning and repentance. In Persia, during Muharran, groups of devotees have long met together in the villages to perform *Ta'zie'* (Passion plays), with texts drawn from a variety of collections made between the seventeenth and early twentieth centuries. Soloists, representing the protagonists, sing in dialogue, interspersed with verses sung by the group. The *Ta'zie'* were once elaborate spectacles: in Tehran, in the nineteenth and early twentieth centuries, they involved choruses and military orchestras. From the 1930s onwards such performances were banned; but Passion plays on a more limited scale still take place, often presented by itinerant troupes.[23]

Poet-Musicians

The dominant position of literature in Islamic culture caused the melodic lines of all vocal genres to be strongly conditioned by the words. In both rural and courtly vocal music, the structure of the melody usually followed the rhythmic structure of the poem. The *qasīda*, for example, a Bedouin folk genre that came to be used in classical suites, may be more than 100 lines long; it is divided into metrical feet, in any one of sixteen traditional metres, and each metre strictly determines the vocal rhythm. However, the singer usually improvises extensively in interpolated melismatic passages, so as to establish the meaning and flavour of the text.

Melodic styles vary from highly intricate, soloistic types, to simple melodic formulas. There are songs for purposes of all kinds: caravan songs and songs of war, epic songs and political songs, processional songs and songs to venerate the saints, dance songs, disputatious songs, and laments.[24] Among the Bedouin, the amateur musician is traditionally

[23] Stephen Blum, 'Iran', *The New Grove* (1980), ix. 301.

[24] Owen Wright, 'Arab Music', *The New Grove* (1980), i. 528 ff.

revered as 'Poet', 'Guardian of the Poem', or 'Man of Letters', whereas the professional poet-musician is regarded as the 'Mercenary Poet'.[25]

In many areas, however, semi-professional poet-musicians are venerated as religious mystics. In Iraq, for example, the *āshuq* ('lovers', 'wandering minstrels') traditionally compose their own words and music, on mystic themes. In Turkey, in Azerbaijan, and among the Kurds in Iraq, *ashik* wander from village to village performing at local festivals, keeping alive a large repertoire of songs, from earlier, named *ashik*, as well as contributing their own improvisations. Throughout Persia, *shāir* enliven social events, such as weddings, circumcision ceremonies, and other important family or community occasions. Minstrel-singing is still a prized art in many parts of Central Asia, and this tradition almost certainly dates back to antiquity.

Musical Theory in Arabic-Speaking Areas of West Asia

From the start of Islam, efforts were made to adapt the various established musical customs of West Asia to the new religious code. Arabs had been predominantly traders and pastoralists and had themselves no large-scale musical traditions on which to draw. They quickly assimilated Persian and Byzantine traditions. Early Arabic sources suggest that pre-Islamic song genres already reflected the characteristic Arab distinction between 'heavy' (prestigious) and 'light' (popular) music, and that entertainment music was often performed by *qayna* ('singing slave girls').[26] Popular instruments included those that derived from the ancient West Asian civilizations: lute, shawm, and frame drum.

After the coming of Islam, with its proscriptions, community entertainment came to be provided by non-Arab *mukhannathūn*, whose music centred on the cult of boy dancers noted for their moral laxity. The association of music with the *qayna* and *mukhannathūn* may have contributed to the hostility towards certain types of music shown by Muslim legists, and to the need to describe Qur'ānic cantillation as 'reading'.[27]

[25] Scheherezade Qassim Hassan, 'Iraq', *The New Grove* (1980), ix. 311.

[26] Wright, 'Arab Music', *The New Grove*, i. 515.

[27] Hostility to popular music, in general, may also have been encouraged because of its association with the poetry of pre-Islamic soothsayers. Hostility still exists in some areas: at the

Nevertheless, with the establishment of the Umayyad caliphate and an increasingly scholarly and artistic ambience, a need for courtly music arose. It is said that famous Umayyad musicians travelled through the territories of the former empires in order to incorporate elements of their musical traditions into the Arab style. There can be little doubt that the melodic and rhythmic structures adopted by the Arabs had their roots in Mesopotamia and their first flowering in Persia; a sophisticated system of modes existed in pre-Islamic Persia, and several mode names are found in both the Persian and Arab-Persian modal systems.[28] On the other hand, early Arab music theory clearly derived from Hellenistic-Byzantine traditions in Alexandria (though there is no way of knowing how far such theory was reflected in practice).

What is beyond doubt is that the amalgamation of cultural systems in the first century of Islam led to a period of innovation, and contributed to the courtly style of music that was to flourish from North Africa to Central Asia. The *ūd* (wooden-bellied short-necked lute, tuned in fourths) was adopted not only for performance but also for demonstrating the intervallic structure of modes. Eight modes deriving from the Byzantine *oktōēchos* were distinguished. There developed an increasingly marked distinction between 'heavy' and 'light' styles; and melodic and rhythmic modes were classified in two sets that reflected these distinctions.[29]

According to Arab-Persian theorists, the most important musical innovation of the time was effected in Baghdad, towards the end of the tenth century. Up to this point, the modes of Islamic art music appear to have been based on the Pythagorean diatonic scale, inherited from Byzantium, and the frets on the lute reflected this. Subsequently, attempts were made to define a musical theory that could reflect the many other types of intervallic patterns in use, not relating to the 'cycle-of-fifths' tuning procedure. The Abbāsid lutenist, Zalzal, introduced additional frets on the lute that made available non-diatonic intervals: one approximately half-way between a minor and a major third; one

time of writing, Kelantan State in Malaysia, for example, in an assertion of Islamic fundamentalism, is attempting to ban song and dance performances, on the grounds that they lead to immoral activity (as reported in the *South China Morning Post*, 16 October 1995, 12).

[28] Harold Powers, review of Owen Wright, *The Modal System of Arab and Persian Music, AD 1250–1300* (Oxford, 1978), in *Journal of the American Musicological Society* (1978), 187; and Amnon Shiloah, 'The Arabic Concept of Mode', *Journal of the American Musicological Society*, 34/1 (1981), 19–42.

[29] Wright, 'Arab Music', *The New Grove*, i. 515.

approximately half-way between a major and an augmented second; and one approximately half-way between a semitone and a tone.[30] The first of these is commonly called 'the neutral third'; its sound is characteristic of traditional music throughout West Asia.

The widespread use of this 'neutral' interval complicated the classification of modes within the octave. The long-necked lute was used for experimenting with the physics of sound—a tradition that goes back to ancient Mesopotamia—to the extent that a leading tenth century theorist, al-Fārābi, referred to such a lute from Baghdad tuned to a scale proceeding in steps of approximate quarter-tones and encompassing a range of little more than a minor third. The same lute displayed another scale in terms of limmas (the diatonic semitone in the Pythagorean system of intervals) and commas (an arithmetically complex Pythagorean interval, now taken to refer to one-ninth of a whole tone).[31]

During the thirteenth century, Arab-Persian musical theory became largely standardized into what became known as the 'Systematist' school. The leader of this school, Safī al-Dīn (Safiaddin Ormavi in Persian), offered a theoretical synthesis of the many expositions of intervals and scales proposed before his time; his system was designed in such a way as to accommodate possible expansions and variations, and it became the chief model for subsequent generations of theorists.[32] Basing his calculations and demonstrations on the divisions of a monochord, Safiaddin divided the octave into two disjunct tetrachords and a whole tone. The tetrachords each consisted of two whole tones and a limma, the whole tones themselves consisting of two limmas and a comma.[33]

Safiaddin (d. 1294) listed twenty different modes. These consisted of units that constituted tetrachords or pentachords. (Other writings, however, showed the importance of units that do not form a tetrachord, and that cannot readily be expressed in terms of the octave.) When such units were used simultaneously, they were usually arranged so that two separate units would together span an octave (or approximately an octave). If two different units were used at the same pitch, their differences would be minimized as far as possible.[34]

[30] Wright, 'Arab Music', *The New Grove*, i. 517. [31] Ibid. 518.
[32] Shiloah, 'The Arabic Concept of Mode', 28, 31.
[33] For a comparison with the ancient Greek theory of tetrachords, see p. 127.
[34] Wright, 'Arab Music', *The New Grove*, i. 519.

Ex. 7.1

Seventeen notes within the octave were identified and named; and various juxtapositions of these formed the basis of named modes (*maqāmāt*). The basic units from which the system was compounded are set out in Ex. 7.1 (after Wright).[35] (In order to fit seventeen notes into staff notation, a flat sign with a line through it is used to denote a slight lowering of the pitch.)

Modes were used in conjunction with repeated rhythmic cycles. These were compounded of beats containing two, three, or four units, derived from poetic metres. The cycles varied in length, occupying a single 'measure', or encompassing a complete tune. In theory, the first and last units of the poetic foot were sounded by a percussion instrument, but the sounding of the second or third units was optional. Following this theory, the eight rhythmic cycles listed by Safiaddin would appear in modern notation as in Ex. 7.2 (after Wright).[36] (The symbol ° above a note indicates that it is a median and that its sounding is optional.)

The continuity of this structural system may be indicated by comparing Safiaddin's modal units with the modal units (*uqūd*) and rhythmic units (*īqā'āt*) of the Tunisian *nawba*, as indicated by Sālah al-Mahdī in his transcription of 'The Tunisian Musical Heritage', published in 1956 (see p. 630) (Exx. 7.3 and 7.4).[37] (Al-Mahdī notated, controversially,

[35] Ibid. [36] Ibid. 520, transcribed from table 4.

[37] Cited in Ruth Davis, 'Melodic and Rhythmic Genre in the Tunisian Nūba: A Performance Analysis', *Ethnomusicologica II: Quaderni dell'Accademia Chigiana XLV* (Proceedings of the VI European Seminar in Ethnomusicology, Siena, 1989; Siena: Accademia Musicale Chigiana, 1993), 71–109; See also Ruth Davis, 'Modern Trends in the Ma'lif of Tunisia, 1934–1984' (Ph.D. diss., Princeton University, 1986).

16/8 (3+3+4+2+4)

16/8 (3+3+2+3+3+2)

8/4 (2+2+2+2+2+2+2+2)

6/2 (4+4+2+2+2+2+2+2+4)

6/4 (2+2+2+2+2+2)

10/8 (2+3+2+3)

3/2 (4+3+3+2)

10/4 (4+2+4+4+2+4)

Ex. 7.2

Ex. 7.3

three different measurements of the 'neutral' interval. Many musicians, however, have declared the 'neutral' interval to be inherently unstable

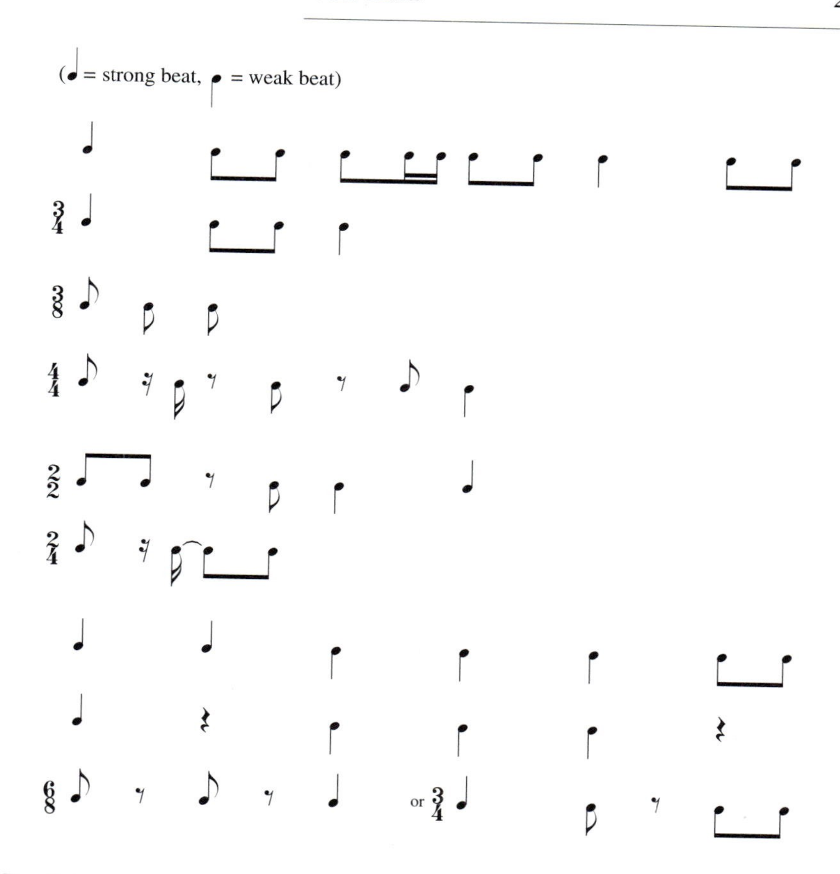

Ex. 7.4

and undefinable: and al-Mahdī's measurements, involving more complex notation, have not been recorded here.)

A feature common to all theoretical sources up to the nineteenth century—and that links Persian-Arabic and Indian philosophies of music—is the specification of multiple affiliations of modes and modal units to ethical and cosmological values. Detailed lists of correspondences involve such categories as the planets, signs of the zodiac, seasons, day and night, hours, elements, humours, temperaments, virtues, classes of people, colours, odours, raw materials, alphabetical letters, and poetry and poetic metres; and the performer was expected to select the appropriate mode for each circumstance.[38]

[38] Shiloah, 'The Arabic Concept of Mode', 38.

Discussion of musical timbre does not feature prominently in theoretical sources; classical theorists appear to have been interested in musical instruments more for their modal possibilities than for their actual sound. An important distinction was made between the lute, with stopped strings, and the zither, with unstopped strings. The most commonly used wind instrument was the *nāy* (end-blown flute), used singly or in pairs. The *zurna* (shawm) was used mainly in popular styles; its name is derived by false popular etymology, from the Persian *sur* (festivity) and *nāy* (pipe). A variety of percussion was in use, the commonest drums being frame drum, and the *naqqārā* (a pair of small kettledrums of unequal size). Islam was essentially a literary culture, and the injunctions against secular music did not encourage the development of purely instrumental forms of music.

No theoretical system has ever provided a wholly accurate description of West Asian modal practice, and there is still no complete list of *maqāmāt* as used in West Asia and North Africa. Classical theorists were mathematicians, astronomers, and philosophers, as much as musicians, and it is unlikely that any major attempt was made to align practice with theory.[39] The most thorough attempt at classification was made in 1932, at the Cairo Congress on Arab Music. Seventeen different tetrachordal and pentachordal units were codified.[40] *Maqāmāt* were classified: by their intervallic structure; by their opening notes and tonics; by their sequences of different units; and by hierarchies of pitches and melodic patterns. The rhythmic cycles were determined by the sequence and length of the beats, and by qualitative differentiation between beats ('strong', 'weak', and various shades between). (See also pp. 204–5.)

An analysis of contemporary Persian performing practice by Hormoz Farhat suggests that the use of non-diatonic intervals, though conforming approximately to medieval theory, is in fact very flexible. It further suggests that the octave is *not* a governing factor of a mode, and that the basic elements of most modes can be expressed within the limits of a tetrachord or pentachord.[41] Indeed, the very notion of a mode as a scale is found to be alien to Persian music: there is no word for it in Persian musical terminology, and most performers would not understand the

[39] Hormoz Farhat, 'Scales and Intervals: Theory and Practice', in Gerard Gillen and Harry White (eds.), *Irish Musical Studies* (Dublin: Irish Academic Press, 1990).

[40] Wright, 'Arab Music', *The New Grove*, i. 521–3.

[41] Hormoz Farhat, 'Iran', *The New Grove* (1980), ix. 295.

concept.[42] This is also true of Arabic music. Modes were delineated essentially in order to describe current practice in theoretical terms. In no music of the world—apart from that of the modern West—have the quarter-tone or microtone been used as separate intervals; they have been used only as increments for raising or lowering larger intervals and thus forming intervals with their own independent identity.[43]

The 'Western' and 'Eastern' Suite Repertoires

The principal form to emerge from Arabic *maqām* theory was the suite or song cycle (see n. 1 for terminology), based on a particular mode, and consisting of a sequence of pieces in contrasting rhythmic metres. The word *nawba*, used in Syria, Tunisia, and Algeria to denote 'suite', literally means 'turn': it may have derived from a court tradition of having a fixed order for the appearance of various performers, or for various instrumental and vocal genres.[44] A suite is usually named after the particular mode to which its repertoire belongs.

Common to all suite-repertoires is the concept that the performance begins with an improvisatory movement, the purpose of which is to establish both the pitch hierarchy, and the principal melodic features of the mode on which the suite is based. In this introduction, the performer gives prominence to important notes by means of ornamentation and vibrato; it usually begins unaccompanied, but part of it may be performed over a slow rhythmic pattern. Because it is the mode that defines the mood of a particular suite performance, with its fixed order of pieces and rhythmic cycles, this expository introduction is, for the musicians, the most important aspect of the performance.

The structure of the movements of a suite varies from style to style, but the tendency is for the more complex pieces to be performed near the beginning, and for the lighter pieces to be performed towards the end. The various movements of a suite may comprise some thirty different pieces, and the *nawba* itself may last for several hours. For modern performances, the suite is usually shortened to around four of five pieces, though these are usually performed in the traditionally

[42] Ibid., and Hormoz Farhat, *The Dastgāh Concept in Persian Music* (Cambridge: Cambridge University Press, 1990), 16.

[43] Farhat, 'Scales and Intervals'.

[44] Wright, 'Arab Music', *The New Grove*, i. 520.

prescribed order, and with an introductory exposition of the unifying mode.

The various pieces that comprise the suite differ in their rhythmic-metric organization. The distinctive character of the suite lies in the contrast it embodies between unity of mode, or melody type, and diversity of metric-rhythmic elements.[45]

Two main aspects distinguish the western (Andalusian) from the eastern styles of suite. The first is that the western suite may be performed with or without melody instruments, and may therefore be performed without instrumental pieces; in Sufi contexts, the movements of a *nawba* may be entirely vocal, using only percussion instruments for accompaniment.

The second is that, whereas in the eastern areas the suite constituted the classical genre of an élite and was performed chiefly by solo virtuosi, in the Maghreb the suite represented, fundamentally, a popular tradition. (This tradition came from medieval Spain, where the suite songs spread from the courts to become a more popular music, using strophic verses from court, *and* popular poetry.[46]) In North Africa, until the advent of modern state patronage, the chief patrons and exponents of classical music were the Sufi brotherhoods: these had become classless, communal organizations, where orthodox Islamic taboos against musical activity were waived. Outside the Sufi lodges, suites were performed by professional musicians in coffee houses, and at family ceremonies, such as weddings and circumcision ceremonies.[47]

Andalusian music is said to have developed after the appointment of the famous Baghdadian musician, Ziryāb, to the court of Cordobá in the ninth century. Ziryāb developed a system of twenty-four modes—one for each hour of the day—each with special cosmological associations according to the symbolic, modal system: *shajara al-tubū* (tree of temperaments).[48] Two centuries after Ziryāb's death, two new genres of poetry, the *muwashshah* (in stanzaic form) and the *zajal* (a colloquial genre with free treatment of metre and form) were set to music, in

[45] Ruth Davis, 'Modern Trends in the Arab-Andalusian Music of Tunisia', *Maghreb Review*, 11/2 (1986), 134–44. See also 'Cultural Policy and the Tunisian *ma'lif*: Redefining a Tradition', *Ethnomusicology*, 41/1 (1997).

[46] Wright, 'Arab Music', *The New Grove*, i. 524.

[47] Davis, 'Melodic and Rhythmic Genre in the Tunisian *Nūba*'.

[48] Sleeve note to *Andalusische Musik aus Marokko*, recorded on EMI, Harmonia Mundi label, IC 2LP 153, performed by the Moroccan Ensemble from Fez, directed by Hagg Abdelkarim Rais.

22. Moroccan musicians performing on violin and long-necked lute

accord with Ziryāb's theories, and formed the basis of the Andalusian suite repertoire.[49]

It was the popular nature of Andalusian music that caused *nawbāt* ensembles to be classified as either 'loud' or 'quiet', according to their outdoor or indoor use (see p. 186). Instruments now commonly found in the Andalusian 'quiet' *nawbāt* usually include the *rabāb* (the 'poet's fiddle', with two strings stretched over a square or trapezoidal, wooden-framed, body, covered front and back with skin), European violin (held upright on the thigh in the viol position) (Pl. 22), *ūd 'arbī* (fretless Maghrebian short-necked lute), and *darabukka* (goblet-shaped drum).

The Andalusian tradition is slightly different in Morocco, Algeria, and Tunisia; divergences exist in terminology, theory, modal practice, and repertoire.

The Moroccan repertoire is known collectively as *al-āla* ('instrumental music'). Its suites—of which less than twelve are still remembered—consist of songs, each divided into five large sections, and based on a different rhythmic mode. Instrumentalists play heterophonically, and often perform the choral part.

The Algerian repertoire is known collectively as *al-san'a* ('work of art'). Its *nawbāt*—of which, again, less than twelve are still

[49] Philip D. Schuyler, 'Moroccan Andalusian Music', *World of Music*, 20 (1978), 33–4.

remembered—consist of nine movements, of which the first is a short instrumental or vocal exposition of the mode, in free rhythm, and the second is an instrumental prelude, performed heterophonically by the entire orchestra.[50]

The Tunisian repertoire is known as the *ma'lūf* ('custom') and is classified by mode into thirteen *nawbāt*, each consisting of a common stock of vocal and instrumental genres, characterized by particular rhythmic metres.[51] Normally, the *nawba* opens with an instrumental prelude played by the entire orchestra, followed by an instrumental overture in triple metre. The main item of the ensuing, predominantly vocal, section is the *qasīda*, a classical poem, typically containing romantic descriptions of love, wine, and nature.[52]

The eastern suite (used principally in Egypt and Syria) usually consists of eight extended movements, the first of which, *taksīm*, is the customary improvised solo, exploring the mode of the *nawba*. (The *taksīm* may occur elsewhere in the suite, in which case it is used for virtuoso display.) The second movement is the *bashraf*, consisting of four or five sections, each containing the same number of rhythmic cycles. The third movement includes four or five sections with asymmetrical rhythmic cycles, all but the last being in quintuple metre. The fourth movement comprises a group of composed songs on strophic poems of Andalusian origin. The fifth, which concludes the classical section of the *nawba*, is a *qasīda*, again the centrepiece of the performance; it is usually accompanied by *ūd*. The three movements that follow are in lighter vein: an instrumental piece in which improvised solo sections alternate with a ritornello; an extended movement for chorus and orchestra based on popular (mainly Egyptian) poetry; and a series of short strophic poems in fast rhythmic modes.

The traditional instruments of the 'eastern' *nawba* are *ūd*, *qānūn* (plucked box zither), European violin, *nāy* (end-blown flute), and *darabukka* (goblet-shaped, single-headed drum). Performances of the 'eastern' *nawba* today usually consist of individual movements or sections, mixed with other more recently composed pieces. The new pieces are often based on Western tunings, and their melodic figuration is apt to suggest underlays of triadic harmony. Strict adherence to traditional principles of *nawba* construction is becoming increasingly rare.

[50] Josef Pacholczyk, 'Arab Music', *The New Grove* (1980), i. 525.

[51] Ruth Davis, 'Links between the Baron Rodolphe D'Erlanger and the Notation of Tunisian Art Music', in *Ethnomusicology and the Historical Dimension* (Philipp Verlag, 1989).

[52] Davis, 'Melodic and Rhythmic Genre in the Tunisian *Nūba*'.

The Classical Style of Persia

As has already been emphasized, Islamic art music was essentially a synthesis of Greek and Persian traditions. If its theorizing derived from Hellenic Alexandria, its musical practice was based on that of Persia. Persians were among the foremost musicians and scholars of the Abbāsid dynasty; and, although Persians adopted the 'eastern' style of classical music, their history and sense of native tradition caused it to develop in distinctive ways.

The first written evidence of Persian music is from the Sassanian period (226–643). Chosroes II was a great patron of music, and his most famous court musician, Bārbod, was said to have developed a musical system with seven modal structures (known as the Royal Modes), thirty derivative modes, and 360 melodies. Following the Arab conquest, Persian musicians were employed throughout the Islamic empire.[53]

Many Persian instruments had their origins in ancient Mesopotamia. And many of the instruments of medieval Europe, such as the shawm, dulcimer, psaltery, and lute, are of Persian origin. The Indian *sitār* was modelled on the Persian lute, and the pot drum and the dulcimer first entered India from Persia. Persian instruments travelled to China along the Silk Road. The instruments now most commonly used in modern Iran are the *setār* and *tār* (long-necked lutes), *santur* (dulcimer), *kamānche* (spike fiddle with four strings), *nāy* (end-blown flute), and *tombak* (vase-shaped pot drum played with the fingers). The *ūd* (short-necked lute) and *qānūn* (plucked box zither) are less used in modern practice (Pl. 23). In recent years, Western instruments such as the violin have tended to replace their Persian counterparts.[54]

With the rise of the Safavid dynasty at the end of the fifteenth century, and the consequent ascendance of Shi'ism, music in Persia declined. The court still patronized musicians, but their art became subject to the precepts of Shi'ite clerics, who viewed it with suspicion. Musical performance became the province of 'labourers of pleasure': illiterate entertainers. The brilliance of the Persian tradition passed to India, where the ruling Moghuls were Turco-Mongols imbued with Persian courtly culture.[55]

[53] Farhat, *The Dastgāh Concept*, 3.

[54] Farhat, 'Iran', *The New Grove*, ix. 297–9.

[55] Ella Zonis, *Classical Persian Music* (Cambridge, Mass.: Harvard University Press, 1973).

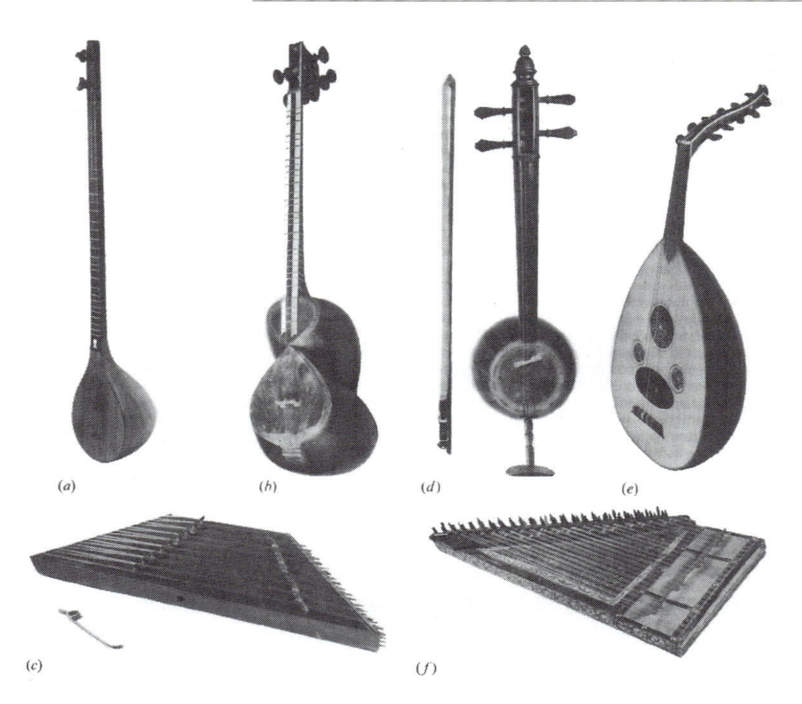

23. Iranian string instruments: (*a*) *setār* (long-necked lute), (*b*) *tār* (long-necked lute), (*c*) *santur* (dulcimer), (*d*) *kamancha* (spike fiddle), (*e*) *ūd* (short-necked lute), (*f*) *qānūn* (box zither)

During the nineteenth century—probably due to the increasing inability of Persian musicians to perform large-scale, improvised structures—what was remembered of the Persian tradition, a repertoire of some 300–400 pieces (known as the *radif*: 'row' or 'series'), was organized into twelve suites *dastgāh-hā* ('organization').

Dastgāh-hā define melodic types. Particular melodic motifs (*gusheh-hā*: modes, in the sense of melody type (see p. 136)) derive from a particular *dastgah* and provide the generic material for a composition; although in essence they are usually confined to a tetrachord, they have developed into melodic types, with a clear final (*ist*: 'stop'), and reciting tone (*shāhed*: 'witness'). Some *gusheh-hā* have descriptive titles associated with the town, village, or society from which they are said to have originated. Because the *gusheh* is used as a framework for improvisation, its form and content differ from player to player, and no one version is universally accepted. An introductory *darāmad* (equivalent to the Arabic *taksīm*) uses the principal *gusheh*, and thereby explores and establishes the mode of the *dastgāh*.[56] Subsequent movements may modulate to different modes, but usually—and invariably in the last piece—they finish with a common cadential formula that re-establishes the basic mode. During the late nineteenth and early twentieth centuries, new Western-influenced compositions, with fixed melodic and rhythmic contours, were added to the traditional repertoire of the *dastgāh-hā*.

Persian vocal quality is distinctive and includes the *tahrir*, a kind of yodelling effect in which individual or repeated notes are articulated, using high falsetto or head-voice breaks: this is a difficult art, now in decline, though sometimes re-created in the modern, light-classical genre, *tasnif* (see p. 632).[57] Another feature of Persian performance style is the use of a strict form of heterophony, in which an instrumentalist 'shadows' the vocalist by imitating the contour of the melody a little behind it, at times repeating a phrase, during a vocal pause. (This practice is used in Iraq, and in some Indian, South East Asian, and Japanese musics.)

The Classical Style of Turkey

By the time the Seljuk Turks established themselves in West Asia, the basic structures of Islamic art music were already in place. Although, from the early fifteenth century onwards, the Anatolian Turks contributed to the theory of art music and played a leading part in the musical life of the Ottoman Empire, they were relative newcomers to a wide zone of cultural influence in which Arabic remained the lingua franca.

The texts on which Islamic art music is based are determined by the prosodic rules of Arabic and Persian verse; these determine standard patterns of long (open) and short (closed) syllables. The Turkish language is agglutinative: it adds syllables to a stem, without change in the stem, to express ideas of declension and conjugation. Unlike Persian and Arabic, it does not have quantity: vowel sounds, and syllables, are not measured as long and short. Accordingly, Arabic-Persian rules of prosody were not entirely suited to Turkish; and in classical song the placing of syllables in their musical framework may strike the foreigner

[56] Ibid. 45–52.

[57] Farhat, 'Iran', *The New Grove*, ix. 298; Peter Manuel, *Popular Musics of the Non-Western World* (New York: Oxford University Press, 1989), 169, 259.

as semantically inappropriate. The most common vocal form is the *sharkī*—a term referring to urban art song, to distinguish it from *türkü* (folk-song)—in a variety of metric structures.

Turkish modes (*makamlar*) theoretically distinguish major and minor seconds and a division of the octave into twenty-four parts;[58] moreover, individual degrees of certain *makamlar* can be varied by a single comma, or two or more commas, and the bridges on *kānūns* (plucked box zithers)—sometimes six to a string—reflect this. In practice, however, bridges are usually altered only in modulation between modes. In the *makam Rast* (for instance) the degree of flattening of the mediant is still not rigidly standardized, and the setting of movable bridges is correspondingly variable.[59] Turkish *makamlar* sound closer in their degree of standardization to Western diatonic modes than do Arab *maqāmāt* or Persian *gusheh-hā*. Of approximately 100 *makamlar* that came to be used regularly in Turkish classical music, thirteen were regarded as *basit* ('simple' or 'basic'); of these, seven correspond roughly—in their intervallic structure, though not in the sequence of their tonics, nor in their dominants—with Western modes; another six are gapped sets with conspicuous augmented seconds. This last feature may be reflected in the standard harmonic minor scales of the West.[60] Melodic constructions are performed in conjunction with rhythmic cycles (*usul*) as short as 'measures', or extended to form longer, through-composed, rhythmic structures. In Turkey, a system of musical notation was developed, using alphabetical symbols for notes, and numbers for durations; and this enabled much court chamber music and music for the Janissary band to be preserved, from the seventeenth century onwards.

During the Ottoman Empire, secular art music came to influence Sufi monastic music, and the monasteries themselves became centres of musical innovation. The most important Sufi sect, in this regard, was the Mevlevi—commonly known as the Mevlevi Order of Whirling Dervishes—founded in Konya in the thirteenth century. This is where classical music in Turkey is held to have started: the Mevlevi order itself has been referred to as the 'Music School of the Ottoman

[58] Kurt Reinhard, 'Turkey', *The New Grove* (1980), xix. 275.

[59] In practice, a singer may flatten the mediant in *Rast* by fewer commas than the *kānūn*; Laurence Picken reports having been present (during the 1960s) at a session at *Radyoevi Istanbul* when the sound engineer, Professor Halil Bedi Yönetken of the Istanbul Konservatuari, confirmed this.

[60] Unpublished comment from Laurence Picken.

Dynasty'. Similar communities spread throughout the empire. In Anatolia, in particular, the instrumentarium was enlarged; and rituals involving complex sequences of music were composed to mystical poems. *Na't* singers introduced the proceedings, during which turning dancers moved in concentric circles.[61] Sufi philosophy also found expression in performances of shadow-puppet theatre, first mentioned in Turkey during the seventeenth century, and popular throughout the eighteenth and nineteenth centuries.[62]

Performances at the sultan's court were given by professional singers and relatively large instrumental groups. The music was transmitted orally, and its form and overall melodic shape were clearly prescribed. Groups performed in heterophony, the individual lines correlated through motivic repetition and sequence and coming together at points of melodic emphasis. The instruments used in Turkish classical music include the *ūd* (short-necked lute), *tanbur* (a special Turkish form of long-necked lute with up to forty-six gut frets), *rabāb* (spike fiddle), plucked and struck trapezoidal zithers, and small pairs of kettledrums.[63]

As early as the sixteenth century, the Turkish court received French musicians as guests, resulting in new forms such as the *frencin* in 12/4 time. During the eighteenth century, an attempt was made to reinvigorate court music through Turkish folk influence; but the appointment (in 1828) of Giuseppi Donizetti, brother of the celebrated opera composer, as director of the court music pointed Turkey in the direction of Europe. Donizetti formed a symphony orchestra, and Western influences came to bear on traditional music.

The Classical Style of Central Asia

In Central Asia a synthesis of courtly music styles began to emerge as early as the eleventh century; by the early fifteenth century it flourished, at a peak of excellence, at the court of Samarkand, in what is now Uzbekistan. That Samarkand was a meeting-point for musical styles across the breadth of Asia is attested by the historian, Hafez-i Abou, describing a pageant during the reign of Sharukh (1405–47): 'Golden-tongued singers and sweet-sounding

[61] Neubauer, 'Islamic Religious Music', *The New Grove*, ix. 343–4.

[62] Eugenia Popescu-Judetz, *Studies in Oriental Arts* (Pittsburgh: Duquesne University Tamburitzans, 1981), 2–10.

[63] Reinhard, 'Turkey', *The New Grove*, xix. 273.

musicians played and sang to motifs in Persian style, to Arab melodies according to Turkish practice, and with Mongol voices following Chinese laws of singing and Altai metres.'[64]

For centuries, the Silk Road across Central Asia had been a transit channel of Asian musical styles. From Chinese sources we know that, from the Han dynasty (second century BC to second century AD), music was carried by the commerce that flowed, east and west, along the Silk Road. Sculpted reliefs indicate that, as early as the third century BC, angled harps, akin to those of ancient Mesopotamia, were used in Central Asia; and that by the fourth century AD there were various types of lutes.[65] A sculpted ceramic camel from a Tang dynasty tomb (seventh to ninth centuries AD)—now in the Shanxi Provincial Museum—has on its back a dancing figure and a musical band consisting of harp, zither, pan pipes, and reed pipes. From the second to tenth centuries, caravans passed through the oasis kingdoms of Kucha, Khotan, and Turfan (now in Xinjiang Province, China) and Samarkand and Bukhara (now in Uzbekistan). The importance of Central Asia to China's musical culture is manifest in the Tang dynasty, by the naming of five of their 'Ten Types of Music' (*c*.640) after these kingdoms (see p. 346).

Islamic court-music style is to be found as far east as Xinjiang, where distinctive traditions developed in Kashgar, Kucha, Illi, Qumul, and elsewhere. The Uighurs of Xinjiang were heirs to the oasis culture of the Tang; they developed a repertoire of twelve large suites (*oniki mukam*) which form a corpus of over seventy instrumental pieces and 170 songs (in the Uighur language), related in style to the court music of Transoxiana (present-day Uzbekistan and northern Tajikistan). The suites finish with a movement in fast tempo, which is often danced; the Uighurs are Turkic-speaking, and it is possible that this practice was originally connected with the mystical practices of Sufism.[66]

The cultural systems of ancient Transoxiana were associated with those of Persia until around AD 500, when the first Turkic incursions heralded a millennium of Turco-Persian intermingling. Uzbeks intruded on the area around 1500, since when the Turkic-speaking Uzbeks, and Persian-speaking Tajiks, have formed a common culture

[64] Cited in Mark Slobin, 'Union of Soviet Socialist Republics', *The New Grove* (1980), xix. 413–14.

[65] Ibid. 418–20.

[66] Laurent Aubert, sleeve note to *Musique sur Les Routes de la Soie*, Auvidis, B 6776.

in the region. (This common culture was divided by an artificial border, following the 1917 Russian Revolution.)

The courtly repertoire of Uzbekistan and northern Tajikistan is known as the *Shashmaqom* ('six *maqom*'); five of the mode names are also names of Persian modes. The *Shashmaqom* are suites of some twenty or thirty vocal or instrumental movements, following a precise sequence of rhythmic modes. The opening piece (*sar-akhbār*: 'beginning of the story') introduces the mode in improvisatory style, sometimes over a slow rhythmic cycle.[67] Subsequent movements are set to different rhythmic cycles, in symmetrical or asymmetrical patterns; and the song-texts are taken from the great lyrical and mystical poets who wrote in Tajik, Eastern Turkish, or a mixture of both. The complex metrics of classical verse may lead to rhythmic cycles of, for example, 15 beats (4+4+4+3); 14 beats (7+7); 20 beats (5+5+5+5); 10 beats (5+5); and 13 beats (5+5+3).[68] Most of the singers and performers of the classical *maqāmāt* are bilingual and perform texts in a mixture of Tajik and Uzbek.

Outside Bukhara, other important centres, such as Khojent, Samarkand, Kokand, and Tashkent, produced classical compositions in similar style, but they were in shorter suites of three or four movements, with less complex modal structures.

Many Tajik and Uzbek musicians still use only the traditional classical instruments. These include: a variety of long-necked lutes with two to five metal or nylon strings, such as the *tanbūr* (called *satār* when played with a bow), and the *dombrak*, a small popular lute with two nylon strings; the *gijak* (a three-stringed fiddle with a metallic body); the *doira* (frame drum), and *tablak* (goblet-shaped drum).[69] The musicians play with ornamentations that have probably characterized the playing of plucked lutes and zithers across Asia since ancient times.

Turkic Peoples as Musical Catalysts

Long before cities such as Bukhara and Samarkand became great centres of Islamic culture, folk styles from western Central Asia were introduced by Turkic peoples into West Asia and

[67] Ibid.

[68] Slobin, 'Union of Soviet Socialist Republics', *The New Grove*, xix. 420.

[69] Jean During, programme note for the Nava Tajik Ensemble, Hong Kong Asian Arts Festival, 1992.

Europe. Centuries of interaction led to broad affinities between folk styles of western Central Asia: the Turkish folk style, in particular, was common to Kazakhs, Kirghis, Turkmen, and Uzbeks. As Turkic peoples moved towards the Bosphorus, they confronted Byzantium, and became heirs to it, as much as to Islam; it is to be remembered that, from the fifteenth century to the second half of the nineteenth century, the Balkans belonged to the Ottoman Empire.

Though the religion of most of the Balkan states remained Christian, the principal form of its Christianity was Orthodox: and the cultural traditions of the Balkans were those of Byzantium, of the East. During the nineteenth century, the attempt (in various areas of Europe) to adopt the character of the dominant Austro-German tradition spread no further south-east than Hungary; the area beyond remained culturally detached. Indeed, a century ago, Greece—the 'teacher of Europe'—was scarcely aware that Bach and Beethoven had ever existed.

The Turks appear to have brought to West Asia the 'limping' (*aksak*) rhythms and declamatory singing techniques of Central Asian folk styles. As Turkish is an agglutinative, polysyllabic, language in which quantity does not exist, verses are constructed on the basis of the numbers of syllables in each line. Verse-lines may consist of any number of syllables, from four to eleven; asymmetrical ('limping') rhythms are common.

In so-called 'long songs' (*uzun hava*)—mostly having eleven-syllable lines—texts are sung in free, declamatory style. Measured songs are known as 'broken songs' (*kīrīk hava*)—'broken' implying the 'shattering' of the large contours of 'long songs' in measured tunes. Dance tunes in irregular rhythms may give the effect of syncopation—but this is because the Western ear seeks completion of non-binary metres. A quaver added to the final beat of a 2/4, 3/4, or 4/4 rhythm creates a 'limping' rhythm of 5/8, 7/8, or 9/8, composed of 2+3, 2+2+3, or 2+2+2+3 units.[70]

Such 'limping' rhythms are found throughout the Balkans and as far north as Hungary. Asymmetrical rhythmic patterns are particularly prevalent in Bulgaria, where units of 5, 7, 8, 9, 10, 11, 12, 13, 14, 15, and 17 pulses are common.[71] Such asymmetrical patterns exist also in the rhythmic cycles of Arab-Persian, and Indian, classical music.

[70] Reinhard, 'Turkey', *The New Grove*, xix. 268–9, and Laurence Picken, *Folk Instruments of Turkey* (Oxford: Oxford University Press, 1975).

[71] Nikolai Kaufman, 'Bulgaria', *The New Grove* (1980), iii. 431.

Turkic traditional 'long songs' are performed in a *quasi*-improvisatory style, with high, syllabically reiterated initial notes, descending—at times by tetrachordal segments—to the final notes. These characteristics apply equally to traditional musics of the Balkans. (They also apply to some folk-songs of North India.) Compare, for example, the transcription of a folk-song from west-central Bulgaria (Ex. 7.5, after Kaufman),[72] with that of a lament from Turkey (Ex. 7.6, after Reinhard, in which the C♯ should be imagined slightly lower in pitch than it would be in equal temperament).[73]

Ex. 7.5

The West Asian Cultural Mix

It is not easy to separate the strands of West Asian music. Its musical styles are linked through ancient history, and through Islam, with the cultural systems of Egypt and North Africa, and with musical traffic along the Silk Road. The peoples of the 'cradle of civilization' came largely from the two main areas of nomad pastoralism: Afro-Asiatic speakers from the deserts to the south, and Indo-Iranian speakers from the deserts to the north. They were joined by Mediterranean-type peoples and, later, by Turkic-Altaic speaking peoples from the steppe. Sumerians, Hittites, Assyrians, Egyptians,

[72] Ibid. 434. [73] Reinhard, 'Turkey', *The New Grove*, xix. 268.

Ex. 7.6

Persians, Greeks, and Romans flexed their muscles in these lands, creating vast and competing empires before Arabs, and then Turks, established hegemonies. The Islamic religion was formed in the ambience of the worship of nature-gods, of Zoroastrianism, Judaism, Hinduism, Buddhism, and Christianity, and the heresies of Manichaenism and Arianism. As a polity, Islam brought the traditions of Arab and African, Persian and Indian, Greek and Roman, Turk and Slav into a great crucible of culture. Though that polity was not to prove durable, Islam—as a code of human behaviour—remains one of the most powerful religious forces in the world today.

So far as nationality has meaning in this context, three different populations with three different linguistic origins—Arabs, Persians, and Turks—placed their stamp on Islamic culture and its music. In but few places are these classical styles widely practised today: many have already succumbed to Western influence, or have been exchanged for Western styles. Yet for all the turmoil that beset the area during this present century, Qur'ānic chanting may be heard, in the great mosques of Iran and Egypt, as though the world had stood still since the eighth century. Islamic resistance to change was to prove both an asset and a liability.

The contradictions of civilization were born and nurtured in West Asia. The interdependence of power, wealth, art, and religion was established in these lands 4,000 years before ever a north European monarch set foot in the Holy Land. So were the chief tools of advanced civilization: writing, arithmetic, monumental architecture, and a legal code. Not even China can rival this ancient achievement. Whatever may be the future of this troubled region, its past influence on the civilizations of India, Europe, and Africa, and to some extent China and South East Asia as well, was decisive in the shaping of the world's cultural systems.

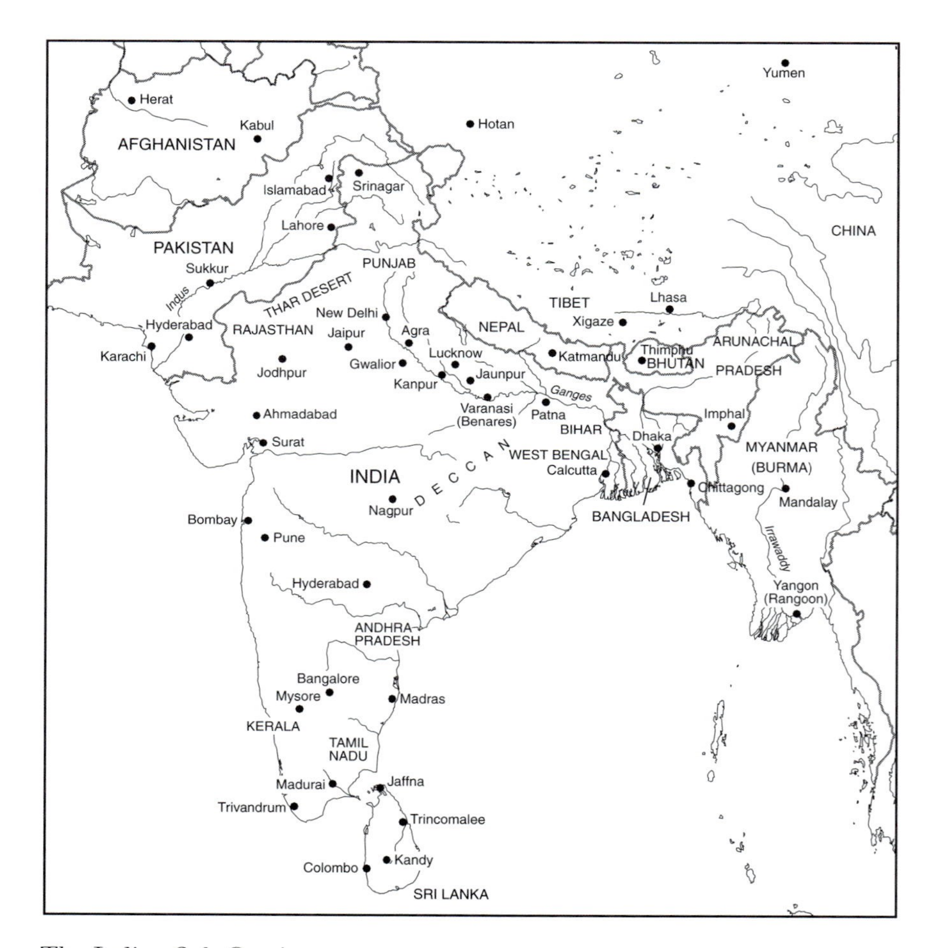

The Indian Sub-Continent

8 The Indian Subcontinent

Aspects of Hinduism and the *Rāga*-System

Of all the civilizations that evolved in the wake of the agrarian revolution, that of India has proved the most durable. Hinduism, the glue that bonded India's diversity of peoples and beliefs, had its origins in pre-Aryan times, and is still a major social force; indeed, in India today, ancient rituals are still to be observed accompanied by chant in the Sāmavedic tradition, dating back to the second millennium BC (see pp. 102–3). Ageing men may still forsake family and worldly goods to become *sādhus*: eternal wanderers, in search of the spiritual, who carry but a bowl, a staff, and a blanket. Cows are still venerated to the extent that they have right of way on major roads. Highly intelligent medical men may deny all the science they ever learned to drink the muddy waters of the sacred Ganges and so purify their souls. Today, throughout the world, and in capital cities, exquisite performances of music and dance take place, aspects of which were first described in the *Nātyashāstra*, a treatise on drama compiled during the first half of the first millennium AD.

India's respect for the authority of tradition is exemplified in the attempt of its thinkers to relate new ideas in religion, and in the arts, to the philosophies of ancient texts. Central to Hindu philosophy is the belief that all forms of creation must eventually merge with *Brāhman*, the indivisible Supreme Being (see p. 97). Music, therefore, as an act of creation, cannot be absolute, for nothing phenomenal can ever be absolute; all forms are regarded as one with the world process of continuous creation and dissolution.

The basis of present-day Indian music is a melodic vocal or instrumental line, governed by a complex system of modes (*rāgas*) and time cycles (*tālas*). The melodic line is usually accompanied by drumming, and always performed over a drone (though the drone is thought to have become a permanent feature of Indian music only in the sixteenth century).[1] An instrument sometimes 'shadows' the principal melodic line; at other times a melodic instrument is used to delineate the time cycle, while the drummer performs complex variations on it.

Not all these features relate to ancient practice, as described in the various treatises. Importantly, in the *Nātyashāstra* (*c.*AD 500, attributed to the sage, Bharata)—the first major treatise to furnish information on musical instruments and playing techniques, scales, tunings, and modal patterns, and on music as it related to drama—no mention was made of the *rāga*-system. The first major description of the concept and structure of *rāga* occurred only in the latter centuries of the first millennium AD, in the *Brihaddeshī*, a treatise on music attributed to Matanga.[2] The distinguishing feature of this *rāga*-system is that a complete, single set of characteristics is prescribed for every mode; indeed it is this that marks the *rāga*-system as a 'classical' tradition, separate from other forms of Indian music.

Matanga's principal concern—like that of most musical theorists who succeeded him—was to reconcile current practice with pre-existing theory. The *rāga*-system had emerged during the middle of the first millennium, apparently in the Aryan heartland of the Ganges Valley, and was initially based on seven basic modal units (called *grāmarāgas*). The system had subsequently expanded to incorporate new *rāgas*, named after peoples living away from this central heartland, and structured on different principles. In the *Brihaddeshī*, Matanga attempted to codify and elaborate such *deshī* ('regional') music so as to conform with *mārga*—the central, *rāga*-based, classical tradition.[3]

Another major work of musical synthesis—Shārngadeva's *Sangītaratnākara* ('Mine of Musical Jewels')—appeared during the thirteenth century, a time when Islamic music was profoundly affecting Indian

[1] B. C. Deva, *Psychoacoustics of Music and Speech* (Madras Music Academy, 1967), 58–86; but the disappearance of harps, during the latter centuries of the first millennium AD, and the prevalence of one-string stick zithers and one-string lutes, suggests that the drone featured in both *deshī-* and *mārga*-music, from early times.

[2] D. R. Widdess, 'Indian Music', *NOCM* (1983). The *Brihaddeshī*, though attributed to Matanga, is a composite work, using various sources, and its date is hard to establish; *c.*AD 800 is a date commonly suggested.

[3] D. K. Widdess, 'The Geography of Rāga', *World of Music*, 35/3 (1993), 35–47. *Mārga* (literally a 'path') implied a set of actions and beliefs leading not only to a universal music but also to liberation from the perpetual cycle of existence (*moksha*).

musical forms. In this important treatise, Shārngadeva summarized the work of many former theorists in the light of innovations in the *rāga*-system then taking place, and, in doing so, he established basic principles of Hindustani classical music for succeeding generations.

The basic meaning of the Sanskrit word *rāga* is 'passion', or 'feeling'. The use of this word to describe a modal system contrasts with the Arabic use of *maqām* ('place'), and the Persian, *dastgāh* ('system'), musically as much as linguistically. The *rāgas* of Indian music are not just theoretical, musical constructs; they are entities with personalities of their own. Their principal purpose is to induce aesthetic delight, according to specific combinations of notes and melodic features. Individual *rāgas* have, at various times, been associated with a particular sentiment (*rasa* (see pp. 103–4)), with a presiding deity, a particular religious festival, a particular role in dramatic music, or with a season, or hour of the day; but, although such associations inspire the performers, they do not define the *process* of performance. Indian music involves a carefully controlled mixture of composition and improvisation that demands musical inspiration on the part of the performer for its effective realization. In Hindu belief, there is no ultimate separation between an act of creation and its creator: creation is seen not as a single event but as a continual process.[4]

For more than two millennia, theorists have described Indian music, both in practical and philosophical terms; they have offered the performer the widest possible set of possibilities, and the performer, in turn, has selected those regarded as most pleasing at a given point in time. Indians have achieved a profusion of forms through an adaptable musical system that aims at inclusion, rather than exclusion. As will be shown later, flexibility lies at the heart of the *rāga*-system.

India's Social Systems

Another link between ancient philosophy and current practice is to be observed in India's social structure, which has been a resilient phenomenon among Hindus; the four classes of the *varna*, described in the *Vedas* (see pp. 95–6), are still considered by many to be eternal. It is, however, the *jātis* (small social groups), as distinct

[4] Lewis Rowell, *Music and Musical Thought in Early India* (Chicago: University of Chicago Press, 1992), 235, 330.

from the four classes, that came to pervade village life. In this context, the so-called caste-system is not so much a system of groups given in nature, as a society of self-monitoring units. (The word 'caste', from the Latin *castus*, meaning 'pure', was introduced by the Portuguese during the sixteenth century.) It appears that the *jāti*-system, in something resembling its modern form, developed only in the thirteenth and fourteenth centuries, and as a *response* to the collapse of Hindu kingship.[5]

Individual groups within the *jāti*-system came to operate both in opposition and in solidarity, to and with each other. Opposition was primarily based on concepts of purity and pollution (still considered important in traditional Indian society), to the extent that elimination of pollution became a task for specialists. Because purification was seen as imitation of the purity of the *brāhman*—and as a necessary antidote to the spread of pollution—rules of purity were applied to the human body (in such matters as food, clothing, cleanliness, and secretions), to the family (in regard to interfamily relationships and marriage customs), and to objects (such as cooking utensils and materials used for building). The degree of purity and permanent pollution attached to the occupations of particular social units came to determine social hierarchies within the four Vedic classes.[6]

Solidarity, on the other hand, was a function of interdependence, arising from the reciprocal relations of patronage. Village families patronized not only the domestic priest but all other specialists in their village; and the intrinsically religious nature of such patronage is still demonstrated when exchange of services and gifts are combined with family rites, festivals, and marriages. A myriad subtleties of status and hierarchy came to exist within the four-class *varna* system. Where 'caste' came to be defined largely by occupation, reflecting at all times the superior ritual status of *brāhman* over other classes, sub-caste came to be defined largely by territory, or locality, with status determined by temporal authority.[7]

India's caste-system proved an enabling factor in its long history of cultural assimilation. It provided each population group with a trade and a social milieu; and, as it expanded, it permitted new groups to emerge. The caste-system as a whole enabled India's extraordinary diversity of peoples, with their widely differing languages and cultural

[5] Robert Inden, *Imagining India* (Oxford: Blackwell, 1990), 82, 219.

[6] Richard Lannoy, *The Speaking Tree: A Study of Indian Culture and Society* (Oxford: Oxford University Press, 1971), 145–56.

[7] Ibid. 163.

systems, to coexist in individual, socially cohesive groups. It permitted a surprising unity of culture, still evident today, even though fifteen major languages and hundreds of regional dialects are spoken, and there are still literally thousands of *jāti*.

Awareness of group identity, and of group interdependence, encouraged tolerance; the emphasis in the system was always on inclusion rather than exclusion. The system encouraged interaction between Hindus and Muslims, and it facilitated the transmission of music and dance traditions through the centuries. Ironically, it encouraged the very flexibility that has largely eliminated barriers of 'caste' and religion in present-day Indian musical life. The notion of *sangam*—of confluence, merging, and meeting—is very strong in Indian culture.

These positive features notwithstanding, the 'caste'-system insitutionalized injustice, and led to corruption and nepotism. Its importance is now fading, particularly in urban areas; but it was a major factor in enabling India to accommodate diverse, and often contradictory, cultural influences.

Geography

The strength and continuity of Indian culture arose partly from the geographical isolation of a subcontinent that incorporates what is now India, the island state of Sri Lanka, Pakistan, Bangladesh, Bhutan, Nepal, and parts of Afghanistan.

In North India, the most populous areas have always been the river valleys of the Indus and Ganges river systems, to west and east respectively. (The Indus Valley area is now in Pakistan.) The Ganges Valley, from Delhi to the delta area (which now incorporates part of Bangladesh), is one of the most heavily populated areas in the world. Between these two river systems lies the Thār, the Great Indian desert. Further north, Delhi is centred on the Indo-Gangetic plain.

This northern area is separated from peninsular India by the high Vindhya mountain range. The geographical heart of the peninsula is the rocky plateau of the Deccan (from Sanskrit *dakshina*: 'south'), but the cultural heart is the southern tip of the peninsula that incorporates Tamil Nadu, Kerala, Karnataka, and Andhra Pradesh. Dravidian languages are still dominant in the peninsula.

South-east of the peninsula, Sri Lanka, source of *Theravāda* Buddhism (and home of Ravana, the demon king featured in the

Rāmāyana), is populated by Sinhalese (the majority group, probably originating from the area north of the Bay of Bengal), Tamils, Muslims, and some Eurasians. Its musical culture belongs largely to the North Indian sphere of influence (though performance of traditional genres tends now to be heavily Westernized); but it harbours distinctive traditions in folk theatre and in drumming associated with the prominent Buddhist temples of Kandy.

A third distinct area comprises the provinces in the arc of mountains that separates the subcontinent from West, Central, and South East Asia. It includes the provinces of Jammu and Kashmir, Himachal Pradesh, Arunachal Pradesh, and what are now the separate countries of Bhutan and Nepal, together with parts of Pakistan and Afghanistan. This area provides a cultural bridge to Central and East Asia.[8]

Bounded by sea and mountain (and to the north-east by jungle swamp), the subcontinent as a whole could be assailed, by land, only from the three north-western passes that now separate Pakistan from Afghanistan: Khyber, Gomal, and Bolan.

Early Empires in the North

The most famous early assailant was Alexander the Great. In 332 BC, at Taxila in Gandhāra (now in Pakistan), an Indian army went down before the Greeks. In this encounter, the cultural systems of East and West were first brought into close contact; and it was in imitation of Western sculptural techniques that the Buddha was given human form. The Greek raid had no immediate military consequence, however; and, following the political vacuum left by the departing Greeks, Chandragupta Maurya established the Mauryan empire from coast to coast; his grandson, Ashoka the Great (reigned 269–232 BC), extended it over the greater part of the peninsula. Ashoka converted to Buddhism and, for some four peaceful decades, promulgated the religion far and wide.[9] The Mauryan is still regarded as the great age of India; no succeeding empire has held such sway.

The Mauryan empire did not long survive Ashoka. During the second century BC, warrior nomads from Central Asia entered the Punjab, and created an empire that reached from Benares on the Ganges to Khotan beyond the Karakoram. For a while this Kushan empire threatened Han

[8] Harold Powers, 'India', *The New Grove* (1980), ix. 69.

[9] Francis Watson, *A Concise History of India* (London: Thames & Hudson, 1974), 50.

24. A relief from Pawaya in North India (*c.*third century) showing court musicians accompanying a dancer: (from left to right) lute, flute (damaged), drums, cymbals, single drum, and arched harp

China; indeed, its greatest king, Kanishka, styled himself 'Son of Heaven'.

This was a time of great cosmopolitan influence on India. As Hellenistic kingdoms gave way before Roman might, ancient trade links were revitalized, bringing prosperity to India's west-coast cities. To the north, Gandhāra became a centre for the gathering and purveying of ideas. King Kanishka was a Buddhist, and it was from Gandhāra that the popular *Mahāyāna* form of Buddhism, incorporating a pantheon of deities from many lands, spread through Siberia into China (see p. 106). (Its doctrine had been formulated under Kanishka's patronage in Kashmir.[10]) The anthropomorphic form of the Buddha image that accompanied it was a synthesis of styles absorbed from the Mediterranean world, infused with the spirit of India.

The Kushan capital of Mathura was sacked in the third century by Sassanid Persians. India then lacked unified control until a native dynasty, the Guptas, building on the cosmopolitan inheritance of the Kushans, seized power in 320, unified the major part of the country, and instituted what is often called India's 'classical age'. It lasted from 320 to 540, though its influence long outlived it.

The Gupta period marked the start of the great period of temple-building and carving in stone, creating institutions that in medieval

[10] Ibid. 57.

times would have a powerful role as centres of religious, political, and social activity (Pl. 24). The Gupta also saw a great development in literature, for the systematization of Sanskrit, shortly before the Mauryan empire, had enabled the literate élites of both North and South to find common cultural ground. Early in the Gupta period, the *Rāmāyana* and *Mahābhārata* were established in an approved Sanskrit version, as were the ancient myths of the *Purānas*. An orthodox form of Hinduism was asserted, evident in the growing rigidity of the caste-system; but this was subsequently tempered by increasing promotion of *bhakti* (devotion), that originated with the Tamil Shaiva hymns from the sixth century onwards, known collectively as the *Tirumurai*. These hymns were to be a constant source of musical inspiration.

It was also during the Gupta period that the *Nātyashāstra* established principles of dramaturgy, aesthetics, dance, and music that would form the basis of all subsequent artistic development. During the six centuries that separated the *Nātyashāstra* of Bharata from the *Brihaddeshī* of Matanga, a period of significant consolidation of Hindu culture and of intellectual advance occurred that would enable Indian civilization to survive not only the ensuing Hunnish invasions but also the advent of Muslim rule.

The Fusion of Hindu and Islamic Cultural Systems in the North

Between the eleventh and sixteenth centuries, India was subjected to a succession of invasions by Turkish, Afghan, and Mongol peoples of Central Asia, all subscribing to Islam. The first major invasion, by Turkic-speaking Ghaznavids, occurred in 1023; a century later, the Ghurids, another Turkic-speaking people (who had recently overthrown their Ghaznavid suzerains), attacked India and, in 1191, defeated the Rajputs. (The Rajputs—literally 'Sons of Kings'—were members of military and landowning classes who dominated much of north and western India; they are commonly held to be descendants of invading Huns.)

In 1206 the Ghurids established the first Turko-Afghan dynasty in Delhi, founding what was to become known as the Delhi Sultanate; and their subsequent push to Bihar and Bengal spelt the death knell to Buddhism in India. By the mid-fourteenth century, the Delhi Sultanate encompassed most of India: only the tip of the peninsula remained independent.

India was spared the worst of the Mongol invasions under Genghis Khan; but the subsequent onslaught of Tamerlane (Tamer-Lenk: 'lame Tamur') led straight through the Punjab to Delhi, and in 1398 the city was sacked. After that, the Delhi sultans controlled little beyond Delhi itself. During the ensuing century the empire fragmented into local kingdoms of Hindus and Muslims; when Tamerlane's descendant Babur invaded from Afghanistan in 1526 and founded the far-reaching Moghul dynasty, only the Rajputs were in a position to offer any resistance.[11]

Islam tested the assimilative power of Hinduism as it had not previously been tested. The two religious cultures had little in common: the one, authoritarian, proselytizing, and opposed to icons; the other eclectic, liberal, and disposed to worship sculpted deities. The two were forced into partnership, and the consequences (once the invaders had become acclimatized) were surprisingly positive.

Islam brought a measure of political unity to India that had not been seen since the sixth century; its spirit of brotherhood helped to loosen the rigidity of the 'caste' system. Guru Nanak (1469–1539), a Hindu by birth who had studied Islam and been on pilgrimage to Mecca, founded the Sikh religion (in the Punjab) on the basis of common aspects he had discovered between the two religions. (It was only when orthodox Muslims harassed the Sikhs and murdered their Second Guru that the Sikhs became a martial community.) The sectarian gods were subsumed in a vision of a universal God of Love; Persian Sufism blended with Hindu *bhakti*; and popular hymns spread the cult of a God who might be worshipped in a mosque or a temple, but who offered mercy and justice to all people.[12]

The twelfth century saw the start of a great outpouring of religious poetry. In the north and east, there was a revival of the cult of Vishnu, particularly as exemplified in his incarnations as Rāma and Krishna; and Krishna's passionate love for Radha was celebrated in Jayadeva's erotic Sanskrit *Gīta Govinda*; its twenty-four verses are still sung throughout India in vernacular tongues, sometimes in the style of classical music. During the fifteenth century, a blending of Sufism

[11] *The Times Atlas of World History*, ed. Geoffrey Barraclough (London, 1989), 131.
[12] J. M. Roberts, *Pelican History of the World* (London: Pelican Books, 1988), 413.

and *bhakti* was epitomized in the poetry of Kabir (*c.*1440–1518), a poet-musician who was born a *brāhman* but brought up a Muslim. (He was a principal inspiration for Guru Nanak.) Hymns written by the poet-saints were carried in regional languages to the remotest villages; they are still sung by millions of Hindus.

The Delhi Sultanate established a *quasi*-Persian court, employing Persian poets and musicians; Persian culture suffused Hinduism. Persian became the official language of India, and remained so until the nineteenth century. Persian vocabulary was tailored to Hindi grammar to form Urdu, promulgated in Arabic script; later, Urdu was blended with Hindi to form the language of Hindustani. The mix of Persian and Indian cultural systems led to a stylistically unified form of architecture, and was to have particularly important consequences for music.

Development of *Dhrupad* and *Khyāl* at the Islamic Courts in the North

The sultans admired Indian music. Amir Khusrau, a Turkish-born poet-musician who served successive sultans in Delhi throughout the thirteenth century, was a lover of things Persian, but also a great admirer of Indian music; he introduced Sufi styles of singing and established the *ghazal* as a North Indian genre.[13] Changes in musical style brought about by the Muslim presence were reflected (as already noted) in the *Sangītaratnākara* ('Mine of Musical Jewels'), by Shārngadeva, a *brāhman* from Kashmir who worked in the Hindu Deccan.

By the fifteenth century, a number of significant changes were under way. The Hindu court at Gwalior had become a leading centre of musical activity and was attracting some of the finest musicians of the day. It was at Gwalior that the famous Mīyān Tānsen learned his craft. He was to become the 'star' of the court of the Moghul emperor, Akbar: it was said that his music could make clouds burst into rain, or cause instant conflagrations. Many of today's musicians claim descent from him. And it was most probably at Gwalior that the development of *dhrupad* as an art-music genre was initiated and that, through it, there developed the exposition of *rāga* in the classical style used today.

[13] Powers, 'India', *The New Grove*, ix. 75.

(The *dhrupada*—from Sanskrit *dhruva* 'refrain' and *pada* 'song'—were ancient Sanskrit verses, many of which were translated into a vernacular language during the fourteenth century.)

The new courtly style of music introduced a new social dimension: effective performance required an appreciative audience, expressing delight at specific instances of artistry through sighs, mutterings of 'bhava, bhava', and appreciative shakings of the head. To this day, classical music is usually performed in the intimate surroundings of a private room. (When performed in a concert hall, it is usually amplified, electronically.)

The *dhrupad* style is formal and austere. At the court of Jaunpur, a Persian ruler developed a more florid style giving greater scope for the imagination. This was to lead to the *khyāl* style of singing (from Persian *khayal*: 'fantasy'), the predominant style in use today. Jaunpur marked the start of a fusion of Indian aesthetics and Persian romanticism that was to characterize the 'Hindustani' music of the north and cause it to diverge, in many aspects of style and usage, from the 'Carnatic' music of the south.

The musical innovations that began with the Delhi sultans were further encouraged by the early Moghul emperors. ('Moghul' is Persian for 'Mongol'; and Babur, the first Moghul, was descended from Tamerlane through his father, and from Genghis Khan through his mother.) The reign of Babur's grandson, Akbar, spanned the half-century between 1556 and 1605 and fostered a 'golden age' of Indian arts. The architecture of Akbar's capital city at Fatehpur Sikri effected a synthesis of Hindu and Islamic elements that would reach its climax in the Taj Mahal, under his grandson, Shahjahan. In the Moghul school of miniature-painting, Hindu and Persian traditions blended in colourful, realistic portraiture, that broke through Islamic conventions.

The long reign of Akbar's third successor, Aurangazeb (1658–1707), was to prove as disastrous as Akbar's was triumphant. Aurangazeb execrated all arts other than calligraphy. He set out to improve, as he saw it, the lot of the peasants, by bringing the whole country under uncompromising Islamic rule, and moved his capital to the Deccan. Thirty wasteful and bloody years later, Islamic influence had been extended over most of the continent; but Aurangazeb left an insecure empire that soon fractured after his death. His continual warring indicated that, because of geographical conditions, the Deccan could not be conquered from Delhi, and the North could not be controlled from the Deccan,[14] a factor that contributed to the maintenance of differences in style between the Hindustani music of the North and the Carnatic music of the South.

Early Developments in the South

Although the cultures of North and South overlapped, their histories differed; and it was not until the nineteenth century that the subcontinent came to be regarded as an 'Indian' entity. The isolation of the South precluded a mixing of peoples such as characterized the North, and ensured that Hinduism would continue to predominate, despite Islamic influence.

As early as the third century AD, wandering minstrels and bards in Tamil Nadu—a principal centre of Hinduism at the time—began to establish a distinctive Tamil literature. Successive bardic meetings in Madurai led to the collecting of over 2,000 poems, known collectively as the *Sangam* literature. From Tamil literature we learn that the bards sang in modes (*pan*), and in specific tunes (*kattalai*: 'mould'), accompanied on the harp. Many of these poems are still performed in the modes of Carnatic music.[15]

During the centuries between the Mauryan and Gupta periods, a burgeoning of art, literature, and philosophy occurred in Maharashtra, in the north-west of the Deccan. It was in South India, too, that the artistic upsurge that followed the Gupta dynasty emerged. The Cholas, who exercised suzerainty over most of the South from the ninth to the thirteenth centuries, built thousands of temples, according with contemporary texts that codified rules for architecture and temple rituals; musicians and dancing girls (*Devadāsī*: 'servants of the god') were attached to the temples. Dance dramas originating some 1,300 years ago are still performed in Kerala; and it was from the South, and from Tamil Nadu in particular, that the *bhakti* (devotional) hymns of the Shaiva and Vaishnava cults originated.

The South was free from Islamic influence until the early fourteenth century, when the Delhi sultans begin to raid the Deccan; thereafter, powerful cities became tributaries to Delhi, and in 1311 Madurai was sacked. Two new powers emerged in response to this threat: the Muslim

[14] Watson, *Concise History of India*, 124.

[15] Widdess, 'Indian Music'; Powers, 'India', *The New Grove*, ix. 75.

Bahmani and the Hindu Vijayanagar. The former was torn by internal strife, though it did much to promote Islamic architecture and culture in the Deccan; the latter became a mighty empire, covering most of the south of the peninsula; it defended the Hindu faith against the onslaught of Islam for over two and a half centuries.

Trade with Europeans brought fabulous wealth to the Vijayanagar, and its kings became energetic promoters of music, dance, and literature, both in temples and courts. Their language was Telugu, and a body of literature in this language came to take its place beside that in Tamil. A genre known as *yakshagāna* ('spirit-song'), consisting of a long narrative poem in Telugu to be sung and enacted, is still performed in temples in Kuchipudi and Melattur (in the south-east), in the style of Carnatic music.[16] Indeed, it was in the Vijayanagar empire that the principles of Carnatic music, as now performed, appear to have been established—though such music was clearly influenced by Hindustani music as practised at the Bahmani courts.[17]

In 1565 Hampi, capital of the Vijayanagar, was sacked by an alliance of sultans from the now-fractured Bahmani empire (making feasible the advance of the Moghul emperor, Aurangazeb, into the Deccan). This threat to the Hindu South was countered by the sudden emergence of a new dynasty, the Marathas, whose rulers soon controlled much of north, west, central, and eastern India. In 1739, however, a Persian army descended through the Punjab, and sacked and pillaged Delhi; and in 1757 an Afghan army did likewise. The Marathas were then called upon to restore order; but, in 1761, at precisely the point when this Hindu dynasty expected to gain control of Delhi, its army was all but annihilated by an Afghan army. The resulting power vacuum was filled, not by Afghans or Persians, but by a people from another continent, the British.

Musical Traditions during British Rule

The British were not the only Europeans in India: they had been preceded by the Portuguese. By the middle of the seventeenth century, Portuguese, Dutch, and British were occupying neighbouring settlements along the south-west coast. The

[16] A form of *yakshagāna*, in Kannada, is also performed in parts of the south-west coast (between Kerala and Goa), by travelling troupes.

[17] Powers, 'India', *The New Grove*, ix. 74, 80.

French arrived later, in 1674, by which time Portuguese power was on the wane, and the Dutch were concentrating their resources on Indonesia. The British were then competing with the French and beat them decisively at the Battle of Plassey in 1757. Subsequently, the British encroached on Indian territory to protect and advance the interests of their East India Company until, by the end of the eighteenth century, their suzerainty was recognized by the country's most powerful rulers.

At first, the British established themselves in Bengal, where, in 1765, after a series of battles, they took charge of the Bengali revenues. Hitherto, Indian goods had been bought by Britain with imported silver and gold. Now they could be bought with the wealth of India itself. Moreover, the British won the support of the landed aristocracy by means of 'Permanent Settlements', which enabled the local landowners to maintain their lands and privileges in return for revenues paid to the state; effectively, this meant to the British government. The mass of Indian peasants, who held their land by right, bore the burden of this exploitative measure. In 1833 the British parliament abolished the East India Company's monopoly on the textile trade. This resulted in raw Indian cotton being exported to Britain, to be manufactured into goods that were then exported to the Indian market. This unscrupulous measure contributed significantly to the wealth of industrial Britain and eliminated the indigenous Indian textile trade.[18]

In 1857 there occurred the 'Mutiny' in Bengal which, with Sikh assistance, the British eventually subdued. As early as 1784, the affairs of the British East India Company had been brought under nominal control of the British parliament, because of corruption among the colonists. Now, because of disaffection of the colonized, power was transferred from the Company to the British Crown. In 1859, the last Moghul 'emperor' was deported to Burma; and, in 1876, Queen Victoria was declared 'Empress of India'.

The principal artistic consequence of British rule sprang from a negative source: the majority of British colonists found Indian arts—and Indian music in particular—incomprehensible, and left them alone. Traditions of music and drama therefore continued at many of the regional courts. (The Indians for their part found little to admire in the music of the British; and to this day there is less promotion of European music in India than in most Asian countries.)

[18] Harbans Mukhia, 'The Years of "The Raj"', in *India* (Hong Kong: APA Publications, 1990), 40.

The patterns in the North and South differed. In 1798 the ruler of Tanjore (in the South) was willing to submit his command to the British, in return for the preservation of his court with its excellent musical traditions. It was in Tanjore—though not at the court—that the 'Trinity' of South Indian composers, the saint-composer Tyagaraja (1767–1847) and his two contemporaries, Shyama Shastri (1762–1827) and Muttusvami Dikshitar (1775–1835), made their outstanding contribution to Carnatic music; their compositions now form the bulk of its repertoire.[19] From Tanjore the Carnatic style spread to other parts of South India; and the preservation of saint-musicians—who traditionally performed for the gods rather than for the court—helped to maintain the status of musicians.

In the North, the development of the *khyāl*, and of the modern-style *sitār* (with movable frets), caused the austere *dhrupad* style to be adapted to a more romantically inclined musical taste. Musicians continued to be employed at certain princely courts, but their status declined. The *sampradāya* (traditions) of Hindustani music were usually family-oriented, and, by the end of the nineteenth century, the traditions themselves were called *gharānā* ('family'). The *guru-shishya-paramparā* (master–disciple-succession) method of transmitting classical music then became specifically associated with family, even though outsiders were often permitted to enter; and the styles of many *gharānā*s—exemplified particularly in the compositions used in *rāga* performances—became jealously guarded secrets. Among the most notable of these *gharānā*s were Agra and Gwalior.[20]

Other *gharānā*s were associated with courts, particularly those that had chosen the winning side in the War of the Mutiny, and thus gained freedom to develop their musical establishments. Among the most notable court-*gharānā*s were those of Jaipur and Rampur.

By the 1880s, the role of the princes as patrons was largely over, and there was a move to make music more widely accessible. In 1887 Vishnu Digambar Paluskar, the leading protagonist in this movement, gave what was probably the first public recital of Hindustani music, to a fee-paying (rather than invited) audience. In 1901 he opened a public music school in Lahore, and branches were soon established in other cities.[21] It was due to Paluskar's tireless efforts that Indian music was promoted, as a unique art form, uncontaminated by European influence, and became associated with the nationalist ambitions of the All-India National

[19] Powers, 'India', *The New Grove*, ix. 81. [20] Ibid. 89–90. [21] Ibid. 90–1.

Congress. When, in 1927, Congress declared national independence to be its objective, funds were provided for the founding of a Music Academy in Madras for research, teaching, and sponsorship, in classical music. Music became a potent symbol of nationalism.

There were, of course, positive as well as negative aspects of British rule. Whatever their motives, the colonists caused the building of roads and railways, hospitals, schools, and universities, and they initiated industrialization. Despite the many atrocities that occurred under British rule, there were some—among the growing class of Westernized Indians—who believed that the British Raj was actually beneficial for India's future. In Britain, argument erupted between 'orientalists' and those in favour of total Westernization. Macaulay famously suggested that 'a single shelf of a good European library is worth the whole native literature of India and Arabia'.[22] Others disagreed: Schopenhauer among them.

In 1847 the East India Company commissioned Max Müller, a naturalized Briton, Professor of Philology at Oxford, to translate the *Rigveda.* Müller it was who first made popular the discovery (by Sir William Jones, in 1786 (see p. 94)) of the relationship between Sanskrit, Greek, and Latin; and he became a champion of Indian culture. His enthusiasm indicates the extent to which the fascination of this culture was beginning to engage some Europeans:[23]

> If I were asked under what sky the human mind has most fully developed some of its choicest gifts, has most deeply pondered over the greatest problems of life, and has found solutions to some of them which well deserve the attention even of those who have studied Plato and Kant—I should point to India. And if I were to ask myself from what literature, we here in Europe, we who have been nurtured almost exclusively on the thoughts of Greeks and Romans, and of one Semitic race, the Jewish, may draw the corrective which is most wanted in order to make our inner life more perfect, more comprehensive, more universal, in fact more truly human a life, not for this life only, but a transfigured and eternal life—again I should point to India ...[24]

[22] Watson, *Concise History of India*, 139.

[23] The racist attitudes that (in general) underlay European veneration of India are discussed in Chapter 13, p. 466.

[24] Cited in Jawaharlal Nehru, *The Discovery of India* (1946; Delhi: Oxford University Press, 1981), 88–9.

Similar words might have been written of other non-Western civilizations. Nevertheless, many have followed Müller's example, and have sought in India an answer to Western woes. One indication of this is that musicians have tended to see, in the apparent freedoms of Indian musical practice, an example of the merits of improvisation over fixed notation. The concept is altogether too facile, however; it ignores—as the following sections will indicate—the extent to which the performance of Indian music is governed by established theory and tradition.

Melodic and Drone Instruments

As with many musical cultures, the human voice is still the principal melodic instrument in India. A singer is valued for vocal agility—allied to knowledge and experience—rather than for vocal tone. A good singer will have a range of three octaves, the capacity to sing fine nuances of pitch, and expertise in applying vibrato and other types of ornamentation.

Instrumental music developed in imitation of vocal music. The most important instruments in both North and South are long-necked lutes: the *vīṇā* in the South and the *sitār* in the North. The term *vīṇā* originally referred to the arched harp, which probably came from Mesopotamia. By the sixth century the harp had been supplanted by the tube zither (an early form of today's *vīṇā*), in use in rural India still (and in South East Asia, in Malagasy, and as children's sound producers in the Balkans). The folk *vīṇā* was originally a bamboo tube to which a single string was attached; later it acquired a gourd resonator and a number of strings and frets.[25] (In early Indian philosophy, the *vīṇā* was related to the human body as the physical equivalent of the human voice, while the vocal tract was regarded as the human *vīṇā*.[26])

The *vīṇā*, as currently used in Carnatic music, has a delicate sound and is in the form of a long-necked lute with a resonator carved out of wood. Twenty-four frets are *fixed* to its hollow fingerboard and there are four melody strings and three drone strings. An ornamental gourd is often attached to the fingerboard.

The North Indian version of the *vīṇā*, known as *rudravīṇā* or *bīn*, has two huge resonators, four metal melody strings, some twenty frets, and

[25] The descriptions of instruments are, in part, adapted from Widdess, 'Indian Music'.
[26] Rowell, *Music*, 115.

three drone strings. A table-shaped bridge causes the strings to buzz when plucked, and, by exciting the generation of high harmonics, adds brightness to the tone.

The *sitār*, named after its Persian ancestor, which has now replaced the *bīn* in Hindustani music, combines features of its predecessor with features of the long-necked lute. Its half-gourd resonator is lute-shaped; its bridge is tabular; and its neck, hollow and long. Sometimes an ornamental gourd is attached to the neck. In addition to five melody and two drone strings, there are some dozen sympathetic strings passing over a separate bridge. A pronounced characteristic of the *sitār* is its capacity for enabling the pitch of a note to be 'bent' by up to a perfect fifth (by lateral displacement), after it has been sounded. Importantly, the frets of the *sitār* are movable, assisting tuning for different modes (Pl. 25).

A plucked instrument, frequently used in Hindustani music, is the *sarod*: a short-necked, pear-shaped lute, derived from the *rabāb*. The resonator and neck are carved from a single piece of wood, and the belly is made of parchment. An unfretted, metal fingerboard enables the fingers to glide along the strings in imitation of vocal style. Four melody and six drone strings are plucked with a triangular plectrum.

Another instrument used in the North in a solo capacity is the *santūr* (dulcimer), of Persian origin. The two, light, wooden hammers (with which the strings are struck) are sometimes used to generate ornamental shakes.

The four-string *tambūrā* is the instrument most commonly employed to provide the complex drone, essential to all *rāga* performance. It is an unfretted, long-neck lute, the strings of which are gently—and continuously—stroked. These are most frequently tuned to the tonic and fifth, though often the fourth, rather than the fifth, is in the drone, and sometimes the seventh is included. A piece of quill or silk may be inserted between the strings and the tabular bridge to induce the generation of harmonics that add to the richness of the sound.

The instrument most frequently used to 'shadow' the voice in Hindustani (North Indian) music is the *sārangī*, a bowed lute made from a block of wood with a parchment belly (Pl. 26). There are four gut melody strings and thirty or more sympathetic strings. The strings are stopped by pressing the fingernail against the side of the string, using glissando to imitate the human voice. The instrument is held upright, on the lap, or on a cushion placed on the ground between the knees. Recently it has come to be used as a principal melodic instrument, in instrumental genres.

25. Pakistani musicians performing on *sitār* and *tablā*. Photo: Jean Jenkins

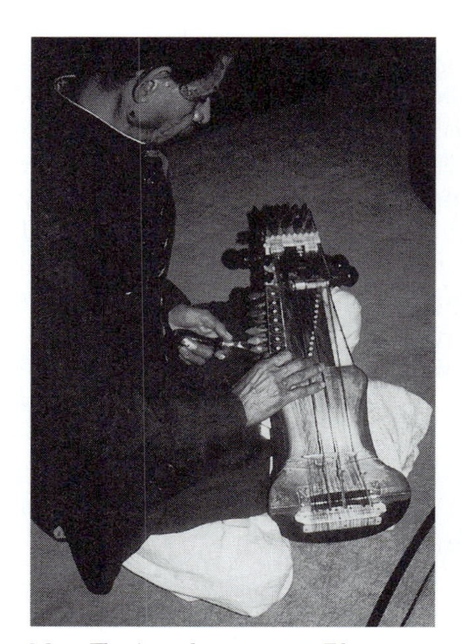

26. Tuning the *sārangī*. Photo: Jean Jenkins

27. Painting depicting *Rāg Meghmalhar*, showing (left to right) *rabāb* (lute), *pakhāvaj* (barrel drum), flute (played by Krishna), *bīn* (stick zither), *tānpura* (lute); Jaipur School (eighteenth century)

In Carnatic (South Indian) music, the voice is now frequently 'shadowed' by a Western violin, held between the player's chest and foot. This enables the left hand to move freely over the fingerboard, with considerable use of glissando. Like the *sārangī*, the violin (held in this position) has come to be used as a principal melodic instrument in instrumental genres.

The bamboo transverse flute has been associated with art music since ancient times, and is the instrument with which Krishna is said to have won the love of the *gopī* (milkmaids) (Pl. 27). Glissando is obtained by carefully graded, lifting and lowering of the fingertips, over the fingerholes.

Shawms were used in India as part of the Muslim *nawba* ensemble, employed for ceremonial occasions. The northern shawm is the *shahnāī*, recently accepted as a melody instrument in art music. The southern shawm—which may pre-date the Muslim shawm—is the larger *nāgasvaram*, regarded as a sacred instrument and played mainly in temples. It has a repertoire of classical music.

The harmonium (a free-reed organ) arrived with Christian missionaries, and Indians have assimilated it, not without controversy, into their instrumentarium. The Indian version is small and portable: bellows are on the back for the left hand, while the right hand plays the keyboard. It is used as a practice instrument by vocalists and, on occasion, as a solo instrument. Although its fixed tuning renders microtonal *shruti*-colourings impossible (see below), its convenience has often caused it to be used as an accompaniment in performance; and it is interesting that singers with fine intonation have managed to coexist with its fixed intonation. In the South, a small harmonium, known as *shruti*-box, is sometimes used for playing the drone.

The instruments described above are those most frequently encountered in the performance of classical music, but many other string and wind instruments are in use in different contexts.

The *Shruti*, and Intonation in Indian Music

Central to the 'passion' or 'feeling' of *rāga*-based music—so most Indian musicians would advise—are the *shruti*, the twenty-two units into which musical theorists divided the octave, in order to delineate intervallic relationships.

28. Shiva, in his celebrated pose as *Naṭarāja*, Lord of the Dance

The term *shruti* has been used in different ways over the ages; the *Vedas*, for example, were called *shruti* because they were 'heard', that is to say, revealed. Definition of *shruti*, in relation to *svara* (notes of a scale), was originally a philosophical issue. In Upanishadic writings, sound was regarded as an omnipresent source of latent energy, inherent in the *ākāsha* (ether); the *Taittirīya Upanishad*, for example, describes the *ākāsha* as 'the audible space that fills the universe'.[27] (Such 'audible space' is commonly represented by the hourglass drum in Shiva's uplifted right hand, in his celebrated pose as *Naṭarāja*, Lord of the Dance (Pl. 28).)

Most sound was considered *un*manifest, beyond the reach of human consciousness; but certain sounds *were* considered manifest, and were subject to the illusions of the phenomenal world. These were the *svara*, which were able to acquire specific attributes, such as pitch, melodic function, and the capacity to give pleasure. *Shruti*, by contrast, were linked with the substratum of sound that lies *within* the *ākāsha*.[28] Thus,

[27] Rowell, *Music*, 3. [28] Ibid. 35.

in the *Nāradīyashikshā* (*c.*AD 500), a set of five *shruti* could be presented as possible *timbral* changes to the Sāmavedic scale (see p. 102).

In writings on musical theory, by contrast, the *shruti* have always numbered twenty-two, and have been presented as units of intervallic measurement; but they were separate from the *svara*: they were never performed, or heard, as individual notes. Their function was—as it still is—to facilitate variation in the pitch of individual *svara*s, according to the context in which these are sounded.[29] (In dealing with the *shruti*, Matanga, in the *Brihaddeshī*, linked music theory with cosmology when he stated: 'the *shruti* are perceived through circumstantial evidence, inference, and/or direct perception, and then become the means for manifestation of the *svara*.'[30])

In the *Nātyashāstra*, Bharata described the two, original, 'parent' scales (*grāma*) of Indian music in terms both of consonance and dissonance, and of *shruti*. These parent scales were the *shadjagrāma* and *madhyamagrāma*, named after the first and fourth degrees of the scale, respectively, and corresponding (approximately) to the Western Ionian and Mixolydian scales. Melodies derived from these parent scales were classified into seven modal groups (then called *jāti*: 'species' or 'class'). Consonance was associated with the perfect fourth and fifth, and dissonance, with the minor second and/or major seventh; each interval contained precise numbers of *shruti*. (Bharata evidently regarded the twenty-two *shruti* as being equal in size, a single *shruti* representing the highest common factor of the recognized intervals.[31])

The concept of 'sonance'—the extent to which different notes agree or disagree with each other—has been pervasive in Indian thought, and four possibilities have commonly been accepted. According to the *Brihaddeshī*:

> That from which the essential nature of a *rāga* arises is the *vādī* [sonant]; that which assists in establishing this nature is the *samvādī* [consonant]; that which promotes it is the *anuvādī* [assonant/neutral]; and that which destroys it is known as *vivādī* [dissonant].[32]

[29] The *svara* were thought to be connected with the *ākāsha* by the vital life-force of human breath (ibid. 40–1); there is similarity here with the Chinese concept of *qi*, the vital life-force associated with the winds and with musical sound (see pp. 330–2).

[30] Cited in ibid. 150–1.

[31] N. A. Jairazbhoy, 'An Interpretation of the 22 Srutis', *Perspectives on Asian Music: Essays in Honor of Dr Laurence E. R. Picken* (*Asian Music*, 6/1–2 (1975)), 38–59.

[32] Cited in Rowell, *Music*, 158.

Later, in the *Sangītaratnākara*, Shārngadeva related these functions to roles and relationships within feudal society: *vādī* as representing the ruler, and *samvādī*, his minister; *anuvādī*, the servant, and *vivādī*, the enemy. The naming of individual *svara* as *vādī* and *samvādī* is still an important characteristic of the Hindustani *rāga*-system, though the *samvādī* is no longer necessarily consonant with the *vādī*, and *vivādī* is used to refer to a note foreign to a given *rāga*.[33]

During the seventeenth century, measurements of string lengths for fixing the position of frets on a lute led to the adoption of a scale of twelve untempered semitones, and this remains the norm today. The octave, however, is still, in theory, divided into twenty-two *shruti*; and the exact tuning of particular *svaras*, sharp or flat to the semitonic scale, remains a defining characteristic of many *rāgas*.

In modern practice, *svaras* are often ornamented with an undulating vibrato (*āndolan*), sufficiently slow and wide as to make precise definition of pitch impracticable. (Early writers described many types of ornamentation—*gamaka*: literally 'a going'—and their function was seen as traversing the [inaudible] *shruti* that lie between the ornamented note and the next note.[34]) In modern Hindustani music (the Persian-influenced music of the North), the most conspicuous form of *gamaka* is still the *mīnd*, a slow portamento from one note to another, though narrow shakes are also common.[35] In Carnatic music (the Hindu music of the South) shakes are used on all long notes, as a means of maintaining musical motion. *Gamaka* is a primary element of all Indian music, and a defining characteristic of a *rāg*, drawing attention to particular notes by making them alternately dissonant and consonant, or by gradually linking a dissonant note to its consonant note of resolution.

Despite the superficial resemblance of present-day Indian musical temperament to that of Western equal temperament, flexibility of intonation remains a primary element in the performance of Indian classical music. Indeed, it could be argued that the very purpose of the *rāga*-system—of modes, with specific orderings of notes (in both ascent and descent), specific phrase structures, intonation, and ornamentation—is to assuage the imperfections inherent in the harmonic series.[36]

[33] Ibid. 158–9.

[34] In both the *Sangītaratnākara* of Sharngadeva (AD 1240) and the *Sangītasamayasāra* of Pārshvadeva (AD 1250); see Rowell, *Music*, 164–5.

[35] Powers, 'India', *The New Grove*, ix. 107.

[36] Wim van der Meer, *Hindustani Music in the 20th Century* (New Delhi: Allied Publishers, 1980), 9–16.

And there is a link, surely, between the merging of dissonance into consonance and the philosophical idea that all forms of creation must ultimately dissolve into the Absolute.

The Modes of Indian Music

In India, only seven notes have ever been named. This contrasts with West Asian music, where seventeen notes were named in an attempt to provide theoretical constructs for all the pitches used in musical performance (see p. 205). In West Asian music, the intervallic relationship between named pitches remains constant; but in India, the intervallic relationship between the seven notes (*svara*) is subject to change. The *svara* are arranged in sequence, according to certain basic scale types. When the seven *svara* conform to one particular scale type they are regarded as 'pure' (*shuddha*); when they deviate from this, they are regarded as 'modified' (*vikrita*). Whether 'pure' or 'modified', however, they keep the same name.[37] The abbreviated names of the seven *svara* (first syllables only)—*sa ri ga ma pa dha ni* (the *sargam*)—are still often chanted in performance (see p. 102).

In North India, during the seventeenth century, the intervals between the 'pure' and 'modified' pitches of the seven *svara* were indicated by new, movable frets on the *sitār*; the positions of the frets allowed for twelve intervals, of approximately a semitone, within the octave. The *svara* are now regarded as 'pure' when positioned as in the diatonic major scale. The second, third, sixth, and seventh may be 'altered' by flattening, approximately by a semitone (*komal*); the fourth may be 'altered' by sharpening, approximately by a semitone (*tīvra*). The first and fifth notes are always 'pure'.

In the Carnatic music of South India, the 'pure' notes are: C, D♭, E𝄫, F, G, A♭, B𝄫. The second, third, sixth, and seventh may be 'altered', by being raised by one, or two, approximate semitones; and the fourth may be 'altered' by being raised by one, approximate semitone. (In Western notation, this means that the third and seventh may be flat or natural, as well as double-flat; the second and sixth may be natural or sharp, as well as flat; and the fourth may be sharp, as well as natural.) As in North India, the first and fifth notes always remain 'pure'.[38]

[37] Powers, 'India', *The New Grove*, ix. 94–8.

[38] Widdess, 'India'.

The scale types of Indian music (*thāt* in the North, *mela* in the South) use the seven *svara* in permutations of these 'pure' and 'altered' notes. Intervallic relationships between the seven *svara* vary, and there has never been a categorization of modes that embraces *all* possibilities of performance; the many attempts to this end tended to be contradictory. However, two comparatively recent systems of categorization, one for Hindustani music, one for Carnatic music, are usually observed in modern practice.

The system used in the North is that propounded by the outstanding musicologist Bhatkhande (1860–1936), whose theoretical distillation of *rāga* practice, following forty years spent in collecting and researching Indian music, has helped to preserve the tradition. Bhatkhande listed ten *thāt* that he believed would accommodate the *rāga*s in common use. The system has been criticized as oversimplified; but no better system has been devised, and most *rāga*s are now named following the ten *thāt* of Bhatkhande (Ex. 8.1).[39]

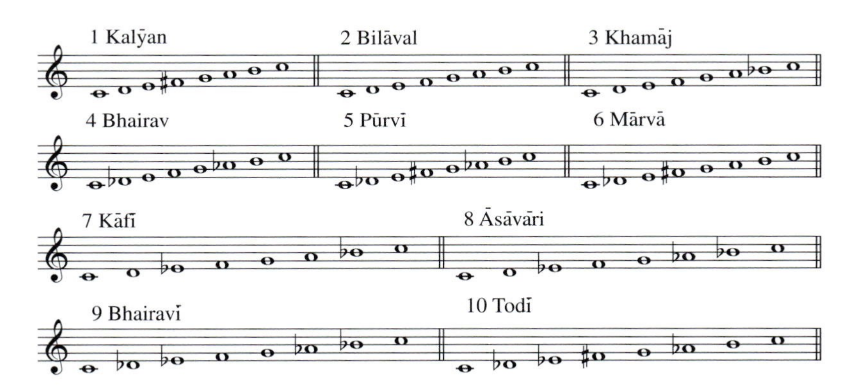

Ex. 8.1

In South India, where greater emphasis was placed on pre-composed (rather than improvised) music, the classification of modes (*melakarta*) was more complex. A seventeenth-century treatise proposed a system of seventy-two Carnatic *melakarta*, that have become virtually synonymous with their *rāga*s. The system provides for the permutation of six possible forms of a tetrachord between C and F, with six possible forms of a tetrachord between G and C. To the resultant thirty-six

[39] Powers, 'India', *The New Grove*, ix. 94–7.

melakarta are added additional permutations effected by sharpening F. The consequent seventy-two *melakarta* are named individually, and there are compositions in all of them. No more than two dozen have real significance, however.[40]

The Theory and Practice of *Rāga*

The concept of *rāga*, as a means of conveying specific feelings through the musical character of a mode, arose from early association of *rāga* with theatre; and it becomes overt in the allocation of specific melodic functions to certain *svara*. Early treatises attached considerable importance to the functions of individual notes within modes.

In the *Nātyashāstra*, four specially important *svara* were designated: the starting note; the predominant note (that acts as a kind of tonal centre); a note that occurs at the end of intermediate sections of the melody; and the final note. Melodies were classified into seven modal groups (then called *jāti*), which could derive from either of two parent scales (*grāma*); and for each group a particular *svara* was specified as the final.[41] If the other important notes corresponded to the final note of the *jāti*, and if no notes were omitted, the *jāti* was regarded as 'pure'. If the other important notes did not so correspond, and one or two notes were omitted, the *jāti* was regarded as 'deviant' or 'transformed'. Other variations in modal organization arose from 'hybrid' *jāti*, and from regional variants.[42]

When the seven-mode system of *grāmarāga*s superseded the *jāti*-system in the middle centuries of the first millennium (see p. 226), and this system itself expanded to include variants, hybrids, and regional additions, the seven 'pure' *grāmarāga*s all came to start on the first *svara*, *sa*. This *svara* then fulfilled a function similar to that of the tonic in Western music; and when a drone on this *svara* was applied, the degree of consonance or dissonance of all other notes tended to be judged in relation to this 'tonic'.

It then became necessary to designate notes other than the first *svara* as 'predominant'. From this emerged the classification of a *vādī*

[40] Powers, 'India', *The New Grove*, ix. 97–8. [41] Jairazbhoy, 'An Interpretation', 216–18.

[42] For a full account of the development of *rāg*, see D. R. Widdess, *The Rāgas of Early Indian Music: Modes, Melodies, and Musical Notations from the Gupta Period to* c.*1250* (Oxford: Oxford University Press, 1995), 29–83, 368–72.

('speaker') and a *samvādī* ('co-speaker') for every *rāga*. This is the system currently in use. The *vādī* and *samvādī* are usually a perfect fifth or perfect fourth apart, and may or may not coincide with the starting note; their differing positions make possible the enormous variety of *rāgas* associated with a particular *thāt*. (In the rather different system of the South, the corresponding term for *vādī* is *jīva-svara*, meaning 'life-giving degree of the scale'; the initial note of the phrase is referred to by the Tamil term *etuppu* ('taking up').[43]

Indian theory uses the generic term *anga* ('limb' or 'component') to account for melodic aspects of individual *rāgas*; *vādī* and *samvādī*, for example, represent just one *anga* of *rāga*. Another is the *āroha-avaroha* ('ascent-descent'); a *rāga* may have different arrangements of 'pure' and 'altered' notes in its ascent and descent. Moreover, the scales of *rāgas* do not always run in stepwise, conjunct motion. Sometimes they appear in 'crooked' motion, incorporating turns of phrase specific to a particular *rāga*. For example, the *āroha-avaroha* of *Rāg Mishra Bhairāvi* may be performed as shown in Ex. 8.2 (after Sorrell).[44] Another *anga* ('limb') of melody refers to range, which is categorized in octaves, or in smaller units of a pentachord or tetrachord. *Rāgas* usually extend over three octaves, and a performer will consciously move from one range to another.[45]

Ex. 8.2

The most important *anga* ('limb') of the modal system is the characterization of *rāgas* by specific melodic elements, such as a rising contour, or a cadential figure (in Sanskrit *mukhyānga*: 'chief component'). From these, there evolved melodic motifs specific to particular *rāgas*. Bhatkhande classified them rather simplistically as *pakad* ('catch-phrases'). The classification provides a helpful guide; but in reality no specific number of 'catch-phrases' defines a *rāga*, because the *rāga* is always open-ended in its realization.[46] Nevertheless, the proper unfolding of a *rāga* must incorporate certain melodic components because, in

[43] Powers, 'India', *The New Grove*, ix. 99–100.

[44] Neil Sorrell, *Indian Music in Performance* (Manchester: Manchester University Press, 1980), 96.

[45] Powers, 'India', *The New Grove*, ix. 91 ff.

[46] Meer, *Hindustani Music*, 24.

Ex. 8.3

association with *vādī* and *samvādī*, they convey its individual essence. Ex. 8.3 (after Powers) shows aspects of *rāg mārva*: (i) in its basic form of ascent and descent (ii) by delineations of range (iii) by its characteristic melodic motifs, and (iv) in a melodic procedure derived from them. The *vādī* and *samvādī* are indicated by V and S.[47]

The performances of Indian music arise from a mixture of fixed composition and improvisation, both of which conform to the melodic implications of a particular *rāga*. (Carnatic music makes substantially greater use of fixed composition than does Hindustani music; flexibility is achieved principally through the *manner* of performance, in particular by the use of ornamentation.)

North Indian musicians practise a large repertoire of melodic configurations (allied to rhythmic patterns) known as *paltās* ('permuta-

[47] Harold Powers, 'Mode', *The New Grove* (1980), xii. 430–1.

tions') or *alankāras* (literally 'making ready', or 'perfections'); and these, adapted to particular *rāgas*, provide the basis for improvisational variation.[48] Early treatises referred to *alankāra* in the sense of ornamentation. According to the *Nātyashāstra*, 'a song without *alankāra* would be like a night without a moon, a river devoid of water, a vine without any flower, and a woman without any ornament'.[49] Shārngadeva, in the *Sangītaratnākara* (thirteenth century), made clear that the composer was expected to be a competent performer; but he also made clear that the composer was expected to know his audience, and how their minds work, rising above his own likes and dislikes, in order to bring delight to everyone. This exemplified the traditional doctrine of non-attachment, propounded in the *Bhagavadgītā* (see p. 97).[50]

Such considerations inform modern practice, in which performers relate their own impulses to the expectations of the audience. No good performer improvises indulgently, and improvisations tend largely to be worked out in practice beforehand. Mostly they are reproductions or reworkings of pre-composed—though unwritten—constructions handed down by particular teachers. At the same time, fixed compositions are often varied in performance, so that composition and improvisation belong to the same process of musical construction.

Many Carnatic musicians claim that the improvisations and ornamentations of Hindustani musicians are considerably more repetitious than are their own performances of fixed compositions. All that can be said, definitively, is that both improvised and composed passages vary from performance to performance, but that improvised passages vary more than do composed passages.[51] Ultimately, the extent of improvisation, and of departure from given models, depends upon the originality—and inspiration—of the performer.

All improvisations take place within a rhythmic framework; and improvisation outside the introductory *ālāpa* section must combine with various cycles of metre and rhythm, and the frequently virtuosic drumming patterns that embellish them.

[48] Gerry Farrell, *Indian Music in Education* (Cambridge: Cambridge University Press, 1990), 50; this book provides a clear account, with musical illustrations, of the process of improvisation in Indian music.

[49] Rowell, *Music*, 162–3.

[50] Ibid. 302.

[51] Meer, *Hindustani Music*, 142.

Percussion Instruments

The patterns and sonorities of Indian rhythms are inseparably connected with the instruments on which they are generated. All such instruments are constructed, and handled, with great care to provide a range of timbres, and precise pitches. Three types of barrel drum are used in Indian classical music: the *mridangam*, the *pakhāvaj*, and the *tablā*.

The *mridangam*—a horizontal drum—is used principally in the South. It is carved from a single block of wood and has a head at each end made of three overlapping rings of leather. The right-hand end is smaller than the left-hand end.

In the North, a larger horizontal drum, the *pākhavāj*, is used to accompany *dhrupad*. The most common percussion instrument, however, is the *tablā*, a pair of single-headed vertical drums, used to accompany most other genres of classical music. The smaller (right-hand) drum is wooden, and barrel-shaped; the larger (left-hand) drum is metal and bowl-shaped. Many legends surround its invention, but it seems likely that it developed from the West Asian *naqqārā*.

One characteristic common to all three drum types is the weighting of the head by the application of a lenticular, black, disk, made from a mixture of lamp black and rice paste. This converts the head to an elastic unit, vibrating in the lower range of audio frequencies, and susceptible of fine tuning, usually to the system tonic. On the *mridangam* and *pākhavāj*, this weighting paste is applied to the end of the smaller, right-hand head; the larger left-hand head is tuned to an indeterminate, stretched-membrane pitch, approximately a sixth below the system tonic. On the *tablā*, the paste is applied to the centre of the head of the right-hand drum; but off-centre on the head of the left-hand drum. The right-hand drum is pitched precisely on the system tonic; the left drum is at a low, but relatively indefinite pitch.[52]

All three drum-types are played exclusively with the hands; by means of different hand and finger positions—pressing the heads with the heels of the hands, striking on different parts of the head, and use of larger and smaller heads, together or alternately—a good player can produce an astonishing variety of pitches and sonorities. Specific drums, and manners of playing to be used, in evoking the eight different *rasa*, are specified in the *Nātyashāstra*.

[52] Widdess, 'Indian Music'.

Rhythmic Cycles

The metric structure of compositions is ordered by rhythmic cycles known as *tāla*. The root meaning of *tāla* pertains to beating with the hands: the claps, finger counts, and silent waves that accompany Indian music. (In ancient times, there were four silent gestures and four audible gestures (see p. 103).[53]) The word *tālam* denotes the small cymbals that beat out the elements of a time cycle in South Indian temple ensembles and some dance ensembles. (Small cymbals are used for the same purpose in many South East Asian ensembles.[54])

Tāla now refers to a specific ordering of beats, repeated cyclically throughout a composition. Each *tāla* contains a specified number of *mātrā* (beats), grouped into *āvarta* (sections) of equal, or unequal, length. The number of sections, and of beats, within each *āvarta* gives the cycle its character, and specific name.

In Carnatic music, all first beats of *āvarta* are stressed. In Hindustani music, the first beats are not always stressed: stress, or its absence, is an important aspect of the character of *āvarta*. The stressed beats (*tālī*) are marked with a clap of the hands; unstressed beats (*khālī*), with a wave. The stressed beats are associated with the undamped resonance of the larger *tablā* drum, while the unstressed beats are associated with lighter strokes on the smaller drum.

In modern performance, a vocalist may perform the appropriate claps and waves at the start of a rhythmic cycle, but will not usually continue with these throughout a performance. In notation, stressed beats are marked X, and unstressed beats, O. The simplest and most widely used *tāl*, *tīntāl*, appears in Western notation as shown in Ex. 8.4.

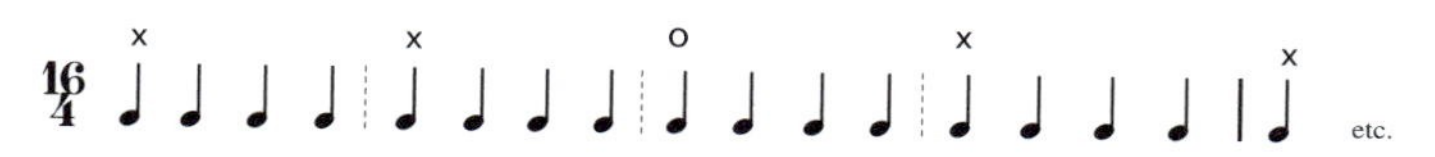

Ex. 8.4

Early theorists recognized five types of rhythmic unit which could form a cycle, or segment of a cycle: 2+2 (quadractic), 1+2 (triple), 3+4 (mixed), 2+3 (broken), and 4+5 (composite).[55] *Tāla* are constructed

[53] Rowell, *Music*, 193–4.
[54] Powers, 'India', *The New Grove*, ix. 118.
[55] Ibid. 119.

from these elements; but in North India, a unit of three may be divided into two units of 1½.

The most common North Indian *tāla* are shown in Table 8.1; the most common South Indian *tāla* are shown in Table 8.2.[56]

Table 8.1. North Indian *tāla*

Name	*Clap pattern*	*No. of beats*
Dādrā	3+(3)	6
Tīvra	3+2+2 or	7
Rūpak	(3)+2+2	7
Kaharvā	4+(4)	8
Jhaptāl	2+3+(2)+3	10
Sūltāl (Sūrphāktāl)	4+2+4	10
Savārī	4+4+1½ +1½	11
Cautāl, Ektāl	4+4+2+2	12
Dhamār	5+2+(3)+4	14
Jhūmrā, Dīpcandī	3+4+(3)+4	14
Pancam savārī	4+4+4+1½ +½	15
Tīntāl	4+4+(4)+4	16

Note: Parentheses indicate *khālī* (unstressed beats).

Table 8.2. South Indian *tāla*

Name	*Clap pattern*	*No. of beats*
Eka	4	4
Rūpaka	2+4	6
Triputa, Mishra Cāpu	3+2+2	7
Ādi	4+2+2	8
Jhampa	7+1+2	10
Matya	4+2+4	10
Dhruva	4+2+4+4	14
Ātā	5+5+2+2	14

56 Widdess, 'Indian Music'.

Rhythmic Patterns

Traditionally, theorists regarded the rhythmic-metric system, and the instructions for drumming, as separate matters.[57] Aspects of technique, still in use in *mridangam* playing, are described in the thirteeenth-century *Sangītaratnākara*. The treatise refers to a basic set of four strokes (*sramavāhani*: 'carrying the burden') in relation to a secondary set of 'flowing' strokes that break the sequence with a stream of rhythm; *mridangam* playing is still based on successive changes of *sramavāhani* in a 'flowing' stream of secondary filler patterns.[58]

Within the Carnatic tradition, the drummer aims primarily to follow the vocal line. Within the Hindustani tradition, however, he aims to elaborate the rhythmic cycle in collaboration—and sometimes in deliberate competition—with the soloist. Specific drum patterns, called *thekā*, are associated with particular *tāla*; as the *thekā* coincide with the *āvarta* (sections) of the *tāla*, they become themselves a method for maintaining the rhythmic cycle. This greater independence in relation to the activity of the soloist has led to increasing musical and technical complexity in expression.

Indian drummers still use a vocabulary of onomatopoeic syllables that correspond to various types of beat strokes and techniques of production. These mnemonics (*bol*s) refer both to temporal duration *and* to sonority. Thus a *thekā* is identified both by its rhythmic pattern *and* by its tone colour. Initially, drummers and dancers learn their rhythms by memorizing sequences of *bol*s; sometimes *bol*s are recited during performance.

Three basic levels of tempo (*laya*) exist in Indian music: slow, medium, and fast. These may be changed in the ratio of two to one (as in South East Asian music), or change may be effected gradually, by means of accelerando. The term *laya* is also used to denote rhythm, in the context of rhythmic passagework.

Form and Genre in Hindustani Music

In Hindustani music, genre and form are indissolubly linked to the process of revealing the essential feeling or mood

[57] Rowell, *Music*, 14.
[58] Powers, 'India', *The New Grove*, ix. 134.

of a *rāga*, in relation to a particular *tāl*. The principal genres, *dhrupad*, *khyāl*, and *thumrī*, differ slightly in structure, but the genre title relates more to performance *style* than to form. All were originally vocal genres; and when *khyāl* and *thumrī* were subsequently taken up by instrumentalists, their styles were based on that of vocal performance.

Most performances in the common genres begin with an improvised *ālāpa* (discourse), the purpose of which—like that of the West Asian *taksīm*—is to set forth the principal notes of the *rāga* and explore the melodic characteristics associated with them. The phrases are presented in a rhapsodic manner without drum accompaniment, though a good performer will be aware of an underlying pulse. The complex tonic drone is played throughout, and is the constant pitch yardstick against which dissonance and consonance are perceived. The *ālāpa* usually ascends and descends, gradually, through the first two octaves of the pitch range.

Ālāpa is usually followed by a transitional passage: *jor* and *jhālā*, that link it to the *tāla*, and to the composition proper. In the *jor*, rhythmic elements gradually emerge, as the outline of the *ālāpa* is repeated, and the tempo increases. In the *jhālā*, rhythmic units and fast repeated notes begin to establish a regular pulse; and phrases from the *ālāpa* may be repeated in successively faster tempo. Plucked instruments usually punctuate the emerging rhythmic cells with percussive strokes on the drone strings.

Dhrupad, the oldest of these genres, is a vocal genre, and is the most subdued and reflective in manner; but—as in Carnatic music, to which it is the most nearly related—it can generate considerable rhythmic excitement. It is usually performed slowly, in twelve-beat *Cautāl*, and accompanied on the *pākhavāj*. A traditional *dhrupad* is in four sections, with a recurring refrain. The refrain usually consists of the first section (*sthāyī*), or the first phrase of that section (*mukhrā*), and may subsequently be varied by augmentation and/or diminution. Other sections are characterized by particular octave ranges, and by emphases on specific, predominant notes.[59] *Dhrupad* has declined in popularity since the eighteenth century, but there is a revival of interest in the genre today, to be compared with the revival of early music in the West.

Khyāl is associated with romantic poetry, and allows the performer greater freedom of expression than does *dhrupad*. In *khyāl*, *rāga*s are extensively ornamented, and the style calls for technical virtuosity more

[59] Powers, 'India', *The New Grove*, ix. 116.

than intellectual rigour. Fast *khyāls* are usually based on specific compositions, followed by rapid, semi-improvised scalic patterns called *tan*; such *khyāls* may dispense with the *ālāpa* altogether. Slow *khyāls* developed at the beginning of this century; their *ālāpa* is based on the *dhrupad* style, and is usually followed by repetitions and variations of the *sthāyī* (first line of the composition), interspersed with improvised variations. These in turn are generally followed by virtuosic *tāns*.

A vocal or instrumental soloist performing a *khyāl* usually indicates that particular sections of the performance are to be improvised by the drummer; such indication is given by a return to the basic *mukhrā* (first phrase of the *sthāyī*); and this is repeated continuously, so as to maintain the rhythmic cycle during the drumming episode. A section of *jawāb-sawāl* (question-answer), in which phrases of increasing rhythmic complexity are exchanged between soloist and *tablā*, is often included to display the virtuosity of the performers. *Khyāl* is usually set to rhythmic cycles such as *Tīntāl*, *Ektāl*, *Jhūmrā tāl*, or *Jhaptāl*, and is accompanied on the *tablā*. It is the genre of classical music most frequently performed today.

The 'light-classical' genre, *thumrī*, developed in the nineteenth century. The word is thought to be derived from the onomatopoeic *thumuk*, indicating the stamp of a dancer's foot: miming of *thumrī* is still a prominent feature of *Kathak* dance.[60] The romantic poetry is expressed through extremely agile ornamentation and *coloratura*; the singer improvises on each line in turn, basing the performance on one of the less profound *rāgas*, and interpreting it with considerable freedom. The *tāl* is usually *Tīntāl*, *Dīpcandī*, or *Dādrā*. An associated Muslim genre, *tappā*, makes yet greater use of ornamentation.

A vocal genre that has remained very popular in Muslim areas of the subcontinent is *ghazal*. It is essentially an Urdu poetic genre, influenced by Sufism, and encompasses the erotic, the mystical, and the philosophical; its Arabic root denotes 'to talk amorously with women'. The genre gained prominence among courtesans of the eighteenth and nineteenth centuries, when it was sung by dancing girls. In recent times, traditional methods of chant have been overtaken by the film and cassette industry, which has popularized *ghazal*, sung in a Western crooning style, accompanied by orchestras that mix Indian and Western instruments.[61]

[60] N. A. Jairazbhoy, 'India', *The New Grove* (1980), ix. 141. [61] Ibid. 142.

Another vocal genre, that has been similarly modernized, is the *bhajan*: the devotional song, associated with *bhakti* since the sixth century. It still forms the basis of temple ritual, where it is usually accompanied by drums and cymbals. Its style was always simple and direct, aiming at clarity. Now, however, *bhajans* appear in the musical style of film songs, accompanied, like *ghazals*, by mixed ensembles of Indian and Western instruments.[62]

The equivalent devotional song of Muslims is the *qawālī*. The genre is associated with Sufism, and its origins are traced to Amir Khusrau in the thirteenth century. The music has affinities with *khyāl* performance: the declamatory style of improvisation makes use of *rāgas* and folk melodies, and is based on a rhythmic cycle. The *qawālī*, however, is no longer associated exclusively with religion and, like *ghazal*, is widely disseminated in popular versions.[63]

Form and Genre in Carnatic Music

In Carnatic music fixed composition plays a much greater role than in Hindustani music. Most of the texts of Carnatic music are devotional, and a majority of compositions are by the 'Trinity' of composers from Tanjore, already referred to (p. 239).[64]

The most important genre of concert music is the *kriti*, a flexible genre of variable length. It developed from the *kīrtanam*, a devotional song for group singing, in verse-refrain form. Extended performances of *kriti* are similar to those of *dhrupad*; but, because composition plays a much greater role than improvisation, the opening *ālāpanam* is shorter than the *ālāpa* in Hindustani music; it is regarded as a formal introduction to the all-important composition, rather than as a demonstration of the essence of the *rāga*, or of the performer's artistry.

The three main elements of *kriti* are the *pallavi* ('blossoming'), a single line of text that recurs as a refrain, and that may be expanded at length through rhythmic and melodic elaboration; the *anupallavi* ('after the blossoming'), that contrasts with this; and the *charanam* ('verse'), usually a more tranquil section, but sometimes a series of

[62] Robert Simon, 'India', *The New Grove* (1980), ix. 144–5.

[63] Regula Qureshi, 'India', *The New Grove* (1980), ix. 146–7.

[64] For a description of the spiritual dimension of Carnatic music, see William Jackson, 'Features of the Kriti: A Song developed by Tyāgāraja', *Asian Music*, 34/1 (1993), 19.

energetic verses that alternate with the *pallavi*.[65] The *kriti* has an almost crystalline form, capable of infinite expansion through contrast and variation of its elements.

Modern concert programmes usually include an extended *rāgam-tānam-pallavi* that provides opportunity for the performers to exhibit skill in melodic and rhythmic improvisation on a particular *pallavi*. (The genre developed from competitions where candidates provided complex *pallavi*, for their rivals to imitate.) Towards the end of the *rāgam-tanam-pallavi*, the *mridangam* player usually improvises an extended cadenza.

Two other South Indian forms are still used widely in concert, and to accompany dance. The *varnam* often opens a concert: it is similar to the *kriti* but it is entirely pre-composed. The *padam* is a slow composition, based on devotional themes.[66]

Classical Dance

Dance, drama, and music form a unity in Indian culture (the word *sangīt* embodies all three components). In certain types of dance, the interaction of drumming with the movements of a dancer's feet is as precise as with the melodic lines of an instrumentalist, and the dancer procures from footwork as much rhythmic complexity and exactitude as drummers procure from drums. Indian systems of mime and of body movement, like systems of music, have their origins in ancient texts; characteristic use of symbolic hand gestures, for example, is described in the *Sāmaveda*.

Three basic elements constitute Indian classical dance. *Nritta* (pure dance) is the abstract movement of limbs of the body to musical accompaniment, referred to above. *Nātya* is the dramatic element: dancers frequently enact stories from the epics and the *Purānas*. *Nritya* (mime) seeks to convey mood and sentiment through bodily gesture, by means of facial expression and hand gestures, and through sung poetry, musical rhythm, costume, jewellery, and physical manifestations of mental and emotional states.[67]

[65] David B. Reck, 'South India', in Jeff Todd Titon (ed.), *Worlds of Music* (New York: Schirmer, 1992), 240.
[66] Powers, 'India', *The New Grove*, ix. 117.
[67] Kapila Vatsyayan, 'India', *The New Grove* (1980), ix. 160.

For dance, the human body is divided on the basis of major and minor parts. The former include the head, torso, arms, and legs; the latter include all parts of the face, from the eyebrows to the chin. Every part of the body is considered for its visual effect, and for its affinity with *rasa*. The *Nātyashāstra* lists 67 hand gestures, and 32 different movements of the lower limbs, along with 108 combinations of these gestures with other parts of the body. Classifications of this sort remain the basis of all classical dance.[68] (The aesthetic theory of *rasa*, as expounded in the *Nātyashāstra*, was described on pp. 103–4.)

In Indian dance, aesthetic shape is considered more important than muscular movement; indeed, the dancer's poses are based on rules for the architecture of the very temples in which the dances were performed. The axis of the vertical and horizontal is of primary importance: thus, for example, a characteristic pose of *Bharatanātyam* has the knees bent, the heels together, toes facing outwards, with arms outstretched and parallel to the ground.

Six dance styles are generally regarded as classical: *Bharatanātyam* (the oldest style, principally performed in the South); *Kuchipudi* (prevalent in Andhra Pradesh, related to *Bharatanātyam* but freer in style); *Kathakali* (a dance drama from Kerala that makes use of heavy make-up and elaborate head dresses); *Odissi* (a dance from the Orissa region, mainly performed by women); *Manipuri* (a dance from the north-east); and *Kathak* (a dance form, the growth of which was closely linked with that of Hindustani music).[69]

Bharatanātyam stands in relation to *Kathak*, rather as Carnatic does to Hindustani music. Both incorporate pure dance and mime; both use stylized facial and hand gestures; both use ankle bells; and both involve precise coordination of footwork with drumming. In *Bharatanātyam*, all aspects of dance relate to devotional texts, and the accompanying chant is continuous. Performances follow set procedures; as with Carnatic music, there is little scope for innovation, and the art lies in the subtlety of interpretation.

Kathak (from *katha*: 'story') is a mixture of mimed story telling and pure dance, with high-speed footwork that can be breathtaking in its virtuosity. Through using the feet flat, and with some 100 bells (*ghungrū*) attached to the ankles, the dancer creates complex rhythms, based

[68] Ibid.; see also Kay Ambrose and Ram Gopal, *Classical Dances and Costumes of India* (London: Adam & Charles Black, 1983).

[69] Vatsyayan, 'India', *The New Grove*, ix. 160.

on specific *tāla*, which are interspersed with rapid *bhramārī* (spins), repeated in multiples of three. The mimed items enact mythological stories of Krishna, or express through bodily gestures the underlying emotion of devotional hymns. These mimed items are usually accompanied by a vocalist, *sārangī*, and *tablā* or *pākhavāj*. A *Kathak* dancer will often include a *jawāb-sawāl* (question-answer) section, reciting the mnemonics of particular rhythms to be taken up by the *tablā*. In this, dancer and *tablā*-player work in competition—each vying with the other in speed and complexity—while the *tāla* is maintained by a melody instrument. *Kathak* dance expresses with particular persuasiveness the combination of form, romance, sentiment, and virtuosity that resulted from the fusion of Hindu and Islamic artistic traditions.

Interaction between Folk and Classical Styles of Music

India is a country of approximately 700 million people, 80 per cent of whom live in some half-million separate villages. The great diversity of folk traditions belonging to the subcontinent has contributed to classical styles, and continues to interact with them.

Just as Hindu culture arose from a mix of Aryan and Dravidian elements, so Hindu music arose from a mix of indigenous folk styles (*deshī*) and the 'sought' music (*mārga*) of the Aryan invaders. The *Nātyashāstra* gave to 'pure' and 'mixed' modes the same collective name as that of castes and sub-castes (*jāti*), indicating the importance attached to interaction between élite and popular culture. The *Brihaddeshī* listed the *rāgas* which indigenous peoples contributed to Aryan music; the process still continues in many areas, particularly in the north-west.

Many folk instruments were incorporated into the classical tradition: the *sārangī*, for example, was originally a folk instrument of Rajastan. Hereditary folk musicians found it advantageous to adopt the styles of classical music, for low-ranking castes could thereby enhance their social status.[70]

Kathakali dance drama developed in this way from folk traditions; it was open to all segments of society, and performed in temple courtyards (Pl. 29). It came to incorporate traditional theatrical symbols: green is

[70] Bonnie C. Wade, 'India', *The New Grove* (1980), ix. 147–8.

29. *Kathakali* dancers in Kerala. Photo: Claude Sauvageot

associated with heroic characters; the sword is a symbol of imperial and melagomaniac pretension; a beard denotes a classic, demonic villain. It includes conventional styles of acting, and of facial make-up. (Similar theatrical symbolism exists in Chinese opera.)

Another southern dance genre that combines folk and classical features is the *Harikathā* ('god-story'). An offshoot of *Kathak*, it is a kind of one-person folk theatre. Accompanied by violin and *mridangam*, the performer wears ankle bells and holds clappers. He or she dances and declaims devotional and folk poetry in a mixture of syllabic and melismatic chant, the ankle bells and clappers providing additional accompaniment. *Harikathā* exhibits a gypsy-like blend of grace, vigour, and virtuosity, in which the sheer variety of speech, song, and dance, and of tempo, vocal inflection, and ornamentation, breathes new life into familiar stories. (Such mixes of technique, which enable a single soloist to capture and hold the attention of the audience, are common throughout Asia: in the *Lam* singers of Laos, for example, or the *P'ansori* singers of Korea.)

The contexts for folk musics are as varied as the subcontinent itself, from Buddhist dance rituals in Leh, to ecstatic, flagellant rituals in

Rajastan. There are hobby-horse dances, dragon dances, and stick dances, all associated with fertility; there are seasonal songs and work songs, buffalo-catching songs, pregnancy songs, wedding songs, and healing songs; and there are possession songs in which the spirits of the ancients are brought to life. Ecstasy may still be induced by drinking the blood of sacred animals. Drum dances may still accompany the search for the soul of an unborn child. In Muslim societies, battles that ended in Muslim victories are still enacted. Acrobatics, snake-charming, and fire-eating add to the entertainment value of folk festivities. In earlier times, in Villukottu in Kerala, ritual musicians were observed playing interlocking patterns in the style of the Indonesian gamelan.[71]

The contexts for folk celebrations are changing, and it is inevitable that music and dance will change with them. In Madras, for example, an Institute for Arts and Crafts is attempting to preserve folk traditions by providing urban performance venues.

Age, magnificence, poverty, and equanimity are bedfellows in Indian culture. To the Westerner, values in India can feel strangely unfamiliar. The Indian's innate belief that the soul may be reborn in a higher status engenders resignation in the face of recurrent adversity; reincarnation is a metaphor for resilience, and confers authenticity upon antiquity. Nor is antiquity a preoccupation merely of the élite: it gives meaning to the lives of millions of peasants, whose income is seldom above that needed for bare subsistence. Uniquely, perhaps, India's spiritual ambience furnishes continuing energy to art forms that have survived the changes and impositions of 3,000 years of history. Ancient India remains with us, as does the ancient past of no other civilization.

[71] A video recording of folk traditions now, in contrast to fifty years ago, 'The Bake Restudy' (1984), is available from: Aspara Media for Intercultural Education, 13659, Victory Boulevard, Suite 577, Van Nuys, California 91401, USA.

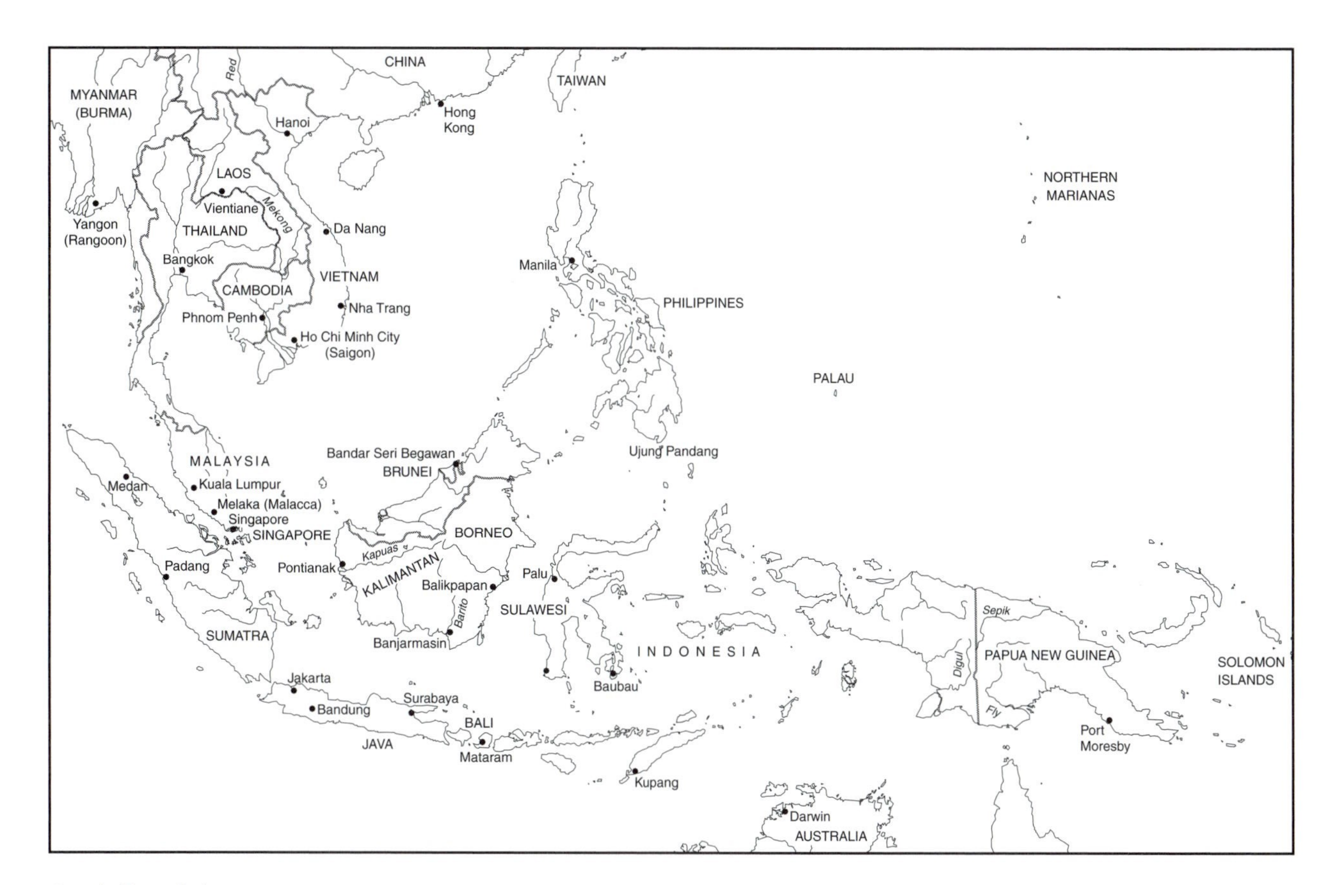

South East Asia

9 *South East Asia*

An Ancient Civilization

The area now known as South East Asia consists of the two archipelago republics of Indonesia and the Philippines, and of a land mass that tails off in a long peninsula. The landmass separates southern India from southern China. Throughout its history, this area has been one of migration, trade, and conflict, involving such peoples as the Malays, Chams, Khmers, Mons, Pyus, Burmans, Laos, Shans, and Thais, as well as traders, or would-be conquerors, from China, India, West Asia, Europe, and, more recently, the USA. The mainland now comprises Myanmar (Burma), Thailand, Laos, Cambodia, Vietnam, Singapore, and Malaysia.

Throughout South East Asia as a whole, there is an extraordinary ethnic mix: in Indonesia alone there are some 3,000 inhabited islands that are home to over 300 cultural groups, speaking over 250 languages. Remarkably, this diverse region, sandwiched between two of the world's greatest civilizations, has nurtured and retained distinctive, cultural systems with homogeneous, musical styles, separate from those of its two venerable neighbours.

Long before South East Asia was influenced by either China or India, it was a region of advanced civilization. As early as the seventh millennium BC, a primitive form of agriculture existed along the Red River Valley in present-day Vietnam; a bronze culture was in existence by the second millennium BC, and ironwork was established by the first millennium BC. In these respects, at least, the civilization of South East Asia is as old as that of China.

The history of the early movements of peoples into the area remains shadowy. Writing was not developed until Hinduism and Buddhism began to spread from India in the early centuries AD; prior to this we are dependent upon Chinese literary sources. Broadly stated, the Bay of Bengal marks a significant divide between peoples of 'Caucasoid' and 'Mongoloid' stock, and between those speaking Indo-European and Sino-Tibetan languages. Other languages spoken in South East Asia include the Khmer language spoken in Cambodia, and the Austronesian languages spoken in Malaysia, Indonesia, and the Philippines.

The distinctiveness of South East Asian cultural systems survived a considerable degree of foreign influence. As early as the third century BC, the Mons (in what is now Lower Burma) were in contact with the Buddhist Ashoka kingdom in India; to the south, Indonesians plied the sea routes to India and China long before the Christian era; and, although the Silk Road linking China to Europe lay to the north of Vietnam and Burma, a more southerly trade route linked China to India via Yunnan, Upper Burma, and Assam.[1] When, during the third century AD, the Silk Road collapsed as a trade route, owing to repeated incursions into Chinese territory by Central Asian nomads, trading by sea came into new prominence. South East Asia then became a focal point of east–west maritime trade. The site of Oc Eo, a recently excavated port city in the Mekong delta region of present-day Vietnam, has yielded evidence of maritime relations with China, Malaysia, Indonesia, India, Persia, and the Mediterranean. It was probably here that Chinese met Indians, the latter shipping goods west, portaging them across the Malay peninsula, and thence to the southern tip of India.[2]

The music and arts of South East Asia were strongly influenced by animistic religion. Before the arrival of Hindu–Buddhist beliefs, the area was steeped in the worship of ancestors and earth-gods; its mythology was imbued with a cosmological dualism between mountains and sea, winged-beings and water-beings, mountain peoples and sea-coast peoples. When the new religions arrived from India, they were syncretized with existing animistic practices. During the twelfth century, a missionary wave of *Theravāda* Buddhism arrived on the mainland from Sri Lanka; but even then the worship of Buddha took place beside the continuing worship of spirits. Even when Islam arrived, during the fifteenth century, and took root in most of Malaysia, Indonesia, and the southern Philippines, it too was tempered by existing animism.

[1] D. G. E. Hall, *A History of South East Asia* (London: Macmillan, 1981), 25.
[2] *The Times Atlas of World History*, ed. Geoffrey Barraclough (London, 1989), 700.

Animistic religion had found strong expression in the arts before ever Hinduism and Buddhism arrived. It is possible that the art of *batik* and a type of shadow-puppet theatre preceded the process of Indianization[3] (the latter, most probably, having spread from China).[4] Certainly this is true of the so-called gong-chime ensembles. With their idiosyncratic tuning systems and their interlocking-ensemble techniques, they are still to be found from the Philippines to Burma. They vary considerably in instrumental composition, tunings, and ensemble techniques, but their timbre is unique to the region. It is music, as much as anything, that establishes the distinctive cultural identity of South East Asia, and it is the 'gong chimes'—that is to say, bronze—that link its culture with that of China. Considerable status attached to bronze in areas to the east of the Indian subcontinent.

Bamboo and Bronze Instruments

It appears likely that the bronze and iron chime metallophones, now found throughout the region, existed as bamboo 'chime' instruments before the bronze age.[5] On the mainland, xylophone keys made with bamboo are still sometimes preferred to those made of other woods, because of their mellower sound quality. (Bamboo can even be made to imitate the sound of bronze gongs: the performer sings a low-pitched note while breathing into an open, bamboo tube placed inside a larger, stopped tube.)

Prime evidence of an advanced bronze culture in South East Asia is provided by the bronze 'drums' that appeared in the Dongson culture (*c.*500–*c.*300 BC) of the Red River Valley in Vietnam.[6] Bronze-working began at *c.*1800 BC and the 'drums' (with metal membrane) represent the last most brilliant phase of the culture. Some of these magnificent artefacts are over 50 centimetres in height, and have *tympana* over 60 centimetres in diameter. The *tympana* are usually characterized by concentric bands of decorations encircling a raised solar star. Figured

[3] Hall, *History of South East Asia*, 9.

[4] Eugenia Popescu-Judetz, *Studies in Oriental Arts* (Pittsburgh: Duquesne University Tamburitzans, 1981), 800.

[5] L. E. R. Picken, 'The Music of Far Eastern Asia', in *The New Oxford History of Music*, i (Oxford: Oxford University Press, 1957), 183–5.

[6] Janice Stargardt, *The Ancient Pyu of Burma* (Cambridge: Pascea, in association with the Institute of South East Asian Studies, Singapore, 1990), 307.

30. Lithophone (*dan ba*) from the southern central highlands of Vietnam, tuned to a pentatonic scale, dating from *c*.4000 BC, at the Institute of Culture and Art, Ho Chi Minh City. Photo: Philip Blackburn

scenes alternate with geometric patterns, and indicate that the drums were first used as percussion instruments, probably to summon thunder and rain; later they became objects of worship, and a means by which to call to the ancestors.[7] They were revered by the Chinese as spoils of war. Also in Vietnam (in the southern central highlands), and dating from around 4000 BC, sets of six stone slabs, tuned to a pentatonic scale (with an accurate octave, and the other notes near to the ratios of just intonation), have been found (Pl. 30).[8] Their function is not clear, but they may have been precursors of the chime metallophones used widely throughout South East Asia.

The Dongson culture spread south and north into what are now the Chinese provinces of Yunnan, Guangdong, and Guangxi. Between the third and second centuries BC, bronze and iron techniques entered Java, and Indonesians subsequently became skilled artisans in bronze and iron. It appears, however, that they were unable to cast the large bronze

[7] Pham Huy Phong (ed.), *Dong Son Drums in Viet Nam* (The Viet Nam Social Science Publishing House, 1990), 262–7.

[8] Information kindly supplied by composer and musicologist Philip Blackburn.

31. Two *angklung*s in a Balinese cremation procession

32. Philippine *kulibit* (tube zither)
Photo: José Maceda

drums. (Modern Vietnamese themselves have been unable to reproduce the ancient techniques.) Instead, Indonesians became expert in producing gongs, the larger ones suspended vertically and the smaller ones suspended horizontally on wooden frames.

These smaller, 'kettle' gongs came to be placed together in groups of three to seven, in varying tunings. Chime metallophones, with keys made of bronze, brass, or iron, were then produced to play in conjunction with them. There is evidence that such instruments were being used, in combination, in Central Java by the eighth century AD.[9] The gongs of modern ensembles are of two main types: individual gongs, or sets of gongs, suspended vertically from frames; and sets of gongs suspended horizontally, on a rack, on a wooden case, or in a frame. Orchestras of mainly bronze instruments, most conspicuous now in Java and Bali, are known as 'gamelans'.

In many areas, bamboo still plays a distinctive role in the musical culture, even though it does not enjoy the same status as bronze. In the poorer villages of Central and East Java, and of Bali, the bars of whole sets of gamelan instruments may consist of lengths of bamboo (mostly tuned to a *slendro* scale). An alternative pitched instrument (in Malay: *angklung*), found widely throughout the region, consists of two or three tongued bamboo tubes, loosely mounted, so as to slide freely, in a wooden frame; one produces the basic note, the other two the octave above. The instrument is sounded by shaking, and a number of players holding one or two such instruments can produce melodic lines (Pl. 31). In Bali, *gamelan angklung* is used specifically in cremation rites, though the ensemble rarely includes *angklung* now. In West Java, however, groups of twenty or more *angklung* players perform a repertoire that includes arrangements of Western marches and dances;[10] and in Malaysia the instrument is used in schools.

Bamboo instruments are still in use in many parts of the Philippines. (In Las Piñas, a three-manual, bamboo pipe organ is in regular use as a recital instrument.) The oldest, Philippine, bamboo instruments are essentially percussive; these include buzzers or 'tuning forks', quill-shaped percussion tubes, clappers, stamping tubes, scrapers, slit drums, Jew's harps, and paired-string zithers. Bamboo flutes, pan pipes, and tube zithers, on the other hand, produce identifiable pitches:

[9] Mantle Hood, 'Indonesia', *The New Grove* (1980), ix. 169.

[10] Eric Taylor, *Musical Instruments of South East Asia* (Singapore: Oxford University Press, 1989), 73.

tube and string lengths are carefully measured to yield note-sets considered appropriate for particular functions (Pl. 32).[11]

Drums play an important part in music-making; indeed, their leading role—in determining tempo, style, and beginnings and endings of a performance—links a line of traditional musical cultures from West Africa to East Asia. Even in the 'gong-chime' cultures, it is normal for two drummers to lead the ensemble. In Burma, uniquely, the 'gong-chime' ensemble (*hsaìng-waìng*) is led by a circular 'drum chime' (*pat-waìng*) of up to twenty-one drums, all tuned to different pitches, in the centre of which sits the drummer.

Other instruments to be found in 'gong-chime' ensembles throughout South East Asia include flutes, shawms, zithers, spike fiddles, and two-string fiddles. In addition, the human voice is often added to the ensemble. The size of 'gong-chime' ensembles varies from as many as seventy-five (in old court orchestras of Central Java) to four or five (in village ensembles).

Tunings of 'Gong-Chime' Instruments

Tuning systems vary throughout the region. No method of generating a scale, such as the cycle-of-fifths procedure, is employed. On the mainland of South East Asia ensembles frequently use an anhemitonic pentatonic scale; but in Indonesia, 'kettle' gongs and other metallophones are usually arranged in individual sets of five notes or seven notes (the modes *slendro* and *pelog* respectively), neither of which is 'tuned' in the sense in which bell chimes in China or Korea were tuned. These two modal types may be used alternatively in different compositions, or alternately in the same composition.

In practice, the difference between these two note-sets lies less in the number of notes they contain than in their tunings. (*Pelog* approximates to a five-note scale with two auxiliary notes sounding a little like the hemitonic pentatonic of Japan.) The five-note *slendro* is anhemitonic; the intervals between the notes are approximately equal, though the ear may tend to rationalize the scale as 'Chinese-like'. The seven-note *pelog* is hemitonic; intervals between notes are unequal, and vary from ensemble to ensemble. (In Thailand, there is a seven-note

[11] José Maceda, 'In Search of a Source of Pentatonic Hemitonic and Anhemitonic Scales in Southeast Asia', *Acta Musicologica*, 3/2 (Bärenreiter-Verlag, 1990), 193.

equidistant scale, from which all tunings derive.) The notes and intervals of both note-sets vary from area to area, and from ensemble to ensemble; but they are consistent *within* an ensemble, because gong-founders copy the pitches of pre-existent instruments. Neither *slendro* nor *pelog* necessarily include the interval of a perfect fifth, on which the modes of China and Europe are based.

Various suggestions have been proposed for the origin of this two-scale system. José Maceda has suggested that the coexistence of hemitonic and anhemitonic note-sets in Indonesian gamelan ensembles may have originated in a 'divisive' system of scaling,[12] applied to vertical, and nose-blown, bamboo flutes, known to be operated in the Philippines, and in the islands of Kalimantan, Java, Nias, and Sulawesi in Indonesia. The first finger-hole is bored half-way along the tube, and yields (approximately) an octave above the fundamental; subsequent holes—usually two, three, or four in number—are bored in relation to this middle hole, and yield notes and intervals within a compass less than an octave. The unit measurement used to determine the length of the flute, and of its finger-holes, is usually the circumference of the flute; and, because the number of circumferential units used to determine the length of the pipe varies—normally 6, 8, 10, 12, 14, or 16—a variety of scales is produced. If after two units a half-unit space is introduced, a semitone step occurs. The resultant 'gapped' scales (scales with intervals larger than a tone) may thus be anhemitonic or hemitonic.

Where this system is operated, both hemitonic and anhemitonic scales are used by the same groups of people, and each has its own distinctive repertoire with separate social applications. In the Philippines, a 'gong-chime' instrument, the *kulintang*, also appears both in hemitonic and anhemitonic tunings, with small and wide gaps at different points among the seven gong pitches. All this suggests that the irregular tunings of Indonesian 'gong chimes' may derive from a 'divisive' method of tuning flutes, perhaps in existence over a much wider area before the development of cycle-of-fifths procedures in Old Babylonia; and that anhemitonic pentatonic tunings in parts of the mainland, which resemble Pythagorean tuning, reflect later, Chinese influence.[13]

Indian influence, on the other hand, was strong in South East Asia; moreover, a two-scale, hemitonic-anhemitonic system is to be found as far north as Burma, and bamboo instruments, tuned to a scale resem-

[12] Ibid. 198–202. [13] Ibid.

bling the Burmese hemitonic (C–E–F–G–B–C, where C is used to define the starting note) is to be found in the central highlands of Vietnam. Richard Widdess has advanced musical evidence from which an Indian basis for the use of *slendro* and *pelog* scales could be deduced (as one possibility). Assuming (for the purposes of comparison) that the largest interval in any *slendro* tuning is always less than twice the size of the smallest, and that the two largest intervals in the pentatonic framework of any *pelog* tuning are more than three times the size of the smallest, the intervals of *slendro* and *pelog* may be compared with those of the two ancient *grāmarāgas* of Indian music, as described in the *Nātyashāstra* in terms of *shruti*-units (see p. 246). (Similarities in rhythmic structure between the music of ancient India and that of Indonesia are also to be observed.[14])

The exact origin of the Indonesian two-scale system is, of course, of lesser importance than the character of the musical styles and genres the system has served. Such arguments make clear, however, that the diatonic scale derived from the cycle-of-fifths procedure is not a special gift of nature, as some Western analysts—most notably Schenker—have maintained (see pp. 476–7), and that tuning systems become acceptable to a society through enculteration (or acculturation), rather than through correspondence with any observable laws of physics.

Musical Structures in 'Gong-Chime' Ensembles

The principles on which the music of 'gong-chime' ensembles are usually constructed may derive, in part, from the limitations imposed by the fixed tuning of the melodic percussion instruments. In essence, however, they do not differ greatly from those used elsewhere. In both *slendro* and *pelog* sets, for example, certain pitches have greater importance than others; and varying 'hierarchies' of pitches and intervals determine the character of particular modes, often associated with times of day and night, with seasons, or with particular aspects of associated dramatic action. Modes—and the 'hierarchy' of pitches associated with them—determine particular melodic

[14] D. R. Widdess, 'Sléndro and Pélog in India?', in B. Arps (ed.), *Performance in Java and Bali* (London: School of Oriental and African Studies, 1993).

patterns which, in turn, affect the melodic and rhythmic organization of an entire piece.

Performances by larger ensembles consist in simultaneous variations on a fundamental 'core' melody, in notes of equal duration. Other melodic patterns (based on the pitch hierarchy) evolve from this melody and give rise to multiple heterophonic structures. The melodic patterns are 'stratified' between different sets of instruments, rhythmic and melodic density being greater in the faster patterns of the upper registers.[15]

In combination, these melodic layers lead to considerable density of rhythm. (In Central Java there may be as many as forty melodic layers; in other areas, as few as three.) The subsections of a piece, and its individual phrase lengths, are delineated by various-sized, vertically suspended gongs; and the most important strokes usually occur on second or fourth beats within the rhythmic structures. This system is commonly referred to as colotomic ('incision in the colon'), because it 'cuts' a composition into its metric subsections. Its effect, however, is similar to the demarcation of rhythmic cycles characteristic of musical systems elsewhere in Asia; indeed, drums are commonly used to support metric structures in this way. In Bali, colotomic punctuation is infinitely varied, and essentially defines form and character in musical compositions.

Interaction, between 'stratification' of melodic material and 'colotomic' delineation of rhythmic structure, is an important feature of many 'gong-chime' ensembles throughout South East Asia. (Whereas in Java and Bali ensembles with a preponderance of metallophones are the norm, on the mainland, in Cambodia, Thailand, and Laos, ensembles incorporate a larger proportion of wooden idiophones, and the heterophony of music performed on them is usually less dense.)

Colotomic delineation of the structure is affected by layering of *tempo*, usually in multiples of two. Thus, in a layer at a tempo twice as fast as that in which the 'core' melody was originally played, the punctuating instruments also play twice as fast. In this way, shifts of tempo are effected in a clearly audible way, but without interruption of musical continuity. (Such techniques of augmentation and diminution of melodic material are not, of course, peculiar to South East Asia, but common to musical cultures around the world.) The beat does not remain constant; within the layered tempos, accelerandos and rallen-

[15] Mantle Hood, 'South East Asia', *The New Grove* (1980), xvii. 764.

tandos are effected, and are often followed by a pause with tremolo of decreasing velocity on a single note. (These features are characteristic of much East Asian music.) Drum patterns are often virtuosic, and may sound improvisatory; but they are customarily related to mood or function of the music, using traditional rhythms, passed down from teacher to pupil. There are usually two drummers, and the rhythms played by the second interlock with those of the first.

The Importance of Theatre and Dance

Religion has played an important part in the maintenance of 'gong-chime' traditions. Because the propitiation of spirits involves frequent enactment of moral tales, together with ceremonies of purification, music is inseparably linked to theatre, dance, and the shadow-puppet play. In many village societies throughout South East Asia, where animistic beliefs still condition the daily routines of life, musical practice remains intimately linked with the religious source of its inspiration.

Theatrical forms acquired regional variants as they spread from area to area; but their origins in animistic belief have ensured broad affinities in style. One pervasive genre is the shadow-puppet play, called, in Indonesia, *wayang kulit* ('leather puppet'), more easily transportable than troupes of singer-dancer-actors and instrumentalists. Although the genre is now most frequently encountered in Indonesia, it was once common across India, South East Asia, and East Asia, having originated, most probably, in China (where it is still practised in Shaanxi province).[16] Even today it is widely practised in Turkey.

The two-dimensional, semi-transparent puppets, cut from thin sheets of leather, are projected in profile on a white silk screen, lit from behind by a flickering oil lamp. The puppets appear in silhouette. They are cut out to show intricate details of costume and ornament, and as many as 100 puppets may be used in a single performance, sometimes in spectacular battle scenes. The puppets are usually managed by a single *dalang* (puppeteer) who, with minimal aid from two assistants (sitting on either side), controls the actions. He manipulates the puppets, narrates the story, and chants (Pl. 33); he also directs the gamelan behind him by means of an elaborate set of cues, which include hitting

[16] Popescu-Judetz, *Studies in Oriental Arts*, 80.

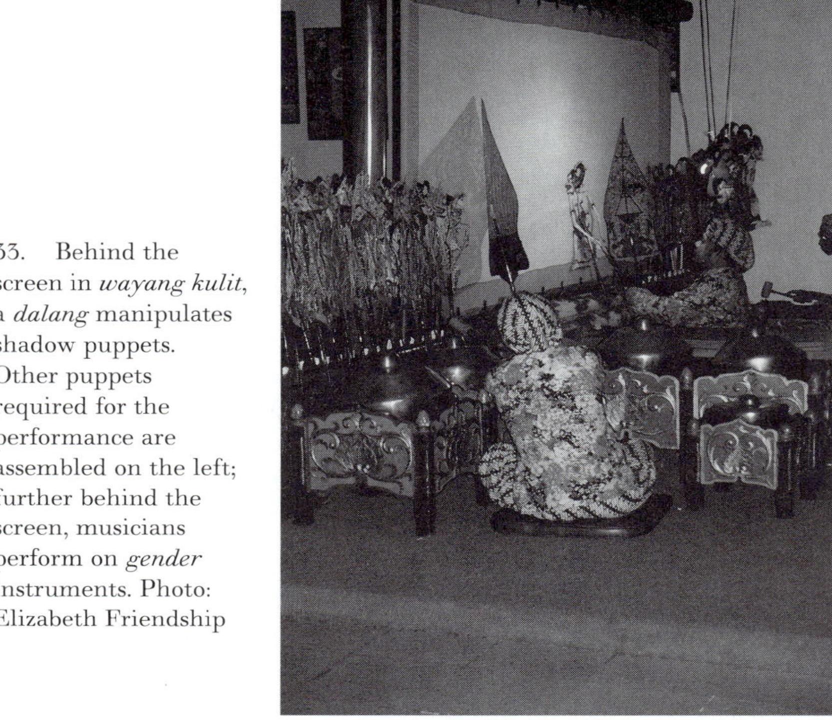

33. Behind the screen in *wayang kulit*, a *dalang* manipulates shadow puppets. Other puppets required for the performance are assembled on the left; further behind the screen, musicians perform on *gender* instruments. Photo: Elizabeth Friendship

the puppet box and a nest of cymbals with mallets held between his toes.[17]

Wayang kulit is performed at temple ceremonies that celebrate special anniversaries, or important stages in seasonal or life cycles. The purpose is mainly didactic. Tales from the *Rāmāyana* and *Mahābhārata* celebrate the triumph of love over hate, and of good over evil, and do so in mixture of high artistry and bawdy humour. The genre offers considerable scope for improvisation, and opportunity for commenting on topical concerns is not the least among its attractions.

The angular movements of the puppets have an affinity with those of traditional dance. South East Asian dance appears to be overlaid with Indian influence, but that influence is in fact restricted. Whereas, in India, dance is usually linked structurally to *chant*, and a detailed

[17] Neil Sorrell, *A Guide to the Gamelan* (London: Faber & Faber, 1990), 21–2.

system of hand and facial gestures is used to illustrate words and ideas, in South East Asia, hand and facial movements do not have the same symbolic significance as in India, and dancers perform to continuous instrumental music.[18] Again, there is no trace in South East Asia of the elaborate footwork that characterizes many Indian dance genres. The greater freedom of South East Asian dance has permitted the evolution of a variety of traditions.

In some areas, dance is still linked to temple ritual; indeed, spirits are thought to reside in masks and costumes. In Bali, for example, the Barong—a fantastic, dragon-type, quadrupedal creature—represents living, protective forces; animated by two male dancers, its body assumes endlessly different shapes and sizes. These Barong-manipulators spend the night nullifying the powers of the creature's traditional opponent—the witch Rangda—only to see her reincarnated in another human being at the end. Caste is still significant in Bali: and only a brāhman may repair a Barong or Rangda mask, because only a brāhman knows how to protect himself from its inherent magic forces.

In many parts of the mainland, speech, song, dance, and comedy combine in all-night festivals of music theatre. Itinerant troupes of professional actors and musicians, often descended from famed families of performers, keep alive the traditions, and are in turn imitated by local, amateur groups. Performances usually take place at the local temple, or in a temporary mat-shed theatre, erected on its premises. Preparations for the festival involve the whole community, and the occasion usually marks some ritual or auspicious period, such as a full moon. Temple festivals, rooted in ancient history, embody a continuing process of affective activity, as inseparable from life as is the religion that still sustains it.

Early Empires in Vietnam and Cambodia

The early history of South East Asia is still unclear, but it appears that, by the second century AD, a state known as Funan was established by Khmers in the lower Mekong delta in what is now southern Vietnam and Cambodia. This state had extensive contacts with China and, in the third century, sent a mission there

[18] Hood, 'South East Asia', *The New Grove*, xvii. 768–73.

with a present of musicians and native products. The mission records the use of an Indian script.[19]

A Hindu kingdom known as Champa emerged to the north of Funan around the second century AD. Early in its history, this state appears to have allied with Funan in an unsuccessful attempt to oust the Chinese from the Red River delta, conquered by them in the second century BC. With the accession of the Tang in China (in the seventh century AD), the whole of what is now Vietnam was brought into tributary relationship with the Chinese empire. China named the area 'Annam': 'The Pacified South'.

Following the fall of the Tang, the Vietnamese secured independence from China (in 928), but the two countries were frequently at war, and it took Vietnam another 500 years to bring Champa securely into its state.[20] (Annam is now known as Trung-Phan; Funan—which the French named Cochin China—is now known as Nam-Phan.)

Early Island Empires

The first clear evidence of statehood in Malaysia and Indonesia dates from the seventh century AD, when the state of Srivijaya began to spread from Sumatra into peninsular Malaysia and Java; it thus gained control of the trade routes through the Malacca and Sunda straits. Srivijaya became famous for ship-building, but its essentially coastal domains were not suitable for wet-rice agriculture, the need for which caused new kingdoms to arise in Central Java, which gradually superseded Srivijaya in strength.

The early rulers of these kingdoms were the Hindu Sanjayas; but during the eighth century, the Buddhist Sailendras took control, and it was during Sailendra rule that the great Buddhist temples of Central Java—the grandest of which was Borobudur—were erected in the shadow of Mount Meru. Around the middle of the ninth century, a Sanjayan king retook Central Java, and commemorated his victory with the building of the great Hindu temple of Prambanan. Sanjayan rule continued until around 930, when the capital was suddenly moved to East Java.

East Java became sufficiently powerful to attract an invasion by the armies of the Kublai Khan (in 1293), then occupying the imperial

[19] Hall, *History of South East Asia*, 27–8.

[20] Ibid. 211–14.

throne of China; but, a year later, the Chinese armies were expelled, and a new empire arose, known as Majahapit. By the mid-fourteenth century, this embraced the entire Indonesian archipelago, claiming suzerainty over the trading ports of the Malay peninsula, Sulawesi, Borneo, Maluku (the Moluccas), and Bali, and spreading Javanese culture in these areas. Conflicts over the royal succession (in the early fifteenth century), however, weakened the empire just at the time when Islam was sweeping the Indian Ocean. By the end of the fifteenth century, the great Majahapit empire had fallen to Islam and—so it is usually claimed—the entire Hindu-Javanese aristocracy had fled to Bali, taking with them the time-honoured Javanese court traditions of music and dance.

Islam in the Island States

Today, Islam is the national religion of both Malaysia and Indonesia: 80 per cent of the population of Indonesia is said to follow the Prophet. This statement must be seen in context, however. Islam spread to South East Asia not through the sword (as it did in West Asia), but through peaceful expansion of trade. As was the case in Sub-Saharan Africa, conversion was as much a matter of convenience as conviction: Arabs dominated the sea routes between South and East Asia, and conversion to Islam enabled Indonesians to join in this lucrative trade. Islam spread throughout the area from Malacca (in present-day peninsular Malaysia), the conversion of which (in 1436) enabled it to capitalize on Islamic trade routes and become the greatest emporium in the East.

When Islam arrived in South East Asia, in the fifteenth century, it was dominated by Sufism, the officiants of which were peripatetic mystics, advocating the merits of asceticism and ecstasy, attended by dance and poetry. Mostly the spread of Islam was peaceful, but in Java it took hold by force of arms. According to Javanese chronicles, however, it was spread across Java by means of the shadow-puppet theatre: confessions of faith, and Qur'ānic prayers, were introduced (apparently) during performances of the *Rāmāyana* and *Mahābhārata*. Islamic chroniclers would characterize the demise of the great Majahapit empire as 'the disappearance of the Light of the Universe'.[21] Clearly,

[21] Eric Oey (ed.), *Indonesia* (Hong Kong: APA Publications, 1986), 30.

Islam syncretized with existing traditions, much as Hinduism and Buddhism had done, over 1,000 years earlier.

The Politics of Hinduism and Buddhism

To appreciate the ritual significance of the ensemble music that developed on the mainland, and in the island states, it is important to understand the political impact of Hinduism and Buddhism on the area in the early centuries AD. These religions proved attractive to petty rulers because they gave authority to kingship; and writing—Sanskrit—enabled that authority to be commemorated in stone inscriptions. A ruler (who had managed to extend his power) would build a *chandi* (monumental tomb) dedicated to his cult deity. The supernatural powers associated with the Shaivite cult of Hinduism, for example, enabled a petty Maharajah to identify with Shiva, and so acquire both immortality and divine legitimacy for his rule.

The transmission of a sacred personality to the king was symbolized in the worship of the Shaivite *linga* (phallus). This *linga* represented the cosmic pillar (see p. 99), and its sanctuary was the summit of a temple mountain, held to be the axis of the universe. It became the duty of a *Deva-raja* (god-king) of the Saivite cult to erect a temple mountain to preserve the royal *linga* and, with it, his 'sacred ego'. The concept of temple mountains had originated in ancient Mesopotamia and, via India, came to fuse with South East Asian belief. Funan, for example, had its sacred hill of Ba Phnom; the Buddhist Sailendras of Central Java were 'Lords of the Mountain'. In Hindu-Buddhist thought, Mount Meru was held to be the centre of the universe and the temple its symbol; the many-tiered temples, characteristic of Bali, are still called 'Meru'.[22]

Mahāyāna Buddhism, as much as Hinduism, enabled rulers to receive divine sanction for their rule, for such rulers could identify with a Bodhisattva, and sponsor the building of temples to act as their mausoleums; indeed, major temples were planned as models of the actual *abode* of the gods. This cult of the 'Buddharaja' motivated the building of the great temple complex of Angkor Wat in Cambodia (twelfth century), one of the largest and most splendid in the world.[23]

[22] Hall, *History of South East Asia*, 113–14.
[23] Michael Freeman, *Angkor* (Hong Kong: Pacific Rim Press, 1992), 11–12.

The four faces that adorn each of the towers of the Bayon Wat—originally there were fifty-two such towers—are actually those of the king, in the guise of the Compassionate Bodhisattva, Lokesvara: a still-observable testament to the awesome power assumed by living god-kings. (Even during the latter half of the twentieth century, Prince Sihanouk could have himself nominally elected by the people, but yet appeal to their hearts and minds as a semi-divine monarch.)

The courts of monarchs naturally became centres of Sanskrit scholarship, for temporal power depended on the visible presence of brāhman priests. The courts also became centres of the arts. Popular religious festivals were consecrated by priests; and, in this way, the brāhmans sanctified socially cohesive animistic practices, while court ceremonies gave public expression to the ruler's legitimacy. Priests, artists, and musicians became indispensable members of the royal retinue. It was at the courts of the Sailendra kings (in Central Java) that the great traditions of dance drama and of gamelan-playing evolved; and it was in Central Java, centre of gong-making, that these traditions spilled over into local communities to create a web of village music-making that is still extant. Only the dance drama was restricted to the courts; commoners learned their *Rāmāyana* and *Mahābhārata* from the ubiquitous village performances of shadow-puppet plays.

The religions of Hinduism and *Mahāyāna* Buddhism, having a common political function, became largely interchangeable. *Theravāda* Buddhism, however, offered no all-powerful god to whom to appeal for benevolent intervention: a king was held to have obtained his position as a result of merit accumulated in a previous lifetime. *Theravāda* Buddhism first became a strong *political* force in the twelfth century, due to a missionary crusade brought by monks advocating austerity and meditation. The resurgence of the creed obviated the need for priests to conduct elaborate ceremonials, and replaced the sacred language of Sanskrit with the sacred language of Pali. *Theravāda* Buddhism spread to the Thai states of the Menam Valley, to Burma, and to Cambodia, where subsequently it destroyed the legitimacy of the Khmer god-kings.[24] *Theravāda* Buddhism would give to the South East Asian mainland a somewhat different character from that of the islands.

[24] Hall, *History of South East Asia*, 128–9.

The Khmer Empire

The Khmer kingdom of Angkor was founded, in the early eighth century, by Jayavarman II, who is thought to have spent some time in Java, either paying tribute, or as a hostage. When he returned to Cambodia, he established his independence through the Saivite cult he had learned in Java; it is likely that it was he who introduced Javanese dance, drama, and shadow-puppet theatre to the Khmer kingdom.

Jayavarman extended his rule to include much of present-day Cambodia, and built mountain-temples at each new city he created. By the eleventh century, his successor had extended the empire south into the Malay kingdom of Tampralinga (Ligor) and west and north into the Mekong Valley. Angkor itself was founded in the twelfth century. By the end of that century, Jayavarman VII had extended the empire's boundaries north into Champa and north-west as far as Vientiane (capital of present-day Laos). It was at this time, however, that *Theravāda* Buddhism spread from Pagan into Cambodia and undermined the sanctity of the monarchy;[25] the sovereign ceased to be the embodiment of Shiva, and was no longer able to gain the religious respect that made possible the development of empire.[26] In the first half of the fifteenth century, Angkor Wat was abandoned by all but a few monks, and the Khmers never recovered their position of ascendancy on the mainland. Nevertheless, the magnificent remains of temples of the ninth to twelfth centuries are a constant reminder—to modern Khmers—of their former greatness.

Early Developments in Burma

During the second or third centuries BC, missionaries from Ashoka's India are said to have been sent to a region referred to in the Buddhist *Jātaka*s as Suvarnabhumi, the 'Golden Land'. Suvarnabhumi probably refers to the fertile area of land that stretches from southern Burma, across central Thailand, to western Cambodia. By the sixth century, a loose network of city states had developed into a kingdom known as Dvārāvāti (the legendary capital city of Krishna in the *Mahābhārata*). Dvārāvāti culture is associated

[25] Hall, *History of South East Asia*, 125–9. [26] Ibid. 135.

with the Mon, who may have been migrants from north-west India, and the kingdom itself became a pre-eminent centre of early *Theravāda* Buddhism.

Northern Burma first enters history with a mention in 128 AD of the trade route from China to the West. This route was used not only by traders, but also by envoys from all parts of the Roman Empire. The Chinese had established a prefecture across the Mekong River, just north of the Burma border area.[27] This was Nanchao, in present-day Yunnan. Shortly thereafter, the Pyu, a Tibeto-Burman-speaking people, made their way south from Central Asia, just west of this Chinese prefecture; they settled in the Irrawaddy Valley, and claimed suzerainty over eighteen Mon states. During the eighth century they moved their capital north to Halin.

In 801 the Pyu sent a formal embassy with thirty-five musicians and thirty-five instruments to the Chinese court. The instruments (as described in a Chinese account) comprised nineteen different types, classified under eight materials (sources of sound): metal (bell cymbals and iron clappers); shell (conches); silk = strings (harps, zithers, lutes); bamboo (flutes and pipes); gourd (mouth organs); skin (drums); ivory (elephant's tusk mouth organ); and horn (two-horned mouth organ).[28]

The Pyu embassy travelled via Nanchao. It stimulated Chinese interest in the Pyu, and it is from the 'Tang History' that we learn that 'rebels' in Nanchao sacked the Pyu capital of Halin in 832.[29] These rebels were Thai who, like the Shan and Lao (to whom they were related), were anxious to escape Chinese domination. The Shan and Lao had already moved south; and throughout the three centuries following the sack of Halin, the Thai slowly infiltrated much of Burma and modern Thailand. The Pyu disappeared from history.

The Burmese themselves arrived from the China–Tibet border area in the ninth century. They moved down the Irrawaddy and established themselves in the rice-producing plains of the north. They made Pagan their capital, and, from there, controlled the trade routes from India to China; in 1057, they established the 'First Burmese Empire'. Temple-building began in earnest towards the end of the eleventh century, and during the twelfth century Pagan acquired the name of 'City of the Four Million Pagodas'.

[27] Ibid. 151–2.

[28] For a full description of these instruments, see Laurence Picken, 'Instruments in an Orchestra from Pyū (Upper Burma) in 802', *Musica Asiatica*, 4 (1984), 245–70.

[29] Hall, *History of South East Asia*, 155.

The court of Pagan became suffused with Mon culture: Pali from Sri Lanka became the sacred language, and the Mon alphabet replaced Sanskrit in royal inscriptions.[30] In 1257, however, Mongol armies defeated the Burmese and sacked Pagan. Thereafter, for some 300 years—until it had to deal with the Portuguese—Burma was divided into petty states. The Mon established a separate kingdom in Pegu in the south; the Shan established sovereignty over Upper Burma from a new capital at Ava; and the Arakanese spread along the Bay of Bengal to Chittagong, in present-day Bangladesh.

The Rise of the Thais

While Burma was in relative disarray, the Thai were strengthening their hold on the Mekong valley area. In 1238 they conquered Sokuthai, and subsequently pushed north beyond present-day Chiangmai, north-east as far as Vientiane (now capital of Laos), west into Pegu (now in Burma), and south down the Menam Valley into the Malay peninsula.

In the mid-fourteenth century, a Thai prince founded a new capital, Ayuddhya, in the south, and had himself crowned as its king. This kingdom consolidated Thai control over the middle and lower Menam as well as over much of the Malay peninsula, and in 1431 the Thais captured the Khmer capital, Angkor. This was a significant event, culturally as much as politically. The victorious Thai carried off the Khmer royal dancers, musicians, actors, and poets, and their culture thus became thoroughly impregnated with Khmer—and, to that extent, Javanese—artistic culture.

Ironically, this military prowess caused the Thai monarch to adopt another Khmer custom by exchanging the title *Dharma-raja* (dharma-king) for *Deva-raja* (god-king) and thereby to assume absolute authority. This was essentially a political gesture that did not greatly affect Thai society, already moulded by *Theravāda* Buddhism. Nevertheless, the power assumed by the monarchy assisted the Thai in adapting to new historical circumstances, brought about by European intervention. Alone, among South East Asian nations, Thailand negotiated independence, as a buffer between British Burma and French 'Indo-China'.

[30] Hall, *History of South East Asia*, 159–61.

The Kingdom of a Million Elephants

From the ninth to the thirteenth centuries, most of the region now known as Laos (but better: Lao) was under the suzerainty of the Khmer empire. During the thirteenth century, southward-migrating Thai began to encroach on the area, establishing the kingdom of Lanna ('Million Rice Fields') in what is now northern Thailand. During the fourteenth century, prior to the Thai sack of Angkor, a prince by the name of Fa Ngum, assisted by the ailing Khmers, brought the area of present-day Lao, as well as much of present-day north-east Thailand, into a kingdom called by him Lan Xang ('Million Elephants'). In so doing, he established Khmer culture in the upper Mekong region. His capital was founded at Luang Phrabang, where he introduced *Theravāda* Buddhism.

In the sixteenth century, Lan Xang embarked on what was to prove a disastrous, two-century-long struggle against Thailand and Burma. At the end of the seventeenth century, part of the area came under Vietnamese rule, while the remainder split into three rival kingdoms that, during the eighteenth century, fell prey to the expansionist Thai; in 1778 the Thai sacked Vientiane and captured the city's expert dancers and musicians.[31] Thai expansionism eventually led to protests from the French, who had turned neighbouring Vietnam into a French Protectorate. By the end of the nineteenth century, on the advice of the British, Thailand began to cede the area to France, and by 1907 the whole area had become the 'French Protectorate of Laos' (the French mistakenly believing Laos to be the plural of Lao).

Successive Burmese Empires

Burma re-enters the historical spotlight with the destruction, by mountain peoples, of the Shan capital of Ava, in 1527, and the subsequent establishment of a 'Second Burmese Empire' with its capital in Pegu. During the seventeenth century, British, French, and Dutch set up trading companies in coastal ports, causing the Burmese to move their capital back north to Ava in 1635. The Second Burmese Empire ended in 1752 when the Mon, with the assistance of French arms, rebelled and retook Ava.

[31] Houmphanh Rattanavong, 'The Lam Lüang, A Popular Entertainment', trans. Amy Catlin, *Selected Reports in Ethnomusicology* (1992), 198.

The establishment of a 'Third Burmese Empire', in 1755, was to have important consequences. From their newly founded capital in Rangoon (now called Yangon), the Burmese attacked Ava and deported the Mon, who then disappear from history, assimilated with the Burmese or Thai. The Burmese then inflicted on Thailand the worst defeat of its history. In 1767 Ayuddhya was sacked, and many of its artists, musicians, and craftsmen deported back to Burma. Just as Thailand had received an influx of Javanese-derived artistic traditions from Cambodia in the fourteenth century, so now the Burmese received an influx of these same traditions from Thailand. (The story was to come full circle in the nineteenth century when, in an effort to legitimize the colonial Cambodian state, the French restored the Khmer court to a splendour unequalled since Angkorian days, and encouraged the restructuring of court performances with the assistance of experts from Thailand.[32])

From the latter part of the eighteenth century onwards, the history of the Burmese people becomes one of increasingly tragic disaster. In 1782 the Burmese moved their capital back north, where they came into conflict with the British in India. In three successive Anglo-Burmese wars the Burmese ceded Arakan and Tenasserim (1826), Lower Burma (1852), and Upper Burma (1886), to the British, at which point Burma—as an independent kingdom—ceased to exist. Only one ray of light penetrated the gloom of this century. Between 1853 and 1878 the enlightened King Mindon made a lone attempt to align the country with Western ideas. His most notable achievement was the hosting of the Fifth International Synod of Buddhism in 1872, the 2,400th anniversary of the Buddha's first sermon. For this he moved the court to his newly founded city of Mandalay. The synod was the first of its kind in 2,000 years; the text of the *Tripitaka* was carved on 729 tablets of stone, and a pagoda was built over each at the foot of the Mandalay hill.

The unity expected as an outcome of this synod did not emerge. Not only did Burma become a British colony; it saw and suffered some of the worst fighting of the Second World War. At the time of writing, its creative and independent-minded peoples are governed by a brutal and oppressive military junta.[33]

[32] Tim Doling and Philip Soden, *Arts Indo China Cultural Development Report: Cambodia* (Hong Kong: Arts Indo China, 1992), 14.

[33] See Bertil Linter, *Outrage: Burma's Struggle for Democracy* (Hong Kong: Review Publishing Company, 1989).

Distinctions between Musical Cultures

The intertwining histories of the various regions of South East Asia have led to certain broad distinctions in culture, between the peninsula and island areas and those further north on the mainland of Asia. There are, however, distinctive differences in practice within these areas, which correspond roughly with present national boundaries. Within these two broadly defined areas, countless individual folk traditions exist which it is beyond the scope of this book to describe. What follows here is a brief description of ways in which particular areas in the two zones have elaborated, and individualized, basic musical elements already described.

Notwithstanding the ubiquity of 'gong-chime' instruments throughout South East Asia, it is only in Java and Bali that large, homogeneous ensembles of mainly bronze instruments, exhibiting many layers of interrelated musical textures, have developed. These are the ensembles known as 'gamelan'. Since persistence of Hinduism in Bali enabled musical traditions to develop idiosyncratically, it is Central Java that now best demonstrates the chief characteristics of the tradition.

The Gamelan Traditions of Central Java

The metal (bronze or iron) instruments of the Central Javanese gamelan are of four main types. The *saron* (normally constructed in three different sizes) is a one-octave metallophone, consisting of thick metal bars, placed over a wooden trough, played with a single wooden mallet covered with felt. The *gender* (normally in two different sizes) is a two-octave metallophone, the thin, ribbed keys of which are laced together and suspended over individual resonating tubes of tin or bamboo; the keys are struck with one—or, in the case of the highest-pitched *gender* two—padded discs, on the end of a short stick. The *bonang* (normally in two sizes) is a two-octave 'gong chime', its bossed 'kettle' gongs disposed in two rows, and played with two cord-bound sticks.

These three instrument groups are all constructed both in five-note (*slendro*) and seven-note (*pelog*) sets. Large gamelans include instruments tuned in both sets; instruments from each set are therefore placed at right angles to each other, and players turn through 90 degrees to change from one to the other. In order to effect a smooth musical transition from the anhemitonic *slendro* to the hemitonic *pelog*, the two note-sets share a single pitch in common (*kumbuk*: 'to collide'). The coexistence of *slendro* and *pelog* is fundamental to the structure of gamelan music.

The fourth type of metal instrument is the vertically suspended gong. As these gongs define the colotomic structure, all but the largest are tuned to coincide with various pitches of the tuned instruments. There are two single gongs and a set of approximately six tuned gongs. The pitches of an entire gamelan may range over some seven octaves.

Up to three wooden xylophones, known as *gambang*, may also be included in the gamelan. The wooden keys rest on the edges of the resonator and may be exchanged for keys of different pitch. As these instruments are less resonant than the metallophones, and the keys are not damped after being struck, they are potentially the most virtuosic of the keyed instruments.[34]

Each of these instrument types has a set function within the ensemble. The *saron* (as well as the lowest-octave *gender*) are used to play the fixed, 'core' melody, in notes of equal duration. The *bonang* are used to reinforce and elaborate this melody. The *gender* and *gambang* instruments, with their larger range, are used to play embellishments of the 'core' melody (which may act as counter melodies); and the vertically suspended gongs indicate the colotomic structure, by punctuating the melody at various points, on the second or fourth beats. In addition, a single 'kettle' gong, the *ketuk*, plays regular strokes as determined by the structure of an individual piece. The instruments are grouped according to musical function: the slower-moving *saron*s, *bonang*s, and gongs at the rear, and the faster-moving *gender*s and *gambang*s at the front.

Also at the front are the singer (usually female), and the *rebab* (two-string spike fiddle), the legato timbres of which bind together the sounds of the idiophones. The vocal part is usually markedly melismatic; the *rebab* blends with the voice, while anticipating the 'core' melody and embellishing it, making use of considerable rubato, and sometimes using differing tunings for expressive effect. In addition, a choir of three of four male singers (*gerong*) sings an ornamented counter melody, with texts whose prosodic form matches the colotomic structure of the piece. A *suling* (end-blown bamboo flute) occupies the rear of the ensemble, and plays independently of vocalist and *rebab*,

[34] Ernst Heins, 'Indonesia', *The New Grove* (1980), ix. 175–8.

usually in short virtuosic bursts imitating birdsong. (The tendency for the flute to perform apart from other instruments is a characteristic of much East Asian music.) Sometimes a zither (*celemping*) joins the *bonang* in expanding and elaborating the 'core' melody.[35]

The centre of the ensemble is occupied by three, hand-beaten, double-headed barrel drums (*kendang*), which provide rhythmic continuity. The large *kendang gending* is used in concert performance, either singly, or in combination with the small *kendang kepitung*. The medium-sized *ciblon* is usually used in dance performance, while for *wayang kulit* performance a separate *kendang wayang* is used. The drummer leads the orchestra: he cues other musicians, establishes tempo, indicates modifications of speed and volume, and underlines the movements of dancers and puppets, all with prescribed rhythmic patterns linked to the various colotomic structures.[36]

Traditionally, there are 'loud' ensembles for outdoors, and 'soft' ensembles for indoors, though the instruments used in each overlap, and the 'soft' style may appear as loud as the 'loud' style. In the latter, the structure is easily recognized, since the 'core' melody is played in four octaves. In the 'soft' style, complex textures tend to obscure the melody. Singing, both solo and choral, adds to this complexity, and occurs only within 'soft' ensembles.

The 'core' melody (*balungan*: 'skeleton' or 'framework') is usually played by between four and eight one-octave instruments at different octave levels, and with different degrees of rhythmic density; it provides the basic melodic material for a composition (*gending*). About 1,000 such melodies are currently in use.[37] The role of the *balungan* is not dissimilar from that of the *thāt* (basic scale sequence) in Indian music, in that it is a *quasi*-theoretical concept that has no musical meaning until given life in expressive sound. The agent for this is *pathet* (mode, literally 'constraint'), the limiting role of which, rather like that of Indian *rāg*, demands a corresponding resourcefulness on the part of the performer. Improvisation, therefore, is important in Javanese music (though not in Balinese music). Short preludes and postludes may be played to establish the *pathet* of the piece. *Pathet* is the spiritual essence of the music, and all elements of the music contribute to it.[38]

[35] Hardja Susilo, 'Indonesia', *The New Grove* (1980), ix. 190 ff.

[36] Heins, 'Indonesia', *The New Grove*, ix. 175.

[37] Sorrell, *A Guide to the Gamelan*, 55–6.

[38] Ibid. 57–62.

One such element is *irama*, the concept of tempo relationships. Changes in the tempo of a given stratum of melody may occur in the proportion of two to one at any given point; and the tempo, in relation to that of the *balungan*, is measured by the pulse of one designated instrument, the *saron panerus* (commonly known as the *peking*). There are five possible *iramas*, with one, two, four, eight, or sixteen notes of the *peking* to one note of the *balungan*.[39] Although *density* is thus formally regulated, the *pulse* itself is subject to frequent variation; and this is indicated by the drummers, whose rhythmic patterns usually relate to particular, set forms. Such forms—they may be joined together to produce larger structures—are classified according to their function: as concert music; to accompany dance; to accompany *wayang kulit*; or for ceremonial occasions.

Javanese legend has it that gongs came into being as signalling instruments at the command of the god Shiva. The early association of the gamelan with the Saivite cult explains much of the magical power still attributed to it. Esteemed instruments are believed to have living personalities and to harbour spirits who must be propitiated with suitable offerings; indeed, special rituals are usually performed before the gongs are forged. It has been believed that gamelan music can induce the gods to provide rain, or induce trance in humans. The gamelan's sacred personality is exemplified in the distancing of the instruments from humans: the hand-held beater acts as intermediary between performer and instrument.[40] Certain gamelans are held to be so sacred that only specially qualified priests may touch them; they may be given proper names and even honorific titles, at special name-giving ceremonies. Such gamelans were horded as regalia by Javanese rulers because of their association with supernatural power. (They are now owned by private families or by the state.)

The great *kratons* (courts) of Jogyakarta and Surakarta in Central Java still house the ancient gamelans, but responsibility for passing on performance skills has passed from the courts to provincial conservatoires and academies. While the courts still provide a venue for many presentations of music and dance, so too do museums, commercial concert halls, broadcasting stations, and private homes.[41] In many villages of Java, however, gamelans still have ritual functions, and they play a significant role in maintaining social cohesion.

[39] Sorrell, *A Guide to the Gamelan*, 62–6. [40] Ibid. 18.
[41] Heins, 'Indonesia', *The New Grove*, ix. 178.

Gong Traditions in Bali

In Bali, gamelans (more often known simply as 'gongs') are still the lifeblood of village society; it has been estimated that there is one gamelan for every 350 people on the island.[42] Because Bali was not Islamicized, its people were free to develop individual musical styles within an evolving, social organization, supported by Hinduism. The Dutch left Bali alone until the end of the nineteenth century; by the time they confronted the Balinese (in the early twentieth century), Hindu traditions of caste, honour, and dignity were so entrenched that many rajas, with their royal retinues, chose to commit mass suicide rather than submit to the enemy. The Dutch, shamed by the manner of their victory, allowed Balinese customs to continue unimpeded. With the gradual decline of the courts, the focus of artistic life shifted to the villages, where musical traditions have evolved individually, and distinctively, over the past century. There are many different types of gamelan in Bali.

The social organization of the island is based on the self-contained *desa* (village), which, through its governing council and its *banjar*s (cooperative groups of neighbours committed to helping each other), caters for the needs and functions of individuals, from birth to cremation. Most villages have at least three main temples, one for official ceremonies, one for honouring the village founders, and one for revering the deities of death and of the afterlife. Many individual, familial compounds also have their own temples.

According to traditional Balinese belief, the island belongs to the gods, and is only on lease to those who live in it. Many still believe it to be inhabited not only by gods, humans, and guardian ancestors, but also by blood-sucking *leyak*s, evil witches, and other demons, who must constantly be placated with offerings, and whose evil influence must be exorcized by purification ceremonies. Life and religion in Bali are inseparable, and neither is possible without art, music, and dance. Frequently, the entire energies of village communities are concentrated on some sort of artistic creation to honour the deities and to ward off evil spirits. No expense is spared. Temples are provided with elaborate decoration for the countless festivals that permeate Balinese life, and culinary delights are prepared for the gods and, subsequently, humans. Music and dance are essential to these proceedings, to entertain both

[42] Ruby Ornstein, 'Indonesia', *The New Grove* (1980), ix. 179–80.

34. Masked dancer with gamelan, in a Balinese temple. Photo: Claude Sauvageot

gods and humans (Pl. 34). All night performances of *topeng* (masked dance) and *wayang kulit* (shadow-puppet theatre) are common, and trance dances survive in some parts of the island.

Sekaha (clubs) that operate out of each *banjar* are formed to regulate nearly every Balinese activity. Each *desa* or *banjar* has its musical *sekaha*, with its own traditions of music and dance repertoire, its own gamelan, and its own rules that govern such matters as attendance and finance. Prominent members of the *sekaha* may be composers and earn a living by teaching other village clubs; but most members are amateurs who enjoy performing and the prestige of belonging to a good *sekaha*. Proceeds from public performances, mainly for tourists, provide a small supplementary income; mostly, however, takings are used for maintaining, and enhancing, the *sekaha*. Traditionally, gamelan-playing has been an all-male activity, but recently women have started their own *sekaha*, and gamelan competitions that are a regular feature of the island's musical activity now exist for women's groups as well as for men's.

Certain aspects of Balinese music immediately distinguish it from that of Java. One is the playing of keyed instruments in pairs, in which one instrument is tuned slightly higher than the other; this generates a resonant, acoustic beat, when the two are played together. (The beat is usually at a frequency of five to eight per second.[43]) Another difference is the greater volume and ferocity of much Balinese music, visually apparent in the use of vicious-looking wooden hammers with which to pound the *saron* instruments. This happens in *gamelan gong kebyar* (*kebyar*: 'to burst open'), a style of performance, introduced in about 1915, which then swept the island like a hurricane. Demanding great virtuosity, it provided opportunity for individual composers, dancers, and musicians to receive recognition as artists, and has pushed virtually every other style of performance into the shade. In a sense, with *kebyar*, Balinese music went 'pop'.

The regal *gamelan gong gede*—now all but displaced by *kebyar*—made use of instruments similar to those of Java. *Saron* and *gender* instruments played the 'core' melody (known in Bali as *pokok*), which was expanded on the *bonang* (known in Bali as *trompong*) and a four-'kettle' chime known as *reyong*. Vertically suspended gongs were similar—though less numerous—to those used in Java, and two drummers led the ensemble. *Rebab* (spike fiddle), *suling* (flute), and vocalist were also used.[44]

The development of *kebyar* coincided with a new importance attached to the bronze instruments. Their pitch range and number in the ensemble were increased, and the pitch range of the ensemble itself was extended to three or four octaves. The *saron* and higher-pitched *gender* instruments, with seven to twelve keys, struck by wooden hammers, came to be known collectively as *gangsa*: ('bronze'). Concurrently, the 'kettle' gongs developed in range and virtuosity. The four-gonged *reyong*, which needed two players, was extended to a twelve-gong instrument requiring four players. The *trompong*, virtually the same instrument, was so named when the *reyong* came to be used as a virtuoso solo instrument. (In *kebyar trompong*, one of the most difficult and virtuosic of modern Balinese dances, the dancer himself plays *trompong* (Pl. 35).) Further impulsive energy came from a cluster of

[43] Michael Tenzer, *Balinese Music* (Berkeley, Singapore: Periplus, 1991), 33.
[44] Ibid.

35. A dancer plays the *trompong* in *kebyar trompong*. Photo: Jean Jenkins

up-turned cymbals, mounted on a base, and struck by cymbals held by the player (known as *rincir*); with this went a more frequent incidence of colotomic punctuation, with a large, single, 'kettle' gong (*kempli*) struck on every beat. Loud cymbals complemented the two sets of conical drums. The shrill, virtuosic *kebyar*-style is unlike that of any other 'gong chime' in South East Asia.

In *gamelan gong kebyar* the 'core' melody (*pokok*) is played on the *calung*s (quieter-sounding, five-keyed *gender*s), supported (an octave lower) by sustained notes on the *jegogan*s (larger five-keyed *gender*s). A developed version of the *calung* part is played on the *ugal* (the lowest-pitched *gangsa*). Above this, *pemade*s and *kantilan*s (seven- or twelve-keyed *gangsa*, pitched one and two octaves higher than the *ugal*, respectively) play extremely fast, interlocking patterns, called *kotekan.*[45] Ex. 9.1 (after Ornstein) illustrates this basic system of melodic stratification, in *pelog* mode.[46]

The *kotekan* is the most virtuosic element in *kebyar*. It sounds like a continuous melodic line, but in fact consists of two interdependent musical lines. In some styles, in the *gamelan gender wayang*, for example (used to accompany *wayang kulit*), the *kotekan* may sound slow and stately. More frequently, however, and particularly in the *kebyar*-style, *kotekan*s are extremely fast. Reaching dazzling speeds, they require superb coordination, and provide a showcase for the talents of their composers.[47] Ex. 9.2 (after Ornstein) illustrates (in *pelog* mode)

[45] Tenzer, *Balinese Music*, 33–7.

[46] Ornstein, 'Indonesia', *The New Grove*, ix. 183.

[47] Tenzer, *Balinese Music*, 46–7.

Ex. 9.1

Ex. 9.2

characteristic *kotekan* figuration for the four players of the *reyong*.[48] The structural principle of the *kotekan* is parallelled by the fast, interlocking patterns performed by the two drummers.

Gamelan gong kebyar is the style in which most dances are now accompanied. In Bali, unlike Java, little music is played on its own. *Kebyar* literally refers to the explosive unison attack with which a performance usually begins. (Frequently the entire gamelan starts or finishes a phrase by crashing down on a single note or on an eight-note chord.) A free-metre introduction may follow the initial outburst, but this will quickly be followed by a *kotekan* on the *reyong*, along with virtuoso playing, solo or group. The music is subject to sudden contrasts of tempo, dynamics, and texture, and may frequently stop just before

[48] Ornstein, 'Indonesia', *The New Grove*, ix. 183.

the end of a phrase, with perhaps a short *kotekan* momentarily filling the sudden silence. The effect is not unlike the opening of a Western, avant-garde orchestral composition of the 1960s or 1970s. It is, however, considerably more precise, for nothing is left to chance and there is little improvisation. From the initial eruption onwards, the style is energetic, dynamic, and impeccably controlled.

Although *kebyar* has overshadowed other gamelan styles, it has by no means replaced them. Performances of *wayang kulit*, for example, are usually accompanied by *gender wayang*; this requires only four musicians, who play interlocking patterns on two pairs of *gender*, tuned in *slendro*, one an octave higher than the other, doubling the music played on the lower instruments.[49] Other extant ensembles include *gamelan semar pegulingan* (a softer, higher-pitched version of the *gamelan gong gede*), the *gamelan angklung* (found in small villages, consisting mainly of four- and five-keyed metallophones, with flute, two small drums, and cymbals), and the *gamelan joged* (a bamboo ensemble).

Thai and Cambodian Instruments and Ensembles

In Cambodia, Laos, Thailand, and Burma, the 'gong-chime' instruments, and many of the techniques of musical construction associated with them, are similar to those of Java and Bali; but the sound gives a different impression. Except in Burma, where the *hsìang-waìng* ensemble consists mainly of bronze instruments and drums, 'gong chimes' and metallophones tend to be subordinate to xylophones; multi-part 'stratification' gives way to heterophonic variation of 'core' melodies, normally involving no more than two layers of different density; and ensembles of mainly homogeneous instruments are less common than those of a more heterogeneous mix. Gone is the insistent, interlocking patterning on multi-layered metallophones. Gone, too, are the distinctive pitch relationships of *slendro* and *pelog* scales. Only in Burma is there a clear distinction between hemitonic and anhemitonic modes; in Cambodia, Thailand, and Laos, the predominant impression is of an anhemitonic pentatonic scale, though all these countries use a seven-note scale.

[49] For a description and transcription of *gendér wayang* music, see Nick Gray, '"Sulendra": An Example of *Petegak* in the Balinese *Gendér Wayang* Repertory', *British Journal of Ethnomusicology*, 1 (1992), 1–16.

The characteristic musical style of the mainland appears to have developed in Cambodia (from Javanese models), and to have spread from Cambodia to Thailand, Laos, and Burma (though early Indian influence may account for some facets of musical style). In these countries, the formation of ensembles, and many elements of musical construction, are similar. In Laos, however, the adoption of the *khaen* (mouth organ) as a symbol of nationality has encouraged the survival of folk traditions that have largely disappeared elsewhere. In Burma, a 'gong chime' culture became joined with other traditions from China and India, traditions that probably pre-date it. It will be convenient, therefore, to describe music and theatre styles of Cambodia and Thailand together, and to consider the peculiarities of Laotian and Burmese styles separately. Vietnam, though sharing certain musical traits of these countries, belongs predominantly to the Chinese sphere of cultural influence; its music will be described at the end.

Cambodian musical styles can be said to date back to the fourteenth century, but almost continuous warfare (during the 1970s and 1980s) has largely destroyed the country's artistic traditions. Thai classical music, on the other hand, can be dated with certainty only to the late eighteenth century, when royal patronage led to a period of musical development that reached a high degree of virtuosity by the end of the nineteenth century. When the Thai monarchy was supplanted with a form of democracy in 1932, the classical music—which, until the mid-nineteenth century, had been restricted to the court—fell into disfavour; but it has since been revitalized, and is now performed in a variety of contexts. Regrettably, however, the Khmer performing traditions of Cambodia have yet to be fully revived; and performance traditions will here be described primarily in the context of Thailand.

In both Thailand and Cambodia, xylophones assume equal importance with 'gong-chime' instruments and metallophones. Xylophones appear in two sizes: the three-octave, high-pitched *ranāt ēk*, and the two-octave, lower-pitched *ranāt thum* (Cambodia: *roneat ēk* and *roneat thung*). The wooden keys are suspended above a boat-shaped resonator, mounted on a pedestal, and are played with wooden hammers. The higher-pitched xylophone plays faster-moving elaborations of a 'core' melody, while the lower-pitched xylophone plays slower-moving extracts from it. The style of playing may be highly virtuosic; on the higher-pitched xylophones, everything is played in octaves. There are also metal-keyed instruments—added in the nineteenth century in imitation of the Javanese *saron* and *gender*—functions of which correspond to those of the two xylophones.[50]

'Gong chimes' are usually suspended on a circular frame, in the middle of which sits the player; they are known, therefore, as 'gong circles'. As with xylophones, two types are normally used: the higher pitched *khōng wong lek* and the lower-pitched *khōng wong yai* (Cambodia: *kong tauch* and *kong thom*). There is also the *gong mon*, a vertically U-shaped 'gong-chime' of Burmese origin, used principally in funeral-rites. (In Cambodia there is, additionally, a racked set of sixteen gongs, *kong vung*.)

In keeping with the essentially solo or 'chamber' character of Thai music, the basic colotomic instrument is the quiet-sounding *ching* (small, cup-shaped finger cymbals of thick metal), but the *chap* (small hand cymbals) and *mōng* (medium-sized gong) are also used. Various drums are used to furnish cyclical rhythmic patterns; these include the *klōng that* (pair of large, barrel-shaped drums) and *thōn* (goblet- or vase-shaped, single-headed drum) (Cambodia: *skor thom* and *skor thaun*).

The Thai two-string fiddle, *sō duang* (Cambodia: *tro so tauch*) entered the South East Asian mainland from China, and has a small resonator, with a leather table at one end, open at the other. A second two-stringed fiddle type, *sō-ū* (Cambodia: *tro ou*), is less clearly Chinese in origin, since its half-coconut resonator has a calfskin table, instead of the thin wooden table that characterizes the equivalent Chinese fiddles, *ban hu* and *yeh hu*. (Both calfskin and wooden tables are found in Cambodia, however.[51]) In Cambodia, two-string fiddles appear in four different sizes. In all instances, the hairs of the bow run permanently *between* the strings (see p. 351).

In Thailand, a three-string spike fiddle with calfskin resonator, *sō sam sui*, leads the *mahori* ensemble; the Cambodian equivalent, the *tro khmer*, is a smaller instrument, and is used principally in village spirit ceremony and wedding ensembles. Another string instrument, perhaps of Chinese derivation, is the *jakay*, a long, three-string crocodile zither (Cambodia: *krapeu*); like the Chinese *zheng*, it is plucked with a plectrum and positioned on two trestles. Ensembles sometimes include a *khim* (trapezoidal hammered dulcimer, similar to the Chinese *yangqin*).

[50] David Morton, 'Thailand', *The New Grove* (1980), xviii. 714–16, and Tran Quang Hai, 'Kampuchea', *The New Grove* (1980), ix, 789–91.

[51] Terry E. Miller and Sam-Ang Sam, 'The Classical Musics of Cambodia and Thailand: A Study of Distinctions', *Ethnomusicology*, 39/2 (1995), 230–5.

36. Students at Chulalongkorn University, Bangkok, perform on *ranāt ēk* (xylophone), *khōng wong yai* (gong circle, behind), *khlui* (end-blown flute)

Two wind instruments appear in Thai and Cambodian ensembles: the *khlui*, a bamboo, vertical end-blown flute, with membrane-covered hole, constructed at four different pitch levels (Cambodia: *khloy*, at only one pitch level); and the *pī*, a shawm, flared at each end, with a bulge in the centre (Cambodia: *sralai*). Each side of the shawm's double reed is made from two layers of a smoked palm-leaf, making it in fact a quadruple reed. (Nepalese, Burmese, and Malaysian shawms have similar quadruple reeds.[52]) The reed permits considerable pitch variation, and the instrument is played with circular breathing.[53]

The *pī phāt* (Cambodia: *pin peat*) is the regional ensemble that most resembles the Indonesian gamelan; it includes two types of *khōng* ('gong circle'), two types of *ranāt* (xylophone), small cymbals, drum (or drums), and *pī* (quadruple reed), from which the Thai ensemble derives its name (Pl. 36). (The Cambodian prefix, *pin*, derives from the Sanskrit, *vīna*, meaning string instrument, but neither *pī phāt* nor *pin peat* currently employs a string instrument.) In the Thai ensemble, the lower-pitched 'gong circle' plays the 'core' melody, while the higher

[52] Carol Tingey, *Heartbeat of Nepal: The Pancai Baja* (Royal Nepal Academy, 1990), 30.

[53] Sam-Ang Sam and Patricia Shehan Campbell, *Silent Temples, Songful Hearts: Traditional Music of Cambodia* (New Jersey: World Music Press, 1991), 41.

pitched 'gong circle', the xylophones, and the *pī* play variants of it. In the Cambodian ensemble, the *sralai* (quadruple reed) carries the 'core' melody, though the vocal part is the most important; 'gong circles' are ascribed lesser importance. The 'gong circles' and xylophones of both Thai and Cambodian ensembles may be played with soft, rather than hard, mallets. In Thailand, the 'soft' ensemble adds a two-string fiddle; in Cambodia, flute replaces quadruple reed.[54] Both Thai *pī phāt* and Cambodian *pin peat* ensembles are used to accompany dance and theatre genres, as well as some religious ceremonies.

The Thai *mahōrī* (Cambodia: *mohori*) ensemble employs string instruments and was used primarily to entertain guests at banquets; in Cambodia, it was also used to accompany folk dances and the *mohori* play, and is now the most widely heard traditional-music ensemble. Thai *mahōrī* ensembles vary in size, but a full ensemble includes both sizes of xylophone and both sizes of 'gong circle', as well as flute, zither, two-string fiddles, and three-string spike fiddle, the last of which usually takes the lead. Finger cymbals define the colotomic structure, and drums provide rhythm patterning. Cambodian *mohori* ensembles do not include 'gong circles', but employ four different sizes of two- string fiddle, as well as dulcimer. Whereas, in the Thai *mahōrī* ensemble, idiophones predominate, it is the strings that provide the basic sonority of the Cambodian *mohori* ensemble.

The *krūāng sāī* is a string ensemble of two-string fiddles and zithers, with flute, the usual idiophones, and optional instruments ranging from three-string spike fiddle and dulcimer to violin and electric organ. It exists only in Thailand.

Many Thai compositions may be performed by any ensemble, regardless of instrumentation, and mixing of Western with traditional Thai instruments is not uncommon. However, certain items of repertoire, intended for use on particular ritual or royal occasions, or associated with particular theatrical genres, are context-specific, and may be played only by the particular ensembles reserved for such occasions.[55]

Thai and Cambodian Musical Styles

In both Thailand and Cambodia, melodic lines are based on either five-note or seven-note scales. In Thailand, the five-

[54] Miller and Sam, 'Classical Musics', 233.

[55] Pamela Myers-Moro, *Thai Music and Musicians in Contemporary Bangkok* (Berkeley and Los Angeles: University of California Press, 1993), 48–9.

note scale, approximating to a Chinese-type anhemitonic pentatonic scale, is extracted from *equidistant heptatonic* octaves. To Thai musicians, equidistance is important, though in practice the intervals vary a little, and tunes may sound conspicuously different when played at different pitch levels. The origin of this (functionally) equidistant seven-note scale is not clear; it may have been in use in Cambodia when the Thais captured the Angkorian musicians; or it may represent a compromise between Indo-Khmer and Chinese tuning systems, developed by the Thais.[56] It is not dominant in other countries of the mainland, where tunings vary from tuner to tuner, and from ensemble to ensemble (as, to a lesser extent, is also the case in Thailand).[57]

In Thailand, two styles of playing exist: the 'Thai' style, which uses only the pitches of the five-note scale; and the 'Mon' style, which uses the two other available notes as auxiliaries, and modulates between modes that start on different degrees of the scale. In both styles, the 'core' melody consists of short motifs or, in more recent compositions, of a short lyrical melody.[58] There are usually three different layers of tempo, each in the proportion of two to one, indicated by the speed of the *ching* strokes (which occur on the last beat of the bar); and playing may reach astonishing levels of speed and virtuosity.[59] In certain compositions, the second layer of tempo may be considered the 'original', the diminished and augmented layers acting as the variants. In Cambodia, however, although three layers of tempo exist, most compositions are played at only one tempo level.[60]

Thai and Cambodian vocal styles differ by virtue of the fact that the Thai language uses segmental tone and the Khmer language does not. Cambodians regard the voice part as the 'core' melody, and those instruments that imitate it most closely—flute, quadruple reed, and fiddle—as playing the purest forms of the melody. In Thailand, by contrast, vocal lines (like instrumental lines) are constructed from a skeletal outline of the 'core' melody, according to complex formulas relating a text syllable to such factors as pitch inflection, degree of scale, and mode. It is because Thai vocal and instrumental lines derive from a

[56] Morton, 'Thailand', *The New Grove*, xviii. 712–14.
[57] Sam and Campbell, *Silent Temples*, 40.
[58] Morton, 'Thailand', *The New Grove*, xviii. 716–18.
[59] For further detail, see Myers-Moro, *Thai Music*, 82–102.
[60] Miller and Sam, 'Classical Musics', 235–6.

skeletal, 'core' melody that the larger 'gong circle', and not the voice, is thought to perform the purest version of the melody.[61]

There is no way of being certain as to which aspects of Thai performance were once those of Cambodia, and which were developed in Thailand; it appears, however, that virtuosic, high-speed playing is peculiar to Thailand, and it is possible that Western influence played a part in this. In Cambodia, ensemble music is slower, and more contemplative; ornamentation is a key element both in vocal and wind-playing styles, and the figurative lines, played by xylophones and 'gong circles', represent an extension of such ornamentation. Where Thai music sounds multi-part, Cambodian music sounds essentially heterophonic. Cambodian elaborations of the 'core' melody are always open-ended in realization, varying from performance to performance; and there is a tendency for the first of a pair of notes to be lengthened, as in the *notes inégales* of European baroque music. Ex. 9.3 (after Sam-Ang Sam), shows one such elaboration.[62]

Ex. 9.3

In Thailand, ensemble music developed into a significant art during the nineteenth century, when a surviving repertorie of suites was varied and expanded into new compositions, demanding skill and virtuosity in performance. Court musicians formed guilds, through which knowledge and skill was passed on, in a master–disciple tradition not unlike that of the North Indian *gharana*-system (though heredity was not an important aspect in Thailand).[63] Many of today's finest living exponents of Thai music achieved their skill in this time-honoured

[61] Miller and Sam, 'Classical Musics', 234.
[62] Sam and Campbell, *Silent Temples*, 98.
[63] See Myers-Moro, *Thai Music*, 103–7.

manner; and it is this tradition that enabled the court music to survive during the early period of democracy, when classical music was in disfavour.[64]

In Thai religious belief, the ability to perform music is imparted not only from an illustrious music master and his predecessors, but also from particular gods, associated with particular instruments. In Bangkok, both master and gods are periodically honoured in a ceremony of homage (*wai khru*), performed on an auspicious occasion by individuals, by a single teacher and pupil, or by an entire music school or university; gods are represented by papier-mâché images of heads, placed on the altar.[65] (An altar, or shrine, is commonly to be found in places where instruments are kept or played.) Recognition of the religious base of special musical ability is considered important, for music is considered a means of achieving peace, purity, and truth.

Typically, a *wai khru* ceremony begins with chanting by Buddhist monks, who bless the food that has been prepared for the gods (in particular the 'giant' god), and for the master's deceased teacher, whose spirit is believed to reside in a drum. An ensemble plays. Alternating with recitation, special music invites the various gods to the ceremony, invites the 'giant' god, brings the gods to the feast, invites the gods and a deceased master to partake of the food, and, finally, *honours* the 'giant' god. Music associated with especially important gods (such as Phra Phirap, the god associated with drama) is considered to be ritually charged with magic forces, and therefore too dangerous for any but the most experienced musicians to perform.[66] When all the designated pieces have been played, the musicians are blessed with perfumed water and petals, and their instruments with necklaces; they are then free to play whatever music they like. The master's disciples, individually, receive ritual blessing and the washing of the head with leaves, from the living master. It is then time for the humans to eat food that has—symbolically—been partaken of by the gods.

Through such ceremonies, gods and humans are united: the god touches the humans through food. More importantly, the essentially religious status of music is confirmed. So too is the uniqueness of the musical clan—for the element of secrecy, habitually characteristic of

[64] For further detail on Thai music repertoire, see ibid. 56–81.

[65] Ibid. 172 ff.

[66] Information supplied by Panya Roongruang, Chulalongkorn University, Bangkok, who kindly enabled the author to attend a 'Homage to the Music Master' ceremony.

master–disciple relationships in transmission, has by no means entirely vanished.

Music Theatre in Cambodia and Thailand

Thai traditions of music theatre reflect those of Cambodia, which, as noted earlier, were restored by the French (during the nineteenth century) under Thai guidance. In Cambodia, until recently, three main theatre genres, all dating back to the Angkorian period—and all based on the Khmer version of the *Rāmāyana*—the *Reamker*—were extant: *lakhon khol* (male masked dance mime); *lakhon kbach boran* (female temple dance); and *sbek thom* and *sbek tauch* (large and small shadow-puppet plays). The male masked dance mime symbolized the divine authority of the god-king, while the female temple dance symbolized the union of the god-king with the chthonic forces of fertility. (When the French restored the full splendour of the Khmer court, it was still widely believed that whoever controlled the dance controlled the people.[67])

The female temple dance had particular importance as the *apsaras* ('heavenly') dance. Inscriptions from the reign of King Jayavarman VII refer to a total of 1,622 dancers at Angkor; they appear to have been divided into 'sacred dancers' assigned to priests, and entertainment-orientated dancers assigned to the public. The temple dancers were believed to make direct contact with the spirit world, so that they could themselves become *apsaras*;[68] images of some 1,700 *apsara*-dancers were carved in relief on the walls of Angkor Wat alone.[69] The temple-dance tradition disappeared at the end of the Angkorian period; but the Khmer court dance continued as *lakhon preah reach trorp* ('theatre belonging to the royal family'). It was renamed *roam kbach boran Khmer* ('Khmer traditional dance') after the monarchy was overthrown in 1970.[70]

Kbach means, literally, 'design'; *roam* means 'to dance'. In Khmer tradition there are eight basic hand gestures that, in various combination with five basic foot positions, form the original dance alphabet.[71] As

[67] Doling and Soden, *Arts Indo China Cultural Development Report: Cambodia*, 14–15.

[68] Chan Moly Sam, 'Muni Mekhala: The Magic Moment in Khmer Court Dance', *Selected Reports in Ethnomusicology* (1992), 93.

[69] Freeman, *Angkor*, 31.

[70] Sam, 'Muni Mekhala', 94.

[71] Ibid. 95.

in Java, the court dancers mime to a sung recitation of the story, accompanied—in this case—by the *pin peat* ensemble. Particular melodies are associated with particular actions or emotions, and the dance patterns are defined by colotomic punctuation, played on drum, finger cymbals, or clappers.[72]

The *pin peat* ensemble also accompanied the shadow-puppet play that existed, until recently, in two forms: the *sbek tauch* (small leather), enacting local legends or topical stories; and *sbek thom* (large leather), enacting episodes from the *Reamker*. The latter are up to 1.8 metres tall, weigh up to seven kilos, and are illuminated by vast burning torches; the puppeteers dance while manipulating them.[73]

Other dance-theatre genres that were extant in Cambodia until recently include: *aiyai*, flirtation songs, in which a man and a woman tease each other in improvised song (a genre common throughout East Asia); *apei*, a combination of episodes from the *Reamker* and from topical themes, presented to villagers after harvesting; and *mohori*, a more recent genre, usually associated with weddings.

The most popular, traditional music-theatre genre in Cambodia today is the *lakhon bassac* (though it is thought that, currently, no more than six troupes exist). *Bassac* theatre developed in the early twentieth century, in the area of the Bassac River, now in southern Vietnam. Itinerant troupes travelled up and down the river in sailing boats, stopping to perform at major centres of population.[74] Usually based on Khmer traditional stories, *lakhon bassac* was strongly influenced (through Vietnam) by Chinese opera, and came also to include many Western, popular, stylistic elements. As in Chinese opera, acting is stylized, and stock characters are associated with particular song types. Some 150 songs are still associated with *bassac* theatre.[75]

In Thailand, until the mid-nineteenth century, only females were permitted to perform masked dance drama inside the court, while only men performed outside. Although male and female performers now

[72] Ibid. 96–7.

[73] Sam-Ang Sam, 'The Floating Maiden in Khmer Shadow Play: Text, Context, and Performance', *Selected Reports in Ethnomusicology* (1992), 118–19. A further, distinctive, form of shadow play, *wayang kulit Siam*, developed in peninsular Malaysia and southern Thailand, and is still extant; see Patricia Matusky, *Malaysian Shadow Play and Music: Continuity of an Oral Tradition* (Oxford: Oxford University Press, 1993).

[74] Doling and Soden, *Arts Indo China Cultural Development Report: Cambodia*, 16.

[75] Information supplied by Catherine Geach, Department of Music and Dance, University of Fine Arts, Phnom Penh.

combine, the genre titles, *lakhōn nai* ('inside drama') and *lakhōn nōk* ('outside drama'), have been retained; and the 'inside' drama is still characterized as being refined and romantic, in contrast to the boisterous nature of 'outside' drama. Another genre, *lakhōn khōn*, performance of which was also formerly restricted to the court, is now regarded as the most highly developed theatrical art of Thailand.[76] All are highly stylized, and are accompanied by forms of *pī phāt* ensemble. In southern Thailand, theatre troupes perform the *lakhōn jatri* (*jatri* means 'sorcery'), a folk genre that originated in shamanism, in which performers now enact the Manora story from the Buddhist *Jātaka*s; this is the oldest theatre genre in Thailand. The ensemble that accompanies it consists basically of gongs, drums, and shawm. A popular theatre genre, *lakhōn likay* (descended from *lakhōn khōn* and *lakhōn nai*), incorporates improvised dialogue and song-texts, and spread from central to north-east Thailand, and into Laos, during the early twentieth century. It now displays Western influence in style and instrumentation, and is performed mainly in provincial towns.[77]

Music and Theatre in Laos

Musicians from the royal palace of Luang Phrabang in Laos, now resident in the USA, claim that their tradition entered the country in 1353 with Fa Ngum and the Khmer, and that it was maintained for 600 years by trained musicians from the palace and from villages, under royal patronage.[78] The tradition was doubtless weakened when the Thai captured leading musicians and artists in 1778 and transported them to the royal palace in Bangkok. It was further undermined under French rule, when Western instruments were introduced.[79] In 1959, a decade after Laos gained independence from France, a National School of Music and Dance was opened in Luang Phrabang;[80] but the country was soon engulfed in civil war. When the Pathet Lao gained victory over the royalists in 1975, many palace musicians

[76] Myers-Moro, *Thai Music*, 238–9.

[77] James R. Brandon, 'South East Asia', *The New Grove* (1980), xvii. 776–7. A related, but distinct, form of dance theatre, *Makyong*, survives on the east coast of peninsular Malaysia; see J. P. B. Dobbs, 'Malaysia', *The New Grove* (1980), xi. 559.

[78] Katherine Bond and Kingsavanh Pathammavong, 'Contents of Dontrii Lao Deum: Traditional Lao Music', *Selected Reports in Ethnomusicology* (1992), 131, 133.

[79] Rattanavong, 'The Lam Lüang', 198.

[80] Bond and Pathammavong, 'Contents of Dontrii Lao Deum', 138.

fled the country; Vientiane became the capital city, palace music was renamed 'traditional music', and the country's rich folk traditions were self-consciously preserved as a 'national art'.[81] In particular, the popular Lao mouth organ, the *khaen*, was adopted as a symbol of national identity, and became prominent in all genres of music, including the 'traditional music' of the *phin phat* ensemble (*phin*, like the Cambodian *pin*, deriving from the Sanskrit *vīna*, meaning string instrument).

The *khaen* is a distinctive instrument of Laos, Burma, northern Vietnam, and the Upper Mekong area of Thailand, though perhaps most widely used in Laos. It is organologically related to the Chinese *sheng* (see pp. 349–50), but, whereas the pipes of the *sheng* end in the wind chest, the seven or eight pairs of pipes of the *khaen* pass *through* the carved, wooden wind chest. Inset into the wall of each pipe is a free reed (at one time made from the bronze of Thai copper coinage, minted in Hamburg and Birmingham between 1887 and *c*.1906). The pitch of each pipe is largely determined by the natural frequency of the reed, and the pipes are vented, both above and below the reed, thus tuning the resonator to the reed. The reed is inserted at one-quarter of the distance between vents, reducing the intensity of the fourth harmonic, and increasing that of the second. Higher harmonics, up to the tenth, are conspicuous in the tonal quality. As a result, the instrument has a richness of sound quality lacking in the acoustically less sophisticated mouth organs of China, Japan, and Korea. (It is probable that the reeds of the mouth organ derive from miniaturized Jew's harps; both instruments are products of a bamboo-culture area.[82])

The *khaen* now comes in a variety of sizes, and its pipes vary between approximately one and two metres in length. By permanently stopping the finger-holes on one or two pipes, a continuous drone can be obtained. The melodic line is played with considerable rhythmic energy, either as single notes, as octaves, or in fourths or fifths; and the *khaen* player often dances while playing. Traditionally, *khaen* players make use of five anhemitonic pentatonic modes (*lai*), each of which has its particular drone and improvisational patterns.[83]

The *khaen* is now played in ensembles of different-sized instruments, and new pieces are still invented; compositions imitating the sound of trains have become a popular means of displaying virtuosity (Pl. 37).

[81] Ibid. 131, 145.

[82] L. E. R. Picken, C. J. Adkins, and T. F. Page, 'The Making of a Kaen: The Free-reed Mouth-Organ of North-East Thailand', *Musica Asiatica*, 4 (1984), 147–51.

[83] Terry E. Miller, 'Laos', *The New Grove* (1980), x. 463–4.

37. A Laotian *khaen* ensemble

Though little performed in urban areas, the *khaen* is widely played in the countryside. The two government-sponsored radio stations broadcast *khaen*-music daily, in the morning to wake people up, and in the evening when work is done.

At the heart of Lao folk tradition is the art of *lam*, a colloquial combination of singing and storytelling, improvisation, action, and dance, accompanied by music.[84] (Singers are called *mawlam*: 'skilled person'.[85]) *Lam* may consist of costumed theatre, singing duels between flirting men and women, competitive singing duels between members of the same sex, or solo singing. In *lam khu*, for example, talented male and female singers tease each other with improvised verses to the vigorous accompaniment of a *khaen*. The session starts with formal exchanges, on such matters as family background and marital status, for which there are traditional words and melodies; after this, each party is free to improvise flirting rhymes, to challenge the other with questions

[84] Tim Doling and Philip Soden, *Arts Indo China Cultural Development Report: Laos* (Hong Kong: Arts Indo China, 1992).

[85] Carol J. Compton, 'Traditional Verbal Arts in Laos: Functions, Forms, Continuities, and Changes in Texts, Contexts, and Performances', *Selected Reports in Ethnomusicology* (1980), 155.

and riddles, and dance together (with the *khaen* player joining in) throughout the night.[86]

In all Lao traditional vocal genres, the music is based on the anhemitonic pentatonic scale, and melodic patterns emerge from exaggeration of the segmental tone of each monosyllabic word of the language, imparting distinctive character to the singing.[87]

Ex. 9.4 (after Miller) shows the music for a formal exchange at the start of *lam khu*. At one time *lam khu* was a common medium of courtship, the boy flirting with the girl in song, as the girl attended to her weaving under the light of the full moon; now *lam khu* is performed only at special village ceremonies, or by companies hired by private families. In order to add interest for modern audiences, the traditional *khaen* accompaniment is often supported by a buffalo bell, a whip (that functions also as a güiro and rattle), a drum, a flute, and a *katchiappee* (three-string lute). Increasingly, microphones are used, and the resultant amplification of the *katchiappee* adds conspicuous rhythmic vitality to the performance. (*Lam khu* is the flirtatious genre of the central region of Laos around Vientiane; similar genres exist in northern and southern regions.)

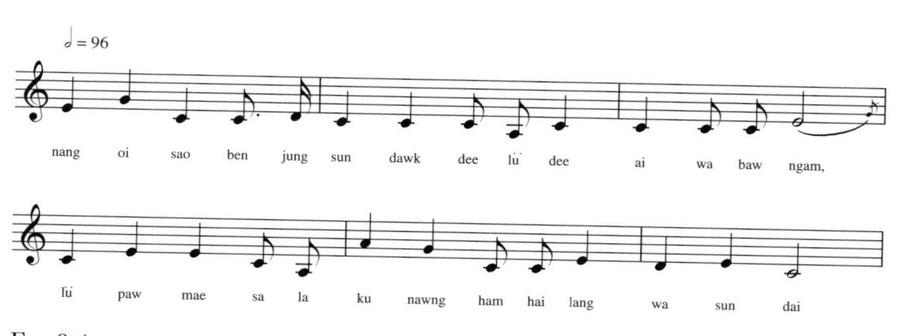

Ex. 9.4

The popular theatre-music genre today is *lam luang* ('sing story'), with up to thirty performers and a *phin phat* ensemble of five to ten players; it enacts stories that derive from ancient legends. With its stock characters and its mixture of song, speech, dance, acrobatics, and slapstick theatre, *lam luang* is similar in style to the *lakhōn jatri* of Thailand. As in other countries of South East Asia, however, the *lam luang* of Lao

[86] Miller, 'Laos', *The New Grove*, x. 460–1, and CD, *Laos, Lam Saravane, Musique pour le khène*, Ocora Records C 559 058.

[87] Miller, 'Laos', *The New Grove*, x. 461.

exists in a version that combines traditional style with Western pop style: *lam luang samay*. This version is performed to the accompaniment of a modern band, usually including electric guitar, bass, keyboards, and drum set, as well as *khaen* and other traditional instruments of the *pī phāt* and *mahōrī* ensembles; its themes are taken from both contemporary and traditional stories.[88]

Music and Theatre in Myanmar (Burma)

Since the early 1970s Myanmar has been ruled by a brutal, totalitarian, military junta that has isolated the country from the rest of the world, and rendered information about it scarce and often ill-informed. Officially, the government encourages many aspects of traditional culture: village *pwe*s (fairs) remain common, for example, and are enlivened by performances of traditional music theatre. In fact, the retention of traditional cultural systems springs from the disastrous economic record of the government, rather than from any disinclination of the people to modernize; and performances of traditional court music presently take place only in the State Schools of Music and Theatre in Yangon (Rangoon) and Mandalay.[89]

A distinctive traditional instrument of Myanmar is the *saùng gauk* (arched harp), the court repertoire of which dates back to the fourteenth century, and makes use of complex tuning systems and modal theories.[90] After the capture of the Thai royal musicians of Ayuddhya in 1767, a virtuoso style of playing developed at the court, and thirteen *kyo* ('string') songs came to be arranged, in order of difficulty, in a course of instruction for apprentice players. There is a large repertoire of song-texts for court use, for spirit ceremonies, as love-songs, and as laments; the repertoire has been passed on orally.

One genre of traditional music theatre that has survived, vigorous and popular, through recent decades is *zat pwe*—Burma's all-night festival of music, theatre, and dance, usually performed by professional troupes in temporary mat-shed theatres, and associated with temple

[88] Doling and Soden, *Arts Indo China Cultural Development Report: Laos*, 14.

[89] Teachers at the State School of Music and Theatre are classed as government officials, and were not permitted to speak to this author (in 1991). It subsequently transpired that for government officials to be seen talking to foreigners without governmental permission could mean losing their job and possible imprisonment.

[90] Muriel C. Williamson, 'Burma', *The New Grove* (1980), iii. 481–5.

38. Burmese *hsaìng-waìng* ensemble, with (left to right) *yagwin* (cymbals), *poat-má* (barrel drum suspended from a pole frame), *pat-waìng* (tuned drum chime, centre), *hnè* (shawm), and *kyì-waìng* (circular gong chime), accompanying a marionette play (above)

festivals. It is a composite of speech, song, dance, and martial acrobatics, accompanied by a distinctive form of 'gong chime'.

The principal Burmese 'gong chime' ensemble is the *hsaìng-waìng*. It is led by its unusual *pat-waìng*, a twenty-one-piece, circular, melodic *drum* chime, with a range of more than three octaves; the use of the Indian method of drum-tuning, by application of paste, suggests that the *pat-waìng* is one of the few Indian instruments to survive the period of Indian influence in South East Asia.[91] The *hsaìng-waìng* ensemble also includes the *kyì-waìng* ('gong circle') and *maùng-zaìng* ('gong chime' arranged horizontally in rows), as well as shawm, finger cymbals, hand cymbals, a six-drum set, slit drum, and clappers to delineate rhythm and structure (Pl. 38).

Hsaìng-waìng musicians, like Javanese and Balinese gamelan musicians, use two basic scales, one essentially hemitonic, the other anhemitonic: C–E–F–G–B (taking C as the starting-point for defining the sequence) and C–D–E–G–A. In both, the two missing notes may be used in auxiliary capacity. The heptatonic scale gives the appearance of

[91] Ibid. 475.

equidistance, with thirds and sevenths slightly flatter, and fourths slightly sharper, than in the diatonic scale.[92]

Present-day *zatpwe* performances usually feature two plays: one modern, one traditional. Each may last more than four hours, and a separate ensemble supports each: one is akin to a Western dance band, typically consisting of electric guitar and keyboards, string bass, trumpet, clarinet, and saxophone; the other is the *hsaìng-waìng*. Each play incorporates a mixture of speech, song, dance, and slapstick comedy, and in each—as is common in performances of music theatre throughout South East Asia—'gong chimes' (or keyboards) improvise during the speech. Whereas the dance-band style uses simple triadic harmony to support melodies that blend Western and traditional traits, the performance on the *hsaìng-waìng* follows traditional 'gong-chime' procedures. The *pat-waìng* (drum chime), punctuated by clashed cymbals, lends exuberant character to the music; and vocal melodic lines tend to display more idiosyncratic rhythms than those elsewhere on the mainland.[93]

The tragic political events in Myanmar, over the past few decades, can scarcely have encouraged confidence in the all-pervading beneficence of the *nat*s (spirits); nevertheless, *zatpwe* appears still to function as a community ritual through which hubris may be exorcised and spiritual strength reborn.

Music and Theatre in Vietnam

Vietnam stands at the crossroads of South East Asian, Chinese, and (to some extent) Indian culture. It also stands at a crossroads of political conflict. Its history has been one of resourceful, heroic—and ultimately victorious—resistance against the might of the Chinese, Mongolian, French, and US empires. Not surprisingly, the Vietnamese retain a powerful sense of national pride and identity, and, despite Chinese domination from the first to the tenth centuries, they have preserved a national language and literature, as well as many distinctive musical and theatrical traditions.

Historically, the Annanite chain of mountains that runs north–south, along the western borders of Vietnam, has tended to separate Chinese

[92] Williamson, 'Burma', *The New Grove* (1980), iii. 480.
[93] Information based on author's observations.

and Indian spheres of cultural influence within South East Asia. Vietnamese philosophy, religion, literature, painting, architecture, theatre, and music all bear marks of Chinese influence. Wooden xylophones survive in the Central Highlands, where they are played melodically, accompanied by bamboo percussion instruments, but gamelan-type 'gong-chime' ensembles are not in evidence. The territory includes fifty-one ethnic minority groups, many of whom have their own distinctive forms of traditional music.[94]

Vietnamese art music manifests the strongly developed sense of mode that characterizes music of South and West Asia. The Vietnamese word for mode is *dieu*, but the word *giong* ('voice' or 'intonation') is also sometimes used. The *dieu* establishes the 'flavour' of the piece, further influenced by *hoi* (modal nuances), which determine special types of ornamentation on particular notes.[95] There are two main *dieu*, both of which derive from the anhemitonic pentatonic scale, though the two additional notes are used as passing notes or ornaments, and in this way condition the *hoi*.[96]

Dieu bac is usually performed in moderate or fast tempo, and its *hoi* are held to express happiness or strength. The sequence of intervals is C–D–F–G–A; the notes C and G are usually accorded greatest importance, but if (less usually) the notes D and A are accorded greater importance, a different *hoi* results. The second main mode, *dieu nam*, is usually performed in slow or moderate tempo, and its *hoi* are held to express tranquillity, melancholy, or grief. The basic sequence of intervals is C–E♭–F–G–B♭; the notes C and G are the most important, and, while the fifth between C and G and the fourth between C and F are stable in pitch, the other intervals may be varied in distance by up to a tone, offering greater variety of *hoi*.[97]

Many of the instruments most commonly used in Vietnam correspond to Chinese instruments (see Chapter 10): the *dan tranh* (sixteen-string zither with movable bridges) to the *zheng*; the *dan ty ba* (four-string, pear-shaped lute) to the *pipa*; the *dan nguyet* (moon-shaped lute) to the *yueqin*; the *dan tam thap luc* (a recently-imported dulcimer) to the *yangqin*; the *sao truc* (bamboo flute with six holes, and a seventh

[94] Tran Van Khe, 'Vietnam', *The New Grove* (1980), xix. 747.
[95] Ibid. 748.
[96] Nguyen Thuy Loan and Sten Sandahl, notes to cassette, *Music from Vietnam*, a joint production by the Swedish National Concert Institute, Caprice, the Swedish International Development Authority, and Vinaconcert (Hanoi), Caprice CAP 21406, 1991.
[97] Ibid.

39. Vietnamese *dan bau* (a monochord, plucked at the harmonics), played by Duc Binh

covered by a thin membrane) to the *dizi*; the *dan nhi* (two-string fiddle) to the *erhu*; and various types of drum, gong, cymbals, and woodblock.

Two instruments are peculiar to Vietnam. The *dan bau* is a monochord played entirely in harmonics. A string is attached at one end to a tuning screw, and at the other end to a curved, flexible rod of cane. One hand plucks the string with a plectrum, while touching the nodal points of the string with the edge of the palm; the other hand varies the tension of the string by bending the flexible rod, altering its pitch by up to a fifth, and making possible a complete chromatic range of plucked harmonics (Pl. 39). The expressive sound of this instrument is now often presented through a small electric amplifier and loudspeaker.

The other instrument peculiar to Vietnam is the *k'long put*, a rural instrument from the central highlands, resembling a bamboo xylophone; it is in fact a wind instrument, excited by handclaps. Bamboo tubes, tuned to different pitches, open at one end and mounted horizontally in a frame, are activated by the player clapping the hands, slightly cupped, in front of the openings.[98] Bamboo xylophones are also to be found in this region. Interestingly, both instruments are tuned to

[98] Nguyen Thuy Loan and Sandahl, notes to cassette, *Music from Vietnam*.

an anhemitonic pentatonic scale, which resembles that used in Burma and the pentatonic framework of Indonesian *pelog*.

The Vietnamese also use the Western guitar, in a form altered to facilitate their use of vibrato. The spaces between frets are excavated to yield a sequence of cavities; notes may be 'bent' by deflecting the string into the resulting depressions, making possible a variety of glissando and vibrato.

An indigenous Vietnamese art-music form, *hat a dao*, dates at least from the eleventh century, when a female singer, Dao-thi ('female of the Dao family'), received an imperial award for her singing.[99] During the fifteenth and sixteenth centuries, under influence from Ming China, *hat a dao* developed into elaborate forms, and was used both in religious and ceremonial contexts. During the seventeenth century, *hat a dao*, as a popular art, was gradually replaced by a style of folk theatre, *hat cheo*; by the eighteenth century it had ceased to be used on public and ceremonial occasions, and had become a poetic form for Mandarin-speaking intellectuals. Subsequently it became associated with the life of brothels and opium dens, and such associations still persist. In recent years, however, attempts have been made to reconstruct *hat a dao* in its original, art-music, form.[100]

The melodic outlines of *hat a dao*, though wide in range, usually correspond to the syllable melody of the language; they centre about three main notes, placing emphasis on timbre, the use of glissando decoration, and different types of vibrato and vocal colour.[101] Such emphasis is also germane to Chinese musical tradition.

Important among extant, traditional songs are the *hat quan ho*. Like *aiyai* of Cambodia and *lam khu* of Laos (and the Mountain Songs of China), they consist of flirtatious 'singing meetings' between men and women. They require a soft quality of voice, with a special kind of vibrato called *rung hot*, meaning 'grains that rebound'.[102] *Hat quan ho* are now practised in this way only in Bac Ninh, in the north, where the style is consciously preserved; nevertheless, the songs are known throughout the country, and are to be heard as street songs, performed in Western intonation and with Western harmonies by teenagers with electric guitars.

[99] Stephen Addiss, 'Text and Context in Vietnamese Sung Poetry: The Art of Hat a Dao', *Selected Reports in Ethnomusicology* (1992), 203.
[100] Ibid. 204–5.
[101] Ibid. 213.
[102] Ibid. 10–11.

Three types of music theatre are still performed in Vietnam. The *hat tuong* arrived from China during the thirteenth century, and closely resembles Chinese opera. It flourished under imperial patronage, but has declined under communist rule.

The preferred genre of music theatre in the north, in the 1990s, is *hat cheo*; this, as already indicated, superseded the *hat a dao* as a popular art form. The earliest surviving text of *hat cheo* dates from the fifteenth century, but the genre itself may be much earlier in origin. It evolved from popular festivities, and constitutes a variety of songs, dances, and instrumental interludes, connected by a narrative thread; the repertoire includes historical plays, but the essential purpose of *hat cheo* is social satire, providing opportunity for criticism of village authorities. (*Cheo* may be a mispronunciation of *trao*, meaning satire.) *Hat cheo* was formerly performed outside village community halls and pagodas; and the musical style is influenced by both *hat a dao* and *hat quan ho*. The art has been kept alive in Hanoi but, in traditional form, is performed mainly for tourists.

The popular *hat cheo* of today is a full-length drama, and uses a wide range of instruments, including such Western instruments as cello, bass, and electric piano. Chordal harmony, however, is used sparingly and usually arises out of heterophony. Acting remains stylized, and plots continue to be based on history and legend, as well as topical subjects. Modern *hat cheo* has adopted use of stage scenery, and a new *hat cheo* theatre has been constructed in Hanoi.

Throughout Vietnam, the preferred genre of music theatre today is the *hat cai luong* ('reformed theatre'). Created (around 1917–20) as a popular entertainment for the new middle class of the Saigon-Cholon area, it juxtaposes Vietnamese and Western musical styles. Its 'reforming' characteristics were the addition of new scripts, modernized costumes, a more natural theatrical style, and a more modern and varied musical style.[103] Traditional *hat cai luong* uses modern as well as traditional instruments (usually amplified); but it largely eschews functional harmony, and retains traditional vocal timbre and ornamentation. With considerable improvisational flair, performers elaborate items chosen from a repertoire of melody types, mostly deriving from folk sources or from *hat tuong*, and already known to performers and audience

[103] Peter Manuel, *Popular Musics of the Non-Western World* (New York: Oxford University Press, 1989), 198–204.

40. Players of Skilled Chamber Music (*Nhac tai tu*): moon-shaped lute (*dan nguyet*); modified guitar (*dan luc huyen cam*); sixteen-string zither (*dan tranh*). The players are members of the Central Renovated Theatre (*Hat Cai Luong*) Troupe, Hanoi. Photo: Philip Blackburn

(Pl. 40).[104] Dramatic themes range from historical subjects to contemporary street life; and because the language is contemporary vernacular, the genre, both musically and dramtically, is highly adaptable.

Traditional songs and instrumental styles are used to accompany Vietnamese puppetry (*mua roi*: 'dancing puppets'). Puppetry has existed in Vietnam for at least a millennium, but a peculiarly Vietnamese form of puppetry, *roi nuoc* (water puppetry), is thought to have developed during the early twelfth century, when determined puppeteers (in the Red River delta) managed to carry on with their show, notwithstanding severe flooding. *Roi nuoc* features puppeteers hidden behind a long screen, who manipulate the puppets with bamboo rods, while standing chest-deep in water. Plots are drawn from the same legendary and historical sources as other forms of Vietnamese traditional theatre, and many of the tunes and instruments used are those of *hat cheo*.[105]

[104] Philip Blackburn, *Stilling Time*, CD of 'Traditional Musics of Vietnam', Minnesota Composers Forum, 1994, tracks 2, 18.

[105] Tim Doling and Philip Soden, *Report of the Arts Vietnam Consultancy Visit* (Hong Kong, 1991).

Music Theatre, Instruments, and Tuning Systems

While clearly belonging to the Chinese sphere of influence, Vietnamese music theatre is not greatly different—in its combination of song, speech, dance, martial acrobatics, and slapstick—from other music-theatre styles of South East Asia, South Asia, and East Asia. Across Africa and Eurasia as a whole, theatrical genres have exploited the use of myth, history, and morality tale, as a means to spread religious and political doctrine among the populace, and to influence the popular reaction in such matters. Theatre has always been an effective vehicle for propaganda.

Differences between music theatre in these different areas lie mostly in modality and timbre. In South East Asia, in a broad sweep of musical styles northwards from Java to Vietnam, the unpredictable tunings of Indonesian note-sets (perhaps deriving from archaic, 'divisive' tuning of flutes) gradually give way to anhemitonic pentatonic scales (deriving from the cycle-of-fifths procedure) and, in Vietnam, to a defined theory of mode. No less conspicuous is the gradual change from the timbres of chime metallophones to those of wooden (including bamboo) xylophones, and thence to a dominance of timbres obtained from stretched silk, nylon, or wire, and non-divisively tuned flutes.

Where string instruments predominate, tunings can be adjusted with relative ease; modes can be defined as much by intervallic relationships between their constituent notes as by melodic patterns derived from them. Particular notes can be emphasized by means such as vibrato, glissando, tremolo, and shakes. Where tuned idiophones predominate, tunings can only be adjusted with difficulty; modes are not susceptible to pitch alteration, and can be defined only by the number of notes in a unique modal set and by particular note patterns deriving from that modal set. Ornamentation can be effected only by movement from one note to another, and effective change of mode only by moving from one set of instruments to another. It may have been such limitations that caused layering of musical material between differing sets of instruments, with differing densities of variation-making, to become characteristic of musical styles throughout much of South East Asia. In any event, it is the change, from such multi-part heterophony on instruments of fixed pitch to heterophony in smaller ensembles, with greater variety of timbre and flexibility of tuning, that most clearly reveals Indian and Chinese influence on what appears to be an essentially indigenous, South East Asian, musical culture.

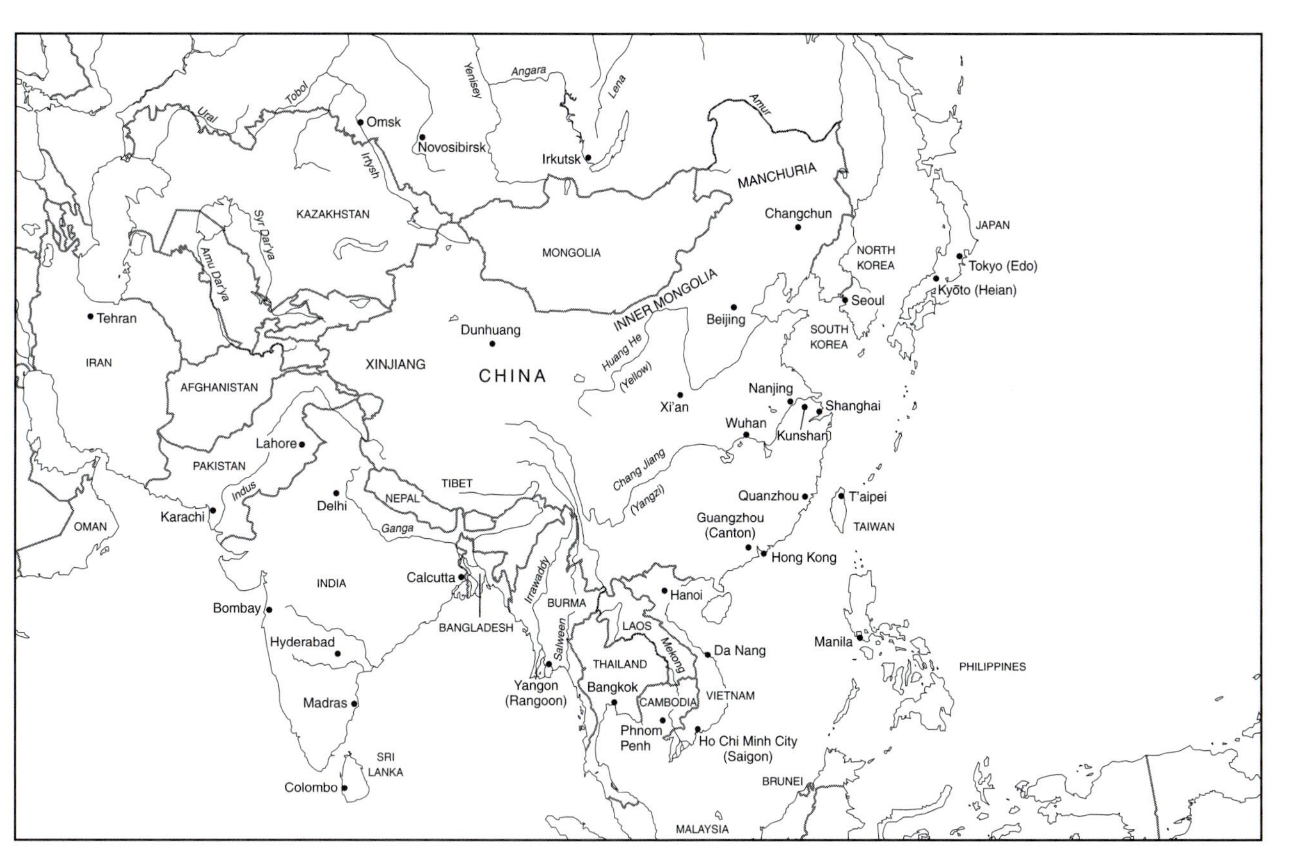
Ural
Tobol
Omsk
Yenisey
Novosibirsk
Angara
Lena
Irkutsk
Amur
Irtysh
MANCHURIA
KAZAKHSTAN
Syr Dar'ya
Amu Dar'ya
MONGOLIA
Changchun
JAPAN
NORTH KOREA
Tokyo (Edo)
Kyōto (Heian)
INNER MONGOLIA
Seoul
Tehran
Beijing
SOUTH KOREA
Dunhuang
IRAN
XINJIANG
CHINA
Huang He (Yellow)
AFGHANISTAN
Xi'an
Nanjing
Shanghai
Wuhan
Kunshan
Lahore
PAKISTAN
Chang Jiang (Yangzi)
TIBET
Indus
Delhi
NEPAL
Quanzhou
T'aipei
Karachi
OMAN
Ganga
Guangzhou (Canton)
TAIWAN
Hong Kong
INDIA
Calcutta
Irrawaddy
Hanoi
Bombay
BURMA
BANGLADESH
LAOS
Hyderabad
Salween
Mekong
Da Nang
Manila
THAILAND
PHILIPPINES
Yangon (Rangoon)
Bangkok
CAMBODIA
VIETNAM
Madras
Phnom Penh
Ho Chi Minh City (Saigon)
SRI LANKA
Colombo
BRUNEI
MALAYSIA

East Asia

10 *East Asia*

China

The Continuity and Spread of Chinese Culture

The most remarkable feature of Chinese civilization is its continuity. Aspects of Chinese culture, still functional today, date back some 4,000 years. Social and governmental systems were integrated by a written language, of which the symbols (the 'characters') were standardized in 221 BC, and still form the basis of the Chinese script. The social and governmental systems themselves, codified towards the end of the first millennium BC, were perpetuated with little essential change until the death of the last empress in 1908; many elements are part of received custom to this day. The roots of this remarkable continuity derive, in part at least, from the use made by Confucius of song-texts with a historical content in teaching the sons of the nobility. Confucius—a sage, but to his countrymen a saint—lived from *c.*551 to 479 BC.

Unlike his Western contemporaries, Confucius did not perceive humankind as the climax of Creation; indeed, for Confucius and his society, there was no Creation. The universe was 'of itself'—self-made and self-being; and humankind, like other species of nature, was a mere fragment of it. A harmonious relationship between humankind and the rest of nature could exist only if there were also harmony between humans themselves—harmony within the family, within the clan, and within the state. The duty of humans, therefore, was to cultivate virtue as an inherent force—and what Confucius meant by 'virtue' was a selfless power of personality. Unlike 'Christian' society, Confucian society was governed by a sense of obligation and duty, rather than of rights. The millennia-long tradition of Confucian teaching still influences the mores of peoples throughout East Asia and the Chinese diaspora.

Table 10.1. Guide to pronunciation of the Pinyin system of Romanized Chinese

a	as in b*a*r
e	as in h*e*r
i	*ee*: *di* 'dee'; but when preceded by c, ch, r, s, sh, z, or zh, then shorter then *er*. Thus, *dizi* 'deedz'
o	as in l*o*rd: *bo* 'bore'
u	as in b*oo*t
ü	as in German umlaut (after x or q, the u is also effectively an umlaut)
c	as in it*s*
q	as in *ch*oose
x	between *ss* and *sh*
z	as in bi*ds*
zh	as in *J*oe
ou	as in *oh*
uo	(after c, d, l, n, r, sh, t, z, zh) same as o (see above): *luo* 'lore'
ian	*ee-en*: *Fujian* 'Foo-jee-en'
ao	as in n*ow*

Source: Stephen Jones, *Folk Music of China: Living Instrumental Traditions* (Oxford: Oxford University Press, 1995).

Notwithstanding their reverence for tradition, the Chinese were immensely innovative and inventive. They were, for example, the first to make paper, the first to use movable type, wheel-carts, boats with a stern-post rudder, to make porcelain, and to carve jade. They were the first to use the magnetic compass, to make grid maps, to understand the technology of accurate time-keeping, and to make clocks with an escapement action. They invented gunpowder and developed sophisticated firearms: the crossbow, the flame-thrower, rockets, land- and sea-mines, guns, cannons, mortars, and repeating-guns. They discovered the circulation of the blood, circadian rhythms ('biological clocks') in the body, and the dietary causes of deficiency diseases, all between 2,100 and 1,800 years before Europeans. They had the decimal system by 1400 BC, a place for zero by the fourth century BC, negative numbers by the second century BC, and were extracting higher roots and solutions of higher numerical equations by the first century BC. And by AD 1584 a Chinese scholar, Zhu Zaiyu, had prepared pitch-pipes of bamboo in a 'well-tempered' scale, calculated on the basis of the twelfth root of 2 (1:1.05946), an invention that was published in Europe some half-century later (by Père Marin Mersenne, in 1736).[1]

When the British attempted to trade with China at the end of the eighteenth century, they could offer nothing—with the possible exception of clockwork—that the Chinese needed; all their products were inferior in quality to those produced in China. The Chinese, understandably, regarded the British as another kind of 'barbarian'. The failure of the British government to reach agreement on trade led private merchants to offer opium—cultivated by the British in India, but illegal in China—and to a series of wars that left China humiliated. The 1842 Treaty of Nanjing—which, *inter alia*, ceded Hong Kong to the British—was the result of collision between cultures with opposite economic and social systems, neither understanding the rules by which the other played the game.

To foreigners, the Chinese court may often have appeared contemptuously aloof, but it was far from being impervious to outside influence. Modern China is a vast land mass. Currently it contains one-quarter of the world's population (subsisting on but 7 per cent of the world's arable land). Population pressure was always great: in the seventh century, the Tang capital, Changan (modern Xian), was said to have over a million inhabitants; in the seventeenth century, by the end of the Ming dynasty, there were about 160 million Chinese subjects.[2] Always vulnerable to attack from the north and west, the Chinese empire gradually absorbed vast areas of these regions, benefiting from the cultural interaction this engendered. (The People's Republic of China has now designated these culturally distinctive areas—Inner Mongolia, Xinjiang-Uighur,

[1] Robert Temple, *The Genius of China: 3000 years of Science, Discovery and Invention* (London: Multimedia Books, 1986); this is a distillation of Joseph Needham, *Science and Civilisation in China* (Cambridge: Cambridge University Press, 1962–).

[2] J. M. Roberts, *Pelican History of the World* (London, Pelican Books, 1988), 427.

Guangxi-Zhuang, Ningxia-Hui, and Tibet—as 'autonomous regions'. These regions embrace fifty-five 'minority' nationalities; but, though these occupy more than 60 per cent of the land, they form only 6 per cent of the population.[3])

Through trade, Chinese cultural influence extended west and south, as far as Europe and Africa. As long ago as the first century BC, the Silk Road provided a trade route to and from China through the 'Jade Gate' in modern Gansu. Chinese silks and lacquer then became available as far apart as Afghanistan, Syria, and Egypt; even Rome had a special market for Chinese silk.[4] The Silk Road itself became a melting-pot of Indian, Persian, and provincial Roman culture; many musical instruments from West Asia came to China along it. (The Silk Road was, however, a hazardous and dangerous route, due to its mountainous terrain and the constant danger from bandits. Its romantic-sounding title was coined only in the nineteenth century, by a German geographer.)

It was writing, as much as anything, that shaped Chinese culture and held the empire together through so many millennia. The Chinese did not develop an alphabet, and this made literacy hard to achieve; widely differing spoken dialects existed throughout the empire. Writing, on the other hand, remained invariant and intelligible, to the literate, everywhere.

Chinese Calligraphy

The unique Chinese form of calligraphy, which spread to Korea and Japan, provides insight into the distinctive mode of thought of the Chinese. The first extensive evidence of Chinese use of characters is on 'oracle bones' of the Shang dynasty; single characters appear on artefacts as early as 8000 BC. Shang rulers based divinations on the shapes of cracks that appear when a red-hot metal skewer is pressed on dried bones from the carapace of turtles, and large mammalian bones. The question asked, and the answer (the diviner's interpretation of the resulting crack), were then recorded in pictorial script on the same bone. Some of our earliest knowledge of musical practices comes from these inscriptions.

[3] Frederic M. Kaplan, Julian M. Sobin, and Arne J. de Keijzer, *The China Guidebook*, 10th edn. (Teaneck, NJ: Eurasia Press, 1989), 20.

[4] Michael Sullivan, *The Arts of China* (Berkeley and Los Angeles: University of California Press, 1984), 78–9.

The characters originated as pictorial representations of *things* and symbolic representations of *ideas*. The notion of representation is intrinsic to all Chinese arts. Chinese music, for example, invariably has an explicit, non-musical reference. Such reference is sometimes directly representational, as, for example, in the well-known *pipa* (lute) solo, *Ambushed from All Sides*, a battle-piece that includes the groans of the wounded and dying, or the *qin* (board-zither) piece, *High Mountains and Flowing Streams*, which contains some seventy-two kinds of sounds to describe the flowing and falling of water.[5] Performers still adjust melodic and rhythmic outlines of well-known melodies—in the *sizhu* ('silk and bamboo') repertoire, for example—in order better to recreate moods or spirits (*yijing*), identified in titles such as 'The Grief of Zhao Jun' or 'Rain Beating on the Banana Leaves'.[6]

Chinese written characters are words; each is read as a single, monosyllabic sound, carrying a basic, concrete meaning. Characters may be relatively simple: a rectangle cut in half by a central vertical line, for example, today depicts 'middle' (originally the character represented an archery target struck centrally). Characters may, however, embody more complex representations: the character for 'country' or 'kingdom' is an amalgam of symbols representing an enclosing boundary, a mouth (to feed), and a spear (for defence). Characters are monosyllabic; because the number of possible monosyllables is limited, Chinese has been forced to develop, *aurally*, into a largely disyllabic language; most words, therefore, are represented by two characters. When the characters for 'middle' and 'kingdom' are joined together, they signify China: the centre of the civilized world. Unlike phonetic, alphabetic, writing of a language, which is a representation of sound, Chinese writing arose, essentially, as a visual representation of objects, gestures, and symbols, as words. The writing itself, therefore, offers scope for imaginative interpretation of the thing or idea represented.

Musical instruments of Chinese origin were originally represented by a single character, in contrast to those from other places, represented by two characters. For example, a character from an early Shang oracle bone shows 'silk' over 'wood', and is believed to refer to the *qin* (seven-string board zither). Today, however, the *qin* is usually referred to as

[5] Mingyue Liang, *Music of the Billion: An Introduction to Chinese Musical Culture* (New York: Heinrichshofen, 1985), 182.

[6] Alan R. Thrasher, 'Structural Continuity in Chinese Sizhu: The Baban Model', *Asian Music*, 20/2 (1989), 81.

the *guqin* ('ancient zither') to distinguish it from other *qin*, such as the 'iron-*qin*' (piano) or 'wind-*qin*' (organ). The name *yangqin* (dulcimer) means 'overseas *qin*', and indeed the instrument probably reached China from Persia, either overland or by sea.

Traditional Chinese calligraphy is written with a skilfully formed, soft brush. To write well requires a good brush, freshly ground 'ink', and, above all, speed: it is necessary to go with the flow of the ink. To the Chinese calligrapher, written characters are infused with the spiritual, life-giving energy of *qi* (see pp. 330–2).

Traditional Chinese painting, like calligraphy, is executed in ink with the writing brush; indeed, it is regarded as an extension of calligraphy. Nature has always been the source of Chinese painting; in this landscape, humans are insignificant, mere constituents within the overall scheme of things. Painting does not aim at a totality of expression: everything cannot be known, nothing is complete.[7] The Chinese concept of perspective places the horizon at an infinite distance. Creating a sense of space is of extreme importance: it facilitates meditation; it imposes a personal journey through the painting on the part of the viewer; and it fixes a moment of eternity.

In Chinese thought, reverence for the arts of calligraphy and painting goes hand in hand with reverence for tradition. Many Chinese traditions were first defined in works attributed to Confucius, one of most famous of which is the so-called 'Analects' ('Words of Discussions'), a compilation of lecture notes made by pupils.

Confucianism and Daoism

That Confucian teaching still exerts a strong influence on Chinese society, some 2,500 years after its origin, suggests that the doctrines of the saint reflected a demand of the Chinese psyche for order, for categorization, and for the codification of behaviour. The Chinese numbered (and still tend to number) everything, from the Three Loyalties and the Five Infinities, to the Ten Types of Music and the Twenty-Four Touches (of vibrato on the *qin*), to the Five Loves and Four Great Freedoms of the Cultural Revolution.[8] Confucius himself, it

[7] Sullivan, *The Arts of China*, 156.

[8] Colin Thubron, *Behind the Wall* (London: Heineman, 1987), which provides a vivid, first-hand account of modern China in the context of its political and cultural history.

is said, categorized the Five Cardinal Relationships: ruler with subject, husband with wife, parent with child, elder sibling with younger sibling, and—the only social relationship where equality was possible—friend with friend.

Two essential concepts in the teaching of Confucius were: *li*, concerned with state rituals and the rituals of ancestor worship, as well as with social interaction and relationships; and *ren*, concerned with personal interrelationships; in short: rites and human-heartedness. Their effect was to instil in individuals both disciplined awareness of their place and obligations in the social fabric, and generosity, as a duty. Such concerns complemented the concept of *le* (delight), usually associated with *yue*, a term that originally encompassed dance, dance properties, gesture, song, and other festal activities. (Only in more recent times was the narrower meaning of 'music' defined by the term *yinyue*.) *Le* and *yue* are represented by the same character, and originally had the same sound.

Confucius was in no sense a religious teacher; he abhorred superstition. An afterlife was restricted to the nobility, and only a nobleman could belong to a clan and so have ancestors.[9] Ordinary people, therefore, were denied the services of learned ritualists, and depended on the psychic powers of shamans, able to make contact with the spirits of the departing or departed. This spirit world came to be appropriated by popular *Daoism*, which, until the arrival of Buddhism, provided the most subtle challenge to Confucian ideology.[10] It still influences many aspects of Chinese life.

Daoists opposed feudalism as upheld by Confucius; they valued rites for their capacity to *affect* the spirits of ancestors, and they investigated nature. Where Confucius symbolized success, *Daoism* provided a refuge for those lacking opportunity for betterment.[11] The tenets of philosophical *Daoism* were set out in the *Daodejing* ('The Way and its Power'),[12] widely attributed to a hypothetical Laozi of the sixth century BC, but probably written some centuries later.

Dao, The Way—the way things are in nature—was the ground of being. In Chinese metaphysical tradition, cosmic energy is relayed through two opposed principles: the *yang* (positive) and the

[9] Roberts, *Pelican History of the World*, 146.
[10] Arthur Cotterell, *China: A Cultural History* (London: Penguin Books, 1988), 34, 77.
[11] Needham, *Science and Civilisation*, ii. 57.
[12] Arthur Waley, *The Way and its Power: A Study of the Tao Te Ching and its Place in Chinese Thought* (London, 1934).

yin (negative). Their ideograms represent the sunny and shady sides of a hill respectively; they are associated with many antithetic concepts, such as masculine and feminine, firm and yielding, strong and weak, heaven and earth, light and dark, rising and falling—even in such everyday matters as spicy and bland cooking.[13] The twelve musical notes of the dodecatonic octave were divided into two groups of six, representing the *yang* and *yin* tones of male and female phoenixes (pheasant-like birds); those obtained from rising fifths represented the *yang*, and those derived from descending fourths represented the *yin*.[14] In *Daoist* thought, the *yang* and the *yin* must always be in balance: one cannot exist without the other. Humankind resides in the middle zone between the two. *Daoism* opened the natural world and its order to the imagination, and harmonized social ritual with nature; but the *dao* could not be defined out of existence: 'The *Dao* that can be told is not the eternal *Dao*', said Lao-zi; 'it is hidden but always present.'[15]

Daoism emerged both as a religion and as a philosophy, and became a cult during the last two centuries BC. As a popular religion, it was rooted in magic. From Shang times, the vital life force was regarded as *qi*: *qi* could rise to heaven with the ancestors and descend with them to earth.[16] Many Chinese still regard *qi* as the vital life force; it is associated with *tai ji* (the pole star around which the earth rotates), the species of callisthenics practised by many Chinese in parks in the early mornings, so as to fill the *tai xu* (great void) with energy for the day.

At a philosophical level also, *Daoism* offered immortality: salvation through faith and works. This linked it with *Māhāyana* Buddhism; in a process of syncretic development, *Daoism* adopted much of Buddhism's ecclesiastical organization. This blend of Buddhism and folk religion is still evident all over East Asia: Buddhas, Bodhisattvas, their guardians, and their spirits often occupy the same temples as popular nature-gods. Their sculpted deities are still adorned with petitions, in couplets that conform to the classic, poetic rules. Temple courtyards are still the locus for elaborate ceremonies in honour of such divinities.

[13] Alan Watts, *Tao, the Watercourse Way* (London: Penguin Books, 1975), 21.

[14] Rembrandt Wolpert, 'Chinese Music', *NOCM* (1983).

[15] Lao-tzu, *Tao Te Ching*, trans. Stephen Mitchell (London: Macmillan, 1988), 2, 4.

[16] Needham, *Science and Civilisation*, iv. 134.

Music, Ritual, and Cosmology

According to the *Daodejing*, 'the greatest music has the most tenuous sounds'. Part of the art of playing the ancient and most revered Chinese instrument, the *qin* (seven-string board zither), consists not in stopping the strings to obtain alternative notes, but in damping them at their acoustic nodes, so as to obtain different harmonics of the *same* note, on a single string. By this means, the different harmonic content of notes of the same pitch, generated in different ways, could be experienced and savoured.

From the earliest times, the Chinese seem to have taken pleasure in syntheses of sounds, colours, and flavours, in response to the syntheses of nature, manifested in storms, rainbows, and spicy herbs. The mixture of scents of the countryside and garden was thought to produce wind, the means by which heaven made music. Herbs, flowers, and the colours of the rainbow were symbols of the climatic processes on which the lives of ancient Chinese depended.[17] A text of *c*.400 BC equates *qi* with musical notes: 'There are six *qi* of heaven. Their incorporation produces the five flowers; their blossoming makes the five colours; they proclaim themselves in the five notes . . .'[18]

The six *qi* were a synonym for the six *lu*, 'channels' through which it was thought the *qi* could be piped off into lengths of bamboo, of the type used for irrigation, as 'humming-tubes'. Such humming-tubes were used to determine the exact moment when the *qi* returned, with an ancestor from heaven: as in many other animistic cultures, shamans were said to 'whistle for the wind'.[19] The pitches and timbres of the *lu* were associated with the *qi* in all aspects of nature. Thus the Eight Winds had to be subject to the Twelve Pitches if they were not to become turbulent. The Eight Winds were each summoned by an appropriate magical dance; and the music for each dance was led by an instrument made from one of the Eight Materials (sources of sound): stone (chimes of lithophonic rocks); metal (bells and bell chimes); wood (boxes to be struck as posed bells, and scrapers in the form of tigers); earth (clay bowls and vessel flutes); stretched skins (drums); bamboo (flutes and pan pipes); gourd (for the air reservoir of free-reed mouth organs); and silk (for zither strings). By such means, correlations were established between notes, colours, winds, and points of the compass.

[17] Ibid. 133. [18] Ibid. 134. [19] Ibid. 150–1.

Of such importance was the correlation of *lu* and *qi* that, in the first century BC, hermetically sealed chambers for 'observing the *qi*' were built. Each of the twelve pitch-pipes was assigned to one of the twelve months, because—according to the official history of the first century BC—'the windy *qi* of heaven and earth correct the twelve pitch-fixations'.[20] Inside such a chamber, the twelve pitch pipes (*lu*) were filled with ashes; it was believed that the appropriate pitch pipe for each month would be 'activated' by the force of subtle *qi*. Human breath, or a wind, would not displace the ashes; but when activated by the emanation of the *qi* from the earth, the ashes would be expelled. This arcane, pseudo-scientific practice persisted into the sixteenth century.

Until the modern period, the Chinese never conceived of a scale as a ladder of rising pitches. The names of the pitches may have referred to original positions occupied by particular instruments about a dance or other performance arena in use in ritual music and dance. These were arranged on either side of the king (the *gong*: the palace and first note). Perhaps because these locations were associated with pitch-giving instruments—bells and stone chimes—they came to refer to pitches. The primary meaning of the word *lu* ('rule'), in transferred sense, referred to the regulation of steps and beats in *yue* ('music with dance').[21]

By the sixth century BC, or earlier, the Chinese were producing finely-tuned *bianzhong* (chimes of suspended bells). The bell may have been developed from metal grain measures; the pitch of the *huangzhong* (yellow bell), the fundamental note, was tested against the appropriate *lu* (pitch pipe), and was directly related to linear measurement, volume, and weight. Without such standards of measurement, it was held that cheating and corruption would spread, trade would be disrupted, and riots and rebellions might ensue.[22] With each dynasty, the state mode, and its final note, changed; no less than thirty-five such changes, with new values for the length of this pitch pipe, were made between the third century BC and the Revolution of 1911.[23]

The Chinese became expert bell-casters; and bell chimes, tuned to a gamut of twelve pitches, provided the starting note for Confucian ritual throughout the year. A tomb in Hubei province has yielded a set of

[20] Temple, *The Genius of China*, 204.
[21] Needham, *Science and Civilisation*, iv. 159, 191.
[22] Temple, *The Genius of China*, 199.
[23] Bell Yung, 'China', *The New Grove* (1980), iv. 261.

sixty-five bells, hung on three frames, with the largest set of bells in the centre. The bells of this tomb garniture are leaf-shaped in cross-section, and the bell vibrates differently when struck on the curve or near the tip of the 'leaf', so that two distinct pitches are obtainable from each bell.[24]

Perhaps because of the persistent association of pitch with cosmological concepts, absolute pitch did not become important in Chinese music; and the five pitches of the anhemitonic pentatonic scale (C–D–E–G–A), based on four steps of a fifth, in sequence, in quasi-Babylonian cycle-of-fifths procedure, became the backbone structure of the music. The five modes available from this scale are named after the starting note of the mode: *gong* (C), *shang* (D), *jue* (E), *zhi* (G), and *yu* (A). Two additional notes, F and B—making up a set of seven—may be used as auxiliaries, as passing-notes, or as ornamental appogiaturas.[25]

The Shang, the Zhou, and the First Emperor

As in many cultures, the origins of Chinese history are associated with the origins of its music. Legend records that Chinese history began in the reign of Huang-ti, the Yellow Emperor. His music-master, Ling Lun, travelling to the west, heard the song of the male and female phoenixes, cut bamboo tubes that yielded the notes of their song, and in this way obtained the twelve perfect pitches.[26]

More certain is the fact that, when the Shang tribe imposed feudal order on the villages of the Yellow River basin about 1523 BC, they developed a great bronze culture. These communities already had calendrical and monetary systems, wheel-carts, the use of the flexible brush for writing and decoration, and the arts of carving in wood and jade. When the Zhou invaded from the north-west and established their long-lasting dynasty about 1126 BC, the barbaric funerary sacrificial practices of the Shang were replaced by animal sacrifices, and the power of magic was progressively replaced by that of moral virtue. Future emperors received a 'Mandate from Heaven' to rule. (Order would

[24] Albrecht Schneider and Hartmut Stolz, 'Acoustics of Chinese Bell Chimes', in Ellen Hickman and David W. Hughes (eds.), *The Archaeology of Early Music Cultures* (Bonn: Verlag für systematische Musikwissenschaft GmbH, 1985).

[25] For a comparison of modes in China, Korea, Japan, and Vietnam, see W. P. Malm, 'East Asia', *The New Grove* (1980), v. 805.

[26] Wolpert, 'Chinese Music'.

become the hallmark of this mandate; disorder and uncontrollable rebellion would legitimize transfer of the mandate to another dynasty.)

The Zhou developed the intellectual and artistic aspects of Shang culture: rituals comprising music, art, and poetry conferred aesthetic dignity on the life of the court.[27] Imperial edicts were cast on bronze vessels; in later Zhou times, documents—such as the *Shijing* ('Book of Songs') and *Shujing* ('Book of Documents')—established a reverence for history and the written word. As the effectiveness of Zhou rule waned during the Warring States Period (sixth to second centuries BC), philosophers such as Confucius would look back to the early period of Zhou rule as a golden age of Chinese civilization.

This artistic culture was all but destroyed when, in 221 BC, the Qin gained unilateral control over the warring states and established a short-lived dynasty. Its leader adopted the name of Qin Shi Huangdi ('First Imperial Ruler of Qin') and was the first emperor of a unified China. He started the building of the Great Wall—eventually 1,400 miles in length—and fostered a legal framework that would guide China for over 2,000 years. (Qin is pronounced 'Chin', and it was this first emperor who gave China the name by which it is known in the West; Chinese, however, refer to their country as Zhongguo, meaning 'The Middle Kingdom'.)

The first emperor's innovations drew criticism from the scholar-gentry and led to his distrusting learning. He is said to have burned books and artworks in the 'Fires of Qin', and to have condemned some 460 Confucian scholars to death.[28] In fact, however, no books known from before his reign are lost; and it is probable that he only forbade writing. Qin Shi Huangdi himself was a megalomaniac tyrant, and arranged for his tomb to be guarded by thousands of lifesize terracotta warriors, so that his dynasty should survive for ever. (Some of these are now on show near modern Xian.) In fact, the dynasty survived his death by a mere three years.

The Han

For all its ruthlessness, it was the Qin that enabled the succeeding Han dynasty (202 BC—AD 220) to re-establish Chinese cultural systems on a firm political base. The classical texts

[27] Sullivan, *The Arts of China*, 31.

[28] Cotterell, *China*, 89–92.

were reinstated as the canon of education; Confucianism became the model for social government; arts and ritual were revived; the Silk Road was opened; and a great flowering of arts ensued. The Han saw the production of books on music and the arts, based on Confucian tradition. They also established the Bureau of Music, responsible for the supervision of ceremonial music and entertainments at court, and for establishing the cosmologically correct, fundamental pitch for the ritual music. (The bureau survived in various forms until the twentieth century.[29]) As early as the first century BC, the Chinese recognized the seven-note diatonic scale, and were aware of the possibility of transposition of modes.[30]

It was during the Han dynasty that the Examination System was created. Scholars who passed these rigorous tests had memorized, and learnt to brush-write, some thousands of a possible 50,000 Chinese characters; they had also memorized legal systems and the Confucian classics, and had acquired the ability to write formal essays on any given subject. Passing a succession of examinations, scholars ascended the ladder of the governmental civil service. Though the mass of the people was largely illiterate, these scholar-civil servants established the tenets of Confucian ethics as the basis of social order throughout the empire. Under the system, any male could present himself as a candidate, and many of peasant stock rose to high office. The Examination System itself led to a reverence for scholarship, still evident throughout East Asia today. The system was abandoned only in 1905.

The Han dynasty lasted until AD 220 and was followed by more than three centuries of political instability. Reunification was achieved in 589 under the short-lived Sui dynasty, followed by the Tang in 618. The Sui developed the incomparable canal system of Central China, a system that contributed greatly to the integration of the population throughout the vast land mass. It was the Tang who then pushed the boundaries of empire into Central Asia, Tibet, and Korea.

During the second to sixth centuries AD, repeated incursions from Central Asia had caused a mass migration of Chinese, south-east from the Yellow River basin to Nanjing, where the great Yangzi River meets the Yellow Sea. With this immigration (into previously non-Han territory) went important aspects of Chinese culture. Although the Tang

[29] Wolpert, 'Chinese Music'.

[30] L. E. R. Picken, 'The Music of Far Eastern Asia', in *The New Oxford History of Music*, i (Oxford: Oxford University Press, 1957).

dynasty re-established its base in the north (in modern Shaanxi province), the unusually cosmopolitan nature of that northern culture caused southerners to regard it as 'foreign'—'barbarian' even—and themselves as superior to it. The cultural divide continues to this day.

From the first century onwards, *Mahāyāna* Buddhism travelled from India along the Silk Road and began to penetrate China in the mountainous west; and when Turkic invasions from the north effectively closed the Silk Road, Buddhism still entered China from the Indianized kingdoms of South East Asia. By the seventh century, Guangzhou (Canton) was already a great trading port; and at the port of Quanzhou (in Fujien province)—already host to Arabs, Jews, Manichaeans, and Nestorian Christians—Chinese and Indians together built Buddhist temples.[31]

The Tang and its Music

The Tang dynasty (618–906) was a golden age of Chinese arts and culture. In the streets of Changan (modern Xian), probably the most advanced capital city of the then world, priests from South East Asia mingled with merchants from Central Asia and Arabia, and with Turks, Indians, Mongols, and Japanese.[32] Architectural and sculptural styles from India, and string and wind instruments from West and Central Asia, were absorbed into Chinese culture. In the early eighth century, some 30,000 musicians and dancers were recorded as being in the employ of the royal household.[33] Musicians were housed in various academies; and at court there were ten different bodies of performers—instrumentalists, singers, and dancers—only two of which were of pure Chinese (Han) origin. The Tang referred to these as 'The Ten Types of Music'; special quarters housed foreign musicians and dancers, from South and South East Asia, Bukhara, Kashgar, Samarkand, Turfan, and other regions.

It was during the Sui and Tang dynasties that *yanyue* ('banquet music') became the principal court musical genre, overshadowing the court ritual or ceremonial music. Although Sui and Tang emperors were considered to be Chinese, many were genealogically related to northern

[31] Sullivan, *The Arts of China*, 115.
[32] Ibid.
[33] Liang, *Music of the Billion*, 98.

tribal peoples, for whom music and dance had been primarily a means of entertainment; and this aspect of music and dance was gradually absorbed into Chinese musical aesthetics.[34]

The Tang banquet-repertoire includes extended suites (*daqu*) appropriate for the most impressive entertainment of guests—including foreign missions—and these, it may be supposed, represent contemporary Chinese taste. Items from this repertoire were played at the imperial court in Japan by musicians from Korea and China; on one occasion, in 838, a payment in gold dust secured copies in tablature for a visiting Japanese musician. Copies of these, made in Japan, and by many scribes over the centuries, still survive. One such copy was even written by a Chinese scribe.[35] Major items of this music were ballet suites in five or six movements, each individually choreographed and costumed.

Large suites were also composed for *qin* (seven-string board zither); those that survived were recorded by Zhu Quan in 1425 (see p. 342). Islamic music, among Uighur, Tajiks, and Uzbeks, was also constructed in large suites (see p. 186); and it is possible that the Chinese suites reflect Central Asian influence.

In 628 a Tang emperor approved a system of eighty-four classified scales.[36] This system theoretically enabled any one of the seven diatonic modes to begin on any one of the twelve pitch pipes, each carrying the name of one of the semitone steps in the octave. Whereas Chinese modal systems had previously been formulated on the basis of relative sizes of tubes, this system was first demonstrated, in the sixth century, on a four-string lute. Around 578, a lutenist from Kuchā had arrived at the imperial court (in the train of a Turkish princess, married to the emperor); the Chinese notes of the basic scale were then equated with the named Kuchean notes.[37] The extent to which this comprehensive system was put into practice in China is not clear; certainly modes of which the initial was an auxiliary were never used. During the Tang dynasty, twenty-eight modes were in use for non-ritual music;[38] but this number was substantially reduced later.

[34] Ibid.

[35] Laurence Picken with Allan Marett, Jonathan Condit, Elizabeth Markham, Yōko Mitani, and Rembrandt Wolpert, *Music from the Tang Court*, i (Oxford); ii– (Cambridge) (1981–).

[36] Picken, 'The Music of Far Eastern Asia', 97–8.

[37] Laurence Picken, *Folk Musical Instruments of Turkey* (Oxford: Oxford University Press, 1975), 604–65.

[38] Wolpert, 'Chinese Music'.

During the Tang dynasty, 'The Hundred Acts' (*baixi*)—popular theatrical performances, known since the second century BC—involving dance, songs, acrobatics, comedy-acting, and puppetry, were much in vogue. The genre provided the basis of popular entertainment in the Sui and Tang, and exerted a formative influence on Chinese opera.

As the Tang empire became overextended, instability threatened again, and intrigues at court distracted attention from victories gained by Muslims against Chinese in Central Asia. The year AD 845 was disastrous for Chinese arts and culture, when the Wu Zong emperor of Tang issued successive orders for the closure and destruction of many thousands of smaller Buddhist institutions, and then turned on the great temples. Buddhist works of art were destroyed on an unprecedented scale, and the wealth of the temples was confiscated. Never again would Buddhism rival the power of the State.[39] Today, it is to Nara, ancient capital of Japan, that one must look for that great fusion of Indian and Chinese art and architecture that was the glory of Chinese Buddhism. (As is now recognized, however, the glory of Nara owed much also to the artistic traditions of Korea.[40])

The Song and Neo-Confucianism

The final demise of the Tang in 906 led to a short period of political unrest, followed by somewhat precarious peace under the Song (960–1279). By this time, foreigners from the north had attained an important foothold in north-east China; only by payment of enormous levies were they kept at bay. The Song sought to revive old Chinese standards in morality, in public life, and in the arts, flanked as they were by enemies, and abhorring the exoticisms of the Tang court. Interest in antiquities was encouraged, and every effort made to eliminate the foreign styles of music and dance, enthusiastically cultivated by the Tang.

Learning was greatly respected, encouraged by emperors themselves keenly interested in scholarship and the arts. The rapid spread of woodblock printing in the tenth century led to publication of the *Classics* (in 130 volumes), the Buddhist *Tripitaka* (in over 5,000 volumes), and the Daoist canon, in some instances in editions of a

[39] Cotterell, *China*, 164.

[40] J. C. Covell and A. Covell, *Korean Impact on Japanese Culture* (Elizabeth, NJ: Hollym, 1984).

million copies and more. By the twelfth century, in the climate of a revival of interest in the entire canon of classical writing in Chinese, a quasi-synthesis of Confucian, Daoist, and Buddhist ideas was realized in the doctrine of Neo-Confucianism, which became the basis of the curriculum for the Examination System.[41] (It was this elaboration of Confucian thought that was subsequently acquired by Korea and Japan.) The principal creator of Neo-Confucianism was Zhu Xi (1130–1200).

At the heart of the new synthesis was the concept of *li*: the invisible, cosmic principle of organization, a concept of *pattern* through which all things are structured, subsuming both larger and smaller patterns. At one extreme, it embraced the universe; at the other, the structure of the natural world, and the phenomena of social life.[42] (*Li*, used by Zhu Xi, is a different word, written with a different character, from *li*, used by Confucius, for ritual ceremony.) Within the concept of a cosmic pattern, applicable to all things, 'The Way'—the *Dao*—was seen as immanent and all-pervading, rather than transcendent and 'super-natural', as Buddhists, earlier, saw it. Zhu Xi's *li* of pattern restored the traditional Confucianist understanding of an *impersonal* heaven;[43] and, by proposing that one component of the *Dao* belongs specifically to human society, Zhu Xi reconciled ancient, divergent uses by Daoists and Confucianists of the term *dao*.[44]

An essential part of Zhu Xi's view of the world was that *li*—the pattern—is inseparable from the substance (*qi*); *li* was non-material, *qi* was matter. To Zhu Xi, however, *qi* was not merely matter in its solid, tangible state, since matter can exist in tenuous, non-perceptible forms, such as gas or vapours; for Zhu Xi, *qi*—matter+energy—comprised 'the tools and raw material from which all things are made'.[45] As Joseph Needham has shown, by refusing to accept that organization ('pure form') could exist separately from matter-energy (postulated by Aristotle, for example), Zhu Xi was in close accord with the organicist view of the world developed during the twentieth century.[46] Moreover, it seems probable that the German mathematician and philosopher Leibnitz (1646–1716) was influenced by Zhu Xi in the development

41 Sullivan, *The Arts of China*, 143.
42 Needham, *Science and Civilisation*, ii. 473.
43 Ibid. 466–7.
44 Ibid. 485.
45 Ibid. 479–80.
46 Ibid. 475.

of his philosophical doctrine known as monadology, which includes as a principal concept the notion of a universe regulated by 'pre-established harmony'.[47]

In Chinese Buddhism, it was the Chan ('meditation') sect (known in Japan as Zen) that flourished in the climate of the new synthesis. Chan monks built temples in beautiful secluded localities, and this stimulated the art of landscape-gardening, whereby unexpected and irregular features stimulate the imagination. Encouraged by the Huizong emperor (1101–25), a great era of landscape-painting dawned. Painting even became an option in the Examination System; candidates might be required to illustrate an excerpt from the *Classics*, or from a well-known poem. The combination of calligraphy, poetry, and painting became known as 'The Three Perfections'.[48]

In this great intellectual revival, music played an important part. In 1101 Chen Yang presented to the Throne a monumental musicological survey, the *Yueshu* ('Book of Music'); and Zhu Xi himself, in his 'General Explanation of the Canon of Rites and Commentaries thereon' (printed posthumously), published what he accepted as Tang tunes of twelve song-texts from the ancient *Shijing* ('Book of Songs', 700–500 BC (see p. 334)).[49] At a popular level, in the cities, huge theatres, capable of holding up to 3,000 spectators, staged song and dance acts, sketches, and music theatre, collectively known as *zaxi* ('Variety Shows').

The Tartars and the Mongols

Meanwhile, political realities were flowing in a different direction. As early as 1127, the northern Tartars had captured the Song capital of Kaifeng, along with the emperor and his retinue. The whole of China north of the Yangzi fell to the Tartar armies, who were only prevented from penetrating further south by the exaction of even greater tribute from what became the 'Southern' Song. Behind the Tartars, the Mongols were preparing to advance from where the Muslims earlier had halted; and, in 1215, the Mongol armies of Genghis Khan began their attack on China. Within twelve years the whole of North China was overrun, leaving only one-hundredth of the former

[47] Needham, *Science and Civilisation*, 478, 496–505.
[48] Cotterell, *China*, 178–80.
[49] Wolpert, 'Chinese Music'.

population alive in the north-west. (Others in the north-east were spared because they were considered more useful alive and taxable, than dead.[50]) China was incorporated into a new 'barbarian' empire that included all Central and Western Asia. The Mongols called their dynasty the Yuan (1260–1368)—'first beginning'—and established their capital in Beijing ('northern capital').

It is a constant feature of Chinese history that its culture—the wealth of which was so alluring to foreign invaders—was strong enough to tame them when they arrived. The Mongols were more changed by China than China by them.[51] The Chinese scholar-gentry gradually penetrated the Mongol civil service, increasing pressure for re-establishment of the Examination System. Their disloyalty, at the heart of the civil service, weakened the entire government, so that, within little more than a 100 years after the invasion, the Mongols were overthrown. Yet the influence was not all one way. The Mongols added sumptuousness and vigour to Chinese art; at court, they established the largest ever ritual orchestras, with as many as 168 musicians and 128 dancers taking part;[52] and the dynamic rhythms of Central Asian music doubtless influenced popular music. The brilliant colours and rough contours of Mongol art removed some of the constraints on Chinese originality;[53] and these qualities were to become ingredients in the formal splendour of the Ming dynasty (1368–1644), successor to the Yuan.

The Ming and its Music, and the Qing

The first Ming emperor established his capital in Nanjing ('southern capital'), quickly regained the lost north, and annexed Manchuria. By the fifteenth century, the power of the Ming was immense: in terms of political and social organization, communications, economic controls, and the organization of a civil service, Ming China was the most advanced civilization in the world. Family feuding, however, forced the third emperor to move the capital back to Beijing—a strategic error from which, ultimately, the empire would never recover. Beijing was a mere 65 kilometres from the Great Wall and

[50] Sullivan, *The Arts of China*, 179.
[51] Roberts, *Pelican History of the World*, 431.
[52] Colin P. Mackerras, 'China', *The New Grove* (1980), iv. 247.
[53] Sullivan, *The Arts of China*, 180.

thus was vulnerable to attack from the north; it was isolated from the hub of Ming culture, in the central and southern regions.

Nevertheless, with military might and over 3,000 years of cultural largess behind it, the Ming court was one of sumptuous splendour. The princes themselves contributed to the flood of learning, and the dynasty contributed substantially to the scientific achievements of Chinese culture. The Ming furnished some of our most valuable sources for knowledge of Chinese music and performance practice.

Following the Mongol invasion, the displaced scholar-gentry and court officials devoted themselves to the study of art and aesthetics, and the writing of novels and dramas. They established the new art form of music theatre, known to the West as opera. Based on heroic themes from China's past, operas were used as a form of anti-Mongol propaganda. Despite frequent bans on opera by the Mongol administration, performances continued, and played a part in the tide of rebellion which overthrew the Mongols. Under the Ming, opera became increasingly popular, and officials again tried to control performances, but not even the threat of the death penalty for actors could prevent performances.[54]

Ming scholars also recreated the Confucian ritual music, and developed the art of the *qin* (seven-string board zither). The fourteenth son of the founder of the Ming, Prince Ning (Zhu Quan, d. 1448), spent his years of retirement collecting and notating such *qin* music as had survived the Mongol invasions. He called his collection *Quxian: Shengi Mipu* ('The Wondrous Secret Treatise of an Emaciated Immortal'); its preface is dated 1425. And in 'A New Account of the Science of Pitch-Pipes', published in 1584—part of a monumental, nineteen-volume 'Complete Books on Music and Theory'—Prince Zhu Zaiyu expounded his system for arriving at a 'well-tempered' scale (see p. 325). It is known that a Jesuit scholar, Matteo Ricci, studying in Macao at the time, was in a position to be aware of this theory; it is possible that it reached Rome through him, and eventually provided the mathematical basis for the 'equal-tempered' scale in Europe.[55]

As the Ming dynasty declined, enemies in the north—this time the Manchu—looked covetously on China; in 1644 they conquered the north and inaugurated the Qing dynasty (1644–1912). The Manchu were great conservers of Chinese culture, and their splendour led to its being much admired in eighteenth century Europe, where the notion of

[54] Wolpert, 'Chinese Music'. [55] Temple, *The Genius of China*, 209.

a country governed by principles of natural philosophy, rather than by revealed religion, found favour among thinkers of the Enlightenment. The Qing emperors, however, were constantly fearful of the independence of thought of their scholar-administrators, now increasingly influenced by the West. They ruled from a position of weakness; and rather than face the realities of the new global politics, they adopted a reactionary posture. Their refusal to heed the increasingly aggressive stance of the West, and their inability to cooperate in trade, was to lead to the ignominious Opium Wars of the mid-nineteenth century, to Russian and Japanese territorial encroachment, and to the 'concessions' (made to Europeans) based on 'unequal treaties'.

The Twentieth Century

The last emperor was but a boy when, in 1911, revolution overthrew the Qing and inaugurated a period of nearly forty years of factional strife. The country was soon run by regional warlords. In 1917 China entered the First World War on the side of the allies; but when the subsequent Paris Peace Conference reinforced Japan's position in Shandung province, nationalist feeling erupted in what became known as the 'May Fourth Movement'. Sun Yatsen, who, after the revolution, had founded the Nationalist Party (Guomindang) in Guangzhou, established a tenuous alliance with the nascent Communist Party. Under Sun Yat Sen's successor, Chiang Kai-shek, this coalition for a while checked the warlords, and a new government was set up in Nanjing. Before moving on to Beijing, however, Chiang attempted to eliminate his Communist allies, forcing them to retreat to remote mountain villages, and to develop a peasant-based party on the Russian model.

Meanwhile Chiang's power had again been threatened by militant warlords and, more seriously, by Japanese encroachment in Manchuria. He nevertheless chose to crush the Communists rather than resist the Japanese: his attacks on Guangxi forced the Communists to undertake their famous 'Long March' of 1934–5, west and north, over the mountains, into Shaanxi province. In 1936 Chiang was compelled to establish a united front against the Japanese in Manchuria, who responded in 1938 by invading China proper. While Chiang Kai-shek and the nationalists retreated to mountainous areas of the south-west, the Communists in the north initiated guerrilla warfare against the occupying Japanese, which they maintained throughout the Second World War. When the war was over, the Nationalists had lost credibility as a government. Civil war broke out and, in 1949, Chiang retreated to Taiwan, taking with him a convoy bearing many of China's most valuable antique and artistic treasures. In the same year, Mao Zedong proclaimed the People's Republic of China from Beijing, and set out to revolutionize the country on socialist lines (destroying, in the process, the landlord class that had been the main employer of village musicians).[56]

Two major catastrophes of Mao Zedong's twenty-seven-year rule should be noted. In 1958 he launched the 'Great Leap Forward', a vast social upheaval, aimed at decentralization of administration, and collectivization of property, intended to transform China into a first-class modern power. Impossible economic goals were set: steel production, for example, was required to be doubled within a year; this involved such measures as smelting private cooking utensils into steel, and causing the entire population to eat in canteens. It was officially estimated that nearly one hundred million peasants were moved from agricultural work into steel production.[57] The Great Leap was a monstrously misjudged operation; it led to the 'Three Years of Hardship', during which, it is estimated, no less than 30 million people died of starvation and disease.

Shortly after Mao recovered from the consequences of this first delusion, he fell into a second. In 1966 he launched the Cultural Revolution, which, to the aims of the Great Leap Forward, added the reform of all aspects of Chinese culture alien to the egalitarian spirit of socialism; in effect, Mao aimed to eliminate every vestige of opposition to his oligarchical rule. The immediate effect was to unleash, against intellectuals, artists, and right-wing sympathizers, senseless violence by the 'Red Guards' (groups of young militants whom Mao himself had set up to spearhead the Revolution). The Cultural Revolution attempted the destruction of almost everything that witnessed—both materially and intellectually—to China's cultural past. The arrest of the 'Gang of Four' in 1976, and the brutal suppression of student uprisings in Tiananmen Square in 1989, were among the aftershocks.

Although Mao Zedong set out to reverse China's social history, he ruled much as China's emperors had always ruled: by exercising abso-

[56] *The Times Atlas of World History*, ed. Geoffrey Barraclough (London, 1989), 262.

[57] Jung Chang, *Wild Swans* (London: Harper Collins, 1991), 293.

lute authority and with a secret police. He attempted to reinstate, in new guise, the pattern of provincial government that China had always known: rule by protégés of the emperor, in this case Communist cadres. Consequently, he was revered by many, as a wise new emperor, sweeping away a rotten dynasty—a status Mao himself enhanced by appearing remote and beyond human approach.[58] Some fifteen years after his death, his memory periodically inspires cult worship.

A sense of history is embedded, however, in the Chinese psyche. Despite the disasters of the twentieth century, many Chinese—inside as well as outside the People's Republic—retain a deep sense of their country's historic culture: it had, after all, survived—in all its proud detachment and exclusiveness—the vicissitudes of some 4,000 years of history.

Confucian and Court Entertainment Music

Central to Chinese musical tradition was the performance of *yayue* (the music of Confucian ceremony). Glimpses occur in song-texts in the *Shijing*, but the first surviving detailed description of *yayue* is an account of Tang dynasty practice, in Chen Yang's *Yueshu* ('Book of Music') of 1101. Two categories of ritual music were specified: 'chime music', consisting of a large orchestra 'outside' (in front of) the main building; and 'chamber song music', 'inside' the building. All the Eight Materials participated in the ritual: two silk and two wind instruments were used 'inside'; all other instruments 'outside' (see p. 331).[59]

The 'outside' music was for the praise of heaven, and the size and disposition of the orchestra varied with the importance of the occasion. Bells, bell chimes, stones, and stone chimes (in sets of up to seventeen pitches) were placed along the four sides of a square, with drums at the four corners. Rows of wind players stood in the centre. At the front were two wooden instruments, used to mark the start and finish of a piece. In front of the musicians were the dancers. All faced the throne. The 'chamber song-music' for 'inside' use extolled the virtues of emperors and their ancestors.

[58] Ibid. 347.

[59] Shigeo Kishibe, 'China', *The New Grove* (1980), iv. 251–2.

41. Palace scene with female orchestra (Ming dynasty, mid-sixteenth century)

Of very different character was the court entertainment music of the Sui and Tang. It consisted largely of 'foreign' music, adapted to some extent to Chinese taste. For its performance, as noted earlier, the Tang established training institutes for slave dancers and musicians. The Tang categorized not only the 'Ten Types of Music', on the basis of country of origin, but also 'Confucian music', Chinese 'popular music', 'foreign music', 'military-band music', 'theatrical music', and '*qin* music'. Distinctions between 'inside' Confucian music, 'inside' popular music, and 'inside' foreign music inevitably became blurred; all were merged into the 'sitting music'. The term *yayue* ('elegant music') was reserved for the music of Confucian ritual in Clan Temples of the Imperial Family, and of the nobility, and the Confucian temples of the suburbs. Entertainment music was subsumed under 'banquet music' (Pl. 41).

The musical *style* of Confucian ceremonial music is exemplified in the tunes of Tang date preserved by Zhu Xi in his 'General Explanation of the Canon of Rites and Commentaries thereon' (see p. 340). Ex. 10.1 (after Picken), shows the melody for the first verse of *Luming Song*

Ex. 10.1

('The Stags Roar').[60] The song is clearly intended to welcome a party of noble guests, and is of the sort that all young nobles were required to learn to sing. It is based primarily on the notes of the anhemitonic pentatonic scale, regarded by Confucianists as *zhengsheng* ('right notes'); but it also uses the sharpened fourth, and the seventh, as *biansheng* ('varied notes'), making a heptatonic scale.[61]

The verse is for the most part in eight-line stanzas of four syllables, but employs additional syllables (though not in the first stanza) at important places in the verse structure. The first verse translates:

> The stags roar,
> Eating wormwood on the open ground.
> I have elegant guests;
> Strike zither, blow mouth organ,
> Blow mouth organ, strike Jew's harp.
> From the baskets we serve each other;
> Those who love me
> Display the manners of Zhou.

It is likely that such tunes were played instrumentally (for the emperor and other nobility) as well as sung; they are to be imagined, therefore, played on sets of bell chimes, stone chimes, large zithers, flutes, mouth organs, and drums, providing parallel lines of tone colour at octave differences, and with mouth organs playing the melody also in fifths.

Han (Chinese) Instruments

The *qin* (seven-stringed, board zither) is traditionally the most honoured of Chinese instruments; indeed, Confucius

[60] L. E. R. Picken, 'Twelve Ritual Melodies of the Tang Dynasty', *Studiae Memoriae Belae Bartok Sacra* (Budapest, 1956). The example has been transposed down a fourth, to facilitate understanding of modal usage.

[61] Kishibe, 'China', *The New Grove*, iv. 252.

42. Playing the *guqin* (seven-string board zither)

himself played on a form of *qin* (Pl. 42). The Han dynasty associated the *qin* with the 'pure Han Chinese' tradition. At this time, the instrument was probably used principally to support the voice, and most probably was played only on open strings and in harmonics. Over the centuries, it became the subject of many treatises, essays, and poems; and during the Song, a repertoire of purely instrumental compositions was developed. The *qin* was considered to be a symbol of correct music and an essential component in Confucian rites. (In modern Chinese, the word *qin* means simply 'string instrument'; the *qin* is now usually called *guqin*: 'ancient *qin*'; or *qixianqin*: 'seven-stringed *qin*'.)

The *qin* was also considered to be a suitable instrument for scholars and officials, and a means of purifying the heart. The body itself was prepared for a performance, through bathing, special styles of dress, and abstinence from food. Savouring the *qin*'s various timbres was held to assist meditation, banish base thoughts, and facilitate communion with the *Dao*; it freed the body from sickness and encouraged longevity.[62]

Many *qin* handbooks appeared during the Ming dynasty, containing scores in tablature and descriptions of the technique. (These describe

[62] R. H. Van Gulik, *The Lore of the Chinese Lute: An Essay in Ch'in Ideology* (Tokyo: Toppan-insatsu-kabushik-kaisha, 1931).

methods of plucking with the right hand, and of glissando and vibrato with the left hand.) The *qin* remained the instrument of the cultural élite during the Qing dynasty; and more than 300 pieces and thirty handbooks have survived from the Ming and Qing. As with most surviving Chinese musical manuscripts, they are written in a form of tablature, known from the twelfth century onwards as *jianzi pu* ('score in abbreviated characters'). This consists of simplified characters to indicate string numbers, stopping positions on the string, and playing instructions.[63]

In scores written before the modern period, the ends of phrases are always marked; but rhythm is unspecified, and much depends upon the knowledge obtained from the teacher. Such knowledge, dependent on oral tradition, is less readily available than before. In this century, attempts have been made to replace the *jianzi pu* by a numerical system of notation. This system, however, ignores the fact that the notes themselves reveal nothing of the technique by which they are obtained; and the beauty of music for *qin* resides in the immense range of tonal colour, resulting from technique, readily conveyed by the *jianzi pu*.[64]

The *qin* is essentially a personal, soft-toned instrument. Like the clavichord, it may appear unsuited to modern performance conditions, but a good instrument can be heard to good effect in a concert hall for 300 or 400. Nevertheless (as with the Vietnamese *dan bau*), it is often amplified through small speakers, in modern performance.

The zither now heard most frequently in performances of Chinese traditional music is the *zheng*, in speech usually qualified (like the *qin*) as *guzheng* ('old *zheng*'). A movable bridge on each string permits fine tuning. Probably a more ancient instrument than the *qin*, it gained popularity during the Han dynasty, when it is said to have replaced the *se*, a large twenty-five-string zither, also with movable bridges. The *zheng* has twelve to seventeen strings. Possibly because it derived from the bamboo tube zither, its ideogram locates it in the category 'bamboo'. (It was therefore categorized as a 'wood' rather than a 'silk' instrument.) Traditionally the *zheng* has been regarded as an instrument for popular entertainment; in literature it is associated with romantic subjects.

Another instrument indigenous to China is the *sheng*; as early as the twelfth century BC, it was represented on oracle bones, and played along

[63] Yōko Mitani, 'Some Melodic Features of Chinese *qin* Music', in D. R. Widdess and R. F. Wolpert, *Music and Tradition: Essays on Asian and other Musics Presented to Laurence Picken* (Cambridge: Cambridge University Press, 1981).

[64] Unpublished comment from Laurence Picken.

with the clapper drum. The *sheng* is a free-reed mouth organ. It consists of a circle of thirteen to seventeen pipes, each with single finger-hole, inserted into a wind chest (originally a gourd) with mouthpiece. It is still widely used in many different contexts, and was traditionally played in chords of melody note, fifth above, and fourth below, where the range of pipes available permitted this.

The instruments so far described are indigenous to China, but from early times other instruments were absorbed into Chinese culture, and many of these are more familiar to the Chinese public than is the *qin*.

'Barbarian' Instruments

Flutes have existed in China from antiquity, but the flute now most characteristic of Chinese music, the *dizi*, is thought to have originated in Tibet. This is a transverse flute with a hole next to the blow-hole covered with a piece of thin membrane, from the lining of a piece of bamboo. The membrane adds a cutting, reedy edge to the tone, and increases the instrument's carrying power in open-air performance. Intonation may be adjusted by altering the angle of the mouth-hole to the lip. The archaic, Chinese flute is the *xiao* (an end-blown, vertical flute). It is less strident that the *dizi*, since it lacks a vibrating membrane (*kazoo*), but is highly expressive. It is commonly played heterophonically with *qin*, but an octave higher in pitch.

The *guanzi*, of which the ancestor, the *bili*, arrived from Central Asia during the Tang, is a double-reed instrument, cylindrically bored, with a relatively large reed. It is highly expressive in its tonal quality. The *suona* (a shawm) originated in West Asia (as its name shows; compare Turkish *zurna*), and arrived some time before the sixteenth century. At first used mainly for military music, it subsequently became the principal instrument of the ritual wind-and-percussion ensembles—recently termed *guchui* ('drumming and blowing')—that became ubiquitous in the north. It is also widely used in dance, and in opera.

With the exception of the zithers, all Chinese string instruments are foreign in origin. The *yangqin* (dulcimer, 'foreign *qin*'), for example, entered China from West Asia, probably during the Qing dynasty, and is still used in a variety of ensembles. It is particularly popular in south-east China, where it is frequently associated with the fiddle, *erhu* (a member of the *huqin* family and a popular solo instrument in the twentieth century).

The *huqin* are two-string, long-necked, bowed lutes that arrived from Central Asia—most probably from a Turkic people—during the tenth century. They are of first importance in the opera orchestra, where they appear in two sizes: the *banhu* (with a resonator made from a half-coconut and a wooden table); and the *erhu* (with a cylindrical resonator of bamboo, with a snakeskin table covering one end) playing an octave lower. In the Beijing opera, the higher pitched *jinghu* (constructed similarly to the *erhu*) is used in place of the *banhu*. The *jinghu* is usually played with the male singers an octave higher, and the *erhu* with the female singers an octave lower. In recent times, new types of *hu* have been introduced to the Chinese orchestra (see p. 356). The *gaohu* is held between the thighs to mute the sound; the *zhonghu* has a range corresponding to the viola; the *gehu* ('reformed *hu*') has four strings and a range corresponding to the cello; a bass *gehu* also exists, having four strings and a range corresponding to that of a double bass.

With the exception of the *gehu*, played with a free bow, the strings of all *huqin* are excited with a bow of slack horsehair (tightened by the fingers) threaded *between* the strings. (The strings were formerly made of silk, but since the 1950s they have more usually been made of nylon or wire.) The various *huqin* have considerable carrying power; and the *erhu*, now frequently used as a solo instrument, is normally played with conspicuous vibrato and portamento.

The lute travelled to China, probably from Persia, as early as the second century AD. It exists in a number of forms. The most common are: the *sanxian* (three-string, long-necked lute); the *yueqin* (four-string, short-necked, circular 'moon-shaped' lute), and the *pipa* (four-string, short-necked, pear-shaped lute). While the first two are used mainly in an accompanying role in ensembles, the *pipa* has a long history as a solo instrument.

The *pipa* arrived in China as a fretted, long-necked, instrument, with a shallow circular body; the modern type, with its pear-shaped outline, and four strings (originally of twisted silk), did not appear until the fifth or sixth century. The name *pipa* refers to the playing technique, with the right hand originally moving a large plectrum, 'forwards' and 'backwards' in successive strokes. Performed at speed, this becomes tremolo, more familiar to Westerners through the technique of Russian balalaika, Hawaiian ukulele, or Spanish guitar. The *pipa*, with four frets on the neck, and with four strings, became the bass instrument of the banquet music in Tang Changan. In much later times, a descriptive type of music of great virtuosity has developed in its use as a solo instrument;

43. Young musicians in Hong Kong play (left to right) *suona* (shawm), *dizi* (transverse bamboo flute), *sheng* (mouth organ), and *xiao* (vertical bamboo flute)

the style incorporates double-stopped glissando with extraordinarily dramatic effects.

A distinctive Chinese percussion instrument, used mainly in folk ensembles, is the *yunluo*, a frame of small pitched gongs (usually ten in number), struck with one or two sticks. It is regarded as a melodic instrument, and its bright, clear timbre imparts a distinctive quality to wind-and-percussion ensembles.[65]

With the exception of the *guqin*, any of these instruments may be found in modern China, in both large and small ensembles (Pl. 43).

Chinese Musical Style

It might be expected that a large body of notated music would have been preserved in a country with so long and cosmopolitan a history, and a culture notable for its refinement and for its literary and artistic accomplishment. This did not occur. Only one

[65] Stephen Jones, *Folk Music of China: Living Instrumental Traditions* (Oxford: Oxford University Press, 1995), 101.

musical manuscript—the *Dunhuang Pipapu*, comprising twenty-five lute pieces—has survived in China from the late Tang; but a substantial body of court entertainment music of the Tang survives in manuscript form in Japan, where, in performance, it has been transformed by Japanese performance practice. As already indicated, a large repertoire of *qin*-music survives from the Ming and Qing dynasties; but it remains of interest to a relatively limited audience. Scores of regional folk-instrumental traditions (dating from the early Qing) exist in *gongche* notation (akin to Western sol-fa); they provide a valuable guide to former practice, but, although *gongche* notation is still used by rural musicians, it is little used by urban professionals.[66]

Many of the earliest Japanese manuscripts of music of Tang date have recently been transcribed into Western staff notation; it is now evident that in Japan (as in Korea) original Chinese music has undergone substantial retardation in performance. Gaps between the notes of slowed-down tunes—played on the lute or zither—have been filled with increasing amounts of ornamental figuration. To this day, the Japanese play their lute (*biwa*) with a large plectrum (limiting dexterity), whereas in China, by the end of the seventh century, the plectrum had largely been discarded in favour of finger-plucking, in imitation of *qin* technique.[67]

Unlike the *qin*-music of the scholar-gentry, entertainment music of the Tang included elements of popular or folk origin.[68] The modes are often hexatonic or heptatonic, and in formal respects (as already noted) the large suites of the repertoire show links with surviving cyclical structures of Central Asia.[69] The scores show that the tunes were given a mildly heterophonic treatment, suited to the characteristics of the instruments: flute, double-reed pipe, mouth organ, lute, and zither. The earliest notations for flute and mouth organ show minimal melodic decoration, very different from the florid decoration that characterizes modern Chinese performance, or performing traditions of Korea and Japan.[70]

The Tang performing tradition did not survive, chiefly because the Song made every effort to eliminate 'foreign' elements introduced by

[66] Ibid. 119–23.

[67] Picken (ed.) *et al.*, *Music from the Tang Court*, i. 11.

[68] Frank Kouwenhoven, 'Bringing to Life Tunes of Ancient China: An Interview with Laurence Picken', *CHIME*, 4 (Autumn 1991), 55.

[69] Ibid. 6.

[70] Ibid. 5.

the Tang; and the destruction of social dance by the Song, as a consequence of Confucian standards of sexual morality, contributed to the loss of the pulse-related drive of music. Later traditions have fared little better. Chinese musical notations are relatively vague, particularly in regard to rhythm; in practice, performers have hitherto made little use of notated scores, as they know their repertoire by heart. During the twentieth century, Communist ideology has substantially weakened oral traditions. Despite such reversals, however, many distinctively Chinese features are retained in modern performance.

Chinese music, like Chinese painting, is essentially incomplete. A scroll-painting is not intended for complete display and viewing, as in a museum; it is intended to be viewed, length by length, as it is unrolled from right to left. Similarly, Chinese music may strike the listener as rhapsodical, as it unfolds in time. There is a sense of latent energy there, sometimes characterized by wide leaps and changes in tessitura; but the music does not create long-term tension. Metre is interpreted very freely (by Western standards), and there is no automatic stress on the first beat of each bar. Rhythmic momentum is seldom maintained for long; accelerandos and rallentandos are frequent. Each note, or melodic pattern, has its own significance; and nuances of vibrato and ornamentation remain important aspects of performance.

Music, also like painting, is often based on literary texts; just as Chinese paintings often include the texts that inspired them, so as to enhance their meaning, so also many notations of instrumental music retain their texts after the words have ceased to be sung. As already indicated, the titles of pieces are invariably evocative, and often programmatic; the music therefore encourages, and assists, reflection on the theme it nominally 'represents'. Instruments themselves may be given evocative names: 'The Dragon's Purr' for a *qin*, for example. Until recently, all music had a non-musical reference and was essentially descriptive.

Because Chinese musical notations of an earlier period left rhythmic detail, and some melodic detail, to be decided by the performer (see p. 349), details of interpretation were passed on from teacher to pupil in the style of a particular regional practice. The modern trend, encouraging the *performer* to interpret the tablature himself, in the process now referred to as *dapu*, was never practised before the 1930s. In those days, only in age, and as an acknowledged master, did a performer presume to depart from the tradition passed on by his own

Ex. 10.2

master.[71] Ex. 10.2 (after Yōko Mitani) shows transcriptions of a piece from an early nineteenth-century handbook as played by two different performers.[72] The same kind of rhythmic flexibility is apparent in many twentieth century compositions, often elaborations of older melodies.

It was during the 1920s—in association with the nationalist 'May Fourth Movement'—that Western techniques were first consciously applied to Chinese traditional melodies, in an effort to forge a national

[71] Unpublished comment from Laurence Picken.
[72] Mitani, 'Some Melodic Features'.

classical tradition.[73] Liu Tianhua (1895–1932), an *erhu* and *pipa* player (for which instruments he subsequently composed), was a leading protagonist of this movement. One of the first collectors of folk music, he founded a 'Society for the Improvement of National Music'. Techniques were then developed on traditional instruments that enabled them to be played with Western-style virtuosity, and chords were added to traditional tunes. The chords were not necessarily used functionally, however; often an accompaniment would shadow a tune heterophonically, playing 'chords' only at moments of particular emphasis. Ex. 10.3 shows a piece for *erhu*, typical of the Repulican period, based on a traditional melody ('Nostalgic Return to the Homeland') with characteristic *yangqin* accompaniment.

During the 1950s, Russian musicians were imported to develop music conservatoires, and their influence was also conspicuous in the development of harmonic practices. Under the regime of Mao Zedong, all music was expected to serve political ends. Village ritual ensembles were discouraged as being 'feudal' and superstitious, while élite tunes—as well as regional folk-songs—were fitted with triadic harmony and Western instrumentation, and, in this form, promoted as popular tunes. New tunes made striking use of non-Chinese, broken-triad phrases. Western influence caused the various scalings of instruments to be brought nearer to equal temperament; and fretted instruments acquired thicker or heavier strings, with nylon or steel replacing silk. The *zheng*, for example, popular in the south, was strung with steel strings. The *pipa*, the popular instrument of the north, received additional frets on belly and neck; its scaling is now closer to that of equal temperament. In ensembles, instruments were doubled, and ensembles became larger in imitation of Western orchestras. As a consequence, heterophonic playing could no longer be tolerated, and musicians learnt to play from 'parts' in fixed notation.

The modern Chinese orchestra—a large ensemble, often of fifty or more players—is set out much like a Western orchestra, with sections of bowed and plucked strings, winds, and percussion. In addition to viola, cello, and bass versions of the *huqin*, chromatic versions of the *sheng* (mouth organ), and, indeed, *sheng* as large as a portative organ, have been devised. Western cellos, double basses, and timpani sometimes support new Chinese instruments. Many Chinese composers—and

[73] Jones, *Folk Music of China*, 39.

Ex. 10.3

some European composers—now compose serial music for the Chinese orchestra, or 'texture' their compositions in a style reminiscent of Penderecki. Since the late 1980s, however, there has been a resurgence of interest in past traditions throughout China, and traditional items are increasingly played on Chinese instruments in a style little influenced by Westernized taste.

Folk and Popular Traditions

Despite the turbulent events of the twentieth century, many regional folk-music styles have survived in China; it has been estimated, for example, that in the mid-1980s, in Hebei province alone, no less than 600 professional or semi-professional folk bands and 200 amateur folk bands existed, comprising some 10,000 musicians.[74] Chinese folk music is currently the subject of active scholarly research, both Chinese and Western.

A broad distinction is commonly made between northern and southern folk tyles. In general, the northern style is characterized by strongly marked rhythms, with angular, disjunct, melodic movement, over a wide compass; the southern style features a more lyrical, gently undulating type of melody, moving within a more restricted compass. Exx. 10.4 and 10.5 (after Han Kuo-huang) illustrate such differences, in the style of lyric-songs.[75] The first is a love-song from Shanxi province: 'Embroidering a Pouch'. The second exists with different texts in various districts of the south; in its Jiangsu version it is a wife's lament for a husband, drafted to the Great Wall by the first emperor.

Three broad (and overlapping) categories of folk-song are usually discriminated: *haozi* (work songs, often in 'call-and-response' form, and

Ex. 10.4

Ex. 10.5

[74] Ibid. 57.

[75] Han Kuo-huang, 'Folk Songs of the Han Chinese: Characteristics and Classifications', *Asian Music*, 20/2 (1989), 108, 111–12.

with largely improvised texts); *xiaodiao* (lyric songs, with relatively clear formal structures); and *shan'ge* (literally 'mountain songs').

The term *shan'ge* dates from the Tang; in certain regions it was associated with mountain-divinity cults, in which only initiates were permitted to participate. During the Ming, the term was used by the scholar-gentry to denote short lyrical folk-songs, usually about love.[76] In more recent times, the term has come to be used for folk-songs with texts on a variety of topics, and in many regions of China, whether mountainous or flat. *Shan'ge* are usually performed by peasants, in free-rhythmic declamation; frequently they are sung in dialogue, a singer (or group of singers) on one hillside answering a singer from across the valley; and in such instances male singers usually employ the far-carrying falsetto voice, reaching a higher range than female singers.[77] Such *shan'ge* may take the form of improvised courtship songs (either as a possible route to marriage or as a celebration of youthful dreams).[78] In the New Territories of Hong Kong, for example, 'battle-songs' used to be sung by lines of boys from one village, confronting lines of girls from another village, when teasing verses would be exchanged for hours, until one side or the other ran out of ideas.[79] Group courtship and group marriage existed in China in ancient times.

Lamentation, by women, provides another occasion for improvised singing. Lamenting has a long history in China; Confucian sexual mores were highly restrictive, and women sang laments at their own weddings, as well as at funerals. Arranged marriages led at times to profound grief; even when there was joy in union, the bride's lament was, in some areas, a necessary ritual, to prevent ill-fortune.[80] In the south, women improvised laments at funerals, and their singing was valued more highly than that of the professional mourners who

[76] Antoinet Schimmelpenninck, 'What about the Singers?', *CHIME*, 4 (Autumn 1991), 34.

[77] Zhang Zuozhi and Helmut Schaffrath, 'China's Mountain Songs', *CHIME*, 4 (Autumn 1991), 24–5, 32.

[78] Long-distance vocal signals are common among mountain peoples worldwide; indeed, in war-torn areas of the Balkans they have been used for centuries to convey information about enemy troop-movements (A. L. Lloyd, 'Europe', *The New Grove* (1980), vi. 306).

[79] Patrick Hase, 'New Territories Poetry and Song', *Sources for Hong Kong Historical Research* (Hong Kong: Museum of History, 1984), and Chan Wing Hoi, *Traditional Folksong and Rural Life in Hong Kong: Overall Report of the General Context of Local Folksongs* (Hong Kong: Museum of History, 1984). See also Antoinet Schimmelpenninck, 'Chinese Folk Singers in Jiangsu Province', *CHIME*, 8 (Spring 1995), 52–8.

[80] Hase, 'New Territories Poetry and Song'. The practice is common worldwide, and is to be observed, for example, in Ethiopia, Russia, and the Balkans.

accompanied the Daoist priests. (The Daoist priests alone can ensure that the dead would not walk.)

Folk-tunes were often preserved by regional instrumental ensembles long after the words had ceased to be sung; indeed, village folk ensembles, often illiterate, performed not only popular folk and opera tunes (of relatively simple, four-square structure), but also certain styles of art music associated with the scholar-gentry. Conspicuous in the repertoire were—and still are—*qupai* ('song-labels'), the type of standard tune for verse-texts of a particular prosodic structure, of Yuan or later date; most notable of these were the *Nan Bei qu* ('Southern and Northern Melodies'), a repertoire of narrative and opera tunes of the Yuan and Ming.[81]

Qupai were so called because the titles of songs were at one time announced on boards, and tunes are today known by these titles, related to the original verse-text.[82] (Current tunes are not necessarily the same as those of former times, but they are still suitable for verse of a particular prosodic structure.) *Qupai* are mainly associated with opera; and the label of the *qupai* indicated to the performer, and still indicates to the audience, not only the tune to be performed but also the dramatic situation and affect associated with it. Singers might be expected to improvise new, topical texts in the heterometric verse structures associated with the particular tune.

A formative influence on the rhythmic structures of the *qupai* was the *ci*, a heterometric verse genre that originated in the Tang and became a sophisticated art form in the Song. It seems likely that poets of the Song began to write song-words for foreign tunes, or for Chinese tunes influenced by tunes of foreign origin. Such tunes were suited to the polysyllabic languages to which they originally belonged, using notes of more than one duration. As Chinese is a monosyllabic language, foreign tunes provided a superfluity of notes for the syllabically economical Chinese verse. It is possible, therefore, that the Song fashion for heterometric verse, with individual lines of a variety of lengths (4, 5, 6, 7, or more, syllables) was a consequence of writing Chinese texts to fit foreign tunes; and it was doubtless the infinite variety of possible, detailed, musical structure, in a fixed metrical framework, that deter-

[81] Stephen Jones, 'The Golden-Character Scripture: Perspectives on Chinese Melody', *Asian Music*, 20/2 (1989), 21–2.

[82] Houyong Gao, 'On Qupai', *Asian Music*, 20/2 (1989), 4.

44. Silk-and-bamboo ensemble in a Chinese tea house , 1987. Photo: Stephen Jones

mined the appeal of the *ci* during the Song, both as verse-form and as text-underlay for songs.[83]

Once established, a complex pattern of line lengths could be used as a plan for composing other song-texts, all of which could be carried by the same tune. Such patterns, named by a fragment of the original text, were known as *cipai* ('*ci*-labels'), and later became the *qupai* ('song labels') of opera melodies. The heterometric verse structures of *cipai*, therefore, influenced the style of song-text associated with the *qupai* of opera.[84]

At the time of the spread of the 'Southern and Northern Melodies', three distinct types of instrumental music were practised: *guchui* ('drumming and blowing'), already developed by the military during the Han, under influences from the Turco-Mongol north, and used for ceremonial occasions at court, in processions, or in warfare (the term is now often used to describe folk shawm-and-percussion bands); *sizhu yiyue* ('silk-bamboo elegant music'), a form of entertainment music that emerged in the south (Pl. 44); and *xiqu* ('opera melodies'), making

[83] L. E. R. Picken, 'Secular Chinese Songs of the Twelfth Century', *Studia Musicologica Academiae Scientiarum Hungaricae Tomus*, 8 (1966), 130–1.

[84] Jones, 'The Golden-Character Scripture', 21–2.

use of selected *qupai*, linked with specific dramatic situations.[85] Extant folk ensembles have been classified under many, overlapping, heads by Chinese scholars; in practice, they fall into two main categories: 'blowing and beating' (wind-and-percussion ensembles, including those led by double-reed instruments), and 'silk and bamboo' (chamber ensembles with strings and winds).[86]

Central to instrumental performance is the process of variation; indeed, variation is an important means of creating large-scale musical structures. A standard melody may be varied by means of ornamentation (known as 'adding flowers'), or by changes to pitch or melodic contour, while retaining its original metrical structure; or it may be varied by changing, or transposing, the mode. Frequently, however, variation involves changes to the metrical structure, by means of augmentation or diminution.[87]

The Chinese word *banyan* means, in English terminology, 'strong-beat, weak-beat', and refers to the basic binary unit. Literally, however, *banyan* means 'beats and eyes', the *ban* referring to the main beat, and *yan*, to subsidiary beats. The *ban* usually denotes a whole bar, the length of which depends upon the number of 'eyes' that follow the *ban*. Thus a bar of 'one beat, three eyes' (4/4 in Western notation) is a slow metre, whereas a bar of 'one beat, no eyes' (1/4 in Western notation) is a fast metre (*liushui*: 'flowing water'). (*Ban* also means 'wooden clapper', the instrument that often accompanies accented beats; not all *liushui* bars are accented, however, and melodies in this metre may acquire distinctively asymmetrical structures.[88]) By increasing the number of 'eyes' in a bar, skeletal melodies in *liushui* metre may be augmented by up to eight times their original length (employing an 8/4 metre), and transformed into highly elaborate versions.[89] Alternatively, a melody in a slow metre may be diminished—by reduction in the number of 'eyes'—into a fast metre. Ex. 10.6 (after Jones) shows an elaborate variation of a skeletal melody, as performed in a northern shawm band, in the mid 1980s.[90]

In traditional scores, 'beats' are marked by dots or circles; most contain only one sign per measure, but some older, classical, scores

[85] Gao, 'On Qupai', 9.

[86] Jones, *Folk Music of China*, 91–3.

[87] Ibid. 142.

[88] See Ibid. 125 for a notated example.

[89] The accentuation of the main beat, often by sounding a gong, is redolent of the marking of 'colotomic' structures in many parts of South East Asia (see p. 290).

[90] Jones, *Folk Music of China*, 123–6, 143.

Ex. 10.6

contain signs for both 'beats' *and* 'eyes'. Since the eighteenth century at least, copies of scores have tended to abandon the diversity of metrical structure inherent in the old system of 'eyes', reducing (for example) 'one beat, seven eyes' to 'one beat, one eye'. Over time, additional notes have tended to be added to the original melody, leading to slower tempos, and more decoration of skeletal notes—echoing similar practices with regard to Tang melodies, both in China and Japan (see p. 353).[91]

In instrumental performance, individual pieces are commonly combined as extended suites (*daqu*: 'large pieces'), with tempi usually progressing from slow to fast. Many such extant suites have their origins in Buddhism; the *Ba datao* ('Eight Great Suites'), for example, derive from the Buddhist music of the Wutaishan mountains (see also p. 218).[92]

One other popular word-born tradition, distinct from opera, is still extant. Storytelling in China, as an art form of spoken narrative and music, is generally traced back to the Tang; literature from the caves at

[91] Ibid. 124–6.

[92] Tian Qing, 'Recent Trends in Buddhist Music Research in China', trans. Tan Hwee San, *British Journal of Ethnomusicology*, 3 (1994), 67.

Dunhuang indicates that Buddhist monks of the Tang used storytelling as a means of disseminating the faith. With the growth of urbanization during the Song, various forms of storytelling became popular in tea houses and entertainment centres in cities. Storytelling developed as a professional art; specialist guilds and schools were established, and particular styles came to be associated with particular regions and dialects. Stories might be told as dramatic monologue, or as a mixture of narrative and singing; and recitation could last for hours, days, or even months. Professional story tellers jealously guarded the details of their own stories and skills, transmitting these only to selected and initiated apprentices.[93] Storytelling was particularly popular during the Qing dynasty, when the major styles of *Suzhou tanci* ('Suzhou story-telling') were established. The art has survived to the present, and incorporates musical elements common to popular instrumental and vocal repertoires.

The Development of Chinese Opera

From a mixture of such folk- and scholar-influenced genres Chinese music theatre, usually termed 'opera', emerged. Its theatrical roots lay in the *baixi* ('Hundred Acts'), popular during the Tang, and the *zaxi* ('Variety Shows'), popular during the Song. In opera, as in storytelling, particular styles came to be associated with particular dialects and regions. Opera was to become *the* entertainment of a rising merchant class—a new social phenomenon in Chinese history—and to be performed: in open-air festival celebrations associated with temples; at the ancestral shrines of the great clans of the south; on the private stages of wealthy families who maintained their own operatic troupes; and at sophisticated tea houses patronized by the 'literati'.

In Jiangxi province, in the early sixteenth century, popular narratives, dance, song, and martial acrobatics developed into a style of entertainment known as *gaoqiang*, a genre with high-pitched melodic lines, now mainly used in Hunan and Sichuan provinces.

In the mid-sixteenth century, a more sophisticated style, *kunqu*, evolved. Originating in Kunshan (also in Jiangsu province), *kunqu*

[93] Tsao Pen-yeh, 'Structural Elements in the Music of Chinese Story-telling', *Asian Music* 20/2 (1989), 130–2.

was based not on folk-songs but on earlier forms of drama, on instrumental music, and possibly also on courtly and military ceremonial music. Although the social status of *kunqu* opera-troupes—like that of opera troupes in general—was low, performances were patronized by the scholar-gentry, who themselves subsequently performed pieces from the *kunqu* heritage, unstaged, at special 'refined gatherings'.[94] *Kunqu* melodies—associated with the 'southern sound' of end-blown flutes as main instruments—were highly melismatic;[95] and the inherent syllable melody of each monosyllable was developed at times into an expressive melodic curve, as shown in Ex. 10.7 (after Tang Xianzu).[96] (The glottal stop of *mo* is represented by a rest; *lǐ* is circumflex and arched; *rén* rises initially; *yōu* is level, with excursions below; *yuàn* descends.) *Kunqu* spread to the major cities north and south, and infiltrated regional opera styles; it remains the most elaborate vocal style ever developed in China.

Ex. 10.7

In the early seventeenth century, the 'Clapper Opera' (named after its principal percussion instrument, a clapper, made of date wood), emerged in northern China as a popular entertainment, and was disseminated by itinerant troupes. By the eighteenth century, it had been absorbed into the local drama of south China; in 1779 it was taken from Sichuan to Beijing.[97]

During the latter half of the eighteenth century, the opera style of Anhui, where more structured melody types had developed—most notably *erhuang* (from Jiangxi province), and *xipi* (derived from the

[94] Mackerras, 'China', *The New Grove*, iv. 253–4.

[95] Rembrandt Wolpert, 'China', *NOCM* (1983).

[96] Tang Xianzu, *Moudan ting* (Beijing: Yinyue chubanshe, 1956), 27, cited in L. E. R. Picken, The Musical Implications of Chinese Song-Texts with Unequal Lines, and the Significance of Nonsense-Syllables, with Special Reference to Art-Song of the Song Dynasty', *Musica Asiatica*, 3 (1981), 35–77, at 64, 65.

[97] Mackerras, 'China', *The New Grove*, iv. 255.

Clapper Opera, of Shanxi province)—travelled north to Beijing and south to Guangdong.[98] In 1790, to celebrate the eightieth birthday of the Qianlong emperor, various companies travelled from South China to Beijing; they featured, in particular, *erhuang* and *xipi* (collectively referred to as *pi-huang*). Imperial enthusiasm for the mixed style caused *pi-huang* to become the core of the Beijing opera.[99]

Anhui opera was sung in a dialect called *zhongzhou* ('central district'), also known as 'stage mandarin'; and all *xipi* and *erhuang* melodies were sung in this dialect. Operas containing such melodies were known as *daxi* ('large spectacles'). Operas sung in local dialects, and incorporating folk tunes, were called *xiaoxi*. *Daxi* narrate historical or legendary incidents, or romantic stories involving rich maidens and talented scholars; troupes of players consist of forty to a hundred members, with an orchestra of ten or twenty players. *Xiaoxi*, on the other hand, are stories of village or urban life, and troupes might be as small as three to eight members, with an orchestra of five to ten players.[100]

Music theatre is a functional aspect of many Daoist and Buddhist ceremonies. In many areas of southern China, for example, at the annual Hungry Ghosts Festival, the ghosts of the childless are entertained with several nights and days of opera; and troupes travel widely to honour birthdays and other festivals associated with particular deities. For such festivals, a temporary mat-shed is built, usually around an open space. At one end is the stage; opposite is an altar before a temporary temple, where the spirits reside. Other areas are occupied by the temporary headquarters of Daoist and Buddhist priests who officiate. For the actor-musicians who perform at such ceremonies, performance has the character of a ritual offering, at times bordering on 'possession'.

Throughout China, traditional dramatic themes have survived the Cultural Revolution, and opera remains popular, particularly among the older generation for whom it is a reminder of old China. Every province has its own opera style, and regional centres have their own opera schools; children are accepted as pupils while young, so as to learn the discipline of dance and acrobatics while their limbs are still supple. The increasing professionalism of operatic performance continues to extend the appeal of the genre, and enables it, even within traditional themes, to react to topical events.

[98] Huang Jinpei, 'Xipi and Erhuang of Beijing and Guangdong Operas', *Asian Music* 20/2 (1989), 152.

[99] Mackerras, 'China', *The New Grove*, iv. 253–8.

[100] Huang, 'Xipi and Erhuang', 152–3.

The Form of Chinese Opera

Typically, a Chinese opera performance uses no scenery; conventions associated with voice, singing style, costume, make-up, deportment, and properties make this unnecessary. A chair on the boards may be a chair or a throne; a chair on a table is a mountain. An actor jumping off a chair is known to have committed suicide. Long, quivering peacock plumes attached to the headdress of actors (or actresses) indicate that they are warriors. Ornate riding crops show that characters are riding horses. Black pennants indicate thunder—and so on. The splendour of the spectacle lies in the richness of costumes, in elaborate mime and dance, and in acrobatic display, martial arts, and swordplay.

One feature, common to traditional drama throughout East Asia, is that assistants, dressed in black costume (rendering them 'invisible'), may appear (or remain) on stage: to make changes in properties, assist actors with their dress, hand them properties, refresh them with tea, or carry discarded properties or items of costume off-stage.

Operatic characters are stereotypes, and are usually recognizable from style of costume, and style and colour of face-painting. Colour of paint is related to character: scarlet for dignity, black for strength, white for treachery, for example. (Face-painting itself probably looks back to the ancient practice of tattooing.)

Four main types of character participate in Beijing opera: *sheng* (male); *dan* (female); *jing* (warriors, bandits, or statesman, conspicuous by their painted faces); and *zhou* (the jester, painted white around eyes and nose). The *sheng* characters are of three categories: the bearded *laosheng* ('old *sheng*') portray distinguished characters, such as generals and court officials, and sing in baritone; the unbearded *xiaosheng* ('young *sheng*') play the roles of scholar-lover, in high pitch (normally falsetto); and the *wusheng* ('military *sheng*') portray warrior roles and must be expert in acrobatics. The *dan* (female) characters may assume military or civilian roles, noble or flirtatious; usually high, quasi-falsetto, singing is required (Pl. 45).[101] Initially, operatic troupes were all male, and actors (such as Mei Lanfang) made great reputations as female impersonators (as still happens in Japanese *Kabuki*). Such male actors sang in falsetto; when women took over the female roles (after

[101] Mackerras, 'China', *The New Grove*, iv. 256.

45. *Dan* (female) characters in the Beijing opera, swaying a pennant. Photo: Claude Sauvageot

about 1910), they imitated the 'squeezed' style of the male falsetto, so that this became the 'traditional' women's style.[102]

The delivery of text normally alternates between speech and song. Two styles of speech are practised. One resembles every day speech, and is reserved for the comic characters of the folk tradition. The other is the delivery of rhymed text, in classical, literary Chinese. This is enunciated in a stylized manner, with accentuation of segmental tone, both in register and in syllable melody.

The feelings of the performers may be expresed through changes of tempo, or variations in melodic line, particularly in the *xipi* and *erhuang* melody types of Beijing and Guangdong opera. Fast tempos usually express anger, slow tempos sorrow; melodic lines may move higher to express joy, or lower to express unhappiness. *Xipi* melodies (from the north) tend to be high and disjunct, and to be sung loudly; *erhuang* melodies (from the south) tend to be lower and more melancholy, and to be sung more softly (reflecting corresponding differences in folk style (see p. 358)). All melody types can be varied to suit the desired emotional expression.[103] Every role-type is distinguished by particular features of vocal style; and many different registers of voice are used. As with baroque opera in the eighteenth century, Chinese audiences know the stories and talk throughout, reserving their concentrated attention for the famous set pieces.

[102] Huang, 'Xipi and Erhuang', 154. [103] Ibid. 154–5, 158.

Traditionally, the opera orchestra is placed to the side of the stage. All tempos are controlled by a percussion player who beats a clapper, and functions as director. (The clapper is played with the left hand; the right hand strikes a small drum.) The melodic section of the orchestra usually consists of *banhu* (or *jinghu*) and *erhu* (two-string fiddles), *dizi* (transverse flute with *kazoo* membrane) or *xiao* (end-blown flute), and *pipa* and *sanxian* (lutes). Sometimes *zheng* (zither) or *yangqin* (dulcimer) is present. The *suona* (oboe) is used in military scenes. Fiddles take the lead, playing the tune in octaves with the singers. Although the 'artificial' vocal registers of the singers may lead to pitch discrepancies with the orchestra, in a good opera orchestra, octaves and unisons are perfectly tuned. The fiddles, in particular, are immensely expressive. In addition to accompanying, and introducing, singer-actors, the opera orchestra plays standard *xiqu* ('opera melodies') known to the audience to give warning of a coming dramatic situation (see pp. 361–2).

Clappers, gongs, and cymbals are used to punctuate, and give rhythmic point to, spoken 'recitative'. The sounds of cymbals slide upwards or downwards in pitch, according to their shape, size, and the point at which they are struck. The constant clatter and boom of the orchestra augment the excitement of dialogue, and are a distinctive feature of the genre.

Regional opera styles may vary considerably in character. In Guangdong province and Hong Kong, for example—the home of Cantonese opera (*yueju*)—the spoken dialect contains no less than five different pitch levels as well as differing syllable melodies, and the language often sounds song-like; spoken song-texts, therefore, predict the melodic line to which they will be sung, and spoken 'recitative' in opera may pass into the singing voice, as it moves between musical pitches. Cantonese opera was banned, during the Qing, as seditious (in part perhaps because Cantonese is unintelligible to most speakers of Mandarin); when it was re-established in the middle of the nineteenth century, it gradually adopted Western features. By the 1930s, it had come to make use of elaborate scenery, and had assumed some of the glitter and vulgarity of Western 'show-biz'; *banhu* and *erhu* had been replaced by violin and saxophone respectively. Today Cantonese opera has still retained backcloths, some scenery, and violin and saxophone; but in recent years scenery, acting, and dance styles have reverted to more traditional Chinese models. Although the old-style, mat-shed performances still occur, most Cantonese opera is now performed in modern auditoria, and makes full use of modern stage resources.

This contrasts with the Clapper Opera, as practised in modern Xian (in Shaanxi province); indeed, the differences between these two styles exemplifies the divide between the 'barbarian' north and the sophisticated south. In Xian, one can still sense something of the cosmopolitan vigour that characterized the great city of Changan. Singing is extremely loud, at times resembling Korean *p'ansori*; clappers play loudly and incessantly; dynamic, sometimes syncopated, rhythms occur; and arias are often accompanied with virtuosic heterophony, on *erhu* and flute. In typical Chinese fashion, however, a given tempo is seldom sustained for long: the pace is constantly increased and decreased. No opportunity is lost to display juggling, stick-twirling, or swordplay, and the stylized gestures of actors are exaggerated, even by the standards of Chinese opera elsewhere.[104]

Perhaps the most stirring element of Chinese music theatre is movement; indeed it could be said to represent the *Dao* of Chinese theatre, whether in the acrobatic skills and superb teamwork manifest in set-piece battles, or the graceful gestures and delicate movements of female characters on, off, and around the stage. Indeed, the Chinese actress moves about the stage with footwork so graceful as to be almost imperceptible. From Tang times, the feet of women dancers were bound, so that they were forced to take exceptionally short and light steps, appearing to hover 'like a lotus in a pool'. (This custom, regrettably, applied to womankind in general; Chinese men were apparently sexually aroused by the sight of tiny feet, and the restriction of normal walking movement prevented concubines from escaping.) The footwork supports a controlled body that moves in curves, with floating arm movements often enhanced by an open fan. This is unique to Chinese theatre. There is nothing here of the sinuous body movements of the Balinese, the controlled energy of the Korean, the heavy symbolism of the Kathkali, or the extremes of body stretch of the European dancer. Grace, vigour and control are subsumed in the spirit of the *Dao*.

Over the past century and a half, the Chinese *Dao* and practical Westernization seem not to have reached accord. The longevity of Chinese cultural systems, once a source of strength, became a liability. Western influence proved corrosive. Many Chinese traditions that survived the upheavals of the first half of the twentieth century were shattered in the madness of the Cultural Revolution, and China is still picking up the pieces. Nevertheless, if the Chinese continue to preserve

[104] As witnessed by the author.

what remains of their past, pursuing a modern enlightenment, they might yet achieve a successful balance between the *Dao* and technology, between the intuitive-spiritual and the cerebral-material, that has so far eluded the West.

Korea

Cultural Independence

The Korean peninsula juts out from the north-east mainland of China between the Yellow Sea on its west and the Sea of Japan on its east. During what is known as the 'Three Kingdoms' period (57 BC–AD 668), Chinese incursions into the northern kingdom of Koguryo brought with them many aspects of Chinese culture; and when the entire peninsula was united in the seventh century (Unified Silla dynasty: 668–936), the Tang-Chinese system of government was added to other elements of Chinese culture already acquired through Buddhism. Notwithstanding this strong Chinese influence, Korea preserved a distinctive cultural personality; and its court traditions differed substantially from those of China.

Mahāyāna Buddhism first entered Koguryo from China during the fourth century AD, and during the Unified Silla dynasty it became the most important cultural influence. Silla's rulers lavished state funds on temples and their carved furnishings, and sent monks to China and India to study the religion; during the early centuries of the Koryo dynasty (935–1392), Buddhism permeated cultural life, and monks occupied a privileged position in society. As in China, however, Buddhism was blamed for political disasters provoked by the Mongols; and with the establishment of the Choson (Yi) Dynasty (1392–1910), espousal of Neo-Confucianism caused Buddhism to decline in importance. Nevertheless, Korea (unlike China) had accepted Buddhism as a state religion—in China, the ethics and rituals of Confucianism performed this function—and, because of that acceptance, the religion and its musical practices have survived.

Silla's success in uniting the Three Kingdoms (AD 735)—Koguryo in the north, Paekche in the south-west, and Silla in the south-east—resulted, in part, from knightly traditions that prevailed in a stratified, hierarchical society. Under Silla's rule, rank (rather than the Chinese Examination System) determined the right to office, and this led to the strengthening of a deeply rooted aristocracy, holding official positions. Korea's aristocrats were less aloof from the peasants than were the examination-orientated official class of China; and greater interaction between court and folk traditions imbued Korean arts with peasant vitality.

The Korean language shows features common to the Ural-Altaic group, to which belong Turkish, Hungarian, and Finnish; but, as with Japanese (to which there are structural affinities), its precise relationship with other languages is unclear. The Chinese language, including the system of characters in their ancient phonetic values, served for a time as the language of official documents; but the ingenious syllabary, instituted by King Sejong in 1443, permitted phonetic writing of Korean (Hangul); and the use of Chinese characters today is in marked decline.

Vicissitudes of Korean History

The history of Korea has been turbulent. Poised uneasily between China and Japan, at a position of strategic importance in East Asia—and with the former USSR touching its north-eastern border—this small peninsula has been trodden by armies from China, Mongolia, Manchuria, Russia, and Japan. Its early history was closely bound to that of China, and its periods of dynastic stability largely coincided with those of China: Unified Silla (668–936) with Tang; Koryo (935–1392) with Song; and Early Choson (Yi (1392–1593)) with Ming. Having reaffirmed Confucian values, prior to the Mongol invasions, Korea—like China—looked inwards rather than outwards during the eighteenth and nineteenth centuries.

Korea suffered equally, if in different ways, from Mongol and Manchu invasions; but it had also to face Japan. In 1592, only a few decades before the Manchu incursions, Japan invaded and overran Korea, burning and looting much of the country's artistic heritage. Because of the gallantry of a small but better-equipped Korean navy, the Japanese were forced to retreat. Five years later, however, they again attacked, capturing many skilled craftsmen, and stealing thousands of books, before ending hostilities a year later.

During the eighteenth century, Western ideas began to reach Korea through China; but during the nineteenth century, Western learning was repressed and foreigners excluded, even after it had been learned that British and French troops had occupied Beijing in 1860. The Koreans refused to enter into trade or diplomatic relations with Russia, America, or Japan. Unhappily, Korea was set to become the centrepiece of Japanese imperial ambition, for Japan reacted to the 'barbarian' threat more pragmatically than her neighbours and sent envoys to Europe to learn the 'secrets' of European weaponry.

In 1894 the Korean government enlisted Chinese help to put down the *Tonghak* ('Eastern Learning') uprising—a social protest movement, based on a syncretic form of religion. Unexpectedly, the Japanese joined in, and inflicted a quick defeat on the Chinese. Subsequently, the Koreans looked to Russia for help. Japan, however, encouraged by a treaty of alliance with Britain, defeated the Russian navy at Port Arthur in 1904, and in 1905 overran Korea. In 1910 Korea was formally annexed to Japan, and its existence as a nation ceased. Koreans were forced to adopt Japanese customs and language, and in the 1930s a process of total 'Japanization' was inaugurated. Resistance was brutally suppressed. For their imperial government, the Japanese erected an imposing building in European colonial style (the Japanese had, after all, learned the art of colonizing from Europe). Ironically—and looking curiously, but rather splendidly, out of place at the head of Seoul's main thoroughfare—the building now houses Korea's National Museum.

When the Japanese capitulated to the Allies in 1945, Koreans did not obtain the peace and independence they had expected. Instead, the peninsula became a focal point of international tensions, anticipating the Cold War. In the North, Russia established both a Communist government and a well-equipped army; in the South, after some indecisiveness by the US occupying command, a legislative assembly was elected. The line of the 38th Parallel of Latitude then became a line of demarcation between Communist and capitalist ideologies. Civil war broke out in 1950; and after three bloody and futile years of fighting, the war finished where it began, with the 38th Parallel separating a free Republic of South Korea from a Russian-influenced Communist North. Because of this, Korean music will be discussed only as it survives in South Korea.

Ritual Music

Korean music was first influenced by Chinese music during the fourth century AD; by the seventh century this Chinese music had become sufficiently Koreanized to be listed by the Tang as a foreign music. With the increasing spread of Chinese Buddhist culture during the Unified Silla period, attempts were made to distinguish between native Korean music and music of Chinese origin; the former (which included music that arrived before the start of the Tang dynasty) was termed *hyangak* ('native music'), and the latter, *tangak*. (The alliance with the Tang caused *tang* to become synonymous with China, generally.[105])

In 1114, and again in 1116, in an attempt to secure an alliance with Korea, the Song court of China sent to Korea the music and instruments necessary for performance of the Confucian Shrine Music, both for the *tungga* (terrace ensemble) and *hon'ga* (courtyard ensemble); also included were instructions for performing the associated 'civil' and 'military' dances. This newly imported Shrine Music was termed *a-ak* (the Korean pronunciation of the Chinese *yayue*); it was soon in use at the Korean Royal Ancestral Shrine, and by 1134 had been incorporated into other sacrificial rites.[106]

During the fourteenth century, political disturbances that led to the founding of the Early Choson dynasty interrupted the performance tradition of *a-ak*: the original Chinese music then came to be mixed with *hyangak* ('native music'), ensembles were altered, and instruments destroyed. It was not until the accession of the fourth Choson dynasty king, Sejong (r. 1418–50), that court ceremonies were rejuvenated.

King Sejong, himself a musicologist, supervised an intensive revision and codification of nearly every aspect of music and rites, and appointed a musical theorist, Pak Yon (1378–1458), as director of the Royal Music Department. Between 1424 and 1430—as indicated in the *Annals of King Sejong*—major changes were made to ritual music, in the light of current understanding of the history and theory of Chinese ritual music:[107] instruments were retuned in accordance with the cycle-of-fifths procedure, based on the fundamental pitch of the *huangzhong* of the Chinese Ming dynasty; new *a-ak* instruments were manufactured;

[105] Byong Won Lee, 'Korea', *The New Grove* (1980), x. 192.

[106] Robert C. Provine, *Early Sources for Korean Ritual Music: Essays on Sino-Korean Musicology* (Seoul: Il Ji Sa Publishing Co., 1988), 10–13.

[107] Ibid. 31, 141.

the terrace and courtyard ensembles began to play in *yin* and *yang* modes respectively;[108] and *a-ak* compositions of doubtful authenticity were abandoned.[109] In 1430 King Sejong ordered a compilation, in notation, of known ritual tunes (*Aak-po*); but, although these appeared during the same year, few of them seem to have been used in rites.[110]

Korean scholars entrusted with these tasks considered only two available Chinese sources to be genuinely authentic: Zhu Xi's 'General Explanation of the Canon of Rites and Commentaries thereon' (*c.*1220) (see p. 340), and Lin Yu's 'Collection of Music of the *Dasheng* Office' (1349), which survives only in fragments, in Korean sources.[111] The twelve melodies recorded by Zhu Xi were revised and orchestrated for performance at banquets and other court ceremonies, but subsequently fell into disuse. Lin Yu's collection included notated melodies (of which sixteen survive), as well as descriptions of Yuan ceremonial practices, current in the early thirteenth century (but probably deriving, in part at least, from the early twelfth century).[112] Two of these melodies, in modified versions, are still performed at the semi-annual Sacrifice to Confucius, at the Shrine of Confucius in the grounds of Songgyun'gwan University in Seoul. (The Royal Department of Music itself survived the vicissitudes of Korean history to become the Korean Traditional Performing Arts Centre.)

Ex. 10.8 shows the second of these melodies (used for the last section of the ritual, 'Ushering out the Spirits'), in heptatonic, Fa-mode, the form in which it is performed today. (Koreans believed, incorrectly, that Zhu Xi had proscribed the use of any of the seven notes available in an

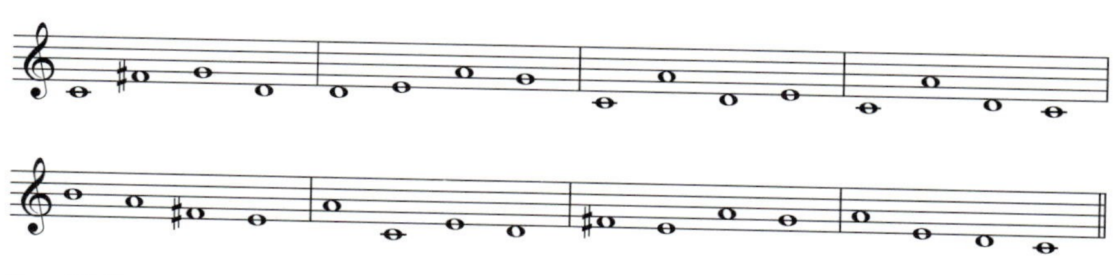

Ex. 10.8

[108] See Robert C. Provine, 'State Sacrificial Rites and Ritual Music in Early Choson', *Journal of the Korean Traditional Performing Arts Centre*, 1 (1989), 276–7.
[109] Lee, 'Korea', *The New Grove*, x. 194.
[110] Provine, *Early Sources*, 42.
[111] Ibid. 145.
[112] Ibid. 118–19, 129–33.

octave set in higher- or lower-octave register.[113]) It is played extremely slowly, with drums beating two pairs of quavers, each followed by a crotchet rest, on the final note of each bar; and an upwards glissando of up to a minor third, effected by wind instruments on approximately the last quaver of each note, imparts a distinctive character to the performance style.[114]

King Sejong himself is credited with the composition of two suites of court music, with vocal texts that extol the accomplishments of Korean royal ancestors; the original scores of these survive in a remarkable form of musical notation in which both pitch and rhythm are defined. King Sejong's son, Sejo (r. 1455–68), subsequently adapted these for use at the Royal Ancestral Shrine; and versions of these are still in the modern repertoire.[115] Although *a-ak* was initially codified for use in state sacrificial rites, King Sejo expressed reservations about the use of Chinese (rather than Korean) music in worship of Korean royal ancestors, and ordered a revision of the shrine music to incorporate elements of *hyangak* ('native music'). In 1493, the *Akhak kwebom* ('Guide to the Study of Music') was published; it provides a definitive account of Korean court music and its context, and marks the culmination of fifteenth-century Korean musical scholarship.[116]

The modern performance style of the 'ancestral-shrine music' (*hyangak*) contrasts with that of *a-ak*, in that the melody is performed with varying durations and is sustained by the use of the nasal-sounding double-reed *piri*; and the vocal line departs from the basic melody by up to a perfect fourth or fifth, rejoining it at apparently random points, as it slowly unfolds in time. These appear to be 'native' musical characteristics, exemplified in modern performance practice of the *Yongsan Hoesang* and *kagok* (see below).

The instruments of ritual music were categorized, as in China, under the eight materials from which they are constructed: metal, stone, silk, bamboo, gourd, clay, skin, and wood. The terrace ensemble of *a-ak* consisted primarily of vocalists and string instruments; the courtyard ensemble, of bells, chimes, and wind instruments (Pl. 46). Chinese custom was followed in the use of ensembles of different size, according

[113] Provine, *Early Sources*, 158, 174.

[114] Keith Pratt, *Korean Music: Its History and its Performance* (London: Faber Music, 1987), 33.

[115] Provine, 'State Sacrificial Rites', 247–50.

[116] Provine, *Early Sources*, 54–61.

46. 'Ancestral-shrine music': the *tungga* (courtyard) orchestra

to the rank of the presiding official. A full courtyard ensemble could include an array of up to eighteen full sets of bells and chimes, with a hundred other instruments; and forty-eight dancers were used for each of the 'civil' and 'military' dancers. In all, as many as 250 musicians and dancers participated in important sacrifices.[117] Subsequent to the Japanese invasions in the late sixteenth century, however, the size of the ritual orchestras was reduced, and the mensurally explicit notation used in the fifteenth century was abandoned, in favour of tablature without mensuration.[118]

It is pertinent to note that the Koreans include in their catalogues of 'National Treasures', 'Intangible National Cultural Assets'. Of these, the 'ancestral shrine music' is asset no. 1. (Masters of particular genres are known as 'human cultural assets'.)

Korean traditional music is now usually divided into two broad categories: *chongak* ('correct music'), which overlaps *a-ak* and covers court music and songs, and *minsogak* ('folk music').

[117] Provine, 'State Sacrificial Rites', 274, 292.
[118] Jonathan Condit, 'Korea', *NOCM* (1983).

Chongak ('Correct Music'): Instrumental Music

The most significant item of surviving Korean court instrumental music is the *Yongsan Hoesang* ('Meeting on Spirit Mountain'), the earliest surviving score of which dates from the fifteenth century. Originally a setting of a Buddhist text, the music gradually abandoned voices, and developed into a long orchestral suite, with movements varying in character and increasing in speed. The suite exists in four different versions, for different types of ensemble.

The Buddhist melody of the *Yongsan Hoesang* is embellished with elaborate heterophony. The instruments vary in their use of vibrato and melodic embellishment, in the melodic path by which they journey from one basic note to the next, and in the precise moment at which they reach it. As in the music of many Asian countries, intervals in Korean music are not rigidly fixed, and performers sometimes lessen or increase an interval by a small amount, for expressive purposes. In Korean court music, a note rarely starts with an exact unison; different instruments 'savour' the note in different ways, usually achieving a precise unison somewhere in the middle, the rest of the time remaining—as Westerners would put it—'out of tune'. The essential element in Korean 'elegant' music is *shigumse* ('living notes'): each note has its own life and shape, while its pitch is altered gradually (by up to a semitone), and its timbre is subtly changed.

A conspicuous feature of *chongak*, that distinguishes it from Chinese and Japanese court music, is the use of ternary units, often in asymmetrical patterns of, for example, five bars of 3/8 or five bars of 6/8.[119]

The melodic lines of all *chongak* belong to the two basic types of mode found in Korean music, both of which (according to the *Akhak kwebom*) were originally played in seven keys, but are now played almost exclusively in E♭ for court music:[120] anhemitonic *p'yongjo* (E♭–F–A♭–B♭–C), and hemitonic *kyemyonjo* (E♭–G–A♭–B♭–D). Within these modes, three or four notes usually predominate, requiring different types of emphasis, or vibrato, according to a given genre or geographical region.[121] It is likely that Chinese melodies originally used in *chongak* were played much more quickly than now, and that increasingly

[119] Condit, 'Korea' *Nocm* (1983). [120] Ibid.
[121] Lee, 'Korea', *The New Grove*, x. 200.

47. Korean traditional music ensemble, with (left to right) *kayagum* (twelve-string zither), *haegum* (two-string fiddle), *tanso* (end-blown flute), *taegum* (transverse flute), *p'iri* (double-reed instrument), *changgo* (hour glass drum), *komun'go* (six-string zither), and (centre) *yanggum* (dulcimer).

elaborate embellishment has accompanied progressive retardation;[122] such retardation is explicit in the temporal sequence of printed scores. (A similar process occurred in the Tang music, *tōgaku*, of Japan.)

The instrumental palette of the Koreans is one rich in tonal variety. The *komun'go*, a six-string zither, resembles the Chinese *qin* in appearance, but is plucked with a short bamboo rod; it was the esteemed instrument of Koguryo in the Three Kingdoms period. From Paekche came the *kayagum*, a twelve-string zither with movable bridges, similar to the Chinese *zheng*; in its turn it travelled to Japan, where one form is known as *koto*. The Koreans make extensive and expressive use of a double-reed, bamboo pipe, *p'iri*; and their horizontal flute, *taegum*, has a membrane-covered hole that extends its carrying power, like the Chinese *dizi*. Nowadays, little use is made of the short-necked lute, *p'ipa*; but to the *komun'go* and *kayagum* is added an equally ancient bowed zither, *ajaeng*: a seven-string zither, bowed with a piece of rosined *Forsythia* wood, and yielding a markedly nasal sound. (This instrument

[122] Jonathan Condit, 'Two Song-Dynasty Chinese Tunes Preserved in Korea', in D. R. Widdess and R. P. Wolpert (eds.), *Music and Tradition: Essays on Asian and Other Musics Presented to Laurence Picken* (Cambridge: Cambridge University Press, 1981).

Ex. 10.9

is also used as a folk instrument; and it survives as such in north China, where it is known as the 'creaking zither'.) The two-string fiddle, *haegum*, is esteemed for its nasal quality, rather than for the melodic expressiveness that is its characteristic attribute in China (Pl. 47). Both *ajaeng* and *haegum* are listed as 'wind' instruments, on account of their sustaining power. In Korea, timbre quality, and manner of performance, appear to take precedence over purely melodic aspects.

In practice, the plucked zithers tend to *follow* the basic melody, while the winds, particularly the flute, execute florid *elaborations* of it; bowed zither and fiddle add their own nasal version of the melody. Ex. 10.9 shows part of the melody on which the *Yongsan Hoesang* is based, bars 1 to 3, as embellished in ensemble, sound approximately as in Ex. 10.10.[123] The notation indicates the range and mix of melodic embellishment, but affords no indication of the essential sound quality. For this the reader is advised to listen to one of the recordings issued by the Korean Traditional Performing Arts Centre.

All court music is based on rhythmic cycles rather than 'bars'; but percussion and melody instruments do not play in active partnership, as they do in India and West Asia. The *changgo* (hourglass drum) indicates, discreetly, the slow passing of a six-, ten-, twelve-, or twenty-beat cycle.

[123] Sleeve notes accompanying the LP set of the *Hyonak Yongsan Hoesang*, played by the National Institute for Classical Music (now called the Korean Traditional Performing Arts Centre), issued in Korea.

Ex. 10.10 (Part I)

Chongak ('Correct Music'): Vocal Music

From the eighteenth century, three traditional genres of vocal music became popular, both within and without the court, and still survive: *kagok*, *sijo*, and *kasa*. All require advanced performance skills.

Kagok is a lengthy song cycle, and is accompanied by a chamber ensemble, in a style similar to that of the *Yongsan Hoesang*. The vocal

Ex. 10.10 (Part II)

style embodies energetic melismas and wide vibrato. The present *kagok* repertoire, established during the seventeenth and eighteenth centuries, consists of twenty-seven songs, each cast in the same seven-section form, two sections being instrumental solos. The *changgo* (hourglass drum) delineates cycles of ten or sixteen beats.[124]

Sijo is the name for lyric songs in the refined style of the scholars. The vocalist usually performs with *changgo* alone as accompaniment; but sometimes *p'iri*, *taegum*, and *haegum* are present, in which case they follow the vocal melody heterophonically, or play during breaks in the

[124] Lee, 'Korea', *The New Grove*, x. 203.

singing. The art of the vocal soloist is paramount, and is characterized by powerful dynamic contrasts, switching between normal voice and falsetto, and employing different types of vibrato, performed either upwards or downwards from the initiating pitch. The rhythmic structure of the songs is composed of various combinations of five- and eight-beat patterns.[125]

The *kasa* are long narrative songs; twelve survive, in a five- or six-beat cycle, usually accompanied only by *changgo*. The vocal style makes extensive use of falsetto; and sometimes the vowels of the text-syllables are transformed into meaningless syllables.[126]

Aspects of vocal technique employed for these court songs are also to be observed in performance of Buddhist chant, described in Chapter 4 (see p. 108).

Minsogak ('Folk Music')

The forms of Korean folk music have their origins in shamanism. In its modern condition, Korean shamanism is akin to Chinese popular Daoism, and Japanese Shintoism. In Korea, rituals are traditionally presided over by female shamans in folk ceremonies, known as *kut*. A *kut* may be sponsored to appease the ancestors of a particular family, or to bring prosperity to an entire community. In earlier times, shamans performed *kut* to the rain dragon in times of drought, and even used their powers to assist political factions.[127]

Museok (rural shamanistic music) used to be performed specifically by *kwangdae*, itinerant folk musicians who enjoyed high esteem before Neo-Confucianism imputed low social status to professional entertainment. During the mid-Choson dynasty, *kwangdae* were spouses of shamans and acted as musical accompanists at shamanistic ceremonies. Subsequently, however, the term *kwangdae* became a generic one, used for folk artists of various kinds.[128] *Museok* now survives as a form of folk music.

Conspicuous among other surviving folk musical forms are the 'farmer's dances' that range from fertility dances to masked mimes. All

[125] Ibid. 204. [126] Ibid.
[127] Laurel Kendall, 'Shamanism', in *Korea* (Hong Kong: APA Publications, 1989), 238–40.
[128] Lee, 'Korea', *The New Grove*, x. 204.

display characteristic Korean grace: in one popular form, the dancer, with *changgo* at waist, wears long paper streamers (attached to a colourful hat), flung about by the nodding head, making acrobatic leaps with body tilted backwards. The dances are accompanied by a *nongak* (farmers' music) ensemble, usually consisting of *taegum* (flute), *p'iri* (bamboo oboe), *t'aep'yongso* (shawm), *haegum* (two-string fiddle), *komun'go* (six-string zither), cymbals, and drums. Characteristically, they are mostly based on cycles in triple metre; indeed, use of triple metre is *the* distinguishing feature of all Korean traditional music.

A recent, urban, genre, *samullori* (literally 'four things play'), derives from both *museok* and *nongak*, and is performed on *changgo*, *puk* (barrel drum), *kkwaenggwari* (small gong), and *ching* (large gong).[129] The music employs complex, asymmetrical rhythm patterns, and develops a state of virtuosic frenzy. The genre has become widely popular, and there are now several dozen professional *samullori* groups practising in Korea.

Sanjo and *P'ansori*

As Western influence gradually undermined the exclusivity of the scholar-gentry during the nineteenth century, two new genres of music developed: the instrumental *sanjo* and the vocal *p'ansori*, both of which developed virtuoso styles of performance, and both of which are rooted in folk styles.

Sanjo (literally 'scattered melodies') was introduced during the 1880s by Kim Ch'angjo. Initially a piece for solo *kayagum* and drum, it may have developed from the improvisations of professional instrumentalists in shamanistic rituals.[130] The *kayagum* (or sometimes *komun'go* or *paegum*), improvises to the accompaniment of a *changgo*, which maintains cycles of six consecutive rhythm patterns, each successively faster than the last;[131] and the soloist's improvisation is further restricted by a framework of modal and melodic conventions. The *sanjo* performance tradition is oral–aural; in modern practice, however, the improvisa-

[129] Keith Howard, Review of Korean Traditional Music, issued on CD, produced for the Korean Traditional Performing Arts Centre, *British Journal of Ethnomusicology*, 2 (1993), 164.
[130] Ibid. 160.
[131] Lee, 'Korea', *The New Grove*, x. 207.

tional element has largely disappeared, and performers tend to play compositions learned from notation, according to particular schools of performance.

P'ansori is a distinctively Korean style of storytelling that achieves a remarkable synthesis of song, speech, and acting. The social origins of *p'ansori* were similar to those of Chinese opera: the original singers were itinerant male performers who, in this instance, are thought to have been blood relatives of the shamans. The stories were transmitted orally until the nineteenth century, when scholars began to show interest in them; texts were then written down, female singers were trained, and the genre became a professional form of entertainment. *P'ansori* singing was never practised by scholars or courtiers, however, as occurred with Chinese opera; it remained a folk entertainment practised by individual folk singers.[132]

P'ansori is essentially a one-person opera, accompanied by *puk* (barrel drum). The singer makes substantial use of modality to denote different moods; the drummer maintains a given rhythmic cycle and responds to the singer by shouting *ch'uimsae* (calls of encouragement, akin to the appreciative *kakegoe* of Japanese *Kabuki* (see p. 404)). The texts have been influenced by current social attitudes in Korea, and some have even incorporated biblical stories.[133] The solitary *p'ansori* singer undertakes the narration, the acting, and the singing. The range of dynamics is extreme: vocal crescendo may amount to a scream. Speech and song—always rhythmical, and with the distinction between them often blurred—are interspersed with grunts and shouts. Tremolo and vibrato are violent, and the range and power of the voice is astonishing. Inevitably it is hoarse and heavy in timbre: *p'ansori* singers train in open spaces, or beside waterfalls, to strengthen their vocal power. As the performance can last from four to eight hours, the physical strain on the vocal chords is considerable, and laryngeal haemorrhages are common. Nevertheless, in this art, speech and song are wonderfully attuned to the dramatic rendering of heroic or romantic stories.

This wealth of traditional music now exists in Korea beneath a suffocating overlay of Western music. Many more schools of Western music than of Korean music are to be found. Yet traditional music of all

[132] Ibid.

[133] Hae-kyung Um, 'Making *P'ansori*: Korean Musical Drama', unpublished paper presented to ICTM UK, 1992.

kinds—farmer's songs and dances, *kuts*, court music, Confucian and Buddhist ritual ceremonies—are still performed at a variety of venues. The orchestra of the Korean Traditional Performing Arts Centre in Seoul is government-sponsored; so too is the associated High School and Primary School, with special courses in traditional music for musically talented children. Around Seoul, on fine days, groups of children may be seen sketching the architectural outlines of Korea's palaces and shrines. Despite the pervasive gloss of Westernization, Korea's traditional arts are still intrinsic to the national culture. Their variety and ubiquity in Korea should fit them to be Global, as much as National, Treasure.

Japan

Peculiarities of Japanese History

The traditional arts of Japan are clearly based on the East Asian model, but they display a marked individuality of style. An island country, Japan developed the characteristic island tendencies to look inwards idiosyncratically, and outwards, aggressively. Nominally, the country was ruled by emperors, but imperial power was always loosely defined. In practice, from the early centuries AD until the end of the sixteenth century, it was ruled, more or less, by the chiefs of warring clans. Nevertheless, this harsh regime resulted in a surprising degree of social cohesion, and a remarkable flowering of the arts and of philosophy.

Japan developed advanced cultural systems long before the arrival of Chinese influence in the sixth century. As, however, until after the Second World War, Japan's official history insisted that its inhabitants had descended from heaven in the year 660 BC, any scientific attempt to trace an earlier history was for long discouraged. Japan's largest prehistoric burial mounds are regarded as imperial tombs and have still not been excavated. Nevertheless, digging to create new buildings and roads has accidentally revealed that, during the Jomon period (10,500–400 BC), Japan was producing the oldest known ceramics in the world. While these appear to have been peculiar to Japan, there is evidence that Jomon lacquerware may have influenced China rather than vice versa. During the succeeding Yayoi period (400 BC–AD 150), Japan produced elaborately ornamented bronze bells (*dotaku*). It was during the succeeding Kofun period (AD 150–600) that material wealth became concentrated in the hands of a few powerful rulers.[134]

References to Japan in Chinese records of the third century AD reveal a country still little affected by developments elsewhere in Asia. Only with the arrival of Buddhism in the early sixth century did Chinese influence begin to be felt; and not until the seventh century, when the Fujiwara clan rose to power, was centralized rule on Chinese lines established.[135] Although the political power of the emperors was severely limited, vigorous artistic activity was maintained at court throughout the Nara (*c*.600–784) and Heian (784–1170) periods. (Heian is the ancient name for Kyōto.) Subsequently, however, military dictatorships began to erode court culture. The imperial court was maintained at Kyōto until the Meiji restoration in 1868, when it moved to the capital: Edo (present-day Tokyo).

During the Nara period, Chinese culture arrived via Korea, and directly and intensively via Japanese missions to China between 632 and 778: Confucianism, Buddhism, art, architecture, sculpture, painting, music, styles of Chinese calligraphy, and paper flowed into the country. By the seventh century, *gigaku*, a masked dance pantomime (of probable Chinese origin), and music of the Three Kingdoms (later classified as *komagaku*: 'Korean music') had been imported from Korea.[136] Tang Chinese music in notation, in manuscript copies from the tenth to the early fourteenth centuries, survive in Japan; this music is still known as *tōgaku* ('Tang Music').

The Nara and Heian were periods of great artistic achievement, but, as political power remained largely in the hands of clan leaders, there was little political stability. With the Kamakura period (1192–1333)—so called because power passed to clans with estates in that area—there emerged a new breed of military dictator, or army general, known as 'Shōgun' ('General of the army'). The Shōguns, in turn, fostered the rise of an élite warrior class, the *Samurai*. (The Chinese character means 'one who serves' or 'waits upon'.) Their loyalty, obedience, and mercilessness subsequently exerted a powerful influence on Japanese culture. When the Kamakura collapsed, a brief attempt was made to restore power to the emperor; but during the ensuing Muromachi period

[134] Holland Cotter, 'Uncovering Japan's Buried Past', review of 'Ancient Japan', exhibition at the Smithsonion Institute in New York, *International Herald Tribune*, 5 September 1992, 7.

[135] Roberts, *Pelican History of the World*, 438.

[136] Elizabeth Markham, 'Japanese Music', *NOCM* (1983).

(1136–1573), neither emperor nor shogunate gained the upper hand. Despite this, two Mongol attempts at invasion were repulsed, the second by a fortunate typhoon that destroyed the Mongol fleet. (The Japanese called this the *kamikaze*: 'wind of god'.) These successes were important because they intensified an already strong Japanese belief in their native superiority and invincibility; they also ensured that Japanese cultural systems were not greatly influenced by the Central Asian traditions of the Mongols.

Not until the end of the sixteenth century did Japan become united, when three powerful generals of the Tokugawa clan established control over their provincial rivals. They established themselves at Edo (present-day Tokyo) and so inaugurated the Tokugawa (or 'Edo') period (1603–1867). This shogunate still feared usurpation by rival clans, and therefore pursued inward-looking policies. Only with the nineteenth-century threat from foreigners—specifically the appearance of the US navy in Edo Bay in 1853—did more outward-looking policies emerge. Japan already viewed European intervention in Chinese affairs with alarm. Spurred on by a sense of 'shameful inferiority' to the West, a revolutionary process of renewal led to the 'restoration' of the monarchy in the Meiji period (1868–); a sumptuous court, and modernization on European lines, would henceforth assist Japan to establish itself on equal terms with other nations of the world.

The course of this history, based almost exclusively on military dictatorship and force of arms, partly explains Japan's more recent history; deriving from European methods of imperialism, it is still within recent memory and need not be described here. It has been touched upon in the context of China and Korea.

Confucianism and Shintoism

The social cohesion that made Japan's cultural achievement possible came from Confucianism, adopted as the basis for Japan's first constitution in the seventh century. Confucian regard for social institutions as the basis of good government and orderly behaviour remains embedded in Japanese culture.

Alongside Confucianism, Shinto—the national religion—is more deeply embedded in Japanese culture. It blended easily with Buddhism, as did Daoism in China, and Shamanism in Korea; indeed, the religion evolved from a form of Shamanism. The word means, literally, 'the way of the *kami*'. *Kami* are local divinities, in places, in rocks, in trees, in wells, in nature, always close to daily life. Many forms of Japanese arts and sports have their origins in the early Shinto belief that man, nature, and *kami* must all be precisely balanced.[137] Shinto is not merely a folk religion, however; it is also a state religion, in which certain *kami* are linked with the origins of Japan and of the imperial family. (Shinto was explicitly separated from Buddhism at the time of the Meiji restoration.) While Shinto festivals take place in association with village shrines with masked dances, elaborate festivals of state are held at the larger shrines—at Kasugu-taisha, for example—with chanting, instrumental performance, and court and other dances. During the long centuries of feudal anarchy, Shintoism, joined with Confucian values, held Japanese society together.

The Tokugawas turned to Confucianism, specifically to a form of Neo-Confucianism borrowed from the Chinese Song dynasty, to assist in the maintenance of political order. Japanese scholars reinterpreted the teachings of Confucius in such a way as to provide a social structure for their newly unified country. The pivotal element of this thinking was the submerging of individuality in prescribed social institutions. Among these, the family was paramount; but there were other important institutions, ranging from fine arts, to ancestral rituals, and athletic activities. In the early Tokugawa period, there must have been many Confucian shrines.[138] Nowadays, most shrines are Buddhist or Shinto. Nevertheless, the elaborate ancestral ceremonies that take place in major Shinto shrines derive in part from Confucian rites of ancestor worship. Japanese nationalism locked Confucianism within a uniquely Japanese context.

From this Japanese Neo-Confucianism a strong sense of group orientation has emerged; the individual is still expected to contribute strongly in the group, without asserting any distinctive individuality. This social characteristic itself owes much to the cult of Zen Buddhism that developed in the thirteenth century.

Zen Buddhism

Zen is the Japanese pronunciation of the Chinese *Chan*, a sect of Buddhism that developed in China, characterized by

[137] Stuart D. B. Picken (1980), *Shinto: Japan's Spiritual Roots* (San Francisco: Kodansha International/USA, 1980), 10.

[138] John Lowe, *Inside Japan* (London: John Murray, 1985), 47.

meditation, the practice of severe austerities, and the development of martial arts (see p. 340). Zen came to demand ruthlessly applied training, aimed at concentrating the mind, no less ruthlessly, towards specific goals. The repulse of the Mongols led to a period of complacency in Japan, during which the nobility became culpably effete: Zen Buddhism exchanged that path for the austere, self-sacrificing ideals of the warrior-*Samurai*.

Like *Dao*, Zen is hard to define. The essence of the discipline is meditation (in the lotus position) according to strict rules; training is harsh, and undertaken under supervision. The objects of meditation are inconceivable concepts (for example, the sound of one hand clapping), or unanswerable questions, known as *koan*s (from the Chinese for a 'judgement'; for example, 'if you meet someone in the street who has reached the truth, you may neither walk past him in silence, nor speak; how then should you meet him?'). Focusing on such impossibilities, the pupil achieves a mental condition in which the mind is void: *satori* (enlightenment).

An enclosed garden in the Ryoanji temple in Kyōto is held to exemplify the quintessence of Zen. In stark contrast to the open, luxurious, cultivated gardens that surround it, this garden, designed by the painter and gardener Soami in the early sixteenth century, is beautiful but austere. Fifteen rocks of varied size and shape are laid out on white, raked, gravel as a garden, 30 metres by 10 metres, surrounded by low, earthenware walls. The garden exists to inspire meditation; and it means whatever you, individually, like to think it means. It demands thought, insistently. Ultimately—and inevitably in the context of Zen—your answer is no answer.

The rocks are of different sizes and shapes and their spacial distribution, in relation to size, is neither logical nor illogical, symmetrical nor asymmetrical. In contrast to other gardens, however, the boundary of this garden is decisively, and symmetrically, fixed. The problem of *meaning* is therefore simple, yet infinitely complex. The size of the fifteen rocks is already fixed: one may juggle with *them* in the mind (or on the ground), but man's control of nature is limited by its independence. There can, therefore, be no one utterly satisfactory, meaningful arrangement of the rocks; yet any one arrangement may seem more satisfactory than another. If nature can be both logical and illogical, there can be no ultimate logic behind human aspiration.

Such thoughts may or may not have been in the head of Soami when he laid out this austere garden—and this writer has not endured the physical and mental rigours of Zen training in arriving at them—but they reveal something of the Zen tendency to compress ideas into very limited but concentrated modules.

Zen strongly influenced *jūdō* ('the way of gentleness'), or *jujitsu* ('the art of gentleness'): allowing one's opponent to lose balance by not resisting attack. Zen explains the apparently inconsequential (but surcharged with concentration) Japanese styles of, for example, archery, *sumō* wrestling, fencing, the tea ceremony, and flower arrangement—not to mention music, painting, and writing. Linked to Shinto *kami*-worship, such activities retain ritual significance; but it is due to Zen Buddhism that they embody such extraordinary *control* of emotion, overwhelming in its sense of formalized discipline. In Japan, relatively simple-seeming action may take a lifetime to perfect.

Japanese compression of thought and feeling is epitomized in the seventeen-syllable *haiku* with its 5–7–5 syllable pattern, the form perfected by the seventeenth century poet Matsuo Bashō. (In Japanese, long vowels are counted as two syllables.) For example:

Sōkai no	Blue sea
Nami sake-kusashi	Waves . . . rice-wine smell . . .
Kyō no tsuki	Today's moon .

Similar compression of thought and feeling applies to certain types of Japanese music. The court music may appear to the Westerner extremely slow, devoid of expression, as drums beat slowly and regularly, and zithers and lutes play occasional notes, often with no attempt at vibrato or other ornamentation. When ornamentation *is* used, it appears to be performed with utter lack of passion, as though every atom of personal feeling were suppressed in the interests of corporate ritual. In fact, such concentrated suppression conceals intrinsic passion.

This Zen-inspired cultural force continues to shape the Japanese psyche. Beneath the layer of hyper-efficient, hi-tech Westernization of modern Japan, a strong respect for tradition remains. The family is still sacrosanct; individual feelings tend to be hidden, while respect for the feelings of others is paramount. It is a super-concentrated form of Chineseness. Conformity is obligatory, and undermines reasoned enquiry: ironically, there was no place in Zen Buddhism for the very flexibility that was a principal ingredient of Buddhism's success. Yet, from Tokugawa times onwards, it generated a distinctive culture, embellished by impressive and beautiful art forms, born (in sum) of suppressed individuality, combined with a native sense of superiority.

This curious blend of Confucianism, Zen Buddhism, and nationalism may help to explain, far better than Western-style, academic, musical analysis, the nature of Japanese traditional music.[139]

Ritual Music

Although the Japanese adopted Chinese governmental systems, they never (unlike Korea) received instruments and scores for the execution of Confucian ritual music from China. They received about 120 items of Tang court-entertainment music, at times performed by visiting Korean or Chinese musicians; but this was banquet music. The true Confucian *yayue* ('elegant music') seems never to have reached Japan.

It may be that the Japanese were misled by the application of the term 'sitting music' to much of the banquet music. Although Japanese envoys to China were permitted to attend court banquets, it is probable that no foreigner would ever have been allowed to assist at Confucian rites, even in suburban temples; and certainly not at the shrines of the emperor's family and those of other noble families. The name *gagaku* (= *yayue*)—that came to be applied to all Japanese court music—is a misnomer. Its use probably came from the overwhelming panache of Chinese palace productions of the banquet music, much of which consisted of individually choreographed and costumed ballets. The items of *tōgaku* ('Tang music') performed in great Buddhist or Shinto temples are banquet music, not *yayue*; they may be associated with items of *komagaku* ('Korean music'), likewise no part of *a-ak*.[140]

Because Shinto—a national religion—operates both at a folk level and at the level of state ceremony, two types of Shinto music (*kagura*) are distinguished. *Satokagura* betrays Shinto's shamanistic origins: its dances are supported by folk instruments, and it is performed at shrines throughout Japan, where priestesses enact purification rituals and frequently pass into trance states. *Mikagura* is the music of Shinto ceremony, solemn in pace, and melismatic in its vocal style. Records of *kagura* musicians as early as the eighth century exist, and the music

[139] For a detailed exposition of Japanese culture and national character, see M. S. Dobbs-Higginson, *Asia Pacific: Its Role in the New World Disorder* (London: Mandarin Paperbacks, 1993), 25–81.

[140] Comment from Laurence Picken.

had already begun to be notated in neumatic notation in the tenth century.[141]

Shinto festivals reflect the Chinese practice of enabling divinities to make excursions from their home shrines, at times to pay homage in the temple of a divine superior, at times to enact a transition from the world of the spirit to the world of mortals. In Japan, as in China, divinities are carried in palanquins (*mikoshi*). At the Gion festival in Kyōto, the palanquins themselves are carried on massive, four-wheel, fixed-base, wooden floats. Each float carries sixteen or more musicians, four of whom may play *taiko* (barrel drums), six *kane* (hand-held gongs), and six *nōkan* (flutes of the type used in the *Nō* theatre). A pair of dancers, as well as officials of the house shrine, may also be accommodated on the float. Flutes and gongs are commonly placed on opposite sides, with drums in the middle; gongs and drums make use of a variety of strokes and sonorities. Drum, gong, and flute parts are notated, in greater or lesser detail. Flutes often play a semitone apart, perhaps to enhance carrying power in the open air or (as is commonly the function of dissonance or noises worldwide) to drive away demons.[142] Similar ceremonies take place throughout Japan.

(The *taiko* has an honoured place in Japanese history, for in ancient times the limits of rural villages were defined not just by geography but by the furthest distance at which the *taiko* could be heard.[143])

The music of the Japanese court, whether of Chinese (Tang), Korean, or Shinto origin, came eventually to be known, as a whole, as *gagaku*.

During the Heian period, the Japanese were playing *tōgaku* ('Tang-music') items in half-a-dozen or so Chinese modes. Such modes came to be classified as either *ritsu* or *ryo*, according to whether they have a flattened ('minor') or natural ('major') third. The six principle *chōshi* (modes) of *tōgaku* are shown in Ex. 10.11.[144]

In the seventeenth century, two new, indigenous scales were introduced, at first into popular Japanese music, associated in particular with solo instrumental music (see p. 405). Both scales are pentatonic: *insen* is hemitonic, and classed as *ritsu*; *yōsen* is anhemitonic, and classed as *ryo*. In both scales, the descent consists of two identical tetrachords; both,

[141] D. B. Waterhouse, 'Japan', *The New Grove* (1980), ix. 507.

[142] Laurence Picken, 'Towards the Archaic Music of Pre-Nara Japan', unpublished paper presented at the Music Centre of the London School of Oriental and African Studies, 10 March 1992.

[143] Sleeve note of tape of *Kodō*, CBS 466629 4.

[144] Markham, 'Japanese Music'.

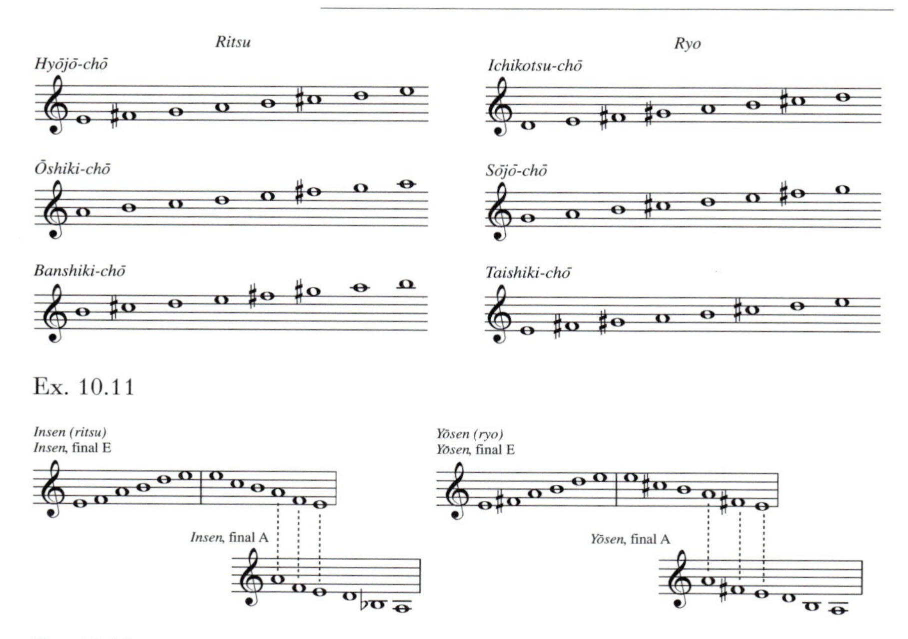

Ex. 10.11

Ex. 10.12

therefore, are susceptible of transposition (as shown in Ex. 10.12), a condition fully exploited in instrumental music of the Tokugawa period.[145]

Each category of *gagaku* has its own instrumentation. The instruments used for court music are broadly similar to the instruments used in China and Korea: the *ryūteki* ('dragon' flute), *hichiriki* (double-reed bamboo pipe), *shō* (mouth organ), *gaku-biwa* (lute), *gaku-sō* (zither), *kakko* (small braced drum), *tsuridaiko* (large standing drum), and *shōko* (gong).[146] The mouth organ plays clusters of up to five additional notes, above the melody note, and the lute sounds its lower open strings as a complex drone with each melody note. Wind instruments tend to follow the voice, while zithers play the notes of the basic melody. In open-air performances of *Bugaku* (associated dances) the *dadaiko* (a huge barrel drum, over twice the height of an average-sized player) is used; the ensemble then consists of winds and percussion alone.

The *komagaku* ensemble uses the 'Korean' flute (*komabue*) in place of the 'dragon' flute, and an hourglass drum (*san-no-tsuzumi*) in place of the small braced drum. The mouth organ is not used.

[145] Markham, 'Japanese Music'.

[146] Robert Garfias, 'Japan', *The New Grove* (1980), ix. 510–11.

The slow beats of the bars are differentiated by the percussion. The main beat is emphasized by a heavy stroke on the barrel drum, always preceded by a softer up-beat; a hanging-gong marks subsidiary beats. The loud stroke on the barrel drum is always the most important beat, but is usually the fifth and seventh beat in an eight-beat measure. In *tōgaku* it is never the first beat.

There are three principal types of musical movement, *jo*, *ha*, and *kyū* (prelude, broaching, and quick), though all three are not necessarily used in one piece. These indications are, however, relative: Japanese court music is seldom very fast and is often, by Western standards, very slow. Increasing elaboration of the original Tang melodies was linked with a slowing in pace, and has completely obscured their melodic outline. In general, embellishment is less vigorous than in Korea, and the music in fact sounds slower.[147]

In the performance of *tōgaku*, retardation has reduced awareness of the modality of the plucked-string and mouth-organ melodic lines; and the hemitonic *insen* scale has come to influence the linear wind parts of flute and reed pipe. The combination of mixed modes, and progressive embellishment of the original melody, along with the mouth organ's 'cluster chords', and the lute's chordal, open-string drone, leads to a harmonically complex ensemble. Though present as the lowest note of the mouth-organ chords, the original melody cannot be heard. (The Japanese tend to think of the embellished line of the *hichiriki* and *ryuteki* as *the* melody.) For example, the first bar of the Chinese Tang melody, *Music for a Thousand Autumns* (Ex. 10.13) is embellished in modern performance as in Ex. 10.14 (after Markham).[148]

Throughout the Nara and Heian periods, *gagaku* was widely performed at court, in Buddhist and Shinto temples, and at the homes of

Ex. 10.13

[147] Allan Marett, 'Banshiki Sangun and Shoenraku: Metrical Structure and Notation of Two Tang-Music Melodies for Flute', in D. R. Widdess and R. P. Wolpert (eds.), *Music and Tradition: Essays on Asian and Other Musics Presented to Laurence Picken* (Cambridge: Cambridge University Press, 1981).

[148] Markham, 'Japanese Music'.

Ex. 10.14

the nobility. During the Tokugawa period, knowledge and scope of the repertoire gradually declined; but, with the Meiji restoration in 1868, guilds of court musicians, who had striven to keep alive traditions of the eighth century, were brought together by the Imperial Household Agency.[149] Since then, performance of this strangely beautiful music has been restored in Japan, though it means less and less to the Japanese of today.

Folk Ceremonies

It is perhaps characteristic of Japan that there was no exact Japanese word for 'folk music' until the mid-twentieth century, when the term used (modelled on a German formula) implied

[149] Garfias, 'Japan', *The New Grove*, ix. 511.

'studies of human traditions'.[150] Many regional folk styles exist in Japan. They include children's songs (it has been suggested that specific melodic features of these songs have influenced modern Japanese pop music);[151] dance songs; drinking songs; geisha songs; work songs (in connection with rice-growing, fishing, and mountain-work, for example); seasonal songs; and songs connected with folk performing arts. Most are linked with dances for specific occasions.

Folk-songs may be accompanied by *shamisen* (three-stringed lute), or by various types of flute, with a variety of percussion instruments. Such ensembles, known as *hayashi*, usually consist of small drum, hand-held gong, and transverse flute. Drumming, as mentioned earlier, has ancient ritual significance in Japan. A popular form of folk drumming adds to the *hayashi* one or two *taiko* (barrel drums), which recumbent players support with their feet by means of wooden grips attached to the underside of the drum. As they beat the drums with increasing concentration and speed, their bodies rise from their recumbent position. The beating of the *taiko*, whether in a standing or recumbent position, involves maximum force and Zen-like concentration. In Saitama prefecture, north-west of Tokyo, this style of drumming is used to encourage those pulling festival floats. Like farmers' drumming in Korea, it is now performed largely for entertainment.[152]

Satokagura (folk performing arts, associated with Shinto ceremonies) occurs in villages throughout Japan. The origin of such ceremonies may predate the introduction of *gigaku* ('masked dance') from Korea in the seventh century. Bird dances exist and may well be of considerable antiquity: cave paintings attest the existence of Palaeolithic bird cults in many parts of the world, and it is known that crane dances existed in China in the fourth century BC. Dancers, costumed and masked as birds, together with bearers of talismanic Shinto-properties, lead a procession in which a divinity in a palanquin is transported from its home shrine to a temporary shrine. A recording of a bird dance at Tsuwano—where the bird is the heron—includes music for two flutes (often playing a minor ninth apart), interspersed with music for drums and gongs.[153]

[150] Fumio Koizumi, 'Japan', *The New Grove* (1980), ix. 540.

[151] Fujita Fumiko, *Problems of Language, Culture, and the Appropriateness of Musical Expression in Japanese Childrens' Performance* (Tokyo: Academic Music Ltd., 1989).

[152] Information supplied by Warabi-Za Folk Song and Dance Company (Japan), based in Akita prefecture, and dedicated to the preservation and performance of Japanese folk arts, as well as to peace and democracy, since its foundation in 1951.

[153] Picken, 'Towards the Archaic Music of Pre-Nara Japan'.

48. Deer dance, in a village near Tokyo

At many village shrines throughout Japan, similar events involve dancers masked as deer: *shika odori* (literally 'deer dancing'; in fact the beasts are mythical, combining features of deer and lion). Accompanied by processions of flute-players, the deer dancers, with drums attached to their waists, indulge in ritual fights (Pl. 48). Oral tradition secures transmission over the centuries; and the ceremonies themselves serve to strengthen the cohesion of village communities.

Nō Theatre

Three principal types of music theatre exist in Japan. *Nō* ('ability') is the oldest; the two later genres, *Kabuki* ('song and dance performance': a more popular genre) and *Bunraku* ('literary music'—puppet theatre) received elements from their predecessor.

During the Heian period (eighth to twelfth centuries) a performing genre called *Dengaku-Nō* ('the *Nō* of field music') developed from rural Shinto music and dance. A different tradition of Chinese origin, involving acrobatics, juggling, and comedy, was the source of *Sarugaku-Nō*, related to the Chinese 'Hundred Acts'. (*Sarugaku* means 'monkey music', monkeys being the animals that imitate human life.) Both led to the comic folk genre, *Kyōgen Nō* ('the *Nō* of mad words'). As *Dengaku* and *Sarugaku* grew in popularity, the two founders of *Nō* theatre, Kannami (1333–84) and his son Zeami (1363–1443), synthesized elements of both—along with forms of dramatic, narrative chants, and Buddhist entertainment dance—into a theatrical form that became greatly esteemed among the *Samurai.* It was to become supreme among Japan's performing arts. The final form of *Nō* owed much to the influence of Zen Buddhism, and *Nō* is now associated more with Buddhism than Shintoism.

Zeami set out the aesthetics and theory of *Nō*, and founded its Kanze school. (The word derives from the 'Kan' of Kannami and the 'Ze' of Zeami.) Many of the plays concern the astute actions of Benkei, a servant, in assisting his noble master in the performance of self-sacrificing, adventurous deeds. *Nō* is still widely performed in Japan, at formal and informal venues, and there is a fine National *Nō* Theatre in Tokyo; *Kyōgen* is sometimes performed between *Nō* plays, but also has a life of its own in certain Buddhist temples.

The skills of *Nō* have been perpetuated through a guild system, the 'secrets' of the art being passed from father to son. As a result, five distinct 'schools' now train *shite* (principal actors) for *Nō* performances. Two other main types of actor are recognized: *waki* (second principal), and *kyōgen* (comic actors). All three must be able both to sing and dance.

Four instrumentalists support the actors. The sounds produced by the instruments, and their functions, are clearly defined, and the exactness in execution is regarded as of paramount importance. A bamboo transverse flute is the only melodic instrument. The other three instruments are hourglass drums, each with very specific and characteristic timbres; the horsehide heads must be heated over charcoal for an hour before each performance. In addition to the four instrumentalists, a unison chorus, usually of eight singers, supports and comments on the action of the principals.

The *Nō* stage is precisely and formally organized. It is made of cypress wood, with a main square stage supported on four pillars. At the rear is the stage for the four musicians and the actors' two assistants. Leading off, stage right, is an entrance passage of approximately half the width, and of the same length, as the main performing arena; it acts as a bridge between the backstage area and that arena. On the wall behind the musicians, a painting of a pine tree symbolizes longevity, and small

49. *Kyōgen Nō* at a Buddhist temple in Kyōto; musical accompaniment is provided by flute, hourglass drum, and suspended gong

pine trees line the ramp. At strategic points under the floor of the main stage, large clay vessels are placed as echo chambers. There is no scenery: only simple properties. The entrance ramp is itself symbolic: walking along the ramp may represent a short or long walk, or even a journey, in different contexts. Most importantly, the ramp provides opportunity for the actors to prepare—and for the audience to be aware of their preparing—to enter the place of action, in a suitably formal and symbolic manner.[154]

Symbolism is the essence of *Nō* aesthetics and informs each mode of acting, intonation, song, and chorus singing. 'Song', however, must be understood in a Japanese way: everything is slow, and the audience is not likely to emerge humming anything that a Westerner would regard as a tune. There are two types of singing: soft and loud. 'Soft singing' is very melismatic in style, and employs a tonal system based on the basic notes of two conjunct tetrachords (ascending: B–E–A), with 'varied' notes between or below; 'loud singing' is most often intoned on one of two basic notes, a minor third apart.[155]

The rhythmic organization of *Nō* music is both measured and unmeasured. The basic, measured cycle is usually one of eight

[154] Shigeo Kishibe, 'Japan', *The New Grove* (1980), ix. 516. [155] Ibid. 517.

beats. Eight- (or sixteen-) syllable text-lines fit readily into this pattern; but text lines of twelve syllables (usually seven-plus-five) impart a degree of metrical freedom. Conversely, when the singing is measured, the hourglass drums and the flute may, independently, play non-metrical patterns of their own. Moreover, the flute line—as in so much East Asian music—often appears to inhabit a tonal world of its own.

In performances of *Kyōgen Nō*, a suspended gong is used along with the drums, in the tradition of *gagaku*. The actors are masked, and movement is somewhat faster and less formal. Although the comic nature of the stories allows for some slapstick, the stories themselves are often morality plays, and *Kyōgen Nō* is still at times performed at Buddhist temples (Pl. 49).

Development of *Kabuki* and *Bunraku*

Perhaps because Zen brought together the tastes of Tokugawa nobility and the austere ideals of the *Samurai*, there was no equivalent in Japan of the scholar-gentry class in China and Korea; but a merchant class developed which, like such classes everywhere, required sophisticated, yet accessible, entertainment. *Kabuki* ('song and dance performance') and *Bunraku* (puppet theatre) fulfilled this requirement.

Kabuki and *Bunraku* both developed, and became prominent, in the seventeenth century; both established guilds of performers; and both imported certain characteristics from *Nō* theatre. Many of Japan's most-loved stories are to be found in all three genres. One such, *Sumidagawa*, concerns the distraught mother, ferried across the river to seek her kidnapped son, only to find his grave—the story adapted by Benjamin Britten in his opera *Curlew River* after he had first seen *Nō* (Pl. 50). This simple but moving story is scarcely less impressive, however, in its *Kabuki* form than it is in *Nō*.

The histories of *Kabuki* and *Bunraku* are intertwined. *Kabuki*, as a music-theatre genre, is said to have started in 1603, after Okuni from Izumo danced her *kabuki* dance (*kabuki-odori*) in a manner that derived from processional dance styles, rather than from those associated with *Nō*. Moreover, this new *Kabuki* was danced by women, whereas *Nō* was performed entirely by men. During the earliest phase of *Kabuki*, when

50. Scene from the *Nō* play *Sumidagawa*

women and young men alike served as actors, the chief function of the performance was as a preliminary to prostitution.[156]

The *Kabuki* theatre and the prostitution quarter were the principal sources of urban popular culture in Tokugawa society. Both were officially regarded as evil, and both were banished to outlying areas of cities. In 1629 'female' theatre was banned; and in 1652, the 'young-boy' theatre that replaced it was likewise banned, on moral grounds. Thereafter, *Kabuki* was performed exclusively by adult males.[157] As in Chinese opera—or, indeed, European pantomime—female impersonation became a major acting skill; and, as acting positions became hereditary,

[156] Masakatsu Gunji, 'The Development of Kabuki', in Chie Nakone and Shinzaburō Ōishi, *Tokugawa Japan*, trans. Conrad Totman (Tokyo: University of Tokyo Press, 1990), 201.
[157] Ibid. 192, 195.

51. *Shamisen* player: coloured woodcut by Hokujei, early nineteenth century

acting roles developed their own particular specializations, so that *Kabuki* came to be distinguished by its stylization.

Enthusiasm for *Kabuki* was kindled by itinerant and regional companies, to such an extent that this music-dance-theatre genre soon became the most popular form of mass entertainment. Nevertheless, the theatre continued to be regarded as a focus of vice and lawlessness: indeed it was subjected to so many governmental restrictions that, in the early eighteenth century, playwrights began to write for puppets rather than actors. Puppet theatre had grown in popularity with ordinary folk, while *Kabuki* was establishing itself with the merchant class. For a while, and among all classes of society, *Bunraku* eclipsed *Kabuki* in popularity. Indeed, Chikamatsu, its major playwright, is often referred to as the 'Shakespeare of Japan'.[158]

[158] Lowe, *Inside Japan*, 44.

Bunraku puppets are rather more than half life-size; they are extremely sophisticated in construction, and even their facial expressions can be altered. Their operators appear below them, kneeling, dressed in black. The text is delivered by a single singer, who accompanies himself on the *shamisen*, in a separate space, usually stage left. (The *shamisen* is a three-string, long-necked, unfretted lute, plucked with a large ivory or ivory-tipped plectrum; its relatively small soundbox has a snakeskin table (Pl. 51).) The playwrights vested in their puppet actors all the emotion and tension, cruelty, love, and pathos formerly vested in living actors. Because the action, though stylized, is at the same time extraordinarily realistic, *Bunraku* can be as gripping in its emotional impact as *Kabuki*.

The music may be declamatory, lyrical, *parlando*, or purely instrumental. The lyrical passages are in the movement types of *tōgaku* ('Tang music'): *jo*, *ha*, and *kyū* (prelude, broaching, and quick); and different patterns of instrumental music represent different moods, places, or situations. *Bunraku* is as lyrical, in the Western sense, as anything in Japanese traditional music, and is sometimes described as the 'Italian Opera of Japan'.

Kabuki recovered its ascendancy in the nineteenth century, by which time a long tradition of playwrights, plays, and 'star' actors belonging to guilds had come into existence.[159] These commonly protected the 'secrets' of the acting style of a family. In performance, actors are still encouraged by *kakegoe* (appreciative calls from the audience); and what is shouted is the stage name of the actor's family—his *yagō*. Appreciation is shown for the recitation of particular lines of the text, or for *mie* (poses performed at climatic moments, with crossing of the eyes, and nodding and rotation of the head). In *aragoto* ('wild matters') acting—the style of ruffians—these movements are exaggerated, as are make-up, costume, and diction. Other styles of acting include *wagoto* ('harmonious matters') and *sewa-goto* ('vernacular matters'). There are marvellous, set-piece, acting scenes—the distraught mother at the grave is one—eagerly awaited.[160] They represent melodrama at its height, as formal in its representation as (for example) the famous death scene of the countess in Tchaikovsky's *Queen of Spades*.

The *Kabuki* stage is wide and shallow and makes use both of scenery and backcloths. Importantly, to the audience's left is the 'Flower Path', a narrow extension running from the stage to the back of the theatre,

[159] W. P. Malm, 'Japan', *The New Grove* (1980), ix. 519. [160] Ibid. 522.

along which actors make their exits and entrances—a structure imitative of *Nō*.

The instruments of *Kabuki* vary according to the style of play and actor. Percussion, flute, and *shamisen* form the basis. Usually, the orchestra plays in a slatted room on stage right, but plays deriving from *Bunraku* have vocalist and *shamisen* player on stage left; while in plays deriving from *Nō*, up to eight each of vocalists and *shamisen* players are disposed on a red dais at the back of the stage, with drums and the *Nō* flute in front. An immense variety of sound effects is used: for example, a different pattern of drumbeat with *shamisen* may indicate a change in mood; and a wealth of gadgets makes possible a vast range of insect and other natural sounds.

Solo and Chamber Music during the Tokugawa Period

Throughout the Tokugawa period, *Kabuki* and *Bunraku* opened Japanese performing arts to a wider audience, by providing a less austere alternative to traditional forms of theatre. This popularization of the performing arts was also reflected in new solo music for three instruments, popular with the merchant class: the *shamisen* (long-necked lute), *koto* (zither), and *shakuhachi* (end-blown flute). During the nineteenth century, these instruments also combined in ensemble playing.

The *koto* is the oldest, dating back to the Nara period, and is the Japanese equivalent of Chinese *zheng* and Korean *kayagum*; it did not receive the special prominence among Japanese courtiers and gentry that it attained elsewhere in East Asia, but it was the instrument for which the blind *koto*-virtuoso Yatsuhashi Kengyō (1614–85) introduced the hemitonic *insen* scale (see p. 393) that was to influence so many genres of Japanese music.[161] The *shamisen* has already been described in the context of *Bunraku*; it was predominantly an accompanying instrument until the mid-nineteenth century, when it left the theatre and became accessible to female performers. The *shakuhachi*—developed from a South Chinese variety of *xiao*—appeared in Japan around the fourteenth century, but did not gain prominence until the mid-nineteenth century.

[161] W. Adriaansz, 'Japan', *The New Grove* (1980), ix. 529.

Instrumental music became popular only after the Meiji restoration (1868), when the standing of the merchant class rivalled that of the declining *Samurai*. As always in Japan, change was slow. Not until the mid-twentieth century was it considered 'respectable' to study *shamisen*; pieces derived from *tōgaku* ('Tang music') items dominated the music; and the *shakuhachi* music of the post-Tokugawa era retains the essentially slow, meditative, dispassionate aura characteristic of so much traditional Japanese music.[162]

Although such music remains popular, it is for the synthesis of music, dance, and drama, found in *Nō*, *Kabuki*, and *Bunraku*, that Japanese performing arts are best known and respected in the West. *Kabuki* may share some common characteristics with Chinese opera, and *Bunraku* with puppet traditions common throughout Asia; but both are peculiarly Japanese. *Nō* is unique. The native capacity for borrowing and absorbing, allied to the relentless discipline of Zen, created there a form that, in its impressively restrained power and elegance, is quintessentially Japanese and unlike anything else in the world.

The musics of East Asia, often lacking in the dynamism that is intrinsic to most other musics of Eurasia, can pose particular difficulties of understanding for Westerners. Of all Asian musics, the music of Japan is likely to seem the most alien. Westerners who wear Japanese watches, drive Japanese cars, and listen to their classical music on Japanese hi-fi (often played by Japanese artists) are not always aware of the traditional mores that support Japan's superstructure of Westernization. For evidence of this support, one need look no further than the cleanliness and supra-efficiency of public-transport systems, the courtesy of behaviour, or the apparent ease with which so many millions of people usually live peaceably and efficiently in a very restricted space. There are, of course, disadvantages to life in such a society, and few would suggest that Japan represents Utopia; but it is something approaching an apotheosis of human *order*, for which Japanese traditional culture has been responsible.

Not surprisingly, beneath the formalities of etiquette, Japan at times appears to be a somewhat confused society. Japanese schoolchildren perform occidental recorder music to the 'um-cha' of an electronic metronome, while 'London Bridge' is, at the time of writing, one of the songs required to be taught in Japanese infant schools. Indigenous music becomes increasingly peripheral in the educational curriculum as

[162] Kishibe, 'Japan', *The New Grove*, ix. 506.

Japanese children become ever more proficient on Western instruments. Yet formalities of behaviour ensure that schools—like trains, elevators, banking systems, and all the paraphernalia of a frenetic yet controlled hi-tech existence—work smoothly; and those formalities have strongly influenced the traditional arts which now, in turn, help to sustain them. Without its Shinto ceremonies, and its Confucian- and Zen-inspired social obligations and restrictions, it is possible to envisage the collapse of the whole structure of successful modern Japan. If for no other reason, Japanese arts, more than those of any other country discussed, are best appreciated in context. The peculiar correlation of past and present in Japan is such that it is the one country of which it seems unnecessary to add: record the past before it is too late.

Part Three

Europe

Western Europe

11 New Horizons

Scholars and Barbarians

In the year 1400, a group of Florentine businessmen returned from a visit to Constantinople with a copy of Ptolemy's *Guide to Geography*, a second-century text that described the world then known to the Greeks. Little of that world was known to Europeans of the early fifteenth century. Included in the *Guide* was the already familiar Ptolemaic understanding of the universe: the sun, the moon, the planets, and 'fixed' stars circling around the earth, with the 'ideal' realm beyond them. But the *Guide* also listed some 8,000 place names in Europe, Africa, and Asia; and it demonstrated the use of grid lines of longitude and latitude, and the calculation of geographical positions within them by astronomical means. Ptolemy's geography was far from accurate, but his *Guide* brought to European cartography a new, scientific, method of viewing the world as an entity. Metrification of the earth's surface enabled all points on a map to be placed proportionately distant from each other, and even unknown locations could be given coordinates.[1]

Ptolemy's *Guide to Geography* created a sensation. European maps had previously depicted small areas of newly discovered coastline, or else they had been illustrative and symbolic. Typically, they had consisted of three continents—representing the Trinity and the three sons of Noah—with Jerusalem at their centre. Towards the end of the fifteenth century, Europeans constructed a 'world map', based on Ptolemaic cartographical principles, mapped with grid lines of longitude

[1] James Burke, *The Day the Universe Changed* (London: BBC, 1985), 85.

and latitude, and displayed as the northern half of a sphere.[2] The map stretched from the Canary Islands to Sri Lanka; to the north was Iceland; to the south *terra incognita.* It contained a considerable element of guesswork; but the fact that its system of griding could be allied to the new science of perspective geometry, and so make possible the charting of a ship's course on the ocean, was of enormous significance to Europeans. It was this fact that gave Columbus the confidence to bid for a western route to the Spice Islands.[3]

Ptolemy's spherical universe was popularly depicted on the weary back and shoulders of the Greek Titan, Atlas, who, as punishment for rebelling against the gods, had been required to prop up the heavens over the earth. When, in 1585, Mercator published a large volume of maps, using his development of Ptolemy's system to project the then vastly increased European knowledge of the world, he called his book an atlas. It was to become a symbol for mastering the world.[4] With the compass from China and with improved maritime technology, mariners from Europe were able to sail the major sea routes of the globe. During the next three centuries, Europeans would dominate world trade and spend much of their time fighting each other over territory that was not properly theirs.

These restless, acquisitive, Europeans, who suddenly burst upon the world at the end of the fifteenth century, were of mixed ancestry. Their genes came not only from Celts, Goths, and Vikings, but also from the peoples of West and Central Asia. During the centuries between Christianity's *entente* with the pagan world in the ninth century and the Great Schism that terminally eroded papal hegemony in the fourteenth century, a synthesis of diverse cultural systems was formed, as invasions from three directions disturbed the calm of Europe's scholastic monasteries.

From the Hungarian plains to the east, Magyars in search of plunder moved quickly through Bavaria, and on through Gaul into Italy; they were beaten by the end of the tenth century and their pagan rites were assimilated into Christendom. To the south, Muslims occupied Sicily, Sardinia, Corsica, and the coastal areas of southern France, from whence pirates pillaged towns and monasteries in Italy. Upon them would shortly be unleashed the energy generated by the third and most vigorous of Europe's intruders, the Vikings.

[2] Until recently, this map was though to have been drawn by Ptolemy himself.
[3] Burke, *The Day the Universe Changed*, 84–9.
[4] *The Collins Atlas of World History*, ed. Pierre Vidal-Naquet (London: Collins, 1986), p. vii.

Norwegians were the first Viking peoples to discover the wealth of European monasteries and the possibility of settlement in more hospitable lands than their own. Britain first felt their force; but it was soon felt also on the northern coasts of France and Spain, and subsequently on the southern coasts of France and Italy. South of the Baltic, Vikings from Sweden traded with Muslims in Kiev, where they were eventually Slavicized. In the north, Danes followed the Norwegians, and then moved inland, establishing colonial bases in Britain and France.[5] These Viking Scandinavians infused Europe with a restless energy, bringing its peoples into warring—though instructive—contact with its more advanced and exalted neighbours. Few at the time could have foreseen that these 'Northmen' or 'Normans' would cooperate with Christian bishops and give their name to a unique form of architecture.[6]

Muslims and Jews were the first victims of the new European restlessness. Not only were Muslims occupying much of southern Europe and the Levant, but the advance of the Seljuk Turks had blocked the pilgrim route to Jerusalem. To Europeans of the eleventh century, Jerusalem was the centre of the world. The Christian Church therefore turned Muslim practice against the practitioners; the pope called for a 'Holy War'—a Christian *jihad*—against the Muslims, and offered a plenary indulgence (forgiveness of all sins) to those who would fight in it. During the following half-century, Christian armies drove the Muslims from Europe; and in 1099 the First Crusade brought Jerusalem under Christian control.

The Crusades epitomized the barbarism of Europe at this time: they were bloody, senseless, and incompetent. During the sack of Jerusalem in 1099, no man, woman, or child was spared; the Jews were burnt alive.[7] A Second Crusade, responding to loss of Levantine territory, began with a slaughter of Jews in the Rhineland, failed to reclaim any land, and disgraced the knightly aristocracy of Europe.

When in 1187 Saladin recaptured Jerusalem for the Muslims, he spared all Christians and permitted them to keep churches for Christian worship. (The Qur'ān recognized the sectarian rights of all 'Peoples of the Book'.) Notwithstanding this, the Christians organized a Third Crusade to recapture the city, which not only failed in its objective but saw the drowning of a German emperor and the imprisonment of an

[5] *The Times Atlas of World History*, ed. Geoffrey Barraclough (London, 1989), 110.
[6] Bamber Gascoigne, *The Christians* (London: Jonathan Cape, 1977), 73.
[7] Ibid. 113.

English king. The Fourth Crusade, at the beginning of the thirteenth century, set out for Egypt in ships provided by Venice. The crusaders were diverted to Constantinople, where they sacked the city, slaughtered its Christian inhabitants, and looted its treasures, many of which finished up in Venice and are now in the Treasury of San Marco. This Fourth Crusade had the effect of completely separating the two halves of the old Roman Empire; henceforth Byzantium and Western Christendom would follow different cultural paths.

Christians and Muslims

The Crusades were an important catalyst in the establishment of a new and distinctive European civilization from a mixture of Judaic, Graeco-Egyptian, and Islamic influences. The Crusaders themselves were a mixed bunch, comprising princes and prelates, knights and aristocrats, mercenaries and conscripts, zealots and criminals, with many conflicting motives for their 'crusading'.

There is evidence, for example, that Godfroi de Bouillon, who instigated and led the First Crusade, and was declared 'Governor of Jerusalem' in 1099, was a direct descendant of a Merovingian, Guillem de Gellone, who had established a renowned academy of Judaic learning at Gellone. (Guillem's father, Theoderic, was recognized both by the Frankish King and the Baghdadian Caliph as being of 'the seed of the royal house of David'.) Both Godfroi and Guillem are associated with the Holy Grail in Wolfram von Eschenbach's romances; in many versions of the Lohengrin story, Godfroi is the son or grandson of Lohengrin's child. Wolfram, writing at the turn of the thirteenth century, makes clear that his *Parzival* romance was originally of Judaic origin and reached Western Europe from Muslim Spain over the Pyrenees.[8] (Wagner visited Rennes-le-Château in the Pyrenees before writing 'Parsifal'.)

Associated with Godfroi de Bouillon was the military Order of the Knights Templar, nine of whose founding members had followed Godfroi to Jerusalem. The Templars—like the later Freemasons, with whom they have been linked[9]—took their name from the Egyptian-

[8] Michael Baigent, Richard Leigh, and Henry Lincoln, *The Holy Blood and The Holy Grail* (London: Corgi Books, 1983), 279, 307, 417.

[9] John J. Robinson, *Born in Blood: The Lost Secrets of Freemasonry* (New York: M. Evans, 1989).

inspired Temple of Solomon. They owed allegiance to no authority other than the pope; by the middle of the twelfth century, they owned substantial estates throughout Europe and the Holy Land, and had established themselves as international bankers. Their contacts with Islamic and Judaic culture kept them aware of new developments in building, surveying, map-making, and navigation; and the Templars had their own sea ports and shipyards, their own military and commercial fleet.[10] They have been credited with providing the impetus for the building of Gothic cathedrals.

The Templars were not alone in having links with the Muslims. Spanish kings of the thirteenth century described themselves as 'Kings of the Three Religions'. So did kings of Sicily, who controlled the Mediterranean sea routes and by the beginning of the thirteenth century were presiding over the richest state in Europe. Frederick II (Holy Roman Emperor 1214–50) was brought up in Sicily, which had been controlled successively by Greeks, Carthaginians, Byzantines, Arabs, and—more recently—Viking 'Normans'. In Sicily, Frederick was host to Greek, Arab, Jewish, and Italian scholars; he maintained a harem and was known as 'the baptized sultan'. The pope excommunicated him, but Frederick led a Sixth Crusade in which, without drawing his sword, he negotiated a treaty that gave Jerusalem to the Christians, on condition that Muslims and Jews could continue working there.[11]

In 1307 the Templars' main body was brutally liquidated by Philip IV of France, but many survived the pogrom against them; a year later, when the Albigensian Crusade was launched against the heretic Cathars of the Languedoc, Cathars swelled the depleted ranks of the Templars. In England, Templar lands were consigned to the more compliant Knights Hospitaller of St John; but Scotland became a refuge for knights from France and England: many fought at the Battle of Bannockburn in 1314, and it appears likely that the Templars instigated the Peasants' Revolt of 1381 (which targeted in particular properties of the Knights Hospitaller).[12] In Portugal, the Templars changed their name to Knights of Christ. Henry the Navigator was a Grand Master of the Order, Vasco da Gama was a Knight of Christ, and Columbus himself was married to the daughter of a former Knight of Christ and so had access to Templar charts and diaries.[13] Were it not for the Templars

[10] Ibid. 73–8. [11] Gascoigne, *The Christians*, 123, 128.
[12] Robinson, *Born in Blood*, 3–46.
[13] Baigent, Leigh, and Lincoln, *The Holy Blood*, 75.

and their Muslim contacts, Columbus might never have reached the Americas.

Poets and Minstrels

If this formative period of European history is largely cloaked in romance, it is because medieval literature and song so often equated chivalric love and duty with Christian love and duty. The medieval concept of *fin' amors* ('refined love')—or 'gentil lovying' as Chaucer put it—centred on *joi*, the joy of a love whose presence brings wisdom and whose absence brings destruction:[14] 'he who has loved faithfully in his own country must keep alive the memory of this love wherever he goes....'[15] *Fin' amors* exalted the status of the individual.

Muslims had developed a similar concept of refined and erotic love which was also expressed through song; the surviving poems have a strophic construction similar to that of European courtly songs.[16] Medieval Europe was not greatly different from the Islamic world that surrounded its southern flanks.

The outpouring of songs reflecting European *fin' amors* was the work of the twelfth century troubadours who wrote in Provençal (*langue d'oc*: old language of southern France); they were followed by the *trouvères*, who wrote in French (*langue d'oeil*: old language of northern France); and then by the *Minnesinger* of Germany. There has been some reluctance to accept direct Islamic influence on these songs, but, in the light of the historical facts, it seems inconceivable that these medieval minstrels—many of whom were indeed 'wandering'—were not influenced by Islamic precedents. The songs became popular in Spain: long before the Jews were expelled from the Iberian peninsula in the late fifteenth century, rabbis were complaining of the popularity of troubadour songs in the Jewish community.[17]

The musical notation of a collection of some 400 Spanish *cantigas*, made during the second half of the thirteenth century under the supervision of Alfonso, King of Castile and León, is similar to that of the songs

[14] John Stevens, 'Troubadours and Trouvères', *The New Grove* (1980), xix. 191.

[15] From an anonymous French *trouvère* song.

[16] Stevens, 'Troubadours and Trouvères', *The New Grove*, xix. 190–3.

[17] Judith R. Cohen, 'The Impact of Mass Media and Acculturation on the Judeo-Spanish Song Tradition in Montreal', in Simon Frith (ed.), *World Music, Politics, and Social Change* (Manchester: Manchester University Press 1979), 90.

of the troubadours and *trouvères*. The poems recount miracles accomplished through the intervention of the Virgin Mary, and the location of the miracles extends from Syria to Scotland. One such tale re-emerges in England as Chaucer's *Prioress's Tale*.[18] The poems deal with everyday, down-to-earth themes, and were sometimes fitted to popular tunes.

Alfonso was an admirer of Islamic as well as of Roman and Visigothic culture, and his court was a meeting place for Christian, Islamic, and Jewish scholars and artists. It was also a refuge for troubadours of the Languedoc fleeing the Albigensian Crusade. Miniatures depict a variety of instruments: bowed fiddle, rebec, and *rebāb*; plucked guitar, lute, psaltery, zither, and harp; shawm, double-shawm, bagpipes, transverse flute, pipe, and recorder; trumpet, horn, and tromba; portative organ; drums, tabors, clappers, castanets, cymbals, and chime bells (Pl. 52). It is known that, of twenty-seven musicians in the employ of Alfonso's son, thirteen were Arabs, Persians, or 'Moors', and one was a Jew.[19]

Many instruments from Islamic West Asia must have filtered into Europe with the *reconquista* and the Crusades. For example, bowed instruments—which, despite their sustaining power, were generally less favoured than plucked instruments in Islamic culture—reached northern Europe via Spain, and eventually became a mainstay of European music.[20] Because instrumental heterophony, drones, and improvised preludes occur in Islamic art music and in much European and Turkish folk music, and indeed in the early practice of Roman and Byzantine chant, it is probable that European courtly songs, too, employed such devices: the sound of a drone is intrinsic to the playing of such instruments as the hurdy-gurdy, and most European bagpipes (Pl. 53). (The hurdy-gurdy lost its social standing during the fourteenth and fifteenth centuries, when solo, monophonic music was going out of fashion.[21]) Folk music from Latvia to Greece can still be found with choral as well as instrumental drones, sometimes supporting two-part polyphony.[22]

The function of the minstrels of medieval Europe was similar to that of the story tellers and folk entertainers across Asia: for example, the

[18] 'Cantigas de Santa Maria', *NOCM* (1983).

[19] Jack Sage, 'Cantiga' and 'Alfonso el Sabio', *The New Grove* (1980), iii. 726; i. 253.

[20] David Munrow, *Instruments of the Middle Ages and Renaissance* (London: Oxford University Press, 1976), 27.

[21] Howard Mayer Brown, 'Performing Practice', *The New Grove* (1980), xiv. 371–5.

[22] Lilija Zobens, 'Parallels Between Balkan and Latvian Folk Music', unpublished paper presented to ICTM UK, 1992.

52. King Alfonso supervises clerical and secular scribes compiling *cantigas*; musicians with bowed and plucked string instruments are in attendance

53. *Music and her Attendants*: fourteenth-century miniature illustrating the *De arithmetica* of Boethius. Above the central figure of Music (playing the portative organ) are players of 'soft' instruments (fiddle, psaltery, and lute); below are the 'loud' instruments (bagpipes, shawn, nakers, and trumpet)

shā'ir of Persia, the *ashik* of Turkey, the Kathkali dancers of India, the *mawlam* of Laos, the *tanci* singers of China, the *p'ansori* singers of Korea. Their mixture of improvised and memorized narrative and song, and of acting, dancing, juggling, and acrobatics, is paralleled in folk theatre and puppet theatre throughout India, South East Asia, and North East Asia: for example, in Burmese *zat pwe*, in Chinese opera, and in Japanese *Kyōgen Nō*. In Europe, such entertainment led to the *Commedia dell'arte* and, subsequently, to opera. Only in Islam was there an injunction against secular performances, but even in the Islamic heartland, folk-singing took place; the lighter styles of *nawba* were essentially popular secular music; and the comic, shadow-puppet play survives in Turkey to this day, as it does in China and South East Asia. As with many of its Asian counterparts, European minstrelsy was a mixture of aristocratic composition and unlettered talent.

The minstrels were of many different kinds, from poor vagabonds—providing rough entertainment in towns and villages—to educated musicians associated with aristocratic society.[23] As early as the seventh century, the Anglo-Saxon *Widsith* ('wide-traveller') referred to minstrels singing of the deeds of past heroes in courts throughout Germanic Europe. The twelfth-century Giraldus Cambrensis described part-singing in Wales and Northumbria, and the accomplishments of instrumentalists in Wales and Ireland.[24]

Throughout the Middle Ages, epics and ballads in the vernacular (*chansons de geste* in northern France, *cantigas de gesta* in Spain), fitted to short, simple musical phrases, were sung by wandering minstrels. Songs in Latin were performed by the Goliards—wandering scholars and ecclesiastics, whose scurrilous poems contained a mixture of polemic, social satire, and bawdy humour.[25] The songs of the troubadours and *trouvères*, by contrast, testified to the growing sophistication of Europe's secular élite; though often *performed* by itinerant *joglars* (*jongleurs* in northern France), they were *composed* by literate aristocrats.

It would be wrong to exaggerate Arab–Persian influence on European music: European counterpoint and harmony developed in the musical culture of the Christian Church; but that culture was certainly in close contact with folk practices of all kinds. It is worth noting the

[23] Brown, 'Performing Practice', *The New Grove*, xiv. 373.

[24] Gerald of Wales, *Journey through Wales and the Description of Wales*, trans. Lewis Thorpe (London: Penguin Books, 1978), 242.

[25] Gordon A. Anderson, 'Goliards', *The New Grove* (1980), vii. 508.

extent to which the music of the troubadours burst the limited bounds of the European ecclesiastical modal system. The songs display a variety of chromatic, non-modal notes, of narrow and wide compass, and they exhibit variety in the relationship between final note and melodic contours. Many of the melodies involve shifts of tonal centre.[26] All these features are to be found in the classical music of West Asia.

Whether the minstrel songs were performed in free rhythm, or according to the ecclesiastical rhythmic modes codified in the thirteenth century, is still not clear. Rhythmic modes were, of course, nothing new to Asia, and it is likely that the European songs were performed in a variety of rhythmic styles. Some may have been performed rhapsodically, reflecting the West Asian *taksim*, or the fact—as observed in the context of Safavid Persia—that practised skill is needed to perform new or improvised material over a complex, regularly recurring rhythmic cycle. Most probably, songs were sung in the simplest rhythm consonant with the scansion of the text.

In literary terms, the troubadour and *trouvère* songs display a high level of sophistication. Dante (1265–1321)—whose choice of Virgil to guide him through Hell, Purgatory, and Paradise most vividly exemplifies the medieval marriage of pagan with Christian—was among those who commented on the construction of vernacular poetry. In his treatise *De vulgari eloquentia*, he stated that 'the *cantio* is the passion or action itself of singing, just as the *lectio* is the passion or action of reading'. He referred to the need for formal melodic structures of stanzas, and for the harmonious proportioning of lines and rhymes. *Armonia*—a concord of sounds—is, he averred, fundamental to the poet's art.[27]

By this time, however, new secular art forms were emerging from the cloisters of the Christian Church.

Theology and Humanism

The most conspicuous symbol of ecclesiastical power, during the Middle Ages, was the building of 'Gothic' cathedrals across northern Europe during the twelfth and thirteenth centuries; it was in the shadow of these great cathedrals that Europeans developed an intellectual and artistic culture that differed in many important

[26] Theodore Karp, 'Troubadours, Trouvères', *The New Grove* (1980), xix. 199.

[27] Stevens, 'Troubadours, Trouvères', *The New Grove*, xix. 196.

aspects from these aspects in other civilizations. The thrusting spires and towers of medieval European cathedrals, and their graceful, soaring interiors, still attest to the extraordinary confidence of those who created them. Imposing temples had been built before; but none had been built quite so high, or with such spacious, lofty interiors. It was intended that the eye should be drawn upwards. 'The dull mind rises to truth from that which is material,'[28] wrote Abbot Suger, the man who was responsible for the first of these Gothic buildings. And on the doors of his Clunaic Abbey of St. Denis, in the suburbs of Paris (*c.*1140), he had inscribed these words: 'The windows will lead you to Christ.'[29]

For the intellectual and technological confidence that inspired these great cathedrals it is necessary to look again to Islam, this time to the reconquest of Spain. The Muslims were the preservers of Greek scholarship, and they added to the knowledge of the Greeks much of their own. The civilization of Andalusia was one of the most splendid in the world of its time. The great library in the Alcazar of Cordobá, for example, contained over 400,000 books covering a wealth of subjects: medicine, astronomy, physiology, zoology, chemistry, pharmacology, physics, mathematics, optics, meteorology, mechanics, hydrostatics, geography, navigation—and music. Similar centres of learning existed throughout Spain.[30] When Toledo passed to the Christians in 1085, a great body of knowledge, newly made available, roused Europe from centuries of intellectual torpor. The most influential aspect of this knowledge was that of Aristotelian logic.

It was Ibn Sina (980–1037), known to the West as Avicenna—a Persian doctor born in Central Asia and also a noted musician—who made clear what Aristotle's philosophy was really about. Not only could—and should—nature be questioned; it was possible to verify this questioning through the logical process of the syllogism, through which two assumed premisses could be used to deduce a conclusion. 'Use systematic doubt and question everything,' wrote Pierre Abelard, leading twelfth-century intellectual and scourge of ecclesiastical dogma: 'By doubting we come to enquiry; by enquiring we perceive the truth.'[31] In a great work of dialectic, *Sic et Non* ('Yes and No'), Abelard questioned the reality of universal truth. For this he was condemned by St Bernard.

[28] Kenneth Clark, *Civilisation* (London: Harper & Row, 1969), 50.
[29] Burke, *The Day the Universe Changed*, 52.
[30] Ibid. 36.
[31] Cited in ibid. 44.

Rational thinking was naturally unattractive to a Church whose dogma was based on revelation; but it proved too compelling to be halted. Paris became a centre for theology and dialectic; by the year 1200, that centre would include a university, with its private army conferred by royal decree.

The effect of the new learning was to bring philosophy and theology to a critical state of conflict. A Muslim philosopher, Ibn Rushd, known to the West as Averroes—or simply 'The Commentator'—had held that the existence of God can be proved by reason. He had then applied reason to the act of creation and challenged the concept of free will. His writings were burned by the Caliph of Cordobá, on the grounds that Allah had decreed hell-fire for those who thought truth could be found through unaided reason.[32] In Christian Paris, where Ibn Rushd's stock was high—even among Dominicans and Franciscans sent thither by the pope to stem the tide of rational thought—the 'Averroists' eventually adopted a doctrine known as the 'double truth', in which theology and philosophy were sundered: reason was henceforth the ground of philosophy; revelation, that of theology.

It was St Thomas Aquinas who applied the 'double truth' to reconcile reason with revelation in a form acceptable to the Church. He held that some things *could* be explained through reason: by way of example he provided five proofs of God's existence. Other things, he averred, could not: he instanced the Christian requirement of baptism, which was revealed in St John's gospel. By the same token, God could do certain things but not others. Among the things he *could* do was to forgive or punish sins; but he could not Himself commit sins, nor could He 'make the sum of the internal angles of a triangle add up to more than two right-angles'.[33] An altar-painting in Santa Caterina at Pisa shows St Thomas receiving the works of Aristotle, along with the Christian precepts of God, Moses, the Evangelists, and St Paul; Averroes lies at Thomas's feet, defeated,[34] though in truth he could lay equal claim to be the 'inventor', *via* St Thomas, of Christianity. The great theological *summa* of this scholastic age may be compared with the great cathedrals—as indeed to the music of the *Ars Nova* written for them—in their great breadth and height, and in the logic of their articulation and subdivision.[35]

[32] Bertrand Russell, *History of Western Philosophy* (Woking: Allen & Unwin, 1946), 474.
[33] Ibid. 480–2.
[34] Gascoigne, *The Christians*, 127.
[35] *Collins Atlas*, 122.

The importance of the new learning to European civilization can scarcely be overestimated. The compromise implicit in the new theology gave juridical consent to humanism. Understanding would no longer arise from belief, for belief became consequent upon understanding. Logic freed education from its episcopal confines: the 'University of Masters and Pupils' in Paris, for example, initially governed by the pope, became independent of episcopal power. Learning passed from monasteries to universities, which grew up alongside cathedrals as itinerant teachers settled in them. Episcopal responsibility for school education then passed to the secular chapters, and subsequently to parish churches.

Humanism—and the secularism it engendered—would lie at the heart of European intellectual and artistic culture. Human beings could henceforth escape the shackles of original sin and exercise their creative faculties in the belief that human nature is innately good; nude male and female bodies, for example, could be seen as the fruit of divine love rather than of an original transgression.[36] Above all, European civilization would—uniquely—evolve in the light of scientific discovery. The notion of 'progress' would become intrinsic to European culture; and the consequent conflict between religious precept, and scientific concept, would provide the essential dynamic of Europe's creativity. Slowly but surely, Western art would become removed from the religious, 'spiritual' source of its inspiration.

Musical Notation and the Composer

The process whereby revealed Christian precepts gave way to rational humanistic concepts was mirrored in the development of ecclesiastical music. It has already been noted (in Chapter 5) that the early medieval theorist, Boethius, classified the consonance of musical intervals on the basis of their mathematical ratios; that he equated music with behaviour; and that his *De institutione musica* was invoked by the Carolingians as the standard theoretical text when they set about unifying Christian chant. Boethius had defined the system of seven diatonic scales and had given to them Greek ethnic names used by Aristoxenus some 800 years earlier for scalic structures.

[36] Ibid. 146.

Two ninth-century treatises developed Boethius' work by attempting a synthesis between what was known of classical Greek theory and the Byzantine *oktōēchos* ('eight melody-types' (see p. 137)). Hucbald's *De harmonica institutione* included the Boethian system of tetrachords within a double octave but, importantly, used a different interval pattern for the tetrachords themselves: D to G (as represented on the white keys of the piano, replacing the Greek model of E to A, with its different melodic feel). The anonymous *Alia musica* categorized the existing eight Church modes and assigned to them the names that they retained throughout the Middle Ages and Renaissance.[37]

A significant feature of this system was that a mode was recognized solely by its *final* note. As polyphonic composition developed, this caused increasing confusion as to what mode was in use; working from Greek and Muslim precedents, theorists could scarcely comprehend a system devoid of modal structure. During the eleventh century, therefore, the pitches used for *intermediate cadences* were discriminated; by the early fourteenth century, Marchettus of Padua's *Lucidarium* (1318) was classifying the *function* of notes in various modes, in an attempt to understand what intervals and progressions are decisive in establishing a particular mode. During the fifteenth century, key signatures of one or two flats were introduced, and this led to another reclassification of the modes; but, by this time, practice was overtaking theory. The modal system was proving incapable of embracing polyphonic procedures. As early as the thirteenth century, the French theorist, Johannes de Grocheo, had indicated that modes and polyphony are incompatible.[38] By the end of the sixteenth century, it would be possible for Church music to exist quite independently of the plainchant from which it evolved.

During the course of the sixteenth century it became clear that the Ionian (major) mode was that most widely used. Major and minor modes—with all their attendant tonal possibilities through harmony and harmonic modulation—would subsequently give to Western music that expressive quality which is today admired throughout most of the world.

This system was made possible by the development of precise musical notation, itself made necessary by the developing complexities of polyphonic ecclesiastical music. In the early eleventh century, Guido of Arezzo conceived the idea of the multi-line staff (originally coloured),

[37] David Hiley, 'Mode', *NOCM* (1983). [38] Ibid.

and also of a sol-fa system. The latter, unknown to Guido, was very similar to that described by Nārada in India, over 500 years earlier—and such syllabic, oral notations were, and are, widespread in Asia. The use of staff notation, however, was a peculiarly European development; and when, towards the end of the twelfth century, European scholars discriminated set patterns of ligatures (indications of slurred notes), in association with the six ecclesiastical rhythmic modes (all in duple compound time), a system for notating rhythm was also developed. The ligatures named by medieval scholars were universal units, used worldwide; but the system of accurate musical notation to which they led caused European music to depend on notation, rather than on oral–aural tradition, for its transmission. It was this development, perhaps more than any other, that marked European musical culture apart from all others.

Exact musical notation led to another phenomenon peculiar to European musical culture: the composer. The silent act of composition became an entity in itself, separate from the art of performance. Other musical systems used predetermined compositions, but they depended for their effect on the exercise of interpretative *manner* by the performer. Only in Europe did notation develop to such a degree of complexity as to make the performer the servant of the *composer*; elsewhere the performer was the servant of *music*.[39] The separation of the roles of composer and performer led to physically overwhelming effusions, in sound, of human thought and feeling: at its best, European music, like so much African and Asian music, represents an indivisible union of mind and emotion. It also created a distinctively European cerebral hierarchy of musical *value*; and it was to lead to a new concept of musical 'genius' as a product of exceptional, and radical, individuality.

The 'Notre Dame' School

Notation was invented in the monasteries. Composers, however, were able to exercise their craft in the shadow of the new Gothic cathedrals. An innovative school of composers was associated with Notre-Dame cathedral in Paris; and the Notre-Dame school is the first in which named composers emerge from the anonymity of the Middle Ages. Work on the construction of the cathedral

[39] Peter Fletcher, *Education and Music* (Oxford: Oxford University Press, 1987), 60.

started in 1163, and the high altar was consecrated in 1182. The *Magnus liber*, a great book of *organa* of the Notre-Dame school, said to have been produced by Léonin and revised by Pérotin, was contemporary with the building.[40]

Organum had originally consisted in the addition of a parallel musical line to a plainchant, at the distance of a fourth or fifth from the melodic line of the chant; by the beginning of the twelfth century, it consisted in the addition of a floridly melismatic part. The speed and complexity of such a part, with ten or more notes to one syllable of the original chant, demanded that the original chant be drawn out into long, held notes. With the Notre-Dame school, the florid part was called *discantus* ('sounding apart'), and the lower part *tenor* (from *tenere*: 'to hold'). By the thirteenth century, Pérotin was composing two or three such *discantus* parts above the *tenor*. Usually these florid polyphonic compositions alternated with choral unison singing of the plainchant.[41]

The practice of polyphony demanded a rhythmic structure in ensemble: the medieval rhythmic modes, as explained by Johannes de Garlandia in his *De mensurabilis musica* of 1240, gave to these great *organa* a dynamic propulsion that appears to have been something new in European ecclesiastical music. Considerably less complex than the rhythmic modes of Asia, the notated rhythmic modes of Europe led eventually to the now ubiquitous barline. The European concern with symmetry of *beat* affords an interesting contrast to, for example, the asymmetrical *aksak* ('limping' rhythms) of much Romanian, Bulgarian, and Turkish folk music, a feature—as already indicated—common to folk and art music from the Balkans to the Bay of Bengal.

A different use of *discantus* was in pieces called *conductus*: Latin songs, with texts in strongly accented rhyming poetry, used for processional purposes. Originating in Sicily and Aquitaine, such songs were taken up by Notre-Dame composers and set, in up to four parts, either with one chord per syllable, or in ornate forms with long melismas. Not all *conductus* settings were religious; some included political and topical comment.[42]

The sacred and the secular constantly interrelate during the Middle Ages. One area of contact was in liturgical drama. Dialogues at Eastertide, relating to symbolic processions to Christ's tomb, had been

[40] Rudolf Flotzinger, 'Magnus Liber', *The New Grove* (1980), xi. 500.
[41] David Hiley, 'Organum', *NOCM* (1983).
[42] David Hiley, 'Conductus', *NOCM* (1983).

common since at least the tenth century; and the rhythmical *conductus* had been associated with such processions. By the thirteenth century, more elaborate dramas became common: the Passion and Easter plays of the *Carmina Burana* (from Austria) and the Play of Daniel (from Beauvais) are among the best known. The Miracle and Mystery plays, performed in England from the end of the fourteenth century onwards, were fully developed dramas, with alternation of pathos and comedy, verse and slapstick, prefiguring Shakespeare and Marlowe. Most of the music is lost, but it seems that soft music was associated with spirituality, loud music with temporal power.[43] We cannot be sure how music dramas in Asia would have sounded at this time—for example, Passion plays in Shi'ite Islam, or *zaxi* (song and dance acts, and plays) in China—but it is evident that, already, the music of European dramatic genres, with its embryonic harmony and counterpoint, was developing in a very different manner from that of corresponding genres elsewhere.

It was in the motet that sacred and secular themes first joined forces. Complex polyphony required professionally trained soloists, and the rise of polyphony enabled both composers and performers to extend their virtuosity. It is important to realize that polyphonic constructions were not originally conceived as whole compositions. The *tenor* was taken—or adapted—from plainchant, and was presented in a given rhythmic mode; above this *tenor*, flowing melodic lines were added at will, according to circumstance and need.[44] 'Troping'—adding new words to long melismas to facilitate memory of the melodic line—was a developed art, applied equally to Latin or vernacular texts. From such troping there developed, in the thirteenth century, a peculiar form of motet, the *tenor* of which was of ecclesiastical origin, while the upper parts might include a mixture of Latin and the vernacular, with devotional or profane content. Some texts even alluded to political matters or attacked the vices of the clergy.[45] It is significant that these developments were spearheaded in Paris (where the university had recently freed itself from papal control), and were contemporary with the writings of St Thomas Aquinas.

[43] John Stevens, 'Medieval Drama', *The New Grove* (1980), xii. 22 ff.
[44] Nino Pirrotta, 'Medieval', *The New Grove* (1980), xii. 19–20.
[45] John Caldwell, 'Medieval', *NOCM* (1983).

The *Ars Nova*

From the emerging humanism of the late thirteenth century, a new school of composition, now known as the *Ars Nova*, emerged during the following century. Many of the conventions that would characterize Renaissance music flowed from this school. An important development was the freeing of ecclesiastical music from ternary rhythm, symbolic of the Holy Trinity. In his *Ars cantus mensurabilis* (*c.*1260), Franco of Cologne had already pioneered a form of rhythmic notation facilitating the freeing of performance from the constraints of modal rhythm. A treatise attributed to Philippe de Vitry (*c.*1322)—from which the term *Ars Nova* originated—introduced shorter time values and, most importantly, the concept of a time signature.[46] Although bar lines were not written until the seventeenth century, the concept of regularly recurring strong and weak beats was henceforth to condition the flow of European music, to the extent that the introduction of a 5/4 time signature in a symphony in the nineteenth century (Tchaikovsky's Sixth) was considered revolutionary. The growing complexity of polyphonic music in Europe affected metre and rhythm in a manner quite different from the rhythm of other musical styles of the world. It still tends to condition the Western response to such styles.

One outcome of fourteenth-century notational developments was an attempt to coordinate increasingly elaborate rhythms with increasingly elaborate melodies. In the motets of the thirteenth century, a rhythmic formula had been superimposed on the chosen *tenor*, but this rhythm—as with rhythmic cycles in many non-European musics—did not necessarily move in conjunction with the upper, melodic lines. Moreover, the swinging *discantus* of thirteenth-century music had thrown into relief the pivotal nature of the *tenor*, which had assumed an increasingly tonal, harmonic, function. A particular feature of the *Ars Nova* was *isorhythm* ('in the same rhythm'), a modern term for the process of repeating a rhythmic pattern, in equal time values, in augmentation or in diminution, in order to effect greater unity in an extended piece, such as a motet. By the end of the fourteenth century, this process was being applied to all the voices; and these now included a *contratenor* to support the *tenor*. This gradually led to an equalization of parts, in terms both of rhythmic density, and of melodic shape.

[46] Pirrotta, 'Medieval', *The New Grove*, xii. 18.

(A similar tendency towards equalization of parts was evident in England, where sequences of 6/3 chords in parallel were already in use in the fourteenth century. During the fifteenth century, the English feeling for chords and chord progressions—probably the most important single development in the course of medieval European music—came to be described in France as the *contenance angloise*, 'English guise', and influenced the Netherlands school of Dufay and Binchois.)

The most acclaimed composer of the *Ars Nova* was Machaut. His Mass is one of the earliest 'one-composer' settings (employing both isorhythmic style, and *conductus*, or note-against-note, style), but his most influential achievement was his secular output. The *ballades* and *rondeaux*, in the tradition of troubadour and *trouvère* song, dealt with themes of chivalric love; but their melodic lines show a song-like expressiveness, new in polyphonic music, that was to influence the rise of the Italian madrigal. His instrumental *tenors*, often supported by a *contratenor*, were no longer drawn from the repertoire of plainchant, but were freely composed, or taken from popular music.[47] In applying to secular genres the formal techniques of church music, Machaut effectively transformed the Latin motet of the Middle Ages into the French chanson of the Renaissance.

Popes, Princes, and Artists

'The Middle Ages' of Europe connotes a period in which the separate offices of priest and king, pope and emperor, failed to establish a coherent relationship. When a grateful Rome gave the imperial crown to the German king who defeated the Magyars in the late tenth century, it also gave away the right to supervise papal elections; and German emperors subsequently arrogated to themselves the right to appoint bishops, whom they then used as instruments of government. Throughout the Middle Ages, the Church—itself no respecter of royal prerogatives—actively resisted this secular usurpation of religious prerogatives.

The Crusades enabled the popes to present themselves as *diplomatic* leaders of the lay rulers, and so to focus the attention of these rulers on Rome rather than on the empire.[48] Gradually, a political structure

[47] Gilbert Reaney, 'Machaut', *The New Grove* (1980), xi. 429–30.
[48] J. M. Roberts, *Pelican History of the World* (London: Pelican Books, 1988), 463.

formed around the Holy See, and decrees came to be promulgated in the pope's name. At the end of the twelfth century—a high point in the fortunes of the papacy—Pope Innocent III had established a papal state, in central Italy, for the protection of Rome. Having won England and France to his side, he elaborated—in his *Venerabilem* (1202)—the notion of a pontifical theocracy, in which the pope would have universal juridical power.[49]

With the accession of Frederick II—the 'baptized sultan'—to the imperial crown in 1214, the Sicilian empire was added to the German and North Italian territories of the Holy Roman Empire, threatening papal hegemony, and causing France to be enlisted in the papal cause. French victories in Italy, however, only brought the papacy into conflict with the nascent nation states of France and England. In 1302 Pope Boniface VIII arrogantly declared belief in the sovereignty of the pope to be essential to salvation. For that, he was arrested by the kings of France and England. Then, in 1309, a French pope was elected to succeed Boniface, and chose to reside, not in Rome, but in Avignon. This marked the end of the Holy Roman Empire as an effective political unit.

The French popes who succeeded Boniface lived in unprecedented luxury while presiding over a world of increasing squalor, superstition, and cruelty. Growing criticism of their worldliness forced the institution back to Italy in 1377. Thereafter, for thirty years, national interests resulted in the election of two popes, each claiming leadership of the Church. In 1409, indeed, there were three. As the moral authority of the papacy entered irreversible decline, the Holy See became just one more Italian state: the feudal inheritance from the barbarian raids of the first millennium was becoming transformed into city and nation states. By the end of the fifteenth century, England, France, and Spain had become 'new monarchies'; Italy was a patchwork of powerful, competitive city states; and the Holy Roman Empire appeared as a conglomerate of principalities and bishoprics, presided over by an emperor who lacked the authority of royal power. Europe was coming of age: popes and princes would in future be counterbalanced by merchants and artists.

Literature had already moved from Latin to the vernacular. The French Romances, in verse, by Chrétien de Troyes, had appeared in the late twelfth century; the tales of the Welsh *Mabinogion* had appeared in

[49] *Collins Atlas*, 98.

writing in the early fourteenth century, to which period belong also Dante, Longland, and Chaucer. All had described a world that accepted, as axiomatic, a distinction between knowledge and belief, between the human and the divine. Moreover, Giotto's statuesque style of painting had given way to one which made use of movement, light, and an advanced knowledge of the workings of the human anatomy, to enable art to imitate nature. In Florence in the fifteenth century, Brunelleschi crowned a Gothic edifice with a monumental Roman-style dome, heralding Renaissance architecture. Through the geometrical and other mathematical studies that this feat entailed, Brunelleschi supplied painters with the means of creating perspective (and mariners—in the sextant—with a reliable means of navigation). In northern Europe, by the end of the fifteenth century, the Gothic style of ecclesiastical building, developed over more than three centuries, was being replicated in the parish churches and guildhalls of prosperous merchant towns.

Until well on into the fifteenth century, musical polyphony was generally thought of as a matter of scholarly training and, therefore, as belonging to the Church; musical entertainment at court consisted largely of un-notated minstrelsy.[50] Nevertheless, Machaut's musical career already presaged an era in which artistic patronage was transferred from Church to court, and in which composers assumed an individual, personal identity. Machaut combined noble birth with a career as a poet-musician and priest; he travelled widely with the court chapel of his patron, John of Luxembourg, and after John's death continued a peripatetic lifestyle. By the end of the fifteenth century, it was expected of any ambitious princeling that he would acquire his own mobile court chapel, staffed by professional singers and instrumentalists. In the matter of composers, there was competition among patrons to acquire those of highest international renown. Ecclesiastical polyphony came thus to be heard by a wider lay audience, one that could appreciate its artistry.[51]

As patronage of music moved from Church to court, the intricacies of earlier polyphony came to be ironed out into a more homogeneous musical style. The *Ars Nova* had tended to bring the various polyphonic strands of a musical piece into a more coherent relationship. During the fifteenth century, such strands were coordinated and subjugated under a single, unifying theme. The 'head-motif' of this theme would be taken

[50] Denis Arnold, 'Renaissance', *NOCM* (1983). [51] Ibid.

up, in 'imitation', by each polyphonic strand in turn; and the use of canonic and other contrapuntal devices led to reduced dependence on a *cantus firmus* as a basis for composition.

Such unification was the achievement of the 'Netherlands' or 'Franco-Flemish' School (emanating from present-day Holland, Belgium, and Luxembourg, then under the suzerainty of the dukes of Burgundy), whose principal composers, such as Dufay, Binchois, Ockeghem, Josquin, and Isaac, worked at various courts throughout Europe, and came to dominate European music-making. The application of musical procedures for placing important thematic material in the foreground of a polyphonic structure, obedient to cogent harmonic principles, was analagous to the increasing use by painters of a mathematical ordering of perspective on a plane surface. Such procedures were applied to forms that ranged from elaborate motets and masses to chansons and madrigals. When such polyphony appeared in print (from movable type), at the start of the sixteenth century, performance of the music spread, from courts to merchant households.

Technology and Musical Instruments

Technological advance in the making of instruments underpinned this development; and instrument-making reached new levels of finesse during the fifteenth century (Pl. 54). A significant and necessary advance came with the construction of bass instruments capable of playing relatively fast-moving melodic lines. The bass shawm, for example, was of an unwieldy length, heavy, cumbersome, and uneven in tone; but the development of the double–bore principle, with two parallel tubes bored in the same block of wood, and joined by a U bend below, provided the bass curtal, or dulcian, with both flexibility of tone and ease of portability.[52] The transformation was revolutionary and unique to Europe.

New alloys, and new techniques in metal-working, which made it possible to produce a copper tube bent through a 180–degree curve, without distorting the bore, similarly reduced the overall length of brass instruments. The development of the slide principle, enabling the length—and hence the pitch of the fundamental—to be altered while playing, conferred a chromatic range on all but treble instruments. The

[52] Munrow, *Instruments of the Middle Ages and Renaissance*, 43.

54. Maximilian with his musicians; woodcut by Hans Burgkmair (early sixteenth century). Bottom left is a portative organ; above are four singers and a cornett; in the centre is a harpist; to the right, an oblong keyboard instrument. On the table are a viola da gamba, flute, recorders, cornett, and crumhorn; on the floor are a kettle drum, tabor, pair of drumsticks, sackbut, lute case, and tromba marina

narrow bore necessary for the pitch range of the slide trumpet (using a *single* slide) required unmanageably large slide movements in treble instruments; and it was necessary to move the whole instrument, not just the slide, to change the pitch of a note. For the alto, tenor, and bass ranges, however, the slide principle proved ideal, when adapted to a *double* slide, on the sackbut, in the sixteenth century. The only important difference between sackbut and modern trombone is the greatly increased flare of the bell.[53] Bands of 'waits' ('watchmen') played shawms, cornetts, and sackbuts on city turrets and walls, or on the streets, as did similar bands in Asia; but in the West, they were now equipped to play the distinctive harmony and counterpoint of Europe.

By the early fifteenth century, keyboards—originally played with the fists rather than the fingers—were being set out in the familiar two-row pattern of black and white notes.[54] The keyboard, when applied to the principle of the monochord—stopping the string with a movable bridge—led to the clavichord. When applied, by means of a mechanical action, to the plucked psaltery, it led to the virginals and harpsichord.

[53] Ibid. 20–1, 68.

[54] Nicolas Meeus, 'Keyboard', *The New Grove* (1980), x. 9.

Organs, originally consisting in 'mixtures' of octave- and fifth-sounding ranks only, now incorporated ranks of stopped 'flue', and 'reed', pipes, permitting contrasts of timbre. During the fifteenth century, individual keyboard players acquired the performance-capability of a group of musicians. Their art became soloistic; and organ, virginals, and harpsichord all acquired large and very varied repertoires. (The development of keyboard instruments substantially influenced the development of harmony.)

Similar refinements and extensions of range were effected on lutes, the resonators of which were no longer carved from solid wood, but fabricated from separate elements. The most important were (and are): the thin pinewood table, strengthened by six or more wooden bars glued beneath, and featuring a carved, circular sound hole; and the hollow, pear-shaped body, built from a series of ribs, shaped and bent over a mould, and glued together, edge to edge, over a paper shell.[55] The resulting lightness of construction greatly increased resonance; and the instrument became the most important Renaissance court instrument, second only to the voice.

The viol—like the spike fiddles of Asia, a bowed lute—was played *da gamba*. The folk fiddle, however, was often played *da braccia*, and was to become the most popular string instrument of Europe. Praetorius wrote in his *Syntagma musicum* (1619): 'Since everyone knows about the violin family, it is unnecessary to write or indicate anything further about it.'[56] The violin appears to have emerged in the mid-sixteenth century. (Praetorius took a lofty view of what he regarded as the superiority of Western over Asian instruments; he referred, for example, to 'a devil's bell and a rubbish pail, together with a squeaking shawm, which are still in high esteem among the Turks . . .'.[57])

The term 'whole consort' is often used to describe ensembles of single-family instruments, such as recorders, crumhorns, or viols; these could now replace voices in the performance of contrapuntal music. The opposite term, 'broken consort', seems first to have been used in England in the 1660s, but is now generally applied to Renaissance ensembles with a mixture of instrument families. 'Broken consorts' emphasized the differences between instrument types. Later,

[55] Munrow, *Instruments of the Middle Ages and Renaissance*, 76.

[56] Cited in ibid. 90.

[57] Frank Ll. Harrison, 'Observation, Elucidation, Utilization: Western Attitudes to Eastern Musics, ca. 1600–ca. 1830', in Malcolm Hamrick Brown and Roland John Wiley (eds.), *Slavonic and Western Music: Essays for Gerald Abraham* (Oxford: Oxford University Press, 1985), 22.

during the seventeenth century, the higher-pitched instruments—notably violin, transverse flute, and oboe—developed further their range, power, agility, and individuality of tone. European music then became a vehicle for technical virtuosity, from which the talented could seek individual fame and fortune. With virtuosity came some of the less attractive aspects of the ensuing tradition: by 1600, for example, castrati had been admitted to the Sistine chapel.

'Rebirth' in Italy

If the forms of European music emerged from Christianity's compromise with Graeco-Islamic scholarship, sealed in the great *Summa* of fourteenth-century Paris, the *ideals* of European music first emerged in the more secular atmosphere of fifteenth- and sixteenth-century Italy. Situated midway between northern Europe and West Asia, Italy had early taken advantage of Islamic knowledge and skills; its economy, for example, was assisted by Arab systems of calculation and book-keeping. It was thus able to recover more quickly than other European countries from the terrible Black Death that killed half the population of Europe during the mid-fourteenth century.[58] Florence, in particular, exploited this advantage to the full; its most powerful family, the Medicis, gained enormous wealth through banking.

Florence acquired a thirst for Greek culture when, in 1397, an envoy from Constantinople accepted a chair of Greek at its university. Contact with Byzantium in turn stimulated an interest in things Roman, and provided inspiration for Brunelleschi's famous dome.[59]

A powerful stimulus towards the acquisition of ancient knowledge appears to have come from King René of Anjou, whose imposing array of titles included Count of Provence, Count of Piedmont, Count of Guise, Duke of Calabria, Duke of Anjou, Duke of Lorraine, King of Hungary, King of Naples and Sicily, King of Aragon, Valencia, Majorca, and Sardinia, and—significantly—King of Jerusalem. A scholar immersed in esoteric tradition, and a prototype of Renaissance princes, René appears to have been instrumental in persuading Cosimo de Medici, from 1439 onwards, to send agents all over the world in search of ancient manuscripts. Cosimo was empowered to commission

[58] Burke, *The Day the Universe Changed*, 57. [59] Ibid. 61, 67.

translations of many Platonic, Neoplatonic, Pythagorean, Gnostic, and Hermetic texts.[60]

In 1444 Cosimo founded the first European public library at San Marco in Florence. Then, in 1470, one Marsilio Ficino, supported by Cosimo's son Lorenzo, established an *Accademia Platonica* just outside Florence. Similar academies sprang up elsewhere in Italy and, subsequently, throughout Europe. Not only did the *Accademia Platonica*, through its proselytization of Graeco-Egyptian thought, conflict with Roman, Christian orthodoxy; it provided a new basis for the consideration of Italian literature, philosophy, drama, and music.[61]

The idea of 'rebirth' (renaissance), which had gained ground in literature and the visual arts during the fourteenth century with forerunners such as Dante and Giotto, now spread to music. With it, music's paramount function was seen to be to heighten the meaning of a text. Plato, in Book 3 of *The Republic*, had asserted that 'the *harmonia* (that is, the modal note-set), and the rhythm, must follow the sense of the words'. This dictum became a Renaissance obsession. For example, in his *Utopia* of 1516, Sir Thomas More stressed the capacity of music to express the inner meaning of words; and in 1558, the Renaissance musical theorist Zarlino considered the music of the ancient Greeks to have reached a 'height of perfection', and medieval music (correspondingly) to have reached the 'lowest depths'. Significantly, he described his own teacher in Venice, Willaert, as a 'new Pythagoras'.[62]

Interest in musical declamation compromised the status of polyphony as the principal means of musical propulsion. By the 1570s Florentine intellectuals were actively studying available sources on Greek music, and promoting monody at the expense of polyphony; by the end of the sixteenth century, Cavalieri, Peri, and Caccini had produced the first through-composed *dramma per musica* in the new *stile rappresentativo*, making the spoken word redundant (Pl. 55). (This term was first used by Caccini in 1600 to denote monodies that employed a variety of musico-theatrical styles.) These developments, in turn, led to the paramount position of the 'continuous' bass line in baroque music.

The Italian Renaissance had its darker side.[63] It was never a popular movement. It was promoted by a small number of scholars and artists who exploited the wealth of liberal aristocrats and humanist popes. It

[60] Baigent, Leigh, and Lincoln, *The Holy Blood*, 142.

[61] Percy M. Young, 'Academy', *The New Grove* (1980), i. 30–1.

[62] Lewis Lockwood, 'Renaissance', *The New Grove* (1980), xv. 737–8.

[63] Russell, *History of Western Philosophy*, 521.

L'EVRIDICE
COMPOSTA IN
MVSICA
In Stile Rappresentatiuo da
GIVLIO CACCINI
detto Romano.

IN FIRENZE
APPRESSO GIORGIO MARESCOTTI
MDC

55. Title page of Caccini's *Euridice*

was attended by a moral and political anarchy that eroded the Church's spiritual authority and encouraged secular doctrines, such as those of Machiavelli. Its inevitable consequence was the Reformation, initiated in Germany, in opposition to the worldliness and perfidy of the papacy. The Counter-Reformation, initiated in Spain and which brought Italy to subjection, was a reaction against the general intellectual and moral freedom of the Renaissance. These movements foreshadowed a century of religious warfare that would undermine the tradition of sacral monarchy and herald the 'Age of Enlightenment'.

The most significant factor of the Renaissance for the future course of European music was that it transferred the arts from the centre of life to its periphery, and from a religious necessity to an expensive ornament. The arts became detached not just from ordinary people but from the spiritual source of their inspiration. The ability to perform music became an essential accomplishment of any aspiring 'gentleman'. As the seventeenth-century English writer Henry Peacham put it: 'I desire in you no more than to sing your part sure at the first sight.'[64] Or, as a contemporary playwright caused an aristocrat to observe of his niece: 'With the voice between her lips and the viol between her legs, she'll be fit for a consort very speedily.'[65] In a famous passage, Peacham encapsulated the late-Renaissance view of music:

> Infinite is the sweet variety that the theorique of music exerciseth the mind withal, as the contemplation of proportion, of concords and discords, diversity of moods and tones, infiniteness of invention etc. But I dare affirm that there is no one science in the world that so affecteth the free and generous spirit with a more delightful or inoffensive recreation or better disposeth the mind to what is commendable and virtuous . . .[66]

European art music had became like jewellery: a luxury trade. It had become an affected attribute of the aristocratic and merchant class; and it could be considered critically, by the eye, as much as by the ear. With the European Renaissance, man—in the memorable line of the Greek philosopher Protagoras—had become 'the measure of all things'.

[64] Oliver Strunk, *Source Readings in Musical History from Classical Antiquity through the Romantic Era, Selected and Translated by O. Strunk* (New York: 1950; London: Faber Paperback, 1981).

[65] Onesiphorus Hoard in Thomas Middleton, *A Trick to Catch the Old One*; cited in Munrow, *Instruments of the Middle Ages and Renaissance*, 87.

[66] Strunk, *Source Readings in Musical History*.

12 *Enlightenment*

The Eighteenth-Century Mould

Just off London's Strand is a house built by John Adam in 1754 for the Society of Arts. The Society—now the Royal Society of Arts, Manufactures, and Commerce—still occupies it. On the panels of its Great Room, a series of paintings by James Barrie, Professor of Painting at the Royal Academy, provides insight into the attitudes and beliefs of the merchant gentlemen who were its members. The purpose of these paintings—in the artist's words—was to illustrate 'one great maxim or moral truth, that the obtaining of happiness . . . depends on cultivating the human faculties'. Man is shown beginning 'in a savage state, full of inconvenience, imperfection and misery'. He then 'progresses through several gradations of culture and happiness, which . . . are finally attended with beatitude or misery'.

First we are shown Orpheus in a 'wild and savage country, surrounded by people as savage as their soil'. These 'hearers of Orpheus' are 'without wisdom and skill to prevent frequent retaliation on themselves and their more feeble offspring'. So the scene moves to a 'Grecian harvest-home', a 'state of happiness, simplicity, and fecundity' in which 'the duty we owe to God, our neighbour, and ourselves is much better attended to . . .'. This is, however, 'but a stage at which we cannot stop'; so the scene changes to one in which Greek athletes, surrounded by gods and great men, are crowned for their 'contest of glory, not of rancour'.

Then—significantly—Father Thames, 'venerable, majestic, and gracious', has 'Europe, Asia, Africa and America . . . pouring their several productions into his lap' (Pl. 56). The 'good river' is 'carried along by our great navigators, Drake, Raleigh, Sebastian Cabot and the late Captain Cook'; Nereids carry 'several articles of our manufactures and

56. *The Triumph of Navigation*, by Sir James Barrie, painted on the ceiling of the Great Room, Royal Society of Arts

commerce', and leading figures of the society appear surrounded by 'specimens of cotton and indigo, gun barrels of white tough iron, maps, charts . . . carpets, and large paper, proper for copper-plate printing'. If, suggests the artist, some of the Nereids appear 'more sportive than industrious' and others 'still more wanton than sportive', they give the picture 'variety and, I am sorry to say, the greater resemblance to the truth'. And, because 'music is naturally connected with matters of joy and triumph', even Dr Burney makes an appearance.

The members of this august society, like many prosperous merchants elsewhere in Europe, believed that theirs was a civilization in which the state of moral, artistic, and scientific development was superior to anything humankind had reached before. The civilizations of Egypt and Greece had been important staging posts in this progress, though they were thought to have slipped into decadence.[1] The higher stages of

[1] Martin Bernal, *Black Athena, the Afroasiatic Roots of Classical Civilization* (2 vols.; London: Free Association Books, 1987), i. 199.

evolution had started with Aristotle, though other civilizations had had certain attributes; Chinese civilization, for example, was admired for a government based on reason rather than superstition (rather than for the scientific discoveries it had made one or two millennia before Europe purloined them); it had even provided a model for the centralizing reforms of the French government. Taste, however, in the words of Voltaire, 'remained the property of certain European peoples'; this was in contrast to 'the peoples of Asia', who 'lacked well-made works of practically every kind . . .'.[2] When the above-named Dr Burney—eighteenth-century music historian extraordinary—undertook his travels around Europe, it was essentially to record the 'progress' of European civilization.[3]

The concept of 'progress' did not originate in the eighteenth century. During the sixteenth century, Europeans realized that they possessed products the ancients had lacked—for example, paper, printing, windmills, sugar, the compass, and gunpowder—even though all of them had come from Asia. But 'progress' could scarcely be asserted of the century from 1560 to 1660, when Europe was destroying itself with religious wars.[4] With the wars over, a chastened Europe, wary—in the north at least—of religious intolerance, recovered its self-confidence. Louis XIV's palace at Versailles was thought by Europeans to be the greatest in the world, and was replicated in lesser form by ambitious princelings in many parts of Europe. During the last quarter of the seventeenth century, French intellectuals fought among themselves the 'Battle of Ancients and Moderns', an imbroglio over whether or not the moderns were morally and artistically superior to the ancients. Under their 'Sun King', Louis XIV, they sided with the moderns, and imposed their view on much of northern Europe.[5]

Philosophy and Aesthetics

With the tide running clearly in favour of 'modernism'—a previously unheard-of concept—European intellectuals

[2] *Encyclopédie, ou dictionnaire raisonné des sciences, des arts et des métiers*, vii (Paris, 1957), 761, cited in Peter Le Huray and James Day (eds.), *Music and Aesthetics in the Eighteenth and Early Nineteenth Centuries*, abridged edn. (Cambridge: Cambridge University Press, 1981), 59.

[3] Daniel Heartz, 'Enlightenment', *The New Grove* (1980), vi. 205–6.

[4] Bernal, *Black Athena*, i. 177.

[5] Benedict Anderson, *Imagined Communities: Reflections on the Origin and Spread of Nationalism* (London: Verso, 1987), 67.

set to work arguing and rationalizing the nicer points of their culture. For example, in 1746, the Abbé Charles Batteux distinguished *les beaux-arts* ('fine arts', as they came to be known in English)—sculpture, painting, music, and poetry—from 'useful' arts (such as cooking), and from 'mixed' arts (such as architecture and eloquence). Views on the nature of art leaned heavily on certain philosophical principles that originated with Plato, or in Egypt.

In France, as early as 1637, Descartes—generally regarded as the founder of modern European philosophy—first introduced the tenets of what came to be called 'Cartesian doubt'. According to Descartes, you can doubt the existence of everything; but what you cannot dispute (or doubt) is that you are actually doubting. You, therefore, exist, even though the external world may not: *Cogito ergo sum*. Descartes followed Plato in separating the mind from the senses. He thought of the mind as a substance, which 'so exists that it needs no other thing in order to exist': the mind is what perceives the self. The senses, on the other hand, perceive the world of matter and cannot perceive the mind; they reveal a world that is complex and untrustworthy. Passions and emotions are, therefore, suspect.[6] The only things to rely on are ideas in the mind.

John Locke (1632–1704), founder of the English 'empiricist' school, took a different view, maintaining that both mind *and* matter are substances. But, he argued, the mind contains only data conveyed to it by the senses; it can analyse such data, but it cannot, of itself, add new materials. Locke was therefore able to adumbrate the convenient proposition that *all* the materials of knowledge are derived from human experience, and no kind of human knowledge is innate.[7]

David Hume (1711–76) subsequently eliminated the Cartesian distinction between the clarity and truth of the mind and the unreliable data of the senses. According to Hume, ideas can be formed only from anterior impressions gained from the senses: 'The faculty of imagination has command over all its ideas ... but as it is impossible that this faculty of imagination can ever, of itself, reach belief, it is evident that belief consists not in the peculiar nature or order of ideas, but in the *manner* of their conception, and their *feeling* in the mind.'[8] Hume, in

[6] Le Huray and Day (eds.), *Music and Aesthetics*, 12.

[7] Ibid. 12–13.

[8] David Hume, *An Enquiry Concerning Human Understanding*, ed. L. A. Selby-Bigge (Oxford: Oxford University Press, 1984), 49.

effect, denied any necessary connection between causes and effects, maintaining that the essential function of reason is to articulate—and thus to 'civilize'—the passions.[9]

Such philosophy engendered a cerebral approach to aesthetics that was singularly European. Interest in aesthetics intensified throughout the eighteenth century; and although—as elsewhere in the world—aesthetic theory did not necessarily accord with artistic practice, in England alone over seventy books on aesthetics were printed in the second half of the century. Among the matters debated were: the nature of aesthetic experience and the factors that determine aesthetic judgement; the nature of the beautiful and the sublime; and the extent to which art should imitate nature. Music, of course, could not imitate nature, but it *could*—or so it was thought—express feelings: indeed, self-evidently it was the art that spoke most directly to the feelings.[10] Thus the relative importance of both expression and proportion to musical composition was much debated, as were the differences between stiff French correctness and supple Italian invention.[11]

The debate soon acquired a moralistic tone: if the search for beauty is a search for truth and perfection, the creation of beauty must itself be a revelation of divine truth. Lord Shaftesbury, for example, in his influential *Characteristicks of Men, Manners, Opinions, Times* (1711), considered that morality and beauty are identical, and that therefore manners, art, and nature can all be measured by the same standard: 'The most natural beauty in the world is honesty and moral truth; for all beauty is truth.' Haydn and Beethoven both took notice of Shaftesbury.[12]

Beauty in music was thought to be achieved by expressing feelings and 'passions'; it was necessary, therefore, for such emotions to be given musical embodiment. The solution was sought in the art of rhetoric. Ancient treatises on rhetoric had purported to analyse the passions systematically, and to deduce means of working on them.[13] Aristotle had argued that the imitation of nature found fullest expression in tragedy, which imitated 'action and life' through the media of plot, language, thought, spectacle, and music.[14] In 1752 J. J. Quantz

[9] F. E. Spearshott, 'Aesthetics of Music', *The New Grove* (1980), i. 126.
[10] Le Huray and Day (eds.), *Music and Aesthetics*, 30
[11] Spearshott, 'Aesthetics of Music', *The New Grove*, i. 125–6.
[12] David P. Schroeder, *Haydn and the Enlightenment* (Oxford: Oxford University Press, 1990), 14.
[13] Spearshott, 'Aesthetics of Music', *The New Grove*, i. 125.
[14] Le Huray and Day (eds.), *Music and Aesthetics*, 3.

suggested that 'the orator and the musician have, at bottom, the same aim'.[15] (This, in essence, did not depart greatly from principles of musical construction used in Asia.)

Descartes, in a treatise on the passions, had elaborated the 'doctrine of affections' by suggesting that complex emotions could be derived from the combination of simple psychological components. He had, moreover, with his friend Père Marin Mersenne, attempted to rationalize the mathematical basis of harmony. (Mersenne it was who propagated the 'well-tempered' scale, calculated on the basis of the twelfth root of two, some half-century after Zhu Zaiyu had propounded the theory in China (see p. 325).) Baroque musical theorists built on these foundations. Johann Mattheson, for example, in 1739, produced detailed analyses of emotions with corresponding musical devices. Each piece of music was intended to portray a single emotion, so that the *manner* in which the emotion was portrayed became the unifying principle of musical construction.[16] (This, again, was in essence compatible with musical procedures throughout much of Asia.)

As instrumental music began to find a life of its own, independently of verbal associations, music was found to be insufficiently precise to handle 'moral' concepts. As late as 1767, Rousseau recalled the 'witty response made by the celebrated Fontenelle after he had been bored to death by an endless succession of instrumental pieces: "Sonate, que me veux-tu?" ['Sonata, what do you want of me?']'. 'To understand what the din of a sonata is all about,' wrote Rousseau, 'we would have to do what the incompetent painter did, when he wrote beneath his works, "This is a tree", "This is a man", and "This is a horse".'[17] It was precisely because the opportunities for imitating nature in music appeared so limited that the medium was held to appeal directly to the imagination and the senses, and that the beautiful in music became equated with the 'sublime'.

That instrumental music—uniquely in Europe and the West—eventually acquired equal or superior status to vocal music was due to the rationalization of harmonic principles. In 1722 Rameau, in his *Traité de l'harmonie réduite à son principe naturel*, assigned to harmony priority over melody in musical construction. Rameau posited a simple harmonic system of triads and their inversions, and this theory enabled music

[15] Spearshott, 'Aesthetics of Music', *The New Grove*, i. 125.
[16] Ibid. 125–6.
[17] Le Huray and Day (eds.), *Music and Aesthetics*, 4.

to be perceived both vertically in terms of chord positions and horizontally in terms of cadential patterns.[18] Such rationalization of the relationship between rhythm and harmony not only transcended local squabbles over the merits of different operatic styles (which were based largely on *melodic* styles); it provided a basic ordering of harmony that would permit themes—themselves often triadic in character—to be extended and contrasted. Composers of outstanding ability would subsequently find means of integrating the musical elements of melody, rhythm, harmony, counterpoint, and motor speed, *independently* of the mood created; through it they would engender and control within a single movement a *variety* of moods, so that a musical 'argument' could be unfolded. Such ability is what set Haydn and Mozart above all other composers of their age.

Philosophy and 'Race'

Eighteenth-century intellectuals invoked Aristotle on other, less enlightening matters. The sage had justified his belief in the superiority of the Hellenic race on the grounds that Europeans, living in 'cold regions', were lacking in 'skill and brainpower'; and that the Asiatic races, though having both brains and skill, were nevertheless 'lacking in courage and willpower', to the extent that they 'remained both enslaved and subject'.[19] The Hellenes, however (according to Aristotle), occupied a 'mid-position geographically', thereby possessing skill and brain power, *and* courage and will power. In this way Aristotle invoked the concept of 'racial superiority' to justify slavery; and, in this way too, Europeans were to link their own notions of racial superiority with their climate.

To many thinkers of the 'Enlightenment'—Locke and Hume among them—Asians and Africans were inferior peoples: skin colour was linked to moral and mental inferiority. Locke's influential political philosophy was built on the notion of a divinely instituted 'state of nature' (as opposed to sacral monarchy); through it—with the aid of a 'contract' between sovereign and civil government—people could live together on the basis of 'reason' and exacted obedience. Locke's philosophy embodied the right to punish attacks on self or property: captives in a 'just' war, for example, could be regarded as slaves, by law of

[18] Ibid. 9. [19] Bernal, *Black Athena*, i. 202.

nature.[20] (Locke's articulation of a system of checks and balances, through which separation of the legislative, executive, and judicial functions of government would—in theory—prevent abuse of power, was to become enshrined in the US constitution.)

Hume took the racial implications of Locke's philosophy a stage further by suggesting that 'such a uniform and constant difference (among races) could not happen in so many countries and ages, if nature had not made an original distinction between breeds of men'.[21] Montesquieu, in his *Persian Letters* (1721), satirized Europe, but nevertheless considered the continent to be the most 'scientific' and 'progressive' because of its beneficent, temperate climate. Rousseau, in his *Social Contract* (1762), denounced slavery, but believed that a people's virtue and political ability depended on climate and topography. In truth, European 'progress' depended absolutely upon the 'several productions' of Asia, Africa, and America pouring into the conveniently placed lap of—among others—'Father Thames'; it also depended upon foreign slave labour.

During the sixteenth century, Africans were imported in large numbers as slaves and servants; and although, in 1598, Queen Elizabeth I ordered the immediate deportation of 'diverse blackamoors brought into this realme, of which kinde of people there are already too manie', the order was not obeyed: by the end of the sixteenth century, it had become fashionable for aristocratic families to own a black houseboy. Nevertheless, in 1601, the queen—who herself used black slaves at court, among whom were seven musicians and three dancers[22]—again expressed her 'discontent' at the 'great number of negars and blackamoors which are crept into this realme', accusing them of being 'infidels, having no understanding of Christ or his Gospel'.[23]

Despite these orders, Africans remained in the kingdom. In 1723 the London *Daily Journal* commented that 'a great number of Blacks come daily into this City, so that 'tis thought in a short time, if they be not supress'd, the City will swarm with them'; and in 1788 it was observed that 'London abounds with an incredible number of these black men... In every country town, nay in almost every village, are to be

[20] Bertrand Russell, *History of Western Philosophy* (Woking: Allen & Unwin, 1946), 647.

[21] Bernal, *Black Athena*, i. 203–4.

[22] Peter Fryer, *Staying Power: The History of Black People in Britain* (London: Pluto Press, 1984), 80.

[23] David Dabydeen, *Hogarth's Blacks: Images of Blacks in Eighteenth Century English Art* (London: Dangaroo Press, 1985), 17.

57. *Grown Gentlemen taught to Dance*: engraving after John Collet (1768). A black musician, merged into the foreground, appears to be playing disinterestedly

seen a little race of mulattoes, mischievous as monkeys and infinitely more dangerous.'[24]

Art of the seventeenth and eighteenth centuries (as David Dabydeen has shown) depicts such 'dangerous mulattoes' as lonely or humiliated, in positions of servitude or subjection. They appear 'as footmen, coachmen, pageboys, soldiers, sailors, musicians, actresses, prostitutes, beggars, prisoners, pimps, highway-robbers, street-sellers, and other similar roles' (Pl. 57).[25] In aristocratic households, ladies posed for their portraits with their pet lamb, their pet lapdog, or their pet black. On occasion, the dog and the black would appear in the same picture, gazing with equal respect at their owner. Comparisons in art between Africans and animals reflected, however unconsciously, the fact that the two were commonly equated.

[24] Ibid. 18. [25] Ibid. 20, 23.

In 1756, for example, an advertisement for 'silver padlocks for Blacks or Dogs...' appeared in the *London Advertiser.* At another level, in 1759, Lord Chesterfield argued that Africans were 'the most ignorant and unpolished people in the world, little better than lions, tigers, leopards, and other wild beasts'. This argument was used to justify buying 'a great number' of Africans 'to sell again to advantage in the West Indies'. Lord Grosvenor likened the 'unamiable' slave trade to the 'unamiable' trade of the butcher.[26] (Egyptians, whose culture was enshrined in Freemasonry, were generally thought not to have the dark skins of Africans, though the matter was much debated. Mozart, in *Die Zauberflöte*, makes striking contrast between the lustful 'Moor', Monastatos, and the philosophical Egyptian, Sarastro.[27])

During the second half of the eighteenth century, such views were modified. Artists adopted a relative view of the merits of English and African countenances. Hogarth, for example, in the *Analysis of Beauty* manuscripts of the 1750s—and anticipating 'Postmodern' attitudes towards aesthetics (see pp. 677–9)—claimed that the 'variety of contradictory opinions' on the nature of beauty caused some to 'discard beauty as a reality, concluding it can only exist in Fancy and Imagination'. He instanced 'the Negro who finds great beauty in the black Females of his own country' but finds, correspondingly, 'as much deformity in the European Beauty as we see in theirs'.[28]

Although not all took this position—Edmund Burke concluded that blackness is 'terrible in its own nature... independent of any association whatsoever'—a growing understanding of human psychology advanced the relativist position. Indeed, in many literary works the 'savage' was used to satirize 'civilization', by expressing amazement or disgust at the grotesque culture of the European; this was a constant theme in Hogarth's satirical drawings. And African music seems to have made some small impact on popular music: by 1787, white and black Londoners were dancing to 'an innocent amusement, vulgarly called *black hops*, where twelve pence will gain admission'.[29] None of this, however, eased the plight of black Africans, who, for the most part, existed on the margins of European society.

[26] Dabydeen, *Hogarth's Blacks*, 30.

[27] Bernal, *Black Athena*, i. 243.

[28] Dabydeen, *Hogarth's Blacks*, 41.

[29] *E. Harris's List of Covent-Garden Ladies—For the Year 1788*, p. 84, cited in Fryer, *Staying Power*, 81.

Nevertheless, there are recorded instances of black musicians achieving success in European music. One such was the violinist George Polygreen Bridgtower, whose father came to Europe from Barbados in the 1770s. Bridgtower made his professional début in Paris, in 1789, at the age of 9, and a few months later was entertaining King George III of England at Windsor. He subsequently became a favourite of the Prince Regent, in whose private band he held the post of first violinist. He is thought to have been favoured also by Haydn,[30] and to have given some fifty concerts as soloist and principal violinist with orchestras at Covent Garden, Drury Lane, and the Haymarket Theatre.[31] More famously, in 1803, on a tour of Germany and Austria, Bridgtower made friends with Beethoven, who described him as 'a very able virtuoso and an absolute master of his instrument'.[32] Beethoven wrote the 'Kreutzer' sonata for Bridgtower, who gave the first performance, with the composer at the piano; and the dedication was changed only after Beethoven had quarrelled with Bridgtower, apparently over a girl.[33] Beethoven, at the time, had not even met Kreutzer.

More poignant is the story of the 'exquisite violinist' Joseph Emidy,[34] who was born in Guinea, and sold to Portuguese slave traders. Emidy was taken by his owner from Brazil to Lisbon, where he played in the opera orchestra. In 1795 he was kidnapped with his violin, and was 'imprisoned' on the ship 'Indefatigable', where for several years he was required to entertain the crew with hornpipes, jigs, and reels. Eventually, Emidy was transferred to another ship, and put ashore at Falmouth, where he made a living performing ('to a degree of perfection not heard before in Cornwall'), teaching, and composing. About the year 1807 a pupil showed some of Emidy's compositions to the London impresario, Salamon; but Salamon's suggestion that Emidy be invited to perform in London was not carried out, as it was thought Emidy's skin colour would cause the undertaking to fail. Emidy received, instead, a 'handsome sum', along with letters of admiration.[35]

Opportunities for black musicians to shine in European art music were, however, rare; more commonly, such musicians played the violin

[30] H. C. Robbins Landon, 'Haydn in England, 1791–1795', in *Haydn, Chronicle and Works*, ii (London: Thames & Hudson, 1976), 66.

[31] Fryer, *Staying Power*, 428–9.

[32] Emily Anderson (ed.), *The Letters of Beethoven*, i (London: Macmillan, 1961), 90.

[33] J. W. Thirlwall, 'The Kreutzer Sonata and Mr. Bridgtower', *Musical World*, 36 (1858), 771.

[34] James Silk Buckingham, *Autobiography of James Silk Buckingham*, i (London: Longman, Brown, Green, & Longmans, 1885), 169–71.

[35] Fryer, *Staying Power*, 431–2.

as street beggars. They were, nevertheless, admired for their performance on the Turkish instruments that were the rage in military bands in the late eighteenth century: large cymbals, bass drums, triangles and tambourines of unprecedented size, and the *chagāna* (soon anglicized to 'johanna' and popularly known as the 'Jingling Johnny'): a pole some six feet high, topped by a horse's tail, decked with crescents, from which hung a profusion of bells.[36]

Art in the eighteenth century may have been seen as a revelation of divine truth, but aesthetics did nothing to ease the plight of black Africans, in Europe or in the Americas. Because the aesthetic object was held to need no moral justification, aesthetics tended to detach art from reality. (This was a far cry from the situation in Sub-Saharan Africa, for example, where music was inseparable from its social context.) The key to aesthetic experience was 'disinterestedness'; as Immanuel Kant expressed it: 'The delight which determines the judgement of taste is independent of all interest.'[37] The French referred to *la sensibilité*. The two terms meant much the same thing: both implied a proneness to emotion and even to sympathy, but in neither was emotion allied to thought. The poor, or indeed the 'savage', might be considered more virtuous than the rich; but they were lauded only because of the *emotions* aroused by their plight.[38]

The Eighteenth-Century 'Middlebrow'

If the equation of art with morality did little to affect human behaviour, it failed equally to provide genuine edification, even among the aristocratic and merchant classes. Audiences themselves became 'disinterested'. Opera, the principal form of public entertainment, embodied the ambiguities of the age. Until the mid-eighteenth century, the dramatic material of opera was taken exclusively from classical mythology, with little obvious relevance to ordinary people. Indeed, the very act of setting dialogue to music as recitative—rather than leaving it to be spoken, as was the case in music-theatre genres throughout Asia—gave to European opera an aura of

[36] Fryer, *Staying Power*, 82–3.
[37] Immanuel Kant, *The Critique of Judgement*, trans. James Creed Meredith (Oxford: Oxford University Press, 1928), 42.
[38] Russell, *History of Western Philosophy*, 701.

pretentiousness that even the subsequent, up-to-date, librettos of opera buffa, could not entirely dispel.

Despite such pretentiousness, however, opera houses themselves developed into something rather less than models of erudition. Many patrons of the opera went to be seen, as much as to listen and watch, and operahouses were duly shaped for this purpose. The larger boxes were furnished like drawing rooms, and it was not unusual for rich patrons to dine and chatter throughout the performance, attending seriously only to favourite arias, sung by favourite singers. 'Star' singers, then as now, could gain fabulous wealth; Farinelli, for example, the most famous castrato of his day, earned the equivalent of over £5,000 a year, an enormous sum for those days.[39] It was not unknown for violence to erupt between supporters of rival singers, nor was it uncommon for the opera-house guards to be required to evict the disorderly from among *hoi polloi* in the 'pit'.[40] Throughout Asia, too, people chattered during music-theatre performances, but Asian music-theatre genres did not pretend to purvey, *through musical art*, any special form of moral erudition. Only in Europe was artistic beauty equated (in theory) with truth.

When not patronizing opera, members of the aristocratic and merchant classes enjoyed a less demanding form of entertainment. In post-Renaissance Europe (until the advent of jazz), popular music differed from art music only in being simpler—for in Western Europe, the separate existence of folk and art music styles was compromised by the propagation of music in print. The printed musical broadside took the popular folk-song from the communal gathering to the individual hearth, and from the country to the town. Broadside ballads streamed off the early eighteenth-century presses, and found their way to such diverse locations as taverns, milking-sheds, boat-cabins, and the book-shelves of students; the English diarist Samuel Pepys possessed a large collection.[41] With printing, 'folk' became 'pop';[42] and the spread of the broadside ballad caused popular music, in urban areas at least, to be conditioned by the same prevailing aesthetic as art music.

In Britain, for example, popular song books, such as *The Musical Miscellany, being a Collection of Choice Songs and Lyrick Poems,*

[39] Angus Heriot, *The Castrati in Opera* (1956; repr. New York, Da Capo Press, 1975), 68.
[40] Ibid. 74–5.
[41] A. L. Lloyd, *Folk Song in England* (London: Lawrence & Wishart, 1967).
[42] Peter Fletcher, *Roll over Rock: A Study of Music in Contemporary Society* (London: Stainer & Bell, 1981), 53.

included tunes with bass line, lyric words, and a part for the recorder. The choice of songs and lyric poems ranged from the beautiful to the banal, from composers such as Purcell to nonentities, and from cant compositions to fake folk-songs. Recorder- and flageolet-playing became popular middle-class pursuits; Pepys was addicted to the flageolet. (Ironically, as the 'penny whistle', the flageolet would become the favourite instrument of militant, black street-marchers in South Africa.)

Such 'manufacturing' of popular music was far removed from the intuitive skills that had engendered rural folk musics; it was also far removed from the rough artifice of the unlettered 'rogues, vagabonds, and sturdy beggars' who, in the words of one British enquiry, 'run about from place to place and entirely win that gain whereby our minstrels [the city 'waits'], not practising any other labours, ought to live'.[43] Already, by the eighteenth century, urbanization, the spread of printed music, and the consequent development of a 'middle-brow' taste, were eroding not only the practice of folk music, but also the veracity of musical aesthetics.

Enlightenment, Revolution, and Romanticism

The fact that prudence was seen as the supreme virtue during the first half of the eighteenth century was the consequence of strong memories of the wars of religion, and of the civil wars in England, France, and Germany.[44] A theory reflecting the conflicting claims of divinity, monarchy, and science was needed; it was supplied in England by Isaac Newton (1642–1727).

Newton—who in religion was a Unitarian and whose interests included alchemy and the Book of Revelation—eventually asserted that matter is passive, and that motion comes only from outside: not to have done so would have been to deny the need for a creator or, for that matter, a king.[45] With blithe disregard for the spherical nature of the earth, Newton declared space to be absolute (that is to say, flat and infinite)—a fallacy that was probably as clearly such to him as to the

[43] H. A. F. Crewdson, *Worshipful Company of Musicians* (London: Constable, 1950), app. 2.
[44] Russell, *History of Western Philosophy*, 703.
[45] Bernal, *Black Athena*, i. 175.

mathematician and philosopher Gottfried Leibnitz (1646–1716), who immediately criticized it.[46] Nevertheless, Newton's orderly cosmos, with the planets revolving in unchanging orbits around the sun, became a symbol for good government.[47] Humans, it seemed, had mastered their universe and could now be responsible for their affairs. 'The proper study of mankind' could—as Pope memorably remarked—be 'man'.

Such ideas were challenged early on by those who saw in them an upholding of aristocratic privilege. Jonathan Swift's *Gulliver's Travels*, for example, satirized the scientific community: his bizarre island of the Houyhnhnms (1726) was published with a phoney map of its South Atlantic location.[48] John Gay, most famous for his parody of government, of morality, and of opera itself, in *The Beggar's Opera* (1728) (Pl. 58), had earlier parodied Newton as the uncomprehending Dr Fossile in his play *Three Hours after Marriage* (1717).[49] As order and stability progressively crumbled before the desire for greater passion and excitement, aesthetic investigation into the nature of beauty came to be superseded by that of the nature of the 'sublime'. In antiquity, the sublime had been equated with 'boldness and grandeur of thought' and with 'the Pathetic, or power of raising the passions'.[50] By the mid-eighteenth century, Edmund Burke could argue that the 'great and sublime in nature . . . is astonishment', a condition he held to be attended by 'some degree of horror'.[51]

A new—and potentially anarchic—social order was adumbrated in the *Encyclopédie*, a massive project that by 1772 had run to 72,000 articles and twenty-eight volumes. The *Encyclopédie* was regarded as one of the great intellectual achievements of the Age of Enlightenment, and its cerebral approach to social, political, and artistic matters was characteristically European. Its most notable contributor, Rousseau, was himself shortly to be denying the divine right of kings.

Rousseau had already achieved prominence in 1750, when he received a prize for answering in the negative the question: have the arts and sciences conferred benefits on mankind? Science, letters, and the arts, he had maintained, created wants, and were the sources of

[46] J. Bronowsky, *The Ascent of Man* (London: BBC, 1973), 240.
[47] Russell, *History of Western Philosophy*, 559.
[48] Anderson, *Imagined Communities*, 68.
[49] Bronowski, *The Ascent of Man*, 237.
[50] The *Peri houpsous*, attributed to Dionysius Longinus, cited in Le Huray and Day (eds.), *Music and Aesthetics*, 4.
[51] Le Huray and Day (eds.), *Music and Aesthetics*, 5.

58. Hogarth's depiction of a scene from John Gay's *The Beggar's Opera*

slavery. Rousseau admired the 'noble savage' and considered everything that differentiated the savage from the civilized to be evil.[52] In keeping with *la sensibilité*, however, such thoughts did not prevent Rousseau from subsequently composing an opera, *Le Devin du Village*, albeit in the style of comic opera fashionable in Italy. Beauty, averred Rousseau, derived from nature, that is to say human nature, and in particular its passionate rather than its rational side. Such radical ideas on the arts were the source of romanticism.

(Rousseau, like some other contemporaries, was not without passing interest in music from beyond Europe. At the end of his *Dictionnaire de musique* (1768) he printed a small collection of what he considered to be non-European tunes, with a comment on the inadequacy of European notational symbols for the purpose. This position was an improvement on that of Rameau, who, in 1760, had concluded—on the basis of third-hand evidence—that three of the five notes used in China gave 'false intervals'; and that it was the difference of the *comma*—which he

[52] Russell, *History of Western Philosophy*, 714.

considered imperceptible to the ear—that made the Greek and Chinese systems so very imperfect.[53])

The *Encyclopédie* advanced Rousseau's concept that beauty derived from nature; but opinions varied as to whether music's non-representational character demeaned the art, or whether (in the words of Jean le Rond d'Alembert, one of the *Encyclopédie*'s editors) music opened up the 'pleasures of the imagination' and encouraged creative genius.[54] It was left to the German, Immanuel Kant (1724–1804), to attempt to mould the conflicting views of the Enlightenment into a new synthesis. Kant considered music to be the most delightful of the arts; but, because it was also the least rational, without cognitive meaning, it must, he averred, be accorded a low position among the arts.[55]

Such demeaning of music's status did not, however, prevent German romantics from subsequently becoming excited by the 'mystery' and 'terror' they experienced through the new musical freedoms, for, to them, the essence of a work of art lay in the *feelings* it aroused.[56] During the nineteenth century, the artist came increasingly to be seen as a visionary revolutionary, exalted as 'spiritual hero'; and the notion of 'genius' came to supersede that of 'talent'. In 1813, E. T. A. Hoffman recognized Beethoven as one such genius; Hoffman could experience through Beethoven's instrumental music fear, horror, suffering, and 'a longing for the infinite', which he described as the 'essence of romanticism'.[57] Beethoven's musical personality would, indeed, hold succeeding generations in musical thrall—and perplexity.

[53] A footnote to his *Code de Musique pratique, ou méthodes pour apprendre la Musique, même à des aveugles* (1760); Frank Ll. Harrison, 'Observation, Elucidation, Utilization: Western Attitudes to Eastern Musics, ca. 1600–ca. 1830', in Malcolm Hamrick Brown and Roland John Wiley (eds.), *Slavonic and Western Music: Essays for Gerald Abraham* (Oxford: Oxford University Press, 1985), 9, 13.

[54] Le Huray and Day (eds.), *Music and Aesthetics*, 14.

[55] Spearshott, 'Aesthetics of Music', *The New Grove*, i. 127.

[56] Le Huray and Day (eds.), *Music and Aesthetics*, 6.

[57] Ibid.

13 *Disintegration*

Language, Folk-Song, and Nationality

Many people would still agree today that the eighteenth century embodied much of what was best in the European cultural tradition; that, in that century, reason and order were blended with judgement and taste, to make possible in music, art, architecture—and, characteristically, landscape-gardening—outstanding creations that still, uniquely, comfort the mind and the spirit. It can be no accident that the music of Bach and Handel, Haydn, Mozart, and early Beethoven emerged during the eighteenth century. The musical formulas that generated this music are still to be observed in music produced according to the pluralist temper of the late twentieth century.

That so much of the eighteenth-century arts continues to appear relevant must, in part, be a consequence of the universalism of that age. 'Enlightened' rulers may have competed for power; but they saw themselves as belonging to a common European culture. The same was also true of artists. In music, for example, many styles, associated with particular European countries, existed; but composers were expected to show facility in *all* the recognized styles, and genres. That romanticism subsequently fragmented the universalism of the eighteenth century into a profusion of different styles was due, to a large extent, to new awakenings of 'nationality'. During the nineteenth century, the nationality of the composer acquired ever-increasing significance.

The collapse of the *Ancien Régime* in France had stimulated (throughout Europe) a view of the present that related, increasingly, to the past; this, in turn, had created a new interest in history. History embodied the notion of 'progression', that each new age could be seen as an advance upon the last; and it encouraged new senses of 'nation-ness' among peoples whose geographical location had placed them at the periphery of the 'universal' culture of the eighteenth century. Such senses of history, and of 'nation-ness', were fostered by both linguistic and musical vernaculars.

As Benedict Anderson has shown,[1] it was primarily the printed book, in popular format, that linked people and events from disparate places and epochs,[2] and that, allied to the clock and the calendar, encouraged a 'consecutive' view of history. When the spread of newsprint subsequently linked events that concerned peoples who speak a particular, common, vernacular language, a sense of 'nation-ness' became a possibility.[3]

Throughout the Middle Ages, the only language taught in Europe was Latin. Like Qur'ānic Arabic, Indian Sanskrit, or, indeed, classical Chinese, Latin was the language through which religious 'truths' had been projected throughout a wide geographical territory, largely irrespective of political boundaries. Such 'truth languages' had been the 'second' languages of bilingual *literati*, for whom they had provided access to communities espousing their particular 'truth'.[4] 'Truth languages' had enabled religious territorial boundaries to override—or supplant—political boundaries.

In Europe, a large majority of the books published before 1500 were in Latin, but by the middle of the sixteenth century the small market of Latin-speakers had become saturated. Encouraged by capitalism, cheap editions were then marketed in vernacular languages, whereupon publishing ceased to be an international enterprise. The expanding vernacular print market created a new vernacular-reading public and, in doing so, destroyed the universality of 'truth languages'. It made possible the spread of Protestantism, for example: within fifteen days of Luther pinning his theses to the Wittenburg chapel door (in 1517), they had been printed in German translation and distributed throughout the country; and between 1522 and 1546, a total of 430 editions (whole or partial) of Luther's biblical translations had been printed.[5]

[1] Benedict Anderson, *Imagined Communities: Reflections on the Origin and Spread of Nationalism* (London: Verso, 1987).

[2] Erich Auerbach, *Mimesis, the Representation of Reality in Western Literature*, trans. Willard Trask (London: Doubleday Anchor, 1967), 64.

[3] Anderson, *Imagined Communities*, 30.

[4] Ibid. 23.

[5] Lucien Febvre and Henri-Jean Martin, *The Coming of the Book: The Impact of Printing, 1450–1800* (London: New Left Books, 1976), trans. of *L'Apparition du livre* (Paris: Albin Michel, 1958).

With the spread of vernacular languages in print, regional dialects gradually came to be subsumed under simplified, *centralized* languages. Such new 'international' languages became major instruments of power. In many countries, they overrode the old 'national' languages; indeed they made possible the centralizing policies of 'enlightened' eighteenth-century monarchs. The court of Frederick the Great in Prussia spoke French, for example—even though Frederick was called 'Great' because he, alone among German princelings, resisted French arms. The Romanov court in Moscow spoke French and German. English became the administrative language of Scotland, Wales, and Ireland. The desire to recover eroded regional vernaculars became a primary element in the development of nationalist feelings during the late eighteenth century. (The survival of such remote languages as Gaelic and Welsh, Basque and Catalan, remains a spur to nationalist feeling in the late twentieth century.)

In this search for national identity, music played an important role. An early instance of this was in Scotland, where the Act of Union with England in 1707, followed by the defeats of the Pretenders and the destruction of Gaelic culture in the Highlands, led to a surge of nationalist feeling. Genuine folk-songs joined with newly composed songs—Lady Jane Scott's *The Bonnie Banks of Loch Lomond* is a well-remembered example—to revive, in musico-literary form, a supposed world of lost innocence.[6] In 1762 James MacPherson published a volume of fragments of archaic Gaelic poetry,[7] and the volume was widely read in Europe; Napoleon took it with him to Egypt. An earlier collection of Scottish and English border ballads, *Reliques of Ancient Poetry*, was also influential throughout Europe; with other Nordic ballads, it had inspired Johan Gottfried von Herder, in Germany in the late 1770s, to collect and publish his *Stimmen der Völker in Liedern*.[8]

'Denn jedes Volk ist Volk; es hat seine National Bildung wie seine Sprache', famously declared Herder ('for each people is a "people"; it has its national culture, as well as its language').[9] During the eighteenth

[6] Martin Bernal, *Black Athena, the Afroasiatic Roots of Classical Civilization* (2 vols.; London: Free Association Books, 1987), i. 207.

[7] MacPherson's sources were never published, and the authenticity of the volume has been questioned; it seems probable, however, that the volume was, in part at least, derived from fragments of ancient Gaelic epic verse.

[8] Bernal, *Black Athena*, i. 207, and Peter Le Huray and James Day (eds.), *Music and Aesthetics in the Eighteenth and Early Nineteenth Centuries*, abridged edn. (Cambridge: Cambridge University Press, 1981), i. 186.

[9] Anderson, *Imagined Communities*, 66.

century, Germany had been eclipsed by the might of France: the language of its courts was French. Language became the principal means by which the German romantics returned Germans to their cultural roots. The *Sturm und Drang* ('Storm and Stress') movement was indicative of this; headed by Goethe, it centred on the novel. (*Romane* is the German for novel, from whence comes *roman*ticism.) As an art form, linked to a specific vernacular, the novel, like the folk-song, inspired a sense of common identity among peoples, linked by language, though not necessarily by national boundaries.

During the late eighteenth century, the increasing interest in languages encouraged a new breed of lexicographers and grammarians to rejuvenate languages marginalized by the new centralized vernaculars. Linguistic dictionaries and grammars provided new senses of national identity, as new vernaculars appeared in print. Romania dispensed with cyrillic script; Hungary and Czech Bohemia dispensed with German; Finland threw off Swedish; Norway rejected Danish; and three distinct languages, both spoken and written, became defined in the northern Balkans: Slovene, Serbo-Croat, and Bulgarian.[10] Vernacular languages were supplemented with national anthems and national flags. Such new senses of 'nation-ness' exposed the irrelevancies to 'nationhood' of the European political map, drawn up in 1815 after the defeat of Napoleon, by Metternich and the Congress of Vienna. (Elsewhere in the world, in South Africa, for example, the colloquial Dutch of the first colonists transformed into Afrikaans; in West Asia, the revival of classical Arabic, and a movement to cleanse vernacular Turkish from Persian and Arabic borrowings, was a symptom of a new nationalism.[11])

Aspects of East and Central European Folk Music

The history of European music makes sense against this background. The German J. S. Bach (1685–1750), for example, in the homogeneous Europe of the eighteenth century, could write with impunity in the Italian style, the French style, or the German ecclesiastical style, albeit with prodigious originality. Jan Dismas Zelenka (1679–1745), a highly original Bohemian composer working at the Dresden court from 1710 until his death, could incorporate

[10] Ibid. 71–2. [11] Ibid. 73.

a folk-inspired melodic style within the Italian instrumental style; indeed, West European folk influences were common in the baroque and classical styles of the eighteenth century. During the nineteenth century, however, the countries of Eastern Europe, marginalized by French and later Austro-German domination, attempted to assert their *regional* musical independence in terms of folk dialects, while remaining *within* the dominant musical tradition. Indeed, it was largely because such countries *were* marginalized, that their folk traditions (in contrast to those of Western Europe) survived, and many are still much alive today.

Folk styles of Western Europe display many regional differences, but, despite this, important unifying features exist.[12] Most song styles tend towards strophic structures, with balanced phrases and rhythms being the norm in northern Europe, and less symmetrical rhythms (involving melismatic vocal style), characteristic of Muslim-influenced areas in the south. The wide embrace of the Western Christian Church (particularly in Protestant areas, where the metrically four-square hymn style affected many aspects of music-making), and the peculiar development of art music in Western Europe, both contributed to this fundamental symmetry of style. In Eastern Europe, however, where feudalism existed for much longer than in Western Europe (in some areas, virtually into the twentieth century), and where social and cultural change was correspondingly slow, an astonishing *variety* of folk styles persisted into the twentieth century. In general, rural populations still predominate throughout the area.

The Slavs, presently numbering over two hundred million people, have made the strongest impact on East European folk musics; but during their expansion into northern Russia, central Europe, and the Balkans (from their original home in present-day Belorussia, in the mid-first millennium AD (see p. 68)), their musics blended in different ways with those of the various territories they settled; and the differing social and political circumstances brought about by their migrations led to disparate musical styles and usages.[13] Across southern Europe, from Portugal to the Bay of Bengal, still extant archaic styles of song, associated with calendrical and life-cycle ceremonies—featuring syllabic melodies of narrow compass, dynamic rhythm, and limited use of melismas—almost certainly date back to the late neolithic, and predate

[12] James Porter, 'Europe', *The New Grove* (1980), vi. 300.
[13] A. L. Lloyd, 'Europe', *The New Grove* (1980), vi. 302–6.

the arrival in Europe of the Slavs and Bulgars. Moreover, drone-based polyphonies, incorporating the synchronous use of major- and minor-second intervals (see p. 42), still common among western Bulgarian, Macedonian, and Bosnian Slavs, are also shared by peoples of longer standing in the region, such as southern Albanians, northern Greeks, and Romanophone Vlachs, and therefore also probably predate the Slavic invasions.

More complex forms of polyphony, and of wide-compassed 'lyric' song, emerged among northern and western Slavs (Russians, Ukranians, Belorussians, Poles, Slovaks, and Czechs), who developed the arch-shaped solo song into an intricate musical form. (The symmetrically shaped strophic song, characteristic of Western Europe, developed only in central Europe, and under West European influence.) In Russia, for example, a distinctive form of 'lyric' song evolved independently of music associated with ritual.[14] In such songs, the melodic lines grow 'organically' from a single melodic unit, either stated at the outset, or emerging as the line unfolds. The lines also make substantial use of melismas (in contrast to the melodic style of Western Europe, the rhythmic structure of which is commonly conditioned by the metrical structure of the song-texts). Russian lyric songs are performed chorally, in types of polyphony formed by the use of descant (*podgolosochnaya*), or heterophony, and in which the various, interweaving, lines merge in a choral unison (or octave) at key points in the form. Only rarely do the lines move in parallel, or with elements of chordal, harmonic structure; and in the harmonic texture, seconds and fourths are more conspicuous than thirds.

A more elaborate form of non-chordal polyphony is to be observed in Georgia, where folk-songs are performed by male-voice groups, with soloists normally performing the upper lines, and the chorus, the bass line. In the isolated, mountainous Svanetia region, for example, songs are performed in three parts, each singer improvising his line according to strict and complex norms of local tradition. The melodic line is usually sung in alternation by the top two voices, but all voices move freely, with seconds conspicuous between the top two voices.[15]

Such idiosyncratic styles contrast with those of central eastern Europe, where, by the nineteenth century at least, predominant folk styles came to be influenced by West European norms of melodic, rhythmic,

[14] Mark Slobin, 'Union of Soviet Socialist Republics', *The New Grove* (1980), xix. 393–4.

[15] Grigol Chkhikvadze, 'Union of Soviet Socialist Republics', *The New Grove* (1980), xix. 362; sleeve-note to CD, *Musics of the Soviet Union*, Smithsonian/Folkways SF 40002.

and harmonic structure. In Czechoslovakia, for example, although more archaic ritual songs persisted in remote areas, and the folk styles of parts of eastern Moravia and Silesia display non-Western features in tonality, rhythm, and singing styles, it was the Westernized folk styles of Bohemia and western Moravia—and in particular, during the nineteenth century, the polka—that came to influence Western art music. In Poland, similarly, the stanzaic song form came to predominate; and it was the clearly defined rhythmic traits (in Western terms) of dances such as the mazurka and polonaise—lack of anacrusis, and a tendency for rhythmic density to occur at the beginning, rather than the end of a bar—that were absorbed by Western Europe.

Central European folk styles, moreover, were influenced by instrumental styles in a way that those of the south, north, and west were not. Small folk ensembles, for example, characteristic of the Carpathian region, include string trios or quartets, the upper first fiddle playing a decorated version of the tune, the second fiddle and (optional) three-string viola marking the rhythm with alternating chords played across the strings, and the three-string cello or bass reinforcing the rhythm. Such groups encouraged a high tessitura on the part of singers, as well as the practice of sustaining the final note of a song, before concluding with a downward portamento of approximately a fourth.

The Eighteenth-Century Musical Synthesis Destroyed

Even so brief a summary of East European folk musics indicates the extent to which these traditions differed from those further west. Given the idiosyncratic nature of folk styles in Russia, for example, and in parts of Central Asia formerly under Russian sovereignty, it is hardly surprising that Russian composers produced a distinctive and extensive body of 'nationalist' symphonic and operatic music that—significantly—was to become a principal mainstay of the 'Western' classical repertoire. Melodic and rhythmic peculiarities of style led, in many instances, to distinctive and original uses of Western-style functional harmony; and the vibrant sonorities of folk singing styles encouraged similarly individualistic uses of orchestration. Early Russian 'nationalist' composers were largely self-taught, and benefited from a certain naïvety in fusing dissimilar musical styles. (Similar naïvity would occur again in the USA, when composers such as Cowell,

Partch, Ives, and Copland sought to forge a distinctively US musical style (see pp. 552–5).)

With hindsight, Mussorgsky appears the most wilful and 'Russian' of the so-called 'Russian Five' (Borodin, Balakirev, Cui, Mussorgsky, and Rimsky-Korsakov). Debussy recognized this as early as 1901, when he likened the composer's art to 'that of an inquisitive savage', and described his music as 'free from artifice or arid formula . . . this form is so manifold that it cannot possibly be likened to the recognised forms. It is achieved by little touches, linked by a mysterious bond and by his gift of luminous intuition.'[16]

The more Westernized nature of central European folk styles encouraged less idiosyncratic attempts at musical fusion. Czech and Polish composers, like Russian composers, produced oustanding works that entered the core repertoire of Western music, but they too experienced difficulties in fusing folk and classical styles. Dvořák's Ninth Symphony, for example ('From the New World', 1893)—as popular a 'nationalist' work as exists—is full of rousing bombast and gentle melancholy. But there are also wilful eccentricities, of scoring and of accompanimental rhythms, that reflect folk idioms, and conflict with the otherwise sonorous, Western, style of orchestration. Furthermore, because the work is built on themes, rather than on motifs, attempts to develop the themes may sound contrived, with intrusive, chromatic modulations that detract from a sense of 'organic' development, ideally associated with the symphonic genre. The symphony includes fine melodies, rhythmically pointed, and effectively harmonized; but the elements of melody, harmony, and rhythm are not held in balance: the dominance of melody, with its *own* harmonic implications, subverts the function of harmony as a basis for thematic development.

That many attempts to fuse folk music with the nineteenth-century symphonic order—like many 'crossover' styles in our own century—were not entirely satisfactory was due not only to the unsuitability of much folk-song for harmonization in the Western classical style, but also to problems of musical structure and 'content', bequeathed by the eighteenth century.

Beethoven, with magnificent daring, and mostly infallible judgement, had already transformed the style he inherited. By allowing his main themes, or motifs, extreme contrasts of both tonality and texture,

[16] 'La Chambre d'enfants de M. Moussorgsky', *Revue blanche*, 1 April 1901, cited in Leon Vallas, *The Theories of Claude Debussy* (London: Dover, 1967), 152.

he had undermined the eighteenth-century concern for carefully balanced key relationships: ambiguous use of tonality was already evident in the First Symphony, which opens with a dominant seventh formed on the tonic note (and in the key, therefore, of the subdominant). Beethoven's fondness for the use of a tonic pedal—in the Allegro theme of Leonora Overtures nos. 2 and 3, for example, or in the opening theme of the String Quartet in F, Op. 59 No. 1—enabled rhythm and melody to lead lives of their own, with reduced dependence on harmony as an agent of musical propulsion. His use of unaccompanied melodic material to open both the Fifth and the Sixth symphonies took this process a step further; and the 'modal' writing in his 'late period'—such as the chorale 'in the Lydian mode' that opens the slow movement of the String Quartet in A minor, Op. 132, or the Et incarnatus in the *Missa Solemnis*—further obscures the relationship between melody, rhythm, and tonal harmony. Such innovations were worthy of all Burke's 'astonishment' and 'horror' over the sublime, let alone Hoffman's 'longing for the infinite' in romanticism.

Throughout the nineteenth century, Beethoven's achievement was, though much discussed, only partly understood; and an increasing tendency to use melodies rather than motifs as the basis of symphonic structure—by 'romantics' as much as by 'nationalists'—made it harder to sustain musical interest by means of musical 'argument'. Nineteenth-century nationalist composers entered a system that, through the force of astonishing genius, had been thrown into disarray.

In fact, the 'nationalist' music of the nineteenth century took a considerable time to flower. In Russia, for example, a vogue for native folk-song occurred in the 1770s (in reaction to large-scale importation of Italian musicians and music earlier in the century), but the first 'nationalist' work of universal acclaim, Glinka's *A Life for the Tsar*, was not produced until 1836, nor published in its entirety until 1881; and the Imperial Russian Music Society, that was to transform the country's musical life, was founded only in 1859.[17] In Czechoslovakia, the first publication of native folk-songs took place in 1800, but it was not until 1866 that Smetana produced the first Bohemian work of universal acclaim, the opera *The Bartered Bride* (Pl. 59).[18]

Rhythmic inadequacy in relation to harmony was not merely a feature of nationalists' music; it affected nineteenth century music as

[17] Gerald Abraham, 'Union of Soviet Socialist Republics', *The New Grove* (1980), xix. 381–2.
[18] John Clapham, 'Czechoslovakia', *The New Grove* (1980), v. 121.

59. Scene from a production of Smetana's *The Bartered Bride*, to mark its hundredth performance, Prague National Opera (1882)

a whole. On the one hand, accompanied melody, so germane to nineteenth-century musical style, became self-sufficient in the song and the drawing-room piece, for which the nineteenth century showed a predilection. On the other hand, the nineteenth century showed a conflicting predilection for the grandiose; and in grandiose music, accompanied melody alone is inadequate. Nor was the association of 'programmes' with large-scale symphonic works a substitute for structures allied logically to harmonic propulsion. In 'nationalist' music, which was usually driven by themes rather than motifs, sustaining a musical 'argument' was a particular problem, though in Finland the problem was circumvented by Sibelius's system of thematic evolution. In German romantic music, the problem was solved by Wagner's system of thematic metamorphosis.

German Idealism and Hegel

'Nationalist' composers—and that means French and Italian, almost as much as East and north European—had to contend not only with a system in disarray, but with a Germany that had developed a considerable sense of cultural and racial superiority. This was, in part, a reaction to French cultural dominance throughout the eighteenth century. It was kindled, in particular, by the discovery in the late eighteenth century that Indic and European languages share common roots. As observed in Chapter 4, Europeans came to regard themselves as descendants of conquering 'Aryans' from the highlands of Central Asia. It was here, according to J. F. Blumenbach, who first publicized the word 'Caucasian' in 1795, that the white 'race' had originated, and from it, all others had subsequently degenerated. German linguists claimed a particularly strong connection between their language and Greek, and came to regard themselves as the purest of 'Aryan' descendants;[19] they subsequently found it expedient to attribute the origins of Greek culture not to Egyptians but to conquering Indo-European-speaking Dorians.

Throughout the first half of the nineteenth century, there was much speculation on the origins of different 'races'. By the middle of the century, it was popularly believed that the 'yellow' races ranked below the white races; and that, according to the Compte de Gobineau, 'the black variety is the lowest and lies at the bottom of the ladder'.[20]

A 'progressive' view of history was articulated at length by Hegel (1770–1831) in his *Philosophy of History*. According to Hegel, in the historical development of spirit (the opposite of matter), there were three main phases.[21] As Martin Bernal has summarized them, the first of these moved from the 'theocratic despotism' of Mongolia and China to the 'theocratic aristocracy' of India and the 'theocratic monarchy of Persia', with Egypt as a point of transition between East and West. The second, the 'adolescence of humanity', was represented by Greece, where, for the first time, there was moral freedom. The third started with Rome and climaxed in the Prussian state.[22] Hegel's theory of history, to quote Bertrand Russell, 'if it was to be made plausible, required some distortion of facts and considerable ignorance. Hegel, like Marx and Spengler after him, possessed both these qualifications'.[23]

As with most philosophers of his day, Hegel also wrote on aesthetics; as a student he had read theology, and he linked his aesthetic system

[19] Bernal, *Black Athena*, i. 193, 219.
[20] Ibid. 241.
[21] Bertrand Russell, *History of Western Philosophy* (Woking: Allen & Unwin, 1946), 763.
[22] Bernal, *Black Athena*, i. 256.
[23] Russell, *History of Western Philosophy*, 762.

with his system of metaphysics. His contemporary Arthur Schopenhauer, in *Die Welt als Wille und Vorstellung* (1819), had expounded the notion that music's non-representational character causes it, uniquely among the arts, to reveal the Will. For Schopenhauer (echoing Buddhist thought), the only escape from the cycle of desire and partial satisfaction that the Will creates lay in the renunciation of desire. This could best be achieved through aesthetic contemplation, of which music offered the highest form. Hegel took this philosophy a stage further, by subsuming art under religion.

In classical art, according to Hegel, beauty, proportion, and harmony had represented only the outward expression of the Spirit; in romanticism, however, new freedoms enabled the arts to become unified in the concept of a single God: a single self-sufficiency.[24] The Greeks had reached the highest point in art in sculpture, by wedding sensuous matter with intelligible form. Romanticism, however, had enabled *music* to reach a yet higher manifestation, because music could resolve tensions;[25] art had—uniquely—acquired the means of expressing the Image (*Erscheinung*) of God, through human form and activity. In this way, Hegel linked what he perceived as the omniscience of German culture with the omniscience of Christianity. (Following the anarchy of the French Revolution, Protestant Europe had again invoked Christianity as an essential bastion of social order.)

German Idealism and Wagner

Whereas, during the eighteenth century, the underlying consensus had caused philosophy to underpin art, during the nineteenth century, the cult of the individual—and in particular of genius as embodying the most radical originality—enabled art to become independent of philosophy. During the second half of the nineteenth century, the authority of philosophy was undermined by advances in technology and the natural sciences, while musical aesthetics suffered correspondingly from advances in empirical studies of acoustics and of the psychology of musical perception. Increasingly the task of interpreting the world fell to the artist. This, like the musical aesthetics of the eighteenth century, was a distinctively European phenomenon.

[24] Le Huray and Day (eds.), *Music and Aesthetics*, 225–6.
[25] F. E. Spearshott, 'Aesthetics of Music', *The New Grove* (1980), i. 127.

No artist fulfilled the task more comprehensively than Wagner; and no artist was more condemnatory of the world he interpreted; the 'Ring' cycle embodied a wholesale denunciation of capitalism, and of European 'progress'. Wagner immersed himself in contemporary politics and philosophy, but his art itself took absolute precedence over them.[26] Audiences he made art's servants. He did not entertain them: he edified them. Where Hegel had considered religion to have manifested itself in art, Wagner considered religion to have been usurped by art:[27] 'Music', he averred, 'reveals with unparalleled precision and certainty the unique essence of religion.'[28]

The view that *instrumental* music, more than other arts, could express feelings and aspirations without the use of words was essentially a German phenomenon. Neither Italy nor France had developed a purely instrumental music: Italian opera of the period, notwithstanding the skill of Rossini, had aspired to be little more than entertainment; and the French had shown small support for the romantic leanings of Berlioz. (Wagner himself regarded Italian opera as a 'trollop' and French opera as a 'coquette with a cold smile'.[29]) German composers, however, could not escape the shadow of Beethoven. The sheer fact of his extraordinary output—which by the middle of the century had become the staple of serious-minded symphony concerts—was overwhelming, as were the problems of symphonic construction it bequeathed.

In purely musical terms, the process of allowing instrumental music an expressive life of its own, independently of words, had found its first major expression with J. S. Bach. More than any composer before him, Bach had cultivated the art of thematic development: the breadth and diversity of his instrumental writing had been without precedent. Nevertheless, instrumental music, with formal structures peculiar to it, did not flourish until the second half of the eighteenth century; and the proposition that a purely instrumental music might possess a unique

[26] Not unusually among artists of the day, Wagner imbibed current racialist theories; and it was his posthumous misfortune to have Hitler make use of a misguided, anti-Semitic article to justify his own obsessive anti-Semitism. Wagner admired Mendelssohn and Halévy; and Hermann Levi, who conducted the first performance of *Parsifal*, ascribed Wagner's 'attacks on what he calls Judaism in music and literature' to 'the noblest motives' (Curt von Westernhagen, 'Wagner', *The New Grove* (1980), xx. 111 ff).

[27] Carl Dahlhaus, 'Wagner', *The New Grove* (1980), xx. 115–17.

[28] Klaus Stichweh, 'Awareness through Compassion', in *Programmheft III, Parsifal* (Bayreuther Festspiele, 1977), 23.

[29] Dahlhaus, 'Wagner', *The New Grove*, xx. 115.

capacity to affect the mind and spirit only gained public attention with the philosophical writings of the early German romantics. With Beethoven's instrumental music, the proposition had become a belief; and the belief had sustained romantic music during the first half of the nineteenth century.

Beethoven's distinctive musical syntax had, nevertheless, proved inimitable. Brahms, on the one hand, attempted to enlarge the symphonic canvas in a traditional mould, by expanding motivic themes in the course of their exposition. Wagner, on the other hand, attempted, through drama, to create a new style of 'infinite melody'. He sought to 'redeem' the symphony by bringing to what he perceived as a Greek ideal of dramatic, artistic, and musical integration, the same integrity as Beethoven had brought to the symphony and string quartet.[30] Wagner's *Gesamtkunstwerk* ('complete art-work') elevated art to what many Germans regarded as the loftiest plane of their intellectual and moral achievement. It is perhaps significant that Wagner's supporters admired the first Bayreuth Festival (1876) more for the example it set than for its actual artistic achievement.[31]

In fact, the plot of *Der Ring des Nibelungen* embodied a subversion of German intellectual culture, even though its music was a direct product of that culture.[32] In this cycle of four operas, Wotan—ruler of the world—has acquired knowledge and insight through drinking from the Well of Wisdom. The price to Wotan has been the loss of an eye and, by implication, of his 'natural' state. The heroic Siegfried, born into the 'perfect' *Wälsung*—or 'Aryan'—race, symbolizes that 'natural' state; in German racial theory, Siegfried represents Grecian man, at the 'adolescent' stage of humanity. But Siegfried's heroic role is, symbolically, to destroy capitalism and the modern state.[33] By the end of *Götterdämmerung*, gods, heroes, villains, and workers have all been eliminated. There remain only the Rhinemaidens, guardians again of the gold that had been stolen from them. Power has been transferred from God back to nature (Pl. 60). A new order, based on compassion, could be created only from a state of total innocence, as exemplified by *Parsifal*.

This was hardly a metaphor for Hegelian philosophy. Hegel had seen in the Prussian state the consummation of God's purpose for humanity.

[30] Ibid.

[31] Westernhagen, 'Wagner', *The New Grove*, xx. 110.

[32] Mozart had done precisely the same thing for the courtly culture of the eighteenth century in his operas, *Le Nozze di Figaro* (1786) and *Il Don Giovanni* (1787).

[33] Deryck Cooke, *I Saw the World End* (London: Oxford University Press, 1979), 279.

60. Hagen attempts to seize the ring from the Rhinemaidens: Hoffman's set for the original production of *Götterdämmerung*, Bayreuth (1876)

Wagner, as a relatively young man, loathed the Prussian state:[34] he was, in any event, more naturally inclined to Schopenhauer's philosophy than to Hegel's. Not least among Wagner's achievements was to enable art itself to challenge the *status quo*, giving it a more powerful subversive potential than Beaumarchais's play *Les Noces de Figaro*—of which Napoleon quipped that it was 'the revolution in action'[35]—or Verdi's opera *Nabucco*, used to further the cause of Italian nationalism.

Through the technique of constantly transforming *leitmotifs* ('leading motifs' associated with particular aspects of the drama) into 'infinite melody', Wagner developed—arguably more than any composer before or since—the capacity to project through his music the *psychological* implications of the drama. His appeal to the subconscious was made in purely musical terms. In the 'Ring' cycle, the opening, mainly arpeggiated, motif is the source of all the succeeding motifs. It was no longer

[34] As indicated in his article 'Revolution', published as the leader of the *Volksblätter* (People's Paper), 8 April 1849; cited in Cooke, *I Saw the World End*, 259.

[35] R. B. Moberley, *Three Mozart Operas* (London: Gollancz, 1967), 51.

necessary for Wagner to incorporate musical ideas habitually associated with, for example, the military or the ballroom; instead the composer could establish and develop musical symbolism relating specifically to the drama in question. Orchestra and voice became equal partners in turning declamation into infinitely extended, symbolic melody, the continuity of which was fundamentally symphonic ('organic') in nature. The drama was always conditioned by the musical syntax. 'The acts of the music made visible' was how Wagner, retrospectively, described the drama.[36]

This ability owed much to Wagner's mature harmonic system, in which chromatic harmony (chords progressing by means of semitonal shifts) alternated with traditional, root-progression harmony. This ambivalence subverted tonality, without eliminating it. Generally, a tonal direction was implied, but the pursuance of it was constantly interrupted by shifting, chromatic harmonies. Motifs could assert their presence over a relatively simple bass line, or, by intermingling, they could generate a contrapuntal texture that engendered less conventional harmony.[37] The process was illuminated by the orchestration; few composers have had a more compelling sense of instrumental colour and of its capacity to irradiate harmony. Where Beethoven had made *harmonic* rhythm non-essential, Wagner made the whole tonal system itself non-essential. Implicit in Wagner's harmonic system was the cycle of stimulation and relaxation that Schopenhauer had attached to the Will.

Wagner's harmonic system led to organized atonality. With a little licence, it is possible to extract from the opening bars of *Tristan* a 'note-row': an ordering of the twelve semitones in such a way that none recurs until the others have sounded in-between. 'Atonal' composers who succeeded Wagner—most notably Schoenberg and Webern—moved from Wagner's *partial* abandonment of tonality to a total abandonment of tonality (and so of functional harmony). (In similar fashion, 'romantic' composers who succeeded Beethoven—most particularly Berlioz and Liszt—had accepted his *partial* abandonment of harmonic rhythm, and had allowed mood and gesture to take precedence over it.) With 'serial' music, rhythm severed its connection with harmony; indeed, the *sound* of the music severed any obvious connection with that of Wagner.

[36] *Über die Benennung 'Musikdrama'* (1872), cited in Dahlhaus, 'Wagner', *The New Grove*, xx. 121.

[37] Dahlhaus, 'Wagner', *The New Grove*, xx. 123–5.

Wagner's music was to prove, in the perceptive words of Claude Debussy, 'a glorious sunset that was mistaken for a dawn'.

Modernism

For many of his successors, Wagner's system of harmony and orchestration provided a basis for music of great emotional intensity, often constructed on a heroic scale. Two composers in particular—Gustav Mahler and Richard Strauss—appeared to adopt this mantle. Yet Mahler's self-conscious, contorted chromaticism, often superimposed on conventional tonal structures, seemingly parodied romantic harmony; and his use of quotations from vernacular musical vocabulary satirized a tradition with which the composer was always instinctively uneasy. In Strauss's music, the constantly shifting tonality, sometimes bordering on polytonality, led to a sense of tonal instability, opposed to the essentially affirmative use of key by Wagner. Mahler and Strauss, in their different ways, were both masters of orchestral effect, and of the creation of subtleties of mood in music. Neither, however, offered a durable solution to the problems of large-scale musical construction, initiated by Beethoven's adaptation of eighteenth century formal structure to incorporate extreme contrasts of tonality and texture, and exacerbated by Wagner's ambivalent use of tonality (Pl. 61).

Debussy, who nursed a life-long, love–hate relationship with Wagner's music, was acutely aware of the need to extricate himself from what Erik Satie mockingly described as the 'Wagnerian adventure'. His response was to retain the vertical, harmonic logic of chord structures, but to deny the *necessity* of a horizontal relationship between them. He thus precluded both the tension *and* the release of the Schopenhauerian Will, and the notion of musical causality implicit in functional harmony. This, too, offered no durable solution, though it influenced the anti-élitist tendency of the French School, which, in the words of Erik Satie again, was 'the only possible opposition to an epoch of excessive refinement'.

Satie made this remark in connection with the scandalous Parisian première of his surrealist Ballet *Parade*, that included in its orchestral percussion section both a siren and a typewriter (Pl. 62). However, the first known performance of Satie's now infamous 'Vexations'—a short passage required to be repeated 840 times—was organized not in France, but in the USA, by John Cage. It was in the USA, too, that

61. Caricature of a Straussian orchestra by A. Schmidhammer

Edgar Varèse (1883–1965), having observed that radicalism and French taste seemed not to be in accord, 'fathered noise into the twentieth century'. Another false dawn was to arise in the USA.

Paradoxically, continuity with Wagner—in theory at least—was embodied in the 'Second Viennese' School of Schoenberg, Webern, and Berg. Schoenberg was committed to the Austro-German tradition; indeed, he claimed that his dodecaphonic, 'serial' system of composition, so far from being a rejection of that tradition, was in fact a continuation of it. When, however, in 1908, he accepted that his increasingly chromatic harmonies could no longer be accommodated within tonal forms, he abandoned tonality entirely.[38] Atonality was first evident in his *Piano Pieces* of 1909–10.

Schoenberg's subsequent rationalization of 'serialism'—an essentially *abstract* system of composition—was a function of the tonal impasse; it was first fully applied in his *Piano Pieces*, *Serenade*, and *Piano Suite* of 1923. He saw his method of composing with twelve notes

[38] O. W. Neighbour, 'Schoenberg, Arnold', *The New Grove* (1980), xvi. 711.

62. Picasso's design for the American Manager in Satie's *Parade*, as revived by Massine in 1974

as 'growing out of necessity'.[39] It fell to Webern, however, in his miniature forms, to remove (most thoroughly) all traces of past aesthetic, by denying to music not only functional harmony, but also rhythmic impulse. Thereafter, a later generation of composers would subject every parameter of musical composition to purely formalist serial procedures. Arguably the early works of Pierre Boulez—*Le Marteau sans maître*, for instance—took this process of 'integral serialism' to its furthest practicable limit.

Beauty and the Beast (1)

Modernism—a term originally attached to architecture, but now suggestive of all the formalist artistic movements

[39] *The Composition with Twelve Tones* (1950), cited in Sam Morgenstern (ed.), *Composers on Music* (New York: Pantheon Books, 1956), 378.

of the twentieth century—finally called into question a view of music that, deriving from Aristotle, had informed the course of European music since the early seventeenth century: that, whether of itself, or through its association with the rhetoric of words, music has the power to express something outside itself. This view had already been strongly challenged by the music critic Eduard Hanslick, in 1854. Hanslick had averred that music neither depended upon models, nor served external goals: 'Music consists of successions and forms of sound, and these alone constitute the object' (see also p. 688).[40]

Over 2,000 years earlier, a similar view had been held by Aristoxenus, who had formulated his theory of scales precisely because he considered music to be a self-contained phenomenological system. Aristoxenus had recognized that music could be judged only by what is audible; self-evidently, for example, the mathematical ratios that determine intervals between pitches (as ascertained by the Pythagoreans) were *not* audible.[41] During the early twentieth century, the course of European music led to the reassertion of a similarly formalist, abstract view of music. Underlying 'serial' theory was the notion that a concord differs from a discord only by association, that the difference is not inherent in the laws of nature. Even Stravinsky, after moving from his exuberant, early ballet style to his pre-war neo-classical style—and long before he espoused serialism—felt it necessary to postulate that music 'by its very nature is essentially powerless to express anything at all'.[42] Composers from Erik Satie to Pierre Boulez appeared to adopt this attitude.

The underlying philosophy of musical modernism was linked with Wagner, in that it accepted the superior standing of the creative artist: that where the daemon leads it is the audience's duty to follow. But, as Kandinsky pointed out with reference to Schoenberg, modernism had made it the duty of the artist to express himself as intensely and directly as possible, even if in so doing he refused to employ 'the habitual forms of the beautiful'.[43] Modernism caused *ugliness*, as well as beauty, to be loved—or at least invoked—in the name of art.

By the early twentieth century, with the individuality of style that then characterized the great composer, it had become possible for

[40] *Vom Musikalisch-Schönen*, cited in Nancy Kovaleff Baker, 'Expression', *The New Grove* (1980), vi. 326.

[41] R. P. Winnington-Ingram, 'Aristoxenus', *The New Grove* (1980), i. 592, and Spearshott, 'Aesthetics of Music', *The New Grove*, i. 123.

[42] *Chroniques de ma vie* (1935), cited in Morgenstern (ed.), *Composers on Music*, 442.

[43] Arnold Whitall, 'Expressionism', *The New Grove* (1980), vi. 333.

Puccini to extract, from the music of *Tosca*, the last drop of beautiful emotion from as lurid a plot as had ever struck the operatic stage. Subsequently, there was a tendency for lurid plots to be dressed in music that departed so far from 'the habitual forms of the beautiful' that it too could be considered lurid. And the place of action moved increasingly from such idealized contexts as heaven, the Church, the palace, or the 'noble' battlefield, to what is commonly called 'the gutter'. Bartók, for example, in his ballet *The Miraculous Mandarin*, took the dramatic elements used by Wagner in *Parsifal*—magic, the destructive power of love, and the need for compassion—and placed them not in the temple of the Holy Grail, but in a brothel. John Gay had done something similar nearly 200 years earlier, but his parody was in a musical style that could be understood as well by ordinary people as by aristocrats. This was hardly the case with Berg's *Lulu*, for example. In the early twentieth century, the association of morality with a love of beauty appeared to be finally discredited.

Are there natural laws in music that define, universally, the beautiful in music? That music affects the emotions remains self-evident. But, since the understanding of music seems not to be expressible in linguistic form, no one has yet been able to show how music achieves its effect, despite all the words that have been expended on the subject.[44] Only in Europe, with its symmetries, its printing presses, its accurate musical notation—and its vertical harmony—was the question ever addressed with any enthusiasm. Africans and Asians have been more concerned to examine the function of music in *controlling*, rather than imitating, nature. The emotions said to be stirred by European art music came to depend less upon geographical or ethnic origin of a *melody type* (which, to some extent, had characterized all the musical cultures of Asia, as well as of early Europe) than upon melodic types as conditioned by harmony and rhythm. (This was true, even of nineteenth-century nationalist composers whose melodic material reflected distinctive regional styles.) European harmony had engendered melody types based on *triadic* intervals, fundamentally different from melody types of other musical cultures.

Harmony—an ordering of triad-based chords, placed in relation to key, to each other, and to the elements of melody and rhythm, which they largely control—was a uniquely Western concept. Thus an analyst such as Schenker, who considered that chords and tonics are in some

[44] Roger Scruton, *The Aesthetic Understanding* (Manchester: Carcanet Press, 1983), 59.

way guaranteed by natural order—he referred to the major triad as the 'chord of nature'—can appeal, if at all, only within the Western tradition. On the other hand, many non-Western peoples, when confronted with Western harmony, have adopted it with enthusiasm. And Westerners, who, for a short time, were denied harmony in much of their contemporary music, can now scarcely escape it. The stern didacticism of modernism has given way to the pluralist pleasures of Postmodernism, where formal discipline runs amok before such a diversity of styles and genres as has never previously been available in one part of the world, let alone in one piece of music. Art music's élite base has been fatally undermined: the popular now aspires to be élite as the élite engages with the popular.

The spread of literacy in Europe made the distinction between popular and élite musical cultures different in kind from that distinction elsewhere. Art music became complex to the eye as much as to the ear; and popular music, though less complex, was also perceived by the eye. Only the folk music of peasants, where it continued to exist, remained strictly an oral–aural tradition. No art music outside the European tradition was notated with such exactness or, for that matter, with the intention that the notation would be used in performance. Nor did any art music undergo such radical change.

It would be misleading to suggest that, because of this, European music became more complex than musical systems elsewhere: the rhythms of traditional African music, for example, are as complex and specific as anything in the French 'mannerist' school of fourteenth-century Europe, or the integral serialism of Boulez. Nor was European music more virtuosic: it is doubtful if any European percussionist has ever equalled the virtuosity of the South Asian *tablā*-player at its best. Nor was European music more responsive to natural beauty: arguably, no music in the world evokes more subtly the serenity of a natural landscape than the slowly moving notes and graces of the Chinese seven-stringed zither. And in Bali, where even the pigeons are made to fly carrying delicate whistles around their necks, the music of the gamelan blends with its topography with a naturalness that Europe probably never experienced, even before St Thomas Aquinas married the religious to the profane with his manipulation of the doctrine of the 'double truth'. The difference between European and other musical cultures became essentially one of function.

During the European Middle Ages, the basic function of art music was theocratic: music supported the dogmas of religion. As that theocratic base was increasingly undermined from the fourteenth century onwards, the function of musical art changed to that of aristocratic service, involving mutual exploitation between servant and served. Art music became a political accoutrement, tied to a contemporary, ever-changing aesthetic, to an extent very much greater than, for example, occurred at Islamic, Indian, or Chinese courts.[45]

For European art music to rise above the level of pleasurable amiability that its new function generated, the application of exceptional genius was required. Those few composers thus qualified were able to adapt the style of the past into a style appropriate to the present; to use that style as an expression of contemporary fashions and ideas; and finally to use the experience and confidence thus accumulated, to enter an exclusive, visionary world, creating works of such depth as to deny the past, the present, and the future. The European aesthetic implied a *need* for 'progress', and change; the dynamic of European art was intrinsically—and uniquely—modern.

Outside Western Europe, where change was not a precondition of creative art, musical excellence was apparent in the skill and subtlety with which traditional musical compositions were performed and—(usually) almost imperceptibly—changed. In Western Europe, where musical notation encouraged individuality (often at the expense of tradition), and where excellence could be measured by the eye as well as by the ear, the acts of both composition and listening became intellectual as much as emotional undertakings. As artists and composers entered ivory towers vacated by princelings and philosophers during the second half of the nineteenth century, their offerings became increasingly removed from the artistic and musical experiences of ordinary people. Only in our own time, with the widespread rejection of modernism, has this situation been reversed, and the consequences have not been wholly beneficial. Today, composers rarely even aspire to rise above the various levels of amiable entertainment engendered by a plurality of musical aesthetics.

Despite the reversals of the 'Postmodern' age, however, classical, European, art music remains with us as never before, delighting audiences whose understanding of the composers' intentions is often, at best, only partial. In the final volume of *A la recherche du temps perdu* (1927), Marcel Proust addressed this subject with acuity:

[45] Peter Fletcher, *Education and Music* (Oxford: Oxford University Press, 1987), 66–7.

> Even where the joys of art are concerned, although we seek and value them for the sake of the impression that they give us, we contrive as quickly as possible to set aside as being inexpressible precisely that element in them which ... we sought; and we concentrate instead upon that other ingredient in aesthetic emotion which allows us to suppose that we are sharing it with other art-lovers .... Since (the art lovers) fail to assimilate what is truly nourishing in art, they need artistic pleasures all the time; they are victims of a morbid hunger which is never satisfied. So they go to concert after concert to applaud the same work .... They will shout 'Bravo, bravo' until they are hoarse at the end of a work they admire, and imagine as they do so that they are discharging a duty. But demonstrations of this kind do not oblige them to clarify the nature of their admiration and of this they remain in ignorance.[46]

These words describe a very European phenomenon; the contradictions they exemplify lie at the heart of Europe's artistic achievement. With the spread of Western musical systems around the globe, however, such contradictions have become a more universal problem; and the dilemmas they pose must be faced not only in the West but throughout the world, so long as the classical arts of any zone of civilization continue to engage the interest and enthusiasm of their citizens.

[46] Marcel Proust, *A la recherche du temps perdu*, trans. Andreas Mayor (London: Chatto & Windus, 1927), 256, 258.

Part Four

The New World

The Americas

14 Cultural Mix in Latin America

European Colonization

The appropriation of the Americas by Europeans was one of the most significant occurrences in human history. It marked the first stage of European hegemony over a large part of the planet. It involved the near elimination of urban, agrarian, and hunter-foodgathering societies that had evolved over some 2,000 years, in two entire continents. It brought into the same environment peoples of African, Asian, and European stocks. Within a period of little more than fifty years, the New World became host to a lasting mix of peoples, the interaction of which—or lack of it—has had profound consequences for the history of humankind. Such interaction has also profoundly affected the subsequent course of music.

The early colonization of Latin America involved an extraordinary degree of serendipity. When Christopher Columbus, an Italian, alighted on the island of San Salvador in the Bahamas in 1492, he believed he had reached the mainland of Asia; he therefore referred to the native inhabitants as 'Indians'. He had persuaded Ferdinand and Isabella of Spain that he could open up a new trade route to the Spice Islands of the Orient by sailing west, and had set sail with a royal blessing 'for gospel and for gold' and a letter from *Los Catholicos* addressed to the 'Grand Khan of Cathay'. He was never to know that he had not sighted Asia.[1]

Columbus's second voyage took him to Hispaniola (modern Haiti and the Dominican Republic), Jamaica, and Cuba; he then believed he had reached Japan. His third voyage took him to Trinidad via the coast of Venezuela; recognizing that this latter was a mainland coast, he

[1] Alistair Cooke, *America* (London: BBC, 1973), 32.

surmised that the land contained a 'terrestrial paradise'. His fourth and last voyage (1502–4), along the Central American coastline, showed that there was *no* sea route to the west: a 'proof' that he was sailing the coast of the Malay Peninsula.[2] Ten years later, Vasco Nuñez de Balboa would cross the isthmus of Panama, claim the whole Pacific Ocean and its contiguous lands for Spain, and institute the first Spanish settlements in what is now Panama.

Spanish hegemony intensified in 1519, following the historic encounter between Hernán Cortés and King Moctezuma II in Tenochtitlán, the mountain capital city of the Aztecs. Aztec culture was then at its height. The Aztecs had achieved dominion very quickly: in less than 200 years they had graduated from tribal to imperial status; in 1519 their rule extended over some twenty million people inhabiting most of Mesoamerica. They had consolidated fine traditions in art, pottery, metalworking, and architecture—developed by the earlier Maya civilization—and had established intricate rituals of music and dance. Tenochtitlán itself (the site of present-day Mexico City), some 50 square kilometres in size, was built on a lake, and was as grand a city as any in the world; the Spaniards called it 'another Venice'.[3] It had been built—according to tradition—on the sighting of an eagle, as foretold by the Aztec's sun-god, Huitzilopochti. Aztecs believed their present era could be prolonged by feeding the sun with human blood, and human sacrifice of prisoners of war was carried out on a vast scale. Unlike the rural peoples of Panama, the urban Aztecs must have seemed invincible.

Serendipity was still at work when Cortés approached Mexico. The Aztecs inherited from the Mayans a consummate knowledge of astronomy, and their astronomers had long foretold the return of their god Quetzacoatl (to whom legend had apparently attributed a white skin and a black beard) that very year. Thus, when Cortés landed on the coast of Mexico, he was welcomed as the returning god, and was able to ensnare and capture King Moctezuma. Nevertheless, the final overthrow and destruction of Tenochtitlán was to take two years, and to involve hideous brutality and loss of life.

Among the many factors that contributed to Cortés's success was evangelical zeal: the Spaniards never doubted that the Christian God was on their side. When Cortés made his first landing at Cozumel Island off the Gulf of Mexico, one of his first actions was to read the *requer-*

[2] Alistair Cooke, *America*, 32.

[3] Ronald Wright, *Stolen Continents: The Indian Story* (London: Murray, 1992), 21.

imento to the indigenous peoples. This little-understood document explained that the lands used by these peoples had been 'donated' to Spain in 1493 by the Borgia Pope Alexander VI, that the peoples themselves were to become subjects of Spain, and that they were to take up the 'true faith' in peace, on pain of death or enslavement. This *requerimento* led to the promulgation of the Roman Catholic faith throughout Latin America, and to Native Americans acquiring expertise in European polyphonic music; it also provided justification for some of the most callous perfidy, torture, and slaughter in the history of the human race.

Fortunate timing also contributed to the next great Spanish conquest—that over the Incas of Peru. Like the Aztecs, the Incas had established ruthless control over a vast area: present-day Ecuador, Peru, Bolivia, and parts of Argentina and Chile. The Incas too were superb builders and had also absorbed fine artistic traditions, from neighbouring Moche, Nasca, and Chimu cultures; their temples and palaces were adorned with sheets of gold, silver, or feathered mosaic.

Francisco Pizarro first landed on the coast of Peru in 1524. When he made what was to be his final landing, in 1531, the Inca state was in unprecedented disarray, following a civil war fought by the two sons of the last emperor. Taking advantage of the victor's weariness, Pizarro tricked him into attending a feast unarmed, took him captor, and slaughtered his bodyguard. A year later, Pizarro reneged on a ransom agreement, and had the young emperor killed, on grounds of 'treason'. The consequent demoralization of the Inca enabled Pizarro to sack the Inca mountain capital, Cusco, and plunder the city of its treasure; Inca chiefs were then executed, and millions of Inca people were enslaved. The Spanish buildings in the Cusco of today are constructed on Inca stone foundations; by a nice irony, where Spanish buildings have succumbed to earthquake, the precisely fitting, Inca stonework, needing no cement, has remained intact.

With the defeat of Aztecs and Incas, the Spanish hold on Meso- and South America was virtually assured. Mexico and Peru, the most populous areas, became the chief centres of colonization. The Rio de la Plata in Argentina had already been explored in 1519, and by 1520 Magellan had sailed the straits that separate the Tierra del Fuego from the rest of Patagonia. In 1541 Orellana made his lone sailing down the Amazon; and by 1550 Guatemala, Equador, Venezuela, Colombia, and Chile had been settled. Argentina followed in 1580 (Pl. 63).

63. A new description of America, from Ortelius' atlas, 1570

Other Europeans, besides the Spanish, sought land in the New World, and, with the pope's blessing, the Portuguese secured rights to what is now Brazil. Because this huge area offered no wealthy empires to conquer, the Portuguese began colonization only in the 1530s, for fear that the French would beat them to it. Salvador, Bahia, was established as the first administrative capital in 1549, and was followed shortly afterwards by the first slave-worked sugar plantations and mills. Between 1575 and 1600 the east coast of Brazil became the foremost sugar-producing territory in the world, and a rush of new immigrants increased the demand for slave labour. No less than five million Africans were captured and shipped from West Africa to Brazil, between 1532 and 1850, after which the slave trade was officially abolished. Over one million Africans died on the journey.[4]

North Europeans also coveted land in the New World. By the early seventeenth century they had gained experience of piracy, raiding, and smuggling in the Caribbean. In the 1620s and 1630s the Dutch rose

[4] For a searing, semi-fictitious account of the Brazilian slave trade, see Bruce Chatwin, *The Viceroy of Ouidah* (London: Pan Books, 1982).

against Spanish domination in Europe and obstructed Spanish shipping in the Caribbean, thus providing cover for the English and French to establish settlements in the Lesser Antilles. These islands would soon become prosperous sugar plantations, based on Brazilian methods of slave labour. By the second half of the seventeenth century, there was a string of French, Dutch, and English island colonies in the Caribbean, embracing a mix of European and African cultures. The 'Sugar' islands, prosperous through African sweat, became valuable objects of barter, affecting the treaties that followed European wars; a slice of what was formerly eastern Brazil was subsequently split between France, Holland, and Britain (now the independent states of French Guiana, Surinam, and Guyana respectively).

From the start of colonization, priests had sent complaints to Europe concerning the bestial treatment of the 'Indians' by *conquistadors*; in 1540 the pope was obliged to proclaim that 'Indians' were henceforth to be considered 'members of the human race', and that those enslaving them would risk excommunication. The *conquistadors* responded by setting up the feudal *encomienda* system, whereby the holder of a land grant received a number of 'Indians' to work for him, on condition that he be responsible for the spiritual health of those assigned to him.

Little concern was shown for the nature of this master–servant relationship. Thousands of Native Americans who had not already died of smallpox died of a kind of hard labour to which they were unaccustomed and unsuited. Nevertheless, the Spaniards and Portuguese, with their long multicultural history, were not averse to intermarriage, providing that the 'Indians' had been converted to Christianity. Consequently, large populations of *Mestizos* (part Spanish, part Native American), *Mulattos* (part Spanish, part African), and *Cafusos* (part Native American, part African) emerged. Importantly, however, a powerful 'Creole' aristocracy continued to own most of the land, and to control a predominantly *Mestizo* work force. (Creoles were native-born people of 'pure' Spanish blood.)

Despite social inequities, the colonial period was relatively peaceful, and it lasted for some 300 years. The civil wars that broke out in the nineteenth century, and were fought between royalists and republicans, supposedly in the cause of independence, had the effect of legitimizing Creole hegemony—for independence brought greater gain to the *Criollos*. The two great revolutionary leaders, the royalist General José de

San Martín in the south, and the republican Simón Bolivár in the north, could not ultimately agree on post-war policy. San Martín retired to Europe in 1822, leaving Bolivár to enter Peru in 1824 and defeat the Royalists.

With this defeat, the Spanish administrative apparatus was destroyed and the continent emerged devastated, its internal political boundaries redefined in new 'nation states'. The future aspirations of these states were to shatter Bolivár's dream of South American unity. Towards the end of his life, Bolivár declared the country 'ungovernable', revolution to be like 'ploughing the sea', and emigration the most sensible course of action for South Americans. He predicted—with considerable perspicacity—that the country would 'ineluctably fall into the hands of a mob gone wild, later to fall under the domination of obscure small tyrants of every colour and race'.[5]

History and the mix of peoples has left six relatively distinct groups of states within Latin America:

1. Mexico and the countries of the isthmus, which have been most directly influenced by the USA
2. the Caribbean islands (West Indies), along with Guyana, Surinam, and French Guiana, with differing European backgrounds, but mostly with a majority of African or *Mulatto* peoples, who did not gain independence until the 1960s or later;
3. the countries of Venezuela and Colombia in the north of the South American continent, with their mixed populations divided between mountain and coastland;
4. The Andean heartland of Peru, Bolivia, and Ecuador, the most 'Indian' of the states, separate in culture and economy from the lowland coastal areas;
5. Brazil in the east, with its Portuguese inheritance and predominance of Africans and *Mulattos*;
6. the southern countries of Paraguay, Argentina, Uruguay, and Chile, *gaucho* (cowboy) country, and the most prosperous and European of the South American states.

Although these regions differ in their cultural and musical traditions, they share a common Iberian heritage. Understanding of this cultural backdrop may be assisted by brief consideration of the ascendance, and subsequent isolation, of Spain.

[5] Stephen Birnbaum, *South America* (Boston: Houghton Mifflin, 1989), 109.

The Rise and Fall of Spain

Before becoming part of the Roman Empire, the Iberian peninsula had been invaded by Phoenicians, Greeks, and Carthaginians. The territory was subsequently overrun by the Vandals, on their way to North Africa, and then by the Visigoths, on their way *from* North Africa, after the sacking of Rome in 410. By 711 the Visigoths had, in turn, been ousted by the Berbers of Morocco; by the end of the tenth century the 'Moors' had added Barcelona, León, and the shrine of Santiago de Compostela to their Spanish empire. Spain, therefore, had experienced many cultural influences before absorbing Islamic influences from North Africa and West Asia. During the tenth century, under Umayyad rule, *El Andalus* was a cultural jewel in the Islamic crown, rivalling Baghdad and Damascus.

Christian resistance to the 'Moorish' invasion intensified during the eleventh century; by the mid-thirteenth century, Christians had reconquered all the peninsula except the kingdom of Granada. In the process, they had founded a number of small Christian kingdoms which, by the thirteenth century, had been absorbed by Castile and Aragon. These domains were brought together for the first time in 1469 with the marriage of Ferdinand of Aragon to Isabella of Castile, sponsors of Columbus's first voyage to America. The country was finally unified in 1492 with the reconquest of Granada. The *reconquista* was essentially Christian; it caused Spanish religion and politics to become unshakeably allied.

The new nation state had nevertheless to absorb large numbers of non-Christian subjects, both Moor and Jew. Its institution for achieving this was the Inquisition, which inflicted torture and burning upon 'heretics'. Established by papal bull in 1478, it began to operate in Castile in 1480; when Charles I became sole ruler of Castile *and* Aragon in 1516, the Inquisition was the only institution that exercised authority over Spanish domains, in the Americas as well as in Europe.[6] It gave Spain an unbreakable religious unity which, in 1519, with careful dynastic planning, was to enable Charles I of Spain to become Charles V, Holy Roman Emperor. Charles then inherited from his mother the Spanish kingdoms of Sicily and the newly discovered Americas, and from his father the Burgundian Netherlands. From his grandfather, Maximilian, he inherited the Hapsburg lands of Austria and the Tyrol,

[6] J. M. Roberts, *Pelican History of the World* (London, Pelican Books, 1988), 543–4.

Alsace, and some city states in Italy. His brother Ferdinand would add the crowns of Bohemia and Hungary. This Spanish hegemony was rightly perceived, throughout Europe, as a threat; Aztec and Inca gold was spent on futile attempts to maintain the unreal pretensions of this vast Hapsburg empire.

Set against this empire was the French House of Valois-Bourbon. A series of Hapsburg–Bourbon wars in Italy from 1494 to 1559 not only drained the Spanish purse, but temporarily redefined the map of Europe. In 1556 Charles V abdicated and divided his estates between his brother, Ferdinand, and his son, the ruthlessly fanatical Philip II. From this division of the Hapsburg empire there followed a century of brutal European conflict, during which, incidentally, Portugal passed both in and out of Spanish control, and the Burgundian Netherlands gained independence from Spain as Holland.

When the European wars ended with the Peace of Westphalia in 1648, Spain, whose power had already been severely eroded by the British defeat of its Armada in 1588, entered the backwaters of European history. It became a feudal society, tied to an unwieldy, corrupt bureaucracy; its isolation protected it from the political and social contradictions that stimulate cultural development. Throughout the following three centuries there was 'unchanging poverty and a terrible equilibrium'.[7]

Music and other Arts in Spain

The most conspicuous legacy of Iberian arts in Latin America is the array of baroque churches and cathedrals that still grace much of the Latin American landscape. Towards the end of the sixteenth century, Spain had copied the new baroque architectural style from Italy and, with the help of Aztec and Inca gold, had made this style more lavish and ostentatious there than elsewhere in Europe. The style was reproduced throughout Latin America, and a Brazilian gold boom in the early 1700s made possible the building of the great baroque cities of the province of Minas Gerais in Brazil.

The churches and cathedrals were built by the Jesuits, a fanatical religious brotherhood, founded in 1534 in the shadow of the Inquisition. The objectives of the brotherhood were the promotion of education, the

[7] John Berger, *The Success and Failure of Picasso* (London: Penguin Books, 1965), 22.

suppression of heresy, and missionary work among the heathen. 'Heathen' existed in abundance in the New World; and for 200 years (before they were suppressed in 1773, because of political intrigue) the Jesuits continued to build baroque churches, and to preach Christianity to Native Americans.

By the time most of the baroque cathedrals were completed, their architectural style had been superseded in other parts of Europe. Spain, even in its heyday in the sixteenth century, had never been in the artistic vanguard. The country nurtured a few artistic personalities whose idiosyncrasies placed them somewhat outside the European mainstream. The revolutionary Cretan artist, El Greco, for example, found refuge there; and the Spanish-born Velasquez was able to incorporate Flemish and Italian influences into an unprecedentedly naturalistic style. Mostly, however, Spanish art was derivative.

Though often individualistic, Spanish music was also largely derivative: even during Spain's 'great century' there was little indication of the sense of 'modernity' that characterized the music of the Italian Renaissance and early baroque styles. Spanish organs, for example, following a fine tradition of instrument-making in Seville, inspired a large body of native organ music; but the music—even that of the great Cabezón—was based on the Italian *toccata* style. Early Renaissance Spanish vocal music developed as a result of frequent visits to Spain by leading Flemish composers—though Victoria's music displays marvellous passion and individuality, through its harmonic colour and use of expressive melodic leaps. Later, an unusual dissonance in a Mass by Valls (1702) would inspire a musical controversy that involved some fifty of Spain's best musical minds, but its style was modelled on Italian polychoral and *concertato* styles. When opera became dominant in the early eighteenth century, Spanish composers were commissioned to set *Italian* opera librettos in Spanish translation: there was never such a thing as 'Spanish opera'. Nevertheless, Spain had a rich tradition of folk and popular music, and this, more than its art music, ultimately influenced the course of Latin American music.

The ballad genre, the Romance, developed from the *cantiga*, originally a sacred song. By the thirteenth century the *cantiga* was showing the influence of French troubadours, incorporating secular tunes for satires and epic stories. The subject matter of these epics consisted largely of stories of wars between the 'Moors' and the Christians, and

Ex. 14.1

the enactment of these stories was to become common in the New World. By contrast with the *cantiga*, the *villancico* (from *villano*, a peasant), originally a rustic song, began to attract literary themes; and during the sixteenth century it became a polyphonic genre.

The Romance and *villancico* were major influences in Latin American popular music, and it was through them that many features of Spanish folk music—some embodying African and Asian traits—were transplanted to the New World. Such features included alternation between major and minor thirds, use of sharpened fourths and unresolved sevenths, and a proclivity for melodies in parallel thirds. A common rhythmic feature was alternation between 3/4 and 6/8 (known in Spain as the *sesquialtera*). Many of these features are demonstrated in the Andalusian folk-song shown in Ex. 14.1.[8]

The *vihuela*—a plucked instrument resembling the guitar in shape, but with six courses of strings tuned in the manner of a lute—appears to be of Spanish origin. It is referred to as early as the thirteenth century, but its greatest period of popularity was during the fifteenth and sixteenth centuries. A four-string guitar (in something approaching its modern shape) developed during the fifteenth century, and is

[8] B. Gil Garcia, *Cancionero Popular de Extremadura*, cited by Martin Cunningham, 'Spain', *The New Grove* (1980), xvii. 793.

thought to have originated in Spain and from the *vihuela.* (The modern, six-string guitar appeared only in the 1780s.) The guitar and *vihuela* were to become ubiquitous in Latin America, the latter in the form of the *charango,* a mandolin-size, four- or five-course, metal-strung guitar.

At about the time the Spaniards started arriving in the New World, the Gypsies, who are thought to have originated in Rajastan (in North India), were arriving in Spain. They brought with them elements of Indian music and dance. The virtuoso footwork of Indian *Kathak* dance is also thought to have originated in Rajastan, and its influence is clear in the *zapateado* footwork of Spanish flamenco. Flamenco itself did not become standardized until the eighteenth century, but many of the features from which it evolved—hemiola rhythms, hand-clapping, finger-snapping, and *zapateado* footwork—were present in Spain at the time of New World settlement. These features, likewise, were copied in Latin America.

Although musical influence from Spain was assertive, it did not prove overwhelming; indeed—during the twentieth century in particular—its very assertiveness stimulated peoples throughout Latin America—whether of European, Native American, or African descent—to blend features of their different musical traditions so as to create novel and diverse musical styles. A distinctive Latin-American voice is to be heard in classical European genres, and in a wide variety of traditional, folk, and pop music genres.

European-Derived Polyphonic Music in Latin America

One of the most remarkable features of Spanish colonization of Latin America was the speed with which polyphonic ecclesiastical music, in the European tradition, was established in the new churches and cathedrals. *Maestros de capilla* were quickly appointed to found choir schools, and to institute ensembles of singers and players; by the end of the sixteenth century, such establishments existed in Mexico City, Puebla, Guatemala City, Lima, Cusco, La Plata, Bogotá, Quito, Bahia, and the island of Puerto Rico. By the end of the seventeenth century, the same was true of Buenos Aires, and by the end of the eighteenth century, of Cuba. In Brazil, following the removal of the Portuguese court to Rio de Janeiro in 1808 (resulting from

Napoleon's annexation of Portugal), a new Royal Chapel could boast fifty professional singers, including some Italian castrati.[9]

By the mid-seventeenth century, a well-endowed cathedral would have one, if not two, good organs, and access to players of stringed instruments, trumpets, sackbuts, and shawms. As early as 1572, Lima cathedral had on its permanent payroll six singers and six instrumentalists; and in 1638 Quito cathedral acquired a new 600-pipe organ. About the same period, the musicians of Bogotá cathedral were performing polychoral baroque music, as well as the music of Morales, Victoria, and Palestrina. By the eighteenth century, the baroque cities of Minas Gerais had acquired organs of the finest European quality.[10]

Significantly, the musicians involved in all this activity were by no means wholly European. Teaching of European choral skills was a common means of conversion to the Catholic faith, and Native Americans responded with enthusiasm to the free, metrical structures of psalmody. (This phenomenon extended beyond Latin America; for example, in French Canada, the native Hurons responded more enthusiastically to Jesuit psalmody than to the boisterous songs of the Huguenot sailors.) In Mexico City, as early as 1530, there was a Native American polyphonic choir, noted for its 'remarkable musical accomplishment'.[11] In Lima, in 1549, a law was passed requiring 'Indians' to accept such 'good things' as singing according to the rules of art, and using sol-fa. By 1622, Lima's Jesuit *Indian* church had two organs, four sets of shawms, two trumpets, many viols and other instruments; and the singing was said to be as fine as that in many Spanish cathedrals.[12]

From early colonial times, *Mestizos* became *maestros de capilla*. In Peru and Chile, indigenous slaves were taught the construction and performance of Western instruments, and in Buenos Aires, 'Indian' and African slaves were taught together. By 1622 the Jesuit church in Buenos Aires had a primitive organ and a choir consisting wholly of African slaves.[13]

Native Americans and Africans, therefore, contributed substantially to the development of polyphonic music, though in truth they had little choice in the matter: the Inquisition supported the work of the Jesuits as

[9] Gerard Béhague, 'Cuba' and 'Brazil', *The New Grove* (1980), v. 84–5; iii. 221–2.

[10] Gerard Béhague, 'Peru', 'Ecuador', and 'Colombia', *The New Grove* (1980), xiv. 558; v. 829; iv. 569.

[11] Gerard Béhague, 'Mexico', *The New Grove* (1980), xii. 227.

[12] Robert Stevenson, 'Lima', *The New Grove* (1980), x. 861.

[13] Gerard Béhague, 'Argentina', *The New Grove* (1980), i. 564.

much as the rule of the *Criollos*. Moreover, there were advantages to both Native American and African slaves in cooperating: throughout Latin America, slaves who showed talent in the arts of music, painting, or carving could anticipate freedom and a privileged social position. Nevertheless, the slaves' own indigenous traditions could scarcely be ignored; as early as 1551 *African* drummers were hired in Lima to welcome the new viceroy. The drums were draped in vermilion—the Inca colour—and the Native Americans were amazed at the size of the drums. In 1568 a *Mulatto* was contracted to teach singing and dancing in Bolivia. In 1598, in Mexico, African drums were so much better known than those of Aztecs that a native historian was obliged to describe the *tlapanhuehuetl* (Aztec death drum) as being similar to 'the drum used by the negroes who now dance in the plazas'.[14]

In any event, the religious impulse was not to last. By the beginning of the eighteenth century, church music was in serious decline; when the Jesuits were expelled in 1767, church-building ceased. As in Spain, polyphonic music gave way to baroque instrumental and operatic music.

Operatic and Symphonic Music in Latin America

During the eighteenth century, new European styles reached Latin America direct from their countries of origin, for, when the Treaty of Utrecht (1713) awarded the Spanish crown to the Bourbon Philip V, Spanish influence in the New World gave way to that of France. Chileans, in particular, began to import French spinets and clavichords, anticipating a craze for French salon music. By the end of the eighteenth century, well-to-do Chileans were succumbing to the easy charm of such music in *tertulias* (upper-class social gatherings).[15] In Argentina in the 1880s, French influence appeared more dramatically, when Hispanic colonial buildings in Buenos Aires were replaced by buildings in the French style.

During the eighteenth century, operatic music replaced ecclesiastical music as the favoured style. As early as 1711, for example, an opera was performed in the vice-royal palace in Mexico City; in 1776 the Havana

[14] Gerard Béhague, 'Peru', 'Bolivia', and 'Latin America', *The New Grove* (1980), xii. 558; ii. 872; x. 522–3.

[15] Juan A. Orrego-Salas, 'Chile', *The New Grove* (1980), iv. 231.

Playhouse in Cuba opened with a Metastasian opera by Piccini, and at the Teatro del Circo in the same city, between 1811 and 1832, eighty performances of European operas were given annually.[16] During the eighteenth and nineteenth centuries, theatres and opera houses became almost as common in Latin America as churches and cathedrals.

This change of taste placed ecclesiastical music in terminal decline. In 1826 Bogotá cathedral, for example—once a centre of musical excellence—issued a simple monophonic Mass, composed 'for those days in which there are no singers'. In 1844, at the same cathedral, a 'Hymn to Saint Peter' was set in *tempo de valse*; and, in 1860, a setting of the Lamentations was described as an 'Air de Valse'.[17]

In fact, few opera houses developed artistically; most presented excerpts from scaled-down operas by Rossini, Bellini, and Donizetti. Individual cities played host to touring 'operatic' groups from Europe. Nevertheless, sufficient operatic performance took place to stimulate production of locally composed operas. By the end of the nineteenth century, for example, indigenous operas had been performed in Cuba, Colombia, and Chile; and the opening of the Teatro Colon in Buenos Aires (1908) induced indigenous operas on nationalist subjects, inspired by the *verismo* style of Puccini. Such enterprise was, however, the exception rather than the rule; and the more usual pattern was for operatic excerpts to be performed by touring companies with piano, or a few instruments.

As far away as Manaus, some 2,400 kilometres miles into the Brazilian interior, in the heart of the Amazon jungle, a Teatro Amazonas was built in 1892, at the height of the rubber boom. Designed in classical style, with four levels of Corinthian columns, its materials were all imported from Europe: white marble from Italy, porcelain and wrought iron from England, polished wood from France. Caruso was booked to open it, though he cancelled at the last moment and was replaced by a substitute. A further 800 kilometres upstream, in Iquitos—which started life as a Jesuit mission—where the head-streams of the Amazon have only just united after their tortuous fall from the Andes, they had French Grand Opera. It was performed in the Gran Hotel Malecon Palacio, imported in pieces from Paris. It is now the headquarters of the police. In Rio itself, in 1909, the Teatro Municipal

[16] Béhague, 'Cuba', *The New Grove*, v. 85.
[17] Béhague, 'Colombia', *The New Grove*, iv. 569.

was modelled on the Paris Opéra, except that it was one-quarter the size. It is, of course, inadequate for large-scale opera, and it is now used for occasional concerts, its basement operating as a famous lunch-time restaurant.

Although opera did not generally thrive, there were sufficient musical foundations in nineteenth-century Latin America to generate an interest in symphonic music. The inspiration for this was not, however, Bach, Mozart, and Beethoven, but composers like Piccini and Rossini, along with the waltzes, quadrilles, mazurkas, and polkas that were as fashionable among the upper classes of Latin American cities as of those of Paris and London. Nevertheless, this vogue for the clichés of Italian and French fashion served to stimulate an interest in musical performance. Pianos were imported in quantity. As early as 1820, it could be said of Chile (generally the most European of South American countries) that 'the love of music is amazing; there is no house that lacks a piano'.[18]

Operatic excerpts, salon music, and visits by European virtuosi stimulated interest in symphonic music, as well as the foundation of conservatoires. By 1929, conservatoires had been established in all the main republics: Brazil (1847), Chile (1849), Mexico (1866), Ecuador (1870), Argentina (1872), Colombia (1882), Venezuela (1887), Bolivia (1908), Uruguay (1908), and Peru (1929). Many cities founded 'Philharmonic' societies. In most countries there followed attempts to found nationalist styles of music based on Native American, African, or syncretic popular styles. During the twentieth century, many universities established music departments; and, as European influences were more fully absorbed, nationalist styles gradually gave way to more avant-garde styles.

The nationalist schools produced a body of symphonic and other music, often highly original in style, that has been little performed in the West. In Mexico, for example, the Revolution of 1910 was a forceful spur to nationalism, and encouraged Mexicans to look back to their Aztec roots. A nationalist style was pioneered by the prolific Carlos Chávez (1899–1978), whose *Sinfonia India* incorporated themes from the Yaqui, Seri, and Huichole peoples, but whose style was influenced essentially by Mexican folk styles. Perhaps the most original talent among the composers of the so-called 'Aztec Renaissance' was Silvestre Revueltas (1899–1940); during a tragically short career, Revueltas

[18] Orrego-Salas, 'Chile', *The New Grove*, iv. 231.

developed a personal and eclectic style, rooted in Mexican folk music, and evocative of ancient tradition. *Sensemaya* (a tale of the sacrificial killing of a snake), one of his most popular works, is almost Stravinskian in its rhythmic ferocity, but it also displays a rich melodiousness. Its assured spontaneity contrasts with the contrived complexity of, for example, Copland's *ersatz* simulation of Latin American rhythms in *El Salón Mexico*.

The Latin American composer of this period best known in Europe was the Brazilian, Heitor Villa-Lobos (1887–1959), whose music created a sensation in Parisian avant-garde circles in the mid-1920s. A versatile and highly original, if uneven composer, Villa-Lobos researched Native American music and incorporated aspects of African-influenced, Brazilian popular music into his style, as in the fourteen *Chôros* of 1920–9. In Cuba, the hugely talented and innovative composer Amadeo Roldán (1900–39) incorporated Afro-Cuban rhythms and sonorities into symphonic music, notably in his ballet *La Rebambaramba*; his *Ritmicas V and VI* were among the first Western pieces for percussion ensemble. In Argentina, Alberto Ginastera (1916–83) reflected the solitude and immensity of the pampas in his early work, most notably in the ballet *Estancia* (1941).

Notwithstanding such examples of musical originality and accomplishment in the European, classical, tradition, a strong base for European arts did not develop in Latin America, as it did in the USA. The Mexican writer Octavio Paz has compared the influence on his country of the Counter-Reformation and Neo-Thomism, which condemned it to 'immobility and backwardness', with the influence on the USA of the Reformation and the Enlightenment, which 'orientated the country towards the future'.[19] In Latin America, indeed, there was none of the lively experimentation that characterized the eighteenth-century Singing Schools of Massachusetts (see pp. 542–3), and that in turn was to generate such radically original composers as William Billings and Charles Ives. In Latin America, general economic impoverishment, and a disparity in wealth between the minority *Criollos* and majority *Mestizo* and *Mulatto* populations, tended to isolate both the *Criollos* and their European musical styles, while encouraging a diversity of popular styles, compounded from features of Spanish, African, and Native American musics.

[19] Octavio Paz, 'Mexico and the United States', in *The Labyrinth of Solitude*, new enlarged edn. (London: Penguin Books, 1990), 370–1.

Spanish-Influenced Popular Music

Across Latin America, traditional folk styles have retained unmistakable Spanish traits; although post-civil-war rivalries caused individual republics to seek their own 'national' folk styles, the common Spanish derivation is seldom far to seek. (That derivation usually remains apparent—though less readily so—in many highly original folk styles that have developed, south of Mexico, since the late 1960s.)

The *zambacueca*, for example, which started life in colonial Peru, travelled south to Chile, where, as the *cueca*, it became the national dance. In Argentina, the *zamba* and *cueca* became separate dances, while, in Peru, the *zambacueca* was renamed *marinera* to distinguish it from the Chilian dance. In the small republic of Paraguay the national song became the *polca*, but this was effectively a slowed-down *cueca*; later, however, as Paraguayan songs and dances came to reflect Native American customs and religious syncretisms, the national style was represented by the *guarania*, named after its principal people.[20] In Argentina, the romantic ballad became the speciality of the *payada* (wandering ballad-singer) of the pampa, who improvised romantic songs and dances (*contrapunto*), often in competition with others. All, however, display the features of Spanish folk music described earlier. Ex.14.2 (after Aretz) shows a characteristic Argentinian ballad.[21]

In many areas of the Caribbean, and in South American states with large African populations, Spanish traits blended with those of Africa. A typical hybrid genre that came to pervade Latin American music and

Ex. 14.2 (Up)

[20] Béhague, 'Latin America', *The New Grove*, x. 220–1.
[21] I. Aretz, *El Folklore Musical Argentino* (Buenos Aires: El Folklore, 1952), 144.

THEME
Poco meno ♪ = 90
Tu - ve uncla - vel en mis ma - nos y el
tiem - po me lo - qui - to
Allegro
poco più
Sin re - llex - io - nar lie - go
Por
alarg.
quien loha - bia cau - ti - va - do
Por
FINAL
Poco meno
quien loha - bia cau - ti - va - do.
D.S.

Ex. 14.2 (Lp)

dance was the *son*, which originated in eastern Cuba towards the end of the nineteenth century and combined African rhythms and instruments with European harmonies and verse-forms (see pp. 518–19). In Cuba, the *son* retained many of its African features; in Mexico, however, where African musical influence was minimal, *son* became a generic title for rural, Spanish-influenced song and dance styles. Accompanied by harp or guitar (the latter featuring *rasgueado* strumming), the Mexican *son* developed a *machismo* image: it was danced by individual couples; *zapateado* footwork added rhythmic energy to the instrumental interludes; and the couplets of its texts dealt directly with women and love, the final verses often depicting passionate *despedidas* ('leave-takings').

During the 1930s the *son* came to be used more for entertainment than for social dance, and female singers were introduced, usually with low, husky voices. At that time, the 'smoochy' sounds of Parisian salon music were pervasive in Latin America, and the *son*, now combining French sentiment with Spanish passion, became popular in Europe as much as in Latin America.

The Parisian music that spread to Latin America was not French in origin: the polka and mazurka came from Eastern Europe, and the quadrille from Italy and Spain. Nevertheless, the rustic folk style of these dances had been refined to suit Parisian taste, and the tunes had been arranged for a variety of ensembles: café bands, dance bands, military bands, and orchestras. Influenced by the more robust Spanish tradition, the *polca*, *mazurca*, and *cuadrilla* became fashionable in urban centres throughout Latin America.

Music in Mexico

The Spanish influence was perhaps felt most strongly in Mexico, where the majority *Mestizo* population has always tended to regard both its Spanish and Native American ancestries as essential characteristics of its national identity. In most areas of Latin America, the Spanish conquest effectively caused the stratified societies of indigenous populations to level into an overall peasantry; such populations came to emphasize the cultural *differences* between themselves and the Spanish invaders. (This contrasted with *Mestizo* populations, who tended to model themselves on Europeans.) A similar situation occurred in Mexico; but, because the *Mestizo* population was dominant, and some aristocratic Native families were assimilated into European society, an exceptional degree of cultural blending occurred.

As Ronald Wright has shown, Aztec society was, in many ways, similar to Spanish society: both societies were hierarchical, mercantile, and martial, and both espoused militant religions. Moreover, the new capital of Mexico was built directly over the site of Tenochtitlán; and, although the Spanish language superseded Aztec *Náhuatl* as the national language, it became heavily Mexicanized in the process.[22] Such blending also occurred in music: the *tocotin*, for example, an Aztec *villancico*, was usually sung in *Náhuatl*, and is thought to have developed from pre-Conquest traditions.[23] Mexicans developed a distinctive cultural aesthetic, in language, music, and art.

Mestizo Mexicans still regard their Spanish-influenced folk styles as *national* folk styles. Many regional variations in style exist, but even those belonging to the Native American-dominated areas of Oaxaca and the Yucatán peninsula have obvious Spanish roots. The words of Mexican folk songs evoke romantic, *machismo*, and at times violent, images: the *corrido*, for example, which took its name from its light, running, style of guitar accompaniment, came to depict heroic or sensational deeds.

It was in Mexico that the characteristic accompaniment-ensemble of the *mariachi* band developed, usually consisting of two violins, *vihuela* (small, five-course, guitar), *jarana* (larger five-course guitar), and harp. (The harp is now sometimes replaced by a *guitaron*, a large guitar with four strings.) In the 1930s two trumpets were added to the ensemble; they usually play in thirds, and punctuate the ends of each couplet. *Mariachi* bands were first formed in the eighteenth century, when they were used at weddings; and they still perform throughout the country, sometimes in public squares or on river boats, their songs 'bought' by parties, or by romantic couples. The *mariachi* sound is associated with many song genres, most notably the Mexican *canción*, a sentimental song genre that was popularized during the 1930s by the mass media as the *ballada romantica*.

Mariachi-style music is also played by marimba bands, particularly in Chiapas, Oaxaca, and Tabasco: in modern performance, a single instrument with double keyboard is usually played by three or four people, using rubber-tipped sticks. The modern marimba developed in

[22] Wright, *Stolen Continents*, 157–8.

[23] Thomas Stanford, 'Mexico', *The New Grove* (1980), xii. 231.

Latin America from an African calabash-resonated xylophone, and was popularized in African–Cuban music;[24] African influence is not apparent in Mexico, however. Although African slaves contributed significantly to Mexican urban culture during the seventeenth and eighteenth centuries, there are relatively few people of African descent in Mexico today.

Three folk dances, indigenous to particular regions, have become widely popular in Mexico. The vigorous *huapango* comes from the Gulf coast province of Veracruz and the central *Regiòn Hasteca*. The usual ensemble consists of a vocalist, a violin, *jarana* (five-course guitar), and *huapanguera* (large, five-course guitar); the violin plays fast passage work, the *jarana* strums the harmonies, the *huapanguera* plays the bass line, and the singer frequently uses falsettos.[25] In contrast to the *huapango*, the more melancholy *jarana*, from the Yucatán peninsula, is not usually accompanied by singing, but rather by an ensemble composed of *jaranas*, drums, cornets, and sometimes a güiro. From Jalisco state comes the *jarabe*; originally danced to a song narrative in traditional costume, it was subsequently associated with the nineteenth-century independence movement, and with Mexico's second revolution of 1910, aimed at democracy. It is still the favourite dance of the *charros*, Mexican cowboys, whose skills were turned to competitive showmanship in city 'Charro Rings', when large cattle ranches were expropriated after the revolution of 1910.

The *charros* of northern Mexico had proved fine cavalrymen during Mexico's various wars, and they came to symbolize the new *norteño* culture. Dressed in *Charro* boots, sequined jacket, gold-embroidered pantaloons, and traditional *sombrero* (wide-brimmed hat), they embodied the image of Mexican *machismo* and romance. The *canción ranchera*, usually accompanied by a *mariachi* ensemble, in *corrido* style, developed in association with this image; and its diffusion by the media during the 1930s caused it to become the most popular folk style of Mexico.[26] Its hemiolas, rubatos, and augmented fourths are Spanish in style, but its accompaniment of *mariachi* fiddles, trumpets, and guitars, often in quite elaborate counterpoint, gives it a distinctively Mexican flavour.

[24] The development of the marimba can be traced back to the early seventeenth century; but the first fully chromatic marimba appeared only at the end of the nineteenth century; see Laurence Kaptain, *The Wood That Sings* (Everett, Pa.: Honeyrock, 1992).

[25] Stanford, 'Mexico', *The New Grove*, xii. 232.

[26] Peter Manuel, *Popular Musics of the Non-Western World* (New York: Oxford University Press, 1989), 55–6.

The *canción ranchera* was also associated with Mexicans living in Texas (until 1848 part of Mexico). It was from Texas that the great US cattle drives started; Texas became US cowboy country *par excellence*, and a natural home of Country Music. It was in Texas, therefore, that the Mexican *canción ranchera* joined with US Country Music in a style that became known as *conjunto* ('ensemble'). The distinguishing feature of this style was the use of the accordion, introduced to Texas by German immigrants during the 1840s. To the accordion was added a twelve-stringed *bajo sexto* (bass-chordal guitar) and a string bass. During the 1950s, the addition of drum set and saxophone caused this modern style of *conjunto* music to be associated with 'Tex-Mex' culture.[27] Mexican *rancheros*, however, tend to consider themselves separate from US cowboys; thus a more traditional style, the *norteño ranchera*, still using the accordion but eschewing the drums and saxophone, became associated with Mexican *norteño* culture. The *canción ranchera*, and the *ballada romantica* have become the most popular traditional folk styles of Mexico, though, in the 1990s, US rock music rivals Mexican styles in popularity.

Indigenous Musical Influences

Attempts have been made by nationally minded Mexicans to recreate the sounds of Aztec music, though there is, regrettably, scant documentation to support its supposed authenticity. Aztecs attached great importance to music. Musicians belonged to a professional caste. They were required to learn a huge repertoire of ritual songs associated with specific times, places, and occasions, and total accuracy was demanded of their performance. At court, however—as is common in music cultures worldwide—creativity was encouraged, because court musicians were required to compose ballads extolling the accomplishments of their chiefs.[28]

Aztec instruments included drums, flutes, and carefully tuned idiophones, and they were produced in a variety of sizes. Certain instruments were thought to be of divine origin; and two drums, the *huehuetl* (a singled-headed drum made from a sacred tree, covered with jaguar

[27] In Cuba, the term *conjunto* implies a standard dance band of two to four horns, piano, bass, and percussion (Manuel, *Popular Musics*, 267).

[28] Robert Stevenson, 'Aztec Music', *The New Grove* (1980), i. 760–1.

64. The Mexican *teponaztli* slit drum, carved in the shape of a dog, is here tied to a string to prevent its being stolen

skin), and the *teponaztli* (a large slit drum made from a section of a tree trunk, into which the blood of sacrificial victims was poured on royal occasions) were considered to be actual gods, temporarily forced to endure earthly exile (Pl. 64). Around these drums, hundreds of dancers would move in concentric circles.

All Aztec youths, male and female, were required to attend schools of dance. It was important that they treated their studies seriously: the punishment for making mistakes during a ritual dance (*tlakoa*, to 'sin' or 'lie') was instant execution. The fact that all Aztec citizens were accustomed to musical activity must have eased the transition to a new musical culture. Colonists instituted Christian ceremonies on the dates of pre-Conquest ceremonies: the dances in celebration of Huitzilopochti, for example, were adapted to celebrate the Feast of Corpus Christi.[29]

From the start of the colonial period, missionaries encouraged Native Americans to perform religious dramas. In Mexico, these retained certain elements evident at the time of the Conquest, such as

[29] Stanford, 'Mexico', *The New Grove*, xii. 229 ff.

predominance of flutes and drums, use of high-pitched falsetto in ceremonial song, ceremonies for the blessing of crops, street decorations of paper, use of feathers in headdresses, dancers costumed as animals, and the use of masks and props. Dance dramas would include elaborately costumed processions with papier-mâché figures, and armies of 'Christians' and 'infidels'; indeed the theme of *Moros y Cristianos*, taken from Spain, was used also to represent Cortés's conquest of Mexico. In rural Mexico, *villancicos* were later adapted for use in the carnivals that developed from such processions.[30]

A different situation developed among descendants of the Incas on the *altiplano* of the Andes, who retained many of their indigenous customs. Annual pilgrimages are still made to Quyllur Rit'i ('The Star of the Snow') at the foot of the glaciers at Sinakara, near Cusco, 4,500 metres above sea level. The site overlooks the steep descent of the Andes into the jungle, where the Incas' ancestors are believed to have evolved, and where, at the annual fiesta, participants dance incessantly to an ostinato rhythm.[31] At Tocquille, an island in Lake Titicaca, fiestas are held on special days of the Christian calendar; but many of the indigenous islanders still worship the pre-Columban gods of sun, moon, and mountains, and transform Christian fiestas into Inca rituals.[32] Similar fiestas occur in many communities on the *altiplano* (Pl. 65).

The traditional instruments of the Incas were similar to those of the Aztecs, the main instruments being pan pipes and drums. Pre-Columban peoples of the Andes were particularly proficient in ceramics, and many societies developed a technology for constructing pan pipes of clay (Pl. 66). Pan pipes were also constructed from wood, cane, and the bones of dead enemies. Importantly, the instruments were made in pairs; the notes of a particular scale—then as now—alternated between each individual set, so that a tune could be played only by *pairs* of players. Subsequently, the instruments were constructed in different octave-registers. In Tocquille, four such registers are now played by forty people, accompanied by enormous sheepskin drums, normally beaten by four players.[33]

The numbers four and eight had particular significance to the Incas, who made ritual distinctions between the number, size, colour, and 'sex' of an instrument. At important feasts, four llamas would be sacrificed to

[30] Stanford, 'Mexico', *The New Grove*, xii. 231.

[31] Peter Cloudsley, 'The Living Inca Heritage', *Geographical Magazine* (Feb. 1985).

[32] Ibid.

[33] Ibid.

65. *Quena* (notched flute) and harp players in procession in an Inca sun-worshipping festival, Cusco

66. Detail from a clavy vessel depicting a procession of musicians; Moche culture *c.*100 BC–AD 800.

the accompaniment of four drums, the enormous heads of which would each be played by four chieftains. In 1552 the *maestro de capilla* of Cusco cathedral adapted an Inca praise-song in European polyphonic style, and dressed eight *Mestizo* choirboys in traditional Inca dress to sing the verses; the body of participants responded, as a refrain to each verse, '... to the great content of the Spaniards and the supreme delight of the Indians at seeing their own songs and dances used by the Spaniards to celebrate Our Lord's festival (Corpus Christi)'.[34]

Modern, urban, Andean music contains both indigenous and European elements.[35] The most conspicuous indigenous element is that of the pan pipes (called *siku* by the Aymara peoples and *antara* by the Quecha); each note produced is preceded by a cough-like sound (a 'chuff') which articulates each note played—a percussive effect that contrasts with the rich, legato obtained from the end-blown notched flute (*quena*), used lyrically. Another indigenous element is the widespread use of the anhemitonic pentatonic scale (though this often extends to six notes). European elements include the use of triadic harmony and string instruments. The original settlers brought from Spain the *vihuela*, harp, mandolin, and violin. Missionaries made wide use of the harp for musical instruction, and the instrument is still used frequently in folk styles, playing arpeggiated harmonies; for marches and fiestas, however, Andeans now use a portable, thirty-six-string harp. Another popular string instrument is the small, guitar-like *charango*, which (as noted earlier) has four or five courses of double strings and is heavily strummed in *rasgueado* style.

The most widely popular traditional genre of Andean music is the *huayno*, which incorporates repetitions of syncopated rhythmical phrases, and may be used as a song or a dance. Ex. 14.3 is typical.[36] The *huayno* was produced in a commercial form, in Lima, during the 1950s and 1960s, where it was diffused by radio and on records.[37]

Andean peoples in Peru remained somewhat isolated from the *Criollos* and *Mestizos* of the lowland areas, both culturally and economically, until the 'Revolutionary Government of the Armed Forces',

[34] Garcilaso de la Vega, *Primera parte de los commentarios reales* (Lisbon, 1609), fo.101^{v}, cited in Stevenson, 'Inca Music', *The New Grove*, ix. 57.

[35] For an account of Peruvian music, and changes to it arising from urban migration, see Thomas Turino, *Moving Away from Silence: Music of the Peruvian Altiplano and the Experience of Urban Migration* (Chicago: University of Chicago Press, 1993).

[36] Guzman Caceres (1929), cited in Isabel Aretz, 'Peru', *The New Grove* (1980), xiv. 563.

[37] Turino, *Moving Away from Silence*, 170.

Ex. 14.3

under President Juan Velasco (1968–75), undertook sweeping social and economic reforms that included the legalization of Quecha as an official language, and encouragement of Peruvian music on radio and television. By the mid-1970s, pan pipes had come to symbolize Native Andean identity; and a pan-pipe movement that combined traditional and Western-influenced musical traits developed in urban areas of the *altiplano*, and spread to the coastal cities when Native Americans subsequently migrated there in large numbers.[38] Participation in large pan-pipe ensembles furnishes a powerful sense of 'national' identity among Andean peoples living in the lowland cities; and Andean 'folk' groups, typically consisting of violin, flute, pan pipes, *charango*, and double-barrelled drum, are now to be found 'busking' in countries far beyond their homeland.

In many rural areas of the highlands, the melancholy tones of the shepherd's ballad, the *yaravi*, can still be heard. Played on the *quena* (end-blown notched flute), it is often used as an introduction to the modern *huayno*.

African Musical Influences

While native musical influence was restricted mainly to the Andean highlands, African musical influence was pervasive throughout much of Latin America. (Africans were most numerous in Brazil, in the circum-Caribbean coastal areas, and in the West Indies.)

[38] Ibid. 34, 152–5.

From earliest colonial times, Africans' innate need for song and dance influenced Latin American music. The Iberian colonists had been accustomed to African mores, and they were willing, within limits, to allow their African slaves to retain their traditional customs; indeed, they instituted African 'confraternities', on similar lines to 'negro chapels' in Andalusia that from the early fifteenth century had been sponsoring vocal and instrumental instruction. These 'confraternities' encouraged memory of the countries from which Africans had been transported; in Buenos Aires they were actually named after those places: Angola, Benguela, and Conga. References to such places were included in *villancicos* composed by Africans in African-dialect texts, called (in Latin America, as in Spain) *negros*.[39]

Like Native Americans, Africans became adept at performing European church music. By the mid-seventeenth century, there were complaints in Mexico City that 'a choir under a negro took the bread out of the mouths of cathedral singers'. Church music began to show the influence of African music; *negros*, for example, often incorporated African call-and-response structures.

Despite the tolerance of African musical traditions shown by missionaries and priests, the exuberance of African music was seen as a possible stimulus for insurrection. Thus, while the *Criollos* clearly enjoyed African music, they constantly placed curbs upon it. In 1643, for example, 'oratorios'—nocturnal music parties directed by Africans, ostensibly in honour of Catholic saints, but in practice consisting of music and dancing—were officially forbidden in Mexico City, but they continued in spite of this; indeed, their popularity overrode complaints of irreverence and indecency, so that, by the eighteenth century, African bands of trumpets and drums would be visiting the local wine shops to advertise the evening's entertainment. In Peru, as early as 1551, the Lima town council hired African drummers to welcome the new viceroy; twelve years later, however, African drumming was confined to specific plazas.[40]

Despite restrictions, the exuberance of African music made its influence ineradicable, and African musical traditions are to be found in many parts of Latin America. In south-western Colombia and north-western Ecuador, for example, the *currulao* (marimba dance) is a social ritual that incorporates symbolic behavioural patterns, and preserves many African features. Two musicians improvise melody and accom-

[39] Robert Stevenson, 'Latin America', *The New Grove* (1980), x. 522–4. [40] Ibid. 524.

paniment, in 6/8 time, on the lower and upper parts of a marimba, respectively, while four other musicians perform on two pairs of drums, also in 6/8 time, and a fifth plays on rattles, in binary rhythm; the text alternates between male solo and female chorus, performing in ternary rhythm, as the lead singer indicates (by shouts) the points at which the audience should participate.[41]

In Salvador, Bahia (Brazil), in public places, Bahaians perform the traditional dance figures of the *copoeira angola* (mock kick-fighting), to the accompaniment of two or more *berimbaus* (gourd-resonated musical bows, with single wire strings), rattles, tambourines, and conga drums; and specific songs and rhythmic patterns accompany the various 'strokes' of the dance.

In Latin America, there was no single fusion of African and European musical styles, as in the blues and jazz of North America; Creole and African musics were mutually influential, and from the 1930s onwards both were influenced by popular musical styles from the USA. Both, however, maintained separate existences; from the early days of slavery, many African musical traditions were retained, and developed in association with syncretist religious cults.

One such is *umbanda*, a Brazilian syncretist cult in which Christian saints are equated with 'Indian' and African gods. Here, the Catholic Santa Barbara may appear as Iansa of the Afro-Brazilian cults; the indigenous sea-goddess, *Iemanja*, may appear as the blond, light-skinned Saint Anne, or as the Virgin Mary herself; while the African Xango, god of thunder, may appear as Saint George. *Macumba* is a similar cult, but is based on deities brought to Brazil by the Yoruba-speaking peoples. By linking African deities to Christian saints, slaves were able to disguise their traditional cult worship under a cloak of Christianity. Syncretist cults, involving incessant drumming, trance, and spirit possession, exist throughout South America and the Caribbean.

Music in Brazil

Brazil is a state with a population of predominantly mixed African and Portuguese stock; intermarriage was common from the start of the colonial period, and many aspects of culture

[41] William Gradante, 'Currulao', *The New Grove* (1980), v. 99.

represent a synthesis of Portuguese and African traits. Brazil is especially noteworthy for its pre-Lenten carnivals, and for its syncretist religious cults.

The most celebrated of the carnivals is that held annually in Rio de Janeiro (though carnivals take place in other areas of Brazil, and in many other states of Latin America); and the musical style particularly associated with this Carnival is the 'samba' (though the style originated as a folk dance). Rio, like many cities in Latin America, now embraces vast inequalities of wealth: huge *favelas* (hillside slums) leer down upon the apparently affluent commercial and tourist centres. Although the relaxed atmosphere of Rio's beach culture belies a growing social tension characteristic of many Latin American cities, at Carnival time people of all classes and colour join the streets in communal street festivity, dancing their joys and sorrows for days and nights on end.

Carnival developed towards the end of the nineteenth century, when costumed dancers 'marched' down the streets to brass-band music, and indulged in many forms of revelry. By the early twentieth century, the event was a popular annual diversion from the routine of work; and, during the 1920s, the original country dances were replaced by the urban samba. In 1928 samba groups were organized into 'schools', and an element of competitiveness emerged as schools competed for prizes. Preparation for Carnival has become a year-round activity, particularly among *favela*-dwellers.

In the 1950s Carnival developed into an international event, with processions ever more extravagant, costumes ever more sumptuous, and floats ever more elaborate, with topical themes a feature of both pageantry and music. Many variants of the samba emerged, but the basic form consists of solo vocal lines alternating with unison refrains, accompanied by a *bateria* of percussion instruments. Harmonies are strummed on guitars (sometimes augmented by brass instruments), but these are often inaudible, due to incessant drumming of ostinato patterns. Although the style embraces African-derived rhythms, the tunes are European in flavour. Ex.14.4 shows the outline of a typical samba tune.

One offshoot of the *samba* was *bossa nova*, *bossa* being a slang word for 'special ability'. The style was initiated during the late 1960s by Antonio Carlos (Tom) Jobim (composer and pianist), with João Gilberto (guitarist and vocalist), and a group of university students in search of a 'cooler' form of samba. It is characterized by a somewhat angular melodic line, incorporating intervals not normally used in the samba,

Ex. 14.4

such as diminished fourths and minor sixths. Sung in a deliberately easy-going style, melodic lines were integrated with chromatic harmony and complex rhythms, in order that the melodic line would no longer predominate.[42] In 1962 *bossa nova* reached the USA, where, for a while, it became extremely popular; dances were adapted to it in ballroom style, even though the music was not intended for dancing. The laid-back ambience of the style is typified by such enervating tunes as 'The Girl from Ipanema', a song that subsequently sold over 25 million copies. Regarded as an essentially élitist music, *bossa nova* did not become a feature of Carnival; but in the early 1990s there was a revival, and the style was specially featured in the 1992 Rio Carnival.

A subsequent style *tropicalismo*—a reaction to the cool *bossa nova*—was inaugurated at the 1967 São Paulo Festival. An eclectic style showing influence of US rock music, *tropicalismo* represented political opposition to a right-wing military government; in 1969 its two most prominent leaders, Gilberto Gil and Gaetano Veloso, were temporarily exiled. By 1972, however, when they returned, rock styles had permeated Brazilian popular music.[43]

Gil was also influential in the re-Africanization of Bahia, where, in the mid-1970s, *afoxés* (groups of dancers belonging to the *condomblé* cult) joined in the city's Carnival, not in frilly costumes and with sambas, but dressed in flowing white robes, and moving to the accompaniment of Angolan drumming. As the *afoxés* proliferated, they became the centre of a growing black-consciousness movement, the music of which is based on elemental African drumming and call-and-response singing. 'Afro-blocos'—huge marching percussion bands—performed Africanized variants of the Rio-style samba, the

[42] Gerard Béhague, 'Bossa Nova', *The New Grove* (1980), iii. 77.
[43] Philip Sweeney, *Directory of World Music* (London: Virgin Books, 1991), 236–7.

first Afro-bloco, *Ilé Ayé*, soon gaining 2,000 members; over twenty Afro-blocos subsequently emerged, most of them promoting their own marching bands. Under the leadership of Gilberto Gill, Bahaian drumming developed into an amalgam of rock, funk, and Caribbean rhythms, known as 'samba-reggae'.[44]

Angolan traditions were kept alive in Bahia through *condomblé* ceremonies; officially, these take place in *terreiros* (temples regarded as sacred ground), but, in practice, they are performed in simple neighbourhood homes, where they provide purposeful social gathering with a mixture of fun, spiritual cleansing, and the hope of renewed 'positive forces' with which to endure the debilitations of *favela* living. The 'priest', wearing a leather hat, and affecting the cross eyes of the crooked angel, dispenses 'beer' liberally to himself, and to others, while he dances. As the drumming intensifies, a forceful pelvic thrust from the priest causes a woman, chosen from the group, to be possessed. (There is symbolic echo here of the ancient cult of the mother-goddess, and of the deflowering of virginity by a priest acting as surrogate for divinity.) The woman is then convulsed by spasms, staggering around the room from one participant to another, until the 'priest' impulsively plants his elbow on a drum, signalling the music to stop. In the strange silence that follows, the woman is helped to the back of the building to recover from the ordeal; then the drumming resumes to enable another person to become 'possessed'.[45]

Music in Trinidad and Tobago

Carnivals, originating in cultic practices, are conspicuous in the islands of Trinidad and Tobago, lying just 16 kilometres off the coast of Venezuela. Trinidad was first a Spanish and then a French colony, until it was captured by the British in 1797. Tobago was ceded to Britain by France in 1814, and amalgamated with Trinidad in 1888. After emancipation in 1838, the substantial African population of the islands was supplemented by a nearly equal number of 'East' Indians (migrants from the Indian Subcontinent), hired as 'indentured' labourers. The islands have therefore been subject to Spanish, French, British, African, and East Indian influence. (Trinidad and Tobago gained independence in 1962.)

[44] Sweeney, *Directory of World Music*, 236–7.
[45] Description of a ceremony attended by the author.

Musically, the islands are known internationally for two indigenous syncretizations: calypso and steel bands. Trinidad's Carnival originated in processions of torch-bearing Africans, re-enacting plantation fire drills to the accompaniment of drums. When drums were banished in 1883, topical songs—deriving from the African cult, *belair*—assumed greater importance. These songs were improvised, and their verses consisted of praises, insults, or topical commentary.[46] By 1900 such songs had acquired the name 'calypso'.

From 1914, recordings of calypso popularized the genre, and led to the introduction of calypso competitions, at which spectators paid to hear groups of rival calypso singers performing topical and satirical texts. As rivalry between competitors grew, the state began to finance the competitions; and by the 1930s great calypso singers, such as Chieftain Walter Douglas and Roaring Lion, turned the calypso into a 'creative' folk genre. By the 1940s calypsos commenting on the previous day's events were being transmitted daily by local radio stations, so that political statements made through calypso came to represent popular opinion, and to be discussed in parliament. Carnival still has a strong political content.

Calypso competitions became the most important events during the Trinidadian Carnival period. Gradually, higher standards of studio production increased calypso's potential for dancing; in the late 1970s the word *soca* (from 'soul calypso') was coined to describe a new type of calypso, oriented towards disco.[47]

Carnival was originally a high-society affair: it only became a street festival of African drumming after the abolition of slavery in 1838. When drums were banned, African rhythm returned to the streets in the form of 'tambour-bamboo', in which bamboos of different lengths and pitches were struck, or notched and scraped. When Bamboo Bands became associated with the traditional *calinda* cult (stick-fighting dances), they too were banned, only to be replaced in 1937 by 'Steel Bands', which then consisted of dustbins, buckets, car hubs, frying pans, and any other suitable noise-making objects that could be found.[48] Gradually it was discovered that indentations of differing size made in metal lids produce different pitches; but it was not until the US military left behind large quantities of oil drums after the Second World War (Trinidad prospered on oil during the mid-twentieth century) that the

[46] Helen Myers, 'Trinidad and Tobago', *The New Grove* (1980), xix. 147–50.
[47] Ibid. 149.
[48] John Bartholomew, *The Steel Band* (Oxford: Oxford University Press 1980), 15–17.

67. Trinidadian Philmore Davidson performs in London on steel pans formed from oil drums, 1951

characteristic sound of the modern steel pan was born (Pl. 67). Although, initially, steel pans were feared by the authorities as much as had been 'tambour-bamboo', they were eventually recognized as being musically invigorating and, following Independence, were encouraged by the Trinidad government.

In contrast to the syncretist music of Africans, East Indians in Trinidad and Tobago developed their own, separate, musical culture. Indian folk-songs, accompanied by *dholak* (double-headed drum), clappers, small cymbals, and hand-clapping, are still sung for religious ceremonies, and at weddings, at childbirth, and when rice-planting; and Vedic texts, accompanied by harmonium and *tambūrā* (string-drone instrument), are sung at Hindu worship. Indian films have been imported to the islands since the 1930s, and these were the principal source of popular music. Syncretized 'orchestras' subsequently developed, consisting of electric organs, electric guitars, Hawaiian guitars, conga drums, bongos, and drum sets.[49]

[49] Myers, 'Trinidad and Tobago', *The New Grove*, xix. 149–50.

Recently, East Indian traditions have merged with calypso, and East Indians sing Indian melodies to Afro-Caribbean rhythms in the calypso tents.[50]

Music in Cuba

One of the most important sources of African musical influence in Latin America is the island of Cuba, which gave birth to the *habañera*, *son*, rumba, *mambo*, *cha-cha-chá*, and to 'salsa'. Cuba's commercial development was relatively late, and its slave trade lasted until the 1870s; African traditions, therefore, were constantly reinvigorated; and in urban areas, African cooperative societies, similar to the 'confraternities' on the South American continent, provided opportunity for the development of an Afro-Cuban style.[51] This music was tolerated by the colonial authorities, and, because Europeans came to consider music-making a degrading occupation, Africans became the sole professional musicians: in 1831 it was reported that music in Cuba—where, in 1776, the Havana Playhouse had opened with a Metastasian opera by Piccinni—was 'in the hands of people of colour.'

During the early decades of the nineteenth century, Cuba was still an important centre of European music, but, as the century wore on, light music associated with ballroom dancing superseded the taste for ecclesiastical and operatic music. Among the popular dances was the *contradanze*, a Breton form of the English country dance, introduced by Franco-Haitians fleeing the Haitian revolution (1804).[52] Gradually, its style became Africanized (Ex.14.5). It became known as the *contradanza habañera* and, as it grew in popularity, simply *habañera*. It adopted the distinctive rhythm shown in Ex.14.5*a* as a kind of ostinato and, later, the rhythm shown in Ex.14.5*b*. (This latter rhythm has become widely, and erroneously, associated with the 'rumba'.) By the end of the nineteenth century, a European-style, couple dance in rondo form, the *danzón*, had replaced the *habañera* as the most popular dance, having adopted a further syncopation known as the *cinquillo* (Ex. 14.5*c*), later shortened into the *tresillo* (Ex.14.5*d*). (The *cinquillo* rhythm was of Haitian origin, and a prominent characteristic of Haitian 'voodoo'

[50] As reported by Stuart Hall in *Redemption Song*, a TV series shown on BBC 2 during 1992.
[51] Manuel, *Popular Musics*, 28.
[52] Ibid. 27.

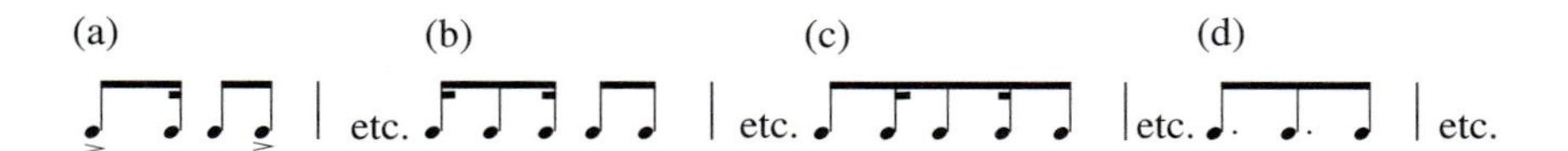

Ex. 14.5

music.[53]) The *danzón* was primarily an instrumental genre; originally played by an 'outdoor' ensemble including timpani and brass instruments, it subsequently became the property of the *charanga* ensemble, typically consisting of a large rhythm section (piano, string bass, timbales, and other percussion), two violins, and flute.[54]

By the end of the nineteenth century, the 'rumba' ensemble emerged, comprising a vocalist, chorus, and three percussionists. The essential features of the rumba were the three basic ostinatos shown in Ex.14.6 (after Manuel); over them, rhythms with shifted accents were improvised on a higher-pitched conga drum, in the style of African master drumming.[55]

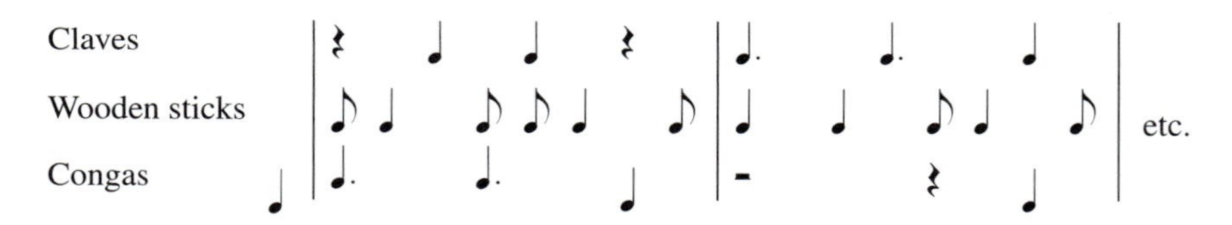

Ex. 14.6

As was shown in Chapter 6, traditional African music makes no intrinsic distinction between melody and rhythm. The conga drums, used in Cuba, yield great variety of pitch; and small bongo drums and tuned *timbales* add to these melodic possibilities. Sticks played on chairs, tables, boxes, or any other convenient objects to hand provide a further variety of pitches and resonances. The improvisations of Cuban drummers are therefore as much melodic as rhythmic.

Nevertheless, not all Cuban music remained distinctively African. The Cuban *son*, for example, though more African than the Mexican *son* (see p. 501), was always a hybrid form. It adopted African-style shifted accents (Ex.14.7), and it used claves, bongos, *botija* (a blown jug), and *marimbula* (a large lamellaphone) in the accompaniment; but it

[53] Carlos Borbolla, 'Cuba', *The New Grove* (1980), v. 86.

[54] Manuel, *Popular Musics*, 27.

[55] Ibid. 29.

Ex. 14.7

also used European harmonies, guitars, and four-line verse-forms. As its popularity increased, rhythmic elements were simplified, the lamellaphone was replaced by a string bass, and a trumpet was added to the ensemble, which quickly superseded the *charanga* ensemble in popularity. During the 1930s (when radio and the gramophone were beginning to dominate pop music), piano and saxophone were added, the percussion section was enlarged, and brass improvisations gave way to tight, pre-composed, short interludes. Such features were to become the basis of 'salsa'.[56]

As the distinctive features of Afro-Cuban music were popularized by US radio stations and record companies, they tended to become clichés. The innocuous rhythm of the *habañera* was disseminated as the rumba, owing to such stylistic simplifications as Harry Belafonte's 'Jamaica Farewell'. Rumbas and *mambos*[57] then became a craze, and the catchy, syncopated tunes on which they were based were thought of as being essentially African. As Emilio Grenet has put it: 'our sister nations, the United States and Spain, distort the characteristics of our music and invest it with an alien spirit . . . the rumba, that creature of our robust virility, is diluted and emasculated.'[58]

Music in Jamaica

Less emasculated were—and are—the hybrid genres that emerged from Jamaica. The island was first colonized by the Spanish (who exterminated the indigenous peoples), and was subsequently captured by the British, to whom the Spanish ceded it in 1670. The Spaniards fled to Cuba, but before doing so freed and armed their slaves, who took to the mountains, organized themselves as the Maroons, and (with other escaped slaves) harried the British with guerrilla warfare for two centuries. Nevertheless, the subsequent trans-shipment

[56] Ibid. 30–1.

[57] The *mambo* is a fast, predominantly instrumental genre, featuring antiphonal writing for horn and reed sections.

[58] Emilio Grenet, sleeve note to *Yambu*, Globe Trails Records, ORB 036.

to Jamaica of huge numbers of African slaves caused Jamaica to become one of the most commercially valuable European colonies in the New World. Jamaica's population is now mainly of African descent; a census taken in 1970 showed that nearly 80 per cent of the then population was unmistakably black, and 95 per cent claimed some measure of African ancestry.[59]

As slaves, Jamaicans kept alive traditional African dancing to drums, and syncretist cults abound throughout the island. The *kumina* cult, for example, based on music and dance of the African *myal* cult, was designed to counteract the sorcery of the legendary 'Obeah man'; 'Pocomania' (thought by some to derive from 'poco-kumina') is a magic cult that involves the sanctification of a drum and the bleeding and sacrifice of a goat. Eschewing magic, however, are the 'Revivalist' cults that flourish in Kingston and in peasant hill communities and that attest the widespread Africanizing of Christianity. To this day on Cudgoe Day—6 January, the day on which John Cudgoe escaped from his plantation, henceforward to harry the British for fifty years—Maroons join from all parts of the globe for a 'Coromantee' ceremony, that involves African music and dance. The tradition has been unbroken since the departure of the Spaniards in 1655.

Unlike the Spanish in Cuba, the British 'Plantocracy' of Jamaica did not establish a vigorous European-based artistic culture. No great cathedrals or opera houses were built; a few eighteenth-century churches and colonial houses are the only architectural legacy of British colonial rule. The work of the Institute of Jamaica, founded in 1879 by a colonial Governor 'for the encouragement of literature, science and art', was either unknown or considered irrelevant to the vast majority of Jamaicans when independence was gained in 1962.[60] Nevertheless, during the half century that preceded independence, the British laid down precise systems of government, education, health, trade, and industry, that would make for a smooth transition of power.

Though little interested in the classical-music tradition of Europe, the 'Plantocracy' of Jamaica promoted European salon music, and encouraged slaves to learn to perform it on European instruments. Slaves, however, soon adapted the music to their own tastes: in the case of the quadrille, for example, the addition of banjos and drums to

[59] Rex M. Nettleford, *Caribbean Cultural Identity: The Case of Jamaica* (Institute of Jamaica, 1978), 51–2.

[60] Ibid. 111.

Ex. 14.8

European fiddles, flutes, clarinets, and trumpets led, by the 1820s, to an Africanized style of Quadrille Band.[61]

The first distinctively African–European folk style to emerge in Jamaica was 'mento', the origins of which lay in rural dance festivals and Trinidadian calypso. The basic instrumentation was guitar, banjo, and rumba box. (This last was an instrument modelled on the African lamellaphone, but large enough to play the bass line; that it did so as a *melodic line* was to prove an important influence on reggae.) To these were added bongos, shakers, and other percussion instruments. To a tune such as 'Island in the Sun' (Ex.14.8) would be added the rhythms shown in Ex.14.9.[62] Mento is still valued as the source of indigenous Jamaican music and dance.

Early Jamaican radio stations relayed European classical music and American pop, but by the 1950s more powerful equipment enabled

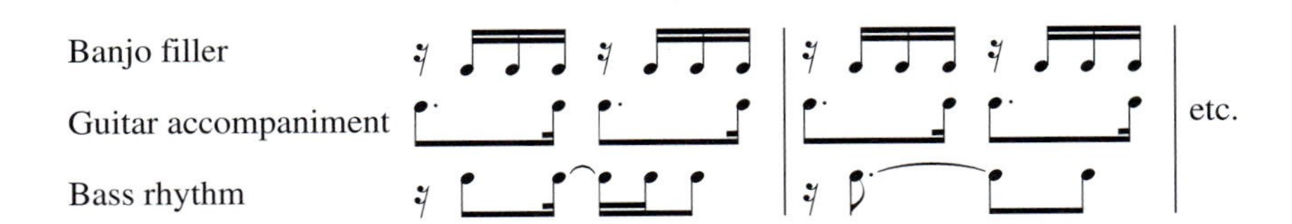

Ex. 14.9

[61] Pamela O'Gordon, 'An Approach to the Study of Jamaican Popular Music', *Jamaica Journal*, 6 (1972), 7.

[62] Ibid.

Jamaicans to hear music of the southern USA, and so to develop a taste for the danceable music of southern rhythm 'n' blues.[63] Such music was further popularized through the institution of Jamaican 'sound systems', powerful PA systems that were driven in pick-up trucks to villages and towns all over the island. They were accompanied by a peculiarly Jamaican type of DJ, identified by comic *noms de plume* such as V-Rocket, Sir Coxsone Dodd, Prince Buster, Duke Reid, and the like. Duke Reid, for example, would arrive at dance gatherings wearing a golden crown and flowing ermine garments; and after being carried through the admiring crowd to his control desk, he would encourage full acceptance of the latest records by typical Jamaican 'raps' such as 'wake it up' or 'jump, shake-a-leg'.[64] This 'rap' language, arising naturally from the inflections of Jamaican *patois*, was to be a major influence on 'dance-hall' reggae, or 'DJ' reggae as it is sometimes called.

As rivalries broke out among DJs, systems began to compete with each other, offering ever increasing volume and musical 'exclusivity'. When DJs ran out of 'exclusive' singles, they imported records from New York, blacking out labels in the hope of disguising the identity of the music. The spread of such records encouraged Jamaicans to develop their own indigenous musical styles, and the two main competing DJs, Coxsone and Reid, were obliged to turn from sound systems to recording studios.

Jamaican musicians, many of whom received their early musical training in military bands, had already begun to develop a new style that was neither mento, nor rhythm 'n' blues, nor calypso. It included short jazz riffs (encouraged by the presence of a 'horn' section), a rhythm characteristic of mento played on the bass, and a more elaborate boogie played on the piano. The latter was partly obscured by heavy accentuation of the second and fourth beats on the guitar (a modified version of the 'banjo filler' of mento); and there were additional syncopations on the trap drums. Ex.14.10 (after O'Gordon) shows the basic rhythms.[65] An onomatopoeic representation of the sound of a piano—ska-ska-ska-ska-ska—provided the name for this new Jamaican sound, popularized from 1959 by a new 'Jamaican Broadcasting Company'. Coxsone then created a group called 'The Skatellites'. Though short-lived, this band

[63] Dermott Hussey and Paul Zach, 'The Red Hot Rhythms of Reggae', in *Jamaica* (Hong Kong: APA Publications, 1988), 236.

[64] Ibid.

[65] O'Gordon, 'An Approach to the Study of Jamaican Popular Music'.

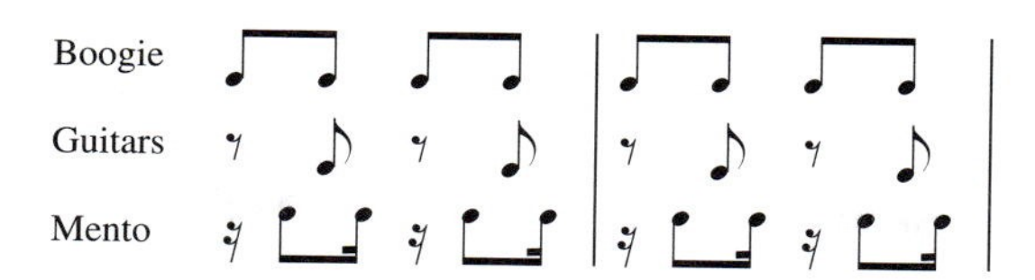

Ex. 14.10

established ska as an indigenous Jamaican form, in which vocals and melody were largely subordinate to instrumental rhythm.

By the mid-1960s, ska had peaked, along with the euphoria that followed independence in 1962. The pace of the music slowed, allowing increased emphasis on the off-beat quaver; vocalists took over from instrumentalists, and lyrics turned to social protest. The bass took over the melodic function of the mento rumba box, and was repeated in ostinato; guitars and keyboards gradually replaced the brass section, and the harmony was confined largely to two chords. The bass melody from Alton Ellis's 'Take it Easy' is a typical precursor of reggae (Ex.14.11).[66] The title of Ellis's first hit, 'Rock Steady', provided the name for the new style. The volume of the melodic bass line was increased; and it was broadcast on sound systems throughout Jamaica.

Ex. 14.11

Reggae and Rastafarianism

'Toots' Hibbert of 'Toots and the Maytals' claims to have first introduced the word reggae:

> I invented reggae. Wrote a song called 'Do the Reggay' in 196– I don't remember when . . . Reggae just mean comin' from the people. Everyday t'ing, like from the ghetto. So all of our music, our Jamaican rhythm, comin' from the majority. . . . When you say reggae you mean regular,

[66] Ibid.; see also Dick Hebdige, *Cut 'n' Mix: Culture, Identity, and Caribbean Music* (London: Routledge, 1987), 70–3.

> majority. And when you say reggae it mean poverty, suffering, Ras Tafari, everything. Ghetto. Its music from the rebels, people who don't have what they want.[67]

The advent of reggae around 1968 coincided with restlessness among Jamaica's majority poor, and with the popularization of Rastafarianism. The seeds of the Rasta movement were sown as early as 1924, when the crowning of a 'Black King' in Africa who would be 'The Redeemer' was prophesied to the poor people of Kingston, Jamaica. In 1930 Ras Tafari Makonnen was crowned Emperor of Ethiopia, adopting the title 'Haile Selassie' and claiming descent from King Solomon; the shanty-town dwellers of Kingston then believed that a prophecy had been fulfilled, and that Haile Selassie would be the saviour of the African diaspora.[68]

Rastafarianism appears to have been based on the 'Holy Piby', the 'Black Man's Bible', compiled by an Anguillan and published in 1924. The Holy Piby was introduced into Jamaica in 1926; it was supplemented by the 'Royal Parchment Scroll of Black Supremacy' (which included the famous prophecy of a redeeming 'Black King'), as well as the 'Rasta Bible' (plagiarized from the former, and sold to converts as an ancient text originating in Accra). From these beginnings the Rastafarian movement grew, developed a religious doctrine, and established dietary and hygienic laws that included the smoking of 'ganja' (marijuana), regarded as 'wisdom weed'.

The Africanism of Rastafarianism brought it into natural partnership with the Africanism and aggressive socialism of reggae. 'Toots' Hibbert may have coined the word reggae, but Bunny Livingston of 'The Wailers' offers a fuller explanation of the phenomenon:

> Well mek me tell you a little history about Africa and reggae. Africa a one nick-name; Ethiopia is the real name fe the whole a dat place. Reggae means the King's music from the latin *Regis*: e.g. like Regal. Now Ethiopia (Africa) is a place with plenty King so they have to be entertained with the king's music. So from you a play reggae with the heavy emphasis pon bass and drums, you a mingle with the spirit of Africa. The rhythm is connected to the heartbeat.[69]

In reggae, the melodic bass line of rock steady became rhythmically more varied; and, in Bob Marley's lyrics, the social protest that had

[67] Hussey and Zach, 'Red Hot Rhythms', 239.

[68] Timothy White, *Catch a Fire: The Life of Bob Marley* (London: Corgi Books, 1983), 26.

[69] Hussey and Zach, 'Red Hot Rhythms', 240.

characterized the lyrics of rock steady hardened into anger, causing lyricism to disintegrate into repetitive rhythmic units. To quote Pamela O'Gordon: 'The woes suffered by the citizens of Kingston are always refracted through the single rhythmic cell';[70] or, as another writer has put it: 'Reggae is not just a music, it is more a philosophy, with the advice handed out to a danceable beat.'

At the entrance to the National Stadium in Kingston there is a statue of Bob Marley. Since his death from cancer in 1981, Marley has been regarded in Jamaica as a national hero. He and his group, The Wailers, rose to international fame from the shanty hovels of Trenchtown, Kingston. It was the promotion of the LP *Burnin'* in 1974 (containing, *inter alia*, images of dreadlocks and 'ganja'-smoking on the record sleeve) that, in particular, furnished Marley with cult status, and made of reggae a symbol of black power worldwide. The Jamaican politician Michael Manley subsequently visited Ethiopia for an audience with Haile Selassie, to receive a 'rod of correction' and be promoted as a modern Joshua who would lead his people to the promised land.[71] Later, during violent election campaigns in 1976 and 1980, Marley promoted peace, through reggae, among the contenders; indeed, before a special 'Smile Jamaica' concert in 1976, Marley himself was shot at, but bravely continued with the concert. As a direct result of this concert, leaders of the two political parties were forced to sign a pledge of peace, prepared by one of the churches.

After Marley's death, the character of reggae began to change. In DJ (also called 'dance-hall') reggae, Marley's seemingly throwaway melodic growls were transformed into a continuous 'rap' of nonsense verse in Jamaican *patois*. The rap was vocalized in an incessant quaver rhythm—to which the *patois* is perfectly attuned—often embracing little more, melodically, than the root and third of a major chord. Because it reflected the largely monosyllabic injunctions of Kingston's daily life, it appeared essentially Jamaican—far removed from the 'rap' of US 'hip-hop' that derived from it (see pp. 589–90). Although the characteristic Jamaican DJ style of the 1990s, 'Ragga' ('raga-muffin'), tends to celebrate the less salubrious aspects of street life, and reggae itself has embraced a variety of social themes and musical styles, the distinctive rhythms of reggae continue to permeate the island.

[70] O'Gordon, 'An Approach to the Study of Jamaican Popular Music'.
[71] White, *Catch a Fire*, 273–6.

In Jamaica's modern resort hotels, however, reggae bands alternate between reggae and US pop, so that the guests, who dance awkwardly, if at all, to the reggae music, can 'smooch' with their partners on the dance floor. The USA has dominated the Caribbean for more than half a century; and when US dollars enter, so too do other aspects of culture. To the poverty-ridden peoples of the Caribbean, a plethora of US television stations dispense images of a brash, consumer society, with values that undermine Afro-Caribbean identity. For many young Caribbeans, the US has become a new 'El Dorado'. As Professor Rex Nettleford, director of the Jamaican National Dance Theatre Company, has expressed it: 'Centuries of psychological conditioning and the inescapable on-going cultural bombardment from the North Atlantic sometimes transforms what is at one moment an object of national pride into a product of doubt, ridicule and low worth.'[72]

Reggae developed in Jamaica from religious and social custom, and in response to a pervasive sense of African identity; its Africanness, therefore, lies in its function as much as in its form. In the 1990s—as occurred earlier with the blues and jazz in the USA—its essentially African identity is in danger of being impaired by the US-dominated recording industry, with its insistence on 'new sounds'. Reggae cannot easily 'develop', in the Western sense, without compromising its Africanness; only time can tell whether its uniqueness will survive Western commercial pressures.

The Tango

A more hybrid genre, the tango, developed on the South American mainland, and became the national symbol of Argentina and Uruguay. The tango owed its popularity, in part at least, to Afro-Cuban music, because of its use of the relatively innocuous *habañera* rhythm of Cuba. In Argentina, however, this rhythm—along with the sensual choreography associated with the dance, involving substantial bodily contact—caused it initially to be scorned as a 'negro' aberration by upper-class Argentinians still chasing the illusive dream of a 'pure' national culture.[73]

The tango appears to have been influenced both by the Cuban *habañera*, popular in mid-nineteenth century Buenos Aires, and by

[72] White, *Catch a Fire*, 52. [73] Manuel, *Popular Musics*, 61.

the Andalusian tango, brought to Argentina by Spanish theatre groups in the 1870s. The tango originated in the *arrabales* (slums and brothels) of Buenos Aires, populated by former soldiers and peasants, and by immigrants from Spain and Italy. (The population of Buenos Aires tripled in the last half of the nineteenth century.) The tango gave identity to this new and alienated urban group, and the shortage of women in the *arrabales* gave to the genre its fatalistic texts and its aggressive, *machismo* choreography.[74]

The early tangos were played by trios of violin, guitar, and flute, in the popular *habañera* rhythm in 2/4 tempo. During the second decade of the twentieth century, the tango became the most popular ballroom dance of British and Parisian bourgeois society and was then taken up by élite society in Argentina. At the same time, the tango was recast as the *tango canción*, a vocal song with instrumental accompaniment, and the original trio was augmented by piano, cello, string bass, and accordion.[75] This line-up was the *orquesta typica* of recordings of Latin American music in the 1920s and 1930s.

The tango's popularity slumped in the 1930s, but its fortunes revived in the 1940s, in its association with the working class movements that led to Peron's rise to power in 1945. With Peron's fall a decade later, the working class was again alienated, and the tango no longer reflected their circumstances. It was superseded in popularity by new forms of rock music; and, as Buenos Aires became the disco capital of the world, the tango was relegated to the realm of folk music.[76] As such, it is still performed, and retains its special sensuality and charm. (It has also, curiously, become a popular dance of Finland.)

New Syncretic Styles

The displacement of the tango in Argentina reflected the dying spasms of the old, colonially inspired culture that had pervaded Latin America for more than three centuries. Among a majority of Latin Americans, frustrated by the inequalities in wealth to which European cultural systems had given rise, a growing awareness of cultural roots has caused inherited European cultural systems to appear increasingly anachronistic. To those of Native American and African stock, in particular, the most relevant musical styles are populist,

[74] Ibid. 59–60. [75] Ibid. 61–2. [76] Ibid. 63.

compounded of Native, African, and European elements. To many in Latin America, music has become a symbol of both national and political identity; the disjunction between the Western classical tradition and more recent populist styles is symptomatic of a wider search for meaningful cultural identity among displaced and underprivileged peoples throughout the world.

In the late 1970s, a new musical movement, with its roots in politics, started in Chile. Known, loosely, as *Nueva Canción*, it rejected US influences; displaying marked originality, it used Andean traditional music and instruments, brought together Native American, Spanish, and African folk influences, and created a pan-Latin American awareness. *Nueva Canción* reflected an increasing opposition to political repression and social injustice, as well as a rejection of North American imperialism. In Chile it became associated with Salvador Allende's *Unidad Popular* party, until, in 1973, Allende was killed in a military *coup* and his democratically elected government was displaced. Under the repressive regime that followed, *Nueva Canción* was suppressed, and its leading exponents were imprisoned or exiled; one, Victor Jara, was tortured and killed. The media were again flooded with North American music. Nevertheless, *Nueva Canción* continued to live on in exile, and the availability of cheap cassette recorders ensured that it would still be heard in Chile.[77]

The development of specifically Latin styles had been hindered during the 1960s by the importation to Latin countries of US rock styles, and by the enlargement of Puerto Rican-dominated *barrios* (Spanish-speaking quarters) in the USA by Cubans, following the Communist *coup* in Cuba in 1959. Latin styles had increasingly blended with US styles, making musical assertion of cultural identity increasingly difficult. Cuban dance music had been popular in New York since the 1940s, when *mambo* was promoted as an up-tempo big-band music, an Africanized version of swing subsequently taken up by US jazz musicians such as Dizzie Gillespie.[78] During the 1950s, *cha-cha-chá*, a style featuring Cuban *charanga* ensemble (see p. 518), had also became fashionable in the USA, but was subsequently superseded by rock 'n' roll.[79]

The Latin successor to *cha-cha-chá*, both in the USA and Latin America, was 'salsa'. This pan-Latin genre grew out of the Cuban *son* in the late 1960s, but was created primarily in Puerto Rico and New

[77] Manuel, *Popular Musics*, 68–72. [78] Ibid. 32, 47.
[79] Sweeney, *Directory of World Music*, 255.

York; and it was New York recording companies that effectively controlled it. The term 'salsa' (meaning 'hot chilli sauce') came to refer to Latin- inspired music generally, but was initially associated with a move away from big-band ensembles to the more authentic *conjunto* format, consisting of a rhythm section of piano, bass, guitar, and percussion, with two to five horns in the lead.[80] Though out of fashion in the USA during the 1960s, salsa acquired a rock flavour during the 1970s, and began to appeal to both Anglo and Latino audiences.[81] Its Latin American vitality was compromised, however, by the record companies, which, in the words of one US Latino, 'want to dominate the market with a bland salsa sound, (while) our music, almost insidiously, takes on a *status quo* role'.[82] As Peter Manuel has observed, New York's three million Latinos were part of a politically heterogeneous consumer group; and the commercial interests of the music industry would scarcely have been served by promoting them as a culturally separate entity.[83]

During the 1970s, salsa was eclipsed in popularity by the Dominican *merengue*, the promotion of which was aided by destitute Dominicans, willing to perform for low wages. It was revived during the 1980s in a bland, sentimental, style, known as *salsa romantica*, or *salsa erotica* (depending on the explicitness of the lyrics).[84]

The late 1980s witnessed a craze for 'lambada', the origins of which have been attributed to Madagascar, Cuba, and Amazonia. It seems, rather, to be linked with a hybrid, Caribbean-influenced dance form that had existed for many years along Brazil's north-eastern coast.[85] Featuring powerful styles of solo singing, incorporating the melodic turns of Spanish folk music and the clear textures of Cuban percussion, its 'hot' style was popularized not in Brazil, or even in the USA, but in France, by a TV company, supported by a soft-drinks company. A lambada single, performed by the Koami studio group, and based (without attribution) on the Bolivian tune 'Llorand Se Fue', became a hit in Europe; it was then replicated by thousands of ensembles, in Latin America and elsewhere, in countless regional stylistic variations.[86]

[80] Manuel, *Popular Musics*, 48, and Sweeney, *Directory of World Music*, 255.

[81] Ibid. 203.

[82] Felipe Luciano, cited in Jeremy Marre and Hannah Charlton, *Beats of the Heart: Popular Music of the World* (New York: Pantheon Books, 1985), 82.

[83] Manuel, *Popular Musics*, 49.

[84] Sweeney, *Directory of World Music*, 256.

[85] Ibid. 239–40.

[86] Ibid.

The first hybrid style to come out of Peru, *chicha*—named after the maize beer of the Andes—was brought into being as a result of massive immigration of Andean peasants into the coastal areas; since 1940 the population of Lima has risen from a little more than half a million to more than five million. The immigrants huddle in outlying shanty towns, in shacks built from waste materials and matting, a contradiction to all that Westerners expect of civilization. While the first generation of immigrants tended to preserve their regional cultural identity, their descendants adopted the lowland, urban, Peruvian mores. These immigrant, urban communities of Peru then created a pan-Andean music, *chicha*, incorporating the fast rhythms of the Colombian *cumbia*, traditional pentatonic *huayno* tunes, and the unmistakable sound of the Andean pan pipes.[87] *Chicha* is now to be heard not only in the suburbs of Lima, where thousands dance to it all day, but on recordings, throughout Latin America.

Political disunity, as well as constant intermarriage between peoples of European, Native American, and African stocks, have contributed to the diversity of cultural traditions to be found throughout Latin America. Yet that diversity also springs from contradictions implicit in the imposition of a quasi-European culture on Native and African peoples, from the start of the colonial period. Such contradictions are apparent in the great baroque cathedrals and churches that still dominate so much of the landscape today. Though aged, un-tuned organ pipes still grace many interiors, there is little evidence today of a once highly developed choral tradition. The faithful attend Mass and sing plainchant; but Native peoples and Africans have their own versions of Christianity. In the imposing cathedral of Cusco, for example, whose carved 'Great Saints' might be idols for the idolatrous, in their vivid reds and golds, 'Inca' celebrations of saints' feast days take place. Female singers, with low-pitched, nasal, voices, perform a Miserere to a reiterated, descending motif, with a largely monochordal accompaniment on harp, *quena* (notched flute), folk fiddle (using wide glissandos), and harmonium, a world apart from Christian plainsong.

In Lima's Museo de Arte, which houses works from both the pre-Columban and colonial eras, the figurative, brilliantly coloured totemistic art of Inca times is displayed only a few paces from paintings of agonized crucifixion, of hell, and of the oppressed, anticipating heavenly rapture. Yet there are links: saints wear Inca earrings and bracelets,

[87] Peter Cloudsley, 'From Creole to Chicha', *Geographical Magazine* (May 1987), 232.

Virgins are clad in flowing Inca costumes, and paintings of Christs could be mistaken for Inca chieftains.

Syncretist religious cults may not be so far from Christian worship as they seem, for a Christian worshipper receiving the Eucharistic host may similarly be possessed, according to the intensity of the belief. Many gods and saints started their spiritual journeys with 'visions' or 'possessions', and sacred shrines also have their origins in paranormal appearances. Three centuries ago, an apparition of a broken terracotta image of Nossa Senhorade Aparecida, the patron saint of Brazil, appeared to a fisherman. The three million pilgrims whom the Virgin receives annually at the Basilica of Aparecida (between Rio de Janeiro and São Paulo) are exceeded in number only by those who visit the Church of the Virgin of Guadalupe in Mexico City, patron saint of the country and the mystic force behind its revolution. The Christ whose outstretched arms embrace the world from the summit of Rio's Corcovado (the statue, completed in 1931, is 30 metres high) embraces a myriad religious customs, with a common, if tenuous, link. In Latin America, religion and politics have been closely intertwined, and music is inseparable from both.

There is some parallel between the relatively sudden forcing together of peoples and cultural systems in the New World in the sixteenth century and the interaction of peoples and cultural systems that is taking place around the world today, as a consequence of the facilitation of contact. In its cultural plurality, Latin America has experienced many characteristics of 'Postmodernism' for at least two hundred years; multiculturalism has a long history in the region. Differing ethnic, social, and political group interests have constantly sought expression through music and the other arts; and, like artistic expression everywhere, they needs must do so in terms of what is currently familiar. In an international market, the 'familiar' needs defining in international terms; and in the musical climate of the late twentieth century, it is not so much the piper as the business executive who calls the tune. The authentic sounds of Latin American musics have frequently been compromised by US and European dominance of the music industry. Yet Latin America has contributed greatly to popular styles today; it has bequeathed a great body of early polyphonic music as well as nineteenth- and twentieth-century symphonic music, that is only now, in the 1990s, being explored by fellow 'Westerners'.

The rival claims of Western convenience culture and indigenous identity culture remain problematic in many areas of Latin America, and the widespread equation of Western arts with social status is unlikely to disappear quickly. Paradoxically, the very cultural diversity that prevented consolidation of artistic accomplishment in the past may be a source of strength in a future in which plurality is *de rigueur.* The interests of the US music industry aside, only economic underdevelopment prevents urban centres in many states of Latin America from achieving the excellence within plurality that frequently appears to be eluding the economically developed West. Given economic development, and independence from cultural conditioning by US media, Latin America could be the vanguard of classical- and popular-music styles of the future.

15 Europeans North of Mexico

Colonization

Few would have thought, when a motley bunch of British adventurers landed on a swamp in Chesapeake Bay in 1607, that their settlement would mark the start of a new and momentous chapter in colonial history. The survivors of this expedition named their settlement, optimistically, Jamestown, after their king. Earlier, Elizabethan mariners had explored this stretch of North America's eastern seaboard and named it Virginia, after their then queen. Before them, in 1540, a Spanish land expedition from Mexico had penetrated as far north as the border of what is now Nebraska, in search of the ever-elusive 'Seven Cities of Gold'; and before the Spanish even, as early as 1504, Bretons had started fishing the cod banks off Nova Scotia, and moving inland up the St Lawrence River to trade in furs. Fur generated income; but fur was not gold. For almost two centuries after Cortés first plundered the wealth of Mexico, settlement north of Mexico was seen as inferior to settlement further south.

British settlers came to America not as conquerors but as seekers of a new and better life. Many came to escape religious persecution, poverty, or criminal prosecution; and they emigrated as communities of men, women, and children. The 'gentlemen unused to work, gallants, and lascivious sons'—as visiting colonial governors described the men of Virginia—were by religion of the Anglican faith; they took to cultivating tobacco, and then indigo, cotton, and timber. The 'ruder and sterner' religious dissenters, who first settled Plymouth, Massachusetts, in 1620, intended to create 'Cities of God';[1] but after providing for their immediate needs, they traded fur, fished 'the sacred cod', and, later, built ships to provide sustenance for the slave-holding planters of Virginia and the West Indies.

[1] Alistair Cooke, *America* (London: BBC, 1973), 73.

The Separatists' dislike of differing religious persuasions forced Quakers, Baptists, and others to settle further south; this encouraged more tolerant communities of Catholics and Protestants to occupy the 'Middle Colonies'. Scots Nonconformists, Irish Catholics, German Lutherans, Swedish Protestants, Moravians, Jacobites, Mennonites, and Jews gradually added to their ranks, so that, by 1733, thirteen British colonies occupied the Atlantic littoral, from New Hampshire in the north to Georgia in the south.[2]

From its outset, the colonization of what was to become the USA differed in important respects from that of Latin America. Settlers from northern Europe were the product of the Reformation and the Enlightenment, not of the Counter-Reformation and Neo-Thomism. These 'protestants' inherited a progressive tradition of rationalist criticism, and were willing to depart radically from British social, religious, and artistic practices.

Such radicalism was soon evident in the espousal of local democracy: in Jamestown, as early as 1619, a 'House of Burgesses', elected by 'the inhabitants'—effectively, all able-bodied males over 16—became the first self-governing body in America. Landowners could govern only by consent of the governed; and any residual notion that a 'luxurious living' could be handed on 'to idle generations' was soon eradicated by the legal abolition of primogeniture.[3] The 'Thirteen Colonies' were not, therefore, burdened with hereditary rights and privileges, such as beset Latin America (and brought France to a state of chaos), nor with an illiterate and backward peasant population. Enterprising and industrious colonists could achieve personal advancement to an extent that would have been inconceivable in their home countries.

The colonies encompassed a great variety of climate, economy, and terrain, but their total size was relatively small: approximately one-third the size of Argentina, for example. Gradually, market centres, such as Boston, New York, and Philadelphia, became accessible to one another; and, as they did so, the 'Thirteen Colonies' grew interdependent. The colonies also became increasingly interconnected by print: between 1691 and 1820, no less than 2,120 newspapers were published, of which 461 continued to publish for more than ten years.[4] Print-

[2] Alistair Cooke, *America*, 90. [3] Ibid. 66–8.

[4] Lucien Febvre and Henri-Jean Martin, *The Coming of the Book: The Impact of Printing, 1450–1800* (London: New Left Books, 1976), trans. of *L'Apparition du livre* (Paris: Albin Michel, 1958), cited in Benedict Anderson, *Imagined Communities: Reflections on the Origin and Spread of Nationalism* (London: Verso, 1987), 62.

journalism was a North American phenomenon: in alliance with the postmaster, the printer dispersed commercial news throughout the length of the Atlantic littoral, and in doing so stimulated a sense of unity among the colonies.[5] Capitalism, radicalism, and a pervasive quest for self-advancement gave to the 'Thirteen Colonies' the confidence to rebel against British attempts to impose taxation, to bid for Independence, and subsequently to become the first republic of the modern era.

Independence and Expansion

North America's success in the War of Independence owed much to the outcome of Britain's century-long rivalry with France. French possessions in the New World initially encompassed a vast sweep of lands, from Nova Scotia west to the Great Lakes, and south along the east bank of the Mississippi. The fur trade did not encourage dense settlements, however; and the population was thinly dispersed, except in Quebec and the St Lawrence Valley. Britain stormed Quebec as early as 1629, and Nova Scotia changed hands many times throughout the seventeenth century. Later, in 1713, it and Newfoundland were ceded to the British, who by then had created a successful fur-trading company in Hudson Bay. France, however, soon established a chain of strategically situated forts that prevented the British from expanding westwards.

In the seven years of near global conflict that flared up in 1756, France found itself overcommitted in Europe, and Britain was able to destroy French seapower in the Atlantic. In 1763 (at the conclusion the Seven Years War), France was forced to cede Canada to Britain, as well as all land east of the Mississippi; at the same time it ceded Louisiana to Spain, in compensation for its earlier transfer to Britain of the once-Spanish Florida. France then exacted retribution by siding with the Americans in the War of Independence (1775–83): it was the French blockade of Yorktown that finally persuaded the British commander, Cornwallis, to surrender to the American General Washington. In 1783 Britain was forced to recognize all lands to the south of the Great Lakes and east of the Mississippi as an independent United States.[6]

[5] Anderson, *Imagined Communities*, 62.
[6] *The Times Atlas of World History*, ed. Geoffrey Barraclough (London, 1989), 164, 195.

During the nineteenth century, leading European states would pursue their imperial ambitions in Asia and Africa, while the USA secured an empire situated on its doorstep.

The North American colonists created a Constitution that owed much to Locke and the British experience, but replaced a hereditary monarch by an elected president. Nevertheless, the theory that all governments derive their just powers from the consent of the governed was a radical one: it would subsequently send the French king, Louis XVI, to the guillotine.[7] Radical too was the idea of federalism. The American Constitution was to prove sufficiently flexible for the thirteen original states to expand (within 100 years of its drafting) to forty-eight (the forty-ninth, Alaska, was admitted in 1959, and the fiftieth, Hawaii, in 1960); and it facilitated the change of an early agricultural economy to an industrial economy, with a level of productivity unmatched in the world. When the War of Independence began in 1775, the American interior was known as the 'back country'; after 1800 it was known as the 'frontier'; by 1890, the frontier had disappeared.[8] In the century and a half following the War of Independence, some forty million people migrated to the USA.

US territory increased dramatically in 1803, with Jefferson's cunning purchase of Louisiana from Napoleon. (The territory had been restored to France by secret treaty with Spain.) Louisiana was then a vast area comprising what later became Arkansas, Missouri, Nebraska, Iowa, South and part of North Dakota, Minnesota, Kansas, Oklahoma, Colorado, and Wyoming, as well as Louisiana. Its purchase increased the size of the USA by 140 per cent, at a cost of approximately four cents an acre.[9] Florida was then bought from Spain in 1819. Further imperial ambitions brought the USA into conflict with a Mexico still struggling for political stability after revolution. At the end of these hostilities, in 1858, huge territories that formerly belonged to Mexico—present-day California, Utah, New Mexico, and Texas—were added to the North American empire. By 1890 the USA comprised a huge part of the North American continent, from the Great Lakes in the north to the Gulfs of California and Mexico in the south.

[7] J. M. Roberts, *Pelican History of the World* (London: Pelican Books, 1988), 673.
[8] *Times Atlas*, 220, 224.
[9] Cooke, *America*, 163.

Manifest Destiny

An aspect of US colonization that differed markedly from that of Latin America—and that also owed much to the European Enlightenment—was the attitude of colonists to indigenous peoples. In Latin America, notwithstanding appalling atrocities of conquest and enslavement, Native Americans who converted to the Catholic faith could be assimilated into the new order; and, in the centres of the old Aztec and Inca empires at least, native populations greatly outnumbered colonists. In the USA, native populations were relatively small, and could be isolated, or eliminated, to make way for farms and plantations; and although, in 1763, a 'Proclamation Line' was established (running vaguely along the crest of the Allegheny mountains) with the intention that all land west of it should be retained as an 'Indian' Reserve, that line forever crumbled before the westward surge of settlers.[10]

English methods of dealing with Native Americans were more subtle than those of the Spanish. The settlers of Jamestown placed a golden crown on the head of a Powhatan chief to persuade him to work for them; but when the Powhatans eventually rose against the British, superior British weaponry reduced their number from 8,000 to less than 1,000.[11] In 1662 New Englanders similarly crowned a Wampanoag Chief as King Philip of Pokanoket; but when 'King Philip' subsequently led a rebellion, the peoples of his confederation were eliminated, and his head was displayed in Plymouth for the next twenty years.

In Native American belief, land could not be owned: it was as endless as the sky, and belonged to the Great Spirit. Thus, when a Native chief in 'New England' first placed a mark on a piece of paper handed to him by white settlers, it was simply to humour these strange intruders.[12] For over a century, active Native Americans would be tricked or wearied into signing away their lands before what a later chief would call the 'advancing banners of the same greedy host'.[13] Those who resisted invariably fell before the superior weaponry of the colonizers; the Pontiacs of Ottawa, the Miamis of Ohio, and the Winnebagos of Illinois were amongst those who resisted and were reduced to remnants. One

[10] *Times Atlas*, 164.

[11] Dee Brown, *Bury my Heart at Wounded Knee* (New York: Bantam Books, 1972), 2–4.

[12] Ibid. 3.

[13] Ronald Wright, *Stolen Continents: The Indian Story* (London: Murray, 1992), 218.

reason for Jefferson's keenness to purchase Louisiana was that it could provide a 'wilderness' into which unassimilated 'Indians' could be herded.[14]

In 1830, in defiance of a Supreme Court ruling that no constitutional right to remove Native Americans from their ancestral lands existed, Congress passed an Act that forced all such peoples to move beyond a 'Permanent Indian Frontier', west of the Mississippi. The largest Native people east of the 'Permanent Frontier' was the Cherokee; and in 1835, after much deliberation, Cherokee leaders signed away the last 50,000 square kilometres of their land; three years later, 16,000 Cherokees were rounded up and placed in concentration camps; and throughout the next winter they were force-marched on a thousand-kilometre journey into 'Indian Territory'. One-quarter of them died on the way. The journey was known as 'The Trail of Tears'.

As elimination of the Native population increased, and as 'Indian Territory' shrank forever before the inexorable westward movement of whites, justification had to be sought (Pl. 68). Echoing Blumenbach and Hegel in Germany, white US citizens developed the concept of 'Manifest Destiny', by which it was held to be the destiny of Europeans, as the dominant race, to rule the whole North American continent, and to be responsible for its native peoples. Of a battle with the Navahos (in 1864), for example, 'Star Chief' Carleton recalled that, 'having fought us with a heroism which any people might be proud to emulate ... they found it was their destiny too, as it had been that of their brethren, tribe after tribe ... to give way to the insatiable progress of our race'. In 1870 treaty lands of the Sioux were invaded by the Big Horn mining association on the grounds that 'the rich and beautiful valleys of Wyoming are destined for the occupancy of the Anglo-Saxon race ... the advance guard of civilization'.[15]

Native Americans developed opposite views. In 1811 a shaman named Tsali declared that the creator had made different peoples in different lands, and had not intended Native Americans to live like whites; their ills would vanish only when they returned to their traditional ways. During his travels, Tsali had seen the heavens open, whereupon Native Americans had ridden down from the sky on black horses, and their leader had given him this information. A succession of strange cosmic happenings appeared to confirm Tsali's message, and the Che-

[14] Wright, *Stolen Continents*, 209.

[15] Cited in Brown, *Bury my Heart*, 31, 184.

68. John Gast's *American Progress* (1872): Manifest Destiny, an emblem of progress, hovers over the white settlers; Native Americans flee

rokees starting 'Ghost Dancing' to encourage their dead relatives to return. The 'Ghost' cult spread to other Native peoples.[16]

Two hundred years earlier, a similar cult had taken root in Cusco: the 'Sickness Dance' had enabled entranced worshippers to prophesy a plague that would kill the invaders but spare Native peoples. In Mexico, in the 1880s, a series of *Cantares Mexicanos* similarly invoked ancestors to relive the glories of the past.[17] And in 1890, at Standing Rock in the US Mid-West—a year after the Blackfoot Sioux and Hunkpapas had been coerced into signing away their large reservation there—a visitor came to the great Hunkpapa Chief, Sitting Bull, with word that Christ had returned to earth again as a Native American, and had taught various pilgrims the Ghost Dance; those who danced it would be suspended in the air while a wave of new earth buried all the white men. The Ghost Dance was then danced all over the Prairie: all work came to a standstill, as more than 3,000 people in Ghost Shirts danced their way into every night.[18]

Frightened Europeans arrested Sitting Bull and surrounded a group of Ghost dancers; in the ensuing scuffle, Sitting Bull was shot. Some 350

[16] Wright, *Stolen Continents*, 210–11. [17] Ibid. 185, 154.
[18] Brown, *Bury my Heart*, 406–9.

dancers were then taken to a cavalry camp at Wounded Knee Creek, where most of them were slaughtered. 'I did not know then how much was ended,' said a Native American later; 'a people's dream died there. It was a beautiful dream.'[19]

The dream may not have died entirely: the Mohawk Iroquois staged a revolt at Oka in Quebec in 1990, for example; and 'Indian' Reserves throughout the continent are becoming self-governing. It is difficult to imagine, however, the rise of an 'Indian' nation in the USA; that possibility belongs further south, to Mexico. It is one of the great ironies of US cultural development that Native Americans have left so few marks upon it. The rich musical culture of the Native Americans has, however, now been amply documented; it demonstrates an intimate relationship between music and social custom, similar to that of Aboriginal Australian and Sub-Saharan African musical cultures, described elsewhere. The music is too varied to be described in summary here; today, it is mostly to be heard in modernized versions.

Slavery and the Civil War

A more conspicuous running sore in the growth of North America is slavery; indeed, the consequences of this practice only swell with the passage of time. As early as the 1680s, Africans were arriving at the rate of 60,000 per decade; by the time of the American Revolution they constituted half the population of Virginia; in the Carolinas there were two Africans to every European.[20] When the Civil War began in 1861, about 90 per cent of US Africans lived as slaves in the South. In the North, some 200,000 emancipated or fugitive slaves, who had sought protection there, fought for the Union and for their freedom.[21]

Disagreement over the issue of slavery was a symptom, rather than a cause, of the malaise that led the North and South to bloody conflict. By the late eighteenth century, the economy of the South was in decline, to the extent that the importation of African slaves was actually made illegal in 1808. The prohibition was not obeyed, however, because shortly thereafter the Southern economy was transformed by the invention of the cotton gin, and by the discovery that sugar could be crystallized. While the North developed the assembly line and experienced an

[19] Brown, *Bury my Heart*, 413–19. [20] Cooke, *America*, 191. [21] *Times Atlas*, 222.

industrial revolution, the South developed a plantation economy for which slaves were needed in ever-increasing numbers.[22]

As settlers from both North and South moved West, their differing ideologies clashed. Individual farmers from the North were self-sufficient and did not wish to compete with slave labour; the plantation economy, on the other hand, was dependent upon it. Northerners attempted to exclude slavery from the new states, and many gave help to fugitive slaves; Southerners responded by forming the Confederate States of America, and attempting to secede from the Union. In 1860 Abraham Lincoln was elected President on a pro-Union ticket. Five years later—four of them in a war in which more than 20 per cent of the three million combatants died—the Confederates surrendered.[23] That the North eventually won was largely due to its modernizing economy; and it was this that subsequently elevated the USA to a position of world domination. Nevertheless, the sense of 'belonging', engendered by the plantation economy, persisted in the South; and North and South still retain markedly different cultural traditions and senses of identity.

Northern Psalms

Neither the plantation workers of the South nor the Puritans of the North were purveyors of classical Western music. The Southerners brought with them a mixture of Scots and English folk-songs and broadside ballads, as well as Anglican hymns and simple anthems. The Pilgrim Fathers brought Henry Ainsworth's *Book of Psalmes: Englished both in Prose and Metre* (completed in 1612 for the 'Separatists' who had found refuge in Amsterdam) and Thomas Ravenscroft's *Whole Booke of Psalmes* of 1621; and Ainsworth's collection included many tunes with varied rhythms and metres that derived from French and Dutch folk sources.[24] North American music, therefore, developed on an essentially egalitarian base. In contrast to Latin America, where skilled church musicians composed in the styles and forms of the European Renaissance, the USA depended on self-taught composers, who created new styles and forms, based on populist music, that soon departed radically from European precedents.

[22] Cooke, *America*, 188–200. [23] *Times Atlas*, 222.
[24] Richard Crawford, 'Psalmody', *The New Grove* (1980), xv. 345.

To the pious-minded Puritans, music was primarily associated with psalm-singing, of which the standards rapidly declined; and, in the absence of the ability to read music, an orally transmitted style of singing developed, performed at a slow tempo, in a freely embellished style. Known as the 'common way' of singing, it incorporated the technique of 'lining-out', whereby the deacon or precentor intones each line before it is sung.[25] 'Lining-out' originated in Europe, and was used extensively in Britain to teach the hymns of Isaac Watts (1674–1748). Lined-out, those same hymns became popular in the USA, particularly among African Americans, and a distinctive 'lining-out' style was to become widespread among evangelical churches in the South.

The 'common way' of singing was popular mainly in rural areas. In urban centres, however, and in Boston in particular, Harvard-educated clerics advocated 'regular' singing, and efforts were made to bring this about. The result was the foundation of a remarkable institution of 'Singing Schools'. Initially these were no more than classes for instruction in music-reading, one outcome of which was the invention of 'shape notation', in which notes were given different shapes in accordance with their pitches. John Tufts, who compiled *An Introduction to the Art of Singing Psalm Tunes* (the first of many collections of Singing School music), placed the first syllables of the sol-fa names on the staff, and used a system of dots after each letter to indicate duration.[26] Tune books followed, with instructional prefaces; and shape-note collections of psalm tunes were soon taken up in the South.

The Singing Schools were immensely successful: by the end of the eighteenth century there were choirs in village churches all over New England, as well as gallery orchestras. When organs supplanted the gallery orchestras, the players became the nucleus of town bands. The Singing Schools established musical literacy; by 1800, more than 1,000 different psalm tunes had been printed in American tune books, many by US composers. The tune books consisted of 'plain' tunes, 'fuging' tunes (containing brief imitative sections), and anthems. It was customary for the tune to be given to the tenor, while parts for soprano, alto, and bass were added around it.

The Singing Schools became social centres, and they initiated concert-going with 'singing lectures'. A 'New England Music Festival' was inaugurated in King's Chapel, Boston, in 1786. From such initiatives,

[25] Gilbert Chase, 'United States of America', *The New Grove* (1980), xix. 425.

[26] Harry Eskew, 'Shape-Note Hymnody', *The New Grove* (1980), xvii. 223–4.

69. Frontispiece to William Billings's *New England Psalm Singer* (Boston, 1770), showing a canon of six-in-one and a ground

choral and orchestral societies developed: for example, the Philo-Harmonic Society (1809) and Handel and Haydn Society (1815) in Boston, and the Musical Fund Society (1820) in Philadelphia. It was through the populist music of the Singing Schools, rather than the singing of ecclesiastical polyphony, that the European tradition came to be established in the USA.

The first North American composer of distinction was William Billings (1746–1800), and he soon initiated a characteristically US approach to his art. In the Preface to his first tune book, he identified 'the grand difficulty in composition' as being 'to preserve the air through each part separately, and yet cause them to harmonize with each other at the same time'. As if to prove the point, he wrote a short hymn, aptly called 'Discord'. 'I don't think myself confined to any Rules of Composition . . . it is best for every *Composer* to be his own *Carver*', Billings wrote in the same Preface;[27] though he later admitted that rules can exist: 'I come as near as I possibly can to a set of rules which I have carved out for myself' (Pl. 69). These rules were not greatly unlike

[27] David P. MacKay, 'Billings', *The New Grove* (1980), ii. 704.

those that Albrechtsberger would be attempting to instil in the young Beethoven a few years later, though they evidently permitted the use of consecutive fifths, thirdless chords, and unresolved discords. Such individualistic traits became common among 'Yankee tunesmiths'.

Billings composed in a variety of styles and genres: his 'Chester', for example, was the favourite marching tune of the New England regiments. His iconoclastic attitude towards tradition was an early indication of a wilful streak in US music, one that would resurface in composers such as Henry Cowell, Charles Ives, Carl Ruggles, John Cage, and Elliott Carter. It would stand in curious contrast to North America's *alter ego*, that feeds off the Europe of the past.

Southern Spirituals

Alongside 'regular' singing, stimulated by the Singing Schools, the 'common way' of psalm-singing persisted; and, on the frontier, where hymn books were scarce and illiteracy was common, the practice of 'lining-out' was particularly popular. In essence, 'lining-out' was responsorial singing, as common to Africans through 'call-and response' technique as to choristers of the Christian Church. The system was adopted by the Baptists, an evangelical body that originated in Holland among the Separatists, and was first established in North America on Rhode Island, in 1639. 'Lining-out' enabled long and complex texts to be sung by large, illiterate congregations; and the fervour with which congregations trailed their leaders, picking up text and tunes just a few steps behind them, led to a rich form of heterophony.[28] In half-speech and half-song, preachers and converts would improvise 'testimony' or 'witness' concerning the joy brought by religion to a life that was often harsh. The following 'testimony' from D. N. Asher, recorded in the 1970s in Blackey, Kentucky, offers something of the flavour:

> When they first stormed the wild seas they lived hard, they had to clear land, they didn't have any houses at all, just rough little log huts, didn't have no chairs like we have now, nor no beds like we have to sleep on.... But the Lord was with them, Grace divine was with them in such a strong way that evenings they would sit on their little dirt porches ... in

[28] Alan Lomax, sleeve note to *The Gospel Ship: Baptist Hymns and White Spirituals from the Southern Mountains*, New World Records, NW 294, 1977.

> old hog-skin moccasins and coon-skin caps and sing the songs that we've sung tonight: 'Guide me O thou Great Jehovah, Pilgrim through the barren land . . . '. God was with them and blessed them to have all kinds of good fruit in this land and country. . .[29]

The emotional impact of such 'testimony' would be heightened with an improvised performance on a favourite 'lining-out' hymn.

'Lining-out' had also been used to teach northern shape-note tunes to rural congregations. As the tastes of the urban North became increasingly sophisticated, and the music of the 'Yankee tunesmiths' came to be correspondingly scorned, the shape-note tune books travelled South with itinerant teachers. Here, shape-note and other tunes were adapted to suit the more folksy tastes of Southern congregations. Along with the Baptist collections, such as Joshua Smith's *Divine Hymns and Spiritual Songs for the Use of Religious Assemblies and Private Christians* (1794), they became the musical bedrock of the huge camp meetings of the Great Revival that swept the frontier after the Revolutionary War. Revivalist meetings might attract between 10,000 and 20,000 worshippers, and at times lasted for several days.[30] While these great throngs indulged in ecstatic singing, dancing, and shrieking, the tunes were subjected to constant repetition, and were broken up by refrains and 'tag-lines'.

It was from the fervour of these meetings that the Spiritual came into being. Pious critics of Revivalism, such as John F. Watson, bemoaned the fact that the camp meetings encouraged music in the 'merry-chorus manner of the Southern harvest field', and that this example 'visibly affected the manner of some whites'.[31] Blacks attended white camp meetings, in addition to their own; and melodies of black Spirituals appear to have emanated not only from European sources, but also from the oral tradition of African songs, and from African musical invention on acculturated European formulas. Blacks appear to have shown greater rhythmic and melodic variety in performing common tunes, using the shifting accents characteristic of African musical style, and sevenths of varying intonation, that were to become characteristic of the blues.[32] Although there is a substantial repertoire of white spirituals, it was blacks who were to popularize the genre.

[29] Ibid. [30] James C. Downey, 'Spiritual', *The New Grove* (1980), xviii. 1 ff.

[31] John F. Watson, *Methodist Error* (Trenton, NJ: 1819), cited in Eileen Southern (ed.), *Readings in Black American Music* (New York: 1971), 63.

[32] Paul Oliver, 'Spiritual', *The New Grove* (1980), xviii. 4–5.

The Folk Tradition

Because music in the USA developed from a populist base, it was necessarily harnessed to politics; indeed, the Revolutionary War cemented a linkage between politics and music that has endured to this day. When that war was over, people cheered their leader in song with 'God Save Great Washington'; and soon were singing 'Adams and Liberty', then 'Lincoln and Liberty' and—to the tune of 'The Old Grey Mare'—'Old Abe Lincoln came out of the Wilderness Many Long Years Ago.' In the South, many a governorship has since been secured by demonstrating ability in 'country' music; and the style of music still associated with presidential elections is popular US, rather than classical European.

From the earliest colonial times, capitalism formed the basis of economic growth; the class structure that emerged depended, therefore, on the acquisition of wealth, rather than on the good fortune of heredity. The USA's early élite of landowners, merchants, and industrialists emerged from a variety of social backgrounds. They were not greatly troubled by theories of aesthetics or by any need for artistic appearances, and the folk balladeer was equally at home in the mansions of the wealthy as in the cabins and hovels of the labourers.

Although, as in Europe, 'folk' quickly went 'pop' in the wake of urbanization, the constant fluidity of the Western 'frontier' ensured that a distinctive folk style would continue there until the end of the nineteenth century. As labourers from southern cotton fields, or eastern textile mills, set off to find new homelands, and as loneliness continued to haunt the frontier homesteader, new folk-songs came into being.

Men on pack horses blazed the trails that would become routes for ox-drawn wagons. As the trail stretched westward, bound for the 'promised land', and as the traffic swelled with the scent of gold, 'boomers' deserted to settle new homesteads, new frontier towns, new saloons, and new gambling joints, where death was as real as life. Keelboats and steamers then provided transportation along newly excavated canals; and in their wake came the railroads—over 50,000 kilometres of them by 1860—laid by 'hobos', tramps, and 'bums', ever mindful of gunmen like Railroad Bill, and mournful of such disasters as befell Casey Jones.

After the civil war came the long cattle drives, with range cattle herded along such routes as 'The Old Chisholm Trail'. Cowboys sang of a harsh life, sleeping rough on 'the lone prairie', while also—perhaps with a jew's harp or harmonica for accompaniment—extolling the excitements of the carefree life of the 'Buckaroo'.[33] A large repertoire of cowboy songs came into being, later to be joined by guitars, fiddles, basses, and accordions, to furnish a model for 'country' music. The domestication of the West provided material for a folklore that reflected the harsh lives of the frontiersmen.

The melodies of the folk-songs were as diverse as was the ancestry of their creators; many derived directly from European precedents. Some were modal, displaying more remote British origins; mostly they were diatonic, with clear, simple, harmonic implications. Accordion, banjo, and—from the turn of the nineteenth century—guitar accompaniment led to the ubiquitous three-chord harmonic underlay in US folk music. (It also became the harmonic basis of African-American blues.) Folksiness is still associated with the South.

The Beautiful and the Sublime

While religious and secular folk traditions were evolving in the South and West, the tastes of the urban North were becoming more sophisticated. As early as 1795, a *Massachusetts Compiler* was published in Boston, with a preface taken from thoroughbass manuals of Europe. Theory books became increasingly Europeanized, and a corresponding influx of professional musicians from across the Atlantic occurred. Professionally trained composers began to denigrate the 'crude' compositions of the Yankee tunesmiths; Andrew Law, for example, bemoaned 'the pitiful productions of numerous composuists', and viewed admiringly the 'beautiful and sublime compositions of the great Masters of Music'.[34]

By the early nineteenth century, it was German rather than US music that was being championed as the ideal, as Handel, Haydn, Beethoven, and Mendelssohn were successively held up as models. German musicians were welcomed in the USA; indeed, most towns acquired a German music teacher.[35] Gradually, as a result of the tradition established by the Singing Schools, all the trappings of European musical culture—choirs, bands, orchestras, concert halls, and opera houses—were

[33] Charlie Seemann, *The American Cowboy: Image and Reality*, sleeve note to *Back in the Saddle Again*, New World Records, NW 314/215, 1979.

[34] Chase, 'United States of America', *The New Grove*, xix. 427.

[35] H. Wiley Hitchcock, *Music in the United States: A Historical Introduction* (Englewood Cliffs, NJ: Prentice Hall, 1974), 56.

transplanted to the USA. Subsequently, the European classical-music tradition would be established there on a scale dwarfing the rest of Europe.

European opera was first performed in the early nineteenth century. Henry Fry, after hearing Bellini's *Norma*, became the first American to *compose* an opera; he called it, optimistically, *Leonora*, and it was performed in Philadelphia in 1845. Romantically inclined composers attempted, somewhat vaguely, to incorporate Native American and African elements into their music. Louis Moreau Gottschalk, a native of Louisiana, spoke of the 'basic Americanist urge that drives me on'; he drew on the melodies and rhythms of African–American folk and popular music, on the 'Plantation' melodies of Stephen Foster, and on African–Cuban music.[36] Though he studied in Germany, Gottschalk was ambivalent about the presence of so many German musicians in the USA: 'It is remarkable', he once mused, 'that nearly all the Russians in America are Counts, just as almost all the musicians who abound in the United States are nephews of Spohr and Mendelssohn.'[37]

Anglo-German influence was evident in the multiplication of choral societies. A chorus of 10,000, with an orchestra of 1,000, was assembled for a National Peace Festival in Boston in 1869. From the growing taste for choral music there developed a vogue (lasting into the twentieth century) for the composition of historical cantatas.[38] Nevertheless, foreign influence was all-pervasive, and US music became increasingly derivative; much of it was scarcely more original than the polkas, waltzes, mazurkas, quicksteps, and quadrilles that were the staple diet of the ballroom.[39]

Dvořák, during his sojourn in the USA (1892–95), encouraged North American composers to draw on African and indigenous musics to form a nationalist style. Few composers had had more experience in the attempt to graft a folk style on to the West European symphonic tradition, and Dvořák may have been aware of the earlier example of Gottschalk. In fact, American composers of the time can have had very little idea of the true nature of African and Native American musics. An early collection of 'negro' materials, compiled in 1867, depicted the

[36] Chase, 'United States of America', *The New Grove*, xix. 428–30.

[37] Hitchcock, *Music in the United States*, 56.

[38] Chase, 'United States of America', *The New Grove*, xix. 429.

[39] A historical reproduction of this music has been recorded as *19th Century American Ballroom Music*, performed by the Smithsonian Social Orchestral and Quadrille Band, Nonesuch Recordings, H–71313.

'negro race' as 'half barbarous';[40] and Native American culture had been dealt a near mortal blow at Wounded Knee Creek in 1890. It would take the indomitable genius of Charles Ives to cut through European influence, and establish a truly North American style in the tradition of Billings; when he did so, there was little that was specifically African or Native American about the music.

Minstrelsy and Sentiment

Until well on into the twentieth century, white US understanding of African music would in general have been limited to the Southern plantation songs and spirituals, both of which were hybrid genres. This limited understanding was reflected in the practice of 'Blackface minstrelsy', which flourished during the middle decades of the nineteenth century. The genre was popularized in England after one Charles Matthews returned from the USA, fascinated by what he had perceived to be 'negro' musical characteristics. In North America, Thomas Dartmouth ('Daddy' or 'Jim Crow') Rice developed a form of 'Blackface minstrelsy' that provided a stereotype, as whites saw it, of the uncouth, dishevelled, plantation slave (Jim Crow), and the Broadway 'negro' dandy (Zip Coon) (Pl. 70).[41] White singers, their faces blackened with burnt cork, parodied what they saw as the feckless, idle, and musically quaint culture of blacks.

These cork-blackened, white entertainers were accompanied by 'plantation' instruments: banjo, tambourine, violin, bone castanets, and, at times, accordion. The music of their shows derived from plantation songs, frontier songs, and British minstrel songs and dances. To these were added later what became known as 'genteel' songs, the white composers of which for the most part had never been near a plantation. Such a one was Stephen Foster, not a few of whose songs became international hits. For his immortal song about the 'Swanee River', Foster scratched out—in the interests of verbal sonority—the original name 'Pedee', in favour of a river he had never seen. Foster's 'My Old Kentucky Home' remains the official state song of Kentucky; his 'Old Folks at Home' remains that of Florida.[42]

[40] Charles Seeger, 'United States of America', *The New Grove* (1980), xix. 439.
[41] Clayton W. Henderson, 'United States of America', *The New Grove* (1980), xix. 351–2.
[42] H. Wiley Hitchcock, 'Foster, Stephen Collins', *The New Grove* (1980), vi. 730.

Blacks themselves toured minstrel shows, performing in front of both black and white audiences; indeed, W. C. Handy, 'Father of the Blues', who had himself been a band-leader of minstrel shows, claimed that blacks were the originators of this form of entertainment.[43] Often blacks added burnt cork to their skins to accord with the white image of the coal-black 'nigger'; and frequently they parodied the jig, the reel, and the hoe-down—the basic fodder of 'country' get-togethers—by syncopating the rhythms. The resulting dance step came to be known as the 'rag'.[44] White musicians had enlivened their songs by imitating black song and dialect as early as the 1830s, with Micah Hawkins's 'Jump Jim Crow' and 'Old Zip Coon' (Turkey in the Straw), written in the plantation style that was to inspire Foster during the next decade. It was a black composer, however, James Bland, who wrote the song 'Carry Me Back to Old Virginny' that is now the official song of Virginia State.

By the late nineteenth century, minstrel bands were performing hour-long 'classical' concerts in the open air. W. C. Handy described how he led his musicians through a mixture of light European music, such as the overtures to *William Tell* and *Poet and the Peasant*, along with a medley of American plantation airs, and instrumental solos. In the theatre, the soloist would offer the latest tune from Broadway, while the repertoire of the leading actor would range from Shakespeare to popular, tear-jerking songs.[45]

The new sentiment in US popular music, evident in the songs of the minstrel shows, had been stimulated by the Civil War. The sentimental songs of George Root and Henry Work, for example, idealized the loyal citizen. They dealt with such subjects as 'Mother's Melancholy' ('Just before the battle, Mother, I am thinking most of you') or Johnny's military trials that could lead to his marching either 'home again' or 'with the angels in heaven' (Pl. 71). European songs were sometimes adapted: for example, the British tune 'Charlie is my Darling' was taken over as 'Johnny Darling, the Union Volunteer'. And volunteers could became immortal heroes; the infamous John Brown was a historic character, hanged for attempting to arm Southern slaves; and his soul went 'marching on' to a Revivalist camp meeting tune to become the 'Battle Hymn of the Republic'.

[43] W. C. Handy, *Father of the Blues* (1941), cited in Southern (ed.), *Readings*, 211.

[44] Tony Palmer, *All You Need is Love* (London: Futura Publications, 1977), 34.

[45] Abbe Niles, 'The Story of the Blues', foreword to W. C. Handy (ed.), *Blues: An Anthology* (1949; repr. New York: Macmillan, 1972), 24.

70. The cover of *Jim Crow Jubilee*, a collection of 'negro' melodies (1847)

71. The cover of a collection of ballads, on sentimental subjects, by George Root (1859)

A National Musical Style

From a mixture of European and homespun musical elements, a national musical style began to assert itself during the twentieth century. Its distinctiveness sprang partly from the fact that it contained within it a cultural ambiguity. In Chapter 2 (pp. 69–70), the suggestion of the anthropologist Claude Lévi-Strauss was quoted: that a culture embodies facets of an environment that of themselves establish an array of references that determine a system of conduct, motivation, and judgement. This system is confirmed by an educationally reflexive view of the historical development of a civilization, and other cultural systems tend to be perceptible only 'through distortions imprinted upon them by the original system'. It was also noted that, while cultures may borrow from one another, if they are not to perish it is essential that they retain 'a certain impermeability to one another'.[46]

Notwithstanding its espousal of European culture, the USA has retained that 'certain impermeability' to it. Its cultural reference systems developed in a manner very different from those of Europe. Its arts emerged from a populist base, whereas those of Europe developed through an exploitation of aristocratic wealth. The art music of the USA was rooted in Billings as much as in Bach, and it had to hand a distinctive folk tradition, stylistically far removed from the Austro-German folk tradition that had dominated European music during the late eighteenth and nineteenth centuries. Inevitably, US musicians perceived European music 'with distortions imprinted upon it by the original (US) system'. European music has never rested easily on US soil.

The USA, as has already been indicated, was heir to the Reformation and the Enlightenment rather than to the Counter-Reformation and Neo-Thomism: unlike Latin America, it developed within a free-thinking tradition. Its cohesive revolution against the Motherland, made possible by its early espousal of capitalism, and of technological advance, encouraged a sense of nationalism. US musicians did not adopt a condescending attitude to their popular musical base, and their attitude to European music was often ambivalent. Such ambivalence is evident in the work of many of the US composers who operated during the two or three decades before the Second World War, when the USA was achieving world prominence: for example, Henry Cowell, Charles Ives,

[46] Claude Lévi-Strauss, *The View from Afar* (Oxford: Blackwell, 1985), pp. xiv-xv, 11.

Carl Ruggles, Virgil Thomson, William Schuman, Roger Sessions, Samuel Barber, Roy Harris, Alan Hovhaness, Wallingford Rieger, and Aaron Copland.

North American composers of this period, relatively fluent in basic European compositional techniques, did not share the European sense of obligation to a historical tradition; they were more concerned that musical style, as learned from Europe, should take a distinctively US direction. Aaron Copland articulated the aspirations of many North American composers in 1952:

> In order to create an indigenous music of universal significance, three conditions are imperative. First, the composer must be part of a nation that has a profile of its own—that is the most important; second, the composer must have in his background some sense of musical culture and, if possible, a basis in folk or popular art; and third, a superstructure of organized musical activities must exist—to some extent, at least—at the service of the native composer.[47]

Such conditions existed in the USA in the mid-twentieth century—as they had existed, for example, in Hungary in the early twentieth century, and in Russia and Bohemia in the mid-nineteenth century. Copland's aspirations were not greatly different from those of Bartók, Mussorgsky, or Dvořák before him. He sought a North American style that would 'speak of universal things in a vernacular of American speech rhythms . . . to write music on a level that left popular music far behind—music with a largeness of utterance wholly representative of the country that Whitman had envisaged'. The attempt to express in music so nebulous a concept as 'largeness' accounts for the naïvety of some US music. Yet Copland's use of US folk tunes and 'jazzy' rhythms, as in his ballet score *Billy the Kid*, represents the tradition of Billings at its best—a polyglot mixture of populism, descriptiveness, heroics, and harmony-gone-wrong, that belongs as distinctively to the USA as pumpkin pie.

It is significant that Copland could define the requirements for a national musical style some thirty years after Charles Ives, the man who best fulfilled them, had ceased to compose. Ives's music was incomprehensible to his contemporary audiences because it rejected, wholly and without compromise, the ethos of European classical music, while still utilizing many of its basic stylistic formulas. Born in 1875 of an

[47] Sam Morgenstern (ed.), *Composers on Music* (New York: Pantheon Books, 1956), 555.

unusually free-thinking musical father, Ives was driven by a dogged conviction about US independence in relation to US music. 'You'll not get a wild, heroic ride to Heaven on pretty little sounds,' his father had told him.[48] Charles Ives believed he would strengthen his musical instincts if he did not use them to make a living: he spent his life as the head of a successful insurance business. 'Everyone', he said, 'should have the opportunity of not being over-influenced':

> If a bishop should offer a 'prize living' to the curate who will love God the hardest for 15 days, whoever gets the prize would love God least. Such stimulants, it strikes us, tend to industrialize art rather than develop a spiritual sturdiness.[49]

No composer more completely embodied the vibrant US historical experience than Ives; and no composer more unwittingly exposed or anticipated the cracks in its cultural make-up. There is a sense in which nationalist music in the USA lived and died in Charles Ives.

Ives's uniqueness lay in rejecting wholly the aura of pretentiousness and bombast that surrounded the German musical culture, brought to North America by émigrés, and by compatriots who had studied in Europe. From his side of the Atlantic, Ives could not appreciate the great affirmation of German musical culture embodied in Wagnerian opera. (As a student, he had been to a performance of *Götterdämmerung* and found it 'a great deal of work over nothing'.) What he saw, with an acuity denied to Europeans, was the irrelevance of the German tradition to the social and political mores of his time.

It was the 'manner' of German music that Ives found so restrictive. For Ives, 'substance', not 'manner', was the germinating force of composition. 'If nature is not enthusiastic about explanation', he said, 'why should Tchaikovsky be?'[50] Ives perceived that it was the 'manner' of German music that limited its 'substance': the 'manner' could not accommodate representation of life as a whole but only one tiny part of it. That tiny part had become representative of all musical culture. If the 'substance' of art was to be so unrepresentative of life as a whole, the fault must lie with the 'manner': that is to say, with the very concept of 'art'.

Into his musical language, Ives incorporated and blended virtually every aspect of the North American musical ambience he had experi-

[48] Cited in David Wooldridge, *Charles Ives: A Portrait* (London: Faber & Faber, 1975), 70.

[49] Charles Ives, *Essays before a Sonata* (1920; ed. Howard Boatwright, New York: Norton, 1961).

[50] Ives, *Essays.*

enced: songs of the revolutionary war, sentimental songs of the civil war, music of marching bands, spirituals, hymns, anthems, minstrel songs, ragtime, and vaudeville; Ives parodied them all with affection. In the process of pasting together an extraordinary collage of evocative musical 'substance', Ives stumbled upon virtually every musical 'manner' into which European music would subsequently rationalize itself: polyrhythm, polytonality, multi-texture, serial procedure, chord clusters, microtones, and spacial separations.[51]

There was a political intent in Ives's music, but it was achieved only by association; the confidence was based essentially on nostalgia. The integrity of the artistic intent was unshakeable, but the political irrelevance of the musical 'substance' was revealed painfully, in 1917, when Ives was asked to set a war poem, on 'Flanders Field'. Associative tunes, such as 'Columbia, Gem of the Ocean' and 'Battle Cry of Freedom', that had served admirably in modernistic collages, were hardly appropriate to the living horror of the 1917 trenches.[52] Ultimately—and ironically—the importance of Ives's music lay in its 'manner':—that is to say, the anarchic treatment of its 'substance', a feature destined to be very important for the future of US music. His musical art was, arguably, the last—as well as the most distinguished—wholly *affirmative* musical statement of, and about, the USA.

For the USA to reject the essential manner of European music would necessitate, in future, eliminating not only its ethos but also its stylistic formulas. US music would look for inspiration to oriental philosophy and music, which, like that of Europe, would have 'distortions imprinted upon it by the original (US) system'. The USA would establish a hybrid culture that was neither wholly European nor wholly American; it would subsequently be referred to as 'Western'.

Egress from Europe

Music in the USA was, nevertheless, greatly enriched by the immigration of European composers already in search of new solutions to the harmonic impasse thrown up by what Satie

[51] It has recently been noted (Alan Rich, *American Pioneers* (London: Phaidon Press, 1995)) that Ives was seen, in later life, adding dissonances to his sketches so as to enhance his reputation as an innovator; the uniqueness of his style of dissonance, however, dispels any doubts concerning his originality in musical invention.

[52] Wooldridge, *Charles Ives*, 200.

called the 'Wagnerian adventure'. US wealth, based on US technology, led the country increasingly to dominate world politics; in the process, it began, correspondingly, to dominate world music. Professional orchestras multiplied: after 1945, any large city would expect to support a professional orchestra. As European politics made refugees of some of Europe's finest artists and intellectuals, they found welcome at US universities, which became the new international patrons of composers; Schoenberg, Stravinsky, and Bartók, among others, found refuge there. However, one of the first twentieth-century émigrés of distinction arrived in North America not as a political refugee, but to escape from what he saw as the conservatism of French artistic taste. Attracted by US technology, and unable to find a secure post in France, Edgar Varèse left Paris for the USA in 1915.

Few composers in the history of Western music have shown more originality than Varése, and it was characteristic of the USA that such radical originality was able to flourish there, rather than in Europe. Varése's use of urban, industrial, sound anticipated John Cage; his use of semitonal clusters anticipated Ligeti; and his approach to musical form anticipated Stockhausen. Like Ives, he was concerned with breadth of musical 'substance', but, unlike Ives, he was also concerned with musical 'manner':

> I have never tried to fit my conception into any known container. . . . I saw a close analogy in the process of crystallisation. . . . There is an idea, the basis of an interval structure, expanded or split into different shapes or groups of sound, constantly changing in shape, direction, and speed, attracted and repulsed by various forces. The form of the work is the consequence of this interaction.[53]

The huge orchestral work *Arcana* (1927), for example, is built on just such a 'form'. The 'idea' is an eleven-note motif based on a minor third; this is built into a mosaic-like structure, informed by short, rhythmic motifs, articulated by an enormous percussion section.

In 1931, in his now infamous *Ionisation*, Varèse dispensed with conventional melodic instruments entirely, and used instead thirty-five un-pitched percussion instruments, including 'high' and 'low' sirens, and a 'lion's roar'. Although the music now sounds rather like a collage of Western rhythmic motifs with the melody accidentally

[53] Cited in Fernand Oullette, *Edgar Varèse*, trans. Derek Coltman (London: Calder & Boyars, 1973), 91.

omitted, it took over *Klangfarbenmelodie* ('melody of sound colours') where Schoenberg left off, and established timbre as a fundamental element in musical composition. Messiaen said of Varèse that he 'created electronic music with real instruments'.

In 1932, when integral serialism had not yet been thought of, Varèse declared, 'I no longer wish to compose for the old instruments played by men and I am handicapped by a lack of adequate electrical instruments for which I conceive my music.' Had his application for grants for researching electronic instruments not been refused, Varèse might have developed a practicable tape recorder before the start of the Second World War. As it was, Varèse was reduced, in 1939, to recording sounds at different pitches by varying the speed of a gramophone turntable. His ideal was realized only in 1958, when the architect, Le Corbusier, conceived his 'Electronic Poem together with the vessel that will contain it', in place of a standard pavilion, for the Brussels World Fair of 1959. Le Corbusier insisted, against virulent opposition, that Varèse should compose the music; and in this resolution he received the fullest support from the young architect of the 'vessel', the composer-to-be, Iannis Xenakis.

Well into the second half of the twentieth century, the USA's ambivalence towards its European roots proved musically advantageous: at a time of national advancement, the country could accommodate the most radical originality. Whereas Europe, during this period, was feeling its way backwards out of its musical impasse towards a form of musical rhetoric that would hold to ransom the notion of the beautiful in music, Charles Ives was able, in the words of an unusually perceptive *New York Times* critic (1927), to exercise 'a gumption . . . not derived from a *Rite of Spring* or even from anything but the conviction of a composer who has not the slightest idea of self-ridicule and who dares jump with feet and hands in a reckless somersault or two on the way to his destination'.[54] The legacy of Ives, in the USA, was a willingness to avoid traditional yardsticks; the US artist was not required to have, in Stockhausen's words, 'four eyes—two looking into the future and two into the past'.[55] The USA came to spearhead many new artistic movements; but the fact that the eyes of US composers appear, over the past half century, to have been fixed so preponderantly on the future—or, at least, *away* from the European past—may prove as damaging to the

[54] Wooldridge, *Charles Ives*, 214.

[55] Jonathan Cott, *Stockhausen: Conversations with the Composer* (London: Picador, 1974), 99.

continuance of a European tradition of composition in Europe, as in the USA.

It was a US composer, Milton Babbitt (b. 1916), who first anticipated integral serialism; as early as the 1940s, Babbitt was experimenting with the mathematical implications of dodecaphony, and was applying them to other parameters. Babbitt was also a pioneer in electronic sound synthesis.

In Harry Partch (1901–76), however, a very different radicalism appeared. Reared in the deserts of Arizona and California, Partch attempted in his music theatre to imitate the theatre of Asia, as he saw it, by integrating art with life: 'My music is visual; it is corporeal, aural, and visual.' In contrast to Varèse, he believed that 'for some hundreds of years, the truth of just intonation, which is defined in any good music dictionary, has been hidden'.[56] To achieve this 'truth', Partch created a forty-three-note scale; and he constructed new musical instruments to accommodate it. His book, *Genesis of a Music*, first published in 1949 but revised in 1974, was one of the first to question whether the European Renaissance had been wholly beneficial. The music of Harry Partch became a cult in California, but is now little known. The instruments, however, have recently been bought by the composer Dean Drummond, who commissions new music for them.

It would take a yet more iconoclastic composer—philosopher might be a more apt title—to use aspects of oriental philosophy to remove the last vestiges of Europeanness from his music. The importance of John Cage to the progress—or, perhaps more appropriately, egress—of Western music can scarcely be overemphasized. Regarded as a crank in his early years, he became a cult among many in his middle years, and was still treated with justifiable respect when he died at the age of 80, in 1992. Where Partch had merely questioned the values of the European Renaissance, Cage abjured the very notion of self-expression, and attempted instead to fulfil the demanding aspiration of achieving 'nothing'.

According to John Cage, Western music had traditionally created an artificial environment; and people should now become more aware of their real environment. In order to achieve this, music should be created, not artificially, but out of sounds *within* the environment. Cage's infamous piece, *4′, 33″*, which received its first performance in

[56] Harry Partch, spoken introduction to recording of *The Delusion of the Fury*, CBS Records M2 30576.

1952, made the point entirely. The pianist opened the lid of the piano and performed nothing; and, as it happened, the first movement consisted of the distant sounds of the wind in the leaves, the second of raindrops on the aluminium roof of the makeshift auditorium, and the third of the mutterings of a confused audience. Cage expressed himself well satisfied with the performance. Like Rauschenberg's canvas *White Painting*, Andy Warhol's later reproduction of a coke bottle, and Duchamp's sculpture *Inverted Urinal*, it was a statement of total depersonalization.

From his study of oriental philosophy, John Cage concluded that the function of music was to 'sober and quieten the mind, thus rendering it susceptible to divine influences'. This involved the Zen proposition of 'waking up to the very life we are living'.[57] With his friend Morton Feldman, Cage worked on the *I Jing* ('Book of Changes'), with the intent of avoiding the 'straitjacket' of Western music. For Cage, this involved leaving musical composition to chance, and losing all personal control over the musical structure of a composition. This he was prepared to do for the specific purpose of achieving 'nothing'. He used silence as a framework for a collage of sounds within the environment. His *Variations IV* was typical: it mixed, largely by chance, the sounds of street traffic, cocktail-bar conversations, prerecorded tapes, and broadcasts, supposedly to place classical music in the context of contemporary life. Study of Zen, however, scarcely brought Cage's music into line with that of East Asia: it was a far cry from the *guqin* music of China or the *gagaku* of Japan.

No composer went so far in this direction as Cage; Feldman was not prepared to give up his own taste entirely; and Cage's new function for music was by no means generally accepted. 'I like John's mind but I don't like what it thinks,' was what Pierre Boulez said to Feldman about Cage.[58] 'Not a composer, but an inventor of genius', was the more acerbic comment from Schoenberg. In his dedication to the ideal of losing self-expression, Cage retained a unique personality: 'I have nothing to say and I am saying it.' From Cage and his associates would emerge a fundamentally non-expressive music, now known as 'Minimalism'. With it, the European baby would disappear with the European bathwater.

[57] Calvin Tomkins, *Ahead of the Game: Four Versions of the Avant-Garde* (London: Penguin Books, 1968), 98.

[58] Ibid.

One important influence on 'Minimalism' was Cage's performance (in 1949) of Erik Satie's *Vexations*, a fragment for piano to be played 840 times (see p. 472). The sort of hypnotic effect that such repetitiousness induces was then novel; Cage reported on the performance: 'We all recognised that something had been set in motion that went far beyond what any of us had anticipated.'[59] Satie's *Vexations* epitomized a concept of music that was to become germane to 'Minimalism': that music is a process (rather than an object)—one, moreover, to which an audience finds itself compelled to submit, eschewing all subjective judgement.

Other influences on 'Minimalist' composers came from Asia and Africa. Philip Glass, for example, studied South Asian *tablā*, and, from the 'additive' structure of *tāl* (in which a rhythmic cycle may be divided into sections of unequal length (see p. 255)), developed a system of extending and contracting rhythmic patterns. Steve Reich studied West African drumming; his use of such techniques as 'phase-shifting' (developed after noting the effect of an identical tape being played simultaneously on two tape recorders, operating at marginally different speeds), and 'resultant patterning' (caused by allowing particular patterns to achieve temporary dominance within a constantly changing musical texture) reflects such African musical devices as apart-playing (see p. 164), melodic 'binding' in xylophone-playing (see pp. 174–5), and the changes in rhythmic structure that appear to arise when a 'resultant' pattern emerges from two different, interlocking rhythmic patterns (see p. 163). Mesmeric, almost imperceptibly changing use of 'minimal' melodic, rhythmic, and harmonic material, arising from such techniques, has come to characterize much 'Western' music of the late twentieth century, including rock and pop.

Of his *Music in Twelve Parts* (1974)—which lasts four and a half hours—Philip Glass remarked: 'when it becomes apparent that nothing "happens", in the usual sense ... [one] can perhaps discover another mode of listening—one in which neither memory nor anticipation ... have a place in sustaining the texture, quality, or reality of the musical experience.'[60] Glass has applied 'Minimalist' theories and techniques to opera, acquiring in the process almost cult status, in Europe as much as the USA. In an age in which the walkman and ghetto-blaster have caused silence (for many people) to appear—literally—terrifying, repetitive music clearly has the power to induce a state of tranquillity, its

[59] Tomkins, *Ahead of the Game*, 102.

[60] Cited in Wim Mertens, *American Minimal Music* (London: Kahn & Averill, 1983), 79.

very repetitiousness reflecting, perhaps, the reassuring rhythm of the heartbeat.

Charles Ives might have been less than pleased: Glass's operas, for example, retain all the trappings—the 'manner'—of the 'received tradition', while reducing the 'substance' to seemingly mindless repetition of very simple material. Western 'Minimalist' formats do not necessarily permit coherent fusions between Asian or African musical intricacies and those of the West. The music itself caters not for audiences seeking expression of a new-found confidence, nor even for those desirous of the heart-warmingly familiar. Instead it caters for audiences made amnesic by the repetitiousness of reductionist 'sound-bites', of glutinous advertising, of hideous brutality, real and fictional, and of over-worn gestures of pop videos, beamed from TV stations into private living rooms from breakfast time to long-past-bedtime.

Sensational, or politically sensitive, subjects may appear, at times, to mask poverty of inventiveness. Calling a 'Minimalist' opera *Nixon in China*, for example, may be an effective box-office ploy; it may even, as its composer, John Adams, has claimed, reflect the pride of a nation in a particular historical event. But the intricate techniques that made the operas of Mozart and Wagner a living memorial to the artistic pride of Europe, that made *Kathak* dance, *wayang kulit*, and Chinese opera among the most breathtakingly accomplished art forms in the world, or that gave life-enhancing energy to Ghanaian drumming or Cuban *rumba*: these are sadly absent in an opera, the minimal material of which scarcely does justice even to what, in reality, is the minimal importance of its subject matter. Fascination with a subject does not of itself provide the means for its effective realization as an opera. Wilfrid Mellers has aptly described the music of Philip Glass's opera *Akhnaten* as 'a potent auralization of impotency'.[61]

The influence of Cage and the 'Minimalists'—as, in a less damaging way, that of Martha Graham and Merce Cunningham in the field of dance—continues to nag at the 'received' European tradition. 'Western' arts engage in a Jekyll-and-Hyde existence as they slip in and out of their historical past. In music, the reaction against post-Renaissance self-expression was probably as inevitable, historically, as Schoenberg's development of serialism. But it undermined—perhaps fatally—the essential élitism of 'art'. Marshall McLuhan claimed that the Balinese

[61] Wilfrid Mellers, 'Monotonously Minimal', review of Philip Glass, *Opera on the Beach*, in *Times Literary Supplement*, Oct. 1988, 21–7.

say: 'We have no art; we do everything as well as we can';[62] but he failed to add that the Balinese preserve an exquisite and intricate tradition of music, theatre, and dance, the origins of which pre-date the European discovery of the Americas by over 1,000 years. The Balinese do not present coke bottles as 'art', nor the roaring of motor bikes as 'music' (though it is not inconceivable that, for tourists, they may at some point choose to do so). In the end, it may prove to be the 'West' that has no art, or at least, living art; and the 'West' may not always be doing everything as well as it can.

[62] Marshall McLuhan and Quentin Fiore, *The Medium is the Massage* (London: Penguin Books, 1967), 127.

16 *Africans North of Mexico*

Race-Consciousness and African Musical Retentions

It is some indication of the degree of racial segregation that has characterized US history that US Africans are still referred to as 'black'. Throughout Latin America, there was a long history of intermarriage between Europeans, Africans, and American Indians: in Brazil and the Caribbean in particular there developed large mixed populations. In the northern USA, by contrast, marriage between peoples of European and African descent was—as it has remained—comparatively rare. A survey conducted throughout the USA in 1970 showed that only 1.5 per cent of every 1,000 US marriages were between blacks and whites; in 1990, the figure had only risen to 4 out of every 1,000.[1]

In the plantation states, during colonial times, a rather different situation developed. Particularly in the area around Chesapeake Bay, there was a shortage of women, both African and European: this gender imbalance, coupled with the harshness of frontier life and the need to procreate, caused mixed marriages to become more common there than in the North.[2] To colonial whites, however, intermarriage between Africans and Europeans threatened the continuance of slavery, for slavery was justified on the presumed inequality of the two 'races'. Early US legislators decided, therefore, that any person with even a drop of black blood should have the same legal status as a pure African. By the early 1700s, what came to be known as the 'one-drop rule' was firmly entrenched in the upper South.[3]

[1] Ronald Hall, Kathy Russell, and Midge Wilson, *Color Complex: The Politics of Skin Color among African Americans* (New York: Harcourt Brace Jovanovitch, 1992), 116.
[2] Ibid. 11–12.
[3] Ibid. 14.

Such measures did not prevent intermarriage between Africans and Europeans, however; and the *Mulattos* who grew up under slavery were granted special privileges, and were able to advance further, educationally and occupationally, than dark-skinned blacks.[4] When slavery was abolished, such privileges disappeared; Africans and *Mulattos* were thrown together, so that mixed marriages (white and black) became increasingly rare. Nevertheless, the association of light skin colour with social advancement among blacks continued, and contributes to the prevalence of colour-consciousness in the USA today.

Protestant USA actively discouraged the syncretist cults that enabled African musical and religious culture to remain alive in many parts of Latin America. On the US plantations, slaves were forbidden to play drums, on the grounds that they incited insurrection. This, however, did not prevent the retention of African music. Just as nomadic societies in Africa developed complex musical traditions without the use of drums, so African slaves in the USA performed trance-inducing ceremonies with hand-clapping, dance, and singing. Moreover, in the originally extensive territory of Louisiana, the French had allowed greater latitude to former Africans, thus enabling cults to thrive in many cities. In Place Congo in New Orleans, for example, blacks regularly gathered to perform music and dance.[5]

On Sundays on the plantations, whites would often join with slaves in such activities as 'log-rolling', where the gathering of logs into great piles afforded opportunity for mutual competition in feats of activity, strength, and the telling of jokes. At night, whites and blacks might compete together in wrestling, jumping, and foot-racing, for a sip of the 'white eye'. And, in the absence of a fiddle, blacks would 'pats juber': create an anatomical percussion section of foot-stamping, thigh-slapping, and hand-clapping. 'Pats juber' would accompany dancing of increasing velocity, sustained by blacks in their own way long after whites dropped out (Pl. 72).[6]

In a compilation of slave narratives drawn up in the 1930s, accounts of music-making for funerals or entertainments on Sundays indicate considerable interaction of black and white musical styles. A slave from South Carolina recounts, for example: 'We danced and had jigs. Some

[4] Hall, Russell, and Wilson, *Color Complex*, 34.

[5] Willard Rhodes and Doris J. Dyer, 'North America', *The New Grove* (1980), xiii. 292–3.

[6] Lewis W. Paine, *Six Years in a Georgia Prison* (New York, 1851), 177–86, cited in Eileen Southern (ed.), *Readings in Black American Music* (New York: Norton, 1971), 89.

72. Plantation slaves making music and dancing; illustration of 1852

played de fiddle and some made whistles from canes, having different lengths for different notes, and blowed 'em like mouth organs.'[7] Many nineteenth-century writers referred to the popularity of the 'quills'—pan pipes, initially assembled from hollow stems of quills—among the rural blacks of Georgia. Tuned to a pentatonic scale, they encouraged the variation-making characteristic of African music.[8]

Perhaps something of African melody survived, though in much altered form. The militant, northern black leader W. E. B. Dubois describes in his *The Souls of Black Folk* (1903) how:

> The songs are indeed the siftings of centuries. . . . My grandfather's grandmother was seized by an evil Dutch trader two centuries ago; and coming to the valleys of the Hudson and Housatonic, black, little, and lithe, she shivered and shrank in the harsh north winds, looked longingly at the hills, and often crooned a heathen melody to the child

[7] C. B. Burton, cited in Southern (ed.), *Readings*, 117.

[8] Alan Lomax, sleeve note to *The Gospel Ship: Baptist Hymns and White Spirituals from the Southern Mountains*, New World Records, NW 294, 1977, side 1, band 7.

Ex. 16.1

> between her knees [Ex. 16.1]. The child sang it to his children and they to their children's children, and so (for) two hundred years it has travelled down to us and we sing it to our children, knowing as little as our fathers what its words may mean, but knowing well the meaning of its music.[9]

Certainly, on the plantations, slaves were expected to sing as well as to work, for singing spurred productivity. As W. C. Handy put it: 'The singing of these men set the rhythm for the work: the pounding of hammers, the swinging of scythes. And the one who sang most lustily soon became strawboss.'[10] And slaves would praise the great house farm, in the hope of drawing favour from the owner:

> I am going away to the great house farm,
> O yea! O yea!, O yea!
> My old master is a good old master,
> O yea! O yea!, O yea![11]

Boisterous as was the singing, it was essentially melancholic. According to Frederick Douglass, an escaped slave and a widely travelled abolitionist, slaves sang 'more to *make* themselves happy than to express their happiness':

> I did not, when a slave, understand the deep meanings of those rude, and apparently incoherent songs. I was myself within the circle, so that I neither saw nor heard as those without might see and hear. They told a tale which was then altogether beyond my feeble comprehension; they

[9] Cited in Southern (ed.), *Readings*, 195.

[10] W. C. Handy, 'The Heart of the Blues', *Étude Music Magazine* (Mar. 1940), cited in Southern (ed.), *Readings*, 203.

[11] Frederick Douglass, *My Bondage and my Freedom* (New York, 1853), cited in Southern (ed.), *Readings*, 83.

> were tones, loud, long and deep, breathing the prayer and complaint of souls boiling over with the bitterest anguish. Every tone was a testament against slavery, and a prayer to God for a deliverance from chains. The hearing of those wild notes always depressed my spirits, and filled my heart with ineffable sadness.[12]

22 September 1862 was the Day of Jubilee, when slaves were legally freed. Northern politicians set out to impose 'Reconstruction' on the South, and talked of giving forty acres and a mule to every freed slave, as well as the right to vote. The Southern plantations were huge businesses, however, and were not readily susceptible of partition into smallholdings; and the newly freed blacks were scarcely equipped to change from being labourers to landowners—nor were the dispossessed southern landowners in any mood to teach them. Furthermore, the *Mulatto* élite no longer enjoyed the distinction of freedom, or special privilege, separating them from the dark-skinned masses. In order to preserve their status, *Mulattos* began to segregate themselves into separate communities. The 'Blue Vein' Society established in Nashville required applicants to be fair enough for the purplish veins at the wrist to be visible to a panel of 'expert' judges.[13]

As the intended 'Reconstruction' failed, Southern politicians introduced repressive legislation that led to greater racial segregation than had previously existed on the plantations. Blacks were forbidden to travel in white sections of trains, or to stay in white hotels; they could not share white toilets or drinking fountains, or share white doctors or dentists. They could not even share white churches. Black churchgoers themselves tended to congregate by colour and class. At the turn of the century, black families wishing to join a colour-conscious congregation might first be required to pass such tests as placing the arm in a suitably coloured paper bag to ensure than the colour of the arm was lighter than that of the bag. The 'Colored Methodist Episcopal'—a breakaway from the 'African Methodist Episcopal Church'—only caused the 'C' to stand for 'Christian' rather than 'Colored' in 1954.[14] Not least of the reasons for the eruption of black music at the turn of the nineteenth century was the extent to which 'Reconstruction' forced blacks to turn inwards on themselves.[15]

During the period of official slavery, hollers (individual field calls), deriving from African work songs, had helped ease the appalling

[12] Ibid. [13] Hall, Russell, and Wilson, *Color Complex*, 24–5. [14] Ibid. 27.
[15] Tony Palmer, *All You Need is Love* (London: Futura Publications, 1977), 27–9.

physical labour and mental drudgery of plantation work. After the civil war, field hollers proliferated, as groups of former slaves joined construction gangs, moved to individual farms, or were sentenced to the 'chain gang' or jail. The holler enabled the lonely worker to communicate at a distance with his family, or to complain to his mule about his hard lot.[16] In the penitentiaries, a form of slavery still existed into the 1960s; it is from such work prisons that we have recordings of work hollers. Alan Lomax has demonstrated their close resemblance to the work songs of Senegal, the Mississippi songs being, in general, less energetic and more melancholy than those of Senegal; both types were characterized by varied repetitions of short phrases in descending spirals, the varying pitches of sevenths and thirds in the blues perhaps reflecting non-tempered African tuning systems.[17]

At the turn of the century, levees (embankments against river floods) were built along southern rivers, creating millions of acres of rich farm land in Texas, Louisiana, Arkansas, and Mississippi. Ready money drew thousands of blacks into the lawless levee camps; and it was in the Yazoo delta, lying on both sides of the Mississippi, between Nantchez and Memphis, that the evocative cadences of the field holler turned into the dance-entertainment genre of the blues. The Yazoo was where blacks had worked on the levee camps, plantations, and railroads; now, in the early decades of the twentieth century, they worked at 'mule-skinning' (driving a mule team), 'roustabouting' (labouring, often as a deckhand on a river boat), or 'tie-tamping' (connecting railway ties). On Saturday nights, gifted musicians would accompany their work songs on guitar or piano, syncopating the beat for the dance floor, and inventing topical rhymes in the manner of the praise-singers of Africa. Leadbelly is credited with first giving the levee-camp holler a danceable beat and creating the first blues:

> I'm down in the bottom, skinning for Johnny Ryan,
> Writin' my 'nitials on the mule's behind.
> I'm down in the bottom, mud up to my knees,
> Workin' for my woman, she so hard to please.[18]

[16] Alan Lomax, sleeve note to LP record, *Roots of the Blues*, New World Records, NW 252, 1977.

[17] Ibid.

[18] Ibid.

Black Spirituals

This was not the first time that blacks had applied African rhythmic and melodic formulas to European harmony. In the early nineteenth century, blacks had applied African-style improvisation to hymns, and shape-note tunes, which they learnt at Revivalist camp meetings. Here and in the Southern rural churches, the highly emotional forms of religious expression—'witnessing', 'testifying', and 'lining-out' hymn-singing—led to improvised antiphonal singing, shouting, chanting, and stamping, as well as to the involuntary clonic spasms of possessed members of the congregation.[19]

In Southern black churches, priests would 'line-out' the text in a semi-musical wail or shout, independent of the melody, already demonstrating the flattened thirds and sevenths later to become characteristic of the blues. As the congregation followed the priest, the hymn was retarded, resulting in gaps between syllables. Individual worshippers would improvise in their own way, perhaps attracting attention with a note of unexpected pitch or a striking rhythmical figure, taken up by others, the whole merging into chordal harmony.[20] This type of harmonic improvisation became known as the 'church-house moan', and a repetitive, emotional style of oratory remains characteristic of much black preaching and politicking.

When blacks applied similar performance characteristics to spirituals, the special genre of 'negro' spiritual developed. Where whites maintained a steady rhythm within the pentatonic scale, it appears that black versions of white tunes incorporated the shifted accents, dotted rhythms, and variable-pitch sevenths characteristic of African music. Some of the melodies derived from white sources: the spiritual 'Roll Jordan', for example, is an adaptation of Stephen Foster's minstrel-show song 'Camptown Races'.[21] But many of the melodies originated from black musical inspiration, adapted to certain European melodic formulas.

In the early 1860s, Thomas W. Higginson, a white, abolitionist army colonel, in command of a black regiment, noted the words of some of the songs he had heard his men sing. Common among them were songs with alternating lines and refrains; for example:

[19] Ibid. [20] Ibid.

[21] Paul Oliver, 'Spiritual', *The New Grove* (1980), xviii. 4.

I know moon-rise, I know star-rise,
Lay dis body down.
I walk in de moonlight, I walk in de starlight,
To lay dis body down.
I'll walk in de graveyard, I'll walk through de graveyard,
To lay dis body down.
I'll lie in de grave and stretch out my arms;
Lay dis body down.
I go to de judgement in de evenin' of de day,
When I lay dis body down.
And my soul and your soul will meet in de day
When I lay dis body down.[22]

This particularly haunting verse shows the extent to which the Christian promise of a beauteous afterlife helped sustain dispossessed African slaves in the USA (as it does to dispossessed citizens of poverty-torn Africa today). In the words of Higginson: 'Never, it seems to me, since man first lived and suffered, was his infinite longing for peace uttered more plaintively than in that line.'[23]

In the South, it became common for blacks to chant spirituals to hand-clapping in a shuffling circular dance, known as the 'ring shout', a trance-inducing practice that survived into the 1930s. Ex. 16.2 is a transcription of a 'ring-shout', taken from a collection of *Slave Songs of the United States* made in 1867.[24] Verses of this kind became typical of the 'negro' spiritual, and permitted virtually limitless extemporization of words.

This subtle African variation-making was mistaken by pious whites for inane repetition; and because of the tendency of slaves to transfer cheerful matters to a presumed afterlife, the words were often regarded as senseless. John F. Watson, for example, in his *Methodist Error* (1819), referred to

> a growing evil, in the practice of singing in our places of public and society worship, *merry* airs, adapted from old *songs*, to hymns of our composing.... In the *blacks*' quarter, the coloured people get together, and sing for hours together, short scraps of disjointed affirmations,

[22] Noted by Colonel Thomas Wentworth Higginson in his memoirs (1870), and cited in Southern (ed.), *Readings*, 182.

[23] Ibid.

[24] Allen, Garrison, and Ware (eds.), *Slave Songs of the United States* (New York, 1867), cited in Southern (ed.), *Readings*, 159.

2 I meet my mudder early in de mornin',
An' I ax her, how you do my mudder?
Walk 'em easy, etc.

Ex. 16.2

> pledges, or prayers, lengthened out with long repetition *choruses*. These are all sung in the . . . husking-frolic method, of the slave blacks . . . .[25]

This, of course, aptly describes the Africanized spiritual that blacks were turning into a genre of their own. By the late 1860s publication of 'negro' spirituals led to increased interest in the genre; and by the end of the nineteenth century, the genre had reached an international audience. 'Negro' spirituals were propagated during the 1870s by the Jubilee Singers, a group of musicians from Fisk University, Nashville, Tennessee; they started singing spirituals as a fund-raising effort, and finished up touring the USA and Europe as celebrities.[26] 'Negro' spirituals were subsequently influenced by the saccharine harmonies of the evangelical crusaders, Dwight L. Moody and Ira Sankey, so that, by the end of the nineteenth century, 'gospel' song was replacing the spiritual in urban centres.[27] (During the 1930s gospel would merge with the blues, and—largely through the gospel songs of Thomas A. Dorsey, a blues singer who served as choral director of the Pilgrim Baptist Church in Chicago from 1932 to 1972—constitute an African-American voice in the US Baptist Church.)

[25] Cited in Southern (ed.), *Readings*, 63.
[26] Oliver, 'Spiritual', *The New Grove*, xviii. 5.
[27] James C. Downey, 'Spiritual', *The New Grove* (1980), xviii. 1–4.

The Blues

From a mixture of African-derived work-hollers, and Africanizing of hymns and spirituals, the blues genre was born. Its full period of gestation was from around 1890 to 1930, the period when the USA was becoming a powerful industrial nation. It was also a period when blacks were ill-educated, confined to ghettos, and without civil rights. Their labour was casual and often migratory, and they were subject to constant exploitation:

> I'm a poor old boy, jes ain't treated right,
> Freezin' ground was my folding bed last night.[28]

The blues came to be characterized by a simple three-line verse structure: the second line was a repeat of the first, often with a slight variation, and the third line contained a punch that might be humorous, plaintive, or political. The opening stanza of W. C. Handy's 'Memphis Blues' is characteristic:

> You want to be my man (gal) you got to give me forty dollars down;
> You want to be my man (gal) you'll give me forty dollars down;
> If you don't be my man (gal), your baby's gonna shake this town.[29]

The twelve-bar tune came to be supported by a standard three-chord underlay, as illustrated in the classic 'Joe Turner' (Ex. 16.3, after Abbe Niles).[30]

The long notes provided opportunity for improvisation, which might consist of simple repetitions, or interjections (as in Ex. 16.4 after Abbe Niles[31]), or new thoughts and themes. The improvised 'breaking up' of a long note was to develop into one of the most significant features of jazz.

Like most early US black musical genres, the blues was a hybrid form, using both European and African formulas. Hall Johnson (1888–1970), a well-educated chorus-leader who did much to preserve the original style of the 'negro' spiritual, has analysed these hybrid elements with remarkable perception for his time (1965):

[28] Lomax, sleeve note to *Roots of the Blues*.

[29] W. C. Handy (ed.), *Blues: An Anthology* (1949; repr. New York: Macmillan, 1972), 70–1.

[30] Abbe Niles, 'The Story of the Blues', foreword to W. C. Handy (ed.), *Blues: Anthology* (1949; repr. New York: Macmillan, 1972), 17.

[31] Ibid. 19.

Ex. 16.3

Ex. 16.4

> The English custom of music for the *ear* only, without any necessary accompaniment of physical motion, tended to develop in the English only the simple static rhythms; but it did give them a feeling for *melody* and *harmony* hitherto unknown to the African slaves. On the other hand, the African had a much more highly developed sense of *rhythm*. . . . Here was a wonderful opportunity to fuse the basic elements of rhythm, melody, and harmony into a great American music. Only the negro slaves, though quite unconsciously, profited by this opportunity. The American settlers had a country to build—no time to think seriously about music. On the other hand, the slave had no life of his own *except* music—the making of songs.[32]

Hall Johnson's analysis of the musical characteristics the slaves brought from Africa contains no surprises; but his analysis of what the slaves *discovered* in the New World is worth recording:

1. A most serviceable MUSICAL SCALE—with longer range but smaller intervals;
2. A wider view of musical structure by the use of the METRICAL PHRASE;
3. The sensuous delights of RICH HARMONY and COUNTERPOINT;

[32] Hall Johnson, *Notes on the Negro Spiritual* (1965), cited in Southern (ed.), *Readings*, 269.

4. Lastly, the powerful, unifying psychological effects of GOOD PART SINGING.[33]

Hall Johnson can scarcely be blamed for being unaware, for example, of the rich harmony and counterpoint of the Congolese pygmy peoples; and he was, in any event, writing with reference to 'negro' spirituals that were sung in chorus, like hymns. Nevertheless, Johnson neatly summarized the musical elements that slaves took from Europeans, and imbued with their own vocal style, with their dazzling rhythmic sense, and their facility in improvisation and embellishment.

The blues developed essentially as dance music, assimilating the ostinato rhythms of rural, black, square-dance music. Black country music had been played mainly on guitars and fiddle, with perhaps a harmonica; and bands used often to improvise over a single chord, given special character by the use of the 'blue' third and seventh. Left-hand chording could be effected by stopping several courses simultaneously with a bottle neck over the index finger, or by holding the back of a knife between the thumb and index finger, thus leaving other fingers free to pick a melody. With the left hand playing chords and contributing to rhythm and melody, and the right hand playing a bass ostinato while picking melodies on the treble strings, the guitar was Africanized into a one-man band.[34] Such features were carried over into the blues.

W. C. Handy was the first to popularize the blues through print. In his epoch-making 'Memphis Blues' (1909), originally written as an electioneering tune for 'Mr Crump' (its original title), Handy attempted to sum up the folk styles of black itinerant bands, and of 'roustabouts' and 'honky-tonk' singers.[35] In 'The Heart of the Blues' (1940) he referred to the 'blue note' as a 'scooping, swooping, slurring tone'. He considered that this 'curious, groping tonality' derived from the 'quarter tone scale of primitive Africa'. (There is, of course, no such thing.) In the blues, the key note and the third were equally stressed, and Abbe Niles refers to the 'hypnotic effect' of the frequent return to the key note and to the tendency of the 'untrained Negro voice' to 'worry' at the third note when dwelling upon it, 'slurring or wavering between flat and natural'.[36] W. C. Handy also exploited the 'breaking-up' of the long notes. With the publication of the 'St Louis Blues' (1914), Handy became

[33] Johnson, *Notes on the Negro Spiritual*, 271.

[34] Lomax, sleeve note to *Roots of the Blues*, side 1, band 2.

[35] Handy, 'The Heart of the Blues', cited in Southern (ed.), *Readings*, 202–4.

[36] Niles, 'The Story of the Blues', 19.

known as 'Father of the Blues'. Ma Rainey and Bessie Smith were among the many legendary singers who immortalized the genre.

The blues differed from other black musical genres in that it was essentially a one-man affair. It was, moreover, a folk affair that told of everyday concerns; and to blacks, everyday concerns were rejection, suppressed anger, and the summoning of the will to survive. As the great blues singer Big Bill Broonzy put it:

> It takes a man that has the blues to sing the blues. The blues is a kind of revenge. That boss actin' so mean and dirty and you want to say somethin', but you can't, so you go out behind the wagon, pretend a horse stepped on your foot and say, 'Get offa me, god damn it'. That's like a man singing the blues: expressin' what he can't say, in a song. . . .[37]

More, perhaps, than any other African-American genre, the blues depicted the yearning of Africans and the resilience with which they bore the indignities heaped upon them by white US Americans.

Eventually the blues style became urbanized and commercialized. As it became popularized, and as blues singers moved to the cities to make records, it was trimmed to the length of a record side: the traditional drones, bottle-neck techniques, harmonica tremolos, shouts, and falsettos lost their improvisatory character. By the end of the 1930s the urban blues had become a relatively lifeless formula; electrical amplification replaced the shout, and the saxophone at the front of the band replaced the harmonica. The melancholy spirit of the blues evaporated as blues singers were exploited by the white moguls of the recording companies.

Ragtime

Another genre that arose from an Africanization of European music was the 'rag'. As indicated in the previous chapter, the rag appears to have been named after the dance step associated with the syncopating—or 'ragging'—by blacks of white country music (see p. 550). Such 'ragged' music, performed by black country jug bands—five-string banjo, empty liquor jars, fiddle, harmonica, and a 'wash-tub' bass—became popular in the settlements of the Mid-West. Ragtime, which became a craze throughout the USA, was popularized in Sedalia, Missouri, and in particular in a bar on a

[37] Lomax, sleeve note to *Roots of the Blues*, side 1, band 2.

street called 'Maple Leaf'. Here, typically, popular tunes of the day were syncopated over a piano vamp by a vocal quartet in close harmony.

Sedalia was a prosperous town with the best brass band of the Midwest. Like bands all over the USA, the Sedalia band performed marches by John Philip Sousa (1854–1932) and others; on Sunday afternoons, it provided light entertainment with waltzes, schottisches, and popular classical music. Gradually it began to adopt the syncopating style of the Maple Leaf Club. As 'coon' tunes from the minstrel shows were hotted up, and favourite waltzes were embellished with African-style syncopations, overtures were replaced by medleys of 'down-south' songs, and quadrilles and schottisches were replaced by the two-step.[38]

The leader of the Sedalia band at that time was a gifted young pianist called Scott Joplin, who had absconded from his German professor of piano in Texarkana to earn a living by providing entertainment for bar parlours and brothels throughout the southern states. Joplin took a job at the Maple Leaf Club, and it was here, in 1899, that a publisher, John Stark, heard his music. Stark bought Joplin's 'Maple Leaf Rag' for fifty dollars; it sold 400,000 copies, enough to enable Stark to set up in St Louis, and for Joplin to move there with him. For a while, Joplin worked in St Louis as a 'professor'; but he soon became ambitious to improve both his artistic and social status by writing an opera for a St Louis World Fair, planned for 1903. The World Fair was postponed; the opera was never published; and the manuscript does not survive.[39]

Ragtime moved to New York and began to influence the white-composed popular songs of the day. There was a craze for the 'ragged' cakewalk. The cakewalk itself had originated as a slave send-up of the gait and attire of the white masters in the grand house; it subsequently became the 'walkaround' finale of the minstrel shows, at which the best performers won a cake.[40] In New York a successful *white* vaudeville 'negro'-impersonator, Benjamin Harney, advertised himself as 'Inventor of Ragtime'; and a white band-leader, Mike Bernard, won a competition for the title 'King of Ragtime'. Joplin, meanwhile, whose skin colour made him ineligible to enter the contest, poured all his energies into the composition of another opera, *Treemonisha*, on the theme of black regeneration. Performed in Harlem in 1915, without scenery or orchestra, it was a failure from which its composer never recovered; assigned

[38] Palmer, *All You Need is Love*, 34–6. [39] Ibid. 37–8. [40] Ibid. 42.

73. The cover of Scott Joplin's first published collection, *Original Rags*

to a madhouse, he died in 1917.[41] The craze for ragtime died later, but Joplin's rags have remained immortal (Pl. 73).

The publisher John Stark had moved his office to New York, but was forced back to St Louis as a result of the New York craze for ragtime, composed and performed by white musicians—and in particular, an imitation of the rag by a Russian immigrant, Israel Baline, who had changed his name to Irving Berlin. Stark's obituary of Scott Joplin included these words: 'Here is the genius whose spirit—though diluted—was filtered through thousands of cheap songs and vain imitations.'[42]

Vain imitation marked also the history of jazz.

Jazz

As to where precisely jazz arose has been widely debated. New Orleans is commonly regarded as its birthplace, but W. C.

[41] Ibid. 45–6. [42] Cited in ibid. 47.

Handy claimed in 1905 that the music of Memphis differed little from that of New Orleans; similar claims have been made for Texas, Indiana, and even New York. Undeniably, the various elements that came to be intrinsic to jazz were present, perhaps uniquely, in New Orleans.[43] Not least was the existence of a large population of mixed ancestry, excluded from white society by the racist policies of the post-abolition South.

New Orleans was one of the oldest cities in North America and embraced an exceptional ethnic mix; it retained Spanish and French cultural influences, long after Jefferson purchased Louisiana in 1803. There was a large, middle-class population of mixed Spanish, French, and British descent, and many with African or Native American blood. This population was known as Creole, and the Creoles of Louisiana occupied positions of power similar to the *Criollos* of Latin America. The skins of many were light enough for them to 'pass' as whites; indeed, the Creoles of mixed descent were deliberately separated from the black population in order to minimize the danger of black insurrection. Prior to abolition, these middle-class Creoles had held managerial posts in plantations.[44]

By 1850 immigrants from Northern Europe were beginning to swell the ranks of the white lower and middle classes of New Orleans. The racist policies of the post-abolition South now forced the Creoles back into the black communities; and the Creoles then found themselves competing with former slaves, as well as with whites, for middle-class positions.[45] Jazz—a mixture, from the start, of European and African musical formulas—provided a sense of common cultural identity in these new Creole and black communities.[46] Many of the early exponents of jazz were of French Creole ancestry: Jelly Roll Morton, for example, was born Joseph La Menthe.[47]

Originally, jazz was a pot-pourri of existing African-American styles and genres: spirituals, blues, ragtime piano, and European dances. It differed, however, from its antecedents in being an ensemble music, in which the syncopations and improvisations of the various players constituted a polyphonic texture. Most importantly, jazz was a portable music that did not depend upon the piano: it was described, literally, as 'music for all occasions'.[48] With a typical instrumentation of trombone,

[43] Palmer, *All You Need is Love*, 50. [44] Ibid. 50–1.

[45] Ortiz M. Walton, *Music: Black, White and Blue* (New York: William Morrow, 1972), 50–3.

[46] Ibid. 50.

[47] Palmer, *All You Need is Love*, 50.

[48] Walton, *Music*, 57–8.

cornet, tuba, and clarinet, sometimes including banjo, guitar, fiddle, or drums, jazz bands played in parks, on river boats, and in public squares; and they played for civic occasions, as well as for parades, funerals, and weddings. Above all, they played for dancing. Around the turn of the century, the mazurka, the quadrille, and the Irish reel were replaced by dances such as the 'slow drag', the 'buzzard lope' and the 'eagle rock'. The formal distance that separated dancing partners in European dance style was replaced by close bodily contact. As one raconteur put it: 'Couples would hang on to each other and just grind back and forth in one spot all night.'[49]

Storeyville is often claimed as the area in New Orleans where jazz originated. More probably, it was the area of New Orleans where the idioms of African-American music were popularized. Named after a city alderman who, in 1898, proposed that the sex trade be confined to a restricted area, it flourished for almost twenty years before being closed down in 1917. The prostitutes were known by the French community as 'Jazz-belles', a corruption of the Biblical 'Jezebels': that, at least, is one suggestion for the origin of the word 'jazz';[50] others are that it was black slang for copulation, or an onomatopoeic representation of the sound of paddle steamers. Kid Ory and King Oliver were among the musicians who worked in Storeyville, though in essence this music consisted of parodies of European dance music.

The first group actually to call itself a jazz band was a white quintet: the 'Original Dixieland Jazz Band'. Its early hits—'Tiger Rag', 'High Society', 'Muskrat Ramble', for example—were African-style parodies of French tunes. Whatever may be said regarding white exploitation of black musical techniques, the eruption of jazz took place *because* a distinctive African-American musical lingua franca had emerged in the USA from spirituals, blues, and ragtime. It was a natural consequence of the development of a musical lingua franca that it would go international.

By 1917 the members of the Original Dixieland Jazz Band were in New York, cutting records and adding to the fever of syncopated music. A little later they were in London and Paris. Jazz took Europe by storm, and the ballroom waltz was replaced by the 'charleston' and 'fox-trot'. Although US jazz was to alternate, for a few decades, between white and black performing styles, its African-American *lingua franca* led to its subsequently becoming a somewhat cliché-ridden genre.

[49] Ibid. 59. [50] Palmer, *All You Need is Love*, 50.

In the USA of the 1920s, however, black musicians soon brought to jazz the soulful temper of the blues, as well as their distinctive traditions of improvisation, with shifting rhythmic accentuations. The early progenitors of this *African*-American jazz, lacking the allure of the white, Original Dixieland Jazz Band, left New Orleans, not in a blaze of publicity, but on the railroad, in search of work. The railroad took them to Chicago. Here, as in New Orleans, blacks were mostly forbidden to enter the white dance halls and beer parlours. It was, therefore, in Chicago's black pubs and clubs that jazz developed into a style with a predominantly African bias. It was here too that Joe 'King' Oliver worked alongside the young Louis Armstrong. The early 'kings' of jazz developed a virtuosic style that forced collective improvisation to give way to a structure more akin to the 'call-and-response' structure of the holler and spiritual. It led also to a reliance on melody, rather than on the traditional harmonies espoused by Dixieland.

Virtuosity led to a competitive instinct among players, never evident in folk blues or ragtime: each musician would attempt to make his 'break' more ingenious than the last, adding to his improvisations timbral sonorities, such as the 'wah-wah' mute on the trumpet, or the 'half-strangled' trombone. In such ways, instruments imitated the tremolos, growls, and shouts that commonly punctuated African singing. The first players to depart from the printed music, by putting in 'licks' of their own invention, were probably the musicians of W. C. Handy's band; but, whereas the Handy Band's improvisations were non-competitive, and did not attempt to overpower the main theme, in jazz—as practised by Armstrong's 'Hot Five', for example—improvisation became the *raison d'être*.[51]

Bix Beiderbecke was among those who learned their trade at the feet of these early jazz 'greats'; indeed he was one of the first white musicians to be admired and copied by black musicians. Beiderbecke was himself an admirer of classical music; Ravel was a close friend. With Paul Whiteman, Beiderbecke developed the system of 'head arrangements' that characterized 'swing': by repeating rhythmic and melodic patterns, known as 'riffs', a sense of spontaneity could be imparted to music largely worked out beforehand.[52] In its relationship to traditional melody and structure, jazz came to be performed in the manner of 'practised improvisation' that had characterized much traditional musical performance throughout Africa and Asia.

[51] Niles, 'The Story of the Blues', 31, 33.

[52] Palmer, *All You Need is Love*, 58.

74. Duke Ellington at the piano

This 'disciplined' style of playing appealed to the predominantly white record-buying public. Fletcher Henderson, a black musician who had played piano for Handy, and who had also recorded jazz with such outstanding musicians as Bessie Smith, Louis Armstrong, and Don Redman, achieved his greatest success (with Redman) as an associate of the white clarinettist and band leader Benny Goodman. Goodman had started out with a quintet; but his band of 1933, consisting of five brass instruments, four saxophones, rhythm guitar, bass, and piano, became a phenomenon; it inaugurated the era of the 'big band'. The clichés of swing would subsequently form the basis for 'jam sessions', the craze for which began in European 'hot clubs' or 'rhythm clubs'. Though Henderson himself was not similarly acclaimed—the playing of his band was considered 'undisciplined'—his distinctive technique of alternating brass and reeds was to influence all the great 'big-band' leaders, from Benny Goodman to Count Basie, Artie Shaw, and—greatest of all—Edward Kennedy 'Duke' Ellington (Pl. 74).[53]

[53] Ibid. 58–9.

Ellington's group first played in dance halls and for cabarets, but, like Scott Joplin before him, the 'Duke' soon sought to elevate African-orientated jazz to the level of symphonic music. In attempting to fuse an essentially oral–aural musical style with the Western aesthetic tradition, Ellington attempted what Persians, Indians, Chinese, and many others attempted in many genres, at various times in the twentieth century. As in other musical cultures, there were in-built musical incompatibilities, apart from the problems created by racial prejudice in the USA. Ellington himself said that jazz was not jazz if it did not 'swing'. His achievement was to prove that it *is* possible to 'compose' for a large jazz ensemble without necessarily restricting freedom of improvisation. Nevertheless, this was not the course jazz was to take. Black musicians continued to be exploited by the white magnates of the music industry: Ellington had to surrender 40 per cent of his composition and performance fees to a white manager; Louis Armstrong surrendered over 51 per cent of his.[54] Black musicians began to emphasize the African elements in jazz so as to defy imitation by whites.

The improvisations and 'head arrangements' of swing had been executed over a simple harmonic basis. 'Bebop', the new jazz style of the 1940s, was built largely on the chord patterns of the blues but with 'discordant' or chromatic notes and progressions added. The melody moved fast. Dizzie Gillespie and Charlie 'Bird' Parker developed a style of music that at first owed little to European convention, and its impetuous streams of improvisational melody were brought to a halt with a sound like 'bebop'. The reaction to this new sound was at first hostile, but by the time of Charlie Parker's death, in 1955, the style was established; indeed, the 'Birdland' club, at which Parker played his last concert, was named after him.

Bebop was followed by 'cool' jazz, and then, during the 1960s, by the avant-garde jazz of musicians such as Ornette Coleman, John Coltrane, and Charlie Mingus. Unlike Dave Brubeck and the Modern Jazz Quartet, whose 'cool' style of counterpoint was bringing 'third-stream' jazz into the ambience of classical music, Coltrane forged a style of music, the wild arabesques and ingenious harmonies of which were essentially African in feeling. Miles Davis subsequently linked jazz with electronics, thereby instituting jazz rock. Jazz had become, primarily, a music to listen to: as a popular dance music, it was eclipsed by rhythm 'n' blues and then by rock 'n' roll.

[54] Palmer, *All You Need is Love*, 60.

The Profit Motive: Tin Pan Alley and Nashville

Early jazz, like early blues, was essentially folk music; and folk music has always furnished a vehicle for political and personal statement. As blacks became more integrated into white society, and as black and white musicians worked more frequently together, African and European musical styles became less distinct. Popular music owed much to African idioms: Irving Berlin, Jerome Kern, and George Gerschwin were among white musicians influenced by them; Gershwin's opera Porgy and Bess (1935), which he called a 'negro' opera, is a masterpiece of US music. Tin Pan Alley itself (New York's music publishing centre) would probably never have come into being (in the first decade of the twentieth century) but for ragtime and the blues. Isaac Goldberg expressed it thus: 'Before the various types of jazz was the modern coon song; before the coon song was the minstrel show; before the minstrel show was the plantation melody and the spiritual. It is safe to say that without the Negro we should have had no Tin Pan Alley.'[55] Nevertheless, black musicians were frequently obliged to compromise their musical instincts in order to achieve commercial success. The advent of audio technology led to music becoming big business: commercial considerations vied with—and often overtook—artistic considerations. This was what Scott Joplin and Bill Stark had failed to understand.

The best song was the one that sold. If songs did not sell they were 'plugged': in stores, in theatres, in silent movies. Tin Pan Alley established the four-line popular song as a ubiquitous phenomenon. All you had to do was think of a first line, repeat it, think up another eight bars, and repeat the first line; and then 'plug' it. It helped if the subject was sentimental. James Thornton, for example, told his wife that he loved her as he did 'When You Were Sweet Sixteen'; he sold the song for $15; the publisher sold a million copies.

The American Society of Composers, Authors, and Publishers (ASCAP) was founded in 1909. In association with Tin Pan Alley, ASCAP came to control the US musical taste. Technology supported the publishing business: the mechanical piano roll was the first home substitute for the performer; and by 1921 its successor, the phonograph,

[55] Isaac Goldberg, *Tin Pan Alley* (New York: John Day, 1930), 32.

had led to a consumption of over a hundred million records in the USA. By 1922 there were over 500 radio stations.[56]

The early success of the phonograph and radio resulted largely from songs from the musicals, created in the sentimental tradition of the minstrel songs and ballads, by Jerome Kern, Irving Berlin, Cole Porter, and Richard Rodgers, among others; indeed, sentiment and melodrama exercised a stranglehold on US popular taste. To all intents and purposes, six major record companies exercised a monopoly over the record market; and, as ASCAP held a monopoly on music publishing, new styles that might have offended the sensibilities of the mostly middle-class US record-buying public, were excluded.

By the late 1930s, the vogue for swing bands without singers was reducing ASCAP's prosperity, and, in consequence, ASCAP challenged the right of radio stations to broadcast non-ASCAP material. Radio replied in 1939 by setting up its own, rival, Broadcast Music Incorporated (BMI). This offered promotional opportunities to the smaller recording companies, forced by the ASCAP monopoly to cater for minority tastes. During the war years, the smaller companies propagated urban blues as 'race music' or 'sepia music', and white country music as 'hillbilly'; in so doing, they broke the stranglehold of sentiment and melodrama.

'Hillbillies' were Southerners, offspring of the mule-skinners, 'hobos', and cowboys, who blazed the western trail: folk who stuck to the old, mean, hard-hitting ways, because it was the only sort of life they knew (Pl. 75). Their music was influenced by frontier folk-songs, Baptist hymnody, and 'lining-out' traditions, as well as (inevitably) black musical styles; when they imitated the 'finger-picking' techniques of black guitarists, they called it 'nigger-picking'. The music developed in the performing arena of Nashville, the 'Opry'; and it was known as the 'Nashville Sound'. The Opry's imprimatur became the hallmark of success: legendary singers, such as Jimmy Rodgers ('The Father of Country Music') and Hank Williams, were first tested at the Opry.

'Country and western', as the genre came to be called, was as conservative as the generality of southern temperament. It engendered a sense of unity among Southern whites, as jazz had done among blacks and Creoles in Louisiana; and its popularity was undiminished by the growth of African-influenced music. With the advent of rock 'n' roll, however, country and western suffered a slump; side drums and electric

[56] For a fuller account of the influence of the media on music, see pp. 610–15.

75. Texan cowboys having a good time in Kansas City

guitars were then permitted in the Opry, and the music was renamed 'rockabilly'. Thereafter the number of full-time country-music radio stations increased from 60 to 600; by 1970 country music was worth $100 million a year to the economy of Nashville. Tired, and largely cliché-ridden, country music is still the staple musical diet of the South; and it sells in record stores throughout the world, as well as in many non-US, non-European, variants.

The Profit Motive: Rhythm 'n' Blues and Rock 'n' Roll

Meanwhile, in the North, as minority record companies popularized the urban blues, 'sepia music' was renamed 'rhythm 'n' blues' and, during the 1940s, gradually replaced jazz as the music of the dance hall. Black singers began to take over the popular market: singers like Muddy Waters, Big Bill Broonzy, and B. B. King injected new life into the urban blues. Nevertheless, many record companies still refused to use black artists, employing instead white 'covers' who toned down the more explicit features of black music. In

1952 Alan Freed, a DJ who promoted black music, broke through the prejudice. Extracting two common words from blues parlance, he advertised a 'rock 'n' roll' concert in the Cleveland arena, and proved there *was* a white audience for black music.[57] He also established the electric guitar as a ubiquitous element in popular music.

As rock singers such as Chuck Berry, Little Richard, and Bo Diddley propagated rock 'n' roll, it seemed that black musicians might at last be in the vanguard; but the major record companies still aimed their product at a traditional white clientele, increasingly critical of the overt sexuality of rock. DJs were in need of a compromise between the tastes of different generations, and found it in Elvis Presley, a white singer who could approximate to the style and accent of African-American singers, without sounding African. Within two years of being bought by RCA Victor, Presley had produced fifty-five best-selling records. To most rock fans of the 1990s, it is Elvis Presley, not Chuck Berry or Bo Diddley, who started rock 'n' roll.[58] Some black musicians, such as James Brown and B. B. King, have paid tribute to Presley for opening up mainstream opportunities for them; but of the tens of thousand 'pilgrims' who still descend on the late Presley's home in Mephis during the annual 'Elvis Week', to celebrate the singer's life and mourn his passing (in 1976), nearly all are white.[59] Ever since the Elvis phenomenon, the vocal style of African-American musicians has been imitated, often superficially, by white rock and pop singers.

The Beatles were a notable exception. In Britain, at least since the eighteenth century, popular music had evolved in the shadow of art music, and had been heavily influenced by it. At the end of the 1940s, only three British radio networks existed, all licensed by the government. There were no independent radio networks, no DJs, and no small independent record companies promoting minority tastes.[60] There was no easy access to the music of Hank Williams or Muddy Waters, for example, nor any reason even to be aware of their existence. A small audience existed for British imitations of Dixieland and big-band jazz. Into this sea of apparent respectability there dropped, in 1954, the recorded voice of the US rock singer, Bill Haley, inciting a bored youthful generation to 'Shake, Rattle, and Roll', and 'Rock around the Clock'.

[57] Charlie Gillett, *The Sound of the City* (London: Sphere Books, 1970), 15–17.

[58] Ibid. 21.

[59] Ron Rosenbaum, 'Elvis the Healer', *Sunday Morning Post Magazine* (Hong Kong, 29 Oct. 1995), 8–15.

[60] Gillett, *The Sound of the City*, 307–16.

The sound caught on quickly in Britain, particularly in Liverpool, where chance brought together four young musicians whose music would create a sensation throughout the world. Many still regard The Beatles as the most inventive pop group of our time. Beatle music was not, by US standards, aggressive; much of it afforded a playful commentary on everyday life, in the manner of folk-song. The group was therefore able to promulgate its music among a more socially diverse and international audience than any former popular-music group. Beatle music crossed not only the generation and class divides, but also the classical–pop divide. It is now regarded as legitimate folk music in the school environment.

Nurtured in a seaport, one moreover that had been the centre of the British slave trade during the seventeenth and eighteenth centuries,[61] The Beatles experienced blues, country, and rock styles from across the Atlantic. They were not, however, encumbered by a long tradition of commercialism, and were free to be original in a European way: McCartney's delight in unexpected harmonies and in the alternation of minor and major thirds, though essentially intuitive, was as much in the manner of the classical tradition as in that of the bluesmen. His use of a classical-style string quartet as accompaniment for 'Yesterday'—a ballad that also includes some of the most instinctively original harmonic progressions to be found in any popular music—was as novel as it was sensational. Later, The Beatles would hire a forty-two-piece orchestra; indeed, the album *Sergeant Pepper's Lonely Hearts Club Band* heralded what was to prove a false dawn of 'art rock', a style subsequently propagated by groups fashionable in the early 1970s, such as Yes, The Who, and Velvet Underground. Their songs encouraged both musicologists and sociologists to write about pop music.

Of rock, and of the various styles of pop music that followed it, Beatlemania made an international phenomenon. Rock invaded the most exclusive and distinctive of cultural zones. During the late 1960s, it entered the Communist bloc, and, to the youth of that time, rock stood for what was progressive. There was Jugorock in urban Slovenia;[62] in

[61] Gail Cameron and Stan Crooke, *Liverpool—Capital of the Slave Trade* (Liverpool: Picton Press, 1992), 1–10.

[62] Alenka Barber-Kersovan, 'Tradition and Acculturation as Polarities of Slovenian Popular Music', in Simon Frith (ed.), *World Music, Politics, and Social Change* (Manchester: Manchester University Press, 1989), 83.

Hungary, rock became a vehicle for social protest;[63] in Moscow, a black market in rock records and photographs of rock idols developed; in Colombia, rock threatened the future of the folk tradition.[64] In China, by the late 1980s, it became possible for the rock star, Cui Juan, to threaten the entire political establishment (see p. 657).

Meanwhile in the USA, if it seemed to white critics that rock 'n' roll had established an interracial music, it did not always seem that way to black critics. The attitude of Miles Davis was typical: 'In rock groups the guys know so little about harmonies. It's a shame because they don't study.... All the jazz musicians can play any school of music because they have the knowledge. It's usually the rock musicians that don't have a musical background.'[65] The bass player, Charlie Mingus, went further: 'Jazz—it's the American Negro's tradition, it's his music. White people don't have the right to play it, it's coloured folk music.... You had your Shakespeare and Marx and Einstein and Jesus Christ and Guy Lombardo but we came up with *Jazz*, don't forget it, and all the pop music in the world today is from that primary cause.'[66]

It is not possible to compose lasting music without the skill and expertise that comes of arduous training. No music so far described in this book has appeared naked, as it were, like Aphrodite from the sea: whether composed on paper or through oral–aural tradition, it has grown out of the past. In the European classical tradition, to which change was intrinsic, there was always a danger that composers might attempt to be too original. It could be argued of Berlioz, for example, that, because he stepped so far outside traditions comprehensible in his time, his posthumous stature has never quite equalled that of a Beethoven or a Wagner, even though his melodic style exercised an important influence on the latter. Kodály once remarked that the greatest musical changes derive from the innovations of relatively minor composers. Caccini and Stamitz are examples; one might perhaps add Boulez and Stockhausen.

Black critics of early rock 'n' roll had a valid point. A few white musicians such as Eric Clapton and Johnnie McLaughlin developed

[63] Anna Sxemere, 'I Get Frightened of my Voice: On Avant-Garde Rock in Hungary', in Frith (ed.), *World Music*, 176.

[64] Bernard J. Broere, 'El Chambu—a Study of Popular Musics in Narino, South Colombia', in Frith (ed.), *World Music*, 105.

[65] Cited in Walton, *Music*, 121.

[66] Cited in ibid. 156.

substantial performance skills; but much pop and rock music was facile and ephemeral. That The Beatles' music still endures is due partly to the unusual collective talent of the group; but it is also due to the timing and circumstances of the group's emergence, which made it, effectively, an urban folk group. It is perhaps significant that The Beatles' active period coincided with a revival of *old* British folk music; and that The Beatles' songs that remain most popular (often rendered in very uncharacteristic versions by singers of very different temperament) are mostly those that deal with everyday, folk-like, themes.

The African element in rock paid a heavy price for its largely ephemeral success. White rock 'n' roll groups trespassed on a century of African-American experience in the preservation of their own musical uniqueness in European terms. The Rolling Stones, a group that attempted to imitate the sounds of African-American singing in a particularly guttural manner, could no more have found a prototype of their music on the savannah or in the rain forests of Africa than in a Confucian ritual orchestra. It was the black *Europeanizing* of African musical characteristics that made the rock phenomenon possible in the first place. The African element in rock and pop has been heavily diluted by the commercial motivation of most rock 'stars' and their recording companies.

For a period, during the 1950s, the commercial success of the 45 r.p.m. record made it possible for black musicians to exploit the white world of pop. As the all-black Tamla-Mowtown label grew from its modest Detroit beginnings to become, during the 1960s, the largest independent record company in the business, it became possible for black music to be managed by blacks, and for the blues and gospel to merge into 'soul'. In response to the Rolling Stones, Mowtown 'soul' moved from the sweet sentiment of Diana Ross and the Supremes, via the funky sound of Jimi Hendrix, to the Jackson Five and, later, to Stevie Wonder. Stevie Wonder's distinctive style synthesized the rhythm and dance elements of the blues, the sensuous love messages derived from gospel, the riffs of the jazzmen, and the electronic gimmickry of rock. But this too has had no future.

Telling It Like It Is

Since the mid-1970s, black anger, and aspiration, have increasingly been expressed in politically vehement rap music, a part of 'hip-hop' culture that also includes graffiti-drawing and 'break-dancing' (athletic dance routines, performed at 'break' points during a song).[67] Rap, along with hip-hop, emerged in the ghettos of New York's South Bronx. Rap itself evolved from Jamaican DJ reggae (see p. 525); indeed it was a New York Jamaican émigré, calling himself 'Kool Herc', who (in the mid-1970s) first extended instrumental breaks in songs by playing two identical records on different turntables and switching from one to the other during the desired break, generating a continuous beat that he called the 'break-beat'. DJs would encourage the dancing with Jamaican-type 'rapped' injunctions ('toasting' over the rhythm) that gradually developed into rhyming phrases, such as: 'Throw your hands in the air and wave 'em like you just don't care', or:

> You dip, dive, and socialize
> We're trying to make you realize
> That we are qualified, to rectify
> That burning desire to boogie.[68]

Rap subsequently developed into a form of melody-less, rhymed story-telling—characteristically depicting that ambience of crime, drugs, and violent sex which frequently informs life in black ghettos—accompanied by rhythmically energetic, electronic music that includes 'sampling' (extracting, manipulating, and reassembling) fragments of other people's music.[69]

A more anarchic form of rap, 'gangsta' rap, surfaced on the West Coast in Los Angeles County with the release of *Straight Outta Compton* (Ruthless Records, 1988) by the rap group, NWA (Niggaz With Attitude); this started as an 'underground' record, and subsequently sold two million copies. In terms of sexism, racism, and street-*verismo*, the rap-texts of *Straight Outta Compton* went far beyond anything that

[67] Tricia Rose, *Black Noise: Rap Music and Black Culture in Contemporary America* (Hanover, NH: University of New England Press, 1994), 47.

[68] 'Toasts' by Joseph Saddler ('Grandmaster Flash'), cited in S. H. Fernando Jr., *The New Beats: Exploring the Music Culture and Attitudes of Hip-Hop* (Edinburgh: Payback Press, 1995), 11.

[69] That rap vocalists do not sing (in the usual sense), and that those providing the backing do not themselves play instruments, has led some to deny rap the status of music; however, many precedents for rhythmically recited verse classed as song exist: among the Amazonian Suyá people, for example (see pp. 56–7); among the Venda of South Africa (John Blacking, 'The Structure of Musical Discourse: The Problem of the Song Text', *Yearbook for Traditional Music*, xiv (1982), 15–23); and Laurence Picken reports having heard, in recordings made in the Republic of Turkmenistan, songs in rhythmic equi-syllabic monotone delivery, with plucked-string accompaniment.

US music, of any sort, had previously been expected to carry; for example:

> Straight outta Compton, another crazy ass nigga
> More punks I smoke, yo, my rep gets bigger.
> I'm a bad muthafucka and you know this
> But the pussy ass niggas won't show this.
> But I don't give a fuck I'ma make my snatch
> If not from the records then from jackin' a crowd
> It's like burglary, the definition is jackin' [stealing]
> And when I'm legally armed it's called packin'
> Shoot a muthafucka in a minute
> I find a good piece of pussy and go up in it.

However offensive such raw expressions of ghetto life may appear, no understanding of modern black music, or of 'Postmodern', post-industrial Western culture, can be complete without knowledge of their existence. They tell of life, as it is lived in some of the worst poverty- and crime-ridden ghettos of the industrialized West, by people with constitutional rights to freedom of speech: 'When you say they're chauvinists, all I can say to you is, well, if ghetto life is chauvinistic, then that's realism ... that's a way of life and they're talking about it', was the verdict of Jerry Heller, NWA's manager.[70] And NWA's follow-up album, *NIGGAZ4LIFE*, went straight to number two on the *Billboard* pop-chart, indicating that the album had been taken up by white youth of 'Middle America', as well as by blacks.

NWA's début stimulated a wave of west-coast 'gangsta' rap, rehearsing the reality of life as many deprived blacks are forced to live it: NWA-members Ice Cube and Dre, for example, left NWA to set up on their own;[71] Ice-T, Compton's Most Wanted, and Above the Law are just a few of countless groups that developed the genre. Rap—largely through 'gangsta' rap—became a major black-music genre and a multi-billion-dollar industry: by 1995 (according to *Billboard* magazine), it accounted for one in five records sold in the USA; and figures from Time Warner—largest promoter of rap (and particularly 'gangsta' rap) in the

[70] Fernando, *The New Beats*, 101.

[71] The volatile history of NWA ended, suddenly, with the death in May 1995 of group-member Eric 'Eazy E' Wright, founder of Ruthless Records, and initial business brains behind the group.

USA—indicate that, by the same year, one in three of all CDs and cassettes sold to US blacks was rap.[72]

The view that 'gangsta' rap constitutes no more than a realistic expression of street life in US black ghettos was (and is) by no means universal. The spread of such rap to the 'vanilla' suburbs generated attacks on rap by conservative whites, particularly after Ice Cube and Tupac Shakur rapped about shooting police officers. And black critics, in turn, came to see 'gangsta' rappers as participating in their own degradation, encouraging rape, murder, and drugs, in black communities. Sterner critics even accused white-led transnational corporations of promoting 'gangsta' rap in order to encourage death, disease, and imprisonment among young blacks, and so reduce the threat of black power.[73] A lyric by MCEiht, for example, from 'One Less Nigga', includes the following lines:

> So call me a devil
> Cause I kill more niggas than the KKK...
> This ain't the Malcolm and Martin days
> 'Cause I'm a nigga on the motherfuckin' street
> And I've got to get my rent paid
> So I pop you and drop you
> And I figure to myself, one less nigga.

The song is currently available on MCA, one of the largest US record companies.

Not all rap developed in the 'gangsta' vein, however. As the eulogizing of crime, racism, and sexism, in 'gangsta' rap, came to be seen as politically self-defeating, many rappers sought instead to publicize—and politicize—through their genre the black struggle against the white power structure. Ice-T (Tracy Marrow), for example, turned from crime, and its description in 'gangsta' rap, to the rapping of black protest; in the process, he achieved four 'gold' records, prodigious wealth, and sufficient *kudos* to undertake university lecture tours, inciting young white audiences to protest the black cause.[74] The rap group Public Enemy in particular, in such albums as *Fear of a Black Planet* (1990) and *Apocalypse 91... The Enemy Strikes Black* (1991),

[72] Cited in Daniel Jeffreys, 'They're Poisoning our Kids', *Independent*, Section Two, 31 July 1995, 2–3.

[73] Ibid. 2.

[74] Fernando, *The New Beats*, 141–2.

76. Chuck D, Public Enemy

used rap to inspire a grass-roots movement of rap activism; indeed, their leading lyricist, Chuck D, wrote *Fight the Power*, the theme song for Spike Lee's film, *Do the Right Thing* (Pl. 76).[75] The political potency of rap has led many rap artists to consider the genres of jazz and blues to be mere relics of the slave days, no longer suitable for black creative expression.

The *motivation* for the sexism and racism evident in rap—and especially 'gangsta' rap—may be appreciated, without such appreciation extending to the product itself. Rap's raw depiction of sex and violence is arguably no more extreme than that depicted in Berg's *Lulu*, or in Bartók's *The Miraculous Mandarin*, for example (see p. 476); rap

[75] For an analysis of this song, demonstrating the rhythmic complexities inherent in apparently 'music-less' music, see Robert Walser, 'Rhythm, Rhyme, and Rhetoric in the Music of Public Enemy', *Ethnomusicology*, 39/2 (1995), 193.

derives from a timeless African oral tradition, just as *Lulu* and *The Miraculous Mandarin* derive from the storytelling traditions of Western opera and ballet. What assaults the senses in 'gangsta' and other rap is the immediacy of a message that is delivered in speech, lacking the adornment that song provides, but containing pounding rhythms (in both speech delivery and accompaniment) that ensure its acceptance as music. Though not without artifice, rap (of any sort) is utterly without allegory. It communicates the despair of underprivileged African-Americans more explicitly, and potently, than has any previous, US, black-music genre.

Beside such overtly political expression, rock, as though embarrassed by the ubiquity of its own verbal and musical clichés, has placed increasing emphasis on visual appearance and performance histrionics (see p. 613). With song-words often nonchalantly superficial, and music essentially unoriginal, rock is mostly as ephemeral as is the 'throwaway' culture it serves. Only when, as dance music, the music's accelerated pulse and amplified percussion beat lead participant dancers to a wordless state of euphoria does rock music still fulfil an explicit social function.[76] This, however, is properly the domain of disco music. Song-words without social meaning are no more useful than wallpaper; the folk-singer who has lost hope, like the composer who has lost a sense of history, is a medium without a message. The formula-ridden similitude of much current rock music is a far cry from the invigorating Africanization of European forms that lay at the heart of the US phenomenon of popular music.

Jazz itself today incorporates such a wide variety of musical styles that any clear definition of the genre has become impossible. In one form or another it is performed all over the world, virtually by all peoples of the world. There is scarcely a style of traditional music described in this book with which it has not, at some point, been 'crossed'. Africanness in music is now less evident in jazz than in the popular-music genres of Latin America and of Africa itself. The internationalization of jazz was perhaps the first clear indication that a world of distinctive, regional, musical styles was being replaced by one in which 'crossover' styles were eroding the uniqueness of hitherto long-sustained musical traditions.

In the West, the most significant effect of the partial Africanizing of popular music has been to create an even greater gulf between classical

[76] This point is elaborated both in the Foreword (p. 21) and in the final chapter (p. 694).

and popular musical styles. During the eighteenth and nineteenth centuries, the difference was mainly of degree; classical music of the eighteenth century was essentially a more sophisticated version of popular music. Throughout the nineteenth century, the gap widened, but classical music drew even more heavily on the music of ordinary 'folk'. During the early years of the twentieth century, the emergence of a pervasive *African* element in popular music drove a wedge between Western classical and popular styles, creating a wound that even the modern popularization of Western classical music has not healed. The germinating profit motive of modern popular music—which now extends not only to identity-conscious, political genres, such as zouk-music, 'salsa', and rap, but also to the promotion of Western classical genres—threatens the continuing individuality of musical styles and genres throughout the world.

Part Five

The Modern World

17 Tradition and Change

Causes of Musical Change

It is probably fair to suggest that the world has changed more over the past 200 years than it did during the millennia that separated the Industrial Revolution from the Neolithic. This sudden acceleration of change has leant a new slant to the meaning of the word 'tradition'. Tradition tends now to be regarded as being antithetic to change—as representing customs that prevailed, before industrialization, urbanization, and electronic communications rendered them largely redundant. Tradition, however—even as thus defined—was never a stasis. Although throughout most of human history continuity was regarded as the touchstone of stability, things were seldom stable for long. Changes in climate, for example, natural disasters, and frequent intrusion by one society into the affairs of another caused political and social change. With too slow a rate of change, societies stagnate; with too great or too continuous change, societies disintegrate.

From the earliest times, musical styles underwent change as they passed from one cultural system to another; such movement could be due to human migration and conquest, to the deliberate borrowing of music by one country from another, or to the interaction of musical styles associated with particular class-based strata within a single country. There is evidence, for example, of songs passing from Japan to Korea, unaltered in pitch (because both societies shared the anhemitonic pentatonic scale), but substantially altered in rhythm (because the Koreans changed the common Japanese duple metre to their favourite triple metre).[1] Today, however, a US pop song performed, for example,

[1] David Hughes, 'Thai Music in Java, Javanese Music in Thailand', *British Journal of Ethnomusicology*, 1 (1992), 18.

77. Richard Walley (playing a dijeridu and guitar simultaneously), as featured in the festival 'Coroboree-Sights and Sounds of the First Austrialians', at the South Bank Centre, London, 1993. Photo: Leon Morris

by a Thai nightclub singer may remain largely unaltered in pitch and rhythm, but acquire a very different character on account of the change in vocal timbre and style.

Nor do styles need to migrate far to change character in performance. In Europe, for example, the use of vibrato in performances of classical music is now commonplace. Until the early twentieth century, however, vibrato was—as it was, and is, throughout Asia—an expressive ornament. The first edition of Grove's *Dictionary of Music and Musicians* (1889) states that 'when vibrato is really an emotional thrill it can be highly effective . . . but when . . . it degenerates into a mannerism, its effect is either painful, ridiculous, or nauseous, entirely opposed to good taste and commonsense . . .'.

Religious evangelism has been a major cause of musical change. An obvious example is the spread of Islam, which had a profound effect on musical styles throughout a huge area of Asia, Africa, and Eastern Europe. It was probably the most significant catalyst for musical change prior to Europe's assault on the world, and the subsequent spread of European military-band music and Christian hymnody. During the twentieth century, this catalytic role has passed to the recording industry.

Music, nevertheless, has often been an important agent of continuity, active in the preservation of cultural identity. It will be constructive, at this point, to summarize, briefly, aspects of usage and style common to non-European, traditional musics (described in previous chapters), and to compare them with aspects of usage and style in European music.

Traditional Functions of Music

The association of musical styles with peoples and regions is a worldwide phenomenon. Autochthonous peoples of Australia and the Americas, for example, have traditionally associated particular ancestral songs with particular ancestral lands; many societies have jealously guarded individual songs and forms of music-making; the multitude of folk styles that exist, throughout the world, define and give meaning to the multitude of different societies to which they are specific; and over thousands of years, distinctive forms of art music have been characteristic of spheres of cultural influence that have their roots in earlier civilizations.

Worldwide, music has been used in the service of religion; indeed, until the twentieth century, no society believed that music did not, in part at least, derive from a spiritual source. In non-literate and civilized societies alike, music was held to affect the condition of humans and the state of their environment. Whether through devotion, trance, or ecstasy, whether through a spirit entering a human being, or a soul's departure from a living body to communicate with the spirit world, it was common for societies to see in music the essential means of making contact with the deities who control the elements and the fate of peoples. Across the globe, beneficent spirits have been held to reside in musical instruments and in the masks and costumes of ritual theatre; and in many societies, skilled musicians have been accredited with supernatural powers, particularly that of making rain. Civilizations across Eurasia have linked music with cosmology. Music was what held together the perceived world of human beings.

Because religious beliefs affect directly the actions of men and of gods, ritual musicians have often been prominent members of society, accorded correspondingly high status. (Usually it is only where music has been linked to immorality, or paganism—most notably in Islamic societies—that professional musicians have been accorded low status.) In many non-literate cultures, ritual songs were performed only by the old and wise, and were passed on only to specially chosen youths, or from father to son. In many parts of Central Asia, ritual songs were the preserve of the shaman. In Israel, custodianship of the music of the temple was the exclusive preserve of the Levites. In West Asia, *muezzin*s form hereditary guilds. In India, temple music is performed exclusively by brāhmans; and illustrious Indian musicians are still revered as saints.

If music has been indispensable to priests and shamans, it has been no less indispensable to chiefs and kings: it is doubtful if there has ever been a king or a queen on earth who was not, at some time, praised in music. In Africa, genealogies sung by praise-singers gave legitimacy to a king's rule; drums symbolized semi-divine power, and their destruction would augur its erosion. From Morocco to Malaysia, the 'loud' *nawba* ensemble was associated with kingship. In Indonesia and Malaysia, the royal gamelans underwent religious initiation before use, and were played only in the royal palaces. In China, Confucian ritual music existed for the praise of heaven, from whence the emperor received his mandate to rule. The amplitude of musical sounds carries its own authority: the Chinese bell chimes and single bells, stone chimes and single stones, in sets of up to seventeen pitches, must have been as impressive as the scores of African kettledrums that in some societies were used to honour a king. Musical performance itself was often dependent upon royal patronage.

Throughout the world, music has been used not only to propitiate nature-gods and give legitimacy to kingship but also to encourage social cooperation: for example, the responsorial, 'call-and-response' style of singing in Africa exists also in Jewish, Christian, Islamic, and Buddhist chant, and in some of the devotional genres of Hinduism. Musical ensembles are at times so structured as to *demand* equality of individual cooperation within a group. The stopped-flute, or trumpet ensembles of Africa, for example, require each member of a group to contribute a single note to a melody. Similar stopped flute ensembles exist in the Philippines and Latin America; and throughout South East Asia the bamboo *angklung* ensemble is based on a similar technique of musical construction. The interlocking textures of African xylophone and *mbira* ensembles require group cooperation, as do the 'gong-chime' ensembles of South East Asia, and the pan-pipe ensembles of the Andes. In some Andean regions of South America, the pitches of pan pipes are organized so that melodies can *only* be played by pairs, or groups, of players.

Through time, music has fulfilled a range of social functions. It has given cohesion to seasonal festivals and celebrations of rites-of-passage. It has eased the labour of work and improved its productivity. It has assisted courtship: throughout much of Asia, males and females have teased or taunted each other playfully in singing bouts, and in some areas they still do so. Music has also been used to dissipate anger and rivalry: insult songs have commonly provided a peaceful means of giving vent to pent-up hatreds.

Lamenting in music is common to many world cultural systems, from the British Isles to China. Laments have usually been for the dead, assisting the soul in its passage, and ensuring that it does not return to haunt the living. Lamentation at times continued for weeks or months; in Chinese official circles mourning was prescribed for three years. Laments may have other purposes: in Africa, South East Asia, China, and elsewhere, laments are at times sung by girls who have been selected for marriage to an unknown man in a different village.

Poet-musicians have been prominent in many societies, officiating at seasonal and cultic ceremonies, and providing moralistic entertainment through the singing of epic legends, histories, and topical stories. Anansi the Spiderman, brought from Africa to Jamaica, Gilgamesh of Mesopotamia, Manas of western Central Asia, Ge-sur of eastern Central Asia, Pwyll of the Celtic Mabinogion, Odysseus of Homeric Greece, Arjuna of the *Mahābhārata*, Buddha as represented in the *Jātaka*s, and the Monkey Sage of China are some of the heroes whose exploits have been sung by itinerant bards, or enacted in theatres, temples, and market-places, by itinerant players. Myths or topical stories have been sung by singer-actors such as the *harakatha* singers of India, the *lam* singers of Laos, the *p'ansori* singers of Korea, the *tanci* singers of China, or indeed, the *pantomimi* of Ancient Rome. Shi'ite Muslims still enact the martyrdom of Hussein. Masked dances are still used to clear evil spirits from a particular region, as in the 'devil dances' of Sri Lanka and Tibet, the 'barong' dances of Bali, the 'lion' dances of China and Korea, or the 'deer' dances of Japan.

Theatrical entertainment that combines the sophisticated with the popular, the philosophical with the urbane, is to be observed in the Kathkali dance of India, the *wayang kulit* (shadow play) of Indonesia (once common throughout Turkey, India, South East Asia, and China), the *lakhon jatri* of Thailand, the *lam luang* of Laos, the *zat pwe* of Burma, the *hat cai luong* of Vietnam, the Chinese opera, the *Kyōgen Nō* of Japan, and a multitude of folk-theatre genres throughout Africa and Eurasia. Music theatre of this sort provides a focus for community life, and a medium for social commentary. Such combinations of music, dance, and drama, using styles based on popular idioms, are wholly intelligible to their audiences, and induce an immediacy of response that has sometimes been lost in Western music theatre.

Traditional Methods of Musical Construction

If the functions allocated to music in different societies are broadly similar, so too are the means by which music is constructed. Pitched notes have customarily been linked together into sets; and the musical statements generated from such a set have been shaped and developed, in remarkably similar ways. Specific melody types are commonly equated with specific human emotions, or actions; and they are frequently conditioned by standard rhythmic cycles, familiar to the community.

In literate societies, note-sets and rhythmic cycles are often given formal description in technical language; in non-literate societies they are not. But in neither instance are musicians free to invent at will. Conventional manners of performance, whether originating in religious ritual, or in scholarly theory (or both), are scrupulously observed; and any modification occurs within strictly prescribed limits. Sequential development in the rules of performance has usually been the result of natural evolution rather than self-conscious change. The music itself varies slightly from performance to performance, and as a style is passed from master to pupil; and words are sometimes adapted to current circumstances. But the substance of a ritual, whether sacred or profane, has remained essentially the same, sometimes over many centuries.

In non-literate cultures, the absence of theory is significant: it places even stronger emphasis on tradition and imitation. African babes, for example, learn their native rhythms on the backs of their dancing mothers: the traditional rhythms and melodies of their native music are etched on the subconscious before they can speak. In literate cultures, theories of mode have often served to rationalize problems of musical temperament that performers tend to deal with instinctively. But from North Africa to China, musical structures feature contrasts in tempo and pitch range; and the most important pitches of a mode are frequently given prominence, through vibrato, or other types of ornamentation. Indeed, ornamentation is the key procedure in creating variation in melody, worldwide; and the variant *shapes* of a melody tend to be instrument-specific, changing with differing techniques of ornamentation on plucked and bowed-string instruments, and between single-, double-, or multi-pipe wind instruments.

The complexities of rhythmic cycles are often linked with poetic metres. African drum rhythms, for example, are usually derived from speech, and drumming itself is commonly a surrogate for speech; the drumming is both complex and virtuosic, but it always aims at clarity of texture. In Asia, structure in time of rhythmic cycles is usually strictly specified: in India, for example, the classification of rhythmic cycles has enabled the art of drumming to develop with breathtaking virtuosity, both as solo music and in conjunction with a solo performer. Throughout much of West, South, and South East Asia, changes in tempo are layered in proportions of two to one; and form is frequently delineated by sections, or movements, of gradually increasing speed of performance.

Across the globe, traditional music-making has achieved an astonishing degree of subtlety and complexity. Musicians were—and in most places still are—among the most highly motor-skilled members of any society. The 'secrets' of their art may or may not have been received from the gods, and passed on by religious castes, but the music itself survives by the diligent practice of humans. Musical performance has always been subject to censure in the light of tradition. Improvisation, in the sense of ornamentation and simple variation-making, is facilitated by long and disciplined training in a given tradition, rather than by self-indulgent submission to an unstructured impulse. The skills of a musician are not acquired easily.

Peculiarities of European Musical Culture

It is possible that traditions similar to those of Africa and Asia once extended throughout Europe. It is clear, for example, that, in historic time, music was used extensively in relation to religion and royalty. In many regions of Europe, there is substantial evidence of the presence of bardic musicians; the troubadours and, later, *Commedia dell'arte* had much in common with Asian itinerant theatre groups. Where ancient European traditions still survive, unadulterated by eighteenth-century harmony, they show affinities with traditional musics elsewhere.

Remnants of Welsh and Irish harping traditions, for example, and the elaborate musical world of Scottish *pibroch* (from Scots-Gaelic *piobaireachd*, 'piping'), suggest that archaic systems of melodic and rhythmic modes once existed in north and west Europe; and many British folk-songs, recorded in the first half of this century, display pitch modality. *Tvisöngur* ('twin-song') in Iceland (a form of improvised, parallel-fifth, vocal organum)[2] uses certain procedures comparable to those developed in Africa and in medieval Europe. The use of a drone in 'bourdon polyphony' in Latvia and the Balkans is paralleled in West and Central Asian folk musics, in Indian classical music, in certain mouth-organ folk genres across South East and East Asia, and indeed in eighth-century performance practice of both Roman and Byzantine chant (see p. 138); and the use of heterophony in Gaelic psalm-singing on the Scottish island of Lewis and in Irish keening may be paralleled world-wide. Frederick Douglass, a fugitive, widely-travelled, African slave, writing in 1855, claimed never to have heard any songs like those he had heard among slaves 'except when in Ireland: there I heard the same *wailing* notes, and was much affected by them'.[3] He was perhaps reacting to the heterophony of Irish keening, in the light of black 'lining-out' psalm-singing in the USA.

It seems unlikely that folk musics in the north and west of Europe ever included the 'limping' rhythms of the Balkans and Turkey that feature in rhythmic cycles from Morocco to the Bay of Bengal; and it is very unlikely that chromatic tetrachords, such as A–B♭–C♯–D′, present today in the Hicaz *makam* of Turkey, were ever distributed in these areas of Europe. They survive, however, in certain Orthodox modes, and in folk music of Greece and the Balkans, and perhaps in the standard harmonic minor scale of the West.

In other important respects, however, Europe departed substantially from African and Asian traditions. Within the Christian Church, music

[2] R. A. Ottósson, 'Iceland', *The New Grove* (1980), ix. 7–9.

[3] Fredrick Douglass, *My Bandage and my Freedom* (New York, 1853), cited in Eileen Southern (ed.), *Readings in Black American Music* (New York: Norton, 1971), 83.

progressively became an elaborate ornament rather than an intrinsic, magical means of communication with the deity. Folk theatre increasingly accepted the ambience of doctrinaire Christianity (though pagan dances, such as the Abbots Bromley horn dance and Padstow mumming, still survive in England). Liturgical chant replaced epic-singing, since good singers were apt for chapel service. Chant acquired counterpoint and, subsequently, harmony. Notation overtook oral–aural, master–disciple tradition as the essential means of transmission; and print subsequently eroded oral–aural folk traditions.

Dance-based, formal symmetry became intrinsic to popular—and thence to élitist—musical style; the use of harmony tended to limit rhythmic variety; and the regularly recurring, printed barline came to dominate European music. The medieval modes were eventually subsumed under the major and minor modes, rationalized into a system of key relationships, symmetrical about a 'natural' condition. Technological advance made possible bass instruments capable of playing agile melodies; and treble instruments acquired unprecedentedly accurate pitch definition, compass, and manœuvrability. The existence of such instruments reinforced harmony which—until the nineteenth century at least—came to condition rhythm.

Notation encouraged the cult of 'the composer'; and the printed score enabled intricate art music to be heard mentally and studied in silence: it existed apart from performance. Moreover, the exactness of the printed score, in terms of pitch and rhythm, prevented individual compositions from successfully adapting to change. The supple, baroque, melodic lines of Handel's *Messiah*, for example, composed to some extent according to the 'doctrine of the affections', seem uncharacteristically constrained when performed in Mozart's rescoring of the work, designed to adapt it to 'classical' musical taste; and when nineteenth-century musical taste demanded that the work be performed by huge choral and orchestral forces, the flexible interplay between florid *obbligato* and supporting *continuo* lines, and between flowing 'andante' and florid 'adagio' movements, was negated. The greatly increased dynamic range of the large forces employed destroyed aspects of musical structure, intrinsic to the style. Similarly, replacement of *castrati* (required in baroque opera) with alternative singers, male or female, natural-voiced or falsetto, creates problems of tessitura and of vocal register: transposing the melodic lines down an octave leads to juxtaposition of melody and bass in the bass line, while changing the key of the movement disturbs the overall tonal structure of the entire work.

In the West, musical change came (in general) to involve production of new pieces in new styles, by new composers, rather than adaptation of older compositions; and this created the possibility of disjunction between past and present. Elsewhere, by contrast, music was usually classified by genre rather than by individual composer, and was adaptable to the more gradual change to which it was normally subjected. Music theatre in China, for example, not being constricted by precise notation, readily adapted to the introduction of female voices in the early years of this century; and Indian modal systems, being inclusive in structure and flexible in execution, proved infinitely adaptable to outside influence, over centuries, and probably millennia.

The Western use of print, and of science, caused change to become an intrinsic feature of Western culture. Whereas in Africa and Asia continuity generally betokens stability, and change, instability, in Europe continuity suggested stagnation, and change came to be regarded as a necessary phenomenon in a 'progressive' society. Thus, when the pace of change accelerated towards the end of the nineteenth century, Europe was, in part at least, prepared to meet it; but when European influence accelerated change in Africa and Asia, those societies were ill-prepared to meet it. Only in the late twentieth century has change become so rapid that societies throughout the entire world are in danger of losing vital cultural links with the past.

European Influence in Africa and Asia

Intervention by Europeans in the affairs of Africa and Asia did not at first greatly affect the styles of traditional arts: the innate sense of superiority of the European ensured that little attention was paid to indigenous culture in countries colonized. Sometimes, as in West Africa, Europeans marvelled at the skill of local craftsmen;[4] but a majority of early colonists neither cared for, nor altered, the local systems more than was necessary for their own convenience. They were, in any case, scarcely purveyors of the European arts. Only in Latin America did European music engender a vigorous response, and there it was as ancillary to Christianity. Migrations—in

[4] John Collins and Paul Richards, 'Popular Music in West Africa', in Simon Frith (ed.), *World Music, Politics, and Social Change* (Manchester: Manchester University Press, 1989), 19.

particular those forced on Africans—have generally caused greater change than any form of colonialism.[5]

Europeans came to Africa and Asia to trade rather than conquer; and trade was scarcely a novelty in lands where cultural systems had largely evolved in response to mercantile interests. When conquest occurred, it was—with the notable exception of the Americas and Australasia—mainly for the purpose of protecting trading interests. In Asia, such conquest proved necessary by the early nineteenth century; and by the end of the century it had proved necessary throughout Africa.

European domination in Africa and Asia caused many peoples of those continents to lose confidence in their native cultural systems. Western music often came to be associated with modernity and progress, and to be preferred to traditional music, or to become syncretized with it. The forms of notation of traditional musics—when they existed—were insufficiently protective: in Africa they were lacking; in Asia they defined so little. The musics depended for preservation on the continuity that oral–aural tradition provides; and, as European musical styles became increasingly pervasive (for sociological and mercantile reasons), many non-European, traditional styles progressively lost their distinctiveness.

By the early decades of the twentieth century, a wide range of European instruments was in use across Africa, West Asia, and East Asia, both for the performance of traditional musics, and for the variant forms of these that new instruments brought about. European harmony and equal temperament gradually eroded ancient musical traditions, based on untempered scales, on elaborate rhythmic systems, and on heterophony. Large 'orchestras' displaced small ensembles accustomed to playing instrument-specific lines in heterophony. Traditional melodies were often ironed out into 'standardized' versions, and in this condition transcribed into Western staff notation. Newly created 'traditional' tunes acquired triadic melodic movement and, sometimes, triadic harmonic underlays. From here it was but a short step to 'composing' new music of increasing virtuosity for performance on traditional instruments.

Throughout much of Africa and Asia, European music gradually came to be imitated directly, and, by the early twentieth century, numerous institutions for teaching European music had been established. Bands and symphony orchestras followed. Traditional musicians

[5] Ibid. 13–18.

began to compose in Western styles and genres, often attempting to superimpose traditional on Western styles, or to blend Western instruments with traditional instruments. In East Asia today, the composition of Western-style, 'modernist' music, for Western and traditional instruments, separately or in combination, has become an industry. The technical accomplishment of East Asian performers on European string and keyboard instruments is among the most prodigious in the world.

Whether we like it or not, the music of Europe is now dominant in most of the 'developed' and 'developing' world. Throughout much of urban Africa and West Asia, in Sri Lanka, Thailand, Malaysia, Singapore, Vietnam, China, Hong Kong, Taiwan, Korea, Japan, and the Philippines—not to mention Latin America—Western music is taught and performed more than is traditional music. Even in India and Indonesia, where native cultural systems seemed at one time impermeable to those of the West, Western music is now in the ascent. So, too, throughout Asia and Africa, is Western pop music. In imitation, varying forms of indigenous pop music have been developed, and are promoted by the commercial market.

Popular Music and the Mass Media

In Europe and the USA, popular music developed as a commercial activity during the latter half of the nineteenth century, when middle- and lower-middle-class spending power had developed sufficiently to exert influence on the musical-entertainment industry.[6] Upright pianos encouraged home music-making and brought an entrepreneurial dimension to music-publishing; it was discovered that popular songs, disseminated through sheet-music, could become big business. From 1892 until the expansion of radio in the 1930s, sheet music was promoted by 'song-slides' (pictures telling the story of the song); and these had a measurable effect on the categories of song being sold.[7]

The phonograph, first marketed for home use around 1900, stimulated the publishing boom; but as a domestic musical instrument it did not exceed the piano in popularity until well into the 1920s. Never-

[6] Peter Gammond, *The Oxford Companion to Popular Music* (Oxford: Oxford University Press, 1991), p. vi.

[7] Simon Frith, *Music for Pleasure* (Oxford: Polity Press in association with Robert Blackwell, 1988), 12.

theless, it spread rapidly in the USA and Europe, and by 1910 was making an impact in Africa and Asia. Only after the First World War did the phonograph become recognised as a machine for home-entertainment, rather than a coin-operated machine, in use at fairs and on the vaudeville circuit. Records—at first a promotional tool for the phonograph—began to be bought, and valued for the music they would yield. In 1927, 104 million records were sold in the USA.[8]

The record industry suffered badly during the 1930s slump. Ironically, its later recovery was due to the popularity of the jukebox (the mechanical record player), rather than to domestic sales; by 1939 there were 300,000 jukeboxes in the USA, accounting for the sale of 30 million records. By then, however, the radio had superseded the phonograph as the principal medium of home entertainment. In its turn, it too was to become the principal means of record promotion.[9]

Radio and the recording industry together created the mass market for popular music. Although radio was too expensive a commodity to be purchased by individuals in many parts of the world, its continuous use in bars and cafés enabled it to reach a very large public. Radio was not, of course, directly controlled by the market consumer, but in many parts of the world it depended on advertisements for its revenue, and promulgated styles of music most likely to attract audiences for the advertisements.[10] Radio became the lifeblood of the recording-star system; and the source of profits shifted from record sales to performing rights and royalties.[11]

Over a space of little more than two decades, the recording industry changed the circumstances of musical performance over a substantial part of the world. It encouraged passive listening, at the expense of engagement in musical performance. It brought into mutual contact musicians and musical styles formerly separated by distance. It enabled performance groups to listen, detachedly, to the totality of their performance. It created a new audience-less context for music-making.[12] It presented new and sometimes dazzling commercial opportunities for popular musicians; and, in this process, it caused music to be regarded primarily as entertainment. Ultimately, it transferred taste-forming from the educated élite to the market consumer.

[8] Ibid. 14–16. [9] Ibid. 16.

[10] Peter Manuel, *Popular Musics of the Non-Western World* (New York: Oxford University Press, 1989), 4.

[11] Frith, *Music for Pleasure*, 17.

[12] Manuel, *Popular Musics*, 4.

The processes of record production profoundly influenced the development of musical style and timbre. In popular music, the microphone changed the approach to vocal quality, which came to be judged less by carrying power than by intimate vocal nuances, expressive of a particular vocal personality. With the replacement of disc-recording by tape-recording in the 1950s, electrical engineers began to make a significant contribution to the quality of the finished product. Tape became an intermediary in the recording process: mistakes could be edited out; and new sounds could be added by electronic means. In the 1960s, the development of multi-track recording led producers and engineers to play an even larger part in the recording process. Multi-track recording made possible the rock album; and in classical music it altered the previously experienced balance between soloist and orchestra. The quality of the *recording* became as important a criterion of excellence as the quality of the *performance*. By the end of the 1960s, records—rather than concerts—had come to define an 'ideal' performatory.[13]

If multi-track recording transformed approaches to classical and popular musical styles in the West, the rapid spread of cheap tape-cassettes during the 1970s had a marked effect on musical styles elsewhere. Cassette recorders became relatively inexpensive to buy, and could be used without an electricity supply; cassettes themselves, too, could be produced cheaply. In many regions of Africa, Asia, and Latin America, 'cottage' cassette industries propagated local styles of both popular and folk music; at the same time, they enabled marginal musical cultures to be represented on radio and television.[14] Above all, they generated the plethora of regional popular-music styles that have come to complement Western pop and rock, and that have led to a marked decline in the performance of traditional folk-music and folk-dance styles.

Regional cassette industries also disseminated—as they still do—illegal, 'pirated' editions of 'hit'-records, originally produced by large, transnational companies. The transnationals responded by merging with, or taking over, small record companies, thus preserving the (for them) essential link between hardware and software production, and strengthening their influence on the distribution, by electronic means, of regional musical styles. By the 1980s, more than half of all commercial recordings sold worldwide were produced by eight transnational

[13] Frith, *Music for Pleasure*, 21–2.

[14] Manuel, *Popular Musics*, 4.

companies.[15] At the time of writing, a mere five transnational record companies control virtually all major chain-store distribution.[16]

The cinema, like the gramophone record, has profoundly influenced the course of popular music. When sound entered the cinema commercially, in the 'talkies' (in 1927, with *The Jazz Singer*), songs became vital to the success of a film; indeed, film songs were often remembered long after the plots, to which they were usually incidental, were forgotten.[17] With the 'talkies', sales of song scores rose dramatically; and film companies took over sheet-music publishing houses, and began to finance the development of sound technology. Moreover, because film songs needed to be self-contained, and to be of sufficient sound quality to guarantee record sales, the sound of the song came, increasingly, not from the actor or actress shown on the film, but from a separate singer, 'dubbing' the sound. Actors and actresses came to be esteemed on the basis of their visual *image*, more than on their technical skills; and when rock musicians started to perform on film, as 'stars', they too came to be esteemed on the basis of their visual image. The visual (the photograph) was no longer admired separately from the sound (the gramophone record); the song was now seen, as much as heard.[18]

Television endorsed this new, intimate, relationship between sound and vision, and it did so for classical as well as for popular music. It often provided, for both rock fans and classical-music lovers, the only access to 'live' performance; and, for many artists, it provided a principal route to stardom.[19] Performers in opera, symphony orchestras, and rock concerts could be viewed close-up; and, as the definition of television images gradually improved in quality to equal that of cinematic films, audiences became accustomed to the 'unreality' of the television image. At huge rock concerts, fans no longer watch their idol shrunk to a puppet by distance, but follow the finest details of facial expression and of gesture on mammoth video screens; Michael Jackson and Madonna are

[15] Krister Malm, 'The Music Industry', in Helen Myers (ed.), *Ethnomusicology: A Handbook* (New Grove Handbooks; London: Macmillan, 1992), 352–3.

[16] Tricia Rose, *Black Noise: Rap Music and Black Culture in Contemporary America* (Hanover, NH: University of New England Press, 1994), 6–7.

[17] M. Kreuger, 'The Movie Musical from Vitaphone to 42nd Street', *A Great Fan Magazine*, (1975), cited in Jody Berland, 'Music Video and Media Reconstruction', in Simon Frith, Andrew Goodwin, and Lawrence Grossberg (eds.), *Sound and Vision: The Music Video Reader* (London: Routledge, 1993), 28.

[18] Ibid. 26.

[19] Lawrence Grossberg, 'The Media Economy of Rock Culture: Cinema, Post-Modernity and Authenticity', in Frith, Goodwin, and Grossberg (eds.), *Sound and Vision*, 189.

just two who have successfully manipulated the screen image. A similar procedure is currently being introduced at some symphony concerts.

As more families bought second television sets during the 1980s, individual channels assumed specialist roles. Developing technology subsequently enabled television screens to be used for such new purposes as playing computer and video games, watching rented videos, and receiving cable and satellite services.[20] Such developments encouraged the targeting of a youthful audience.

The advent of video, which coincided roughly with that of satellite and cable television, encouraged the music industry to invest in television, and to produce music/TV projects for distribution worldwide. Such projects, crossing national boundaries, brought transnational advertisers into partnership with televised music, for music was able to break through cultural and linguistic barriers. Hit songs (in English) have no need of translation: they are known, and understood, throughout the world.[21] Rock stars, therefore, provide transnational advertisers with a massive audience, while advertisers provide rock stars with a scale of TV promotion beyond the means of most recording companies.[22] Satellite television itself has enabled musical styles to be promulgated in geographically isolated regions: Star TV, for example, has brought Japanese *karaoke* ('empty orchestra') to Lhasa (in Tibet). And the association of star opera singers with televised sporting events has stimulated a new audience, worldwide, for opera 'hits'.

The continuing and widespread propagation of music through the mass media has rendered music-making in traditional contexts increasingly rare, and has discouraged the widespread dissemination of regional musical styles. Music and dance, once the focal points of social cohesion, are now visual/aural entertainment; they vie for attention with pop cassettes, videos, and television soap operas. Traditional artists perform in National Arts Centres, where they present their work in new ways, often based on Western models.

As Western styles of music and theatre spread throughout the globe, their peripheral function in daily life spreads with them. Grandiose performances of Western opera, for example, travel the world as spectacular entertainment. Arguably there is nothing *more* illogical, or

[20] Simon Frith, 'Youth, Music, Television', in Frith, Goodwin, and Grossberg (eds.), *Sound and Vision*, 69.

[21] Ibid. 70–1.

[22] Leslie Savan, 'Commercials Go Rock', in Frith, Goodwin, and Grossberg (eds.), *Sound and Vision*, 89–90.

peripheral, about a monumental staging of *Aida* in a 20,000-seat auditorium in Mexico City, or against the backdrop of the great Egyptian palace in Luxor, than a similar staging in the Roman amphitheatre in Verona or, for that matter, a conventional staging at *La Scala* in Milan. None of these performances is to be regarded as ritually *essential* to the business of living, as still are, for example, the monkey ceremonies of the Suyá people of Brazil or the age-set ceremonies of the Samburu people of Kenya. Notwithstanding attempts by modern opera directors to confer contemporary relevance on the drama, opera—in the twentieth century as much as the eighteenth—remains, to quote the precise and fitting words of Dr. Samuel Johnson, 'an exotic and irrational entertainment'.

Music may still, in some as yet undefined way, contribute to our general sense of well-being, still soothe the spirit in sickness or in love, still affect human behaviour, still have strong historical associations, still be one of the most fundamental elements in religious and social ceremony; but it no longer affords for us direct communication with the god, no longer makes rain or drives it away, very rarely even 'soothes the savage breast'. Its art has become largely synonymous with entertainment.

In examination of the diffusion of myths, ideas on astronomy, musical instruments, and modal systems, Laurence Picken suggested that it may have taken about a millennium and a half for knowledge of the system of seven diatonic modes to travel from Old Babylonia to China; and that a further half-millennium passed before the complete set of heptachordal octave species was displayed at the Chinese Court.[23] Today the transmission of a new musical idea around the globe can be instantaneous. Tradition and change appear to be no longer separable concepts; the speed of change is overtaking human capacity to absorb it. In the words of the anthropologist, Claude Lévi-Strauss: 'The fusion of groups previously separated by distance, language, and culture, marks the end of a world'.[24]

[23] L. E. R. Picken, *Folk Musical Instruments of Turkey* (Oxford: Oxford University Press, 1975).

[24] Claude Lévi-Strauss, *The View from Afar* (Oxford: Blackwell, 1985), 23.

18 *Westernization and National Musical Identity in Africa and Asia*

New technologies, and the new experiences they occasion, affect different societies in different ways, according to prevailing, local, cultural traditions. The new musical technologies and experiences introduced to many countries of the world as a consequence of Western colonization tended to weaken native musical traditions (though the responses differed, in various parts of the globe); but when new technologies of the twentieth century brought far-flung peoples and their musics into both visual and aural contact with each other—creating the impression of a world that is shrinking—it enhanced senses of national cultural identity among different peoples, and led to a revival of 'national' musical styles. It also encouraged the formation of 'national', popular styles that mixed local melodies, instruments, and timbres, with Western musical characteristics—rather as, in the nineteenth century, countries in northern and Eastern Europe attempted to fuse 'national' folk styles with the dominant Austro-German tradition. In order to understand more fully the variety of musical interrelationships that exists throughout the world today, it will be instructive to examine the ways in which various societies have responded both to colonialism and to the impact of electronic media.

Sub-Saharan Africa

In Sub-Saharan Africa, European musical influence was probably first experienced in the Cape regions of South Africa, for European settlement occurred there some 200 years earlier than elsewhere. Colonists bonded indigenous Africans to play music; indeed, slaves able to perform music were priced more highly than those who could not. It appears that, as early as the 1650s, Khoisan ('Hottentot') Africans were playing European melodies on the *ramkie* (a three- or four-stringed guitar brought to Africa by Malabar slaves);[1] and by 1676 the Governor of Cape Town was being entertained by a 'slave orchestra', of musicians from South and West Africa, and some Malays. Owners of country estates might possess 'slave orchestras' of up to thirty musicians; at weekends they could visit taverns to hear 'violins, flutes, hautboys, trumpets, harps, and other instruments', played by slaves. By 1831 an African orchestra, playing Western instruments, resided in Cape Town Castle.[2]

On the West Coast of Africa, European music arrived as a result of trade. There is evidence of African brass bands as early as 1750, and by 1841 Ghanaian musicians were entertaining Europeans with mazurkas, polkas, and marches.[3] Africans soon applied the shifted accents of their indigenous music to European genres; conversely, when they took European instruments back to their rural homes, traditional songs and rhythms became subject to European influence.[4]

In many areas, Christian missionaries used brass bands to encourage hymn-singing; on the east coast, in Kenya for example, missionaries encouraged the formation of European-style choirs, and attempted to suppress traditional singing and drumming. In consequence, traditional musical structures gave way, in many parts of Sub-Saharan Africa, to the limited parameters of Western hymnodic style, using four-square tunes, with harmonies based on the three primary chords.

New styles also derived from European *classical* music. In Lagos, for example, a Handel Festival was founded in 1882;[5] its organizer, Professor R. A. Coker, came to be known as 'The Mozart of West Africa'.[6] The Handel Festival was followed by the foundation of a Philharmonic Society, and similar enterprises were established in Ghana and Sierra Leone. Such institutions mainly benefited Europeans and Creoles; but, because they encouraged Africans to equate European music with

[1] David Coplan, 'The Urbanization of African Performing Arts in South Africa', D.Phil. thesis (Indiana, 1980).

[2] David Coplan, *In Township Tonight* (London: Longman, 1985), 8–9.

[3] Chris Stapleton and Chris May, *African All Stars: The Pop Music of a Continent* (London, Quartet Books, 1987), 8.

[4] Ibid. 8–10.

[5] John Collins and Paul Richards, 'Popular Music in West Africa', in Simon Frith (ed.), *World Music, Politics, and Social Change* (Manchester: Manchester University Press, 1989), 23, 27.

[6] Stapleton and May, *African All Stars*, 12.

elevated social status, European musical instruments and idioms came to be mixed with those of indigenous traditions.[7]

The most influential European instrument was the acoustic guitar. It was introduced into the port of Matadi in Zaire in 1914, where it soon came to be preferred to the Congolese lamellaphone.[8] During the 1920s, the guitar spread widely throughout West Africa, and strumming and finger-picking styles of playing were incorporated in the practice of traditional ensembles, choirs, street bands, and dance bands. Gradually, the guitar replaced traditional lutes and xylophones in urban areas throughout Sub-Saharan Africa; together with records, radio, and film, it became a symbol of modernity. New styles of guitar-based music emerged, incorporating strummed chords, picking techniques, and traditional 'time-lines', performed on bottles. Such syncretic styles were propagated by semi-professional entertainers, and new urban styles were disseminated on radio (which first appeared in Africa in 1924), in association with the recording industry.

As early as 1912 representatives of the Gramophone Record Company (later EMI) were seeking business in West and South Africa. Two years later, recordings of European-influenced music were being made in South Africa, and two years after that, in West Africa. Along the east coast, record companies competed in the recording of Indian music, new songs, and traditional African songs, in Swahili and other local languages.[9] Sales were boosted by recordings of Christian Church music (sung in local languages), and of *tārab*, an African–Muslim genre, with lyrics sung in Swahili, in the style of Islamic cantillation, but accompanied by such instruments as lutes, guitars, accordions, violins, trumpets, and clarinets. Reinvigorated by Latin American music, *tārab* furnished the basis for East African pop music in the 1940s and 1950s.[10]

African–Cuban music, in particular, influenced the development of new urban styles. It entered the continent during the 1930s, but its lasting impact coincided with a surge of African nationalism at the end of the Second World War. African demands for independence reflected a renewed awareness of the heritage of African culture; and the African musical idioms in Cuban rumbas, *boleros*, and *mambos* already reflected this heritage.[11] The introduction of Latin music and jazz to Sub-

[7] Collins and Richards, 'Popular Music', 27.
[8] Stapleton and May, *African All Stars*, 15–18.
[9] Ibid. 257–63.
[10] Ibid. 226.
[11] Ibid. 20–6.

Saharan Africa engendered a sense of pan-African identity both in Africa and throughout the African diaspora; such identity was reinforced during the 1970s when Bob Marley associated reggae with Rastafarianism, and US Soul brought the message of 'Black Power' to Africa.

Pride in Africa's cultural heritage was the force behind the many distinctively African styles of pop music that developed in Africa from the 1930s and, in particular, after the Second World War. Such pride was encouraged by politicians. In Guinea, for example, Sékou Touré's encouragement of African culture resulted in 1953 in the foundation of the African Ballet of Keita Fodeba, which became a model for dance troupes elsewhere. In Tanzania, Julius Nyerere complained (in 1962) that the ambition of young men was 'not to become well-educated Africans but to become black Europeans'; he encouraged them to perform traditional music and wear traditional costume.[12] In Ghana, at about the same time, Kwame Nkrumah was exhorting musicians to explore traditional music and to wear traditional costume; he insisted that every group performing on radio should include at least one traditional song in their programme.[13] Earlier, in Senegal, President Leopold Senghor, himself a poet of consequence, established the concept of 'negritude'—pride in being African—which he propagated through journals such as *L'Étudiant noir* (1939), and *Présence africaine* (1947). From Wole Soyinka in Nigeria came the famous retort that 'a tiger does not need to proclaim its tigritude'.[14]

One of the earliest syncretic pop styles to emerge was 'Highlife'. Originating in the palm-wine bars of the west-coast ports, and popularized during the 1930s by prosperous, west-coast merchants, the style drew on many different sources: European salon music, performed at soirées; 'concert parties' (presenting dramatized, African folk stories); guitar bands; and Western-style dance bands. Highlife was sung in local languages, and it incorporated and adapted traditional songs and rhythms.[15] During the 1950s, claves and castanets were replaced with modern drum sets and bongos, and electric instruments were added to the ensembles. Promoted, most notably, by E. T. Mensah's Tempos Band, this form of Highlife spread to Nigeria, The Gambia, and Sierra Leone. It retained, nevertheless, its African roots, and it was used to

[12] J. K. Nyerere, *Tanzania National Assembly Official Reports (Dar Es Salaam)* (1962), 9.
[13] Stapleton and May, *African All Stars*, 38.
[14] Ibid. 20–3.
[15] Atta Mensah, 'Highlife', *The New Grove* (1980), viii. 550.

support Ghana's independence movement; during the Ghanaian depression of the 1970s, it came to be associated with Gospel.[16]

In the 1970s a proliferation of popular styles occurred, employing Western guitars and harmonies but retaining predominantly African musical idioms. 'Afrobeat' developed in Nigeria; its principal proponent, Fela Anikulapo-Kuti, mixed traditional call-and-response patterns with elements of jazz and rhythm 'n' blues, while inveighing against the West in his texts, in a form of 'broken English', comparable with Jamaican patois.[17] In The Gambia, the Super Eagles rechristened themselves with a Mandika name, Ifang Bondi, and used Senegambian drums in their percussion section. In Senegal, Youssou N'Dour sang with the vocal nuances of Islamic cantillation, at first accompanied by a small 'talking-drum' (as lead instrument), and subsequently by a range of traditional drums (performing Wolof traditional rhythms), with acoustic and electric guitars. N'Dour established himself as a modern-age praise-singer, attracting the famous and wealthy to his concerts.[18]

In Mali and Guinea—which, with Senegal and The Gambia, had formed the backbone of the great Mali empire—new styles were developed by singers such as Mory Kante and Ousmane Kouyate, themselves descended from castes of praise-singers. Such singers accompanied themselves on *kora* (twenty-one-string bridge-harp), and on *balafon* (xylophone), in modern fusions influenced by Latin American music. When Salif Keita, a descendant of Soundjata Keita (who founded the Mali empire in 1240), became a professional singer, and combined traditional songs with electric instruments, he broke, controversially, with a centuries-long tradition in which nobles could only speak to the people through praise-singers *in their employ*.[19] The quasi-ostinato melo-rhythms in Keita's music reflect the clear textures of West African traditional music (though such traits were diminished subsequently, under the influence of French recording studios).

During the 1980s Soukous, a new syncretic style from Zaire, became popular throughout Africa. Soukous was influenced by Cuban music, but its guitar styles imitated the melo-rhythms traditionally played on lamellaphones. Zairean guitarists came to be numbered among the most proficient in Africa; and, because guitars were given musical strands in Soukous that would more normally be played by the wind section, the style acquired a strikingly luminous musical texture. In

[16] Stapleton and May, *African All Stars*, 35–7. [17] Ibid. 63–4.
[18] Ibid. 119–21. [19] Ibid. 111–12.

standard form, Soukous is performed in two sections: a slow, *rumba*-influenced, introduction, and a faster section (*seben*), characterized by improvisation over guitar-based melo-rhythms. The *seben* became a showpiece, and the virtuosity of guitarists facilitated the blending of traditional African melo-rhythms with Cuban rhythms and harmonies.[20]

South Africa

A more complex musical pattern developed in South Africa, in the context of industrialization and the persistence of a racial caste system. South Africa's urban musical styles emerged largely from the mines, slums, and 'slumyards' of Johannesburg. (Slumyards were compounds of corrugated iron rooms, set in private backyards, let at exorbitant rates, without authorization, to blacks.) As David Coplan has shown,[21] urban, 'black' musical culture—separate from the music of white South Africans, and considerably more African than European in its roots—was subjected to constant interdiction (and influence) by mission-educated, middle-class blacks; such blacks associated urban styles with the vice and crime of slum living conditions, forced on a non-enfranchised, segregated, majority proletariat. In South Africa, music was intrinsically linked to racial and social identity. (Many of the social and musical attitudes and activities described in this section subsequently came to be replicated in urban areas in other parts of Sub-Saharan Africa.)

The existence of an urban proletariat was a consequence of the discovery of diamonds in Kimberley (in the Orange Free State) in 1867, and of gold in the Witwatersrand (in the southern Transvaal) in 1886. A conscious mixing of musical cultures occurred, as immigrants from Europe and North America joined with Africans in the mining towns, bringing with them banjos, guitars, concertinas, keyboards, violins, and cornets, and musical styles ranging from country dance music to ragtime. Africans soon became proficient at playing Western instruments in Western dance styles, and acquired enhanced urban status by absorbing certain aspects of European culture.[22]

In 1896 the enactment of pass laws that prohibited black Africans from living in the same communities as the whites (for whom they

[20] Ibid. 135–8, 153. [21] Coplan, *In Township Tonight.* [22] Ibid. 12–14.

worked) caused blacks to move to the slums and slumyards in ever increasing numbers. Impoverished and overcrowded conditions led to rampant alcoholism and crime; by the turn of the nineteenth century, criminal gangs such as the 'Ninevites'—whose initial purpose was to protect black Africans in a 'town without law'—paraded the streets, playing European tunes on the mouth organs for which they came to be known. Their offshoot, the *Amalaita*—whose members, mainly from Christian families, set out to resist the pass laws—imitated Scottish military bands by drilling to their commands and marching to harmonicas and penny whistles. (The penny whistle was a cheap imitation of the six-hole, metal flageolet.) By the end of the First World War the *Amalaita* had become an urban youth movement, combining European military ranking with traditional age-set groupings, and parading to penny-whistle and drum music.[23]

In an attempt to eliminate drinking and factional fighting, compound managers organized dance competitions, with music that combined the styles both of Zulu dance music and Wesleyan hymnody; their success caused commercial employers to follow suit. Such competitions gave rise during the First World War to a new and distinctive style of male-voice choral singing, *ingom'ebusuku* ('night music'); popularized by Reuben T. Caluza—whose syncretic style incorporated elements of Weslyan hymnody, 'negro' spirituals, ragtime, newly arranged Zulu songs, and 'Scottish' penny-whistle bands—*ingom'ebusuku* became acceptable both to working-class and middle-class Africans.[24]

Ingom'ebusuku became the principal entertainment at church-oriented gatherings known as 'tea meetings', such as originated in the Cape in the 1870s. Initially, people bought tea and cakes, so as to hear others perform hymns, popular songs, or variety turns; but tea meetings subsequently became associated with alcohol and sex. Because of Caluza's brand of *ingom'ebusuku*, however, tea meetings were regularized into profitable entertainments; and choral songs, in styles influenced by ragtime and jazz, became endemic in working-class culture. This choral tradition still continues in Johannesburg and Durban; indeed, male-voice choral singing remains popular throughout much of Sub-Saharan Africa.

In the slums and slumyards of the 1920s, however, tea meetings were replaced by *shebeens* (illegal, non-white drinking shops), operated by female entrepreneurs, and these became the focus of urban social life. The *Abaqhafi* ('cultural driftwood') musicians hired to perform in the

[23] Coplan, *In Township Tonight*, 47, 61–2. [24] Ibid. 65–7, 72–5.

shebeens developed an urban style, known as *marabi*, a symbol of working-class solidarity. The style consisted, in essence, of 'ragged' tunes over a three-chord vamp, but also incorporated elements of *ingom'ebusuku* and traditional African, European, and North American musical styles. *Marabi* came to be based on a constantly reiterated four-bar harmonic underlay (chords I–IV–V–V). This underlay was not necessarily synchronized with the African melo-rhythms it supported, however; nor—in keeping with African musical tradition—did the various melo-rhythms enter simultaneously. Ex. 18.1 (after Coplan) illustrates the style.[25]

The influence of *marabi* (as a symbol of working-class solidarity) intensified after the showing of Donald Swanson's film, *The Magic Garden* (1950). This was a product of Sophiatown, a black community developed from freehold land, where black South Africans found the stability to develop a concerted township culture. *The Magic Garden* was the first South African film to use African actors on African locations; it featured, in particular, William Cele playing his own 'Penny-Whistle Blues' and 'Penny-Whistle Ragtime', on the streets of Johannesburg. Its success, and that of subsequent record releases, led to a surge in street music (penny whistles and home-made drums) performed by urban youth, protagonists of a genuinely African culture, in the tradition of the Ninevites and *Amalaita*. Gradually, home-made guitars, milk-tin rattles, and one-string basses made from tea chests came to augment the penny whistles and drums, in the performance of a jazz-influenced, street-music style, known as *kwela*. When saxophones replaced penny whistles, and drum kits replaced rattles, *kwela* jazz became another symbol of black urban identity.[26]

A 10-year-old, *kwela* penny-whistler was featured in a musical play from Sophiatown, *King Kong* (1959), composed, acted, and performed by black South Africans, scripted, produced, and directed by white South Africans. Blending African and Western music and dance traditions, it achieved widespread popularity in Johannesburg. When shown in London, however, *King Kong* was criticized as amateurish and politically insubstantial, and the score was altered to appeal to white taste. This annoyed black South Africans at home; but talented members of the cast—most notably the singer, Miriam Makeba, and the trumpeter, Hugh Masekela—stayed on and achieved celebrity status, outside South Africa.[27]

[25] Ibid. 106, 258–60. [26] Ibid. 157–60. [27] Ibid. 173–5.

Ex. 18.1

Ironically, it was to take a white US singer to bring South African music into the mainstream of Western popular music. Though controversial at the time, Paul Simon's collaboration with Ray Phiri and South African groups—most notably the *ingom'ebusuku* group, Ladysmith Black Mambazo—in his *Graceland* album (1986) had the effect of promoting black South African musicians in the West. A year after the album was released, Ladysmith Black Mambazo's album *Shaka Zulu* moved into the British album charts; and in 1987 the Zimbabwean group, Bhundu Boys, reached number one in the Independent charts of *Melody Maker* with their album *Shabini*; in the same year they appeared with Madonna at the Wembley Stadium in London.[28] During the 1990s performances by South African musicians have become increasingly evident in the Western recording market.

That African popular music continues to walk a tightrope between African heritage and Western assimilation is due, very largely, to the economic inequalities between Africa and the West. The deprivation caused by colonialism is still evident; and tragically severe political turbulence in Central Africa during the 1990s has decimated the music industry in this region. Recordings of African music are produced and promoted mainly by European and US companies, and their commercial success is determined by the tastes of a predominantly Western-buying public. Nevertheless, African 'crossover' styles sound more conspicuously 'African' than comparable styles in Asia sound 'Asian'. It remains to be seen whether an identifiably African—as opposed to African-American—style of music will survive the present need of African musicians to promote themselves in, and out of, a Western ambience; or whether an African-based recording industry, perhaps based in South Africa, will eventually succeed in disseminating African music worldwide.

North Africa and West Asia: Westernization

The effect of colonialism was markedly different in the Islamic areas of North Africa and West Asia from that in Sub-Saharan Africa. Until 1683, when a European army raised the Turkish seige of Vienna, the Ottoman Empire presented a conspicuous threat to Europe, rather than vice versa. Following this Turkish defeat, however, many countries of the Ottoman Empire adopted European technical, political, and philosophical ideas, and thus enabled Europe to gain economic control over their affairs during the latter part of the nineteenth century and, by 1920, political control over most of the Islamic heartland.[29]

As the Ottoman Empire disintegrated politically, and as constituent countries increasingly demanded independence from Ottoman rule,

[28] Stapleton and May, *African All Stars*, 220–2.

[29] *The Times Atlas of World History*, ed. Geoffrey Barraclough (London, 1989), 228.

new forms of trade and communication, largely funded by foreign capital, transformed much of the area. Turkey and Egypt, for example, developed rail networks, tramways, ports, banks, and water and electricity companies, providing ready markets for European goods. Such large-scale adoption of European systems undermined confidence in many aspects of indigenous traditional cultures; and this loss became especially evident in music, as élite Arabs, Turks, and Persians came to esteem European music more highly than their own.

As early as 1797, Sultan Selim III of Turkey founded an Italian-style opera house; himself a noted composer and *ney* (vertical-flute) player, he also introduced a new *makam*, akin to the European major scale, and commissioned the first notational system for Turkish music. In 1826 Salim's successor, Mahmut II, abolished the Janissaries (*yeni ceri:* 'new soldiers') and replaced the Janissary band of drums, shawms, and valveless trumpets with a band on European lines. (European bands, though created from Turkish models, were considered superior on account of their greater modernity.) As noted in Chapter 7, Giuseppi Donizetti (brother of Gaetano) was hired to direct the opera, and was known as 'Donizetti Pasha'. In 1882 Giuseppi's grandson attended a musical performance, given in front of the Sultan on a mixture of Turkish and European instruments, and noted that it began with an air from *Il trovatore*.[30] Turkish music became increasingly virtuosic; and new compositions, most notably those by Tanburi Cemil Bey (1871–1916), incorporated a melodic style with conspicuous sequences of triadic intervals. Bey introduced folk tunes—ostensibly in a *makam* but, in reality, in European style—to provide 'national' flavour.[31]

With the accession of Atatürk as President of the new Republic of Turkey, in 1923, Westernization was officially prescribed: Turks were required to wear European clothes; Arabic script was replaced by Roman script; the language was 'purified' of Arabic and Persian elements; and Turkish music was banned from the state-monopoly radio stations. In 1926 the Traditional Classical Music Conservatory in Istanbul was closed, and was replaced by one teaching Western music.[32] (It has, however, since been revived.)

[30] Karl Signell, 'The Modernisation Process in Two Oriental Music Cultures: Turkish and Japanese', *Asian Music*, 7/2 (1976), 73–4.

[31] Ibid. 75.

[32] Ibid. 76–8.

Ziya Gökalp, the principal architect of Turkish ideology in the early Republican period, considered the *makamlar* of Ottoman art music to be built on the 'irrational' structure of the 'quarter, eighth, and sixteenth tones' of Byzantine music. According to him, the 'real' Turkish music was that of the villages of Anatolia, which consisted of 'melodies, unfettered by rules, systems and techniques, of sincere songs which express the heart of the Turk'.[33] Atatürk himself rejected traditional Turkish art music as being 'insufficient for the sophisticated soul and feelings of the Turk',[34] and encouraged the collection of folk music, and its standardization into styles associated with the regional and provincial divisions of the Turkish state. It was expected that a synthesis of 'folk' and Western styles would lead to a new 'national' music; in the event, the 'folk', deprived of a musical style that accorded with their taste, tuned their radios not to the official Turkish radio stations but to stations in Egypt and the Lebanon. In 1948, in consequence, Arabic language, music, and films were officially banned.[35]

A similar process of Westernization began in Iran in 1862, when Emperor Nāsseraddin Shāh ordered the establishment of a military band, such as he had observed in Europe playing overtures, marches, polkas, and waltzes. A French musician, Alfred Lemair, was hired to turn a traditional ensemble of indigenous shawms, horns, trumpets, and percussion into a Western concert band. His work was so successful that, by the end of the nineteenth century, a music school in Teheran taught Western instruments and music theory.[36]

Westernization in Persia intensified after the accession of the Pahlavi dynasty in 1925. The music school (now a fully-fledged conservatoire) and a School of National Music were both state funded, and by the late 1930s a small symphony orchestra existed. Iranian composers subsequently began to study abroad, and then to compose in nationalist and modernist styles. By the 1970s the Teheran Symphony Orchestra consisted of 100 players, and newly built concert halls were hosting international artists; music departments were instituted in universities, and television beamed Western music at the populace. Pop, rock, jazz, and

[33] Martin Stokes, 'The Media and Reform: the Saz and Elektrosaz in Urban Folk Music', *British Journal of Ethnomusicology*, 1 (1992), 91–3.

[34] Signell, 'The Modernisation Process', 73–4.

[35] Stokes, 'The Media and Reform', 91–3.

[36] Hormoz Farhat, 'Western Musical Influences in Persia', *Musicological Annual*, xxvii (Ljubljana, 1991), 88–90.

Latin-American musical styles were widely disseminated; and, in their wake, the record and cassette industry marketed local pop music and hybrid love-songs that blended Persian modes with Western harmony.[37]

Egypt, likewise, espoused European musical models. The country's first modern contact with Europe occurred when Napoleon invaded the country in 1798; and during the nineteenth century both France and Britain invested heavily in the country's infrastructure. The inauguration of the Suez Canal, in November 1869, was preceded a few days earlier by the inauguration of the Cairo Opera House, with Verdi's *Rigoletto*. In 1871 the same opera house presented the première of Verdi's *Aida*. By the end of the nineteenth century, aristocrats—who had formerly patronized traditional music by maintaining private musical ensembles that performed in their palace courtyards—patronized the opera, as well as performances of ballets and musical plays, some adapted directly from European models.[38] By the 1960s and 1970s, Egyptian composers were composing symphonic works for the Cairo Symphony Orchestra.[39]

The desire to adopt Western cultural institutions as a perceived prerequisite of modernization was prompted by nationalistic feeling, which, in turn, was prompted by a sense of cultural inferiority in relation to the West. Traditional music was a significant element in this cultural Westernization; Islamic élites made a determined effort to 'modernize' their musical tradition, so that it might—as they saw it—gain parity with, or indeed precedence over, European music.

Mention was made in Chapter 7 of the Cairo Congress on Arab Music, held at the Academy of Oriental Music in 1932. The conference was sponsored by King Fu'ād of Egypt himself, 'in order to discuss all that is required to make [Arabic] music civilized, and to teach it and rebuild it on acknowledged scientific principles'.[40] According to the Director of the Academy, the Oriental Music Club had already been 'reviving and systematizing Arab music so that it will rise upon an artistic foundation,

[37] Farhat, 'Western Musical Influences', 92–4.

[38] Virginia Danielson, 'The Arab Middle East', in Peter Manuel, *Popular Musics of the Non-Western World* (New York: Oxford University Press, 1989).

[39] Ali Jihad Racy, 'Musical Aesthetics in Present-Day Cairo', *Ethnomusicology* (September 1982).

[40] Ali Jihad Racy, 'Historical Worldviews of Early Ethnomusicologists: An East–West Encounter in Cairo, 1932', in Stephen Blum, Philip V. Bohlman, and Daniel M. Neuman (eds.), *Ethnomusicology and Modern Music History* (Urbana, Ill.: University of Illinois Press, 1987), 69.

as Western music did earlier'. The king's cultural endeavours, he maintained, would 'bring the country to a zenith of cultural refinement and lead it to compete in the arena of civilized nations'.[41] The Congress on Arab Music was attended by ethnomusicologists from Europe, as well as from West Asia: Hindemith, Bartók, Curt Sachs, and Egon Wellesz were among the participants.

In an echo of problems besetting Greek musical theorists some 2,000 years earlier, when Aristoxenus postulated his 'Perfect Immutable System' of tetrachords (see p. 127), a 'Music Scale Committee' was established, and was required to determine a scalar model that could be adopted as a standard, systematic reference for Arab intonation. Although no such model could accurately cover the variety of existing modal tunings, the committee censured the prevalent use of pianos and Western wind instruments, as being unsuited to the performance of differing *maqāmāt*. Other Egyptians at the congress, however, contended that the piano could help standardize intonation, advance music education, and assist the future development of an 'Arab polyphony'. Many Egyptians believed that their history had reached a peak in the distant past, but that it had since been disrupted by 'decline' and 'stagnation'. Their beliefs prevailed. According to one Egyptian participant, to deprive oriental music of the benefits of tonally fixed instruments would 'gravely threaten the future of our music and even bring about its demise'.[42] Western staff notation was adopted, and Western theoretical models were applied to Arab musical theory. European-based conservatoires were then established to teach traditional music by means of notation, rather than through oral–aural transmission.[43]

The effects of the Arab Congress soon spread to other areas of North Africa. In Tunisia, for example, as in Egypt, musical traditions were preserved partly by aristocrats (who maintained private musical ensembles to perform in their courtyards), and partly by members of Sufi lodges. (The denigration, or proscription, of Sufism during the twentieth century—widespread throughout the Islamic world—contributed greatly to the demise of the classical tradition.) According to the Baron Rodolphe d'Erlanger, by 1917 Sufi lodges, and coffee houses (where traditional music was often played), had been superseded by bars and nightclubs as places of entertainment; and European instruments of

[41] Ibid. 70. [42] Ibid.

[43] Ali Jihad Racy, 'Musical Change and Commercial Recording in Egypt, 1904–1932', Dissertation (University of Illinois at Urbana-Champagne, 1977).

fixed pitch, such as the piano, harmonium, and fretted mandolin, had joined forces with traditional, non-tempered instruments. Moreover, 'the prince had abandoned his private ensemble for a brass band of foreign instruments which vainly blast out notes that grate on the ears'.[44] D'Erlanger subsequently attended the Cairo Congress, but so too did Tunisian musicians who espoused the ideal of integrating traditional Arab music into Westernized, urban society. (D'Erlanger lived in Tunisia from 1914 to his death in 1932, and dedicated himself to the revival of Tunisian music.)

In 1934 the Rashidya Institute was established in Tunisia for the purpose of preserving and promoting the *ma'lūf* (the Tunisian classical repertoire). A regular company of eighteen instrumentalists and seven vocalists was formed, but, because traditional heterophony proved impracticable in so large an ensemble, a *standard* version of each melody had to be formulated. During the 1940s the whole *ma'lūf* was transcribed into staff notation; following Tunisian Independence in 1956, the government published the complete *ma'lūf* in transcription as *The Tunisian Musical Heritage*, and established festivals to encourage its performance.[45]

A similar process of change took place in Morocco; indeed, many traditional musicians and conservatoire teachers came to believe that there were no 'neutral' intervals in Moroccan traditional music. The violin was introduced during the nineteenth century, and became the most important instrument in the Moroccan ensemble, both numerically and in timbre; in consequence, the sound of the Moroccan ensemble came to resemble that of the Egyptian film orchestra rather than that of the traditional *nawba* ensemble.[46]

In Morocco, as in Tunisia, a conservatory system was initiated in the 1930s to counteract the decline in knowledge of the repertoire; and oral transmission was gradually replaced by Western notation. Although new *maqāmāt* compositions are still composed, and conservatoires jealously guard their regional traditions, radio and records promote 'standardized' versions, thus eliminating the element of controlled improvisation at the heart of the *maqām* tradition.

[44] Cited in Ruth Davis, 'Links between the Baron Rodolphe D'Erlanger and the Notation of Tunisian Art Music', in *Ethnomusicology and the Historical Dimension: Papers Presented at the European Seminar in Ethnomusicology*, London, May 1986 (Philip Verlag, 1989), 51.

[45] Ruth Davis, 'Modern Trends in the Arab-Andalusian Music of Tunisia', *Maghreb Review*, 11/2 (1986), 134–44. See also 'Cultural Policy and the Tunisian *Ma'lūf*: Redefining a Tradition', *Ethnomusicology*, 41/1 (1997).

[46] Philip D. Schuyler, 'Moroccan Andalusian Music', *World of Music*, 20 (1978), 40–3.

Throughout North Africa, action to preserve the *maqām* tradition had the effect of undermining it.

North Africa and West Asia: Popular Musical Styles

The process of Westernization in North Africa and West Asia was initiated, and managed, by a wealthy élite, largely isolated from the mass of people who continued to live according to traditional Islamic ideals.[47] In Cairo, for example, the majority of the population could scarcely afford operatic entertainment; *their* musical fare was provided in coffee houses, or at weddings and communal religious occasions, by *mashāyikh* (storytellers, who had been trained to recite the Qur'ān). The repertoire of the *mashāyikh* comprised both religious and secular poetic genres, such as the *qasīda* and *muwashshah*; and many performers, particularly those linked to Sufi lodges, had a thorough command of the *maqāmāt.* They were adept in providing music for new texts, and came to be regarded as important custodians of Arabic culture.[48]

Famous *mashāyikh* became 'stars' of the burgeoning radio and recording industry. The most celebrated was the female singer Umm Kulthum: trained in Qur'ānic recitation during her childhood, her fame rested not only on the quality of her singing but also on her ability to articulate a text in accordance with traditional *maqām* practice. Her popularity became such that she was able to insist that her broadcasts be relayed live and from a concert hall, so that full-length performances would be put on air.[49]

In the early twentieth century, the *mashāyikh* usually performed without accompaniment; but during the 1920s and 1930s they increasingly adopted such Western instruments as clarinet, accordion, cello, string bass, and castanets. As ensembles of such instruments became popular on film, they grew in size, adding violins, saxophones, electric guitars, and electric keyboards. Western musical styles were then incorporated into the music: triadic passages appeared in melodic lines, for example; harmonizations emerged alongside traditional heterophonic

[47] J. M. Roberts, *Pelican History of the World* (London, 1988), 851.
[48] Danielson, 'The Arab Middle East', 184.
[49] Ibid. 148.

ensembles; and Latin American rhythms were incorporated into instrumental interludes. Only the distinctive nasal style of Islamic cantillation preserved an Arabic quality in popular song.

Both records and radio stimulated the performance of Arabic music in popular versions. Phonographs and records entered Egypt as early as the 1890s; and by 1929 some 725,000 records a year, mostly of 'Arabic' music, were being marketed.[50] Recordings offered high financial rewards to popular artists, but the restricted running time of the 78 r.p.m. record limited scope for improvisation, and encouraged new, easily produced genres. Although, during the 1930s, radio became the principal means of disseminating recordings, it was film that came to dominate, and profoundly alter, commercial Arabic music. Film songs tended to be short, in a variety of *maqāmāt*, and to be performed with little or no improvisation. Accompanying ensembles, augmented in particular by violins, came to number twenty or thirty players, modelled on those of Hollywood studios. Cairo-based music became popular throughout the Arabic world; indeed the threat to the Tunisian *ma'lūf* came not so much from European music as from Egyptian popular music, which had flooded the Tunisian record market and created a taste for Tunisian songs of inferior quality.

Records and radio, and exposure to Western light music, had a similar effect in Iran. The *tasnif*, an accompanied vocal genre (incorporated into the *dastgāh-hā* during the nineteenth century), became a popular ballad, composed in Persian modes, but following the ternary structure of Western songs, and sometimes including a harmonic underlay for a mixture of traditional and Western instruments. In this form, it was commonly known as *tarāne*. The *tarāne*'s length of three to four minutes was suited to the 78 r.p.m. record; but, when traditional *dastgāh-hā* performances were similarly reduced in length, fewer modes were used in performance, and many were eliminated. Moreover, the performance tempo was increased, so that more music could be included on the record. Classical music itself underwent considerable change: new songs were composed, many imitating Western love-songs, and programmes of traditional music became tailored to fit fifteen- or thirty-minute slots.[51]

During 1978–9 a popular assertion of both national and religious identity in Iran led to a revolution that conferred political power on the *Wali Faqih* (Theological Ruler). Institutions teaching Western music

[50] Danielson, 'The Arab Middle East', 145.

[51] Farhat, 'Western Musical Influences', 90–2.

were then closed, the Teheran Symphony was disbanded, and—in an attempt to eliminate pop and hybrid love-songs—no music at all was permitted on radio. (This was soon found to be unenforceable.) Such draconian measures have since been partly ameliorated; in particular, there has been renewed activity in traditional music, with the School of National Music back in full operation.[52] The clerical regime has not always been appreciated, even in Iran, but many Iranians were clearly sympathetic to the anti-Western sentiment that brought it to power. Nevertheless, Western music continues to be popular; the sale of pianos, for example, has risen sharply since the revolution, and the demand for private teaching has accelerated.

A popular reaction to Western values—though without inspiring political revolution—also occurred in Turkey. Already in the late nineteenth century, as the Ottoman Empire declined, musical patronage in Turkey had passed from the urban élite to an increasingly affluent merchant class, of non-Muslim Greeks, Armenians, and Jews, who established nightclubs and casinos, offering live musical entertainment. Musicians performed gypsy music and light-classical genres such as the *sarkī* (a pre-composed song on *maqām* principles with instrumental accompaniment). Also popular were imported genres: the *sirto* (derived from Greek island folk music) and the *longa* (adapted from Romanian gypsy music). Such genres still contribute to urban music-making.[53]

During the 1950s large-scale migration from rural to urban areas brought rural influence to urban music. Characteristic of a new, folk-influenced, style was the urban *türkü*, its irregular metres fitted (sometimes rhapsodically) about simple metres of four or eight beats, its melodic lines including 'neutral' intervals. The *türkü* was accompanied by the traditional *ney* (vertical flute) and *saz* (long-necked lute, now frequently used in its electrified form, *elektrosaz*), and also by Western instruments.

An important consequence of the banning of Arabic culture by the Turkish government (in 1948) was that commercial musicians began to imitate Arabic musical style. The new style—now known as 'Arabesk'—featured antiphonal vocal patterns (characteristic of some Arabic music), and a monophonic style of *saz* playing, inspired by the timbre of the *elektrosaz*. Encouraged by a surge of Islamic fundamentalism during the 1970s and 1980s, this Arab-inspired style became immensely

[52] Ibid. 94–5. [53] Manuel, *Popular Musics*, 163–4.

popular; it is estimated that, out of 200 million cassettes sold in Turkey in 1987, 150 million were of Arabesk.[54]

Throughout West Asia and North Africa, the esteem accorded Western arts by élite groups that formerly patronized performers of traditional music seriously weakened indigenous traditions. Essential subtleties of intonation and ornamentation were eliminated in the attempt to preserve repertoires in Western staff notation. Western 'concert-giving' styles changed the contexts in which professional musicians operated, while phonograph, radio, and cassette encouraged the creation of new urban styles. Throughout the core world of Islam, cultural identity in music came to be expressed as much through Islamized, Western pop styles as through the Islamic classical tradition that represents it fundamentally. In this respect, the musical *effect* of colonization has been similar to that in Sub-Saharan Africa.

The Indian Subcontinent

In the Indian Subcontinent, the circumstances that affect modernization and Westernization again differed, in many important respects, from those of other areas. Islam arrived in the subcontinent much later than in these other zones, preceding the advent of Europeans by a few centuries only. When it reached what is now Pakistan, North India, and Bangladesh, conversion—as in west and east Sub-Saharan Africa—was only partial; although Islam became the religion of the rulers and of much of the population, it was not absorbed by the autochthonous cultures.[55] In South India, the influence of Islam was relatively slight; in North India, the Hindustani musical style that emerged after the Islamic invasions was more distinctively Indian than Islamic.

British colonization in India (like Dutch colonization in Indonesia) arose from mercantile and agricultural interests, rather than from the investment interests that spurred Westernization among élite Egyptians, Iranians, and Turks. India was only accessible to Europeans following long sea voyages; colonial rule, therefore, could only be

[54] Cited in Stokes, 'The Media and Reform', 90.

[55] Harold Powers, 'Classical Music, Cultural Roots, and Colonial Rule: An Indic Musicologist looks at the Muslim World', *Asian Music* (Dec. 1980), 13.

effected from local power bases, secured by local rulers. By the second quarter of the nineteenth century, direct rule had expanded into metropolitan capitals, and was supported by a widespread, indigenous, ruling élite.[56] This system of control was, in broad terms, retained until the middle of the twentieth century.

The existence of indigenous ruling élites who valued and patronized the native arts was a crucial element in their survival. Throughout the independence movements of the twentieth century, the great musical traditions of India (as of Java) were powerfully linked with nationalist sentiment; after independence, they were accepted by the new ruling élites as an important indication of indigenous cultural attainment.[57] The élite castes of India never considered native musical traditions to be inferior to those of the West; nor did they create institutions for the performance of Western music.

For centuries, Indian music had been supported by a canon of theoretical treatises, and the canon itself had been supported by generations of master–disciple teaching. Under Western influence, much of the Carnatic repertoire was transcribed into notation, but such notation was used more as a tool for teaching than as a means of preserving a memorized music. Oral–aural transmission was understood to be intrinsic to musical style,[58] and the great musical traditions of India survived through the early decades of the twentieth century.

In more recent decades, these traditions have been exposed to change at a pace such as to affect radically their styles, and the retention of performance skills is by no means assured. Their complexity demands long and arduous training, and they are not readily adaptable to conservatoire methods of teaching; mastery in performance still depends largely on the kind of constant observation and imitation that occurs only within the *guru shishya paramparā* (master–disciple succession). New social and economic conditions are not conducive to the many years of living with a guru that this tradition entails; many gurus have, in any event, become globe-trotting superstars, unable to devote full attention to their disciples. Because, in general, the *guru shishya paramparā* works effectively only within musical castes, genuine musical accomplishment has become more than ever a matter of family tradition. Young adherents of the classical traditions are, increasingly, amateur, and many turn to forms of light-classical music less demanding in execution. Indian classical music only survives, in the 1990s, amongst a

[56] Ibid. 13. [57] Ibid. 19–20. [58] Ibid. 15–17.

plethora of new, popular styles, of which the connection with the canonical tradition is increasingly attenuated.

Such new popular styles were first engendered by the recording industry, introduced into India in 1902; their output increased dramatically with the advent of the film industry in 1912. Reflecting the inseparability of music and theatre in Asian traditions, music became intrinsic to Indian film—between 1931 and 1954 only two commercial films were made without songs—and films eventually came to be judged as much by their songs as by their scenarios and actors.[59]

Initially, songs were sung by actor-vocalists, and the incorporation of traditional songs enabled music to combine with dance and drama in traditional style; indeed, film songs in both folk and classical styles reinforced Indian nationalism, prior to Independence.[60] Subsequently, however, promotion both of songs and of 'star' actors led to the songs being recorded separately by 'playback singers', so that actors could appear to break into song at any point, or location, in the drama. By the 1960s film songs had lost their originality; films became stereotyped and predictable, contrasting with the diversity of folk arts throughout the subcontinent.[61]

A major influence on the songs of the early films was the light-classical, Urdu poetic genre, *ghazal*. In its 'filmi' version, the style of *ghazal* was much altered: improvisation was largely eliminated; orchestral interludes were interspersed between verses; and the strophic structure was replaced by one in which male and female singers sang antiphonally.[62] *Qawāli* singing (Sufi devotional music) also found its way into films, and the forthright style of singing gave way to a crooning style, reflecting the romantic image of the 'filmi' male hero.[63] Moreover, the original accompaniment of *dholak*, harmonium, *tablā*, and hand-clapping was usually augmented by Western string and wind instruments; melodies came to be predominantly diatonic with harmonic underlays; and the literary emphasis was placed on erotic, rather than devotional, aspects of the text.

[59] Manuel, *Popular Musics*, 172–9.

[60] Alison E. Arnold, 'Aspects of Production and Consumption in the Popular Hindi Film Song Industry', *Asian Music*, 24/1 (1993), 122.

[61] Manuel, *Popular Musics*, 180–2.

[62] Ibid.

[63] Regula Qureshi, '"Muslim Devotional": Popular Religious Music and Muslim Identity under British, Indian, and Pakistani Hegemony', *Asian Music*, 24/1 (1993), 111.

From the 1940s onwards, *regional* film-music styles developed, and folk styles were incorporated into Hindi films. In Gujarat, for example, the folk-dance forms of *rās* and *garba* were employed. More commonly, however, local folk styles were syncretized with elements of Western disco music, to such an extent that the only remaining indigenous feature was the Indian vocal style. Conversely, film music was often incorporated into regional folk music: wedding celebrations, for example, came to include film songs, accompanied by drums, harmonium, amplified zithers, and electric keyboard.[64]

Until the 1970s, outside the cinema, film music was only propagated through radio and records. Cassettes transformed this situation. They first appeared in the early 1970s but by the mid-1980s cassette sales accounted for some 95 per cent of the recorded-music market.[65] The low production costs of cassette technology enabled small cassette companies to challenge the dominance of the corporate music industry in general, and that of the Bombay film-music style, in particular.

One effect of the cassette industry was the popularization of a new cross over style of *ghazal*, independent of the cinema. Abandoning the influence of disco music for a style that incorporated sentimental lyrics and languid tunes, the new *ghazal* gradually lost any connection with its semi-classical predecessor, and adopted a simple form of Urdu, and a non-percussive accompaniment. Other forms of devotional music, based on Hindu *bhakti* traditions, adopted similar characteristics. The *bhajan*, which in 'filmi' versions had generated many hits, became an outstandingly successful pop genre in its own right, bringing popular religion and popular music into convenient unity of purpose.

Perhaps the most significant aspect of the burgeoning cassette industry has been the development of recordings of *regional* folk styles, which, by the early 1990s, accounted for between 40 and 50 per cent of all cassette sales.[66] Such cassettes were assembled, in general, from short items, with instrumental groups playing precomposed interludes between verses; but the cassette industry also enabled more extended regional genres to be recorded, as well as genres in regional languages.

The impact of Western classical music in India has been slight in comparison with that in many other countries; but Indian musicians—in India itself as well as in the Indian diaspora—commonly explore

[64] Manuel, *Popular Musics*, 179, 185.

[65] Peter Manuel, 'The Cassette Industry and Popular Music in North India', *Popular Music* (May 1991), 190–6.

[66] Ibid. 198.

syncretic styles that involve jazz or contemporary Western music. Skilled classical sitarists are to be heard mixing the clichés of jazz with the *pakad*s and *alankar*s of Indian music; skilled *Kathak* dancers are to be found performing in the style of Martha Graham, to the beat of American pop music; and, increasingly, Indian and European dancers are to be seen working alongside each other. Nevertheless, Hindu musicians still regard music as a sacred art, and performers seek divine blessing before and after a performance. India remains a land of contradictions—of spirituality and commercialism, tradition and modernity—among which the canonical musical styles appear still to be inalienable components.

Java

In Indonesia, as in India, effective colonial rule (in this case, by the Dutch), depended upon secure local power bases, in alliance with local rulers; and, again as in India, their patronage of traditional music was a crucial factor in its survival. Javanese traditional gamelan styles are still propagated as entertainment, and as an important element in village life, by professional and amateur groups; but popular-music styles have reduced the once-pervasive popularity of the traditional gamelan.

The Dutch in Indonesia (unlike the British in India) did not attempt to foster a Europeanized middle class. In Java (and in Jakarta, in particular), the emergence of a cosmopolitan, urban proletariat, combined with a long tradition of village-based, musical ensembles, caused new, popular-music genres to identify with working-class culture. The cassette industry, in particular, led to the formation of an eclectic range of musical styles.[67]

An early intimation of a developing, syncretic musical culture was provided by *kroncong*, a popular-music genre that originated among trading communities developed by Portuguese sailors during the sixteenth century. When, during the seventeenth century, the Dutch ousted the Portuguese from Java and the Malay peninsula, and established Batavia (present-day Jakarta) as the headquarters of the Dutch East India Company, the city developed into a leading commercial centre, with a racially mixed community.[68] By the nineteenth century,

[67] Manuel, *Popular Musics*, 207–8. [68] Ibid. 208.

kroncong had become popular in the lower-class neighbourhoods of Jakarta; and during the twentieth century it continued to develop as a street and restaurant music.[69] As texts became standardized in Indonesian, *kroncong* became popular over a wider geographical and social range; by the 1930s Indonesian film-makers were using it as a means of reaching the mass of Indonesians, and by the middle of the twentieth century it had become a pan-Indonesian phenomenon.[70]

The term *kroncong* refers to a five-string instrument, resembling the ukulele. By the 1930s a typical *kroncong*-ensemble comprised *kroncong*, guitar, banjo, violin, cello, and bass viol, to which transverse flute, viola, and celesta were sometimes added. The vocal lines were sung in free metre, within a basically diatonic scale; the plucked instruments furnished Western-style harmonies; and violin and flute performed quasi-improvisational melodies, sometimes in heterophony with the vocal line.[71]

In the middle years of the twentieth century, as *kroncong* spread to Central Java, its texts made use of regional languages, and its music was influenced by the gamelan. Under these influences, the genre gained in respectability. Texts and melodic lines then began to reflect the Javanese tradition of *tembang*, in which the verbal meaning of written poetic texts was apparent only when embellished in specific styles of song.[72] The music acquired a colotomic, polyphonic texture: the plucked cello imitated the style of the *kendang* (drum); the violin recalled the heterophonic playing of the *rebāb* (spike fiddle); the guitar reproduced the melodic figurations of the *gambang* instruments (chime metallophones); and the *kroncong* itself played staccato chords on off-beats, in imitation of the *ketuk* (single 'kettle' gong).[73]

A livelier genre of syncretic popular music was *orkes melayu*, which used elements from Indian film music and Arab urban music. During the nationalist rule of Sukarno (1949–65), the style was modernized, and used by film-makers as an antidote to Western pop music. With the accession to power of General Suharto, and a more open policy towards the West, rock music began to displace *melayu* as the preferred popular style. An attempt was then made to foster a new, pan-Indonesian style that would blend *orkes melayu* with imported styles. The result was

69 Martin Hatch, 'Popular Music in Indonesia', in Firth (ed.), *World Music*, 54–5.
70 Manuel, *Popular Musics*, 209.
71 Hatch, 'Popular Music', 55.
72 Ibid. 49.
73 Manuel, *Popular Musics*, 209.

dangdut, a genre that by the mid-1980s had become popular in Malaysia as well as throughout Indonesia, as film and dance music, and as an expression of youthful attitudes.[74]

Dangdut took its name, onomatopoeically, from a characteristic rhythmic pattern, that included a low-pitched drum stroke on the fourth beat, and a high-pitched stroke on the first beat, of a four-beat bar. (This pattern is now usually employed in pairs of half-beats, starting on the half-beat before the third beat, or *on* the first beat, or in both places.) Initially, *dangdut* ensembles consisted of instruments such as Indian flutes, *tablā* (the *dangdut* drum), acoustic guitar, mandolin, and tambourine; but electric guitars, pianos, and organs soon complemented or replaced these instruments. During the mid-1970s, synthesizers were added to the ensemble, and the lyrics began to incorporate social criticism, as well as moral teaching, based on Islamic doctrine. The spread of *dangdut* was paralleled by the spread of cheap cassettes; and, by the end of the 1970s, around half the new cassettes produced in Indonesia were *dangdut*.[75] In the 1990s, *dangdut* is most frequently produced as disco music, and remains popular, in Malaysia as well as Indonesia. It is complemented by *nusantara*, a pan-Malay genre that incorporates elements of rock music and indigenous vocal style, and combines traditional and Western instruments.

Java has a long history of cultural assimilation, and gamelan instruments are sometimes mixed with instruments originating in other parts of the world. In Jakarta, a symphony orchestra, electrified gamelans, Western pop music, pop genres evolving directly from gamelan instruments and techniques, and dance styles that mix Western techniques with traditional martial arts, are all to be encountered. A similar eclecticism pertains throughout the island, though respect for tradition remains strong. Traditional genres no longer occupy the dominant place in Javanese music-making that they once did; nevertheless the gamelan is an entrenched symbol of Javanese culture, and its increasing adoption in Western countries can only enhance its durability.

Bali

In the neighbouring island of Bali, traditional music-making still retains its central place in village life. Bali is no

[74] Manuel, *Popular Musics*, 210–11. [75] Hatch, 'Popular Music', 56–8.

longer quite the tropical paradise described by Western artists who first savoured its beauty: the German painter, Walter Spies, whose introduction of Western painting techniques led to a renaissance in Balinese art and who created the *kecak* dance for a German film company; or the American composer, Colin McPhee, who composed music influenced by gamelan techniques, and who documented traditional Balinese music styles for posterity, before they were swamped by *kebyar*. Much of Bali's southern coastline has become swathed in the crass commercialism attendant upon tourism; the specialist craft villages that punctuate the interior landscape display intricate artefacts of formula-ridden similitude; and exuberant music and dance styles, divorced from their natural contexts, are presented nightly for visitors, and tailored to a limited concentration span. Alongside the 'gamelanization' of tourists, the perpetuation of animist traditions can seem curiously incongruous.

Oddly, however, the essential spirit of Bali appears relatively untouched by such onslaughts. The Balinese still like to believe that they are the blessed tenants of a magic land inhabited by gods and *leyak*s: they remain inseparable from their religion. Village compounds still maintain their private temples; and even the most Westernized youths will be sure to place offerings regularly at the shrines of their ancestors. Such youths may well be rock-music enthusiasts, but they are also likely to have had experience on the village gamelan or to be skilled in dance. Balinese art does not aspire to 'greatness': it is essentially functional. To this extent, all Balinese *have* to be artists.

It may be no accident that two countries where music and dance traditions have survived in particular intensity, and where Western classical music is relatively little appreciated—India and Bali—both espouse forms of Hinduism; this polytheistic religion appears to incorporate the flexibility required for the accommodation of a wide spectrum of spiritual and material needs. The performing arts of Bali survive *in context* more vigorously than do those of India. Three factors contribute to this: the music depends on group participation more than on individual virtuosity; the representational art of dance and the non-representational art of music are virtually inseparable; and the parameters of music and dance, determined by the cooperative nature of the performance and its ritual associations, encourage and restrain individuality in equal measure.

Many Westerners have mourned the passing of old gamelan styles, now replaced by *kebyar*; nevertheless, the sudden island-wide adoption of this vigorous style, after 1915, undoubtedly contributed to the survival of Balinese traditions. Though based on traditional structures, *kebyar* had become sufficiently flexible to accommodate new ideas, while its pyrotechnic virtuosity placed it firmly in the twentieth century.[76] By the middle decades of the century, *kebyar* became somewhat stereotyped; and the years between 1940 and 1965 were dominated by war and political turmoil. Thereafter, President Sukarno, himself partly Balinese, encouraged new, nationalistically oriented compositions. Such a move was hardly compatible with the chimerical nature of Balinese arts; but it led to a renaissance of creative activity, stimulated by the foundation of a High School (SMKI), and College (STSI, formerly ASTI), for performing arts. These institutions form part of an Indonesia-wide system of campuses, entrusted with the preservation of old styles, the creation of new works, and the encouragement of academic research. Under their influence, many Balinese composers now look to older models for inspiration.

Balinese arts remain restricted in *scale*. Temples are built and rebuilt largely according to a traditional pattern that blends harmoniously with the ecological and architectural environment: they do not obtrude in either style or scale. Similarly, the performing arts have not developed élite or grandiose traditions. Gamelans vary in quality and composition, and in the accomplishment of their players; at the annual gamelan competition the performance teams are highly competitive. Nevertheless, all gamelans belong to the same communal tradition: they are essentially village-based. Musicians trained at STSI do not usually aspire to become jet-set virtuosi, nor to become 'crossover' rock stars. Rather, they see it as their duty to assist and enliven music-making throughout the island; they teach new compositions to village gamelan players, and thus ensure that the tradition does not ossify. Yet the essential parameters of the tradition appear not to alter; the sheer noisiness of *gamelan gong kebyar*, for example, discourages experimentation with non-Balinese instruments, or with electronic equipment.

Certain in-built restraints have contributed to the unusual survival of traditional, performing arts in Bali. Because of the importance still attached to religion, dance genres—of which music is an inseparable aspect—invariably involve (in one guise or another) the interplay between good and evil, and the balancing of extremes that lies at the heart of Bali's harmonious village life. This limits the scope for innovation. And because all but the most blatantly tourist-oriented

[76] Michael Tenzer, *Balinese Music* (Berkeley, Singapore: Periplus, 1991), 24–5.

performances take place, if not in a village temple, in a *bale banjar* (meeting hall in the form of an open pavilion), or palace courtyard, the *space* around which the gamelan is positioned (on three sides) is usually restricted. Moreover, the individually idiosyncratic tuning systems of the resounding metal instruments are not conducive to blending with Western instruments; and the instruments lend themselves as naturally to the 'stratified' polyphony of the music as does Balinese architecture to its verdant landscape. Taken together, these circumstances greatly discourage the intrusion of such alien elements as stage scenery, modern trap drums, or saxophones.

How long can this condition survive? Probably for as long as spiritual values continue to influence material values, and as long, therefore, as music continues to fulfil an *actively* social purpose, subsuming its usefulness as a form of entertainment, or symbol of nationalism. Economically, Bali is a relatively poor country, and its people, like any other on earth, seek greater prosperity and material convenience. Only time will tell whether materialism, already disfiguring tourist areas, will erode the unusual degree of social cohesion, reflected in music, that characterizes Balinese village life.

Mainland South East Asia

Notwithstanding the example of Bali, there is widespread correlation between the retention of traditional arts and the presence of economic deprivation. For most of the South East Asian mainland, the post-1945 era has been appallingly turbulent. Of the countries north of Malaysia, Thailand alone, having avoided colonization, did not have to fight for independence; Vietnam, Laos, and Cambodia did so, only to be devastated, subsequently, by civil war, and by US intervention in the area. (Cambodia and Laos gained independence in 1953, Vietnam in 1954.) Burma, at the time of writing, remains under the control of a brutal junta.[77] Remarkably, however, many artistic systems, both traditional and Western, have survived this devastation.

In Cambodia, Vietnam, and Laos, during some ten years of relative calm between the gaining of independence and the start of US bombing

[77] See Bertil Linter, *Outrage: Burma's Struggle for Democracy* (Hong Kong: Review Publishing Company, 1989).

raids on North Vietnam (in 1964), foundations were laid for a revival of traditional music and for the development of Western music. In Cambodia, where the French had established an *École des Arts Cambodgiens* as early as 1917, the court dance troupe was re-established as the Royal Cambodian Ballet, betokening revived Khmer royal power; its establishment stimulated a widespread revival of traditional arts.[78] In Laos (where likewise the French had encouraged traditional arts, to encourage nationalistic feeling in the face of pan-Thai nationalism), traditional music and theatre forms were cultivated as 'national' arts; the *khaen* was adopted as a Lao 'national' instrument; and a National School of Music and Dance opened in Luang Phrabang in 1959.[79] In Vietnam, a modernization programme included the founding of the Hanoi Conservatory of Music (in 1956), with departments in both Western and traditional music. Talented performers of Western music were sent to various musical centres within the Soviet Union for advanced study, and many have taught at the Hanoi Conservatory since their return.

In Thailand, paradoxically, freedom from any colonial yoke had the effect of discouraging retention of traditional performance practice. Many of the Chakra kings and princes took an interest in classical music and dance, but the classical arts were largely confined to the court, the main patron of the performers. Thus when democracy supplanted absolute monarchy in 1932, Thailand was free to advance the speed of Westernization, and its classical arts declined. In recent years, however, as Thailand has developed economic dominance within the area, traditional arts have been re-emphasized as a symbol of 'national' pride and identity. The Department of Fine Arts supports a traditional music and dance ensemble that plays for royal and civic occasions, and at the National Theatre; and universities increasingly support music departments offering both Western and Thai music to prospective music teachers. Thai music forms part of the school curriculum.

Although modernization in Thailand brought about a considerable degree of acculturation to features of Western culture, not until the 1990s was there any significant interest in Western classical music, previously only exemplified in military bands. A new concert hall in Bangkok now attracts visits from international Western musicians and

[78] Tim Doling and Philip Soden, *Arts Indo China Cultural Development Report: Cambodia* (Hong Kong: Arts Indo China, 1992), 17.

[79] Katherine Bond and Kingsavanh Pathammavong, 'Contents of Dontrii Lao Deum: Traditional Lao Music', *Selected Reports in Ethnomusicology* (1992), 138, 145.

ensembles; fledgling conservatoires in major cities provide tuition in instrumental skills; Western music is taught in many university music departments; young Thais achieve advanced instrumental skills; and a nascent symphony orchestra exists in Bangkok. Western classical music appears about to supersede Thai classical music in popularity, though neither is greatly conspicuous in Thai life. Few temples, for example, maintain traditional orchestras, preferring to hire players for the ritual music required to be performed at cremations. It is popular styles, both Western and syncretic, that command overwhelming attention.

Thai songs first combined with Western musical characteristics during the 1930s, in a genre known as *sakon* ('Western' or 'modern'), which has since become the major urban, syncretic, popular-music style. The melodies remain largely pentatonic, and are sung with Thai vocal inflections; but the performance style is influence by rock music, and the music may incorporate Latin American rhythms. *Luk tung*, by contrast, developed as a rural style, and retains a rustic, folk character. It, likewise, features a predominantly pentatonic melodic structure; but its texts are less sentimental than those of *sakon*, and are performed in a melismatic, ornamented vocal style, accompanied by simple triadic harmonies, played on a blend of Western and indigenous instruments. *Luk tung* is often danced in the style of *ram wong* (to dance in a circle), a form of social dancing that became popular during the 1930s (as also in Cambodia (see p. 650)). *Sakon* and *luk tung* are now popular in both urban and rural areas; and the need for Thailand's flourishing record industry to promote apparently original styles of popular music has led to the development of a host of new genres and sub-genres.[80]

In fashionable clubs, restaurants, and hotels, however, Western pop music is the principal attraction; and tastes appear to be as ephemeral as they are throughout the West. During the 1980s, British DJ's set the fashion; and during the same period, Japanese *karaoke* came and went. Now, in the early 1990s, in the affluent venues of Bangkok, it is Western pop music, flamboyantly performed by Westerners, that appeals to status-conscious, newly rich Thais; such groups are expected to perform a mixture of new music and 'top twenty' hits, from the 1960s, 1970s, and 1980s.[81] In a country where economic advancement has led to huge

[80] Pamela Myers-Moro, *Thai Music and Musicians in Contemporary Bangkok* (Berkeley and Los Angeles: University of California Press, 1993), 7.

[81] Ross Blaufarb, 'Foreign Bands Boom the New Trend in Thailand's Expanding Nightclub Scene', *Asiabeat* (Hong Kong, Feb. 1993), 73–7.

disparities of wealth, Western commercial values appear gradually to be corroding traditional cultural systems and values.

Such is not, as yet, the case in Vietnam, Laos, or Cambodia, where economic regeneration has, until recently, been prevented by political turmoil. For each of these countries, the America–Vietnam war, and its bloody aftermath, have had calamitous consequences; and the differing musical environments that each has developed can be fully appreciated only in the light of recent history.

Between 1965 and 1968, US B52 bombers flew some 350,000 sorties over North Vietnam; many areas of central Vietnam were then subjected to chemical defoliants, and to carpet-bombing. In 1975 North Vietnamese, victorious over the USA, but in contravention of the terms of the Paris ceasefire agreement of 1973, invaded and overpowered Saigon (renaming it Ho Chi Minh City), and reunified the country.[82] In 1977, following encroachments on its territory by the Khmer Rouge, Vietnam invaded Cambodia and instituted a new government there. Because that invasion was backed by Russia, and because China supported the Khmer Rouge, China mounted a punitive invasion of Vietnam in 1979, leading to a steep rise in the numbers of 'boat-people' attempting to emigrate. Vietnam was then supported financially by Russia, until the Soviet Union collapsed in 1989. This, and the refusal of the USA to establish trade relationships, led to economic ruin. Subsequently, a more open policy towards the free market, and a relaxation of US trade restrictions, have encouraged economic and cultural regeneration.

Because gifted Vietnamese performers of Western music were able to study in the eastern bloc until the collapse of the Soviet Union, many skilled musicians exist in Vietnam, though without suitable performance outlets. A National Symphony Orchestra came into being in Hanoi in the early 1980s but, in the mid-1990s, is only just beginning to acquire suitable instruments, other equipment, and rehearsal space. At the Hanoi Conservatory, the present emphasis is on the teaching of Western music; but traditional music is also taught, and the conservatory is largely responsible for the preservation of traditional performance skills. Despite chronic inadequacies in both plant and equipment, students from the Hanoi Conservatory have at various times between 1980 and 1992 won prizes in international competitions.

[82] Justin Wintle, *Vietnam's Wars* (London: Weidenfeld & Nicolson, 1991), 134. Some two million to three million Vietnamese lost their lives as a result of hostilities between 1964 and 1975.

The Hanoi Conservatory has also produced many of Vietnam's foremost traditional musicians; and its teachers and students perform as soloists in traditional music ensembles, and in theatre orchestras. Much of the traditional repertoire has survived, through oral–aural tradition, and performances on radio and in concert still conform to traditional tuning systems. Westernization of traditional music is relatively unobtrusive. Nevertheless, it is the modernized versions of traditional music theatre that appeal most widely (see pp. 318–19).

Laos, a country of some 4 million people—as opposed to Vietnam's 70 million—suffered disproportionately during the American–Vietnam war, experiencing (during 1968 and 1969) no less than 378,000 B52 sorties.[83] When the communist Pathet Lao achieved power in 1975—their opposition to a government controlled by a French-educated élite had brought Laos into the war—US financial aid was withdrawn, leaving Laos as one of the poorest countries in the world.

One effect of government by the Lao People's Revolutionary Party has been that many of the Lao performing arts traditions survive, and are supported by state-run, centralized bodies. In Vientiane, for example, there exist (at the time of writing) a *Lam Luang* Troupe, a Drama Troupe, a National Dance and Music Ensemble, a Puppet Troupe, and a National College of Dance and Music (transferred from Luang Phrabang in 1975), all under the aegis of the Ministry of Culture. In theory, the performing groups exist for the purpose of supporting, through touring, surviving *lam* traditions in the countryside—traditions that are rapidly being eroded by access to television and the availability of cassette tapes. In practice, although the Ministry of Culture is eager to promote and advance all these enterprises, it lacks the funding to do so.

The Lao National College of Music and Dance is housed in minimal temporary accommodation, much of it without windows or doors. In these circumstances, dance students fare rather better than music students. The dance curriculum now includes Western classical ballet as well as Lao Folkloric and Classical Dance, and the college contributes positively to the retention of traditional dance forms. Music instruction ostensibly includes Western music, in addition to Lao traditional music and 'popular music'; there are teachers of Western strings, voice, and jazz, trained in East Europe or in Vietnam. There is little evidence of successful teaching, however, made almost impossible by the humid,

[83] Tim Doling and Philip Soden, *Arts Indo China Cultural Development Report: Laos* (Hong Kong: Arts Indo China, 1992).

cacophonous environment, and the lack of properly fitted instruments. The teaching of *lam* is not even attempted, since it is regarded as an art that can be transmitted only through family and community tradition.[84]

An ambitious project for a new National College of Arts, incorporating a *cité des arts* and estimated at over US $9 million, is currently being coordinated by UNESCO. Plans have been drawn up, though funding has yet to be secured. Should this project materialize, with a national *lam luang* troupe to present model performances, in a fully equipped modern auditorium, it is open to question whether *lam khu* and *lam luang* will still be performed in villages, or whether they will become antiquarian forms of entertainment, striving for attention in a sea of Western light-classical and popular genres, and modernized traditional classics. The *khaen* is already yielding to the accordion in many places. Laotian traditional arts are closely related to religious custom, and much may depend upon the extent to which Buddhism and animism continue to condition daily life.

Of the three countries misleadingly termed 'Indochina' (by the French), Cambodia has suffered the most since 1945. Prince Sihanouk, placed on the throne by the French in 1941 (during the Japanese occupation), who subsequently used his perceived status as god-king to secure a popular mandate, maintained his country's neutrality until 1966, but at the expense of alienating left-wing opponents, whom he labelled 'Khmer Rouge'. In 1965 he terminated diplomatic relations with the USA, and permitted the establishment of communist guerrilla bases along the country's borders.[85] In 1969 US President Nixon (secretly, and without Congressional approval) initiated a four-year campaign of 'carpet-bombing' in Cambodia; in 1970 US troops invaded Cambodia, embroiled the country in war, and made some two million Cambodians homeless.[86]

When the Khmer Rouge, under Pol Pot, assumed power in 1975, its leaders instituted a campaign aimed at transforming Cambodia into a Maoist agrarian cooperative. In the process, over a million people—from a population of some eight million—died. Among them were an estimated 90 per cent of the arts community, and the majority of the

[84] Information collected by author.

[85] William Shawcross, *Sideshow: Kissinger, Nixon, and the Destruction of Cambodia* (New York: Simon & Schuster, 1979), 49, 64.

[86] Ibid. 19–35, 399.

country's 70,000 monks. Most of the temples were destroyed. The Fine Arts College, the National Theatre, and the National Museum were abandoned; the librarians of the National Library were executed, and the books thrown into the street. The former Royal Cambodian Ballet, with its long history of court patronage, lost most of its members. The entire education system was dismantled. The calendar was set at 'Year Zero'; currency was abolished; and postal services halted. In 1979 the calendar was *re*-set to universal norms, however, when the Vietnamese ousted the Khmer Rouge. Although Khmer Rouge guerrillas continued virulent harassment, they could not prevent democratic elections in 1993, and these led to an uneasy political alliance, with Sihanouk as constitutional monarch.

Since 1979, great energy has been expended on reconstructing educational and training systems: at the time of writing, an estimated one-fifth of the population receives some education. Both traditional and Western music are taught at the University of Fine Arts (originally the *École des Arts Cambodgiens*). Theoretically, the university incorporates a specialist primary and secondary school; enrolments, however, are few, and attendance is irregular; expertise and equipment are exiguous; and the buildings are wholly inadequate. A National Theatre Company was established in Phnom Penh, in 1980, for the performance of traditional dance drama; this was followed by a Bassac Troupe and a Folkloric Troupe. More recently, there has been a determined effort to reconstruct the Royal Ballet, and the revived company undertook a foreign tour in 1989. Continuing political instability and economic impoverishment have, however, prevented the continued development of such initiatives.

Reconstruction of traditional arts has been hampered by the brutal fact that only a few experienced traditional artists remain alive. A classical dance company, founded by the Ministry of Culture in the 1960s, disappeared under the Khmer Rouge. In Siem Reap, music and dance groups were once attached to the Provincial Bureau of Culture, but the groups are non-functional. Siem Reap was home to the last remaining *sbek thomm* (large leather puppet) troupe; it owned 150 puppets,[87] but the skill of puppet-making is now in near-terminal decline.

In Kompong Cham, north-east of Phnom Penh, a troupe was instituted to perform *lakhon bassac* and a reconstructed form of *lakhon apei*;

[87] Sam-Ang Sam, 'The Floating Maiden in Khmer Shadow Play: Text, Context, and Performance', *Selected Reports in Ethnomusicology* (1992), 119.

but lack of adequate performance space, coupled with the emergence of a generation unused to live theatre, caused the troupe to perform only *lakhon bassac*, now usually presented from the back of an old truck.[88]

Traditional skills may have been eroded, but a modernized version of a traditional dance-music style, *roan vung* ('dance in a circle'), is widely popular. The melodies are based on the anhemitonic pentatonic scale, and are performed in traditional Khmer vocal style; the distinctive rhythmic style is supported by an underlay of simple Western harmonies, performed by lead, rhythm, and bass guitar, electric keyboard, and drum set. More vigorous than the *luk tung* of Thailand, *roan vung*—as recorded abroad—is to be heard in public places throughout Cambodia, and purveys a strong sense of Khmer cultural identity.

Cambodian traditional arts are among the most venerable in mainland South East Asia; Cambodians with knowledge of these skills, now living abroad, lend support to the reconstruction of their country's arts. Many charitable organizations direct their efforts towards Cambodia's homeless children, and encourage them to acquire traditional performance skills. Khmer artistic traditions may yet be revitalized, in the land of their origin.

One advantage of being late to undergo modernization is that there exists a chance to learn from others' mistakes; to achieve material improvement without loss of the spiritual values that contribute to cultural identity. Vietnam, Laos, Cambodia, and Burma stand at a junction, between tragedy and hope. Traditional performing arts have been preserved, and those of each country retain distinguishing characteristics. Economic regeneration seems assured, as the Asia–Pacific region secures dominance in world trade. While foreign investors hover round the ailing economies of South East Asia, opportunity exists to ensure that increasing modernization and Westernization do not eradicate still-relevant, traditional customs that contribute, so productively, to harmonious living and to a sense of cultural belonging.

China

It is a measure of the strength that a civilization draws from its hallowing through time that so much of what is distinct-

[88] Information provided by Som Kim Chuor, Director of Kampong Cham Provincial Bureau of Culture, and kindly passed on by Tim Doling.

ively Chinese has survived the terrible events suffered by Chinese during the twentieth century. Few countries have suffered so much self-inflicted destruction during this century as has China.

When Mao Zedong achieved victory over Chiang Kai-shek in 1949, the result was the replacement of one form of repression by another. Music was consciously manipulated to serve the needs of the state—as, in very different fashion, it had been since the time of Confucius. One of Mao's first acts, after declaring the People's Republic of China, was to establish an All-China Association of Music Workers. Thereupon, a committee was formed for the Improvement of Folk-songs and Balladry; and a Ministry of Culture was established to be responsible to the State Council for music and all the arts. Local bureaux of culture were set up throughout the country. As earlier in Stalinist Russia, the texts of regional folk-songs were revised, and their tunes furnished with Western harmonies, to encourage mass singing and to induce positive attitudes towards revolutionary aims. Professional musicians were sent to live among workers and peasants, to foster amateur music-making and collective techniques of composition.[89]

Such Western musical influence was not sudden: it spread after Britain humiliated China in the Opium War of 1839, and intensified throughout the nineteenth century. In 1879 a group of European musicians founded a band in Shanghai, which by 1907 had become the Shanghai Symphony Orchestra; in 1927 Shanghai saw the founding of the first of many music conservatoires throughout China. Enthusiasm for European music was further encouraged by Russian musicians, of whom the most notable was Alexander Tcherepnin, brought to China in 1934 as consultant to the Ministry of Education; it was further kindled in Shanghai during the 1930s by the arrival of some 18,000 Jewish refugees, many of whom were professional or amateur musicians.[90]

Revolutionary songs in Western military style had been an established aspect of political indoctrination since the 1920s; their texts encouraged militant patriotism, and denounced foreign exploitation. Such exploitation was exemplified, during the 1930s, in 'Yellow Music', a popular style that superimposed Western harmonies on Chinese

[89] A. C. Scott, 'China', *The New Grove* (1980), vi. 279.

[90] Richard Curt Kraus, *Pianos and Politics in China* (New York: Oxford University Press, 1989), 4–6.

pentatonic melodies and was associated with the nightclubs and brothels of Shanghai.[91]

It was in Shanghai, in the mid-1930s, that the 'National Salvation Song Movement' began, when political agitation for Chiang Kai-shek to resist Japanese aggression increased. The central figure in this movement was the composer Xian Xinghai (1905–45). Born to the poverty of a family of boat-people in southern China, but with a musical talent that led to his studying at the Paris Conservatoire, Xian was soon torn between his regard for European musical culture and the demands of China's revolution. He came to believe that the primary purpose of music is to lead people to revolutionary action, but he also displayed genuine interest in Chinese instruments and folk music. He is best remembered for his *Yellow River Cantata*, a work that elevated the status of propaganda music by incorporating Chinese folk music and instruments, as well as Western styles of choral and orchestral writing.[92] It was composed in Yan'an, the small city in the north of Shaanxi Province which the Communists made their capital, at the conclusion of their 'long march', and to which Xian travelled *incognito* to become director (and composer-in-residence) of its 'Arts Academy'.

The Communist Party saw in music an inexpensive means of encouraging the revolutionary spirit; an important element of Xian Xinghai's work was to teach young cadres how to compose songs, and how to organize and train choirs for this purpose.[93] 'When ten thousand people sang at once,' wrote a Korean observer, 'the earth seemed to move and the mountain shake. We sang before class, we sang before eating, and whole units sang on the march. There was solo singing, ensemble singing, and choral singing. Yan'an was not only the sacred place of the revolution, it also became a true city of song.'[94]

Music continued to be an important political tool of the communist party until the death of Mao in 1976. During the Great Leap Forward (see p. 344), the demand for ever-increasing mass production extended, absurdly, to the arts. In 1959, the tenth anniversary of the founding of the Peoples' Republic, it was noted that the number of China's specialist music schools had increased substantially, and that the number of professional musical organizations had increased from 3 to 148; thirty musical periodicals had been published; 32 million records had been pressed, covering 3,500 titles; and ninety-four Chinese had gained prizes

[91] Manuel, *Popular Musics*, 225. [92] Kraus, *Pianos and Politics*, 58.
[93] Ibid. 56. [94] Ibid. 55.

in international competitions. Urged to build on this record of achievement, the Shanghai Musicians' Association set a goal of producing 1,500 new songs, and the Shanghai Conservatory increased its goal from 600 to 1,734. In Beijing, the General Political Department set an initial quota of 500 pieces and increased it to 1,545; and the Central Experimental Opera Theatre planned 1,379 works for the year.[95]

The Great Leap stimulated the search for a 'national' musical style; and, as happened in so many other countries worldwide, folk tunes came to be blended with Western musical techniques. (The use of pentatonic melodies had been encouraged, as early as the 1930s, by Tcherepnin.[96]) The most noted composition of this period—one that remains popular among Chinese everywhere—was *Liang Shanbo and Zhu Yingtai*, commonly known as the *Butterfly Lovers' Concerto*. Composed jointly in 1959 by Chen Gang and the violinist He Zhanhao, it depicts a popular love-story, presenting Shaoxing opera tunes in the style of the Tchaikovsky violin concerto. In it, the solo violin, using wide vibrato and portamento, is made to sound like an *erhu*. The concerto's immediate popularity survived criticisms that, on the one hand, its pentatonic melodic style furnished a too-facile popularity, and, on the other, that its use of a romantic Chinese story and Western romantic harmony honoured the feudal order.[97]

The Great Leap Forward was, effectively, a repudiation of Soviet methods of industrialization; in 1960 it led Russia to withdraw all technical assistance from China, including Soviet and eastern-bloc musicians who served as faculty members, or acted as advisers, in Chinese colleges. The Great Leap temporarily lowered Mao's Zedong's political standing, and more moderate socialists started to dismantle Mao's disastrous collectivist policies. In due course, however, Mao reverted to the 'class-struggle' roots of the revolution, and in 1966 he launched the Great Proletarian Cultural Revolution, in an attempt to achieve the egalitarian, working-class culture for which he had striven so long.

Any genuine understanding of the musical environment of China today must take into account the devastation unleashed by the Cultural Revolution, and its continuing effect on those who experienced it. (It was Mao's Cultural Revolution that inspired Pol Pot's similar destruction of Cambodia in the late 1970s.) Mao aimed to eradicate not only bourgeois Western culture, but also China's traditional culture, because

[95] Ibid. 107. [96] Ibid. 5. [97] Ibid. 109.

of its 'feudal origins'. His militant, young Red Guards were bidden to rid the country of the 'Four Olds': old culture, old customs, old habits, and old ways of thinking. There was no clear definition of 'old'; that was left to the Red Guards to decide.[98]

Between 1966 and 1976 millions of men and women were forced out of the cities into rural areas, where they received 're- education' through physical labour. Huge numbers were executed. In the cities, intellectuals were assigned the work of labourers: medical doctors emptied bedpans in hospitals, professors cleaned the toilets in universities, artists worked on building sites. Such 'intellectuals' were required to attend 'struggle meetings', and political indoctrination meetings, at which they were made to 'confess' their 'crimes'. 'Mao Zedong Thought Propaganda Teams' were organized throughout the country; anyone found reading a book not written by Mao ran the danger of being labelled an opponent of the People's Republic.[99] With utter disregard for human life, or for the loyalty of others, Mao manipulated the party machine so as to blame mass destruction on others, and thus reinforce the cult of his own personality.

During the Cultural Revolution, art became the weapon of class warfare. Previous to this, the content and style of Chinese opera had already been transformed at the hands of the Communists; traditional plays had been abandoned and replaced by others with revolutionary plots. Some original tunes and orchestrations had been retained, but new sections had been added in Western romantic style, with incidental music akin to Western film music. During the Cultural Revolution, under the aegis of Mao's wife, Jiang Qing, the number of permitted 'model operas' was reduced to five. Particular orchestrations were prescribed. *The Red Lantern*, for example, was produced in 1968 in versions for traditional orchestra as well as for piano and Chinese percussion; it was described as a successful example of 'making foreign things fit China'.[100] (*The Red Lantern* was the most popular of the model operas; set in a small town under Japanese occupation, it tells of a railway worker using his lantern to send secret messages to nearby guerrillas.) For nearly ten years, the five 'model operas', and three modern ballets, were almost the only musical activity promoted by the state.[101]

[98] Nien Cheng, *Life and Death in Shanghai* (London: Grafton Books, 1986), 82.
[99] Ibid. 234.
[100] Scott, 'China', *The New Grove*, vi. 281.
[101] Roger Garside, *Coming Alive: China after Mao* (New York: Mentor, 1981), 28.

In 1969, under the personal guidance of Jiang Qing, four members of the Central Philharmonic in Beijing adapted Xian Xinghai's *Yellow River Cantata* as the *Yellow River Concerto* (for piano). It was produced to glorify Mao Zedong's struggle against the Japanese; its four composers spent several weeks living at a former revolutionary base, in caves on the banks of the Yellow River, interviewing older peasants about the war against Japan, and listening to Shanxi folk music.[102] The prelude to the concerto uses a *pipa* (lute), and incorporates 'The Song of the Yellow River Boatmen'. Its second movement makes use of the piano to symbolize the people who have struggled for a living on the banks of the great river. The third movement uses traditional flutes to restore calm, and then depicts the country under the Japanese. The finale incorporates the patriotic songs 'Defend the Yellow River' and 'The East is Red' to depict Mao Zedong's challenge to the enemy.[103]

Yin Chengzong, one of a committee of composers that produced the concerto, described it as 'playing a militant part in uniting and educating the people and attacking the enemy'. Subsequently, however, he defected to the USA and denounced his earlier statements.[104] Like the *Warsaw Concerto*, with which it has much it common, the *Yellow River Concerto* derives from the style of Rachmaninov. It was played about eight times a month by the Central Philharmonic, in its one and only permitted programme.

By 1973, denigration of Western music had abated sufficiently for musicians to be permitted to perform such music; indeed, in that same year, both the London and Vienna Philharmonic orchestras visited China. Nevertheless, members of the State Council's Culture Group—the final arbiters of concert programmes for Chinese performers—disliked what appeared to them as a reversion to Western 'bourgeois' music, and they instituted a move to vilify European 'music without titles' (see p. 653). When the Philadelphia Orchestra arrived in China, Jiang Qing personally requested of Eugene Ormandy, the conductor, that the orchestra play Beethoven's Pastoral Symphony. Beethoven's titles were apparently considered inadequate, for all European music, untitled and titled, was subsequently condemned; untitled works were considered 'a means by which bourgeois composers conceal the class content of their works', titled works as 'concealing the decadent, chaotic

[102] Kraus, *Pianos and Politics*, 148.

[103] Keith Anderson and Ching-wah Lam, sleeve note to CD, *Popular Chinese Orchestral Music*, HK 8.240055.

[104] Manuel, *Popular Musics*, 228.

life, and depraved sentiments of the bourgeoisie that the weird cacophony represents'.[105] 'Class struggle' then led to a complete purge of European classical music.

With the death of Mao in 1976, and the subsequent imprisonment of Jiang Qing (and other members of the 'Gang of Four'), more liberal policies prevailed under Deng Xiaoping. European 'music without titles' was restored, foreign musicians and orchestras were again welcomed in China, and musicians who had emigrated were encouraged to return. There was also a boom in the production, and export, of pianos and other instruments. Deng's 'Four Modernizations' programme, however, downgraded the place of music, encouraged science at the expense of arts, and required musical institutions to become self-sufficient. Both the Central Philharmonic and Shanghai orchestras were forced to perform light music for survival, a situation that still obtains. Nevertheless, students at China's principal conservatoires continue to achieve success in international competitions, and Chinese composers now explore modernist, rather that neo-romantic, styles.

Popular Western musical styles returned to China more by default than by design, as an inevitable corollary of economic liberalization. With the ending of the Cultural Revolution in 1976, rock music began to infiltrate Chinese culture; and pop songs from Hong Kong and Taiwan (based on Chinese popular songs) were officially endorsed, with the Open Door Policy of 1979. By the mid-1980s, a form of rock music showing Western influence had become widely disseminated, as songs incorporating such native instruments as the *suona* (shawm) and *zheng* (zither) were introduced.[106] The music of village bands became absorbed into the new, *quasi* rock culture. Lyrical love ballads, performed by female singers to the accompaniment of piano, bass, electric guitar, and other Western instruments, became popular, while dance bands and discothèques appeared throughout the length and breadth of the Peoples' Republic. By 1985 the China News Agency could announce that China had an estimated ten million guitarists.[107]

Older Chinese saw in this new romantic pop style a reflection of 'Yellow Music', and of China's humiliating treatment at the hands of colonialists. The Party itself periodically attempted to curb artistic freedoms: in 1983, for example, a 'Spiritual Pollution' campaign was

[105] Kraus, *Pianos and Politics*, 171.

[106] For detailed discussion of rock music in China, see Peter Micic, 'Notes on Pop/Rock Genres in the Eighties in China', *CHIME*, 8 (Spring 1995), 76–96.

[107] Manuel, *Popular Musics*, 233.

launched, and eighty-four of Shanghai's 136 dance halls were closed in 1985.[108] Despite such measures, by the late 1980s rock had become widely popular, and its leading proponent, Cui Jian, a national idol. After the Tiananmen Square massacre of 1989, the Party banned rock concerts for nine months; but after that, Cui Jian offered to organize a concert tour to raise money for the Beijing Asian Games, an offer accepted by the Party. Cui's lyrics contained anti-Communist implications, however: his first album had been entitled *Rock 'n Roll on the Road of the Long March.* The Party halted the tour, and banned Cui Jian from giving concerts for almost three years.

Notwithstanding such expressions of Party disapproval, the taste for rock music, both imported directly from the West, and in Chinese-tinged versions, continued. Rock music receives little attention from the Chinese media; but videos by Chinese performers are often seen outside China; MTV Asia, for example, has broadcast videos of Cui Jian, and the groups Black Panther and Tang Dynasty. In the mid-1990s, however, Chinese rock music is in decline. Newer bands have lacked style and technique, while wider variety and availability of consumer goods and activities have dulled the former allure of rock music. Moreover, the political climate has become less confrontational than that which made of Cui Jian a 'star'. And there may be a deeper, cultural explanation: as one commercial-music entrepeneur has put it: 'This is a melodic culture in which ballads sell well but anything with a beat does not.'[109] Throughout the whole of East Asia, and despite heavy promotion of Western rock music, crooners are more widely appreciated than are rock artists.

The effects of the political events of the twentieth century on Chinese traditional music were described, briefly, in Chapter 10 (pp. 355–7). Growing awareness of China's cultural heritage has encouraged the use of small ensembles and of more authentic presentations of Chinese folk music; and the formation of the large 'Chinese orchestra' is increasingly recognized as being contrary to Chinese tradition. In rural areas many musical traditions have survived, particularly those associated with religion. South and south-east of Beijing, for example, village ensembles play types of traditional music, the roots of which lie in local, popular temple music and even in vanished court music. In poorer

[108] Ibid. 233–4.

[109] Kenny Bloom, director of Dragon International Company, as reported by Jasper Becker in *Sunday Morning Post*, Hong Kong, 10 Dec., 1995, Agenda, 3.

villages, a continuing respect for traditional Daoist ceremonies encourages perpetuation of associated ritual music, though in more prosperous areas, Buddhist adherents pay to keep traditional Buddhist music alive. More frequently, however, groups of peasants now perform mixed programmes of folk-songs, opera tunes, and modern pop tunes, to a paying audience.[110]

There has been one recent, ironic, consequence of the inane, revolutionary, musical policies of Jiang Qing. When, in 1977, the 'model operas' were banned and the traditional operas were restored, the latter were patronized mainly by the elderly, for whom they had nostalgic appeal. Many young people who had not experienced the atrocities of the Cultural Revolution could not relate to the shrill vocal style and stylized plots of traditional opera. Increasingly then, since 1986, they preferred disco versions of tunes from the very model revolutionary operas now excoriated by the Communist Party.[111]

Short of reimposing a totalitarian state, there is no way in which any governmental party can impose musical taste, for musical taste—and the emotional response that conditions it—still appears to be formed by a mixture of association and familiarity. Chinese music has constantly been linked with human conduct; although official pronouncements on music, belonging to past ages, could have done little to affect folk styles (or, for that matter, the taste of Tang emperors for foreign musics associated with slave 'singing girls'), music in China has always been an important agent of conservatism. The Cultural Revolution confirmed music in this historic role, and it is a measure of the mass involvement in the Cultural Revolution that musical styles could effectively be proscribed. In this electronic age, musical style can less easily be proscribed. The seemingly inevitable introduction of liberal associations for music to a Chinese populace for long officially denied them has led to a state of musical confusion from which China is unlikely to emerge speedily.

Japan

While Chinese culture atrophied in the throes of Communism, other East Asian countries became increasingly West-

[110] Xue Yibing, 'The Present State of Traditional Village Music Associations in Northern China: Three Case Studies', unpublished paper presented to ICTM UK, 1992.

[111] Manuel, *Popular Musics*, 234.

ernized. Japan, for example, was busy modernizing even before the American fleet appeared in Edo Bay in 1853. The centralized Tokugawa government of the seventeenth and eighteenth centuries had been successful in creating an affluent merchant class, and by the end of the Tokugawa period (1868) about 40–50 per cent of Japanese males were receiving some formal education. Japanese were not hostile to learning from foreigners, and, during the reign of the Meiji emperor (1868–1912), universities and schools were instituted on European models. During the same period, the military was modernized, and the economy advanced. As a consequence of these initiatives, Japan's modernization programme touched the lives of most of the population.[112]

This modernization programme applied equally to the arts, and in 1880 an American school-music supervisor, Luther Whiting Mason, was hired to teach 'modern' music. The intention was to blend the best elements of Western and Japanese musical styles; but enthusiasm for modernization largely displaced Japanese traditions, and school children were soon singing European or American tunes (set to Japanese texts), accompanied by piano. As a result of Mason's work, a Tokyo Music School was founded in 1890; it is now the Tokyo College of the Arts (*Geijutsu Daigaku*), the most prestigious music school in Japan.

Paradoxically, in order to honour the modernizing emperor, the imperial *gagaku* court orchestra was revived, but the musicians were also expected to play waltzes, quadrilles, and marches, in addition to *gagaku*. A national anthem, a setting of a tenth-century poem, was constructed in the anhemitonic pentatonic *ichikotsu* mode, and was subsequently harmonized (Ex. 18.2).[113] It was then performed—as it is now—in two versions: one monophonic for *gagaku* ensemble, the other harmonized and orchestrated for Western band or orchestra.[114] Ex. 18.2 indicates the extent to which Asian harmonization can vary from European norms, much as did the harmonizations of eighteenth-century, US 'Yankee tunesmiths'.

Western influence affected many areas of music. Militaristic songs became popular. The *shakuhachi* (bamboo, end-blown flute), originally associated with mendicant Buddhist monks and still used as an aid to meditation, was now used in secular chamber music. The Chevé,

[112] Karl Signell, 'The Modernisation Process', 83.
[113] Ibid. 99.
[114] Ibid. 85.

Ex. 18.2

numerical system of notation was adopted for traditional music, and spread throughout East Asia. By the turn of the nineteenth century, Japanese composers were already blending European and Japanese musical styles.

During the first half of the twentieth century, a newly Westernized Japan applied Western methods of imperialism to Asia. When this offensive period ended with Japanese defeat, in 1945, the country developed not only its industrial and economic base, but also its musical base, all on Western lines. Tokyo is now home to more symphony orchestras than any other city in the world; Japanese performers occupy some of the world's most prestigious positions; Japanese composers are among the best known in Asia and have written successfully for blends of Japanese traditional and Western instruments, as well as in avant-garde and jazz-oriented styles. Japanese popular musicians draws on virtually every Western style to create Japanese-Western fusions; and *karaoke* ('empty orchestra') clubs and bars, where people sing songs as soloists against a prerecorded backing, have become an international phenomenon. Nevertheless (as noted in Chapter 10), Japanese retain a deep respect for tradition; their indigenous art forms thrive (albeit at times in modernized form), though—significantly—they are less popular with the younger generation.

Taiwan and Korea

Japan's success at modernizing became painfully evident to the outside world in 1895, when military victories in China were followed by colonization of Taiwan, and when subsequent victories in Russia, in 1905, were followed by colonization of Korea. Taiwan and Korea had already experienced aspects of Western culture during the nineteenth century, as a result of Christian missionary activity; but Japanese occupation was to lead to Western-style modernization, laying the foundations of future economic development.

In Taiwan, the arrival in 1949 of Chiang Kai-shek and the Guomindang heralded a period of growing prosperity. In instituting sweeping land reforms, Chiang provided generous rewards for farmers and former landlords, who then became cooperative entrepreneurs, complementing the skills and attitudes of the monks, merchants, scholars, and artists who had crossed the straits with their leader. The educational system was overhauled, and students were sent abroad to study science and technology. At home, an arts infrastructure, embracing both Chinese and Western styles, was developed.

Under the Guomindang, Taiwan assumed the title 'Republic of China' and, with it, the role of custodian of Chinese arts. The Guomindang government sponsored Chinese opera, Chinese music, and Chinese dance companies. Under its aegis, universities developed performing-arts departments, with faculties in both Chinese and Western traditions; and special secondary schools were established to prepare children for careers in all aspects of Chinese opera.

Traditional arts are still admired and widely supported in Taiwan; Chinese musical styles and instruments are frequently incorporated into new compositions and pop styles. Traditional arts, however, are now a minority taste, and it is Western rather than Chinese music that is dominant. Material success is associated with Westernization, and wealthy parents encourage their children to play Western instruments. Western classical music is well developed: Taiwanese performers have achieved success internationally; and a society of composers flourishes, many members of which have studied abroad, and have become expert in blending Chinese musical idioms and instruments with Western, modernist, styles of composition.

In South Korea, a similar dual process of preserving traditional arts, and of developing Western music, occurred, though such initiatives were delayed by civil war and a period of unstable government. From the early 1970s however, the country made considerable economic progress, and developed a strong infrastructure for musical education and performance. A degree in Korean Music was introduced at the National University in Seoul as early as 1959; and the university music department continues to play a prominent role in preserving traditional music. The Korean Traditional Performing Arts Centre (see p. 375) is state funded, and its permanent musicians present frequent performances of traditional music. Nevertheless, Western music predominates, as it does in Japan and Taiwan. The National Theatre in Seoul, for example, is home to a National Symphony Orchestra, a National Ballet Company, and a National Opera Company; universities throughout the country teach Western music; and many regional symphony orchestras have emerged, both professional and amateur. Moreover, Korean musicians, like those from other East Asian countries, number among the world's leaders; and Korea has its society of contemporary composers, whose music embodies both Western modernism and native traditions.

Korea also displays a lively Western-influenced pop-music scene. *Bbongjjahk*, for example, is a Korean form of 'country' music, currently popular among adult record buyers; and young Koreans have developed a native form of rap.[115] Building on the virtuosic drumming techniques of the traditional *nongak* (farmers' music) percussion ensemble, Koreans have also developed a distinctive and influential style of jazz; and the internationally acclaimed percussion quartet *SamulNori* (in fact, the original *Samullori* group, founded in 1978 (see p. 384)) has joined with numerous jazz groups, and attracts students from all over the world.[116] In Korea, as in other largely Westernized societies, it is

[115] 'Republic of Korea', *Asiabeat* (Hong Kong, Feb. 1993), 51.

[116] Carol Scott, 'Korean Jazz has its own Natural Rhythm', *Asiabeat* (Hong Kong, Feb. 1992), 82.

syncretic pop musics, as much as traditional art musics, that (to most Koreans) purvey 'national', cultural identity.

Hong Kong

Hong Kong is unique among Asian cultural centres in having originated, in its modern form, as a crossroads of Chinese and European cultural influence. When, in 1840, Captain Charles Elliot of the British Royal Navy acquired from a recently humiliated China a barren granite island, known to the Chinese as Heung Kong ('Fragrant Harbour'), the island had but 6,000 or 7,000 inhabitants, many of them living in boats. Elliot had the task of supervising some thirty British firms operating from Guangzhou (Canton); his new acquisition was less than 100 miles from Guangzhou, and he envisaged it as a permanent outpost of British authority, from whence Britain could conduct its business with China.[117] Early in 1841 the Union Jack was raised on the island and it was declared a Free Port.

When Hong Kong formally became a British possession in June 1843, its founding governor, Sir Henry Pottinger, prophesied that the island would soon become a 'vast emporium of commerce and wealth'.[118] In 1860 the British acquired Kowloon from the Chinese 'in perpetuity'; and in 1897 they acquired the 900 square kilometres of the New Territories 'for a period of ninety-nine years'. By 1916 Hong Kong had amassed a population of 530,000; by 1941 it had amassed 1.6 million; by 1955, 2.4 million; and by 1988, 5.6 million. A historical collusion of Chinese and 'barbarians' had brought into being a phenomenal entrepôt, with a unique blend of cultures.

Until 1949 Hong Kong was a busy but unexceptional port dealing principally with Chinese trade, eclipsed in importance by the cosmopolitan Shanghai. Mao Zedung's victory over Chiang Kai-shek in 1949 not only sent refugees—many of them industrialists—pouring into Hong Kong; it also caused China to fight against the United Nations in Korea, and led to a subsequent Western boycott of trade with China. As a consequence, Hong Kong was forced to find a new role. Within a few decades, capitalizing on cheap and willing labour from Chinese refugees, and on European, Chinese, and American enterprise, Hong

[117] Jan Morris, *Hong Kong: Epilogue to an Empire* (London: Penguin Books, 1988), 24–5.
[118] Ibid. 25.

Kong had become a world-famous manufacturing and financial centre.[119]

Ninety-eight per cent of Hong Kong's present population is Chinese, a large proportion being derived from rural communities in South China. The transition from the countryside to some of the most densely populated urban areas in the world, together with the need to survive and succeed in a highly competitive society, did not create encouraging conditions for artistic activities. Moreover, the British-led Hong Kong government initially placed its emphasis on European culture, and only during the 1980s did it begin to sponsor Chinese art forms, such as a Chinese orchestra and a Chinese dance troupe.[120]

In South China, the most popular traditional performing art was Cantonese opera; other forms of traditional music took place in tea houses. A similar pattern was replicated in Hong Kong. Until the 1950s, Cantonese opera was the most popular performing art across a wide social spectrum; and until the 1970s, many Hong Kong tea houses featured Chinese music ensembles. The ensembles in tea houses subsequently disappeared. Opera, however, continued to be a major element in entertainment—even after the cinema began to reach large audiences—and its influence was considerable. Operatic melodies were played in contexts outside the opera and remained familiar to most people; they even influenced pop music. Moreover, the melodramatic acting style of Cantonese opera came to permeate film, television, and theatre. Hong Kong developed one of the largest film industries in the world, and its films reflected an increasingly distinctive indigenous culture.

By the late 1970s, Hong Kong had become, both socially and economically, spectacularly successful. Under the aegis of a British administration that developed British-style institutions, a Chinese population had created a cornucopia of capitalism, its cultural roots lying predominantly in the Chinese mainland, its lifestyle corresponding, in many aspects, to lifestyles in the West. Up to this point, Hong Kong had been little concerned with the arts; but a new city, conspicuously successful in its blend of cultural systems, needed an arts profile to match its commercial profile.

[119] Morris, *Hong Kong: Epilogue to an Empire*, 28.

[120] Information (compiled by Dr John Hosier) extracted, with permission, from the introduction to the Hong Kong Academy for Performing Arts' 1992 presentation to the Hong Kong Council for Accreditation.

The government responded by funding, successively, a fully professional Philharmonic Orchestra, a Chinese Orchestra, an International Arts Festival, and an Asian Arts Festival. It also funded an agency for training young people of Hong Kong in Western and Chinese music, and in 1985 it helped to fund an Academy for the Performing Arts. Three university music departments came into being. A performing-arts venue was erected on Hong Kong island, and this was followed by the erection of a vast Cultural Centre in Kowloon. As successive new towns were built in the New Territories, all were equipped with substantial performing-arts venues. Concert programmes by internationally acclaimed artists were subsidized.

In the flurry of activity that followed, Western arts came to predominate. Chinese opera maintained its profile: opera companies continued to be engaged for performances in mat-sheds, attached to temple festivals; a new interest in Chinese opera developed among younger audiences. Nevertheless, by far the greater proportion of interest was in Western music; indeed music-teaching became something of an industry: over 50,000 children a year currently sit British instrumental music examinations, and many acquire exceptionally high standards of technique.

Hong Kong composers played a significant part in establishing an 'Asian Composers League', in 1973; this was a pan-Asian development that aimed to unite Asian composers and foster exchanges between them. In 1983 Hong Kong composers established their own Guild, and the following year the Guild followed Japan and Korea in being accepted as a full member of the International Society for Contemporary Music. In a newly created society, with Chinese roots and British influence, contention developed over the suitability of neo-romanticism or modernism as a way forward for Hong Kong composers; but modernism soon won the day, and many Hong Kong composers demonstrated remarkable facility in using the techniques of integral serialism. Modernist works were also written for the Chinese orchestra, some imitating the textural sound world of Penderecki. As musicians with deeper knowledge of Chinese traditional music moved to Hong Kong from the mainland, many composers were stimulated to assert their Chineseness in music: by using Chinese instruments or texts; by developing a descriptive, rhapsodical style of composition; or by combining Chinese tunes with modernist textures. The idiom of all this music, however, was—and is—essentially Western.

Important developments also took place in popular music styles. 'Cantopop' became a musical symbol of Hong Kong. Consisting mainly of pop or rock versions of popular Chinese folk tunes, or of Japanese or Western popular tunes set to Chinese lyrics, and often employing such traditional instruments as the *erhu* and *dizi*, it was one of the first pop styles to be officially endorsed in China (in the wake of the Open Door Policy of 1979).[121] The Territory is now the leading East Asian centre for the promotion of popular music.

Hong Kong's Western, artistic profile emerged *after* the development of a successful commercial profile. It arose less from a need to *appear* modern than from a need to give recognition to an existing state of modernization. Like the high-rise skyline in the shadow of which they operate, the Hong Kong arts are quite suddenly there, in answer to a perceived need. Nevertheless, a demand for balancing Western modernity with Chinese tradition is always apparent. Hong Kong's dynamism derives, very largely, from an unusually successful blend of potentially incompatible cultural elements; and it was made possible by the relative suddenness of the territory's emergence as a large commercial and cultural centre, and by the combination of Western and Chinese human expertise—both uprooted—that brought it into being.

East Joins West

Throughout East Asia as a whole, modernization has led to rapid economic development, so that the standard of living, in many parts of the region, is now equal to the highest anywhere. The enthusiasm among Asian musicians for Western modernism—at a time when many Western composers are abjuring modernism in favour of neo-romantic styles—suggests a strong sense of association between the material, economic, and artistic aspects of life. Modern arts are seen as indicative of a new, progressive spirit, and, as modernization has become increasingly identified with Westernization, modern arts have become identified with Western arts.

Nevertheless, most Asian artists retain a deep respect for their traditional arts; and many professional musicians have knowledge and facility in both Asian and Western traditions. In new composition, the mixing of the two traditions does not always sound comfortable: penta-

[121] Micic, 'Notes on Pop/Rock Genres', 77–8.

tonic melodies, for example, do not sit easily with atonality. But atonality has its own limitations, amongst which is a reduced role of harmony as an agent of rhythm. Atonality can therefore prove adaptable to a reflective Asian musical style, and can be enhanced by the use of pungent, Asian timbres, and styles of ornamentation.

In Chapter 2 of this book, the anthropologist Claude Lévi-Strauss was quoted as suggesting that, from birth, 'things and beings' in an environment establish an array of references forming a system of 'conduct, motivation and judgement'; that this view is 'confirmed by an educationally reflexive view of the history of a particular culture or civilisation'; that other cultural systems are perceptible only 'through distortions imprinted on them by the original system'; and that 'in order not to perish, they must... remain somewhat impermeable toward one another'.[122] This view was considered in relation to the USA in Chapter 14 (see pp. 531–2). Even more than for the USA, Asian appreciation of European musical style is likely to be marked by such distortions. Chinese music is reflective and programmatic, and Chinese often identify with romantic, nineteenth-century European music to the exclusion of other styles. Some East Asian musicians experience difficulty in acquiring the sense of a steady rhythmic pulse, and coherent phrasing, characteristic of Western music (and of most musics west of the Bay of Bengal), but that is less characteristic of East Asian musics. Similar distortions are, of course, likely to mark Western perceptions of Asian musics, when *Western* composers attempt also to fuse Asian and Western musical styles.

European composers, when attempting east–west fusions, have an intrinsic advantage in being enculterated to *European* musical styles. US composers have an intrinsic advantage of long acclimatization to distortions imprinted upon European musical styles, arising from their transatlantic perspective. Many Asian composers have the considerable advantage of a thorough understanding of both Asian *and* European musical styles, and they will continue to hold that advantage so long as traditional Asian musics are admired and practised. If such admiration and practice should decline, Asia's level of attachment to European music could rise to a level similar to that of the USA, and provide yet greater distortions of European music, distancing that music ever further from its roots. In musical terms, Easterners could become Westerners. Such a process would seem already to be under way.

[122] Claude Lévi-Strauss, *The View from Afar* (Oxford: Blackwell, 1985), p. xiv, 11, 18.

Conclusions

That musical Westernization is now, and universally, an ongoing process seems not to be in doubt. Nor is it to be doubted that the process has had markedly different effects upon different cultural systems. Nevertheless, from the facts presented in this chapter, a few general conclusions may be drawn.

Communal musical activity appears to contribute to the formation of a stable society but does not, of itself, lead to economic or political advancement. Economically poor countries, or peoples, regard their traditional arts as symbolic of 'national', or 'ethnic', pride and aspiration. Economic advance, consequent upon Westernization, tends, however, to devalue traditional arts, in favour of Western styles, or fusions.

A successful modern *political* profile—which, in modern terms, means a successful *economic* profile—seems to demand, *after the event*, a successful *élite* musical profile. (Such a profile rarely precedes the event.) When, as is often the case, that profile is construed in *Western* terms, it appears to need complementing by a 'national' musical profile, in indigenous terms. Music is susceptible of manipulation for political purposes.

Such profiles tend to be instigated by political élites and developed by musical élites. For ordinary people, 'crossover' styles, the 'national' elements of which are usually most conspicuous in timbre and instrumentation, constitute a compromise between these two positions.

Musicians of non-European countries whose interests lie principally in *Western* styles appear to need, additionally, a distinctively 'national' musical profile in order to authenticate their indigenous roots. The blending, in composition, of Western modernism with indigenous traditions links—notionally at least—modernity with specific cultural identity. People in varying social situations, whether due to class, ethnicity, population density, or work patterns, need—and usually develop—musical styles to reflect those situations.[123]

Blending of musical styles tends to weaken the identity of the styles blended. Attempts by African and Asian composers to impart 'local' colour to Western *élite* genres and styles (by means of timbre and, to some extent, specific melodic and rhythmic shapes) have not usually

[123] For detailed examinations of ethnicity and identity in relation to music, see Martin Stokes (ed.), *Ethnicity, Identity and Music: The Musical Construction of Place* (Oxford: Berg Publishers, 1994).

displaced the predominantly Western musical ambience in their compositions. Attempts by *Asian* musicians to effect a similar blending of styles in *popular* genres have not always displayed empathy with African-derived rhythm, an essential element of Western pop music (however much weakened in this role); and, where such 'crossover' styles employ Western harmony and instrumental timbres, a Western musical ambience tends, likewise, to predominate. However, attempts by *African* musicians to effect such blending—notably through the subtlety and vitality of African rhythm—have usually resulted in a predominantly *African* musical ambience.

In general, both African and (to a lesser extent) Asian musical styles have proved permeable to European musical styles, with which, through time, they interacted. Between African and Asian styles themselves—and particularly between those of Sub-Saharan Africa and East Asia—there has been less interaction. Africa and East Asia have remained 'somewhat impermeable towards one another'. Both have retained distinct musical identities. In relation to the apparent permeability of African and European musical styles towards one another and a possible genetic link between Africans and Europeans (closer than that between either and other major ethnic groups (see Foreword, pp. 28–9)),[124] attention may be drawn to suggested interrelatedness between the Niger-Congo, Afroasiatic, and Indo-European language groups, where correspondences between genetic relationships and language groups have been shown to exist.[125] Such matters, however, are beyond the scope of this book.

The traits of a traditional music that enable its region of origin to be determined, even within a few seconds of audition, are primarily concerned with timbre, scalar structure, and rhythm. Differences in melodic structure are less readily distinguished aurally (by those outside a particular region) and are usually linked with place and ethnicity only by association. Timbre has always been a fundamentally important element of monophonic and heterophonic musics. In European music, because harmonic procedures developed and were allied to notation, *interchange* of instruments—of timbre—was facilitated, without thereby causing conspicuous alteration in a given sequence of notes and durations. Accordingly, European music, past and present, has

[124] W. W. Howells, 'The Dispersion of Human Populations', *The Cambridge Encyclopaedia of Human Evolution* (Cambridge: Cambridge University Press, 1992), 398–9.

[125] Steve Jones, 'Genes and Language', in ibid.

tended to emphasize the elements of pitch and rhythm over timbre. In modern genres of music, worldwide, the ubiquity of European instruments and harmonic procedures—notwithstanding their blending with other 'national', or local, instruments and styles—has diminished the association between music and ethnicity and place.

Nevertheless, the evident, general, human need for 'national' identity, and the link between a sense of that identity and music, suggests that some variety will be retained, even within the increasing global mix of musical styles, élite and popular, Western and non-Western. Though music does not have explicit meaning, it can generate shared emotional states and, by association, condition powerful social and political awareness.

19 *The Postmodern West*

Collapse of the Pyramid

For some four centuries—not a long span in human history—educated Europeans believed their political, cultural, and artistic systems were superior to any others, a belief reinforced by the spread of these systems in Africa, Asia, and the Americas. That these systems were built on knowledge and skill generated by much earlier civilizations in Africa and Asia was neither recognized nor understood. When the USA assumed leadership of the Western world after the Second World War, Europe still held most of its Afro-Asian empire. European civilization, believed to have its roots in the unique cultural achievements of Ancient Greece, appeared to demonstrate a level of social and scientific advance with which the rest of the world would for ever be struggling to catch up.

The ensuing half century changed that perspective. Japan's relatively brief emulation of Western colonial methods had already ended, in 1945, in ignominy. Europe's lingering colonial ambitions were fatally undermined (in 1956) by Britain's unsuccessful endeavour to retain control of the Suez Canal; European disengagement from other colonial situations was then only a matter of time. US colonial ambitions in the Pacific were laid to rest in 1975 by a people of South East Asia, in wealth and technology poorer than the USA, but its senior by some 4,000 years. And around the world, once-colonized peoples came increasingly to question the relevance of certain Western values and systems, emulated in the wake of colonial subjugation. Their adoption of Western systems became more selective; they gained confidence in their own cultural traditions.

Conversely, Western peoples experienced a loss of confidence in many aspects of European culture. Growing awareness of past achievements of civilizations in Africa and Asia provoked unease over Europe's colonial history, as it became clear that the concept of cultural superiority was incompatible with that of multiculturalism. Uneven distribution of wealth at home, appalling poverty abroad, and increasing crime and corruption throughout the world revealed the weaknesses of Western democracy. Disillusionment with urban decadence, and the realization that science (in the hands of politicians) can act destructively, with power to eliminate all living species, as well as in the interests of 'progress', led to the questioning of many aspects of Western civilization. 'Progress' appeared no longer a wholly propitious cultural goal.

In Europe, during the post-war years, erosion of social hierarchies, based on class, undermined élitism at the heart of artistic tradition; and a process of acculturation—acculturating ordinary people to classical music and élite groups to popular music—undermined previously accepted value systems. For some cultural arbiters today, eighteenth-century Enlightenment and the artistic achievements that sprang from it no longer appear as a peak of cultural achievement; and modernism—a logical consequence of that Enlightenment[1]—is still regarded as incomprehensible, repugnant even, by many who otherwise espouse the post-Enlightenment tradition. Now, in the mid-1990s, 'Deconstructionist' and 'Postmodernist' discourse denies both the precepts of modernism and the plausibility of aesthetic determinism. The essential building blocks of European arts remain in place, but the values they embody begin to appear only partially relevant to contemporary society. Europe's widespread rejection of musical modernism stands in curious contrast to its enthusiastic adoption in Asia by a musical élite.

In the USA, where a hierarchy based on heredity rather than wealth did *not* develop, but where vast inequalities, between black and white communities, *did*, post-war cultural politics has been dominated by the need to give equal recognition to non-European cultures, and, in particular, to African-American culture. The consequence, again, has been to blur value distinctions, and to reduce confidence in the culture inherited from Europe. Because the USA had already experienced a multicultural history, the African element in popular music, and the African-American element in modern music, appeared less intrusive there than in Europe. In the USA, musical 'modernity' had no essential correlation with 'élitism'; it readily embraced elements of popular music, and even mocked the European tradition. Moreover, immigrants of Asian stock

[1] See Jürgen Habermas, 'Modernity—An Incomplete Project', in Hal Foster (ed.), *Postmodern Culture* (London: Pluto Press, 1983).

were in a position to recreate their 'national' musical traditions in the USA, unfettered by European aesthetics.

Both in Europe and the USA, musical culture today embraces similar incongruities. Both continents consciously promote non-European musics, either in *quasi*-traditional form, or 'crossed' with classical, or popular, styles; yet in neither continent has this development weakened fundamental associations between particular musical styles and groups in the society. 'Crossover' musics still tend to be associated with particular 'ethnic' societies, European classical music still with middle-class attitudes, rock with white anti-authoritarianism, rap with Afrocentrism. Although performance venues themselves have now become multicultural—pop music and non-Western musics are both promoted in concert halls, variety shows in opera houses, operas in huge arenas—the essential functions of such venues, and the social perspectives they represent, remain largely intact.

The most significant effect of growing multiculturalism over the past half century has been the rapid erosion of belief that any one musical style—or, indeed, any one item in a particular style—is 'superior' to another. In the post-structuralist, multiculturalist world of the 1990s, it appears no longer certain that Pavarotti, for example, sings more uplifting music, more proficiently, than Sting, or that New York's Lincoln Centre provides more edifying music theatre than Broadway. By the same token, it is no longer necessarily accepted that Beethoven wrote better music than Hummel, Mozart than Salieri; or that William Shakespeare wrote better English verse than Tim Rice. Such equations prove particularly questionable when they involve non-Western arts: did Caccini, for example, compose better music than the Suyá people of Brazil, Bach than the Balinese, Steve Reich than the *amadinda* xylophonists of Buganda? The difficulty of making an evaluation *between* different varieties of music has made questionable the practice of evaluating *within* a variety. Common consent holds only that all composed, and wrote, not worse nor better than each other, but differently.

The grand concept of a hierarchy of excellence, a cultural pyramid, with élite arts illuminating its apex and popular arts round its base—a concept that sustained the belief of civilizations in themselves, at least since the time of the Old Babylonians—has, it seems, finally been invalidated by the revolution in communications, and by the movement towards democracy in all judgement-making. Although cultural arbiters still invoke 'civilized' values, civilization itself no longer appears to provide a universally acceptable model of social organization; nor do 'the arts' provide universally acceptable icons of excellence. The cultural pyramid has become a multifaceted structure. The arts no longer proceed *de haut en bas* but—like the jewelled images of a kaleidoscope—proceed in all directions at once;[2] and their multifarious manifestations appear side by side in the same dynamic market place, their 'value' indicated by the price tags. The spiritual and social values that, for millennia, were attached to music have been weakened by the quantity of musics on offer, and by the advent of an unprecedentedly materialist culture, craving instant gratification.

Paths to Nowhere

At the heart of the contradictions that beset the present age is the Western cultural imperative to 'change'—change, allied to the concept of 'progress', has traditionally conditioned—and still conditions—the ineluctable development of arts and sciences. Since Guido of Arezzo published his system for notating precise pitches in the early eleventh century, Western composers have delighted in finding new ways of manipulating sound on paper—in theory—before putting it into practice. In such a system, music could scarcely remain static; change became, therefore—uniquely—a touchstone of musical excellence. Elsewhere in the world, musical performance conformed to traditional structures, generally varying only slightly from performance to performance and from master to disciple; but Western musical style changed consciously, each significant exemplar of change—in the nineteenth century in particular—being seen (by cultural arbiters of the day) as an apotheosis of musical achievement.

When, at the beginning of the twentieth century, 'modernism' reined in the freedoms of romanticism, paths of musical 'progress' in the Western system of tonality appeared to be exhausted. Nevertheless, change and 'progress' were still regarded as cultural imperatives, and alternatives had to be found. In Vienna, serialism provided one possible path, even though its atonal basis was essentially incompatible both with triadic harmony and with modally derived melody. Serialism, however, denied musical memory as a component in the comprehension of musical structure—denied, that is, the very attribute that had sustained all musical cultures, including that of the West, in time and

[2] Charles Jencks, 'Leapfrogging the Cultural Pyramid', *Observer*, 16 Jan. 1992, 25.

place; and it subverted the natural, speech-influenced, flow of melody and rhythm, as practised over millennia. The sounds of serialism seemed shocking; and, as the élite art of modern music spilled down the cultural pyramid, the subject matter of this music, when allied to words, also became associated with shock. 'To shock' became an apparent function of the new music; and, as shock depends on novelty, novelty, rather than systematic change, became at times the touchstone of the avant-garde.

As this book has established, music has been intimately associated with—and largely shaped by—language; even within non-tonal languages, language has conditioned both melodies and rhythms. Wagner and Verdi, in their different ways, even though they made demands on vocal physical stamina that were unprecedented in European music, both allowed words their natural musical contours; and both allowed words, with luminous clarity, to dominate the musical texture. Their use of language in music was complex, but the text was usually comprehensible in its musical context; indeed, Wagner's *Der Ring des Nibelungen* might justly be described as the apotheosis of syllabic chant.

If melismatic chant in its day, in Europe and throughout Asia, intruded upon the natural speech relationship between words and music, serialism subverted this. Serialism broke radically, not only with the European past, but with all other musical styles. No previous modal system in the world had made use of scales of more than seven basic notes within the octave; and, with the exception of Thailand, none had used an *exactly* equidistant scale of more than five notes.[3] The equidistant scale of twelve notes that characterized serialism, in which, moreover, there was no 'hierarchy' of pitches, not only destroyed the natural relationship between music and language but removed all audible foci from the music. When, with 'integral serialism', all the parameters of music came to be serialized, the only remaining musical determinant was texture. Modality—from the earliest times, and throughout the world, the touchstone of musical structure in time—appeared finally subverted.

As suggested in Chapter 1, the reversion to a music based on texture may have been an unconscious reversion to an archetype. Ligeti-type pianissimo string-clusters, for example, might be likened to the

[3] Proposals for a twenty-four quarter-tone scale in Syria and Persia during the nineteenth century were theoretical constructs, aimed—unsuccessfully—at rationalizing Persian/Arab modal systems; see Hormoz Farhat, 'Scales and Intervals, Theory and Practice', in Gerard Gillen and Harry White, *Irish Musical Studies* (Dublin: Irish Academic Press, 1990), 220.

unheard *shruti* of the Indian *ākāsa* (ether): and the emergence of shafts of sound, or colour, within such textures, to the revelation of individual *svara* out of the *ākāsa*. Less restrained modernist textures might be likened to the melody-less use of wind and percussion in Lamaist ensembles (with only the shawms providing notes structured, in limited form, as melody), or to the use of bells in the Shang dynasty in China. Nevertheless, modernist musical textures often were (and often still are) so largely devoid of differentiated textural sounds—as well as of melody, metre, and harmony—that they failed to connect with the symbolism of any established musical aesthetic; they denied, therefore, any purpose to the music. Such music undermined vocal music. It neither entertained nor uplifted. In the end, it even lost the power to shock.

Of course, not all contemporary composers embraced an exclusively modernist aesthetic. Many composers have discerned a cultural imperative towards greater universality, and have incorporated perceived elements of non-Western musical style, of jazz, or of other popular styles, into their music. Stravinsky and Tippett, for example—arguably two composers of the twentieth century who most successfully avoided the various straitjackets made ready to encase them[4]—both, at times, incorporated elements of blues and jazz into an essentially tonal musical language. Britten and Shostakovitch, composers more nationalist in sentiment and therefore less typical of their time, both developed personal, and distinctive, means by which to manipulate triadic harmony. Messiaen's system of 'modes of limited transposition'[5] was, again, essentially tonal. Such individuality of style was the consequence of a *unique* balancing of different musical styles, made possible by adjustments to, rather than abandonment of, established aesthetic criteria.

The pluralist temper of the late twentieth century has rendered such uniqueness in musical composition elusive; not only has the validity of established, 'syntagmatic' aesthetic criteria been contested, but a wide variety of 'paradigmatic' musical structures has been accepted.[6] A paradigm favoured by many composers of the late-twentieth century centres on a 'neo-romantic' type of harmony, at times manipulated so as

[4] See Peter Fletcher, *Education and Music* (Oxford: Oxford University Press, 1987), 76–93, for further discussion of this subject.

[5] Created by dividing an equal-tempered, dodecaphonic scale into two, three, or four equal intervals, each further divided into identical arrangements of tones and semitones; see Robert Sherlaw Johnson, *Messiaen* (London: Dent, 1975), 16.

[6] In structuralist terminology, 'syntagmatic' units are those that conform to logical syntax; 'paradigmatic' units, by contrast, are developed according to patterns of 'associative' words, or ideas lacking inherent grammar.

to incorporate elements of popular or non-Western musical style. In contrast to modernism, such 'neo-romanticism' affords the easy listening that a large fraction of the concert-going public is thought to desire, embodying an apparent resemblance to music 'as it was', with only an occasional nod to modernity.

That such music is based largely on parody is not, of itself, an impairment—for parody, in the sense of quotation, imitation, or reworking of the music of others, has had a long and honourable history. Obrecht and Ockeghem, Bach and Handel, Ives and Tippett, all used musical material from the past, either to rework it, or to present it in new light by changing its musical context; in doing so, they usually treated their borrowed material with respect. Even when parody has been used to *satirize* music and styles of the past—a trend that, in modern times, may be said to have started with Mahler—the use of parody has had clear artistic purpose. In much 'neo-romantic' composition, however, the use of parody appears gratuitous, reflecting a 'Great *Ennui*' at the end of the twentieth century comparable to that shown by George Steiner[7] to have existed at the end of the nineteenth century (to which, in part, Steiner attributes the Holocaust). It augurs, perhaps, the final dissolution of a unique, European artistic culture.

The Postmodern Compromise

This essentially anti-aesthetics stance is in accordance with the Deconstructionist, Postmodernist viewpoint, represented by writers such as Derrida, Lyotard, and Baudrillard: that a world of stable structures has made way for one of flux and indeterminacy; and that, because criticism renders any sequence of ideas subject to plurality of meaning, texts are inherently unstable and indeterminate. There can therefore (according to this viewpoint) be no hierarchy of value; criticism is without authority, and no one text can claim precedence over another.[8]

Already in the 1970s (as Stuart Sim has shown[9]), structuralism had blurred the distinction between the aesthetic and non-aesthetic by treating all phenomena equally (advertising and artistic texts, for

[7] George Steiner, *In Bluebeard's Castle: Some Notes towards the Re-definition of Culture* (London: Faber & Faber, 1971), 13–27.

[8] Stuart Sim, 'Structuralism and Post-Structuralism', in Oswald Hanfling (ed.), *Philosophical Aesthetics: An Introduction* (Oxford: Blackwell/Open University, 1992), 425, 433–5.

[9] Ibid. 413, 424.

example); and attempts by Lévi-Strauss and others to reduce all aspects of culture to a multi-dimensional grid limited the scope for evaluative interpretation.

Structuralist analysis presupposed that any system is amenable to semiotic analysis (analysis according to a theory of signs), and that behind every text (or musical score) lies an essential structure, whether this be well or badly realized by its creator. For Jacques Derrida,[10] however, architect of Deconstructionism, such presupposition was false; for Derrida it is 'signs without fault, without truth, and without origin' (essentially, signs that are arbitrary) that are 'offered to an active interpretation'. In Derrida's world of Deconstructionism, it is *re*ception, not *con*ception, that provides the key to interpretation of meaning, because for Derrida the meaning given to a text depends upon the ingenuity of the reader's 'active interpretation'. This, in essence, is a reaffirmation of Hume's famous declaration that there is no necessary connection between causes and effects (see pp. 442–3).[11]

In the Postmodernist world of Jean-François Lyotard all 'grand narratives' (Lyotard's term for large-scale, all-embracing theories of explanation) are rejected. Lyotard's stance is at the heart of Postmodernist rhetoric. Stuart Sim has described it thus:

> Lyotard is excluding the possibility of discourses being grounded in any traditional philosophical manner.... Inasmuch as there is a concept of grounding in *The Postmodern Condition*,[12] it is to be found in 'narrative' (*petit récit* as opposed to *grand récit*). By 'narrative' Lyotard seems to mean any sequence of ideas. The virtue of narrative to Lyotard is that it is self-justifying and self-validating: 'it certifies itself in the pragmatics of its own transmission',[13] as he puts it. Narrative simply *is*; it requires no further justification or license from any 'grand narrative' for its operation or existence.... Under such a reading, narrative is perceived to be liberating on a personal level, while grand narrative is totalitarian and authoritarian.[14]

[10] Jacques Derrida, *Writing and Difference*, trans. A. Bass (London: Routledge & Kegan Paul, 1978), 292; cited in Sim 'Structuralism and Post-Structuralism', 426.

[11] Sim, 'Structuralism and Post-Structuralism', 426, 422.

[12] Jean-François Lyotard, *The Postmodern Condition: A Report on Knowledge*, trans. G. Bennington and B. Massumi (Manchester: Manchester University Press, 1984).

[13] Ibid. 27.

[14] Sim, 'Structuralism and Post-Structuralism', 434.

Jean Baudrillard[15] takes the anti-aesthetics argument to a point at which judgement of any kind is rejected; in the process, he almost reverts (though for different reasons) to a Hindu form of metaphysics. According to Baudrillard, image has taken over from reality, because the television image is more 'real', and more authoritative, than the real object. In a world where there is no contact with objects and beings, but only with their simulations, there can be no judgement, only experience.[16]

Postmodernist theory is essentially a *post hoc* rationalization of a highly complex and confusing world. As expounded in texts, Postmodernism experiences the very dilemma for which it criticizes philosophy—that narrative is without authority. Taken literally, Postmodernism is an impossible condition, because continuing modernity is intrinsic to European culture (as it now is to most other world cultures); 'Post-*European*' would provide a more accurate, less implausible, epithet for the contemporary condition. *Post*modernism implies that historical continuity is no longer guaranteed, that a complete break with tradition has occurred (though self-evidently this cannot occur). Inevitably, Postmodernism precludes the exaltation of artistic genius; it denies, therefore, the traditional role of the artist, formerly regarded by the West, as in many other societies, as a kind of seer.

The readoption of traditional European harmony, by 'neo-romantic' composers, represents not so much a move *beyond* modernity as a fatal compromise with it. Where the greatest European music transcended the spirit of its age, 'neo-romantic' music panders to its age. It releases composers from the intellectual and musical rigour demanded, if integration of multifarious musical styles is to be achieved, encouraging instead the packaging of mixtures of stylistic clichés. It stands on its head the assertion of the symbolist French poet, Paul Valéry, for example, that 'You can measure the worth of an artist by the quality of his refusals'. The predictable 'entertainment' such music provides is supported by public and private institutions, because it offers a token of modernity without facing it. It reflects a body politic that pays lip-service to *égalité* without getting to grips with global poverty and anarchy. It creates a world of music that is heard, but seldom *listened to*, and that fails to affect people, emotionally.

[15] Jean Baudrillard, 'The Structural Law of Value and the Order of Simulacra', in J. Fekete (ed.), *The Structural Allegory: Reconstructive Encounters with the New French Thought*, trans. C. Levin (Manchester: Manchester University Press, 1984), 89.

[16] Sim, 'Structuralism and Post-Structuralism', 435–6.

Spirituality goes 'Pop'

It has been a constant theme of this book that music has a special attribute, in words non-definable, but attested in its constant use as a primary element of religious and social ceremony. It is still possible to encounter, in the West, exquisitely refined religious chant and polyphony, performed in context. For the most part, however, music no longer registers man's awe before divinity, and the voice approaching the god no longer attempts to appear 'other-worldly'. The music of modern religious ceremony belongs unequivocally to the human, modern world; and the style of performance, so far from aiming at a special quality, suitable for divinity, frequently imitates the most secular of human music. Spirituality has gone 'pop'. The egalitarianism at the heart of the Reformation appears today to have reached its logical end.

So too does the secularism at the heart of the Renaissance. Throughout the world, as civilizations advanced, they tended increasingly to use music for entertainment rather than for ritual; but the apparent merit-acquiring attributes of music continued to be recognized to a degree, both at court, and among the common folk. Although on occasion, music is still to be witnessed performed in its ceremonial context, any merit-acquiring property still ascribed to it is more commonly of a commercial rather than a spiritual nature. Recording, radio, and television industries have made of music a consumer commodity.

Gone, in most Westernized societies, are the manifold, communal, musical celebrations of seasonal change and of rites-of-passage that sustained professional and amateur musicians in local communities, and gave life and purpose to musical genres and styles specific to local regions. Gone, likewise, are communal performance practices that required of all performers equal participation in a musical ensemble (though the intrinsic need for such is still apparent in the espousal of gamelan-playing in Europe and the USA, for example). It is evident that, for humans, music is still strongly associated with season, with place, and with social and national identity, and that it is still capable of powerfully affecting the emotions; but most people no longer *make* the music they listen to. Nor do they court (or insult) each other in song; they do so, non-musically, non-collectively, in their living space.

A society that regards music as the 'voice' of the ancestors provides, of course, no more rational explanation of the effect of music on humans than does a society of unremitting commercialism and consumerism.

Ultimately, all art, including musical art, is valued on the basis of communal acceptance; but where in societies throughout the world a basis for acceptability—for classical canons, at least—was formerly defined by a cultural élite, trained to that purpose (often as a result of hereditary caste), acceptability is largely defined today by the consumer market. Music is seldom judged on the basis of its fitness for religious or social ceremony, because—to an unprecedented extent—consumption has replaced tradition as the empirical arbiter of value. As a leading UK recording manager has stated: 'There are four main areas of music that chart: music as seen on TV, including theme music; local heroes such as Nigel Kennedy or Lesley Garrett; TV-advertised albums such as *The Essential James Galway* or *Sensual Classics*; and accessible contemporary music like Gorecki or Taverner.'[17]

That the 'accessible' music of Gorecki and Taverner is commonly regarded as 'spiritual' suggests that 'spirituality' is a quality that many still seek in music; and if the music of Gorecki and Taverner is the prototype of such 'spirituality', this would seem to lie in slow-moving music, with minimal variety of rhythm and harmony (presumably in contrast to the fast-moving, though equally minimal, harmonies and rhythms of most pop music).

In 1993, Gorecki's Third Symphony (its prolonged, uneventful, monochordalism aptly characterized by its title, *Symphony of Sorrowful Songs*) reached number four in the UK album charts. In 1994, however, a different 'spiritual' product, a two-disc recording of plainchant, *Canto Gregoriano*, sung by a choir of Spanish Benedictine monks,[18] likewise became an international best-selling album. The music of both albums is slow-moving and apparently uneventful; but, whereas Gorecki's music relies for variety almost entirely on timbre and amplitude, the plainchant—even though performed in the homogenized, Solesmes style authorized by the Roman Catholic Church—yields exquisite variety by means of a highly refined system of pitch modality. That the commercial success of the plainchant was as much a surprise to the personnel of EMI Records (who produced it) as to the monks (who performed it) suggests that consumerism and spirituality are not necessarily at variance.

Nevertheless, commercial organizations seldom exist for altruistic reasons; and any special, merit-acquiring attribute still to be ascribed to

[17] Cited in Nicolas Soames, 'A Crush on New', *Classical Music*, 9 Oct. 1993, 25.

[18] *Coro de monjes del Monasterio Benedictino de Santo Domingo de Silos*, EMI records: CMS 5 65217 2.

the Western equivalent of what Chinese, Koreans, and Japanese aptly termed 'elegant music' is essentially flawed by the techniques by which such musical elegance is commonly advertised. Advertising is done to attract sales, not to distinguish critically between commodities. Advertisements for classical music, pop music, ginseng, candyfloss, fast cars, and holidays for two in the Bahamas—to take a random selection—attract essentially the same techniques. That candyfloss may be less nourishing than ginseng, that fast cars kill more readily than slower cars, or that affordable holidays in the Bahamas may be facilitated by the poverty that surrounds them, is of little consequence to the advertiser. Nor is the possibility that a performance of *Fidelio*, for example, or a performance of an Indian *rāg*, might prove more spiritually nourishing than a performance by Ice Cube or Madonna, or for that matter, Philip Glass. All, essentially, are commodities. The commercial success of *Canto Gregoriano* was largely due to its being advertised, not as a musical experience, but as an aid to relaxation.

The Global Market Place

Advertising is a function of retailing; and retailing—whether of ginseng or of new music—depends for its success upon effective distribution. A fine new musical sound created in Uruguay or Morocco will have little international influence unless it appears on discs or cassettes, displayed in international retail outlets. A handful of transnational recording companies now hold a monopoly on disc and cassette distribution, and it has become increasingly difficult for small countries, with small language areas and markets, to make disc and cassette production commercially viable (see pp. 612–13).[19]

So-called 'independent' recording companies are now mostly owned (or otherwise controlled) by transnational companies. That they are usually permitted to operate with relative autonomy, while receiving access to production facilities and major distribution networks, has undoubtedly facilitated the spread of regionally successful minority-taste genres internationally (as well as assisting the issuing of CDs of specialist Western styles): cultural diversity can be turned to economic advantage in many areas of international trade; and the major recording

[19] Roger Wallis and Krister Malm, *Big Sounds from Small Peoples: The Music Industry and Small Countries* (London: Constable, 1984), 11.

companies have seldom been slow to exploit the commercial potential of minority musics, from the tango and *bossa nova*, to reggae and rap.[20] The present trend, however, is for transnational companies to use their 'independent' subsidiaries to test the potential marketability of new, minority genres; and, if a new, minority style is accepted for a major label, it is usually reproduced in second-hand versions, adapted to the taste of the mainly Western, international disc-buying public, acculturated to US and European pop styles. A new product needs to achieve international sales if it is to prove viable, commercially: African soukous, Jamaican reggae, Latin American lambada, and Antillean zouk[21] are just a few of the 'local' styles, the 'local-ness' of which has been compromised by transnational record companies.

'Transnational corporations', in the words of Wally Olins, 'aim at creating a single, bland, homogenised world-market-place, in which everyone buys more or less the same things. They operate on the principle that anything can be made anywhere and sold everywhere.'[22] The global market place that emerged in the 1980s was a consequence of the deregulation of international currencies in the early 1970s (authorized by US President Nixon), as set up by the Bretton Woods conference in 1944 (and effectively managed by the USA through the International Monetary Fund). The subsequent elimination of all capital controls led to a huge increase in the size of the world's capital and financial markets, and to a corresponding change in the proportion of foreign exchange used for trade and long-term investment, and in that used for speculation (from approximately 90/10 per cent to 10/90 per cent, respectively).[23] Moreover, the enormous concentrations of capital that the global economy generated overwhelmed both national institutions and government constraints. Power—political as much as economic—passed from parliamentary institutions to transnational corporations: national economies became interdependent, and global media empires, lacking both national loyalty and effective international control, were enabled to bargain with governments across the world.[24]

[20] Krister Malm, 'The Music Industry', in H. Meyers (ed.), *Ethnomusicology: An Introduction* (New Grove Handbooks in Musicology; London: Macmillan, 1992), 353.

[21] See Jocelyne Guilbault, *Zouk: World Music in the West Indies* (Chicago: University of Chicago Press, 1993).

[22] Wally Olins, 'The European Global Company', *RSA Journal* (June 1994), 18.

[23] Noam Chomsky, *World Orders, Old and New* (London: Pluto Press, 1994), 158–9.

[24] See Anthony Sampson, *The Essential Anatomy of Britain* (London: Coronet Books, 1993).

The revolution in communications greatly facilitated the mobility of capital, and caused labour to become increasingly immobile.[25] It enabled employers to play one national workforce against another by switching places of production from high-wage to low-wage areas of the world (the latter often characterized by high rates of repression and low environmental standards). This commonly had the effect of reducing the living standards and expectations of a majority of a population, while enabling a privileged minority to reap inordinate benefits from escalating profits.

At the time of writing, it is estimated that the richest 20 per cent of the world population (largely comprising countries of the industrialized North) earns about 150 times more than the poorest 20 per cent (mainly in the South); moreover, it consumes about 80 per cent of the world's processed mineral and energy resources, controls 80 per cent of all global trade and domestic investments, and holds 94 per cent of research and development facilities worldwide.[26] The poverty of Third World countries is compounded by international debt demands (themselves often caused by bank initiatives to stimulate borrowing); in 1988, for example, the poor peoples of the South were required to pay the rich peoples of the North about $132 billion in debt-servicing.

In countries where merely to survive is the principal preoccupation, to spend money on artistic development is both impracticable and unthinkable, though such may be the very countries where meaningful, innovative musical styles are evolving. In 'developing' countries, where Westernization has all but eliminated traditional musical styles, and where a firm base for European art music has not been established, the imperative towards industrialization and economic growth overrides, inexorably, the need for publicly funded artistic provision; at the same time, materialist ambition on the part of individual citizens discourages active involvement in the arts. The transnational recording corporations—operating from Europe and the USA (still the major world centres of power and influence)—are therefore able to exploit, for their own financial gain, the musics of small, economically underdeveloped countries; and they influence substantially who hears what, in various parts of the world, and the formation of musical preferences

[25] Chomsky, *World Orders*, 160–2.

[26] Figures quoted from the Just World Trust, cited in Sanen Marshall, 'Reasons for Concern over Population Conference', *New Straits Times*, 27 Aug. 1994, 13.

among youth groups.[27] They are a major factor in the reduction of musical diversity around the world.

Multiculturalism goes 'Pop'

No less important, as a factor in reducing the range of musical variety, is the Postmodern fashion for 'fusing' musical cultures. There is, of course, nothing inherently new in the process of one musical culture interacting with—or being dominated by—another. Given that all musical styles develop from shared means of manipulating musical statements, the borrowing of musical ideas is, and always has been, widespread and commonplace, as well as beneficial. Nor has such borrowing necessarily compromised individual musical styles.

Within the European tradition, for example, the persistent borrowing of Spanish melodies and rhythms by French composers during the nineteenth century did not prevent their music sounding essentially French; nor did Tippett's use of the blues style in his Third Symphony, and in *The Knot Garden*, or his use of Javanese gamelan instruments and scales in the Triple Concerto, make the music sound any less Tippettesque. Western classical music has borrowed persistently from folk music; the examples are endless. Indeed, it can be argued, as did Kodály on occasion, that most new developments in the field of Western classical music have been due to some infusion of elements from popular music practice—as, for example, with the rise of the clarinet, fostered by Mozart.

The use of musical notation in the West makes borrowing evident; but it is plain that musical borrowing has, from the earliest times, taken place throughout the world. The greater musical traditions that spread as the distinctive civilizations of cultural zones in Eurasia developed all benefited from such borrowing, because it facilitated variety within a kind of unity. Like 'language families', the cultural unities of these greater traditions developed over long periods of time, and their distinguishing traits were seldom compromised when historical events led to their being influenced by other *musical* 'families'.

Sometimes, as a consequence of historical events, persistent interaction between particular musical 'families' caused them to 'fuse', over

[27] Wallis and Malm, *Big Sounds from Small Peoples*, 74–109.

time, and so create new and distinctive styles, or 'families' of styles. Such was the case with the emergence of Hindustani music in the fifteenth century and of jazz in the twentieth century, to take two dissimilar examples; the former was essentially a fusion of Hindu and Persian musical traditions (sharing similar features), the latter a fusion of American–European and African musical traditions (with dissimilar features). Both emerged from a process of musical sharing and blending over centuries. So long a passage of time allowed for amalgams of individual traits to be tested, accepted, or rejected.

Fusion of musical cultures does not impair a musical tradition unless a new influence causes loss of confidence in indigenous musical culture, accompanied by decline in associated skills; such loss occurred in many parts of Africa and Asia with the spread of European music from the sixteenth century onwards. In the 1990s, ironically, the influence of African and Asian musics—reflecting a new cultural assertiveness among African and Asian peoples—is contributing to a corresponding loss of confidence among *Western* peoples. Western enthusiasm for multiculturalism is one consequence of this loss, and the fusion of musical styles has became a Postmodernist, Western obsession.

It is a commonplace today to witness—and not only in the West—Indian dance styles, for example, blended with European styles, performed to a mixture of Indian classical and Western popular musics (even though the approaches of the two styles to symbolism, physical movement, and integration with music are utterly dissimilar); or to hear Javanese gamelan music interspersed with music by Western composers, or amalgams of Javanese and non-Javanese styles. Few jazz performers resist the impulse to explore fusions with non-Western traditional styles; likewise, few exponents of non-Western traditional musics resist the impulse to explore the possibilities inherent in fusions with Western music, particularly the clichés of jazz. Jazz has even been fused with Western, Renaissance polyphony.[28] Such fusions are created suddenly, and are not tested by time.

One consequence of this sudden merging of musical styles is that the original components of a mixture become scarcely distinguishable. When Hindustani and jazz musicians join together for a 'fusion' event, for example, they create an immediate hybrid of European, African, Hindu, and Persian musical styles—not allowing for the varied

[28] Jan Gabarek ((saxophone)/Hilliard Ensemble) *Officium*, an ECM-label CD that sold 50,000 copies in six months in the UK alone, 1994.

influences that brought these styles into being in the first place. The mixing of such a multiplicity of musical styles reduces the potency of all: aspects of style that blend most readily are usually the simplest and most basic; and the need to find common ground quickly places emphasis on experiment, more than on skilled technique. Novelty—if such there be—lies more in a particular mix of clichés than in any innovative unfolding of pre-existent systems.

Because fusion-performances are gradually taking precedence, both in quantity and in popularity, over tradition-based performances of individual musical styles, features of traditional musical styles that have developed over hundreds or thousands of years are disappearing; and the skills of those who have contributed to their hallowed status are being discarded. The status of Western classical music is also being undermined. Plurality is a virtue only if its individual constituents retain, within the pluralist ambience, their essential defining character. To quote Lévi-Strauss again:

> The great creative years were those in which communication had become adequate for mutual stimulation by remote partners, yet was not so frequent or so rapid as to endanger the indispensable obstacles between individuals and groups, or to reduce them to the point where overly facile exchanges might equalise and nullify their diversity.[29]

Like spirituality, multiculturalism has gone 'pop'. Electronic communications and the Western-dominated mass media have led to the ultimate change in artistic culture: value judging in commercial terms. A market-orientated entertainment industry that judges quantitatively, rather than qualitatively, has little room for élite artistic culture; profound human experiences, such as the arts provide, are not susceptible of quantitative measurement. If all artistic forms and styles are to be accepted as potentially of equal value, the very concept of value (in anything other than quantitative, commercial, terms) becomes meaningless. It is this difficulty that provides the fuel for the anti-aesthetics rhetoric of Postmodernism.

Beauty and the Beast (2)

Value in the arts has never been easy to determine, least of all in music. In most societies, specific musical genres

[29] Claude Lévi-Strauss, *The View from Afar* (Oxford: Blackwell, 1985), 24.

were—and in many cases still are—related to specific social functions, causing aesthetic and social values to be determined conjointly. This contrasts with the West, where, unusually, aesthetic criteria were established and developed from age to age, enabling music and the arts to be judged independently of other functions. Postmodern discourse conceals the fact that many of the world's arts, now afloat in the same cultural orbit as Western arts, are incompatible with Western, deterministic, value systems, essential to the appreciation of Western classical arts.

As was shown in Chapter 12, Western philosophy encouraged the valuing of beauty in art, on the grounds that the search for beauty is a search for truth (beauty, in this connotation, may be defined as a combination of qualities that pleases the intellect, or moral sense); and, as this held true for music, the emotions music aroused were subject to rational analysis. The concept that the source of aesthetic value in music can lie in an extra-musical phenomenon, such as an emotion, has maintained a persistent hold on European musical thinking, despite being challenged, repeatedly, by musical aestheticians.

As noted earlier (p. 475), the first, and most important, challenge to this concept came from Eduard Hanslick; he asserted that, because music is neither conceptual nor mimetic and cannot therefore generate a predicate, and because emotion embodies not only an affective state but also a set of beliefs concerning the *object* of the emotion, music is fundamentally unsusceptible of embodying emotions and feelings.[30] With remarkable prescience, Hanslick considered that music could generate emotion only through a form of symbolism peculiar to itself. In essence, this view of music has never been conclusively opposed (as early as the third century AD, the Daoist, Xi Kang, asserted that music is 'without sadness or joy').

Aesthetic theory has always been least satisfactory when applied to the non-representational art of music. Modernism in music, in its various forms, and later, popular music, posed acute problems for musical aestheticians. The more recent challenge from world musics appears to have conferred the *coup de grâce* on aesthetic theory itself. It is questionable whether any analytical technique or aesthetic theory can be devised to evaluate, in comparative terms, musical styles that have evolved in different cultural environments, embracing different social

[30] Robert Wilkinson, 'Art, Emotion and Expression', in Hanfling (ed.), *Philosophical Aesthetics*, 208–9.

and artistic value systems. (It is for this reason that the task of musical analysis has become a major concern of sociologists, with emphasis placed on musical function rather than on musical structure.)

This is the central musical predicament of the 'Postmodern' age. Beauty is a cultural construct. Whether applied to music, art, or nature, it means different things in different contexts; it cannot be *validated* on universal principles. It can, however, be validated on the basis of value systems operative within specific societies and contexts; and, because it appeals to both mind and senses, it is susceptible of varying intensity of appreciation. It can only exist, however, if it has cultural meaning; it is for this reason that aesthetic and social aspects of a culture have usually been linked.

That the quest for beauty has been a concern of societies worldwide, and that concepts of beauty can vary radically from one society to another (see p. 476), may be attested by the constant efforts of humans to 'beautify' their bodies. All societies are concerned with bodily appearance, and all take certain steps to embellish, or substantially alter, the natural bodily condition. Beautification of the human body has taken startlingly different forms in different societies.

Many peoples in Africa and in the Americas regard the insertion of plates—round or trapezoidal, of wood or of clay—into a hole punctured in the lower or upper lip (or both) as an act of beautification. The size of the plates is increasingly enlarged, as the size of the punctured hole expands. Young men of the Suyá people of Brazil, for example, whose musical practices were referred to in Chapter 1, insert discs up to three inches in diameter into their lower lip, in preparation for adulthood and marriage. Throughout the world, large, heavy, ornamental objects, are used to alter the natural shape of various parts of the body, and are usually inserted into lips, ears, or nose. All are considered means of beautification.[31]

Even without the addition of ornaments, the natural shape of various parts of the body has frequently been altered so as to conform to concepts of beauty within a particular society. Women of the Padaung people of Myanmar (Burma), for example, wear neck bands of brass rod to elongate the shape of their necks. The shape of the human skull has been flattened, rounded, or elongated, for aesthetic purposes, by pressing small boards against it, or constricting it with bandages, in infancy.

[31] Information in this section taken from the booklet accompanying exhibition, *Enduring Beauty*, at National Museum, Kuala Lumpur, Malaysia (June 1994); contributors include YBhg Dato Sharum bin Yub, Nigel Barley, Encik Ruza bin Elias, Angela Fisher, and Carol Beckwith.

Such practice took place in the Americas, Melanesia, parts of Asia, Africa, Greece, Rome, and modern Europe; the practice itself dates from before the Neolithic. (In Nazi Germany, during the 1930s, some parents bound their infants' heads, in order to assume the elongated shape of head thought to belong to the 'master race'.) In China, at least from the tenth century AD onwards, women endured the painful process of foot-binding, so as to develop the small feet that Chinese men found sexually arousing.

A common—and painful—beautification procedure was that of tattooing (from the Tahitian *tatau*: 'to puncture'), a practice with a long history and widespread distribution. Although tattooing was considered a beautification of the body, it had a further practical advantage of purveying information concerning status, age, and tribal affiliation. In Africa and Australia, where tattooing would be ineffective on dark pigmented skin, scarification has been widely practised: the skin is punctured, as with tattooing, but the wound is then irritated and becomes inflamed, so that a hard scar is left when it heals. Where scarification has been practised, it has been considered to enhance bodily beauty, and scarification designs have been punctured extensively over face, body, and limbs.

In Europe, from the mid-fifteenth to the mid-twentieth centuries, various forms of corset were worn by females in order to lower, heighten, and contract the waistline, according to current fashion; and the position of the waistline at any time was reflected in the clothing of upper-class women. In the 1970s, punks in Europe and the USA pierced ears and nose for the wearing of earrings, safety pins, and other objects. The use of earrings by males was as common in Europe in the sixteenth and seventeenth centuries as it is in the West today. It may be significant that it is principally Western males who keep alive the fashion for body-tattooing, though the tattoos are now acquired through relatively painless techniques.

To the reader who has persisted with the descriptions of peoples and their musics in this book, this brief digression on differing forms of body beautification should not appear irrelevant. All the body alterations described above fulfilled—and in some cases still fulfil—for the peoples who practised them both social and aesthetic functions, as do virtually all the musics described in these pages. And, just as one musical style may, at first hearing, appear strange and 'discordant' to those enculterated to a different style, so body adornments that appear beautiful to one set of people may appear ugly to another.

The appreciative evaluation of beauty is a function of enculteration to specific value systems, or of acculturation to new value systems. It pre-supposes the existence of such value systems, for, without them, beauty cannot exist. In all arts, different varieties share common traits; equally, however, varieties develop differing traits. In association with the value systems of particular cultures, such traits acquire symbolic meaning; and, in association with such meanings, particular aesthetic systems arise, permitting assessment of beauty. Symbolism is an essential means of preserving ideas. Without the symbolism inherent in the art, architecture, and music of eighteenth-century Europe, for example, our understanding of the spirit, and genius, of that age would be greatly diminished; this holds true of all societies and cultural systems.

By examining the means by which a given society uses dance and the plastic arts to symbolize—visually—things, sensations, and events that belong mainly to the visual world, it is possible for an 'outsider' to perceive cultural values associated with such arts; and by such a process of acculturation, the 'outsider' may learn to discriminate the excellent from the commonplace. This is as true of music as of dance and the plastic arts, even though its symbolism is non-visual. Beauty, it is to be repeated, is a cultural construct, and cannot exist without symbolic meaning. Much of what is produced in the name of art today lacks symbolic meaning; it therefore lacks beauty. A multicultural world needs cultural value systems to be understood, and shared, not obliterated.

The process of acculturation to new value systems cannot be achieved without sustained effort, over time. Nor should it be overlooked that such value systems have usually developed in association with consummate skill acquisition. Nevertheless, if multiculturalism is to have lasting benefit, and concepts of beauty are to be retained, acculturation to a diversity of aesthetic concepts is imperative; merely to adapt non-Western aesthetic constructs so as to blend with Western cultural norms is wholly insufficient. The arts, and the musics, of non-Western cultures will be *valued* only when they are appreciated *on their own terms*, in accordance with the value systems under which they evolved. This is unlikely to happen on any significant scale as long as the musical fare offered by radio stations, TV stations, and record stores is dominated by best-selling Western pop styles, performed primarily by people of 'Caucasoid' stock. At the time of writing, MTV Network International broadcasts a near-continuous diet of mainly Western pop music to one quarter of the world's TV households; 'The even better thing is we have three quarters of the world to go,' says Bill Roedy, current President of the Network.[32]

Recovering the Numinous

The gains to be accrued from our new world of fast communications and cultural sharing are inevitably offset by loss of much that was distinctive and instructive. It may, nevertheless, be necessary to accept that, in a culturally anodyne world of fast communication and cultural sharing, the differences between musical cultures will assume less and less significance; that traditional styles may survive precisely because they are only *partially* relevant to the modern world, and exist contiguous with 'non-national' styles, both influencing either.

It would be delusive, however, to believe that increasing homogeneity of style necessarily diminishes the essence of music. As Laurence Picken demonstrated in the Foreword to this book, it is a particular attribute of music that universals exist, worldwide in their significance:[33] that pitch descents in extended sequence, for example, are felt, universally, and fundamentally, to be soothing and comforting;[34] and that for those who participate in the creation (in any sense) of music, that act of creation may still engender the catharsis of ritual.[35] In our modern world, music is seldom employed in its primal function of mediating between gods and humans; but it retains the power to transport the human mind beyond the verbal analysis that informs daily life to a state of stillness that is essentially wordless, beyond logic, beyond reason.

Bernd Schwarze has suggested that whoever hears music is never wholly in the world, but instead is either approaching it, or withdrawing from it.[36] A similar concept of music was evident in the world-view of ancient India (see pp. 98–9) that placed man at the centre of an expanding and contracting universe, seen from without by the theatre director and from within by the priest. Universally, the performer on stage—in Indian terminology, the *sūtradhāra* ('he who holds the

[32] As reported by Alex Spillius, *Independent on Sunday*, 28 May 1995, 23.

[33] Foreword, p. 10.

[34] Foreword, pp. 10, 17.

[35] Foreword, pp. 25–6.

[36] Bernd Schwarze, 'Popmusik und Gnosis: aus dem "Gesangbuch" einer wiederentdeckten Weltreligion', *Acta Musicologica*, 66/2 (1994), 113–21.

strings')—views the world from without, approaching its chaos with radical vitality, controlling the actions of its players by the pacing of the rhythms; but in this performance is disclosed the complementary need for a mystical view from within, the domain of the priest and seer, whose music leads to withdrawal, to a condition of total stillness.

This contrasting, complementary, outward/inward flow of musical process was exemplified in descriptions of the *gisaló* dance and wept-song lamentation of the Kaluli people of Papua New Guinea (see pp. 16–19); and it is revealed no less in today's frenetic world, in the dichotomy between disco hall and concert hall. The participant dancer at a Western disco (or rave) is transported to a state of ecstasy (bordering, perhaps, on euphoria), by acceleration of musical pulse, amplification of the percussion beat, and elevation of respiratory rate. Conversely, for the rapt, relatively motionless listener to profound works of the Western classical repertoire (or of any other repertoire intended to induce meditation rather than movement), ecstasy may approach the Zen-like peace of *samādhi* (see p. 27), the condition of total stillness—'body and mind fallen off'—as the heartbeat slows, and oxygenation lessens.

In this latter aspect, perhaps, is revealed that magical, 'other-worldly' voice of music, that voice that has been employed by humans, universally, for communication with the spirit world, that non-rational voice, surcharged with emotion, that communicates so effectively where words fail. And if it is in this kind of withdrawal that spiritual rejuvenation is to be found, it is perhaps because music is essentially 'the same kind of language as weeping, sobbing, shrieking, laughing,'[37] a universal means of non-verbal communication, the ultimate effect of which is cathartic.

That music is an immanent, life-affirming phenomenon appears now to be appreciated more readily in economically poor communities (whether rural or industrialized) than in industrialized communities of the West; in economically depressed communities, music provides an antidote to material hardship, whereas in affluent communities music is regarded primarily as a consumer commodity. It is fact, however, that music affords an incomparable resource for the emotions; and as such, it can provide an antidote to the unprecedented materialism that shapes the lives of those fortunate enough not to be living in the Third World.

[37] Foreword, p. 6.

To the youth of the affluent West, it is at discos and raves, rather than in performances of classical canons, that this resource is most frequently experienced; and the fact that *Canto Gregoriano* has been played at the end of raves suggests that *samādhi*, as well as euphoria, is sought at them. Discos and raves are, nevertheless, essentially hedonistic occasions, 'one-night stands', geared to the consumer market. They lack the formalities, the subtle vocabularies of music and dance routines, that give meaning to life-renewing ceremonies—those of the Kaluli or Suyá peoples, for example—and to the profoundest items of classical repertoires. As Terry Eagleton has put it: '... the role of culture is not only to reflect social practice, *but to legitimate it.*' He continues: 'If you erode people's sense of corporate identity, *reducing their common history to the eternal now of consumerist desire*, they will simply cease to operate effectively as responsible citizens' (emphasis added).[38]

One benefit of the advanced communications of the late twentieth century is that, for diasporic peoples in particular, their common history *can* now be celebrated, communally, in music: in traditional genres, or in such hybrid genres as jazz, reggae, and souk music, as modern *ghazal* and *bhajan*. And it is precisely this affirmation of a common culture, legitimated by history, that distinguishes many such genres from those of Western, commercial pop, so often characterized by fundamentally a-historic, rudimentary, histrionics.

Enduring art, however, seeks not only commonality, but also transcendence, beyond the topicality of its age. That is why Beethoven's *Wellington's Victory*, for example, Tchaikovsky's *1812 Overture*, Xian Xinghai's revolutionary songs, commercial Western pop music, or the (understandably vehement) diatribes of Afrocentrist rap are unlikely to achieve the status of 'great art'. This is not a question of popular *versus* élite; for 'folk' poetry as song-text, rural or urban, may well achieve such transcendence, when it transports us from observation of the transient to contemplation of the eternal; and the most (seemingly) unsophisticated musical structures may appear to plumb the very wellsprings of our personal being. Art—and, in particular, music—indeed functions as a source of ethnic and social identity; but in its highest manifestations it attempts also to position that identity in a wider, *quasi*-cosmic, framework. This is fundamentally true of all societies.

[38] Terry Eagleton, Inaugural Lecture as Thomas Wharton Professor of English Literature at Oxford University; cited in Robert Saxton, 'Where Do I Begin?', *Musical Times*, Oct. 1994, 631.

It is one of the great dangers, in our synthetic, fast-moving, 'Postmodern' society, that the significance of this highest manifestation will be overlooked. Revitalized artistic creativity, cultivated through universally available education, based on rigorous learning, application, *and judgement*, is necessary to counter the many trivia that in the here-today, throw-away culture of the West have come to be accepted as creative arts (and often imposed as such upon the rest of the world). True recognition of established artistic traditions is indispensable to any such process. No musician, no poet, no dancer, in any culture, ever achieved standing without painstaking intellectual and physical effort, based on perceived models, and nurtured by belief. In a cultural ambience that views élitism with suspicion, such qualities are hard to achieve; they will be achievable only when creative artists, grasping the present and admitting the past, are again *expected* to display *unique* mastery and vision, and are permitted to hew at least a semi-determinist path beyond the detritus of 'Postmodern' society.

In his *Modern Man in Search of a Soul* Carl Jung defined the essence of art and the universal role of the artist in terms that are as relevant now as then:

> The personal idiosyncrasies that creep into a work of art are not essential; in fact, the more we have to cope with these peculiarities, the less it is a question of art. What is essential in a work of art is that it should rise far above the realm of personal life and speak from the spirit and heart of the poet as man to the spirit and heart of mankind....
>
> The artist is not a person endowed with free will who seeks his own ends, but one who allows art to realise its purposes through him. As a human being he may have moods and a will and personal aims, but as an artist he is 'man' in the higher sense—he is 'collective man'—one who carries and shapes the unconscious, psychic life of mankind.[39]

These words apply to artists throughout the world. To restore the role of the creative artist to that of being 'man, in the higher sense'—seer, creator, and skilled 'magician'—should be the major responsibility of our age.

[39] C. J. Jung, *Modern Man in Search of a Soul* (London: Routledge & Kegan Paul Ltd., 1933), 168–9.

Bibliography

ABRAHAM, GERALD, 'Union of Soviet Socialist Republics', *The New Grove* (1980).

ADDISS, STEPHEN, 'Text and Context in Vietnamese Sung Poetry: The Art of Hat a Dao', *Selected Reports in Ethnomusicology* (1992).

ADRIAANSZ, W., 'Japan', *The New Grove* (1980).

ALLEN, W. F., WARE, C. P., and GARRISON, L. M. (eds.), *Slave Songs of the United States* (New York, 1867).

AMBROSE, KAY, and GOPAL, RAM, *Classical Dances and Costumes of India* (London: Adam & Charles Black, 1983).

ANDERSON, BENEDICT, *Imagined Communities: Reflections on the Origin and Spread of Nationalism* (London: Verso, 1987).

ANDERSON, EMILY (ed.), *The Letters of Beethoven*, i (London: Macmillan, 1961).

ANDERSON, GORDON A., 'Goliards', *The New Grove* (1980).

ANDERSON, ROBERT, 'Ancient Mesopotamian and Egyptian Music', *NOCM* (1983).

ANDERSON, WARREN, 'Ethos', *The New Grove* (1980).

APPLEYARD, BRYAN, *Understanding the Present: Science and the Soul of Modern Man* (London: Pan Books, 1992).

ARETZ, ISABEL, *El Folklore Musical Argentino* (Buenos Aires: El Folklore 1952).

—— 'Peru', *The New Grove* (1980).

ARISTOPHANES, *The Clouds*, trans. Alan H. Sommerstein (London: Penguin, 1973).

ARNOLD, ALISON E., 'Aspects of Production and Consumption in the Popular Hindi Film Song Industry', *Asian Music*, 24/1 (1993).

ARNOLD, DENIS, 'Renaissance', *NOCM* (1983).

AUERBACH, ERICH, *Mimesis, the Representation of Reality in Western Literature*, trans. Willard Trask (London: Doubleday Anchor, 1967).

AVENARY, HANOCH, 'Jewish Music', *NOCM* (1983).

BACHMANN, WERNER, *The Origins of Bowing*, trans. Norma Deane (London: Oxford University Press, 1969).

BAIGENT, MICHAEL, LEIGH, RICHARD, and LINCOLN, HENRY, *The Holy Blood and The Holy Grail* (London: Corgi Books, 1983).

BAINES, ANTHONY, *The Oxford Companion to Musical Instruments* (Oxford: Oxford University Press, 1992).

BAKER, NANCY KOVALEFF, 'Expression', *The New Grove* (1980).

BANERJEE, ASHIS, 'The Caste System', in Shalina Saran (ed.), *Southern India* (Munich: Nelles Verlag GmbH, 1990).

BARBER-KERSOVAN, ALENKA, 'Tradition and Acculturation as Polarities of Slovenian Popular Music', in Simon Frith (ed.), *World Music, Politics, and Social Change* (Manchester: Manchester University Press, 1989).

BARTHOLOMEW, JOHN, *The Steel Band* (Oxford: Oxford University Press, 1980).

BATES, DANIEL, and RASSAM, AMAL, *Peoples and Cultures of the Middle East* (Englewood Cliffs, NJ: Prentice Hall, 1983).

BAUDRILLARD, JEAN, 'The Structural Law of Value and the Order of Simulacra', in J. Fekete (ed.), *The Structural Allegory: Reconstructive Encounters with the New French Thought*, trans. C. Levin (Manchester: Manchester University Press, 1984).

BÉHAGUE, GERARD, 'Argentina', 'Bolivia', 'Bossa Nova', 'Brazil', 'Chile', 'Colombia', 'Cuba', 'Ecuador', 'Latin America', 'Mexico, and 'Peru', *The New Grove* (1980).

BERGER, JOHN, *The Success and Failure of Picasso* (London: Penguin Books, 1965).

BERLAND, JODY, 'Music Video and Media Reconstruction', in Simon Frith, Andrew Goodwin, and Lawrence Grossberg (eds.), *Sound and Vision: The Music Video Reader* (London: Routledge, 1993).

BERNAL, MARTIN, *Black Athena, the Afroasiatic Roots of Classical Civilization* (2 vols.; London: Free Association Books, 1987).

BLACKBURN, PHILIP, *Stilling Time*, CD of 'Traditional Musics of Vietnam', Minnesota Composers Forum, 1994.

BLACKING, JOHN, 'The Structure of Musical Discourse: The Problem of the Song Text', *Yearbook for Traditional Music*, xiv (1982), 15–23.

BLADES, JAMES, 'Cymbals' and 'Xylophone', *The New Grove* (1980).

BLAUFARB, ROSS, 'Foreign Bands Boom the New Trend in Thailand's Expanding Nightclub Scene', *Asiabeat* (Hong Kong, February 1993).

BLENCH, ROGER, 'The Morphology and Distribution of Sub-Saharan Musical Instruments, of North African, Middle Eastern, and Asian Origin', *Musica Asiatica*, 4 (1984).

BLUM, STEPHEN, 'Iran', *The New Grove* (1980).

BOND, KATHERINE, and PATHAMMAVONG, KINGSAVANH, 'Contents of Dontrii Lao Deum: Traditional Lao Music', *Selected Reports in Ethnomusicology* (1992).

BORBOLLA, CARLOS, 'Cuba', *The New Grove* (1980).

BRANDON, JAMES R., 'South East Asia', *The New Grove* (1980).

BRANSCOMBE, PETER, 'Pantomime', *The New Grove* (1980).

BRINGARD, MARIE-THÉRÈSE (ed.), *Sounding Forms: African Musical Instruments* (American Federation of Arts, 1989).

BROERE, BERNARD J., 'El Chambu—a Study of Popular Musics in Narino, South Colombia', in Simon Frith (ed.), *World Music, Politics, and Social Change* (Manchester: Manchester University Press, 1989).

BRONOWSKI, J., *The Ascent of Man* (London: BBC, 1973).

BROOKS, GEORGE E., 'African "Landlords" and European "Strangers": African–European Relations to 1870', in Phyllis M. Martin and Patrick O'Meara (eds.), *Africa* (Bloomington, Ind.: Indiana University Press, 1986).

BROW, ROBERT, 'Origins of Religion', in *The Religions of the World* (London: Lion Publishing, 1982).

BROWN, DEE, *Bury my Heart at Wounded Knee* (New York: Bantam Books, 1972).

BROWN, HOWARD MAYER, 'Performing Practice', *The New Grove* (1980).

BUCKINGHAM, JAMES SILK, *Autobiography of James Silk Buckingham*, i (London: Longman, Brown, Green, & Longmans, 1885).

BURKE, JAMES, *The Day the Universe Changed* (London: BBC, 1985).

CALDWELL, JOHN, 'Medieval', *NOCM* (1983).

CAMERON, GAIL, and CROOKE, STAN, *Liverpool—Capital of the Slave Trade* (Liverpool: Picton Press, 1992).

CHAN, WING HOI, *Traditional Folksong and Rural Life in Hong Kong: Overall Report of the General Context of Local Folksongs* (Hong Kong: Museum of History, 1984).

CHANG, JUNG, *Wild Swans* (London: Harper Collins, 1991).

CHASE, GILBERT, 'United States of America', *The New Grove* (1980).

CHATWIN, BRUCE, *The Viceroy of Ouidah* (London: Pan Books, 1982).

—— *The Songlines* (London: Picador, 1987).

CHENG, NIEN (1986), *Life and Death in Shanghai* (London: Grafton Books, 1986).

CHERNOFF, JOHN MILLER, *African Rhythm and African Sensibility* (Chicago: University of Chicago Press, 1979).

CHING, FRANK, *Ancestors* (London: Pan Books, 1979).

CHKHIKVADZE, GRIGOL, 'Union of Soviet Socialist Republics', *The New Grove* (1980).

CHOMSKY, NOAM, *World Orders, Old and New* (London: Pluto Press, 1994).

CLAPHAM, JOHN, 'Czechoslovakia', *The New Grove* (1980).

CLARK, KENNETH, *Civilisation* (London: Harper & Row, 1969).

CLOUDSLEY, PETER, 'The Living Inca Heritage', *Geographical Magazine* (February 1985).

—— 'From Creole to Chicha', *Geographical Magazine* (May 1987).

COHEN, JUDITH R., 'The Impact of Mass Media and Acculturation on the Judeo-Spanish Song Tradition in Montreal', in Simon Frith (ed.), *World Music, Politics, and Social Change* (Manchester: Manchester University Press, 1989).

The Collins Atlas of World History, ed. Pierre Vidal-Naquet (London: Collins, 1987).

COLLINS, JOHN, and RICHARDS, PAUL, 'Popular Music in West Africa', in Simon Frith (ed.), *World Music, Politics, and Social Change* (Manchester: Manchester University Press, 1989).

COMPTON, CAROL J., 'Traditional Verbal Arts in Laos: Functions, Forms, Continuities, and Changes in Texts, Contexts, and Performances', *Selected Reports in Ethnomusicology* (1980).

CONDIT, JONATHAN, 'Two Song-Dynasty Chinese tunes Preserved in Korea', in D. R. Widdess and R. P. Wolpert (eds.), *Tradition and Change: Essays on Asian and other Musics Presented to Laurence Picken* (Cambridge: Cambridge University Press, 1981).

—— 'Korean Music', *NOCM* (1983).

COOKE, ALISTAIR, *America* (London: BBC, 1973).

COOKE, ANDREW, 'Reconstructing the Etamiivu Ensemble', unpublished paper presented to ICTM UK (1992).

COOKE, DERYCK, *I Saw the World End* (London: Oxford University Press, 1979).

COOKE, PETER, 'Pygmy Music' and 'Stopped Flute Ensembles', *The New Grove* (1980).

—— 'Exploring Musical Pitch Systems', *ICTM UK Bulletin*, 27 (1990).

—— *Play Amadinda: Xylophone Music from Uganda* (Edinburgh: K. and C. Productions, 1990).

—— and WACHSMANN, KLAUSS, 'Africa', *The New Grove* (1980).

COPLAN, DAVID, 'The Urbanization of African Performing Arts in South Africa', D.Phil. thesis (Indiana, 1980).

—— *In Township Tonight* (London: Longman, 1985).

COTT, JONATHAN, *Stockhausen: Conversations with the Composer* (London: Picador, 1974).

COTTER, HOLLAND, 'Uncovering Japan's Buried Past', review of 'Ancient Japan', exhibition at the Smithsonian Institute in New York, *International Herald Tribune*, 5 September 1992.

COTTERELL, ARTHUR, *China: A Cultural History* (London: Penguin Books, 1988).

COVELL, J. C., and COVELL, A., *Korean Impact on Japanese Culture* (Hollym, 1984).

CRAWFORD, RICHARD, 'Psalmody', *The New Grove* (1980).

CREWDSON, H. A. F., *Worshipful Company of Musicians* (London: Constable, 1950).

CROCKER, RICHARD L., 'Melisma', *The New Grove* (1980).

CROSSLEY-HOLLAND, PETER, 'Buddhist Music' and 'Central Asia', *The New Grove* (1980).

CUNNINGHAM, MARTIN, 'Spain', *The New Grove* (1980).

CURRY SMITH, CLYDE, 'The Ancient Religions of Greece and Rome', in *The Religions of the World* (London: Lion Publishing, 1982).

DABYDEEN, DAVID, *Hogarth's Blacks: Images of Blacks in Eighteenth Century English Art* (London: Dangaroo Press, 1985).

DAHLHAUS, CARL, 'Wagner', *The New Grove* (1980).

DANIELSON, VIRGINIA, 'The Arab Middle East', in Peter Manuel, *Popular Musics of the Non-Western World* (New York: Oxford, 1989).

DAVIDSON, BASIL, *Africa in History* (London: Paladin Books, 1984).

DAVIS, RUTH, 'Modern Trends in the Arab-Andalusian Music of Tunisia', *Maghreb Review*, 11/2 (1986), 134–44.

—— 'Modern Trends in the *Ma'lūf* of Tunisia, 1934–1984' (Ph.D. diss., Princeton University, 1986).

—— 'Links between the Baron Rodolphe D'Erlanger and the Notation of Tunisian Art Music', in *Ethnomusicology and the Historical Dimension: Papers Presented at the European Seminar in Ethnomusicology*, London, May 1986 (Philip Verlag, 1989).

—— 'Melodic and Rhythmic Genre in the Tunisian *Nūba*: A Performance Analysis'; *Ethnomusicologica II: Quaderni dell'Accademia Chigiana XLV* (Proceedings of the VI European Seminar in Ethnomusicology, Siena, 1989; Siena: Accademia Musicale Chigiana, 1993), 71–109.

—— 'Cultural Policy and the Tunisian *Ma'lūf*: Redefining a Tradition', *Ethnomusicology*, 41/1 (1997).

DERRIDA, JACQUES, *Writing and Difference*, trans. A. Bass (London: Routledge & Kegan Paul, 1978).

DEVA, B. C., *Psychoacoustics of Music and Speech* (Madras Music Academy, 1967).

DIAMOND, JARED, *The Rise and Fall of the Third Chimpanzee* (London: Vintage, 1992).

DOBBS-HIGGINSON, M. S., *Asia Pacific: Its Role in the New World Disorder* (London: Mandarin Paperbacks, 1993).

DOLING, TIM, and SODEN, PHILIP, *Report of the Arts Vietnam Consultancy Visit* (Hong Kong, 1991).

—— —— *Arts Indo China Cultural Development Report: Cambodia* (Hong Kong: Arts Indo China, 1992).

—— —— *Arts Indo China Cultural Development Report: Laos* (Hong Kong: Arts Indo China, 1992).

DOUGLASS, FREDERICK, *My Bondage and my Freedom* (New York, 1853).

DOVER, KENNETH, *The Greeks* (London: BBC, 1980).

DOWNEY, JAMES C., 'Spiritual', *The New Grove* (1980).

DYEN, DORIS J., and RHODES, WILLARD, 'North America', *The New Grove* (1980).

EDWARDS W. H., 'The Aborigines', in *The Religions of the World* (London: Lion Publishing, 1982).

EINHARD, *The Life of Charlemagne*, trans. in Lewis Thorpe, *Two Lives of Charlemagne* (Harmondsworth: Penguin, 1979).

ELIADE, MIRCEA, *Shamanism: Archaic Techniques of Ecstasy* (London: Penguin, 1964).

ELLIS, CATHERINE I., 'Australia', *The New Grove* (1980).

ESKEW, HARRY, 'Shape-Note Hymnody', *The New Grove* (1980).

FARHAT, HORMOZ, 'Iran', *The New Grove* (1980).

—— 'Scales and Intervals: Theory and Practice', in Gerard Gillen and Harry White, *Irish Musical Studies* (Dublin: Irish Academic Press, 1990).

—— *The Dastgāh Concept in Persian Music* (Cambridge: Cambridge University Press, 1990).

—— 'Western Musical Influences in Persia', *Musicological Annual*, xxvii (Ljubljana, 1991).

FARMER, GEORGE HENRY, 'The Music of Islam', *The New Oxford History of Music*, i (Oxford: Oxford University Press, 1957).

FARRELL, GERRY, *Indian Music in Education* (Cambridge: Cambridge University Press, 1990).

FARUQĪ, LOIS IBSEN AL-, 'Ornamentation in Arabian Improvisational Music: A Study of Interrelatedness in the Arts', *The World of Music*, 20 (1978).

FEBVRE, LUCIEN, and MARTIN, HENRI-JEAN, *The Coming of the Book: The Impact of Printing, 1450–1800* (London: New Left Books, 1976), trans. of *L'Apparition du livre* (Paris: Albin Michel, 1958).

FERNANDO, S. H., Jr., *The New Beats: Exploring the Music Culture and Attitudes of Hip-Hop* (Edinburgh: Payback Press, 1995).

FLEISCHHAUER, GÜNTER, 'Rome', *The New Grove* (1980).

FLETCHER, PETER, *Roll over Rock: A Study of Music in Contemporary Society* (London: Stainer & Bell, 1981).

FLETCHER, PETER, *Education and Music* (Oxford: Oxford University Press, 1987).

FLOTZINGER, RUDOLF, 'Magnus Liber', *The New Grove* (1980).

FOSTER, HAL (ed.), *Postmodern Culture* (London: Pluto Press, 1983).

FRANSSON, F., and TJERNLUND, P., 'Statistical Tone Measurements of the Tone-Scale in Played Music', STL-OPSR, 2–3, Department of Speech Communication, KTH, Stockholm, 1970.

FREEMAN, MICHAEL, *Angkor* (Hong Kong: Pacific Rim Press, 1992).

FRITH, SIMON, *Music for Pleasure* (Oxford: Polity Press in association with Robert Blackwell, 1988).

—— 'Youth, Music, Television', in Simon Frith, Andrew Goodwin, and Lawrence Grossberg (eds.), *Sound and Vision: The Music Video Reader* (London: Routledge, 1993).

—— (ed.), *World Music, Politics, and Social Change* (Manchester: Manchester University Press, 1989).

—— GOODWIN, ANDREW, and GROSSBERG, LAWRENCE (eds.), *Sound and Vision: The Music Video Reader* (London: Routledge, 1993).

FRYER, PETER, *Staying Power: The History of Black People in Britain* (London: Pluto Press, 1984).

FUMIKO, FUJITA, *Problems of Language, Culture, and the Appropriateness of Musical Expression in Japanese Childrens' Performance* (Tokyo: Academic Music Ltd, 1989).

GAMMOND, PETER, *The Oxford Companion to Popular Music* (Oxford: Oxford University Press, 1991).

GAO, HOUYONG, 'On Qupai', *Asian Music*, 20/2 (1989).

GARFIAS, ROBERT, 'Japan', *The New Grove* (1980).

GARSIDE, ROGER, *Coming Alive: China after Mao* (New York: Mentor, 1981).

GASCOIGNE, BAMBER, *The Christians* (London: Jonathan Cape, 1977).

GELB, L. J., '*Homo ludens* in Early Mesopotamia', *Studia Orientalia*, 46 (1975), 43–76.

GERALD OF WALES, *Journey through Wales and the Description of Wales*, trans. Lewis Thorpe (London: Penguin Books, 1978).

GERSHEVITCH, ILYA, 'The Sound of Avestan Verse-Lines', Ratanbai Katrak Lectures (unpublished, Oxford, 1968).

GILLETT, CHARLIE, *The Sound of the City* (London: Sphere Books, 1970).

GOLDBERG, ISAAC, *Tin Pan Alley* (New York: John Day, 1930).

GOUZOULES, S., GOUZOULES, H., and MARLER, P, 'Rhesus Monkey Screams: Representational Signalling in the Recruitment of Agnostic Aid', *Animal Behaviour*, 32 (1984).

GRAME, THEODORE, 'Morocco', *The New Grove* (1980).

GRAY, NICK (1992), '"Sulendra": An Example of *Petegak* in the Balinese *Gendér Wayang* Repertory', *British Journal of Ethnomusicology*, 1 (1992).

GREWAL, BIKRAM, and ISRAEL, SAMUEL (eds.), *India* (Hong Kong: APA Publication, 1990).

GRIFFITHS, ANN, and RIMMER, JOAN, 'Harp', *The New Grove* (1980).

GROSSBERG, LAWRENCE, 'The Media Economy of Rock Culture: Cinema, Post-Modernity and Authenticity', in Simon Frith, Andrew Goodwin, and Lawrence Grossberg (eds.), *Sound and Vision: The Music Video Reader* (London: Routledge, 1993).

GUILBAULT, JOCELYNE, *Zouk: World Music in the West Indies* (Chicago: University of Chicago Press, 1993).

GULIK, R. H. VAN (1931), *The Lore of the Chinese Lute: An Essay in Ch'in Ideology* (Tokyo: Toppan-insatsu-kabushik-kaisha, 1931).

GUNJI, MASAKATSU, 'The Development of Kabuki', in Chie Nakone and Shinzaburō Ōishi (eds.), *Tokugawa Japan*, trans. Conrad Totman (Tokyo: University of Tokyo Press, 1990).

HABERMAS, JÜRGEN, 'Modernity—An Incomplete Project', in Hal Foster (ed.), *Postmodern Culture* (London: Pluto Press, 1983).

HALL, D. G. E., *A History of South East Asia* (London: Macmillan, 1981).

HALL, RONALD, RUSSELL, KATHY, and WILSON, MIDGE, *Color Complex: The Politics of Skin Color among African Americans* (New York: Harcourt Brace Jovanovitch, 1992).

HAN, KUO-HUANG, 'Folk Songs of the Han Chinese: Characteristics and Classifications', *Asian Music*, 20/2 (1989).

HANDY, W. C., 'The Heart of the Blues', *Étude Music Magazine* (March 1940); repr. in Eileen Southern (ed.), *Readings in Black American Music* (New York: Norton, 1971), 202–7.

—— *Father of the Blues* (1941), excerpts repr. in Eileen Southern (ed.), *Readings in Black American Music* (New York: Norton, 1971), 202–7.

—— (ed.), *Blues: An Anthology* (1949; repr. New York: Macmillan, 1972).

HANFLING, OSWALD (ed.), *Philosophical Aesthetics: An Introduction* (Oxford: Blackwell/Open University, 1992).

HANNICK, CHRISTIAN, 'Christian Church, Music of the Early' and 'Ethiopia', *The New Grove* (1980).

HARRISON, FRANK Ll. (1985), 'Observation, Elucidation, Utilization: Western Attitudes to Eastern Musics, ca. 1600–ca. 1830', in Malcolm Hamrick Brown and Roland John Wiley (eds.), *Slavonic and Western Music: Essays for Gerald Abraham* (Oxford: Oxford University Press, 1985).

HASE, PATRICK, 'New Territories Poetry and Song', *Sources for Hong Kong Historical Research* (Hong Kong: Museum of History, 1984).

HASSAN, SCHEHEREZADE QASSIM, 'Iraq', *The New Grove* (1980).

HATCH, MARTIN, 'Popular Music in Indonesia', in Simon Frith (ed.), *World Music, Politics, and Social Change* (Manchester: Manchester University Press, 1989).

HEARTZ, DANIEL, 'Enlightenment', *The New Grove* (1980).

HEBDIGE, DICK, *Cut 'n' Mix: Culture, Identity, and Caribbean Music* (London: Routledge, 1987).

HEINS, ERNST, 'Indonesia', *The New Grove* (1980).

HENDERSON, CLAYTON W., 'Minstrelsy, American', *The New Grove* (1980).

HERACLITUS, *The Presocratics*, trans. Philip Wheelwright (New York: Odyssey Press, 1966).

HERIOT, ANGUS, *The Castrati in Opera* (1956; repr. New York: Da Capo Press, 1975).

HERMAN, MARILYN, 'Ethiopian Zefen and the "Band of Blossoming Hope" in Israel', unpublished paper presented to ICTM UK 1992.

HILEY, DAVID, 'Conductus', 'Mode', 'Organum', and 'Plainchant', *NOCM* (1983).

HINNELLS, JOHN, 'Mithraism: Cult of the Bull', in *The Religions of the World* (London: Lion Publishing, 1982).

HINZ, W., *The Lost World of Elam: Recreation of a Vanished Civilisation*, trans. Jennifer Barnes (London: Sidgwick & Jackson, 1972).

HITCHCOCK, H. WILEY, *Music in the United States: A Historical Introduction* (Englewood Cliffs, NJ: Prentice Hall, 1974).

—— 'Foster, Stephen Collins', *The New Grove* (1980).

HOOD, MANTLE, 'Indonesia' and 'South East Asia', *The New Grove* (1980).

HOWARD, KEITH, review of Korean Traditional Music on CD, *British Journal of Ethnomusicology*, 2 (1993).

HUANG JINPEI, 'Xipi and Erhuang of Beijing and Guangdong Operas', *Asian Music*, 20/2 (1989).

HUGHES, DAVID, 'Thai Music in Java, Javanese Music in Thailand', *British Journal of Ethnomusicology*, 1 (1992).

HUME, DAVID, *An Enquiry Concerning Human Understanding*, ed. L. A. Selby Bigge (Oxford: Oxford University Press, 1984).

HUSSEY, DERMOTT, and ZACH, PAUL, 'The Red Hot Rhythms of Reggae', in *Jamaica* (Hong Kong: APA Publications, 1988).

INDEN, ROBERT, *Imagining India* (Oxford: Blackwell, 1990).

IVES, CHARLES, *Essays before a Sonata* (1920; ed. Howard Boatwright, New York: Norton, 1961).

JACKSON, WILLIAM, 'Features of the Kriti: A Song developed by Tyāgāraja', *Asian Music*, 34/1 (1993).

JAIRAZBHOY, N. A., 'An Interpretation of the 22 Srutis', *Perspectives on Asian Music: Essays in Honor of Dr Laurence E. R. Picken* (*Asian Music*, 6/1–2 (1975)).

——'India', *The New Grove* (1980).

JING, MIAO, and JIANZHONG, QIAO, *Lun Hanzu Minge Jinshi Secaiqu de Huafen (A Study of Similar Color Area Divisions in Han Folk Songs)* (Beijing: Wenhua Yishu, 1987).

JOHNSON, ROBERT SHERLAW, *Messiaen* (London: Dent, 1975).

JONES, STEPHEN, 'The Golden-Character Scripture: Perspectives on Chinese Melody', *Asian Music*, 20/2 (1989).

——*Folk Music of China: Living Instrumental Traditions* (Oxford: Oxford University Press, 1995).

JONES, STEVE, *The Language of the Genes* (London: Flamingo, 1994).

JORDAN, PAUL, *Egypt, the Black Land* (London: Phaidon Press, 1976).

JUNG, ANGELIKA, 'Maqām and the Cyclic Principle', in Harold Powers (ed.), 'First Meeting of the ICTM Study Group on *Maqām*', *Yearbook for Traditional Music*, 20 (1988), 199–218.

JUNG, C. J., *Modern Man in Search of a Soul* (London: Routledge & Kegan Paul Ltd., 1933).

KANT, IMMANUEL, *The Critique of Judgement*, trans. James Creed Meredith (Oxford: Oxford University Press, 1928).

KAPLAN, FREDERIC M., SOBIN, JULIAN M., and KEIJZER, ARNE J. DE, *The China Guidebook*, 10th edn. (Teaneck, NJ: Eurasia Press, 1989).

KARP, THEODORE, 'Troubadours, Trouvères', *The New Grove* (1980).

KATAMBA, FRANCIS, and COOKE, PETER, 'Ssematimba ne Kikwabanga: The Music and Poetry of a Ganda Historical Song', *The World of Music*, 2 (1987).

KATZNER, KENNETH, *The Languages of the World* (London: Routledge, 1977).

KAUFFMAN, ROBERT A., 'African Rhythm: A Reassessment', *Ethnomusicology* (September 1980).

——'Lamellaphone', *The New Grove* (1980).

KAUFMAN, NIKOLAI, 'Bulgaria', *The New Grove* (1980).

KENDALL, LAUREL, 'Shamanism', in *Korea* (Hong Kong: APA Publications, 1989).

KIDSON, PETER, 'The Figural Arts', in M. I. Finley (ed.), *The Legacy of Greece* (Oxford: Oxford University Press, 1981).

KISHIBE, SHIGEO, 'China', *The New Grove* (1980).

KNAPPERT, JAN (1979), *Myths and Legends of the Swahili* (Kenya: Heinemann, 1979).

KOETTING, JAMES (1986), 'What Do We Know About African Rhythm?', ed. Roderic Knight, *Ethnomusicology*, 30/4 (1986).

KOIZUMI, FUMIO, 'Japan', *The New Grove* (1980).

KOUWENHOVEN, FRANK, 'Bringing to Life Tunes of Ancient China: an Interview with Laurence Picken', *CHIME*, 4 (Autumn, 1991).

KRAUS, RICHARD CURT, *Pianos and Politics in China* (New York: Oxford University Press, 1989).

KREUGER, M., 'The Movie Musical from Vitaphone to 42nd Street', *A Great Fan Magazine* (1975).

LAMPHEAR, JOHN, 'Aspects of Early African History', in Phyllis M. Martin and Patrick O'Meara (eds.), *Africa* (Bloomington, Ind.: Indiana University Press, 1986).

LANDON, H. C. ROBBINS, 'Haydn in England, 1791–1795', in *Haydn, Chronicle and Works*, ii (London: Thames and Hudson, 1976).

LANNOY, RICHARD, *The Speaking Tree: A Study of Indian Culture and Society* (Oxford: Oxford University Press, 1971).

LAO-TZU, *Tao Te Ching*, trans. Stephen Mitchell (London: Macmillan, 1988).

LE HURAY, PETER, and DAY, JAMES (eds.), *Music and Aesthetics in the Eighteenth and Early Nineteenth Centuries*, abridged edn. (Cambridge: Cambridge University Press, 1981).

LEE, BYONG WON, 'Korea', *The New Grove* (1980).

LÉVI-STRAUSS, CLAUDE, *The View from Afar* (Oxford: Blackwell, 1985).

LEVY, KENNETH, 'Plainchant', *The New Grove* (1980).

LIANG, DAVID M. Y., YANG, RICHARD F. S., and YANG, MYRTLE L., 'Poetic Songs of the Yuan', *Chinese Culture*, 11/1 (1970).

LIANG, MINGYUE, *Music of the Billion: An Introduction to Chinese Musical Culture* (New York: Heinrichshofen, 1985).

LINTER, BERTIL, *Outrage: Burma's Struggle for Democracy* (Hong Kong: Review Publishing Company, 1989).

LIVINGSTONE, FRANK, 'Did the Australopithicenes Sing?', *Current Anthropology*, 14/1–2 (1973).

LLOYD, A. L., *Folk Song in England* (London: Lawrence & Wishart, 1967).

—— 'Europe', *The New Grove* (1980).

LOCKWOOD, DOUGLAS, *I, the Aboriginal* (Australia: Rigby, 1962).

LOCKWOOD, LEWIS, 'Renaissance', *The New Grove* (1980).

LOMAX, ALAN, sleeve note to *The Gospel Ship: Baptist Hymns and White Spirituals from the Southern Mountains*, New World Records, NW 294, 1977.

—— sleeve note to *Roots of the Blues*, New World Records, NW 252, 1977.

LORTAT-JACOB, B., 'Berber Music', *The New Grove* (1980).

LOWE, JOHN, *Inside Japan* (London: John Murray, 1985).

LYOTARD, JEAN-FRANÇOIS, *The Postmodern Condition: A Report on Knowledge*, trans. G. Bennington and B. Massumi (Manchester: Manchester University Press, 1984).

MACEDA, JOSÉ, 'In Search of a Source of Pentatonic, Hemitonic and Anhemitonic Scales in Southeast Asia', *Acta Musicologica*, 3/2 (Bärenreiter-Verlag, 1990).

MacKay, David P., 'Billings', *The New Grove* (1980).

Mackerras, Colin P., 'China', *The New Grove* (1980).

McLuhan, Marshall, and Fiore, Quentin, *The Medium is the Massage* (London: Penguin Books, 1967).

Magowan, Fiona, 'The Land is our *Märr*, It Stays Forever: The *Yothu-Yindi* Relationship in Australian Aboriginal Traditional and Popular Musics', in Martin Stokes (ed.), *Ethnicity, Identity and Music: The Musical Construction of Place* (Oxford: Berg Publications, 1994).

Mahdi, Salah El, 'North Africa', *The New Grove* (1980).

Malm, Krister, 'The Music Industry', in H. Meyers (ed.), *Ethnomusicology: An Introduction* (New Europe Handbooks in Musicology; London: Macmillan, 1992), 349–64.

Malm, W. P., 'East Asia' and 'Japan', *The New Grove* (1980).

—— *Six Hidden Views of Japanese Music* (Berkeley and Los Angeles: University of California Press, 1986).

Mallory, J. P., *In Search of Indo-Europeans: Language, Archaeology and Myth* (London: Thames & Hudson, 1989).

Manuel, Peter, *Popular Musics of the Non-Western World* (New York: Oxford University Press, 1989).

—— 'The Cassette Industry and Popular Music in North India', *Popular Music* (May 1991).

Marett, Allan, 'Banshiki Sangun and Shoenraku: Metrical Structure and Notation of Two Tang-Music Melodies for Flute', in D. R. Widdess and R. P. Wolpert (eds.), *Tradition and Change: Essays on Asian and Other Musics Pre-sented to Laurence Picken* (Cambridge: Cambridge University Press, 1981).

Markham, Elizabeth, 'Japanese Music', *NOCM* (1983).

Marre, Jeremy, and Charlton, Hannah, *Beats of the Heart: Popular Music of the World* (New York: Pantheon Books, 1985).

Marrou, H. I., *A History of Education in Antiquity* (London: Sheen & Ward, 1966).

Martin, B. G., 'The Spread of Islam', in Phyllis M. Martin and Patrick O'Meara (eds.), *Africa* (Bloomington, Ind.: Indiana University Press, 1986).

Martin, Phyllis M., and O'Meara, Patrick (eds.) *Africa* (Bloomington, Ind.: Indiana University Press, 1986).

Massey, Reginald, and Massey, Jamila, *The Music of India* (London: Stanmore Press, 1976).

Matusky, Patricia, *Malaysian Shadow Play and Music: Continuity of an Oral Tradition* (Oxford: Oxford University Press, 1993).

Mazrui, Ali A., *The Africans* (London: BBC, 1986).

Meer, Wim van der, *Hindustani Music in the 20th Century* (New Delhi: Allied Publishers, 1980).

MEEUS, NICOLAS, 'Keyboard', *The New Grove* (1980).

MELLERS, WILFRID (1988), 'Monotonously Minimal', review of Philip Glass, *Opera on the Beach*, in *Times Literary Supplement* (October 1988).

MENSAH, ATTA, 'Highlife', *The New Grove* (1980).

MERTENS, WIM, *American Minimal Music* (London: Kahn & Averill, 1983).

METZ, WULF, 'One God, Many Paths', in *The Religions of the World* (London: Lion Publishing, 1982).

MICIC, PETER, 'Notes on Pop/Rock Genres in the Eighties in China', *CHIME*, 8 (Spring 1995).

MILLER, TERRY E. (1980), 'Laos', *The New Grove* (1980).

—— 'A Melody not Sung: The Performance of Lao Buddhist Texts in Northeast Thailand', *Selected Reports in Ethnomusicology* (1992).

—— and SAM, SAM-ANG, 'The Classical Musics of Cambodia and Thailand: A Study of Distinctions', *Ethnomusicology*, 39/2 (1995).

MITANI, YŌKO, 'Some Melodic Features of Chinese *qin* Music', in D. R. Widdess and R. P. Wolpert (eds.), *Tradition and Change: Essays on Asian and other Musics Presented to Laurence Picken* (Cambridge: Cambridge University Press, 1981).

MOBERLEY, R. B., *Three Mozart Operas* (London: Gollancz, 1967).

MORGENSTERN, SAM (ed.), *Composers on Music* (New York: Pantheon Books, 1956).

MORRIS, JAN, *Hong Kong: Epilogue to an Empire* (London: Penguin Books, 1988).

MORTON, DAVID, 'Thailand', *The New Grove* (1980).

MOUNTFORD, J. F., and WINNINGTON-INGRAM, R. P., 'Ancient Greek Music', *NOCM* (1983).

MOYLE, ALICE M., 'Australia', *The New Grove* (1980).

MUKHIA, HARBANS, 'The Years of "The Raj" ', in *India* (Hong Kong: APA Publications, 1990).

MUNROW, DAVID, *Instruments of the Middle Ages and Renaissance* (London: Oxford University Press, 1976).

MUNSON, PATRICK J., 'Africa's Prehistoric Past', in Phyllis M. Martin and Patrick O'Meara (eds.), *Africa* (Bloomington, Ind.: Indiana University Press, 1986).

MYERS, HELEN, 'Trinidad and Tobago', *The New Grove* (1980).

—— 'African Music', *NOCM* (1983).

MYERS-MORO, PAMELA, *Thai Music and Musicians in Contemporary Bangkok* (Berkeley and Los Angeles; University of California Press, 1993).

NEEDHAM, JOSEPH, *Science and Civilisation in China* (Cambridge: Cambridge University Press, 1962–).

NEHRU, JAWAHARLAL, *The Discovery of India* (1946; Delhi: Oxford University Press, 1981).

NEIGHBOUR, O. W., 'Schoenberg, Arnold', *The New Grove* (1980).

NELSON, KRISTINA, 'Reciter and Listener: Some Factors Shaping the Mujawwad Style of Qur'anic Reciting', *Ethnomusicology* (January 1982).

NETTL, BRUNO, 'North America', *The New Grove* (1980).

NETTLEFORD, REX M., *Caribbean Cultural Identity: the Case of Jamaica* (Institute of Jamaica, 1978).

NEUBAUER, ECKHARD, 'Islamic Religious Music', *The New Grove* (1980).

NGUYEN THUY LOAN and SANDAHL, STEN, notes to cassette, *Music from Vietnam*, a joint production by the Swedish National Concert Institute, Caprice, the Swedish International Development Authority, and Vinaconcert (Hanoi), Caprice CAP 21406, 1991.

NIKIPROWETZKY, TOLIA, 'Tuareg Music', *The New Grove* (1980).

NILES, ABBE, 'The Story of the Blues', foreword to W. C. Handy (ed.), *Blues: An Anthology* (1949; repr. New York: Macmillan, 1972), 12–45.

NKETIA, J. H. KWABENA, *Music in African Cultures: A Review of the Meaning and Significance of Traditional African Music* (University of Ghana, 1966).

—— *The Music of Africa* (London: Gollancz, 1979).

NYERERE, J. K., *Tanzania National Assembly Official Reports (Dar Es Salaam)* (1962).

O'GORDON, PAMELA, 'An Approach to the Study of Jamaican Popular Music', *Jamaica Journal*, 6 (1972).

OEY, ERIC (ed.), *Indonesia* (Hong Kong: APA Publications, 1986).

OTTÓSSON, R. A., 'Iceland', *The New Grove* (1980).

OLIVER, PAUL, 'Spiritual', *The New Grove* (1980).

OLIVER, ROLAND, *The African Experience* (London: Weidenfeld & Nicolson, 1991).

OLINS, WALLY, 'The European Global Company', *RSA Journal* (June 1994).

ORREGO-SALAS, JUAN A., 'Chile', *The New Grove* (1980).

OULLETTE, FERNAND, *Edgar Varèse*, trans. Derek Coltman (London: Calder & Boyars, 1973).

PACHOLCZYK, JOSEF, 'Arab Music', *The New Grove* (1980).

PAINE, LEWIS W., *Six Years in a Georgia Prison* (New York, 1851).

PALMER, TONY, *All You Need is Love* (London: Futura Publications, 1977).

PAZ, OCTAVIO, *The Labyrinth of Solitude*, new enlarged edn. (London: Penguin Books, 1990).

PEGG, CAROLE, 'Mongolian Conceptualizations of Overtone Singing (Xöömi)', *British Journal of Ethnomusicology*, 1 (1992).

PÉRÈS, MARCEL, 'Old Roman Chant, 7th–8th Centuries', sleeve note to *Chant de L'Église de Rome*, performed by Ensemble Organum, Harmonia Mundi 901218, 1989.

PHAM HUY PHONG (ed.), *Dong Son Drums in Viet Nam* (The Viet Nam Social Science Publishing House, 1990).

PICKEN, L. E. R., 'Twelve Ritual Melodies of the Tang Dynasty', *Studiae Memoriae Belae Bartok Sacra* (Budapest, 1956).

——'The Music of Far Eastern Asia', in *The New Oxford History of Music* (Oxford: Oxford University Press, 1957).

——'Secular Chinese Songs of the Twelfth Century', *Studia Musicologica Academiae Scientiarum Hungaricae Tomus*, 8 (1966).

——*Folk Musical Instruments of Turkey* (Oxford: Oxford University Press 1975).

——'The Musical Implications of Chinese Song-Texts with Unequal Lines, and the Significance of Nonsense Syllables, with Special Reference to Art-Songs of the Song Dynasty', *Musica Asiatica*, 3 (1981).

——'Instruments in an Orchestra from Pyū (Upper Burma) in 802', *Musica Asiastica*, 4 (1984).

——'Towards the Archaic Music of Pre-Nara Japan', unpublished paper presented at the Music Centre of the London School of Oriental and African Studies, 10 March 1992.

——ADKINS, C. J., and PAGE, T. F., 'The Making of a Kaen: The Free-reed Mouth-Organ of North-East Thailand', *Musica Asiatica*, 4 (1984).

——(ed.), with Allan Marett, Jonathan Condit, Elizabeth Markham, Yōko Mitani, and Rembrandt Wolpert, *Music from the Tang Court*, i (London: Oxford University Press, 1981); ii– (Cambridge: Cambridge University Press, 1985–).

PICKEN, STUART D. B., *Shinto: Japan's Spiritual Roots* (San Francisco: Kodansha International/USA, 1980).

PIRROTTA, NINO, 'Medieval', *The New Grove* (1980).

POPESCU-JUDETZ, EUGENIA, *Studies in Oriental Arts* (Pittsburgh: Duquesne University Tamburitzans, 1981).

PORTER, JAMES, 'Europe', *The New Grove* (1980).

POSTGATE, J. N., *Early Mesopotamia: Society and Economy at the Dawn of History* (London: Routledge, 1992).

POWELL, ANDREW, *Living Buddhism* (London: British Museum, 1989).

POWERS, HAROLD, review of Owen Wright, *The Modal System of Arab and Persian Music,* AD *1250–1300* (Oxford, 1978), in *Journal of the American Musicological Society* (1978).

——'India' and 'Mode', *The New Grove* (1980).

——'Classical Music, Cultural Roots, and Colonial Rule: An Indic Musicologist looks at the Muslim World', *Asian Music* (December 1980).

PRATT, KEITH, *Korean Music: Its History and its Performance* (London: Faber Music, 1987).

PROUST, MARCEL, *A la recherche du temps perdu*, trans. Andreas Mayor (London: Chatto & Windus, 1927).

PROVINE, ROBERT C., *Early Sources for Korean Ritual Music: Essays on Sino-Korean Musicology* (Seoul: Il Ji Sa Publishing Co., 1988).

—— 'State Sacrificial Rites and Ritual Music in Early Choson', *Journal of the Korean Traditional Performing Arts Centre*, 1 (1989).

QURESHI, REGULA, 'India', *The New Grove* (1980).

—— ' "Muslim Devotional": Popular Religious Music and Muslim Identity under British, Indian, and Pakistani Hegemony', *Asian Music*, 24/1 (1993).

RACY, ALI JIHAD, 'Musical Change and Commercial recording in Egypt, 1904–1932', Dissertation (University of Illinois at Urbana-Champagne, 1977).

—— 'Historical Worldviews of Early Ethnomusicologists: An East–West Encounter in Cairo, 1932', in Stephen Blum, Philip V. Bohlman, and Daniel M. Neuman (eds)., *Ethnomusicology and Modern Music History* (Urbana, Ill.: University of Illinois Press, 1987).

—— 'Musical Aesthetics in Present-Day Cairo', *Ethnomusicology* (September 1982).

RATTANAVONG, HOUMPHANH, 'The Lam Lüang, A Popular Entertainment', trans. Amy Catlin, *Selected Reports in Ethnomusicology* (1992).

REANEY, GILBERT, 'Machaut', *The New Grove* (1980).

RECK, DAVID B., 'South India', in. Jeff Todd Titon (ed.), *Worlds of Music* (New York: Schirmer, 1992).

RENFREW, COLIN, *Archaeology and Language* (London: Penguin Books, 1987).

RICH, ALAN, *American Pioneers* (London: Phaidon Press, 1995).

ROBERTS, J. M., *Pelican History of the World* (London: Pelican Books, 1988).

ROBINSON, JOHN J., *Born in Blood: The Lost Secrets of Freemasonry* (New York: M. Evans, 1989).

ROSE, TRICIA, *Black Noise: Rap Music and Black Culture in Contemporary America* (Hanover, NH: University of New England Press, 1994).

ROSENBAUM, RON, 'Elvis the Healer', *Sunday Morning Post Magazine* (Hong Kong, 29 October 1995), 8–15.

ROWELL, LEWIS, *Music and Musical Thought in Early India* (Chicago and London: University of Chicago Press, 1992).

RUFFLE, JOHN, 'Ancient Egypt, Land of the Priest-King', *The Religions of the World* (London: Lion Publishing, 1982).

RUSSELL, BERTRAND, *History of Western Philosophy* (Woking: Allen & Unwin, 1946).

SAGE, JACK, 'Cantiga' and 'Alfonso el Sabio', *The New Grove* (1980).

SALÉE, PIERRE, 'Gabon', *The New Grove* (1980).

SAM, CHAN MOLY, 'Muni Mekhala: The Magic Moment in Khmer Court Dance', *Selected Reports in Ethnomusicology* (1992).

SAM, SAM-ANG, 'The Floating Maiden in Khmer Shadow Play: Text, Context, and Performance', *Selected Reports in Ethnomusicology* (1992).

—— and CAMPBELL, PATRICIA SHEHAN, *Silent Temples, Songful Hearts: Traditional Music of Cambodia* (New Jersey: World Music Press, 1991).

SAVAN, LESLIE, 'Commercials Go Rock', in Simon Frith, Andrew Goodwin, and Lawrence Grossberg (eds.), *Sound and Vision: The Music Video Reader* (London: Routledge, 1993).

SCHIMMELPENNINCK, ANTOINET, 'What about the Singers?', *CHIME*, 4 (Autumn 1991).

—— 'Chinese Folk Singers in Jiangsu Province', *CHIME*, 8 (Spring 1995).

SCHNEIDER, ALBRECHT, and STOLZ, HARTMUT, 'Acoustics of Chinese Bell Chimes', in Ellen Hickman and David W. Hughes (eds.), *The Archaeology of Early Music Cultures* (Bonn: Verlag für Musikwissenschaft GmbH, 1985).

SCHROEDER, DAVID P., *Haydn and the Enlightenment* (Oxford: Oxford University Press, 1990).

SCHWARZE, BERND, 'Popmusik und Gnosis: aus dem "Gesangbuch" einer wiederentdeckten Weltreligion', *Acta Musicologica*, 66/2 (1994).

SCHUYLER, PHILIP D., 'Moroccan Andalusian Music', *World of Music*, 20 (1978).

SCOTT, A. C., 'China', *The New Grove* (1980).

SCOTT, CAROL, 'Korean Jazz has its own Natural Rhythm', *Asia Beat* (Hong Kong, February 1992).

SCRUTON, ROGER (1983), *The Aesthetic Understanding* (Manchester: Carcanet Press, 1983).

SEEGER, ANTHONY, *Why Suyá Sing: A Musical Anthropology of an Amazonian People* (Cambridge: Cambridge University Press, 1987).

SEEGER, CHARLES, 'United States of America', *The New Grove* (1980).

SEEMANN, CHARLIE, *The American Cowboy: Image and Reality*, sleeve note to *Back in the Saddle Again*, New World Records, NW 314/215, 1979.

SEYFARTH, ROBERT M., 'Vocal Communication and its Relation to Language', in Dorothy L. Cheney, Robert M. Seyfarth, Barbara B. Smuts, Richard W. Wrangham, and Thomas T. Struhsaker (eds.), *Primate Societies* (Chicago: University of Chicago Press, 1987).

SHAWCROSS, WILLIAM, *Sideshow: Kissinger, Nixon, and the Destruction of Cambodia* (New York: Simon & Schuster, 1979).

SHILOAH, AMMON, 'The Arabic Concept of Mode', *Journal of the American Musicological Society*, 34/1 (1981).

SIEGEL, J. A., and SIEGEL, W., 'Categorical Perception of Tonal Intervals: Musicians Can't Tell Sharp from Flat', *Perception and Psychophysics*, 21 (1977).

SIGNELL, KARL, 'The Modernisation Process in Two Oriental Music Cultures: Turkish and Japanese', *Asian Music*, 7/2 (1976).

SIM, STUART, 'Structuralism and Post-Structuralism', in Oswald Hanfling (ed.), *Philosophical Aesthetics: An Introduction* (Oxford: Blackwell/Open University, 1992).

SIMON, ROBERT, 'India', *The New Grove* (1980).

SLOBIN, MARK, 'Union of Soviet Socialist Republics', *The New Grove* (1980).

—— 'Central Asian and Siberian Music', *NOCM* (1983).

SONAM, THE VENERABLE, *The Yongsanjae Ritual*, published privately in Korea.

SORRELL, NEIL, *Indian Music in Performance* (Manchester: Manchester University Press, 1980).

—— *A Guide to the Gamelan* (London: Faber & Faber, 1990).

SOUTHERN, EILEEN (ed.), *Readings in Black American Music* (New York: Norton, 1971).

SPEARSHOTT, F. E., 'Aesthetics of Music', *The New Grove* (1980).

SPENDER, NATASHA, 'Psychology of Music', *The New Grove* (1980).

STANFORD, THOMAS, 'Mexico', *The New Grove* (1980).

STAPLETON, CHRIS, and MAY, CHRIS, *African All Stars: The Pop Music of a Continent* (London: Quartet Books, 1987).

STARGARDT, JANICE, *The Ancient Pyu of Burma* (Cambridge: Pacsea, in association with the Institute of South East Asian Studies, Singapore, 1990).

STAUDER, WILHELM, 'Mesopotamia', *The New Grove* (1980).

STEINER, GEORGE, *In Bluebeard's Castle: Some Notes towards the Re-definition of Culture* (London: Faber & Faber, 1971).

STEVENS, JOHN, 'Medieval Drama' and 'Troubadours and Trouvères', *The New Grove* (1980).

STEVENSON, ROBERT, 'Aztec Music', 'Inca Music', 'Latin America' and 'Lima', *The New Grove* (1980).

STICHWEH, KLAUS, 'Awareness through Compassion', in *Programmheft III, Parsifal* (Bayreuther Festspiele, 1977).

STOBART, HENRY, 'The Sirens of the Andes', *Musical Times* (February 1992).

STOCK, JONATHAN, 'Contemporary Recital Solos for the Chinese Two-Stringed Fiddle', *British Journal of Ethnomusicology*, 1 (1992).

STOKES, MARTIN, 'The Media and Reform: The Saz and Elektrosaz in Urban Folk Music', *British Journal of Ethnomusicology*, 1 (1992).

—— (ed.), *Ethnicity, Identity and Music: The Musical Construction of Place* (Oxford: Berg Publishers, 1994).

STONE, I. F., *The Trial of Socrates* (London: Jonathan Cape, 1988).

STRINGER, C. B., 'Evolution of Early Humans', *The Cambridge Encyclopedia of Human Evolution* (Cambridge: Cambridge University Press, 1992).

STRUNK, OLIVER (ed.), *Source Readings in Musical History from Classical Antiquity through the Romantic Era, Selected and Translated by O. Strunk* (New York, 1950; London: Faber Paperbacks, 1981).

STUBINGTON, JILL, sleeve note to *Les Aborigènes: Chants et danses de l'Australie du Nord*, CD, Arion ARN 64056. 1980.

SULLIVAN, MICHAEL, *The Arts of China* (Berkekey and Los Angeles: University of California Press, 1984).

SUNDBERG, JOHAN, 'Acoustics', *The New Grove* (1980).

SUSILO, HARDJA, 'Indonesia', *The New Grove* (1980).

SWEENEY, PHILIP, *Directory of World Music* (London: Virgin Books, 1991).

SXEMERE, ANNA, 'I Get Frightened of my Voice: On Avant-Garde Rock in Hungary', in Simon Frith (ed.), *World Music, Politics, and Social Change* (Manchester: Manchester University Press, 1989).

TAYLOR, CHARLES, 'Sound', *The New Grove* (1980).

TAYLOR, ERIC, *Musical Instruments of South East Asia* (Singapore: Oxford University Press, 1989).

TEMPLE, ROBERT, *The Genius of China: 3000 years of Science, Discovery and Invention* (London: Multimedia Books, 1986).

TENZER, MICHAEL, *Balinese Music* (Berkeley, Singapore: Periplus, 1991).

TERHARDT, E., 'Pitch, Consonance and Harmony', *Journal of the Acoustical Society of America*, 55 (1967).

THIERING, BARBARA, *Jesus the Man* (London: Corgi Books, 1992).

THIRLWALL, J. W., 'The Kreutzer Sonata and Mr Bridgtower', *Musical World*, 36 (1858).

THORPE, W. H., *Bird Song: The Biology of Vocal Communication and Expression in Birds* (Cambridge: Cambridge University Press, 1961).

THRASHER, ALAN R., 'Structural Continuity in Chinese Sizhu: The Baban Model', *Asian Music*, 20/2 (1989).

THUBRON, COLIN, *Behind the Wall* (London: Heinemann, 1987).

TIAN, QING, 'Recent Trends in Buddhist Music Research in China', trans. Tan Hwee San, *British Journal of Ethnomusicology*, 3 (1994).

The Times Atlas of World History, ed. Geoffrey Barraclough (London, 1989).

TINGEY, CAROL, *Heartbeat of Nepal: The Pancai Baja* (Royal Nepal Academy, 1990).

TITON, JEFF TODD (ed.), *Worlds of Music* (New York: Schirmer, 1992).

TOMKINS, CALVIN, *Ahead of the Game: Four Versions of the Avant-Garde* (London: Penguin Books, 1968).

TRACEY, ANDREW, 'Mozambique', *The New Grove* (1980).

TRAN QUANG HAI, 'Cambodia', *The New Grove* (1980).

TREWIN, A. MARK, 'The Court Ceremonial Music of Tibet', *CHIME*, 8 (Spring 1995).

TSAO PEN-YEH, 'Structural Elements in the Music of Chinese Story-telling', *Asian Music*, 20/2 (1989).

TURINO, THOMAS, *Moving Away from Silence: Music of the Peruvian Altiplano and the Experience of Urban Migration* (Chicago: University of Chicago Press, 1993).

UM, HAE-KYUNG, 'Making *P'ansori*: Korean Musical Drama' (unpublished paper presented to ICTM UK, 1992).

VALLAS, LEON, *The Theories of Claude Debussy* (London: Dover, 1967).

VATSYAYAN, KAPILA, 'India', *The New Grove* (1980).

—— *The Square and the Circle of the Indian Arts* (New Delhi: Roli Books International, 1983).

VEGA, GARCILASO DE LA, *Primera parte de los commentarios reales* (Lisbon, 1609).

WALEY, ARTHUR, *The Way and its Power: A Study of the Tao Te Ching and its Place in Chinese Thought* (London: Allen & Unwin, 1934).

WALSER, ROBERT, 'Rhythm, Rhyme, and Rhetoric in the Music of Public Enemy', *Ethnomusicology*, 39/2 (1995).

WALLIS, ROGER, and MALM, KRISTER, *Big Sounds from Small Peoples: The Music Industry and Small Countries* (London: Constable, 1984).

WALTON, ORTIZ M., *Music: Black, White and Blue* (New York: William Morrow, 1972).

WATERHOUSE, D. B., 'Japan', *The New Grove* (1980).

WATSON, FRANCIS, *A Concise History of India* (London: Thames & Hudson, 1974).

WATSON, JOHN F., *Methodist Error* (Trenton, NJ: 1819).

WATTS, ALAN, *Tao, the Watercourse Way* (London: Penguin Books, 1975).

WERNER, ERIC, 'Jewish Music', *The New Grove* (1980).

WEST, M. L., *Ancient Greek Music* (Oxford: Oxford University Press, 1992).

—— 'The Babylonian Musical Notation and the Hurrian Melodic Texts', *Music and Letters*, 75 (1994), 161–79.

WESTERNHAGEN, CURT VON, 'Wagner', *The New Grove* (1980).

WHITALL, ARNOLD, 'Expressionism', *The New Grove* (1980).

WHITE, TIMOTHY, *Catch a Fire: The Life of Bob Marley* (London: Corgi Books, 1983).

WIDDESS, D. R., 'Indian Music', *NOCM* (1983).

—— 'The Geography of Rāga', *World of Music*, 35/3 (1993).

—— 'Sléndro and Pélog in India?', in B. Arps (ed.), *Performance in Java and Bali* (London: School of Oriental and African Studies, 1993).

—— *The Rāgas of Early Indian Music: Modes, Melodies, and Musical Notations from the Gupta Period to c.1250* (Oxford: Oxford University Press, 1995).

WIDDESS, D. R. and WOLPERT, R. P. (eds.), *Music and Tradition: Essays on Asian and Other Musics Presented to Laurence Picken* (Cambridge: Cambridge University Press, 1981).

WILKINSON, ROBERT, 'Art, Emotion and Expression', in Oswald Hanfling (ed.), *Philosophical Aesthetics: An Introduction* (Oxford: Blackwell/Open University, 1992).

WILLIAMS, RAYMOND, *Keywords: A Vocabulary of Culture and Society* (London: Flamingo, 1983).

WILLIAMSON, MURIEL C., 'Burma', *The New Grove* (1980).

WINNINGTON-INGRAM, R. P., 'Aristoxenus', *The New Grove* (1980).

WINTLE, JUSTIN, *Vietnam's Wars* (London: Weidenfeld & Nicolson, 1991).

WOLPERT, REMBRANDT, 'Chinese Music', *NOCM* (1983).

WRIGHT, OWEN, 'Arab Music', *The New Grove* (1980).

WRIGHT, RONALD, *Stolen Continents: The Indian Story* (London: Murray, 1992).

YIBING, XUE, 'The Present State of Traditional Village Music Associations in Northern China: Three Case Studies', unpublished paper presented to ICTM UK, 1992.

YOUNG, PERCY M., 'Academy', *The New Grove* (1980).

YUNG, BELL N., 'China', *The New Grove* (1980).

—— 'Creative Process in Cantonese Opera 1: The Role of Linguistic Tones', *Ethnomusicology* (January 1983).

ZOBENS, LILIJA, 'Parallels between Balkan and Latvian Folk Music', unpublished paper presented to ICTM UK, 1992.

ZONIS, ELLA, *Classical Persian Music* (Cambridge, Mass.: Harvard University Press, 1973).

ZUOZHI, ZHANG, and SCHAFFRATH, HELMUT (1991), 'China's Mountains Songs', *CHIME*, 4 (Autumn 1991).

Credits for Illustrations

Thanks are due to the following for permission to reproduce illustrations on the plates indicated. Every effort has been made to contact copyright holders; we apologize to anyone who may have been omitted.

Dust-cover, Popperfoto; 1 Artia; 2 Collection Musée de l'Homme, cliché Jean Guiart; 3 British Museum; 4 National Museums of Scotland; 5 Artia; 6 Archaeological Survey of India; 7 Ven. Sonam; 8, 9 Popperfoto; 10 Staatliche Antikensammlungen und Glyptothek, München; 11 National Archaeological Museum, Naples; 12 Musée Royal de l'Afrique Centrale, Turvuren; 13–16 National Museums of Scotland; 17 Uganda Protectorate Public Relations Photographic Department; 18 P. R. Cooke; 19 National Museums of Scotland; 20 Victoria and Albert Museum; 21 Topkapi Saray Museum, Istanbul; 22 Music Village; 23 Iranian Embassy, London; 24 Syndics of Cambridge University Press Library; 25, 26, National Museums of Scotland; 27 Shri Bhavani Museum and Library, Aundh; Department of Archaeology and Museums, Bombay; 29 Claude Sauvageot; 30 Philip Blackburn; 31 author; 32 José Maceda; 33 Elizabeth Friendship; 34 Claude Sauvageot; 35 National Museums of Scotland; 36 author; 37 Ministry of Culture and Information, Vientiane, Laos; 38 Museum für Völkerkunde, Leipzig; 39 Saigontourist; 40 Philip Blackburn; 41 Kunsthistorisches Museum, Vienna; 42, 43 Music office, Hong Kong Government; 44 Stephen Jones; 45 Claude Sauvageot; 46 Embassy of the Republic of Korea; 47 Korean Traditional Performing Arts Centre; 48, 49 author; 50 Japan Foundation, Tokyo; 51 Artia; 52 Patrimonio Nacional, Madrid; 54 OUP, Scholes collection; 56 RSA, London; 57 OUP, Scholes collection; 59 Smetana Museum, Prague; 60 Nationalarchiv der Richard-Wagner-Steftung Bayreuth; 62 Succession Picasso/DACS 1997; 63 British Library; 64, 65 Popperfoto; 66 Museum für Völkerkunde, München; 67 Popperfoto; 69 Wm L. Clements Library, University of Michigan; 70, 71 Bodleian Library, Oxford; 72 Peter Newark's Western Americana; 74 Redfern's Music Picture Library; 75 Peter Newark's Western Americana; 76 Redfern's Music Picture Library, 77 Leon Morris.

Index